ABNORMAL PSYCHOLOGY
The Perspectives Text/Anthology

ABNORMAL PSYCHOLOGY
The Perspectives Text/Anthology

James D. Smrtic

Mohawk Valley Community College

The McGraw-Hill Companies, Inc.
College Custom Series

*New York   St. Louis   San Francisco   Auckland   Bogotá
Caracas   Lisbon   London   Madrid   Mexico   Milan   Montreal
New Delhi   Paris   San Juan   Singapore   Sydney   Tokyo   Toronto*

McGraw-Hill's College Custom Series consists of products that are produced from camera-ready copy. Peer review, class testing, and accuracy are primarily the responsibility of the author.

McGraw-Hill

A Division of The McGraw·Hill Companies

ABNORMAL PSYCHOLOGY: The Perspectives Text/Anthology

1 2 3 4 5 6 7 8 9 0 DOW DOW 9 0 9 8 7

ISBN 0-07-059456-2
Library of Congress Catalog Card Number 96-78909

Editor: M.A. Hollander
Printer/Binder: R.R. Donnelley & Sons Company
Cover Design: Jeffrey G. Boyd
Cover Photograph: James D. Smrtic

DEDICATION

In loving memory of, and appreciation for, my parents:

My father, who taught me how to work and play.
My mother, whose courage I can only approximate.

The Collaborates

Left to right: Donna L. Sawyer, *Research Coordinator*, James D. Smrtic, *Author*, Carmelita M. Lomeo, *Consulting Editor*, Jim Rooney, *Photographer and Illustrator*, Jeanette Bridenbecker, *Administrative/ Technical Writer*. (Photograph by Jim Rooney.)

Acknowledgments

This book is the result of over twenty years of work in abnormal psychology. During this time, a multitude of friends, colleagues, and students have made contributions and influenced my thinking. This book would not have been possible without them.

Special thanks to my children, Jennifer and Jim, for your support and tolerance. You give my life purpose and meaning. The encouragement and support of my brother, George, and his family, Joni, Mike, and Tom, are greatly appreciated.

There are four people who made essential contributions. Donna Sawyer did a tremendous amount of the research. Not only was she able to locate obscure references, but sense material of relevance. Jeanette Bridenbecker's dedication, perseverance, and loyalty to this project was matchless. Her contribution surpassed technical support. She helped me write. Carmelita Lomeo lent her professional expertise to the writing and editing process. Jim Rooney's unique artistic abilities captured abstract concepts on film or paper.

I greatly appreciate the willingness of my colleagues, from many disciplines, to share their expertise or information, often on short notice. It was amazing how the answer to virtually any question could be found by walking down a hallway.

The members of the Human Services and Psychology Department provided moral support and guidance. Josephine Alexander, Jan Barber, Elin Cormican, Mary Ann DiMeo, Andrew Kinney, James Rotenberg, Michael Sewall, George Strong, Joseph Zizzi, and Professor Emeritus Joseph E. Riley offered support and assistance in their areas of expertise.

Members of the Health Services Department, especially Civita Allard, Anna Diana, George May, and Mary Ann Nasuta provided valuable assistance in issues of medical and physiological areas.

From the Social Science and Criminal Justice Department, Sarah Coleman, Ethel Fine, Russell Hoffman, Dennis Lee, Kenneth McConnell, Beverly Quist, and Charlie Rogers assisted in legal and sociological areas.

The faculty of the Life Science Department was consulted in areas of physiology, biology, and neuroscience. Among them are Thomas Capraro, Paul Davidson, Sam Drogo, Ron Janowsky, Robert Jubenville, Angelo Lattuca, William Perrotti, and Richard Thomas.

Mathematicians Gary Kulis, Don Willner, and Richard Meili provided guidance on statistics. Pat Merry and Rita Ellis provided technical support in computer generated documents. Wayne Freed procured videos incorporated into the text. Dawn DeBuvitz contributed by providing student support. English professors George Searles and Steve Mocko helped with grammar.

Learning Resources specialists Fred Bauer, Sherry Day, June Knapp, Mary Kopel, Bonnie Mitchell, and Audrey Sotendahl could be counted on to locate and procure arcane references. I'm sure they're glad this project is finished. Secretaries Diana Mims, Janet Henderson, Toni Carbone, Juliet Sweet, and Pat Bennett offered technical support and encouragement. Students Jennifer North, Laurie Miller and Robert R. Moore were very helpful.

I am indebted to the authors and publishers whose works are included in this book, and have graciously permitted their use.

A special thanks to Margaret Hollander, who listened to me as no one else did, and McGraw-Hill for having confidence in the perspectives approach and this book. Mary Lea Gray was invaluable in obtaining permissions, attending to detail, and offering moral support.

For those I have forgotten, please forgive me. You were there when I needed help. I have been remiss.

Preface

While studying abnormal psychology as an undergraduate, I wondered why the text was organized around mental disorders and not the perspectives that explain them. By approaching the subject in this fashion, I found it difficult to appreciate the unique nature of each perspective. Without a prior understanding of the theory, orientation, and model of a perspective, it was difficult to understand why a treatment would be employed. It seemed more logical and pedagogically sound to present the perspective first, and then offer its explanation. Theory drives treatment.

I halfheartedly vowed that when I wrote my abnormal psychology text, it would employ a perspectives approach. Years later, I found my students experienced the same frustration. My interest was rekindled. This book represents my continued commitment to the perspectives approach.

With this approach, students wrestle with each perspective, trying to decide which is best for understanding abnormal behavior. They become convinced of the superiority of one, only to find their opinion changes when they study the next. They realize that the experts don't agree—that there are many ways to view a problem. They are guided into making *their* evaluations.

Many abnormal psychology texts claim to employ a perspectives approach, but ultimately employ the traditional. This one maintains it. It tells a complete story, with a logical beginning, body, and end. It is a text/anthology, and offers the advantages of each. You will find the content current, but not at the expense of excluding classic works that have not become dated. Thousands of sources were examined. Original works of the field's masters are alongside those of contemporary researchers, theorists, and professional writers. The text is opinionated, but not without empirical justification.

I am convinced of the superiority of the perspectives approach. This book is intended for those of similar conviction. Adoption of this approach involves a shift of focus from centering on pathology to theories that explain it. Ultimately, the benefits are worth it.

James D. Smrtic

Contents

ABNORMAL PSYCHOLOGY

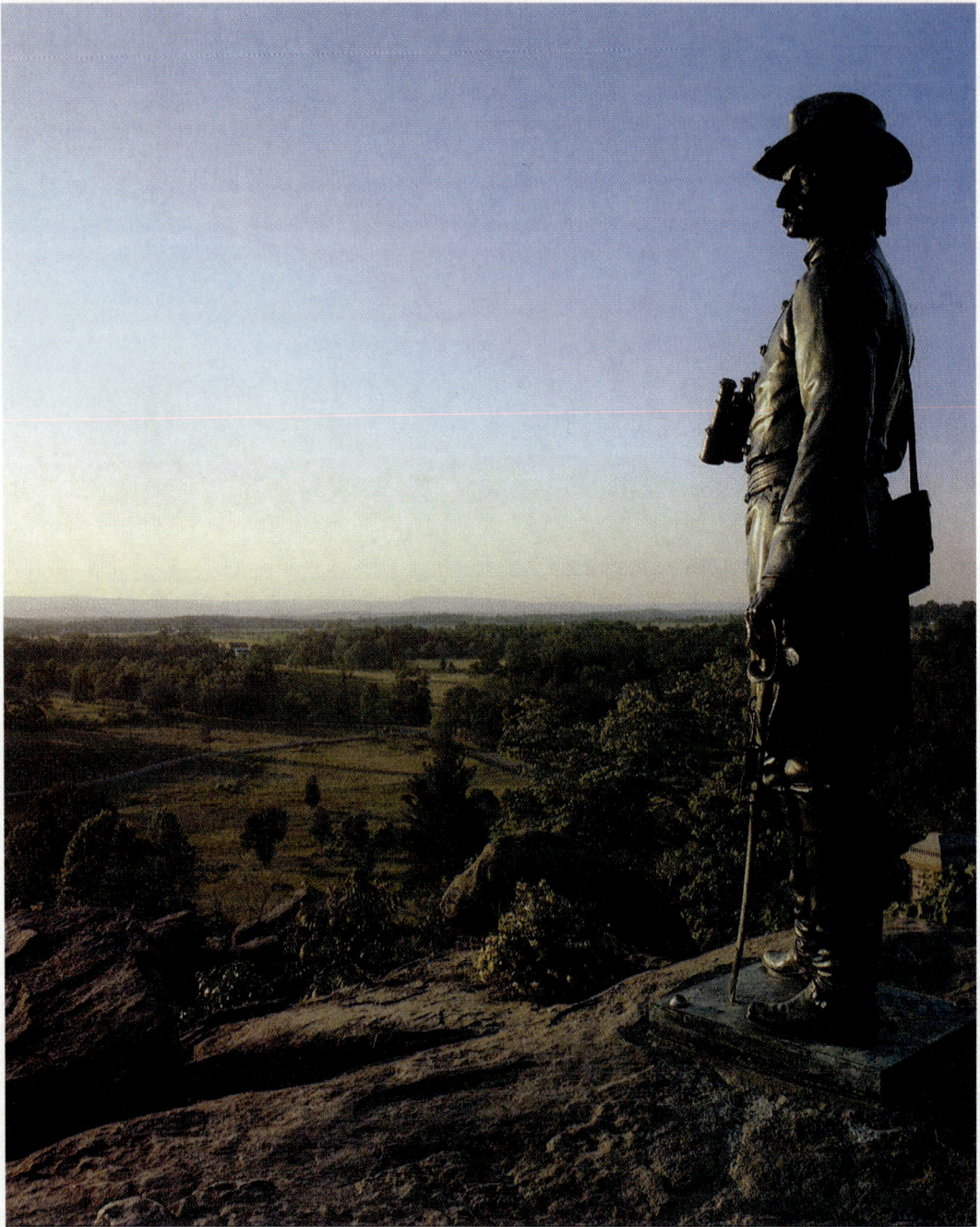

General Warren plans Union strategy as he overlooks the Gettysburg Battlefield from Big Round Top. Gettysburg was the turning point of the Civil War.

Chapter 1

DIRECTION

Lenny Bruce, social and cultural commentator, was thrown in jail in the 1960s for saying things in his comedy routines that today could be heard on prime-time television. Lenny made some interesting comments about his friends' reactions to the first televised debate between John Kennedy and Richard Nixon during the presidential campaign of 1960. There was tremendous interest in the debate. A very close election was predicted. *Life* magazine reported in September of 1988 that nine of ten of the 46 million American families with television watched the debate and 57% of those interviewed said the debate influenced their vote. Bruce commented:

> I would be with a bunch of Kennedy fans watching the debate and their comment would be, "He's really slaughtering Nixon." then we would all go to another apartment, and the Nixon fans would say, "How do you like the shellacking he gave Kennedy?" And then I realized that each group loved its candidate so that a guy would have to be blatant—he would have to look into the camera and say, "I am a thief, a crook, do you hear me, I am the worst choice you could ever make for the Presidency!" And even then his followers would say, "Now there's an honest man for you. It takes a big guy to admit that. That's the kind of guy we need for President." (Bruce, 1966, pp. 232-233.)

Bruce, whose life was tragically cut short by a heroin overdose, probably never anticipated that his comments would be used to begin an abnormal psychology text. However, he made a very significant point. Each of the spectators witnessed the same debate. The picture on the television that each saw was the same. Each heard the exact same dialogue at the exact same time. Although each of the spectator's sensations of the debate was identical, it is important to note that spectator's *perception* of the event could be drastically different. This same phenomenon can be observed in the judging of subjective athletic events. The results of some of the classic fights of Muhammad Ali, like those with Joe Frazier in the 1970s, are still debated. Nancy Kerrigan's Silver Medal finish in women's figure skating in the 1994 Olympics was extremely controversial. Whenever human beings are exposed to any event, it is likely that each individual's subjective perception of that event will be unique. Perception is an individual process.

Within American politics are thousands of politicians. Although all are politicians, they are further designated by party affiliation. There are Democrats, Republicans, Liberals, Conservatives, and a variety of smaller parties. But, as we all have probably observed, Democrats don't agree with Republicans, and Liberals don't agree with Conservatives. It is a wonder anything gets done. While all politicians are concerned with the same objective problems like inflation, unemployment, or foreign affairs, their subjective ways of interpreting these problems, and their recommendations for dealing with these issues, are different. It is difficult to find political "experts" who agree.

I had previously thought that if we were to find experts consistently agreeing among themselves in any field, it would be medicine. After all, one person's hernia is probably similar to the next's. But, alas, this is not the case. While watching a television talk show involving a panel of medical experts, I was shocked by what I heard. Since childhood I had been told that meat was a good source of necessary protein. One doctor immediately alerted me to the fact that I was clogging my blood vessels with cholesterol by eating meat. The point was made that large amounts of vitamin E should be taken to promote good health, prompting another expert to rebut that vitamin E is merely a placebo and large doses can be toxic. Although many doctors recommend medication to control high blood pressure, a doctor on the panel said that these drugs have serious side effects and that proper treatment of high blood pressure can be accomplished through dietary regulation and exercise. Finally, another specialist advocated the sticking of pins into the human flesh to cure whatever ails the person. Emotionally drained and frustrated, I slumped back into my chair wondering, "Who is right? Who really knows? Can we ever find experts in a field who agree?"

The Gospels of the Bible tell the story of the life of Jesus Christ. However, each tells the story in a unique way, as perceived or inspired, through the eyes of Matthew, Mark, Luke, and John. Although each book provides different accounts, interpretations, and emphases, all portray the life of Christ.

This is a book about abnormal psychology. I would really like to be able to tell you in this book that within the field of abnormal psychology, there is universal agreement regarding the causes and therapeutic treatment of abnormal behavior and mental disorders. However, as you may already anticipate, such is not the case. A common saying among psychologists is that "wherever there are two psychologists, there are three opinions."

Within abnormal psychology, we are faced with one undeniable, common objective phenomenon for study and investigation. For whatever reasons, there are some people whose behavior, thoughts, and emotions are qualitatively and quantitatively different from those of most other people. We may call this behavior abnormal, maladaptive, or self-defeating. The abnormal behavior may represent a serious problem for the individual or it may not. However, experts in the field of abnormal psychology will disagree as to how and why this person's abnormal behavior developed in the first place. They will also disagree about how to best treat him so that his symptoms diminish and his life becomes more satisfying.

As previously mentioned, there are a variety of American political parties whose members are in general agreement on important, fundamental political issues. Conservatives, in general, desire to limit the powers and expenditures of the government. They are likely to disagree, however, on which particular powers and expenditures to limit. Within abnormal psychology, there are also groups of scientists who adhere to a common model regarding the causes and proper treatments for mental disorders. Because human behavior is so complex and not readily understood, scientists have endeavored to explain what makes people act the way that they do by using models, or analogies. A good model accurately represents the real phenomenon. It loses its "as if" quality and creates a reality of its own. Imagine a child who has tediously labored building a model of a Corvette. The model lost its "as if" quality as he "drove" it across the dining room table. It *is* his Corvette.

In order to enable us to understand something as abstract as human behavior, scientists have created models to account for human behavior. By using models to represent their conjectures, scientists are able to study new phenomena. Scientists can then verify whether their explanation for human behavior is consistent with actual cases. If not, the model can be modified. Typically, models are neither completely wrong or right. They help us understand abstractions, like abnormal behavior. According to the model that a particular group of scientists follows, certain metaphors can be used to compare human behavior with other things. A metaphor is a figure of speech in which a term is transferred from the object or situation it ordinarily describes to a novel situation. "Mental Illness" is a powerful metaphor. In abnormal psychology, a group of scientists share a common perspective when they advocate a certain model for the cause and treatment of abnormal behavior, agree on which metaphors and scientific vocabulary are acceptable, and share a common theoretical orientation. Those sharing a particular perspective concur in regard to the fundamental causes and treatments of mental disorders.

They are likely to disagree, however, on the specifics. The debate and controversy among the various perspectives employed to study abnormal behavior is every bit as real and emotionally charged as that among the various political parties.

The purpose of this book is to familiarize students with the perspectives approach to the study of abnormal psychology. Each of the perspectives will be presented separately, so that you can appreciate its unique nature. A description of the theory and history of the perspective will be followed by selected readings, written by the experts of the perspective to extend your understanding. Questions follow each article so that you can test your understanding of the material.

However, before we can delve into the study of the various perspectives on abnormal behavior, some preliminary information and clarification is required. Chapter 2, *"Abnormality,"* investigates the essential nature of the phenomenom we will study—abnormal behavior. Chapter 3, *"The Diagnostic Manual,"* explains and describes the *Diagnostic and Statistical Manual of Mental Disorders.* Chapter 4, *"The Mental Disorders,"* will describe the behavioral, emotional, and cognitive symptoms that characterize the major disorders. An understanding of the classification and diagnosis of these disorders is crucial for understanding the study of abnormal psychology. The official document which classifies and categorizes the mental disorders is the *Diagnostic and Statistical Manual of Mental Disorders.* Once you are familiar with the classification system and the symptoms of the disorders, the study of the perspectives can begin.

Chapter 5, *"The Illness Perspective,"* presents the viewpoint that abnormal behavior is appropriately described as mental illness, and therefore requires medically oriented interventions and treatments. This perspective is most familiar to the layman. It is also the most powerful and influential of the perspectives, and has flourished since drug treatments for mental disorders became widespread during the 1950's. There have been many incredible technological advances in this perspective in the past few decades.

Chapter 6, *"The Holistic Perspective,"* is the newest of the perspectives. Instead of dissecting man into his "mind" and "body" components, it views him as a complex, integrated, interdependent organism, which can be best perceived and understood in holistic form. Whereas other perspectives are primarily concerned with providing treatment for existing disorders, an important emphasis of this perspective is upon their prevention.

Chapter 7, *"The Psychoanalytic Perspective,"* is based upon the theories of the incomparable Sigmund Freud, the most influential person in psychiatry and clinical psychology. Freud believed that unresolved, unconscious conflict, often dating back to childhood, was a significant factor in later psychopathology.

Chapter 8 is entitled *"The Learning Perspective"* and presents the behavioristic model of abnormality. The learning perspective views all behavior as a product of learning. Abnormal behavior is learned in the same manner as any other behavior. Abnormal behavior is viewed as the result of faulty reinforcement and conditioning. Therapy involves helping the patient learn more adaptive behaviors and unlearn those behaviors that are maladaptive.

Chapter 9, *"The Humanistic Perspective,"* is another of the more recent to emerge. The humanistic view of man is optimistic and enthusiastic. It stresses the unique quality and innate goodness of every human being. Humanism is ever mindful of the importance of personal integrity, autonomy, and freedom for the effective functioning of man. It is concerned with our existential dilemmas, and is relevant in a society where many ask, "Who am I? What is the meaning of my life?" This perspective is very much concerned with the subjective experience of the individual.

The final perspective, "*The Social Perspective*," is the subject of Chapter 10. Unlike the other perspectives, which had their roots in psychology or psychiatry, the social perspective applied sociological theory to aid in the understanding of abnormal behavior. This perspective has had a tremendous impact on the delivery of mental health services in the past forty years. Originally, this perspective was highly critical of the illness perspective and conventional psychiatry. It argued against labeling people "mentally ill" simply because they don't conform to social convention. The social perspective advocated alternatives to long-term mental hospitalization, and was the driving force behind the Community Mental Health Movement.

Each of these perspectives offers a unique understanding of abnormality. Each uses its own model and metaphor, vocabulary, and theoretical orientation. Each offers its own type of treatments. Again we see that it is difficult to find experts in agreement. After reading about the various perspectives, you may find yourself asking, "Who is right? What is the best way to conceptualize abnormal behavior? What is the best way to treat it? Does anyone really know?" If you find yourself more confused about abnormal psychology after you have read most of the book than you did before—don't dismay. You feel exactly like a serious student of abnormal psychology should feel—confused. Besides, how compelling could the study of abnormal psychology be if every question had only one answer?

Chapter 11, "*Clarification*," is designed to "put the perspectives into perspective." Various strengths and weaknesses of each perspective will be discussed, so that we might finally arrive at some conclusions regarding the relative merit of each. We will discuss specific circumstances in which particular perspectives have demonstrated their applicability and success. We will also discuss their limitations.

But, if after completing the book, you are still somewhat confused about abnormal psychology, don't dismay. You see, you just can't get the experts to agree.

REFERENCE

Lenny Bruce, *How to Talk Dirty and Influence People* (Chicago: Playboy Press, and New York: Pocket Books, 1966).

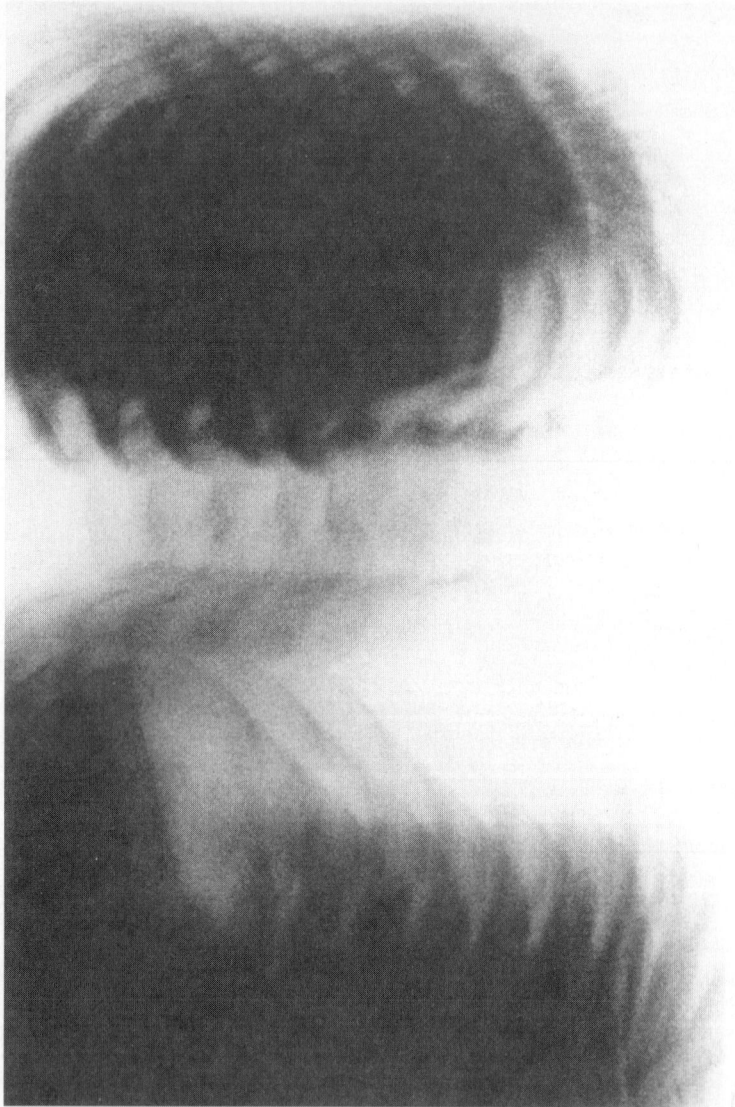

Multiple Exposures of a Young Woman. (Photograph by Jim Rooney.)

Chapter 2
ABNORMALITY

In Chapter 1, the words "normal" and "abnormal" are used a number of times. All of us have some general idea of what is meant when we describe behavior as normal or abnormal. When we assess our own behavior or that of others, we often try to evaluate the normality of the behavior. But specifically, what does it mean to be normal? Is it normal to smoke marijuana or use cocaine? Is it normal to get married or divorced? Is it normal to find religious fulfillment by joining a sect, shaving your head, begging in the street, and giving your solicited money to a total stranger? Is being normal good? Is being abnormal bad? These are very difficult questions to answer.

Unfortunately (or perhaps fortunately), there is no easy, clear-cut way to distinguish normal behavior from abnormal. There is no clear-cut dividing line that has normality on its left and abnormality on its right. As black is distinguished from white by an infinite number of shades of gray, it is difficult to precisely distinguish normal from abnormal. The situation is not hopeless, however. There are some useful ways of looking at the concept of normality that can help us determine if behavior is normal or abnormal. In our society, very important decisions are often based upon an assessment of the type and extent of the abnormality of the individual. Should a person be involuntarily committed to a mental hospital? Does a person represent potential harm to himself or others? Is a criminal suspect capable of knowing right from wrong? Does he understand the charges against him? We shall now begin to explore a variety of approaches to the understanding of abnormality, so that your understanding of it can surpass the general level.

This chapter will examine a number of issues related to normality and abnormality. First, we will describe how abnormal people have been viewed and treated throughout history. Next we will distinguish normality from abnormality on a variety of dimensions. Finally, we will examine the relationship between abnormal psychology and the criminal justice system, a branch of psychology known as forensics.

THE HISTORY OF ABNORMALITY

Since the beginning of mankind, there have been abnormal people. They have been perceived and treated in a variety of ways. Today, a dominant view is that abnormal people are "mentally ill", a metaphor in which the concept of illness is applied to conceptualize abnormal behavior. However, this view is relatively recent.

Groups of people evolve sources of social authority. They are people who are assumed to have special abilities and talents and have the confidence of the public. The sources of authority are typically afforded great status and prestige. They are expected to provide explanations, or attributions, for life's problems, and means for dealing with them. They are empowered to perform rituals to help us cope with things over which we feel powerless. Historically, these sources of authority have assumed the responsibility for the attribution of abnormality and method of dealing with abnormal people. The attributions are typically consistent with the present social climate, or prevailing social attitudes, and the existing technology. In today's society, science and medicine are major sources of social authority.

We will examine four distinct periods in the history of abnormality. In each, we will describe the sources of social authority, the prevailing social climate, the attributions for abnormality, and the methods for dealing with it. These periods are the ancient, classic, middle, and modern.

Figure 2-1. The Shaman. Illustration by Jennifer North.

The Ancient Period

This period of history is sometimes called the primitive period and occurred before 500 B.C. It is difficult to ascertain what was done with abnormal people, and why, because assumptions are based largely on archeological relics and remains. The source of social authority during this period was the shaman. The shaman was the equivalent of today's religious, educational, and medical authority combined in one.

Abnormal behavior was believed to result from a breakdown of a magical-religious system, such as taboo violations, neglect of ritual obligations, or spiritual possessions.

The selection and training of the shaman was a rigorous process, and usually began in adolescence. Omens, such as an unusual physical appearance, unexpected recovery from a severe illness, or extreme psychological symptoms, such as hallucinations, altered states of consciousness, and unusual dreams and visions would identify the potential shaman (Walsh, 1994). Mohave Indian shamans were lesbians called Berdache. They were revered by their people and the only ones allowed to bury the dead, as they were believed to be specially equipped to deal with such danger (Roscoe, 1988).

Afflicted tribespeople would attend a shamanatic seance. The shaman induced a state of frenzy and excitement through rhythmic music, dancing, smoking, drinking, drugs, and incense. With spirits present, the disturbed would reveal their sins and violations and have peace of mind restored through sacrifice and atonement. In extreme cases, trephining was employed. A hole was dug or drilled in the center of the forehead, the location of a mystical, or evil, third eye. This allowed evil spirits to escape. Trephined skulls evidence regrowth of bone, indicating that patients survived the ordeal. Apparently, the patient consented to this practice, which was performed not with malice, but compassion, as the shaman did the best possible with an extremely primitive technology.

Shamanism is practiced in many areas of the world presently. It is often referred to as "traditional medicine" by those who embrace it to avoid the scorn of scientific Westerners who perceive it as "witchdoctory." However, we have learned, and continue to learn from the shaman. Many pharmaceutical discoveries have been made possible through knowledge possessed by shamans of the therapeutic properties of rare plants. Such was the theme of the contemporary motion picture, "The Medicine Man."

Mark Plotkin is an ethnobotanist who has spent years studying how tribal people use plants in the Amazon rain forest for medicinal purposes. For example, the roots of shiny-leaved Brunfelsia guianensis are steeped in liquid to produce a hallucinogen used by the shaman to gain revelation regarding the plights of his disturbed patients. He has a sense of urgency, as civilization encroaches destructively into the rain forest, which could conceivably contain cures for cancer and AIDS. As he said, "If the jungle is a drug store, closing time is near." Comparing his modern scientific perspective with that of the shaman, he said, ". . . most important is that there are different realities, and none is necessarily more valid. You can't discount anything, no matter how silly it might sound. And because you have a Ph.D. and the other guy can't read, it doesn't mean you know more about botany than he does." (Jackson, 1989.)

The shamanatic seance provides a mechanism to deal with shame, guilt, and matters of conscience. These are fundamental concerns to many modern religions and variations of psychotherapy.

As shamans trephined to release evil spirits, a contemporary study of European, Near Eastern, Hispanic, and African cultures revealed that 36 percent of those sampled believe in the hexing power of the evil eye (Kaplan and Sadock, 1985, p. 258). In March of 1993 The Associated Press reported that shortly following the theft of Hopi Indian rite-of-passage ceremony relics, Jimmy Lee Hinton suffered kidney, liver, and gall bladder failure and experienced haunting nightmares of Hopi gods. An accomplice was nearly killed in a motorcycle accident and lost use of an arm and leg. Hinton's advice to other potential thieves was, "Set aside your greed for awhile. It's not art you're collecting. It's life. It's a people's soul. It's their religion."

Contemporary musicians, such as Jim Morrison, have mimicked shamanatic procedures to create frenzied excitement in the audience.

Ultimately, the treatment of abnormal people during the ancient period was characterized by a compelling source of social authority in the shaman, who practiced a therapeutic process with limited technology, with the consent and confidence of the people. The legacy of shamanism is conspicuous in modern religion, psychology and medicine.

Figure 2-2. The Rock of Gibraltar. (Corbis-Bettman.)

The Classic Period

This period of history occurred from approximately 500 B.C. to 400 A.D. We will concentrate on how abnormal people were viewed and treated during the "golden ages" of Greek and Roman civilization. During this period, there was keen interest in religion, literature, and medicine. There was a definite interest in trying to help abnormal people. Generally, the social climate was one of compassion. Two dominant attributions were employed; mythological, and medical.

Greece and Rome had their own mythologies. Earthly events were attributed to the desires of various gods. People had faith in these myths, and they provided guidance and meaning in life. Earthly transgression brought retribution from the gods.

The Greek mythological figure Hercules, son of Jupiter, was well known for his extraordinary strength. While in the process of completing his twelve labors that would sanctify him to the gods, he wrenched apart a mountain creating the Pillars of Hercules, which are today known as the Rock of Gibraltar, which stands at the entrance to the Mediterranean Sea, and Mount Hacho on the African coast (Herzberg, 1928, p. 225). Fear of retribution from such a power for the commitment of earthly transgressions created an atmosphere of mutual respect and social reciprocity among people.

According to humanist Rollo May, there is practically no discussion of anxiety during the early Greek classical period. It wasn't until during the second or third century B.C., when belief in the myths declined, that evidence of psychological problems and social decay appears in literature (Hall, 1967). Apparently, the mythology served to prevent alienation and anxiety, and promote prosocial behavior.

Following the decline of mythology, a medical attribution evolved, and this period represents the antecedent of today's illness perspective. During the 4th century B.C., Greek physician, Hippocrates proposed that an ideal balance and interaction of four bodily humors (blood, yellow bile, black bile, and phlegm) were essential for personality stability. Excesses of particular humors caused specific disorders

Figure 2-3. St. Catherine exorcising a possessed woman, painted by Giralamo di Benvenuto of Siena (1470-1524). (Denver Art Museum. Samuel H. Kress Collection.)

(Kaplan and Sadock, 1985, p. 2035). An excess of black bile, for instance, predisposed to melancholia, or extreme sadness. Treatment involved ridding the body of the excess humor through purgation (forced excretion) and emetics, which produce nausea, hopefully restoring balance (Halgin and Whitbourne, 1993, p. 9). In contemporary terms, Hippocrates hypothesized a biochemical theory of depression, which is presently receiving intense research. His work was limited by a lack of technology.

Hippocrates disdained mythological attributions. For example, epilepsy was known as the "sacred disease." He cynically commented, "If you cut open the head, you will find the brain humid, full of sweat and smelling badly. And in this way, you may see that it is not a god that injured the body, but disease" (Zilboorg & Henry, 1941, p.44). This may represent history's first "perspectives clash."

Ultimately, the classic period was characterized by a sincere concern with helping abnormal people, a benevolent social climate, with progress limited by a lack of technology.

The Middle Period

The middle period occurred approximately between the year 400 and the firm establishment of the Renaissance, which progressed during the 15th and 16th centuries. This period was characterized by extreme fear and superstition, perhaps paranoiac, and is often referred to as the "dark ages". With the decline of the Greek and Roman civilizations, interest in science, literature, and medicine waned. Treatment of abnormal people was often very cruel, and the social climate regressed dramatically, when compared with the enlightened classic period.

The Christian church, particularly the Roman Catholic, was the primary social institution, and religious leaders were the source of social authority. The church was extremely powerful, and performed judicial and governmental functions, in addition to religious. Powerful institutions desire to maintain control, and are swift to deal with challenges to their authority. Institutional priority supersedes individual rights and integrity, inviting degradation and abuse of the people. Because of this, formulators of American government, many who fled from Europe, demanded the separation of church and state, which exists today.

Abnormal behavior was attributed to witchcraft. Disturbed people were assumed to be possessed by the devil. In some cases, the possession was voluntary, as the person had made a pact with the devil. In others, the possession was involuntary, and the devil had simply invaded the individual.

The church developed procedures to rid people of the devil, ultimately allowing them to enter heaven. Historically, oppressive regimes have justified persecution of out-groups by developing a psychology in which treatment becomes a euphemism for persecution. Procedures included, "beating the devil" from the person, exorcism, or ultimately, burning at the stake.

In 1484, Pope Innocent VIII published the edict Summis Desiderantes Affectibus. It expressed his official position in favor of witchhunting, and served as the handbook for the Inquisition for the next two centuries (Sadock and Kaplan, 1985, p. 204). Confessions of witchcraft were often obtained under the duress of torture. Those designated as witches were typically unusual in some way; physical abnormalities like birthmarks, perceived as "devil patches," speech impediments, speaking in unknown languages, unexplained paralyses, hallucinations, and premonitions. Religious leaders could not adequately explain such phenomena, so riddance of the "witches" discouraged potential public doubt, and served as a poignant warning to potential dissidents. Thus, the political and social order was maintained.

Persecution of witches was not restricted to Europe. The infamous Salem Witch trials occurred in what is now Salem, Massachusetts in 1692. A group of young girls gathered at the village minister's house, and naively discussed the supernatural. Their behavior became more bizarre, as they had frequent "fits," convulsions, barked, mewed, and danced wildly. Mass hysteria resulted. Allegations of witchcraft prompted the trials in which 250 persons were arrested, 50 were condemned, 19 were executed, 2 died in prison, and 1 died of torture (Deutsch, 1949, pp. 34-35). Arthur Miller wrote the definitive novel on the Salem Witch Trials, called *The Crucible*. Writing about *The Crucible* in 1967, Miller said, "When irrational terror takes to itself the fiat of moral goodness, somebody has to die." (Ferres, in Ferres, 1972, p. 12)

An interesting alternative explanation was offered by L.R. Caporael (1976). By examining historical records, she determined that weather conditions were conducive for the growth of the rye fungus ergot during this period. One of the components of ergot is a hallucinogen related to LSD, leading to the speculation that the bizarre behavior of the "witches" resulted from the ingestion of bread contaminated by the hallucinogen.

In conclusion, the middle ages were characterized by ignorance, persecution, superstition and self-righteous brutality. It was not a good time to be abnormal.

The Modern Period

This period began during the latter half of the 1700s. Significant occurrences made it inevitable that the way the abnormal were viewed and treated would change. Many of the early American settlements were established as religious colonies. Following the Revolution of 1776, Americans now had state and national identities. The industrial revolution had begun, and there was rekindled scientific and medical interest. These factors contributed to the decline of the absolute authority of the church.

Gradually, a trend emerged in which abnormal people were relegated to institutions called asylums. There were many reasons for social isolation. It had been learned that certain diseases, like leprosy, were contagious. For the protection of society, lepers were isolated in colonies, setting a precedent for the isolation of the abnormal, who were perceived as possibly ill. Sixteenth century Swiss physician Paracelsus employed homeopathic plant remedies to treat tuberculosis and syphilis, which were common in the asylums (Nash, 1982, p. 284). He also claimed that the moon could affect behavior. The asy-

Figure 2-4. Mohawk Valley Psychiatric Center, Utica, New York, was originally established as the New York State Lunatic Asylum in 1843. The imposing structure belies the meaning of asylum. (Photograph by Jim Rooney.)

lum was an appropriate place for "moonstruck lunatics." For example, the Mohawk Valley Psychiatric Center in Utica, New York, was originally founded as the New York State Lunatic Asylum in 1843. Although somewhat weakened, belief in witchcraft persisted. As the execution of witches ceased, they were likely to be placed in asylums. Thus, placement of the abnormal in asylums became the norm, regardless of whether the attribution was illness, lunacy, or witchcraft.

Although intended to be places of safety and refuge, the asylums were not. They became prisons characterized by cruel and inhumane treatment. Believed to be like animals and insensitive to cold and hunger, inmates were routinely beaten, starved and tortured.

A movement began for more humane treatment. In 1793 Philippe Pinel proposed a compassionate program for the treatment of the insane at the Hospital of La Bicetre in Paris. He removed the chains from 49 inmates, making a significant symbolic step toward humanitarian reform. American reformer, Dorothea L. Dix, was horrified by conditions in the asylums, and spent 30 years lobbying for humane treatment. She was responsible for the creation or expansion of 32 institutions in which humane treatment, or moral therapy, was employed (Kaplan and Sadock, 1985, pp. 1577-1578).

The beginning of today's illness perspective can be traced to Benjamin Rush, "the father of American Psychiatry." In 1783 he introduced moral treatment to the Pennsylvania hospital. In 1812 he wrote *Medical Inquiries and Observations upon the Diseases of the Mind*. He rejected witchcraft and lunacy, and advocated medical attributions. He employed blood letting, purges, emetics, diet, and drugs in a "healthful environment" in which old ideas were removed from patients through conversation with a sympathetic physician (Kaplan and Sadock, 1985, p. 1577). An incredible man, Rush was also a sign-er of the Declaration of Independence, surgeon general to the Continental Army, Treasurer of the United States Mint, and founder of the first antislavery society in America (Bootzin, 1993, p.15).

Other treatments included the tranquilizing chair, in which a patient was confined with a translucent veil covering his eyes. A commode was attached to the seat, since a patient would remain confined for days. An ovary compressor was used to hinder abnormal wanderings of a woman's uterus for the prevention of hysteria. A "bath of surprise," in which an unsuspecting patient fell through a trap door into a tub filled with cold water, was intended to restore his wits. The Utica safety crib, a cage-like bed which kept the person in a horizontal position, was used to calm patients at the New York State Lunatic Asylum until the 1870s. Although today these treatments may sound primitive, at the time they were considered state of the art. An 1800 painting, *General Washington in His Last Illness Attended by Doctors Craik and Brown*, by an unknown artist, depicts Washington in a comatose state. His pulse is being taken, and various medicinals, including port, are on the bedside table. He had undergone an immense series of bleedings prior to his death. Such was the treatment afforded the president.

Unfortunately, these treatments and moral therapy seldom resulted in cure. Retrospectively, we can speculate that many of the patients suffered from serious physical illnesses, brain infection, trauma, disease or atrophy; conditions which today remain resistant to treatment.

The latter half of the twentieth century can be characterized by a gradually improving technology for the treatment of mental disorders. Subsequent chapters will describe significant advances in both medical and psychotherapeutic methods.

Today's social climate is an enigma. The quality of a society can be measured by the way that it cares for its least capable or desirable members. Evidence for an enlightened social climate can be found in the care and treatment provided to the mentally disabled in quality institutional or community-based settings. Per patient expenditures are often as high as $70,000 annually.

However, demand for such services dramatically exceeds supply. It is difficult to estimate the number of homeless Americans. According to the 1990 census, 200,000 people are homeless. The Urban League estimates the number to be 600,000, and others speculate the number is over 1,000,000 (cited in Woodside and McClam, 1994, p. 124). Approximately one half of this population has serious mental disorders and receive little, if any, treatment.

We have covered four distinct periods in the history of abnormality. Each was characterized by its technology, source of authority, attribution, and social climate. Today, we look to science and medicine as sources of social authority to provide medical and psychotherapeutic treatments for mental illness. In the past, spiritual, religious, mythological, or elementary medical procedures were employed. We can only speculate about future attributions and treatments.

DISTINGUISHING ABNORMALITY FROM NORMALITY

As stated earlier in the chapter, the distinction between normality and abnormality is typically not precisely defined. However, there are a number of dimensions on which they can be compared and analyzed. We will examine them.

The Statistical Approach To Abnormality

One way that an understanding of abnormality can be approached is from a statistical point of view. Quite simply, we can use statistics to define normal behavior as frequently occurring behavior. It is common, usual, frequently occurring behavior. It is the type of behavior most people demonstrate most of the time. Conversely, abnormal behavior is statistically infrequent in its occurrence. It is relatively uncommon and rare. Normality implies usual behavior. Abnormality implies unusual behavior.

The statistical approach can be quite easily understood by analyzing the possible outcomes of flip

Figure 2-5. Fish eating fish. Refer to the normal curve of probablity on page 16. Note that the tails do not touch baseline. Theoretically, the normal curve accounts for all possible outcomes. Consider the probability of the photographer capturing this picture. (Cy DeCosse Incorporated.)

ping ten coins simultaneously a great number of times. Since there are two sides to a coin, there is a one in two chance a coin will show a head when flipped, and a one in two chance it will show a tail (neglecting the remote possibility the coin will stand on its edge). If we had a lot of spare time and the perseverance to see it through, we would find that if the coins were flipped one million times, outcomes of five heads and five tails would be the most frequent. Somewhat less frequent would be outcomes of six heads and four tails or six tails and four heads. Somewhat less would be seven heads and three tails or seven tails and three heads. Lesser yet would be the outcome of eight heads and two tails or eight tails and two heads. Still lesser would be outcomes of nine heads and one tail or nine tails and one head. The least frequent outcomes, occurring very rarely, would be all ten heads or all ten tails. Statistically speaking, it would be relatively normal to toss the ten coins and have an outcome of five heads and five tails, as this is a relatively common event. It would be very abnormal to have an outcome of ten heads or ten tails, because these occur extremely rarely.

At the outset of this chapter the question, "Is being normal good?" was asked. That was a loaded question, as the answer depends on the specific situation involved. We could substitute terms like "conformist," "mediocre," or "typical" for normal and some would reason these are undesirable, as they connote lack of individuality and blandness. Conversely, descriptive terms like "team player," "well-adjusted," and "acceptable" have more positive connotations. Depending upon the situation involved, being normal or abnormal may be either good or bad. Nationally, millions of people buy lottery tickets. Only a small proportion of those purchased are winners. It is normal to buy a losing ticket. I think we can see that being normal in this situation has no advantage. Conversely, to have purchased a winning ticket is statistically abnormal, but obviously desirable in this instance.

Is being abnormal bad? Again, it depends on the situation. A genius is abnormal. It is also abnormal

Percent of scores in interval	2.27	13.59	34.13	34.13	13.59	2.27
Wechsler IQ	55 70	85	100	115	130 145	

Negatively Abnormal   Normal   Positively Abnormal

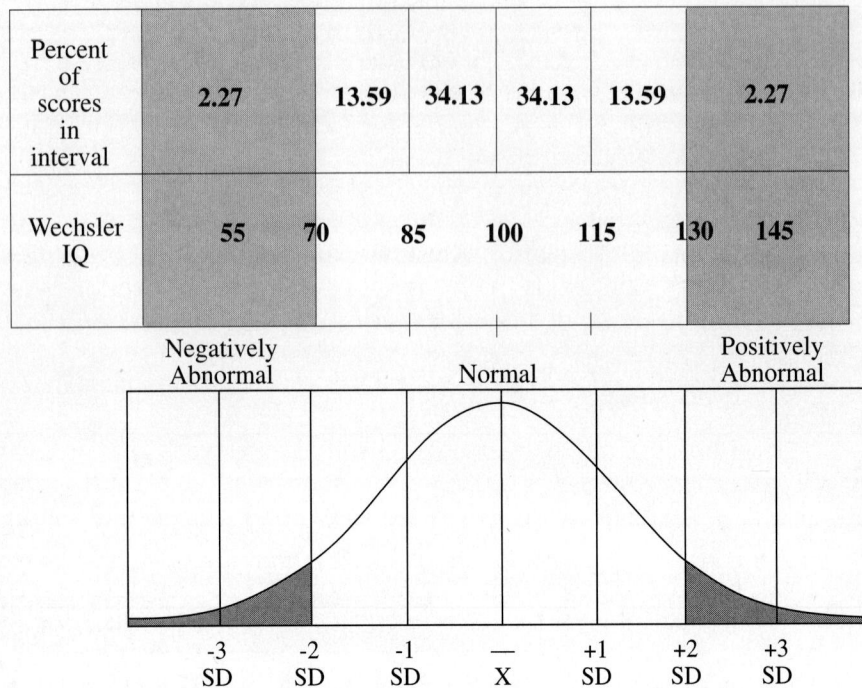

| -3 SD | -2 SD | -1 SD | — X | +1 SD | +2 SD | +3 SD |

for a football player to be on the winning Super Bowl team. Both of these are desired abnormalities. Lemmings are rodents noted for their mass migrations into the ocean, resulting in their deaths. I can see no advantage in being a normal lemming who jumps into the sea. The "radical," "deviant" lemming, who dawdles while the others leap, survives. There is a clear advantage to being a "deviant" lemming. However, there are also negative aspects to abnormality. This is particularly true in people who lack the ability to function in a normal routine, derive little satisfaction from life, and are alienated from the world around them. These people will be covered much more extensively later.

Do You Have Normal Intelligence?

For any specific human trait or ability, it is likely that any individual will demonstrate that trait or ability to relatively the same extent as do most other people. Human intelligence is a good example of such a trait. It is very probable you have taken an **intelligence quotient** (or **I.Q.**) test. A score of 100 is typically considered normal intelligence. Statistically speaking, the score 100 should divide the population in half, if the population were to take the intelligence test. Although technically 100 is defined as normal, the actual range of scores that are considered normal is much broader. It ranges from 85 to 115. About 68 percent of the populations' scores fall within this range. I.Q. scores between 70 and 85 are considered low normal. About 13.6 percent of the population scores within this range. Likewise, I.Q. scores between 115 and 130 are considered high normal. Approximately 13.6 percent of the population also scores in this range. Thus, if we include all levels of normal intelligence, about 95 percent of the population has normal intelligence.

Those who exhibit the most extreme deviations from a score of 100 are designated as mentally retarded or gifted. Those with scores of 70 or below are designated as retarded; those with scores of 130 or higher are considered gifted. About 2.27 percent of the population falls in each of these categories. It is important to note that a retarded person with an I.Q. of 70 is equally abnormal statistically as the gifted person with an I.Q. of 130, as each represents an equal deviation from the normal I.Q. of 100. Graphically, the distribution of intelligence scores appears as shown in Figure 2-7.

The population of the United States was estimated to be 258,300,000 in mid-1993 by the Census Bureau. Based on this estimate, about 175,644,000 Americans have normal intelligence. If we include those with low and high normal intelligence, the number of people with normal intelligence increases to about 245,385,000. Most people have normal intelligence.

Since in theory, only the lowest 2.27 percent of the population based upon I.Q. score is considered retarded, it is statistically abnormal to be retarded. Statistics also show how uncommon it is for a person to be gifted, as this category is designated by only the highest 2.27 percent of the population based upon I.Q. Both groups are statistically abnormal. However, retardation is considered a negative abnormality because the person demonstrates intelligence to a lesser extent than the normal person, and giftedness is a positive abnormality, as the person demonstrates the trait to a greater extent than normal. Since you are able to comprehend this text, you most probably have normal intelligence. Some readers may be gifted.

Do You Enjoy Social Activities?

The same analysis that was just made with intelligence can be made with any human trait or ability. Let us examine human affiliation, or the need to be near people. Normal people spend much of their time with their immediate family. They have a spouse or an intimate relationship with a significant other, a few very good friends, and a large group of casual acquaintances from work, school, or the community. Most people belong to a few social, civic, or professional organizations. Many meet with others of their faith through church membership. Distant relatives are seen less frequently. Aunt Martha visits only on Thanksgiving, Christmas, and Easter. If this roughly describes your affiliation, you are normal for the trait.

However, there are also some extremely introverted people with very low affiliation needs. These people have very few social contacts, do not belong to any social organizations, do not affiliate with family, and live alone. The reclusive hermit may live alone in a cabin in the mountains with virtually no contact with the outside world. His actions are statistically abnormal, because he demonstrates affiliation to a lesser extent than the population. Note that no value judgement was placed on his behavior. The statistical approach does not make this type of judgement. It only makes a statement about the statistical frequency of the behavior.

In 1988, adventurer Francis Le Guen, descended 262 1/2 feet into an underground grotto in an attempt to set a new Guiness Book record for an underground stay by a woman. She spent 111 days in total isolation. She committed suicide the following year (Hall, 1991).

The other extreme is demonstrated by those who are extremely extroverted and have very high affiliation needs. They feel compelled to belong to numerous organizations. They demand continual contact with family and friends. They continually give others what they feel is badly needed advice and serve as carriers of news among many people. They feel that they should always be consulted by their associates and included in all their plans. They are stung if they are not. These people may be called busybodies, gossips, or nosey. Consider Aunt Martha.

How Clean Are You?

We can analyze the trait of cleanliness in the same manner. Based upon my casual polling of students over the years, most people wash their face and hands between five and eight times a day. They bathe daily, or perhaps more frequently in hot, humid weather. Most people change their clothes daily. This basically describes normal cleanliness.

It is essentially abnormal never to wash, bathe, or change clothing. It is also abnormal for a person to wash his hands seventy times a day, change his clothes ten times a day, take numerous lengthy baths using caustic detergents, avoid wastebaskets, and turn off light switches with his elbows to avoid contamination. The latter demonstrates the symptoms of obsessive-compulsive disorder, which will be more thoroughly described later.

How Generous Are You?

Let us examine the trait of generosity. Most people devote some time to a charitable activity, donate some money to a few favorite causes, give presents to relatives and close friends on special occasions, loan friends money if there is a great need and if the probability of return is high, and put a couple of dollars in the collection plate at church. This describes normal generosity.

A miser demonstrates a minimum of generosity. *The Guinness Book of World Records* describes the world's greatest miser as Henrietta Howland Green. She left an estate of 95 million dollars at the time of her death in 1916 and was the world's richest woman. Despite her wealth, she often ate only cold oatmeal, as she was too cheap to heat it. She wore the same black dress, which often concealed millions of dollars in negotiable stocks and bonds, for 20 years. She only had the dirtiest parts cleaned, and paid proportionally for the laundering.

To Henrietta, doctors were only money-grubbing quacks. Her only son, Edward, injured his leg while sledding. She tried to treat it herself, but the leg worsened. Dressed as paupers, they reluctantly went to a doctor, who requested a pauper's pittance for payment. She refused treatment, instead applying sand to the festering leg. Gangrene set in. His leg was later amputated (Nash, 1982). Logically, it doesn't seem as if anyone could be that cheap. Behold "negative infinity."

Some people demonstrate what could be considered excessive generosity. Members of cults often willingly sacrifice their worldly possessions, live in unnecessary poverty, dress and eat poorly, and without question surrender the money they have solicited to their leaders.

Ultimately, normal people demonstrate a multitude of traits, behaviors, and characteristics to roughly the same extent as do most other members of the population. They fall in the middle part of the curve on an accumulation of traits. Abnormal people demonstrate a multitude of traits on the extreme ends of the curve. It is the cumulative effect of a variety of abnormal behaviors that leads others to perceive the individual's overall behavior as abnormal. Consider the mentally retarded person, who lives alone in a one-room shack in an isolated area, avoids social interaction, and washes and bathes in ritualistic fashion many times daily. He is excessively miserly and hoards pennies in a sack hidden beneath his bed. This person is statistically abnormal.

Analyze your degree of intelligence, affiliation, cleanliness, and generosity. Are you statistically normal?

THE CULTURAL APPROACH TO ABNORMALITY

Another way of approaching abnormality is from a cultural viewpoint. To present this approach it is helpful to borrow a term from sociology. *Cultural relativism* means that what is considered normal is a function of culture and, therefore, varies among cultures. Upon examining cultures throughout the world, it becomes evident that different groups of people often have very different ways of doing essentially the same thing. That groups of people have different techniques, traditions, customs, or systems of social organization is not really important. Of great importance is that these groups are able to function, survive, and socialize their children into the culture, regardless of their methods. It is also important for a culture to adapt to changing conditions and circumstances.

Ethnocentrism

The tendency to view one's culture as inherently superior, and therefore the one against which others should be judged, is called ethnocentrism. Americans often have the reputation of being highly ethno-

Figure 2-7. The isolation of the Hopi demands cooperation for survival. (Photograph by Jerry Jacka.)

centric. When in foreign countries, Americans are often perceived as unwilling to learn the native language and customs. There is probably some truth to this. Do you take any foreign languages? Ethnocentrism seems a natural tendency, and other cultures are also highly ethnocentric.

Within contemporary American society we have developed complex codes of conduct that constitute normal behavior. We are so accustomed to our way of life that we often have a tendency to view the culture, traditions, and customs of others as inferior, primitive, weird, threatening, or abnormal. Our eyes become surrounded by "cultural blinders" that make us view behavior within a very narrow perspective. We perceive our way of doing things as normal, moral, logical, and right. We see theirs as abnormal, immoral, illogical, and wrong. Let us now examine how normality varies from culture to culture, so that you can better appreciate cultural relativism and ethnocentrism.

Family System of the Hopi

The Hopi Indians of northern Arizona have a family system that is organized around the mother. Driving through the Hopi reservation takes the better part of a day. Until recently, its vastness has prevented rapid cultural change. It is common for a mature woman, her daughters, and her grand-daughters to occupy the same residence. This arrangement may last throughout life, with all of the children living in this residence. In fact, the Hopi term "mother" applies not only to a child's biological mother, but to aunts and other women of the same generation within certain family guidelines (Queen and Habenstein, 1974, pp. 50-51). Thus, if the child's biological mother were to die, the child would not be displaced into a new, strange environment. He would stay where he had been living. There would also be an ample supply of caretakers, all of whom the child was already used to calling mother, to take over the child's care. This family arrangement provides a built-in child care mechanism for the Hopi.

In American culture, if both biological parents of a child die, the responsibility for the care of the child is often uncertain. Brothers, sisters, or parents of the deceased may assume the responsibility, but this often imposes an undue hardship on them. There is no legal obligation for them to do so. Regardless of where the child is ultimately placed, he will have to cope with his loss in a different, strange environment. The availability of quality child care remains a problem in American society.

As previously mentioned, a culture must be able to adapt to changing conditions. Historically, many groups of people throughout the world have established family systems in which multiple sex partners were the norm. Sexual relations are typically regulated by caste, class, and family restrictions, and these societies functioned reasonably well. However, since Acquired Immune Deficiency Syndrome (AIDS) has become a major menace to world health, many of these groups have become ravaged by this disease. Their traditions will have to change in a way that reduces the chance that the disease will spread, if they are to survive.

Gender Roles

The designation of gender roles is also culturally relative. Gender roles have changed dramatically in American society since the 1950s. The feminist movement challenged traditional role stereotypes. For example, female college students were once a slim minority. Today they are a majority. Gender roles change over time.

They also vary among cultures. In her classic work, *Sex and Temperament, In Three Primitive Societies*, anthropologist Margaret Mead (1963) analyzed societies on the island of New Guinea—the Arapesh, the Mundugumor, and the Tchambuli—to determine if there were universal differences in role and temperament between the sexes.

The Arapesh, regardless of sex, is expected to be gentle, responsive, and unaggressive. Both parents share in the rearing of children. Both parents are said to be pregnant, to have labor pains, and to "give birth" to the baby. In the Arapesh society, men are said to look tired, haggard, and worn out when rearing children. In some cases in our culture, statements like, "Why shouldn't he look good? She had, and takes care of, the children!" apply. In some families, rearing practices are similar to those of the Arapesh. In others, where fathers assume primary parental responsibility, the example applies.

Mead was warned upon leaving the gentle Arapesh that the next tribe, the Mundugumor, would be much different. Indeed, they were. They were head-hunters and cannibals. She was warned not to visit them, but went anyway, as head-hunting was recently made illegal. Mead encountered some risk in her pursuit of knowledge. The Mundugumor men and women are sexually aggressive and violent. Children are not wanted and, within cultural guidelines, routinely killed. Sexual relations are characterized by much biting, scratching, and fighting. Unfortunately, similar examples of abandoned, "throw-away" children exist in our culture, as does an increasing problem of sexual violence.

Among the Tchambuli, Mead found that the women assume the role of provider and the men take care of domestic concerns. Women work together in groups and men arrange social activities, devote themselves to hobbies, and gossip. Women are sexually aggressive and the men's emotional satisfaction centers around them. How does American society compare? This analysis demonstrates that gender roles are a function of culture and time.

Why Do Some Practices Appear Abnormal?

All cultures throughout the world use cosmetics, jewelry, clothes, or other adornments to decorate the body. Unusual techniques of decoration, in comparison to our standards, are practiced by the Tchikrin, a little known group of people from the central Brazilian wilderness. Their existence has been threatened by the incursion into the rainforest. Plugs of wood are inserted in their infants' ear lobes. These plugs will eventually be replaced by larger ones to make the holes larger. Dowels are inserted in boys' lower lips. Mothers save the plugs as the children outgrow them and also save the babies' desiccated umbilical cords. At puberty boys are given penis sheaths as a symbol of manhood. They will be given their first lip plugs, which will eventually be replaced by saucer-like plates that are four inches in diameter and will dramatically change the shape of their face. Although both men and women have elaborately painted bodies, potential suitors can identify those girls who have reached the age of marriage by the broad black stripes that have been painted on their thighs, breasts, and upper arms. These girls soon learn that it is intensely sexually stimulating to pluck an eyebrow from their boyfriend's face with their teeth while engaging in sexual foreplay (Turner, 1971).

The practices of the Tchikrin appear unusual, if not bizarre, to us. However, equivalents to these customs exist in our culture. Although the holes made are not as large, ear piercing is common in American women and men. Regardless of how it is done, ear piercing is a form of body desecration. Whereas Tchikrin mothers save their children's outgrown plugs and umbilical cords, American mothers have an affinity for baby teeth and locks of hair. The pride that the Tchikrin youth feels when he is given his first penis sheath at the time of puberty is analogous to the exhilaration that the American male feels when he puts on his athletic supporter for the first time in eighth-grade gym class.

It may sound cruel to make children wear plugs and saucer-like plates that will make their lips beautifully protrude as adults, but, as I can attest, it is no more cruel than making American children wear braces because of an aversion to teeth that are not perfectly aligned. Tchikrin parents have good intentions when they stretch their children's lips. We bend our children's gums and alter the alignment of their teeth. Pity the American child whose teeth are not straight, the same as you would the Tchikrin with a flat lip.

Sexually eligible Tchikrin women are designated by bodies that are painted in stripes. American women also communicate eligibility by dress and decoration. They are likely to attend "singles' nights" and "happy hours" in groups. Absence of wedding rings and subtle non-verbal cues often indicate eligibility of men and women. Single women are also likely to dress in a more conspicuous manner than married women and apply cosmetics (many of which are made from by-products of urine) more heavily. Tattooing, another form of body desecration, is fairly common among American women and men.

The point of all of these examples is that normality and abnormality are culturally determined. What is normal in one culture may not be normal in another. However, when an individual's behavior is clinically evaluated, the criteria for evaluation are traditionally those of the native culture.

We must also consider subcultural differences. Subcultures are groups of people within a society that are characterized by unifying factors such as common customs, values, social status, ethnic or racial background, residence, or religion. The sub-culture is readily identified as a distinct segment of "American" society.

Subcultures coexist within most American cities. Although seldom officially designated, sub-cultural areas can be identified by casual observation. Bridges, streams, and roads often separate them. Significant differences in values and attitudes are common among subcultures. In some, family is clearly defined as an enduring relationship among biological relatives. A strong work ethic exists. Education is a high priority. In others, family is more abstract, and often consists of the present members of the residence, regardless of biological relationship. Work is not highly valued, and education is a low priority. These examples represent extremes. Consider your subculture. How does it affect your likelihood of succeeding in college? Consider the connotative differences between "punk," "biker," "yuppy," and "country." Standards for normality vary among these groups. As we will explain later, the present *Diagnostic and Statistical Manual of Mental Disorders* attempts to recognize subculture in defining abnormality.

By combining the statistical and cultural approaches, it follows that abnormal behavior is that which is infrequently demonstrated within a particular cultural and subcultural setting. The person who demonstrates a multitude of abnormal behaviors which are inconsistent with his culture and subculture, is more likely to be considered abnormal. Of critical importance is the cultural context in which the person is being evaluated.

Figure 2-8.
A radio-recorder enables this Kayapo Indian of the Brazilian Amazon to tape tribal songs. Outside infiltration occurred with the discovery of gold. The very existence of the Kayapo is threatened. (Photograph by Miguel Rio Branco, Magnum Photos.)

SUCCESS AND NORMALITY

The success of an individual can often be an important factor in determining society's perception of the acceptability of behavior. Two people may behave in a very similar manner, but the interpretation may be a function of the success of each. The adage that rich people who behave unusually are eccentric, whereas poor people who behave in the same manner are just plain crazy, bears truth. The wealthy may dabble in a variety of business endeavors and be considered diversified entrepreneurs. The less affluent, who work a second job, "hustle" and "moonlight."

Money Talks

Success can be defined in a variety of ways, but some likely elements of it are fame, wealth, popularity, personal satisfaction, and expertise in some area. Howard Hughes, an American billionaire who died in 1976, is a prime example of an individual whose unusual behavior was largely excused as eccentricity. At the age of twenty, Hughes was earning an annual income of two million dollars. He later became famous for the transcontinental and around-the-world flying records he set in the 1930s. He was a successful motion picture producer, aircraft manufacturer, and real estate investor. He had affairs with many of Hollywood's most beautiful actresses. Throughout his life there were some very abnormal aspects of his behavior. However, at the peak of his fame, nonoffensive words like shy, reticent, and secretive were used to describe Hughes (Current Biography, 1941). Reclusive, asocial, and bizarre might have been used to describe someone not as successful as Hughes.

On April 19, 1976, shortly after Hughes' death, Time reported that for the last ten years of his life, Hughes lived as a recluse in a twentieth floor penthouse in Acapulco, Mexico. He was sheltered from the light of day by black curtains sealed with masking tape around the windows of the one room in which he spent most of his time. The room included a glass partition to protect him from germ contamination from his servants. He often ate only cakes that were measured with a ruler to make certain they were perfectly square. One of the world's richest men was malnourished.

He refused to cut his hair or fingernails, would not allow removal of hypodermic needle fragments that were broken off in his arms, stored his urine, and scooped up flaking skin that fell from his emaciated body (Nash, 1982, pp. 190-191).

An Associated Press story of June 14, 1978, describing the legal proceedings for the determination of Hughes' estate, reported that "Hughes' condition in these last years of his life resembled that of a chronic psychotic patient in the very worst of mental hospitals." A patient in any mental hospital in the country who showed behavior as "aberrant and as regressed as Hughes would be classified as psychotic." It is interesting that it was only after his death that words such as psychotic were used to describe him. Perhaps there was no longer the fear of reprisal from a powerful, vindictive Howard Hughes.

Ray Kroc, founder of the multi-billion dollar McDonald's fast-food empire, was admired by the business community for his innovative genius. Starting with a single restaurant in Des Plaines, Illinois in 1955, he built the multinational giant of today. Throughout his life, Kroc was very impulsive and seemingly irrational. He was an alcoholic. Kroc was selling milk shake mixers when he was impressed by an efficiently run hamburger stand operated by Maurice and Richard McDonald. The purchase price for the franchise was 2.7 million dollars. Kroc borrowed the money at exorbitant interest rates that forced him to repay 14 million dollars. Although his was not the typical business loan, Kroc's impulsive gamble worked.

In 1974 Kroc bought the San Diego Padres. The team had been doing poorly and attendance was sagging. Thanks to an aggressive promotion campaign that included the famous San Diego Chicken, attendance soared. However, the poor play of the Padres continued. When he became frustrated and dismayed over his team's performance, Kroc would chastise his team and apologize to the fans over the stadium's public address system. When his team was not a success on the field, the fans began to question his state of mind.

Figure 2-9. Mark Fidrych lectures the baseball prior to pitching. (Sports Illustrated/J. Iacona.)

Fleeting Fame

Mark "The Bird" Fidrych was a baseball pitcher for the Detroit Tigers during the late 1970s. He was the American League rookie of the year in 1976. When pitching, he would often kneel on his hands and knees and would pat the dirt on the mound. He would talk to the ball and give it instructions. He would talk to himself. He was idolized by the fans who perceived him as a genius who could "psyche out" the opposing batters. Typically the games would be attended by 5,000 fans, however when "The Bird" pitched, 50,000 would attend. Then Fidrych suffered an arm injury and was sent to the minors.

Fans then came to ridicule him. Apparently the difference between genius and insanity for "The Bird" was a few miles per hour on his fast ball. In 1989, The Associated Press reported that Fidrych was a turkey farmer in Lexington, Massachusetts, and pitched for the Marlboro Orioles of the Musial League. In his first start in seven years, the dozen fans marveled as he began his trademark one-sided conversation with a baseball.

The distinction between genius and insanity may be a fine one. The artist is capable of transforming his creative idea into a musical, literary, or physical work of art. The madman, lacking such talent, is merely perceived as hallucinating.

QUALITIES OF NORMALITY

The cultural and success approaches both stress the importance of society's interpretation of behavior. Let us now look at some qualities of normality from the individual's point of view. People desire to be happy. Personal satisfaction with one's behavior is an important determinant of normality. By personal satisfaction I do not mean that the person is always pleased with his behavior and the way that his life is going. Being normal does not mean being perfect. Normal people have financial, employment, marital, and health problems. Despite these everyday problems, the normal person is generally satisfied and content with life.

Normal people are able to experience pleasure. The inability to experience pleasure is called anhedonia, or melancholia. It is common in people with mental disorders. Although media stereotypes often characterize people with disorders as being in a blissful world of their own, such is typically not the case. They are in a perpetual state of subjective distress.

Normal people are generally in control of their behavior and emotions. They can decide whether and how to act in a given situation. Their behavior is intentional and goal directed, and they can successfully execute a daily plan. Despite personal difficulties, they are able to control their emotions so that they can function in a normal routine. People with disorders often are unable to control their behavior. They frequently act impulsively. They often fail to act. They may be too sad or agitated to function in social settings. Their lives lack predictability and the exercise of voluntary control.

Normal people are flexible. Flexibility may well be the key to survival in our modern society. It is a less than perfect world, and life is often unfair. Bad things happen to reasonable people at inopportune times. Normal people accept these axioms and can adapt to changing or unexpected situations. If plan "A" fails, they undertake plan "B." Many people with mental disorders are very rigid. They have inflexible perceptions about their lives. They have difficulty coping when things happen contrary to plan. Their rigidity causes them much anxiety. Anxiety is a symptom of many disorders.

Ultimately, the normal person is able to function in a daily manner that is acceptable to him. He is generally satisfied, but not without problems.

We have now distinguished normal behavior from abnormal. But what does all this have to do with the individual? At what point does a person's condition become sufficiently abnormal to warrant professional attention? At what point should a person be placed in a mental institution, perhaps against his will? Once again, these are complex issues that warrant closer examination. Professional attention is given to people for a variety of reasons. Most people voluntarily seek help. They realize that they are neither content nor functioning acceptably. They periodically visit their psychologist or psychiatrist as outpatients. Others become patients in private or state mental hospitals. Most patients return to the community, and hopefully receive adequate follow-up care.

People become patients in mental hospitals in a variety of ways. Before describing them, the structure of the staff in a mental hospital should be explained.

Mental Hospital Staff

Psychiatrists typically make the most important treatment decisions. They are medical doctors with additional training in psychology. They can prescribe drugs and perform other medical treatments in addition to psychotherapy. Psychologists have graduate training in psychology and typically have Ph.D.'s. They cannot prescribe medication or perform other medical treatments, but they have thorough training in psychotherapy, personality theory, and psychological testing. Psychiatric social workers have contact with the patient and his family and may perform psychotherapy. Psychiatric nurses have the responsibility for direct patient care. Psychiatric aides assist the patients in their daily routine and have the most direct contact.

How Do People Become Patients in Mental Hospitals?

Voluntary admission occurs when the patient appears at the hospital and requests treatment. He will sign papers to make his request official. He may leave when he wishes. Members of the staff, of course, request being informed of the patient's intent to leave, and they may inform the patient that he is leaving against medical advice. However, he is free to leave. If a patient is being committed, he is compelled to enter the hospital. He must remain there for a specified time. He may stay there as little as three days or indefinitely. The person may be committed by court order or by the directive of physicians. (Interestingly, the physicians need not be psychiatrists). Historically, patients have been more likely to be committed to state hospitals than to private ones. The staffs at private mental hospitals often pride themselves on the fact that their patients are admitted, not committed, to their hospitals. However, as the number of state hospital beds declined, the care of patients is often contracted to private hospitals.

The number of patients who are involuntarily committed to mental hospitals in the United States has declined dramatically in the past four decades since the implementation of deinstitutionalization. In 1955 there were 558,000 patients in American mental hospitals. In 1990 there were 98,400. The nation's population has increased by roughly 85 million people since 1955, when 339 of every 100,000 Americans resided in a state mental hospital. Today, it is only 41 per 100,000. It has become increasingly more difficult to receive institutional care (Bachrach, 1992).

When Does Someone Need Professional Help?

People enter mental hospitals under a variety of circumstances. Generally, people do not desire hospitalization as long as they are reasonably satisfied with their behavior, thoughts, emotions, and everyday life. The most important factors in making a decision to commit are the degree of the person's subjective distress and the likelihood he will bring harm to self or others. Many people are not satisfied with their lives and voluntarily seek inpatient treatment. Clinicians must also assess the likelihood that the person will bring harm to himself or others. It is very difficult to determine one's potential for harmful behavior. However, prior injurious behavior best predicts future. For example, half of completed suicides have made prior attempts.

There are many clear-cut instances of individuals who demonstrated a threat to the safety of others. For example, John W. Hinckley, Jr., was committed indefinitely to a mental hospital following the jury's verdict of not guilty by reason of insanity for his attempted assassination of President Reagan on March 30, 1981. Others are convicted of their crimes and sentenced to prison. Charles Manson (cult murderer of pregnant actress Sharon Tate), Kenneth Bianchi ("Hillside Strangler"), and Mark Chapman (killer of John Lennon) were judged to represent a threat to society and separated from it by imprisonment. Their personal satisfaction was irrelevant.

Other instances are not so clear-cut. An important issue involves the extent to which the state has the right to protect an individual from potential harm to himself. On September 29, 1975, Newsweek reported the classic case of Robert Friedman. Friedman was arrested for begging near a city bus station. Questioning of Friedman revealed that he was carrying $24,087 in small bills in his attache case. With the support of Friedman's family, a judge signed a commitment order that placed him in Chicago-Read Mental Center for an indefinite period. Although Friedman was content with his actions and did not represent a threat to others, it was apparently felt that it was not in his best interest to roam the streets of Chicago carrying many thousands of dollars in small bills. Such commitments demonstrate the "thank you" proposition, which assumes a presently disturbed person will later be thankful he was committed. Chicago authorities were severely criticized. However, had he been allowed to remain free and been either robbed or murdered, there would have also been strong criticism. "Didn't anyone care about this sick individual?" might have been the public outcry. Obviously, these are difficult decisions. Ironically, because Friedman was not poor, he was charged top rates for his care. Upon his release, most of his savings were required to pay for his treatment.

Unless an individual publicly demonstrates his potential for harm or bizarre behavior, the responsibility for initiating commitment proceedings typically rests with the family or close associates. Seldom do authorities intervene without invitation. This is particularly true in cases of substance abuse and domestic violence. The likelihood of intervention is a function of the family's tolerance. Family members are often reluctant to bring the problem to the attention of the authorities, and often wait until the situation can no longer be tolerated. Often, they wait too long.

Forensic Psychology

Forensics is the study, or practice, of formal debate or argumentation. Forensic psychology is the involvement of psychology in the criminal justice process and system. A person's mental condition is often germane in determining a legal decision. Forensic psychologists provide psychological evidence and interpretation relevant to the making of important judicial decisions.

In 1992, Jeffrey Dahmer pleaded guilty and insane for the murders of 15 young men and boys in Milwaukee, Wisconsin. His apartment was crammed with the remains of his victims. He had dismembered them, and preserved, froze, cooked, and consumed the remains. A jury judged him to be sane. "How could a man who could commit such heinous acts be judged as sane? He must surely be sick," reacted many stunned Americans. In the course of the following discussion we will examine factors involved in rendering this decision, as well as in other notorious cases.

Mental illness is a psychological concept. Generally, it is a term that is used to describe any of a multitude of mental disorders included in the *Diagnostic and Statistical Manual of Mental Disorders.* Insanity is a legal concept. It signifies a degree of mental unsoundness or pathology sufficient to render a person legally not responsible for acts he has committed. Mental illness is diagnosed and treated by psychologists and psychiatrists. Insanity is typically determined by a jury in a court of law. Psychological evidence is employed in making this determination.

Obviously, what constitutes insanity is subject to debate. Although standards change with time, and vary across jurisdictions, there are essentially four conditions which could result in a judgement of insanity. They are:

1. *The inability to appreciate the wrongful nature of the act.*

   In 1843 Daniel M'Naghten killed an official of the English government. He believed he was being commanded by God, and saw nothing wrong with what he had done. Thus, he was judged insane because he was "laboring under such a defect of reason, from disease of the mind, as not to know the nature and quality of the act he was doing . . ." (Melton, et.al, 1987, p.115).

   In general, people who do not appreciate the wrongful nature of an act do not deny it. They do not evade detection nor attempt to conceal or destroy evidence.

2. *Acting upon an irresistible impulse.*

   This criterion states that a person who is compelled by an irresistible impulse may not be responsible for an act, even if he appreciated its wrongful nature. The impulse is judged to be so obligatory it renders the individual unable to control or conform his actions to the laws

Figure 2-10.

Above: The profiling staff of the Behavioral Science Unit at the Federal Bureau of Investigation Academy, Quantico, Virginia, in 1983. Roy Hazelwood, now retired, stands at the top left. (Photograph by Terry Arc.)

Left: Jeffrey Dahmer. Hazelwood said he was so bizarre he was diagnostically "unclassifiable." (AP photograph.).

of society. Typically, acts compelled by an irresistible impulse are spontaneous. They are singular acts in which prior planning is absent, and consequences are not contemplated.

3. *Cannot understand charges against him.*

A person may be judged insane if by virtue of a "mental disease or defect" he is unable to comprehend the nature of the crime with which he is charged, does not understand the judicial process, or cannot contemplate consequences, like imprisonment, if convicted.

This determination might apply in cases of severe mental retardation, brain disease or injury, or in psychotic individuals who are out of contact with reality.

4. *Cannot assist in his own defense.*

This determination results when a person is judged to be incompetent to defend himself in a court of law. Although trials are adversarial by nature, they are intended to be fair.

Again, retarded or psychotic individuals lack the capacity to participate in the judicial procedure and testify in a manner that is in their best interest. Depressed, despondent, or distraught individuals may lack the desire and tenacity to adequately defend themselves.

Let us now examine more closely the decision that Jeffrey Dahmer was sane. First of all, Dahmer knew right from wrong. The Associated Press reported that he had been questioned by police at least four times, and skillfully evaded detection. Incredibly, police saw a bleeding, naked 14 year old boy with Dahmer outside his apartment. Dahmer convinced the police the boy was his drunken lover. He was left in Dahmer's care and was later killed. He primarily chose victims without cars, as disposal of vehicles presented a problem. He disposed of body parts by soaking them in acid, which enabled him to flush the evidence down the toilet.

Dahmer was not controlled by irresistible impulse. He worked in a chocolate factory during the week, and only killed on weekends when he could savor the killings. He used condoms when having sex with the corpses, demonstrating a degree of control.

Although emotionally reserved and surprisingly calm throughout his trial, he understood the charges against him and was capable of assisting in his defense. The evidence showed he failed the aforementioned tests for insanity. Certainly, the behavior was abhorrent. However, legally he was sane. Dahmer was beaten to death by another inmate at the Columbia Correctional Institute in Portage, Wisconsin in November of 1994. He had recently returned to the main body of the prison population after having been kept in protective custody.

In 1990, Delbert Ward was accused of smothering his 64 year old ailing brother, William, while he slept. The Ward family lived on a dilapidated farm in rural Munnsville, New York, and were described by the police and other officials as the ultimate "hillbillies." The family was described as outcasts in their own community, and some residents would shy away from them in a diner because of the odor (Kover, 1992). As portrayed in the 1992 film, "Brother's Keeper," Delbert was semi-literate, unkempt, and void of interpersonal skills. However, when charges of murder were brought against him, the community rallied to his defense.

Citing a rural practice of killing sick or diseased animals, his defense argued that if Delbert killed William, it was from compassion for his languishing brother. Of critical importance was whether Delbert appreciated the wrongful nature of his alleged act. During the trial, he was asked if he knew the difference between the truth and a lie. His vague, and perhaps clever, response was, "Maybe. Maybe not." He was acquitted.

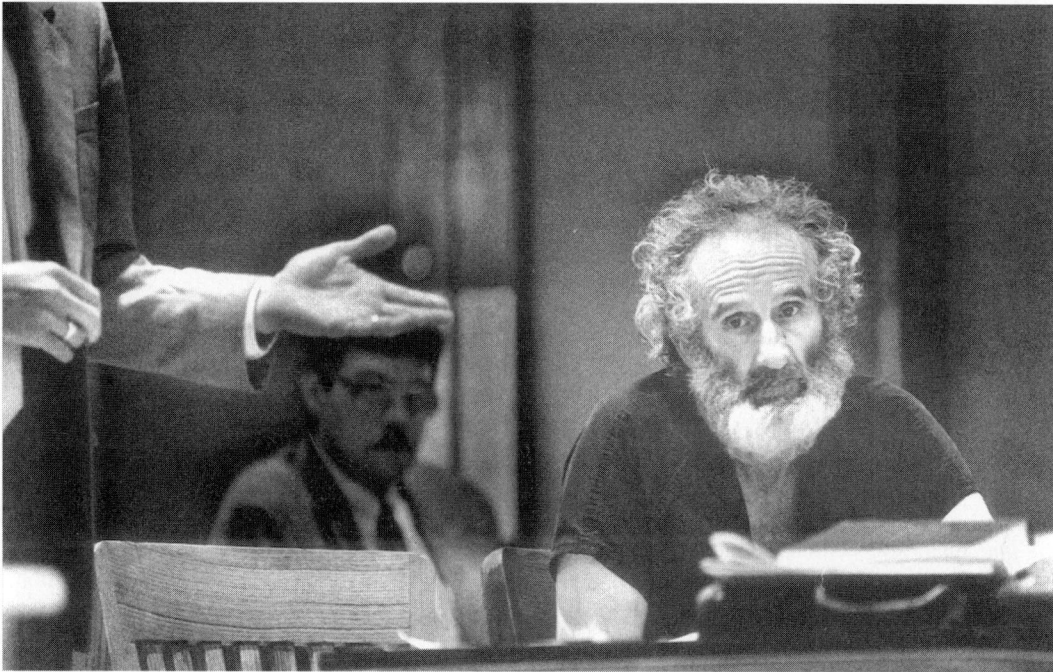

Figure 2-11. Delbert Ward sits before a jury as his lawyer pleads his defense. (Observer/Dispatch.)

In 1993, in a case of national notoriety, Lorena Bobbitt cut off her husband John's penis. She claimed her husband was abusive and violent, and that he had raped her prior to the mutilation. John Bobbitt was acquitted on charges of marital sexual assault. Lorena Bobbitt was acquitted by a jury that found her temporarily insane, and was temporarily committed to a mental hospital (Associated Press, Jan. 22, 1994). Apparently, the jury felt she acted on an irresistible impulse under extreme physical and psychological duress. There was no past history of similar behavior, and recurrence was unlikely. John Bobbitt spent fifteen days in jail in the Fall of 1994 for hitting another woman.

In May of 1993, a jury ruled that 15 year old April Dell'Olio, was not criminally responsible for killing her 17 year old boyfriend, David Eccleston, because she had a mental defect and diminished mental capacity. She was sentenced to five years of weekly outpatient psychotherapy. Dell'Olio had admitted she had stabbed Eccelston 23 times near New Berlin High School because Eccelston taunted her about affairs he was having with her classmates.

Chenango County Judge Kevin M. Dowd apologized to the mother of the slain student saying, "Never in my entire legal career have I had a case which had more disturbing overtones than this one. A young man is dead, and basically I am hamstrung on the situation where I have to treat it like the psychological equivalent of, 'April had a bad hair day on October 20, 1992.'" (Associated Press, Dec. 5, 1993).

In 1975 in rural Missouri, Bobby Shaw shot and killed his good friend Calvin Morris. While imprisoned at Missouri's Potosi Correctional Center, he fatally stabbed a prison guard in 1978. He was sentenced to be executed by lethal injection on June 9, 1993.

Shaw had been described as psychotic, schizophrenic, retarded, and brain damaged since childhood. His family and prison associates dismissed his reports of "people" in his room and cell. He stated, "voices" had ordered him to commit the killings, as well as other acts of violence. Regardless, an insanity plea had not been considered.

In December of 1992, Shaw's pro bono lawyer, Sean O'Brien, was concerned that Shaw was insane, and should not be executed. Malingers will often feign psychotic symptoms, like hallucinations, to create an impression of insanity. In Shakespeare's Hamlet, Hamlet is on trial for the murder of Polonius. Of Hamlet, who had been depressed and hallucinating when the murder occurred, it was said, "Though this be madness, yet there is method in it." True schizophrenics often try to hide their symptoms to avoid ridicule. Georgetown neurologist, Jonathan Pincus, was called in to interview Shaw. On June 7, 1993, Time reported Pincus' deft interview with Shaw:

> "Do you have hallucinations?" asked Pincus.
> "No," said Shaw.
> "Do you hear things that aren't there?"
> "No."
> Pincus, talking in a gentle, take-your-time manner, shifted to other
> questions. Then he asked,
> "Do you hear things that are there, but other people don't hear?"
> "Well...yeah," said Shaw.

This interview, combined with tests that revealed brain damage from childhood abuse, convinced Pincus that Shaw was insane, and should not be executed. Just prior to his scheduled execution, Missouri Governor Mel Carnahan commuted Shaw's death sentence to life imprisonment, citing that "Shaw suffers from varying degrees of mental illness," a fact left out of his trial (*Time*, June 14, 1993).

The previous cases demonstrate how insanity can be a mitigating factor in criminal cases. Public perception is often that insanity pleas can be successfully used by sane and guilty individuals to avoid prosecution. However, only 10 percent of serial and mass killers, and 1 percent of felony defendants, employ insanity pleas. Only a third are successful (*Newsweek*, February 3, 1992).

As we have seen, forensic aspects of criminal cases can be very complex and controversial. Consider this issue. A sane person has been found guilty of murder and sentenced to death. While awaiting execution, he develops mental disorders sufficient for him to be judged incompetent to be executed. Should this person be given treatment that would help him regain competency for execution? A debate on this issue concluded that treating incompetent prisoners is ethical if the patient consents to the treatment (Heilbrun, et al, 1992, pp. 596-605). Some interesting questions emerge. Would a sane malingerer consent to treatment that would make him well enough to be executed? Is a person who is judged incompetent for execution capable of providing "informed consent" for treatment?

We have closely examined the concept of normality from a variety of perspectives, its history, and forensic issues. How normality and abnormality compare should have more specific meaning for you. We are now ready to describe specific mental disorders.

REFERENCES

Bachrach PhD, L.L. (1992, May). What We Know About Homelessness Among Mentally Ill Persons: An Analytical Review and Commentary. *Hospital and Community Psychiatry*, 43(5).

Block, M., (ed.) (1941) *Current Biography: Who's Who and Why*. New York: The H.W. Wilson Company.

Bootzin, R.R., et.al, (1993) *Abnormal Psychology: Current Perspectives*. New York:McGraw-Hill, Inc.

Caporael, L.R. (1976) Ergotism: The Satan Loosed in Salem? *Science*, Vol. 192, 21-26.

Deutsch, A. (1949) *The Mentally Ill In America* - 2nd Ed. New York: Columbia University Press.

Ferres, J.H., (ed.) (1972) *Twentieth Century Interpretations of the Crucible*. New York:Prentice-Hall, Inc.

Halgin, R.P., and Whitbourne, S.K. (1993) *Abnormal Psychology: The Human Experience of Psychological Disorders*. Fort Worth: Harcourt Brace Javanovich College Publishers.

Hall, M.H., (1967, September) An Interview With "Mr. Humanist," Rollo May. *Psychology Today.*

Hall, S.S. (1991, Mar/Apr). *Journey Out Of Time.* Health.

Heilbrun, K., et.al. (1992, May). The Debate on Treating Individuals Incompetent for Execution. *American Journal of Psychiatry*, 149(5).

Herzberg, M.J. (1928) *Myths and Their Meaning.* New York:Allyn and Bacon.

Jackson, D.D. (1989, February) Searching For Medicinal Wealth In Amazonia. *Smithsonian.*

Kaplan, H.I. and Sadock, B.J., (eds.) (1985) *Comprehensive Textbook of Psychiatry/IV*, 1, (4th ed.). Baltimore: Williams & Wilkins.

Kovar, J. (1992, November 20) Brother's Keeper: Documentary on Delbert Ward Murder Trail Premieres. *Observer-Dispatch* Utica, New York, 1B.

Mead, M. (1963) *Sex and Temperament in Three Primitive Societies.* New York: Dell Publishing Company, Inc.

Nash, J.R. (1982) Zanies: *The World's Greatest Eccentrics.* New Jersey: New Century Publishers, Inc.

Queen and Habenstein, (1974) *The Family in Various Cultures.* Philadelphia: B. Lippencott Company.

Roscoe, W., (ed.) (1988) *Living the Spirit.* New York: St. Martin's Press.

Turner, T.S. (1969, October) Tchikrin: A Central Brazilian Tribe and Its Symbolic Language of Bodily Adornment. *Natural History,* 50-59, 70.

Walsh, R. (1994, Summer) The Making of a Shaman: Calling, Training, and Culmination. *Journal of Humanistic Psychology*, 34(3). Sage Publications, Inc.

Woodside, M. and McClam, T. (1994) *An Introduction to Human Services* - 2nd ed. California: Brooks/Cole Publishing Company.

Zilboorg, G. and Henry, G.W. (1941) *A History of Medical Psychology.* New York: Norton.

The 1994 Information Please Almanac. (1994) Boston and New York: Houghton Mifflin Company, 3.

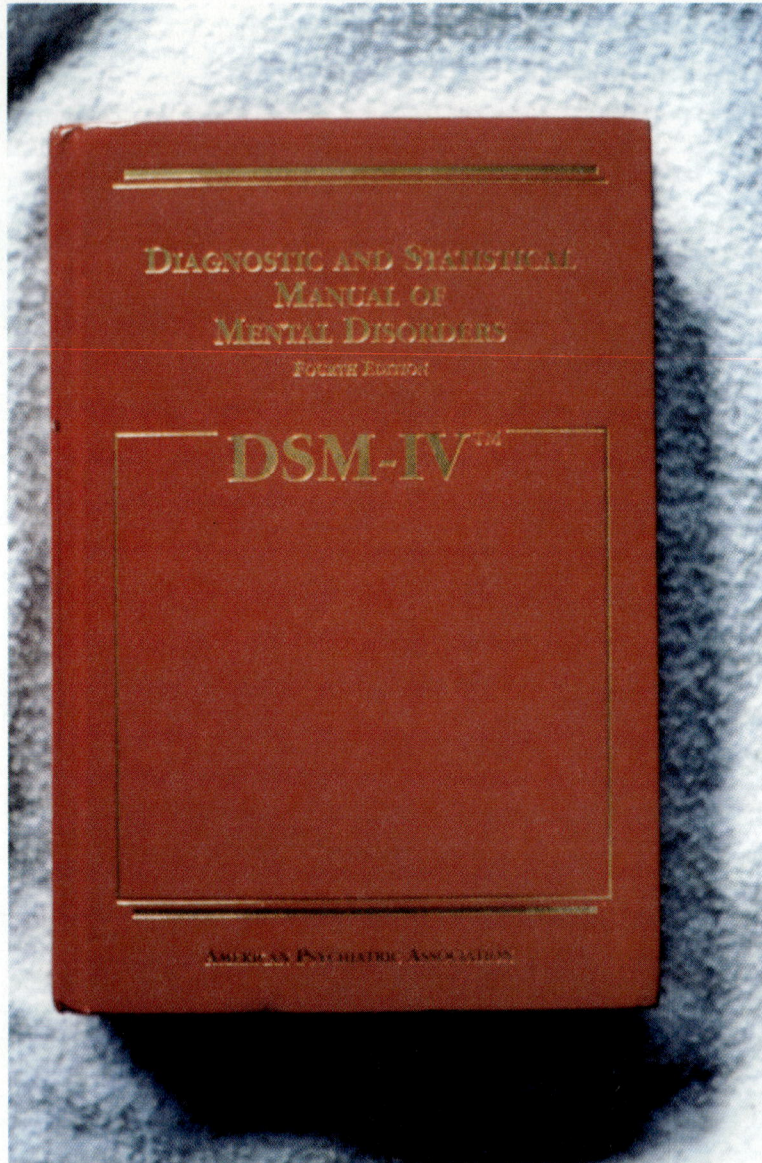

Diagnostic and Statistical Manual of Mental Disorders, Fourth Edition, 1994. (Photograph by Jim Rooney.)

Chapter 3

THE DIAGNOSTIC MANUAL OF MENTAL DISORDERS

El Nino, Spanish for the child, is a climatic condition which results from abnormal warming of the Pacific Ocean off the coast of South America. The warming usually occurs around Christmas, and causes the diversion of major weather patterns. Deserts receive torrential rain; jungles are parched. Such was the case in January, 1995. Parts of usually arid California were deluged with twenty inches of rain. Temperatures in the usually frigid Adirondack mountains of New York State were at times one hundred degrees higher than the previous year. When meterologist Dr. Jerome Namias was asked about predicting the next El Nino following the one of 1983, he said, "Weather is always abnormal. . . . Perhaps the only thing more complex is human behavior itself." (Canby, 1983.) Our task is even more arduous, as we attempt to develop a sense of understanding, order, and predictability regarding *abnormal* human behavior.

However, there is often a degree of predictability and order in the most disturbed of minds. Logically, serial killers, who wish to avoid detection, should not visit the scene of the crime, nor seek contact with the families of their victims. However, they often do. Wayne Williams, convicted Atlanta child murderer, and Arthur Shawcross, who murdered eleven women in Rochester, New York, became suspects when found at points where bodies were discovered. David Meirhofer, who kept body parts of his victims frozen and labeled "Dear Meat," called to taunt one of his victim's parents on the anniversary of her abduction. The conversation was recorded, and ultimately lead to his apprehension.

Oliver Zink, former FBI agent, collected data for profiles of serial killers used by the FBI's National Center for the Analysis of Violent Crime, centered at Quantico, Virginia, and popularized in the film *Silence of the Lambs*. At a conference, he graphically described the profile of the serial killer. I asked him if disseminating such information at a public forum could be used by a serial killer to avoid detection. He smiled and said, "I used to worry about that, but you see it doesn't matter. They're going to do it anyway. They can't help it." Such is the order sought.

Human behavior is a variable phenomenon. It does not lend itself easily to clear-cut diagnostic classification. It is presumptuous to hope that human behavior can be neatly and easily plugged into precise diagnostic categories, which are mutually exclusive, and yet encompass all forms of psychopathology. Psychology is challenged by the variable, abstract nature of human behavior. Other sciences do not have such a complex problem. A chemist may analyze a particular compound and definitely classify it based upon its characteristics. He may examine a tasteless, colorless, odorless liquid and discover that this compound is composed of two parts hydrogen and one part oxygen. He may also discover that this compound can exist as a solid and as a gas. He will determine that this compound is water. He will also know that any other compound that has the same characteristics and composition must also be water. This method of analysis does not work as well with human behavior. Although the classification of the mental disorders is a difficult task, it has been undertaken by clinical psychology and psychiatry.

Our society is in a continual state of change. The mental health field must keep pace. As times change, so must our perception and description of the mental disorders. New research continually indicates the need to reexamine the classification system. Because of new findings and cultural change, some categories outlive their usefulness. New classifications are created as the situation dictates. Some advocacy groups argue that certain symptoms warrant the addition of a new disorder to the classification system; others advocate the exclusion of some that exist. Although helping people with their mental disorders is the main concern of all mental health professionals, psychiatrists, psychologists, and social workers often have separate professional interests that lead to disagreement in the classification of abnormal behaviors. For all these reasons, it is not surprising that the classification of abnormal behavior is a difficult task.

The American Psychiatric Association is composed of medical doctors who treat mental disorders. With assistance from psychologists and social workers, it produces the official document for the classification and diagnosis of mental disorders in the United States. This document is called the Diagnostic and Statistical Manual of Mental Disorders. It is intended to be compatible with the mental disorders section of the International Classification of Diseases, published by the World Health Organization.

The first edition of the Diagnostic and Statistical Manual of Mental Disorders, DSM-I, appeared in 1952. It was replaced by DSM-II in 1968. In 1974, the American Psychiatric Association began work on DSM-III. It was felt that DSM-II provided insufficient information to make accurate diagnoses. It was also felt that it was too heavily based upon Freudian theory. DSM-III was published in 1980.

The work to revise DSM-III began in 1983. The Diagnostic and Statistical Manual of Mental Disorders (Third Edition-Revised), or DSM—III-R, was published in 1987. In the introduction to DSM—III-R, Robert Spitzer, chairman of the work group to revise DSM-III, stated that DSM—III was " . . . one still frame in the ongoing process of attempting to better understand mental disorders DSM-III—R represents another still frame" (DSM-III-R, 1987, pp. xvii-xx).

The "ongoing process" continued. Work began on DSM-IV in 1988. Major goals of the Diagnostic Manual are: to make clinical treatment and management decisions consistent, based upon reliable diagnostic categories; to be acceptable to clinicians and researchers of the various perspectives; and to be useful in educating health professionals. These are very ambitious goals. DSM—IV was scheduled to be published in 1992. Because of the monumental task of collecting and analyzing the research, and disagreement and controversy among the authors and their constituencies, publication was delayed. Preliminary drafts were published for scrutiny and reaction in 1991 and 1993. DSM—IV was finally published in the Spring of 1994.

Political Controversy Over the DSM

The American Psychiatric Association estimates that forty million Americans suffer from some form of mental illness each year, and that the direct cost of treating all mental disorders was sixty-seven billion dollars in 1990. The Diagnostic and Statistical Manual is used to differentiate the different forms of mental disorders, and is a tremendously difficult document to compose. As mentioned, to differentiate something as nebulous as abnormal human behavior into distinct diagnostic categories is an ambitious task. Ultimately, the composition of the DSM is a political process, and the result is a political document. The diagnosis of mental disorders is based upon symptoms that are behavioral, emotional, or cognitive in nature. The American Psychiatric Association votes on which behaviors, emotions, or thoughts represent mental disorders and, therefore, warrant treatment. Physical medicine often has diagnostic tests that can definitely diagnose a disease. An X-ray can be used to determine whether a bone is broken. There is little need to vote on whether physicians should treat broken bones. In psychiatry there are few definite diagnostic tests, and diagnoses are based on behavioral, emotional, and cognitive symptoms. The mental health professionals vote on what constitutes a disorder.

The political aspects of the composition of the DSM are very complex. Because the American Psychiatric Association publishes the document, nonmedical mental health practitioners fear a DSM that is tied too closely to the medical model If the causes of mental disorders are assumed to be medical or biological, they would require medical treatments. Psychiatry has typically resisted attempts by psychologists to gain hospital privileges and prescribe medication. Said Win Schacter, Executive Director of the California Psychological Association, regarding psychiatry's effort to block hospital privileges for psychologists in California, psychiatry's behavior "acts to serve as a declaration of war, and psychology will proceed accordingly" (quoted in DeAngelis, 1992, p. 22). Psychologists are concerned that a DSM built around the medical model could lessen the demand for nonmedical practitioners. They, therefore, desire a more behavior-oriented document.

In the eyes of others, psychiatry has attempted to take under its wing the treatment of certain disorders that have traditionally been the provinces of other disciplines. Learning and language disabilities have been traditionally dealt with by nonmedical educational specialists such as school psychologists, special education teachers, speech pathologists, and audiologists. Problems in academic skills such as speech, reading, mathematics, and writing are considered mental disorders. Psychiatrists are therefore eligible to treat these disorders and receive third-party insurance payments, which are typically more difficult for nonmedical specialists to receive. The competence of psychiatrists in these areas, whose training is largely medical, has been questioned by those specifically trained in these skill areas. In brief, nonmedical specialists are suspicious of a "power play" by psychiatrists to describe mental disorders in a way that best suits the economic interest of their profession.

Specific lobbies have exerted their influence on the DSM. In DSM—I (1952), homosexuality was considered a type of "pathologic sexuality." Because of the efforts of the gay rights lobby, DSM—II (1968), considered homosexuality a "sexual-orientation disturbance." In DSM—III (1980), one type of homosexuality remained. It was called ego-dystonic homosexuality, and described a sustained pattern of homosexual arousal that is unwanted and a source of distress. This category was eliminated from DSM—III-R (1987). It was argued that people are distressed by many personal characteristics, like nose shape and size, but such discomfort does not constitute a disorder. Homosexuality is no longer considered a disorder. Furthermore, if a person is afraid of homosexuals, he could be considered homophobic. These are indications of cultural and political change.

Feminists had been in general agreement regarding many DSM—III and DSM—III-R issues. For example, they successfully resisted the inclusion of a proposed disorder for DSM—III-R called paraphilic rapism, which would have described men who compulsively commit rape. Fearing legal defenses built around the disorder, they successfully argued that rape is a crime, and should not be "psychiatrized" as a mental disorder. Also suggested, but not included, was a category to be called marital rape. It would have described sexual assaults perpetrated against spouses. Had this condition been included, it might have been raised by the defense in the previously mentioned case of John Bobbitt.

However, feminists have been divided since the mid-1980s regarding premenstrual syndrome. Some argued that inclusion of the category would legitimize study of the syndrome for research and treatment purposes. Others contended it is a gynecological, not mental condition, and should not be included. Politically concerned feminists argued that "raging hormonal imbalances" would serve as an excuse to discriminate against women (APA *Monitor*, 1986). To strike a compromise in DSM—III-R (1987), the condition was called late luteal phase dysphoric disorder, or "L2D2" by Dr. Thomas A. Widiger, DSM—IV Task Force and Research Coordinator. It was placed in a category at the end of the document called Proposed Diagnostic Categories Needing Further Study.

Continued dissention over the condition contributed to delaying the publishing of DSM—IV until 1994. Ultimately, it was called premenstrual dysphoric disorder, and placed in an Appendix in the back of the book called Criteria Sets and Axes Provided For Further Study. However, it can also be coded as a mood disorder not otherwise specified, found in the mental disorders section of the document. This compromise was intended to appease both feminist factions. At a conference on DSM—IV held in March of 1994, I asked Dr. Widiger if the condition was a mental disorder. "It has 'quasi' official recognition," was his response. The debate continues.

Posttraumatic stress disorder was included as a disorder in DSM—III (1980). It was created largely due to the efforts of the Vietnam Veterans lobby. Prior to this, those with the syndrome had often been treated for substance dependence, schizophrenia, or depression. The veterans argued that it was the trauma of the war that created these conditions. Creation of the category legitimized the syndrome, and stimulated funding for research and treatment.

DSM-II was criticized for being too brief and incomplete. Conversely, DSM—III and DSM-III—R seem to embrace the philosophy that it is better to include a disorder and let further research prove it unnecessary than to fail to include a legitimate disorder. This practice leads to the criticism that the document is overly zealous in considering some very common and minor conditions as disorders. For example, nicotine withdrawal, a substance-related disorder, can be diagnosed when a person has used nicotine for several weeks, ceases abruptly, and becomes irritable, anxious, restless, or depressed. A person who becomes anxious after drinking as little as two cups of coffee, four cups of tea, or six cola drinks can be diagnosed as suffering from caffeine intoxication. Drinking decaffeinated coffee can cure this disorder. A good student who finds herself having trouble studying or writing a term paper can be described as having an adjustment disorder. This disorder seems to reach epidemic levels around final exam period. Returning to New York from California can cause circadian rhythm sleep disorder (jet lag). Children who say "pasghetti" instead of spaghetti, or "aks" instead of ask, may have an expressive language disorder. Normal children, who test poorly in math, may have mathematics disorder.

Using the term "mental illness" to describe just about anything that causes people distress has obvious economic implications for psychiatry. In my "not so wildest" dreams I imagine an enterprising psychiatrist "treating" the wretched coffee drinker, smoker, or college dropout at a posh mountain resort, and then submitting the bills for third-party payment. Many questions posed by clinicians at conferences on new editions of the DSM regard insurance payment for treating disorders.

DSM—IV is nearly nine hundred pages long. It is easy to find something to criticize in any document of this magnitude. The *Diagnostic Manual* is designed to be atheoretical, and not employ the language of, or advocate, any particular perspective. The fact that the document can be used by clinicians with diverse backgrounds, training, and theoretical orientations is definitely to its credit. The advantages and strengths of DSM—IV outweigh its flaws.

What Is Meant by "Neurosis"?

Before we can describe the multiaxial evaluation system and the mental disorders, some further clarification is required. A major diagnostic category of DSM-II was neurosis. The term has a 200 year history and is an integral part of a century-old theory—psychoanalysis. Sigmund Freud devoted much of his career to working with neurotics. He developed his own theory on the origin of neurotic personality. However, the DSM, as mentioned, professes to be atheoretical. It was argued that to continue to use neurosis would give the document a psychoanalytic bias. Thus, neurosis has been virtually eliminated since DSM—III (1980). Obviously, these disorders cannot be eliminated by the executive decree of the American Psychiatric Association. Traditional neurotic disorders have been renamed and reclassified throughout the document. If "a rose by any other name smells as sweet," neurosis by any other name remains equally distressing.

Some of the articles included in this book were written before the elimination of neurosis from the DSM. They discuss and employ the concept of neurosis. Despite its virtual exclusion, neurosis remains a valuable and useful psychological concept. Therefore, it will be described.

Neurosis Versus Psychosis

One way to understand neurotic personality is to compare it to psychotic personality. The concept of psychotic personality is maintained in the present *Diagnostic Manual*. Although the distinction between neurosis and psychosis is not precise, there are some reliable ways to distinguish them.

One dimension of distinction is severity. The overall condition of the neurotic is neither as severe nor as debilitating as that of the psychotic. The neurotic certainly has his share of difficulties, but he can still maintain relationships with others and struggle through life. The psychotic, on the other hand, may cease functioning socially, and may find himself either incapable or disinterested in conducting his daily routine. Despite any difficulties, it is likely that the neurotic will continue to work. The psychotic won't. Whereas the neurotic's overall ability to function is impaired, the psychotic's is virtually destroyed.

Degree of contact with reality is another distinction. Neurotics are generally in touch with reality. Although judgement may be impaired, neurotics have reasonably accurate perceptions of time, place, and identity. They know the correct time of day, day of the week, and month of the year. They realize that their ability to function is impaired. They are aware of their condition. Psychotics, however, are characterized by a break with reality. They may not have accurate perceptions of time, place, or identity. Their perceptions of the world around them are very different from those of normal people. They may not be aware of their impaired condition. Although most psychotics are not always out of touch with reality, episodes of breaking with reality are common in this condition.

The condition of the neurotic is typically more stable than that of the psychotic. The neurotic may exist in his impaired condition for years. He may be able to function relatively normally for extended periods, with episodic aggravation of his condition during periods of stress. There is an element of consistency in the condition of the neurotic. Psychotics frequently undergo abrupt, drastic changes in their condition. They may lose touch with reality for a period of time. At times they may be capable of carrying on meaningful conversation, while at other times they may be incapable. The emotional condition of the psychotic is also likely to be unstable. At times he may be extremely depressed and may cry out loudly. Within a few moments he may be in a state of euphoria. The neurotic may have the long-range goal of getting back in control of his life so that he can be more satisfied. The psychotic may express specific wishes and goals in one breath, and contradict himself in the next. Statements such as, "I have big plans for the future! I love life!" may be immediately followed by, "My life is miserable. I wish I were dead."

Psychotics are more likely to be hospitalized than neurotics. Neurotics typically spend briefer periods in hospitals than psychotics. Since deinstitutionalization during the past few decades, periods of hospitalization have become briefer for both groups. Only the most severely impaired patients spend years in hospitals They typically remain in the hospital because of their inability to care for themselves, lack of attention to personal health and hygiene, and tendency for potentially dangerous behavior, such as the throwing of lit matches into wastebaskets.

Disturbances of the affective domain refer to problems of an emotional nature. Disturbances of the cognitive domain refer to disturbances of logic, thought, and reasoning ability. The neurotic is likely to experience intense, irrational feelings of guilt, anxiety, sadness, or fear. These are impairments of the affective domain. Not only is the psychotic likely to experience these same feelings, but he will also demonstrate cognitive disturbances such as illogical thought, delusions (false beliefs), and defective reasoning. He may have hallucinations in which he has perceptions of sight, sound, touch, taste or odor, despite the absence of stimuli, or illusions, which are faulty perceptual interpretations, such as perceiving the shutting of a door as a gunshot. The neurotic's major impairment is in the affective domain. Psychotics are likely to experience both affective and cognitive impairment.

The Multiaxial Evaluation System

A major improvement that was implemented in DSM—III, and modified slightly in both DSM-III-R and DSM—IV, is the multiaxial evaluation system. An axis is a source of information about a specific aspect of the patient's condition or existence. A complete diagnosis provides information on five axes, each of which provides additional insight into the overall clinical picture. For the skilled clinician, the information contained on each of the axes fits together like the pieces of a puzzle. As each piece is added, the clinical picture becomes increasingly clear. Ultimately, the axes combine to help the clinician plan treatment and predict outcome. A description of the axes follows.

Axis I: Clinical Disorders
Other Conditions That May Be a Focus of Clinical Attention

Axis I includes the specific mental disorder(s) that is (are) the focus of clinical attention and treatment. There are fifteen major categories of Axis I disorders. All have code numbers, which are used for statistical and reimbursement purposes. They are further subdivided into hundreds of clinically distinct diagnostic categories. Those who either ask for, or are recommended for treatment, typically receive at least one Axis I diagnosis.

Certain general assumptions can be made about mental disorders. That one exists is a statement that there is pathology in the way the individual thinks, feels, or acts. These conditions are typically a source of discomfort and distress for the person. For example, a depressed person may become troubled by his suicidal thoughts, and voluntarily seek treatment. Since people with these conditions willingly present for treatment, they are referred to as *presenting* conditions. In other cases, family members, friends, or the authorities may encourage or compel presentation for treatment. Although mental disorders may be long lasting in some cases, they are generally assumed to be temporary. They are also assumed to be treatable, although treatment may bring merely symptomatic relief.

Some common Axis I disorders include schizophrenia, mood disorders, sexual disorders, anxiety disorders, and substance-related disorders. Each disorder is described in great detail in DSM—IV, giving the clinician valuable information about its symptoms, associated features, likely course, prevalence, and complications. Each new edition of the DSM is increasingly more detailed than its predecessor.

Axis II: Personality Disorders
Mental Retardation

Axis II lists personality disorders and mental retardation. In DSM—III-R (1987), developmental disorders, such as mental retardation, speech, language, and reading disorders were coded on Axis II, rather than Axis I, for reasons that were unclear. In DSM—IV (1994), all with the exception of mental retardation are coded on Axis I. Mental retardation remains on Axis II because of insistance by the mental retardation lobby, which wants it to remain distinct.

Personality disorders are deeply ingrained character flaws that are typically evident early in life. "Personality traits are enduring patterns of perceiving, relating to, and thinking about the environment and oneself that are exhibited in a wide range of social and personal contexts. Only when personality traits are inflexible and maladaptive and cause either significant functional impairment or subjective distress do they constitute Personality Disorders" (quoted. in DSM-IV, 1994, p. 630).

General assumptions can be made about personality disorders. Although people with them are distressed and impaired in their ability to function, they seldom perceive their personality disorder as a source of their problems. They will often deny the disorder, and claim there is nothing wrong with them. They are unlikely to perceive the relationship between their personality and the chronic types of problems they experience. If they recognize they have such a disorder, they see nothing wrong with it, because they feel "everyone is like that." They have very poor self-esteem. When compared to people with mental disorders, they are less likely to present for treatment. Whereas mental disorders are assumed to be temporary, personality disorders are chronic and endure inflexibly, and pervasively, across a broad range of personal and social situations. They are stable and of long duration, and onset can be traced to at least adolescence or early adulthood (DSM—IV, 1994, pp. 630-633). They are very resistant to treatment.

Recall the case of Jeffrey Dahmer, judged to be sane and guilty of fifteen murders in Milwaukee. It was decided that he be imprisoned and not treated as he had a severe antisocial personality disorder that could not be helped. Dahmer had said prior to his death in 1994 that he still had violent urges, and would commit further crimes if released.

It is very important for the clinician to know when a patient has a personality disorder. This diagnosis can provide a "blueprint" for understanding the pattern of behavior of the patient. It can help the clinician to understand the types of problems and conflicts that the patient has experienced in the past, and help him to anticipate those likely to occur in the future.

DSM—IV lists ten personality disorders, which are grouped into three clusters based upon common theme. Two examples from each cluster are presented.

Cluster A

Cluster A contains disorders in which people seem odd or eccentric. Paranoid and schizotypal personality disorder are classified in this cluster.

Paranoid personality disorder: must have four or more of the following:
- Expects to be exploited or harmed by others.
- Questions, without justification, the loyalty of friends and relatives.
- Reads threatening meanings into benign remarks.
- Bears grudges and is unforgiving.
- Is reluctant to confide in others.
- Is easily slighted and quick to react with anger.
- Questions, without justification, the fidelity of spouse or sexual partner.
- Perceives character attacks that are not apparent to others, and is quick to angrily counterattack (DSM—IV, 1994, pp. 637-638).

Schizotypal personality disorder: must have five or more of the following:
- Ideas of reference (the feeling that incidents and events have particular and unusual meaning for the person).
- Magical thinking (extreme superstitiousness, belief in clairvoyance, or a "sixth sense").
- Unusual perceptual experiences, like body illusions ("My mind is a computer").
- Odd thinking and speech ("I think my thinking needs to be thunk more").
- Suspicious or paranoid ideas.
- Inappropriate mood (purposeless giggling).
- Behavior, dress, or appearance that is odd, eccentric, or peculiar.
- Virtual social isolate with few contacts beyond first-degree relatives.
- Excessive social anxiety that does not diminish with familiarity (DSM—IV, 1994, p. 645).

Cluster B

Cluster B contains disorders in which people are highly emotional, dramatic, or erratic. Narcissism and antisocial personality disorder are contained in this cluster.

Narcissism: must have five or more of the following:
- Has a grandiose sense of self-importance.
- Is preoccupied with fantasies of unlimited success, brilliance, or ideal love.
- Believes that he or she is "special," and can only be understood by, or associate with other special people.
- Requires excessive admiration, and acts in a way that demands attention (strategically entering a meeting or class seven minutes late).
- Has a sense of entitlement; believes he should be given especially favorable treatment (parks in handicapped spots, occupies multiple parking spaces, and "cuts and skips" waiting lines).
- Is interpersonally exploitive and manipulative.
- Is unwilling, or unable, to recognize the feelings and needs of others.
- Is highly envious and believes others envy him or her.
- Demonstrates arrogant, haughty, behavior and attitude (DSM—IV, 1994, p. 661).

Figure 3-1: Tonya Harding's solicitation of favorable treatment from an Olympic judge demonstrated an attitude of entitlement. (Courtesy of Corbis-Bettman.)

Antisocial personality disorder: must have three or more of the following since age 15, but must be 18 to receive diagnosis:
- Habitual violation of social norms and laws (theft, vandalism, and destruction).
- Deceitfulness, use of aliases, conning for profit and pleasure, and pathological lying, often without purpose.
- Impulsivity without regard for future.
- Irritability and aggressiveness, as indicated by repeated fights or assaults.
- Consistent irresponsibility and failure to honor obligations or commitments.
- Reckless disregard for safety of self or others, as indicated by senseless risk taking.
- Lack, or lack of inclination, of empathy for victims, and absence of guilt or remorse for clear ly antisocial acts (DSM—IV, 1994, pp. 649-650).

Cluster C

Cluster C contains disorders in which people are overly anxious or fearful. Dependent personality disorder and avoidant personality disorder are contained in this cluster.

Dependent personality disorder: must have at least five of the following:

- Cannot make everyday decisions without excessive advice.
- Needs others to make his/her most important decisions.
- Agrees with others because of fear of rejection, or loss of social support.

Figure 3-2. The slanting, sinister eyes of "Patches" betrayed the evil intent of John Wayne Gacy, who used a clown ruse to lure victims during the 1970s in Chicago. Gacy pathologically denied responsibility and showed no remorse. When he was executed, the crowd chanted "Kill the clown!" (Chicago Tribune photograph.)

- Has difficulty doing things alone.
- Does unpleasant or demeaning things to gain acceptance.
- Is very uncomfortable when alone.
- Urgently seeks another relationship for support and care when one ends.
- Unrealistically preoccupied with fears of being left to take care of himself or herself (DSM—IV, 1994, pp. 668-669).

Avoidant personality disorder: must have at least four of the following:
- Avoids activities that involve significant interpersonal contact for fear of criticism or rejection.
- Unwilling to enter a relationship without certainty of being liked.
- Shows restraint in intimate relationships for fear of shame or ridicule.
- Is preoccupied by being criticized or rejected in social situations.
- Feels interpersonally inadequate ("Why ask her out? She won't like me anyway.").
- Views self as socially inept, personally unappealing, or inferior to others.
- Shies from new activities for fear of embarrassment (DSM—IV, 1994, pp. 664-665).

Axis III: General Medical Conditions

Axis III provides information regarding any current general medical conditions that are potentially relevant for understanding and treating the individual. This information can be very useful. In some cases it is evident that a general medical condition is causally related to the development or worsening of mental symptoms. It is understandable that a previously active person, who suffers a serious heart attack and must curtail most of his activities, or a woman who was recently diagnosed with breast cancer, would be vulnerable to depression. A person with an ulcer listed on axis III may have some type of anxiety disorder listed on axis I. If the condition of a person with schizophrenia and diabetes worsens such that hospitalization is necessary, the notation of diabetes on axis III indicates that management of insulin is required.

Among general medical conditions are: infectious and parasitic diseases; diseases of the nervous system and sense organs; diseases of the circulatory, respiratory and digestive systems; injury; and poisoning (DSM—IV, 1994, p. 28).

Figure 3-3: Homeless people, stuck outdoors on the Washington Mall during a blizzard, huddle under blankets atop a heating grate. Homelessness is the extreme of housing problems. (Reuters/Corbis-Bettmann.)

Axis IV: Psychosocial and Environmental Problems

Axis IV provides information regarding psychosocial and environmental problems that may affect the treatment and prognosis of mental disorders. Information on this axis typically describes negative life events which are sources of distress for the individual. Generally, as psychosocial and environmental problems become more severe, the likelihood is greater they will precipitate or exacerbate mental, personality, or developmental disorders. In some cases, the problem serves as a "trigger" for a mental disorder. Agoraphobiacs are reclusive people who fear leaving the relative safety and security of their home. Receiving an eviction notice could conceivably precipitate a panic attack in such an individual.

Psychosocial and environmental problems are grouped in the following categories:

- Problems with primary support group—e.g., distruption of family because of divorce.
- Problems related to the social environment—e.g., adjustment to life-cycle transition, such as retirement.
- Educational problems—e.g., discord with teachers or classmates.
- Occupational problems—e.g., harassment or discrimination in the workplace.
- Housing problems—e.g., discord with neighbors or landlord.
- Economic problems—e.g., poverty.
- Problems with access to health care services—e.g., inadequate health insurance.
- Problems related to interaction with the legal system/crime—e.g., a victim of assault.
- Other psychosocial and environmental problems—e.g., war, epidemic, or natural disaster.

The clinician identifies the relevant psychosocial and environmental problem(s) and indicates the specific factors involved (DSM—IV, 1994, pp. 29-30). However, there is no mechanism to rate the severity of the problem, as was the case in DSM—III-R. It employed a six-point scale ranging from none to catastrophic to rate the perceived impact of the stressor on the individual. For example, having to move because of a company relocation could either be anticipated and welcome, or a source of considerable distress.

Axis V: Global Assessment of Functioning

Axis V, the Global Assessment of Functioning Scale (GAF), provides a judgement of the patient's overall functioning level (psychological, social, and occupational) at the time of the assessment. This axis is useful in planning treatment, measuring its impact, and making a prognosis. The following is a brief description of the scale:

Code	Description
100	Superior functioning in a wide range of activities. No symptoms and the person is sought by others because of his/her positive qualities.
90	Absent or minimal symptoms, active social and occupational functioning.
70	Some mild symptoms, but generally functioning fairly well.
50	Serious symptoms and serious impairment of function (inability to keep a job or maintain relationships).
30	Behavior is influenced by delusions or there is serious impairment in communication or judgement.
10	Unable to function or serious danger of harm to self or others (DSM—IV, 1994, pp. 30-32).
0	Inadequate information.

This scale is used to plan treatment. For example, a change in the GAF from 100 to 30 following a sexual assault would indicate an acute need for intense treatment, whereas a slight decrease in the GAF of a mentally retarded person who lives in a group home would not.

It is also used to measure the impact of treatment. An increase in the GAF of a patient with schizophrenia from 30 to 50 within a two-week period after taking a new drug may indicate the treatment is working.

The GAF is also used in making a statement of prognosis, or predicting the outcome of treatment. In general, patients can be expected to return to their premorbid, or prior, level of function following a course of treatment. Consider a man who has become acutely anxious upon filing for bankruptcy because of a business failure. Had his GAF been 100 prior to the bankruptcy, his prognosis would likely be better than had it been 70.

Imagine yourself as a clinician, social worker, or psychiatric nurse. You are assigned responsibility for the care of the following patient.

> Marilyn R. is a 33 year old caucasian female. She is married to Ron R., 35, and has two children, Jason, 7, and Heather, 5. Her marriage has progessively deteriorated over the past year. A week ago, Marilyn apparently attempted suicide by overdosing on a combination of medications and slashing her wrists in the middle of the night. She was unconscious when brought to the hospital. She has regained consciousness and her medical condition has stabilized. She and her family have been interviewed, and a provisional diagnosis has been made as follows:

DSM—IV Multiaxial Evaluation

Axis I: Clinical Disorders
Other Conditions That May Be a Focus of Clinical Attention

Dysthymic Disorder:

- Chronic depression for the last two years.
- Poor appetite, insomnia, low self esteem, and feelings of hopelessness.
- Has not been without symptoms for more than two months during the past two years.
- Another form of mood disorder is excluded.
- Patient is without psychotic features.
- The symptoms are not the result of a substance or a general medical condition.
- Patient experiences significant distress and functioning is impaired.

Axis II: Personality Disorders
Mental Retardation

Dependent Personality Disorder:

Axis III: General Medical Conditions

Carcinoma of the Breast: mastectomy performed two months ago.

Axis IV: Psychosocial and Environmental Problems

Problems with primary support group—her husband, who had been threatening to leave, packed and left in the early evening proceeding her suicide attempt. Marilyn R. is very concerned with the care of her children who are presently staying with her mother. Ron R. has been physically abusive toward Marilyn R.

Problems related to interaction with legal system/crime—Ron R. has served two years in prison for drug offenses. He has been under treatment for cocaine dependence, but continues use.

Axis V: Global Assessment of Functioning

GAF = 70 (6 months ago) Some minor symptoms, but generally functioning fairly well.
GAF = 10 (present) Unable to function or serious danger of harm to self or others.

Think about the information contained on each axis. Each axis provides another "piece to the puzzle." Contemplate the interaction of the information contained on the various axes.

Marilyn R. has dysthymic disorder, so we know she has been chronically depressed for at least two years. As mentioned earlier, people with dependent personality disorder fear rejection and abandonment. They are devastated when important relationships end. Having a mastectomy produces great stress. The patient may worry whether the cancer has really been stopped. Loss of a breast may represent a threat to her femininity and further diminish her already poor self-esteem. Depression often follows loss. Although she had been depressed for two years, she had not previously attempted suicide. Her husband leaving was likely the "trigger" that precipitated her attempt. Despite her present GAF of 10, the 70 six months ago is reason for cautious optimism regarding her prognosis. Ultimately, the "pieces fit." It is understandable that a depressed woman with dependent personality and concern for her health would attempt suicide following separation from her husband. A major strength of DSM—IV is the multiaxial system.

Having explained the perspectives approach, distinguished normality from abnormality, and described the *Diagnostic Manual of Mental Disorders*, we are ready to study the specific mental disorders.

References

APA Monitor (1986, February). *American Psychological Association.*

Canby, T. (1984, February). El Nino's Ill Wind. *National Geographic*, 183.

DeAngelis, T. (1992, March). Psychiatrists Ambushing Hospital Privilege Efforts. *American Psychological Monitor*, 22.

Diagnostic and Statistical Manual of Mental Disorders (1952). Washington, D.C.:American Psychiatric Association.

Diagnostic and Statistical Manual of Mental Disorders (1968) (2nd ed.). Washington, D.C.:American Psychiatric Association.

Diagnostic and Statistical Manual of Mental Disorders (1980) (3rd ed.). Washington, D.C.:American Psychiatric Association.

Diagnostic and Statistical Manual of Mental Disorders (1987) (3rd ed. rev). Washington, D.C.:American Psychiatric Association.

Diagnostic and Statistical Manual of Mental Disorders (1994) (4th ed.). Washington, D.C.: American Psychiatric Association.

Chapter 4

THE MENTAL DISORDERS

DSM—IV contains fifteen major categories of mental disorders. Each category contains many disorders. There are hundreds of disorders. To discuss each would be an exhausting task beyond the scope of this book. Therefore, I will present those disorders that are the most common, significant, or compelling. One purpose of the following discussion is to allow the reader to develop an appreciation for the vastly different nature of the disorders. Although they are all mental disorders, they differ greatly. Another aim is to enable the reader to recognize the collection of symptoms that characterize each particular disorder, called its syndrome. Two case studies, A Portrait of Neurosis and A Portrait of Psychosis, detail the experiential aspects of these conditions and will be presented at the end of this chapter. They are designed to help you speculate about what having the disorders would really be like.

CATEGORY I. DISORDERS USUALLY FIRST EVIDENT IN INFANCY, CHILDHOOD, OR ADOLESCENCE

A. Mental Retardation

DSM—IV defines retardation as "significantly subaverage general intellectual functioning that is accompanied by significant limitations in adaptive functioning." The diagnosis must be made before age eighteen. As previously mentioned, it is the only mental disorder coded on axis II.

It is important to distinguish the *subnormal* condition of the retarded person from the *abnormal* condition of people with other mental disorders. The mentally retarded person functions at a lower intellectual level than normal. He cannot perform as much or as well mentally as a normal person. Deficit areas include thought, logic, language, general knowledge, and specific academic skills. People with other disorders often have normal intellectual ability, but are impaired in other areas. A psychotic person may have the delusion he is Hitler. A retarded person most likely would not know who Hitler was. The degree of mental retardation is assessed through an intelligence quotient test. Lower I.Q. scores indicate lower intellectual and adaptive functioning. There is a measurement error of approximately five points in assessing I.Q.

Least impaired are the *mildly* retarded. The I.Q. scores for mild retardation range from about 50 to 70, which distinguishes low normal intelligence. Normal I.Q. is 100. The mildly retarded comprise about 85 percent of the retarded population. They are often called "educable" because they are capable of learning basic vocational skills. The academic level of the mildly retarded is about sixth grade; a level at which some newspapers are written. Mildly retarded people usually live in the community. Changes in business and industry have enabled many of them to be successfully employed in the community. For example, fast-food stores have cash registers with pictures of menu items on keys and automatically dispense change. Clinicians should exercise judgement in making this diagnosis. The connotative difference between "low normal intelligence" and "mild retardation" is significant.

Moderate retardation is determined by I.Q. scores between 35 and 50. The moderately retarded are likely to progress to about a second grade level. They can generally use language to communicate and learn simple vocational skills in supervised "sheltered workshop" situations. Although considered dated and derogatory by some, the term "trainable" conveys that they can benefit from educational programs with sufficient structure, support, repetition, and supervision. They may be capable of independent travel on public transportation to familiar places, like their work place. However, they may have difficulty adapting to change in routine, such as a bus made late by snow.

The I.Q. range for *severe* retardation is from 20 to 35. People in this category often have poor motor development and little communicative speech. Reading is limited to "survival" words like "stop" and "men", and may only represent recognition. They may develop minimal personal hygiene skills, but vocational training usually fails. In the community, they require either the support of their families or that provided in a group home.

The *profoundly* retarded have I.Q. scores below 20. Sensorimotor functioning is greatly impaired. Intellectual development is minimal. Whether in an institution or home, they require constant supervision. Language is usually absent or unintelligible. Since measurement of intelligence requires language, assessment of non-verbal persons is difficult. In the absence of language, diagnosis is often based upon inferences of intelligence according to psychomotor activity, such as "Client can use a fork and spoon." Institutional populations are composed primarily of the profoundly retarded. Thankfully, this group comprises only about one percent of the retarded population.

There can be many causes of mental retardation. About forty percent is caused by a general medical condition or substance. The remaining sixty percent of the mentally retarded are considered to have a primary mental disorder, or one that is not due to a general medical condition or substance (DSM—IV, 1994, p. 43 & 123). Primary mental retardation is likely the result of "soft" neurological impairment, which is of insuffient severity to be measured by laboratory tests, combined with environmental deprivation, abuse, or neglect.

Let us examine some types of mental retardation that are the result of a general medical condition or substance. **Down's syndrome**, or *trisomy 21*, is a condition that results from the abnormal doubling of the 21st chromosome. Very young mothers and those over thirty-five (particularly having their first child) have a higher risk of having a child with this disorder. If blood tests reveal proteins that correlate highly with Down syndrome, amniocentesis (surgical withdrawal of amniotic fluid which can indicate genetic abnormalities) can be used to pinpoint the disorder early in pregnancy (The Associated Press, 1992). A test for Down syndrome called chorionic villus sampling can be employed in the tenth week of pregnancy, a month before amniocentesis. It was proven to be safe in a study of 150,000 women (Raeburn, 1994, p. 11A).

Tay-Sachs disease is characterized by a baby's failure to flourish, progressive retardation, and death in early childhood. It occurs primarily among children of Ashkenazi Jewish parents; one in thirty carry the gene, and one in three thousand six hundred children of Ashkenazi Jewish parents will inherit the disease (Gannett News Service, 1989). The disease is caused by a deficiency of the enzyme N-acetyl hexosamindase. The deficiency can be detected in amniotic fluid during the first trimester, providing the parents opportunity to chose between terminating the pregnancy, or having a terminally ill child. Major screening programs exist in metropolitan centers of the United States (Wright, et. al, 1976). This disease has been virtually eliminated in the United States and Canada.

Substances can also cause mental retardation. Eleven percent of all U.S. infants in 1988 tested positive for cocaine or alcohol (Dorris, 1990). Maternal consumption of alcohol during pregnancy can lead to **fetal alcohol syndrome**, a condition that leaves the child with retarded nervous system development and physical deformities. The New York State Council on Alcoholism states that fetal alcohol syndrome

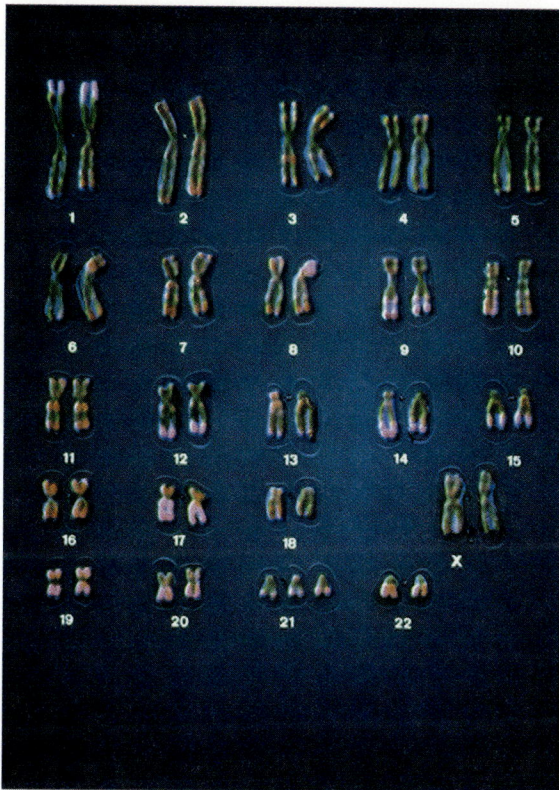

Figure 4-1: The chromosomes of an individual with Down's Syndrome. There are three sets of chromosome number 21. X (bottom, right) determines sex. What is the sex of this person? (CNRI/Science Photo Library/Custom Medical Stock Photo, Inc.)

is the third leading cause of birth defects with accompanying mental retardation, and the only one that is preventable among the top three. The syndrome affects one in 750 live births. 36,000, newborns each year may be affected by a range of less severe alcohol-related fetal alcohol effects.

Research on babies born to mothers who use **cocaine** documents the negative effects this drug has on the developing fetus. Some are so impaired they die shortly after birth. Others survive. Cocaine use during the first trimester, when the nervous system is very rapidly developing, can inhibit the production of neurotransmitters norepinephrine and dopamine, thus retarding neuronal development. Twenty-five percent of women who use cocaine during pregnancy have low birth-weight babies which are prone to retardation, developmental lags, and perceptual disabilities (Adler, 1989). The cost of intensive neonatal care for the sickest of such infants can be $150,000 per year.

Primary mental retardation can be caused by neglect, abuse, or environmental deprivation. The literature is replete with case studies of children who were kept locked in closets or basements for much of their early development. Even when rescued from these terrible conditions, intellectual development is typically permanently impaired. Researchers Renee Spitz and Wayne Dennis have well documented the devastating effects of austere institutional rearing. Such children often fail to thrive, and are developmentally and intellectually retarded. Approximately twenty percent of mental retardation is caused by environmental deprivation (DSM—IV, 1994, p. 43).

About forty percent of mental retardation has no clear cause and is likely the result of a combination of medical and environmental factors. A typical child with retardation who receives special education in a public school likely comes from a home characterized by lack of parental care, stimulation, and supervision, but not of sufficient degree to be considered abusive or neglectful. The child's mother likely used some drugs and alcohol during pregnancy. The child may have consumed paint chips (a source of lead), received blows to the head from falls, and had an extremely high fever during infancy. Although these factors are not sufficient to produce positive laboratory test results, they imply "soft" neurological impairment, or minimal brain dysfunction. Such children are likely to demonstrate poor eye tracking, motor and coordination difficulties, tics, and distractibility, along with retardation.

Although the retarded person's overall level of functioning is subnormal, some may have truly remarkable abilities in a specialized area. Such is the case with the idiot savant (literally the "clever idiot"). Whereas normal intelligence is relatively "shallow" but "wide," the idiot savant's is incredibly "deep," but extremely "narrow." Despite their retardation, some savants have the ability to memorize calendars and quickly tell what day of the week a particular date fell on thousands of years ago.

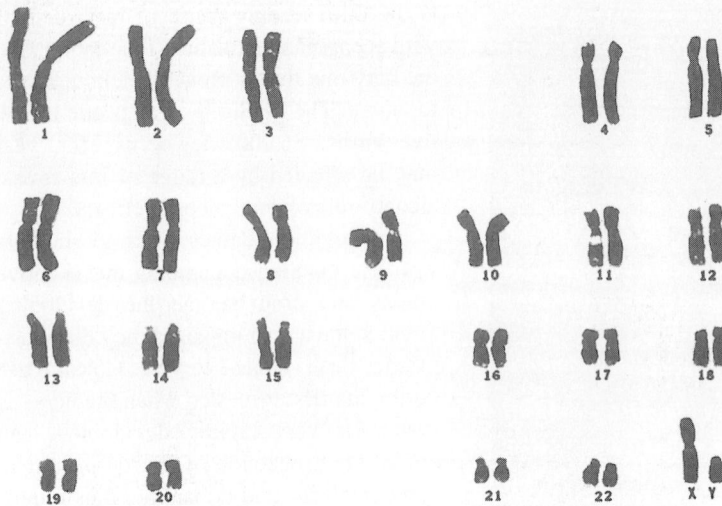

Figure 4-2. The person whose chromosomes are shown on page 49 is a female. Note the two long X chromosomes. XY (bottom, right) is a male. (Photograph courtesy of John B. Jenkins.)

Jedediah Buxton could quickly and correctly multiply 23,145,789 by 5,642,732 by 54,965 in his head, but was of "dull mentality" (Asimov, in Hamacheck, 1973). Thomas Fuller, a Virginia slave, could calculate the number of seconds in seventy years, seventeen days, and twelve hours in a minute and a half.

Although this condition is very rare, the triad of retardation, blindness, and musical genius often occur together. The condition also occurs six times as often in males than females. In 1964 at a meeting of the American Psychiatric Association, a discussant concluded, "The importance, then, of the Idiot-Savant lies in our inability to explain him; he stands as a landmark of our own ignorance and the phenomenon of the Idiot-Savant exists as a challenge to our capabilities" (quoted in Treffert, 1988). It remains an enigma. Raymond, as portrayed by Dustin Hoffman in the critically acclaimed film *Rain Man*, was an idiot savant.

B. Communication Disorders

Included within this category are a variety of communication disorders. Examples include:

- **Reading Disorder** Reading achievement, as measured by standardized tests, is substantially below the person's chronological age, intelligence, or level of education.
- **Disorder of Written Expression** Writing skills, as measured by standardized tests are substantially below the person's chronological age, intelligence, or level of education.
- **Developmental Coordination Disorder**. Performance in activities that require motor coordination is substantially below the person's chronological age and intelligence. There are marked delays in achieving motor milestones, such as crawling, sitting, and walking. Such children are likely to drop things, perform poorly in sports, and are reputed to be "clumsy."
- **Phonological Disorder.** Failure to use developmentally expected speech sounds appropriate for age and dialect. Such children make errors in sound production and organization. They may substitute "T" for a target "K" sound, or vice versa; "I want to fly my "tike." There may be maladaptive excesses, such as lisps and whistles.
- **Stuttering**. Disturbance in the fluency and timing of speech. Examples are sound repetitions, prolongations, and pauses. There may be circumlocutions, or substitutions to avoid problem words (DSM—IV, 1994, pp. 48-65). When asking for a Coca-Cola, a child might say, "I want a Co-Co-Co-Co-drink."

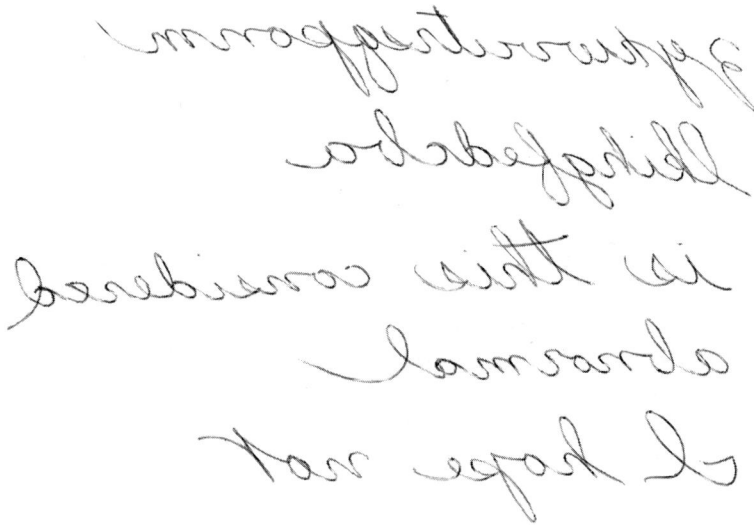

Figure 4-3.
Can you read this? If not, view through a mirror.

C. Autistic Disorder

Autism is a very controversial and puzzling disorder. Autistic children neither relate to nor interact with other people. They often are more intimately involved with inanimate objects such as dolls or puppets. Because of their lack of responsiveness to others, they may be mistaken for deaf or retarded. DSM—IV states that the diagnosis must be made before age three. Failure to make eye contact, babble, imitate gestures (waving bye-bye), or differentially respond to gain or loss of attention are early indicators of autism. It should be obvious at an early age that the child is abnormal.

Other symptoms include gross deficits in communication skills. Language may be absent or echolalic. When asked, "How are you today?" the child may respond, "How are you today?" with the same tone and inflection as that which was used with him. Unlike children with selective mutism, who have demonstrated age appropriate language but fail to speak in specific social settings like school, these children have never used language effectively.

Autistic children often display self-destructive behaviors like head banging, gouging, biting, and scratching. They may become preoccupied with one activity, such as riding a tricycle in circles. Stereotypic behaviors, like rocking in a mechanical fashion, spinning, and hand flapping, are common.

As with the profoundly retarded, it is difficult to assess the intelligence of autistic children because of their lack of language skills. As might be expected, they score considerably lower than average. However, sometimes they have unusually good musical abilities, such as perfect pitch or other artistic talents.

The distinctions between autistic disorder and schizophrenia, a serious psychotic disorder that will be discussed later in this chapter, need clarification. Whereas schizophrenia is very rare in children, autism is evident by early childhood. Psychotics are typically incoherent, detached from their surroundings, and out of touch with reality. Autistic children seem to selectively interact with the environment or recognize reality. Parents are ignored, yet the child is greatly disturbed if separated from a favorite toy. Unlike schizophrenics, autistic children typically do not have hallucinations or delusions.

The behavior of autistics is relatively more odd, bizarre, and peculiar than the retarded. A retarded child will be an active participant in a group activity. He may hit the baseball, and mistakenly run to third base. An autistic child may pick up the bat and twirl it, flapping and spinning as he walks off the field.

Autistic disorder occurs about five times more frequently in boys than in girls, and about fifty times more frequently among siblings of a child with the disorder than among the general population.

D. Attention-Deficit/Hyperactivity Disorder

The essential feature of this disorder is a persistent pattern of inattention and/or hyperactivity/impulsivity considerably more frequent and severe than normal. Aspects of the syndrome are evident before age seven. Such children require little sleep, and have an acute propensity for making messes. "Challenging" to parents is an understatement.

Symptoms of inattention, or hyperactivity/impulsivity define the disorder. Symptoms of inattention include difficulty sustaining attention, carelessness, difficulty following through on instructions, forgetfulness, and difficulty in task organization and completion. Indicators of hyperactivity/impulsivity include fidgeting and squirming, inability to sit still when expected to, excessive talk, interruption of others, and unnecessary climbing or running.

Obviously, the hyperactive child is likely to have difficulty in school. The child's behavior is incompatible with a need for order, compliance, and conformity in the classroom. He is likely viewed as a nuisance by the teacher and an annoyance by peers. The condition is four to nine times more common in boys than girls (DSM—IV, 1994, pp. 78-85).

Figure 4-4. In March of 1996, Mahmoud Abdul-Rauf refused to stand for the national anthem. A compromise allowed him to stand while praying. [Photograph by David Walberg/Sports Illustrated © Time, Inc.]

E. Tourette's Disorder

This syndrome, initially described by Gilles de la Tourette, is characterized by multiple motor and vocal tics. The disorder must be diagnosed before eighteen years of age. However, initial symptoms typically develop between ages two and ten, and have appeared in ninety-six percent of cases by age eleven.

Tics are sudden, rapid, recurrent non-rhythmic movements or vocalizations. The tics occur many times a day, often in bouts, for a period of more than a year. There is never a tic-free period of more than three consecutive months.

Vocal tics include involuntary sounds such as grunts, yelps, barks, snorts, or clicks (DSM—IV, 1994, pp. 101-103). Coprolalia, the involuntary uttering of obscenities, occurs in about sixty percent of individuals with this disorder. Palilalia, or the repetition of one's last words or phrases, is common. Utterances are made in sing-song fashion with varying pitch. "I want to ride my bike, bi-i-i-ke, bi-i-i-ke, bi-i-ke, bike."

Motor tics are involuntary, recurrent, repetitive, purposeless body movements which affect multiple muscle groups. The person may impulsively touch things, and perform complicated movements, like squatting, deep knee bends, retracing steps, and twirling (Kaplan & Sadock, 1985).

Mahmoud Abdul-Rauf is a professional basketball player for the Denver Nuggets. He is a perfectionist and diagnosed with Tourette's disorder. He is dissatisfied with baskets that are not swishes and made sixty-seven consecutive foul shots. He cries "whoops" all the time. During one game he sat next to teammate Reggie Williams. Rauf involuntarily and repeatedly punched him so hard he had to have his arm iced. He has received technical fouls for verbal and motor tics. In 1991, he converted to Islam. Islam's quest for perfection and repetition of prayers five times daily suit him well (Reilly, 1993, p. 84).

CATEGORY II. DELIRIUM, DEMENTIA, AND AMNESTIC AND OTHER COGNITIVE DISORDERS

DSM—III-R (1987) distinguished organic disorders (those caused by a general medical condition or a substance) from functional disorders (those with unspecified cause). DSM—IV (1994) no longer makes this distinction. Such language implies that "mental disorders are unrelated to physical or biological factors or processes, or that general medical conditions are unrelated to behavioral or psychosocial factors or processes" (quoted in DSM—IV, 1994, p. 165). Present research is indicating that biological and psychological factors interact in many disorders. Disorders previously called organic have been regrouped into three separate categories, this being one of them.

A *syndrome* is a collection of symptoms that characterize a disorder. This category includes disorders whose symptoms are primarily cognitive. Cognitive disorders are characterized by faulty mental activity in such areas as memory, perceiving, thinking, knowing, reasoning, and awareness. A specific cognitive syndrome can result from different causes. Disorders in this section are assumed to be caused by a general medical condition, a substance (abuse of drug, medication, or toxin), or a combination of these factors. This category describes three cognitive syndromes: *delirium, dementia*, and *amesia*. It also includes cognitive disorder not otherwise specified, for cognitive dysfunction that does not satisfy criteria for the other three.

A. Delirium

Delirium is demonstrated by a person who is in a clouded state of consciousness, has a reduced awareness of the environment, and has difficulty focusing, sustaining, or shifting attention. The person may respond with a blank stare to direct questions posed in face-to-face interaction. The delirious speak incoherently, are disoriented in space and time, and suffer memory lapses. The condition is often accompanied by fever, tremors, and convulsions. Delirium usually develops over a short period of time, and may occur abruptly, or over a course of hours or days.

A general medical condition that can cause delirium is hypoglycemia, or low blood sugar. Episodes can be prevented by promptly eating a food with sugar, like a candy bar, upon first awareness of symptoms. However, sometimes the delirium occurs so abruptly the person fails to take preventive action. Other causes include systemic infections (blood poisioning), kidney or liver disease, or head trauma. Delirium can also be caused by substances such as cocaine, hallucinogen, and alcohol. Phencyclidine (angel dust) can cause pernicious delirium accompanied by severe convulsions.

B. Dementia

Dementia is characterized by a loss of intellectual abilities to the degree that it interferes with social and occupational function. The person has multiple cognitive deficits that must include memory impairment. Abstract thought processes are typically impaired. The person would likely appreciate only the literal meaning of common sayings like "what goes around, comes around." If asked would he rather be a "big fish in a small pond, or a small fish in a big pond," he might respond, "That's stupid, I'm not a fish." Typically dementia is insidious, or gets progressively worse. In some cases it is static, or stable. Sometimes, it may remit, if detected early and promptly treated. Unlike delirium, there is no clouding of consciousness.

Dementia requires one of the following cognitive disturbances:
- **Aphasia.** A disturbance characterized by difficulty speaking or understanding language.
- **Apraxia**. The inability to carry out motor activities, despite intact motor function. (Trying to comb one's hair with scissors.)
- **Agnosia**. The failure to recognize or identify objects. (Perceiving fire hydrants as small children.)
- Disturbance in planning, organizing, sequencing, and executing activities. (Becoming disoriented when making a routine trip to a nearby store.) (DSM—IV, 1994, p. 133-146)

The following are specific types of dementia:

1. Dementia of the Alzheimer's Type
Reasonably synonymous with what was once called senilty, this condition affects between two and four percent of the population over age sixty-five. The prevalence increases significantly after age seventy-five. Laboratory findings indicate brain atrophy, neuronal loss, and larger cerebral ventricles than would be expected given the normal aging process. Along with common symptoms of dementia, the person may demonstrate personality change and irritability. Autopsies of patients with this condition reveal lower than normal levels of the neurotransmitter acetylcholine in the brain. This implies either a reduction in the brain's ability to produce the neurotransmitter, or decreased receptivity. Furthermore, drugs that enhance acetylcholine production have resulted in improved memory in old normal volunteers (Karasu, 1989, vol. 2, p. 829).

2. Dementia Due to Syphilis
This condition, commonly called neurosyphilis or general paresis, is a type of presenile dementia, as the symptoms occur before age sixty-five. The disorder results from untreated syphilis, a venereal disease spread by intimate sexual contact with an infected person. Because of spirochetal invasion, the brain and nervous system suffer severe, permanent damage. Signs of neurological damage, such as slurred speech and a trailing gait, begin about five to fifteen years after the initial infection. Along with common symptoms of dementia, like loss of intellectual function and impaired judgement, the victim may exhibit bizarre delusions, paralysis, poor reflexes, and extremely poor hygiene.

At one time paresis accounted for ten percent of all admissions to mental hospitals (Mulder and Dale, 1967, p. 781), and was likely common in the lunatic asylums of the 1800s. In 1939 it was discovered that penicillin could cure syphilis and, therefore, prevent general paresis (Arnold, 1984). In 1972, public health investigator Peter Buxtun revealed evidence of a shocking story. Since 1933 a group of four hundred black men with syphilis from Tuskegee, Alabama, had treatment purposely withheld from them to study the course of untreated syphilis. Only when they began to demonstrate the symptoms of dementia were they given penicillin. Much was learned through the study, for example, victims apparently become less likely to infect partners the longer they have had the disease. Despite public criticism of the study on moral, ethical, and legal grounds, it was allowed to continue (Brown, 1994).

Cases of syphilis and general paresis were dramatically reduced as a result of penicillin. However, cases of syphilis have been on the rise. In 1987, the Center for Disease Control reported a twenty-three percent increase in cases of syphilis, reaching its highest rate since the 1950s. This trend continued into the 1990s. In 1992, in New York State, reported cases of early syphilis declined twenty-four percent to

8,709 cases from the previous year 1992. However, levels are still above those of 1984 (Farrell, 1994).

Apparently, since some people realize that there is a cure for this disease, they do not always seek immediate treatment and, therefore, continue to spread the infection to others. People are more aware of the dangers of AIDS, which may lessen their concern with syphilis. Others, like the homeless, may be ignorant of the matter, or incapable of seeking treatment. Regardless of the reasons, any case of syphilis that results in dementia is an unnecessary tragedy.

It is interesting to note that only five to ten percent of syphilitics who do not receive treatment for it develop neurosyphilis (Carson and Butcher, 1992, p. 488). Most infected people are fortunate enough to have some other type of infection that is treated with penicillin which "accidentally" kills the spirochete.

3. Dementia Due to Huntington's Disease

Huntington's disease is a progressive, degenerative nervous disorder that is ultimately fatal. There is no known cure or effective treatment for this genetic disorder. All those with the disease have an afflicted parent. The disease is passed on through a dominant gene, which means there is a fifty percent chance that a child of an afflicted parent will develop the disorder.

Along with the typical symptoms of dementia, the disorder is characterized by gradually increasing difficulty in movement, loss of coordination, depression, tremors, and impaired speech. The condition was called Huntington's chorea (latin for dance), describing the spastic writhing of the victim. Muscular emaciation is so extensive that injecting a pain killer is difficult. Death follows agonizing deterioration. The disease usually begins to afflict victims when they are between the ages of thirty-five and forty-five, often after they have had children of their own. However, symptoms may begin as early as four, or as late as eighty-five years.

Huntington's disease is particularly tragic. People who have a parent with the disease often suffer extreme anxiety wondering if they will get it. Because they do not experience symptoms until adulthood, they will agonize over whether to have children, who may possibly inherit the trait. Amazing breakthroughs have recently been made regarding this disorder. They will be described in Chapter 5, "The Illness Perspective."

4. Dementia Due to Head Trauma

Recent literature has demonstrated the extensive brain damage suffered by professional boxers. The "punch-drunk" fighter syndrome is technically called dementia pugilistica. Ira Casson found that eighty-seven percent of a sample of professional fighters had definite evidence of brain damage (et al., 1984). Also, the amount of brain damage has been found to correlate positively to the number of bouts (Ross, 1983).

In January of 1983, Duk Koo Kim died from injuries suffered during a professional boxing match. Despondent, his mother committed suicide by drinking poison. *The Journal of the American Medical Association* published a series of articles condemning boxing on moral, ethical, and medical grounds. Quotes from the articles include, "When animal fights are outlawed by civilized society, where does that leave professional boxing?", "Boxing is not a sport, but a gladiatorial contest in which two men try to beat each other senseless," and "Boxing is a sacrifice of living flesh to the mere titillation of spectators." ("Boxing", 1984, p. 2696.)

Muhammad Ali, arguably the best professional fighter in history, courageously withstood a multitude of brutal punches to the head from such boxing greats as Joe Frazier, Ken Norton, and George Foreman. At his prime, his fists and tongue were matchless. His opponents were typically slower and methodical. Ali's motto was, "Float like a butterfly, sting like a bee." When stripped of his championship and convicted of refusing to enter the Army during the Vietnam war, he quipped "I ain't got no quarrel with those Viet Cong. They never called me nigger." He threw his Olympic gold medal into the Ohio River after being refused service in a Louisville diner. When he retired, his face was still unmarked. However, head shots from 228 career bouts left him with a form of Parkinson's disease (*Life,*

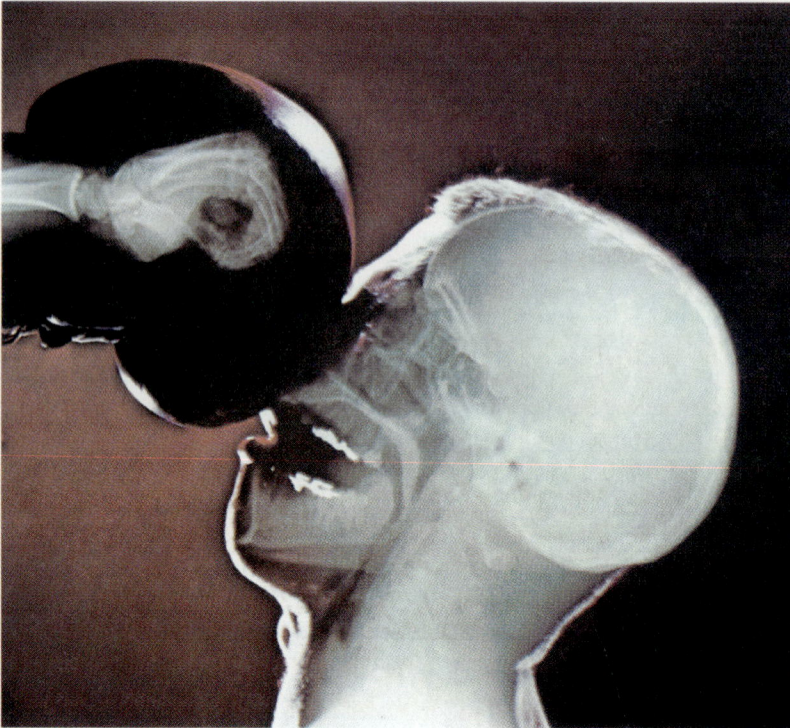

Figure 4-5. Brain of a boxer being displaced at the moment of impact. (California Medical Publications.)

1990, p. 47). His once glib speech has slowed, and his movements are carefully measured. However, he has continued courageously in humanitarian pursuits, such as negotiating with Sudam Hussein for the release of American hostages in Iraq during 1990.

Postconcussional disorder is described in the DSM—IV Appendix category called Criteria Sets and Axes Provided for Further Study. It describes people who have a history of head trauma specifically caused by cerebral concussion. The trauma is sufficient to smash the brain, which floats in fluid, into the skull. Symptoms include loss of consciousness, amnesia, seizures, disordered sleep, changes in personality, and irritability.

Professional football players who have experienced numerous concussions are susceptible to the condition. Sometimes the condition is merely temporary. In 1986, Buffalo Bills quarterback Jim Kelly suffered a blow that made him so woozy that he called the same running play four consecutive times because he couldn't remember any pass plays (Freeman, p. C2). ESPN reported that Dallas Cowboy quarterback, Troy Aikman, was struck in the head with a knee of a 330-pound defensive lineman. He returned to his sideline and asked his former center, who had been out for eight weeks and was in street clothes and on crutches, "Why aren't you playing?"

Sometimes it persists. Harry Carson, a cornerstone of the New York Giants 1986 Super Bowl team, complains of a condition that he likens to having Alzheimers disease. "I don't think as clearly as a normal person," he said. Former New York Jet wide receiver Al Toon retired because of the effects of damage from numerous concussions. He admittedly has contemplated suicide (Campbell, p. D1).

5. Dementia Due to HIV

The essential feature of dementia due to HIV disease is dementia judged to be the direct consequence of human immunodeficiency virus. Laboratory findings indicate diffuse destruction of the white matter and subcortical structures of the brain. The condition is highly infectious. Although seriously ill, victims may demonstrate brief episodes of assaultive anger called "AIDS rage," in which they may spit at, bite, or attempt to prick with needles those who care for them. "AIDS blankets" are often used to restrain an agitated victim and protect the caretakers from infection. Anyone employed in the medical, human services, or criminal justice field must be aware of the threat AIDS poses.

According to the U.S. Department of Health and Human Services, as of 1992 AIDS had accounted for 166,211 deaths in the United States. 30,579 new cases of the disease, an all time high, were reported in 1991. The number declined to 22,660 in 1992. Hopefully, public education and awareness have motivated people to modify behaviors that put them at risk for the disease.

Among the victims of AIDS have been pianist Liberace, tennis star Arthur Asche, and movie stars Rock Hudson, Anthony Perkins, and John C. Holmes, who performed in more than one-thousand pornographic films and peep-show loops. Amanda Blake, who played the feisty "Miss Kitty" on television's "Gunsmoke," and Robert Reed, the reassuringly calm father of situation comedy "The Brady Bunch," died from the disease *(Newsweek,* 1993, pp. 22-23).

C. Amnestic Disorders

Amnesia refers to a loss of memory. Amnestic disorders are characterized by both short-term memory impairment (the inability to learn new information) and long-term memory impairment (the inability to recall information that was previously known). *Confabulation*, in which someone with amnesia makes up events or information to fill in memory gaps, is common. He is likely to deny or minimize his condition, demonstrate apathy, lack initiative, and be emotionally bland. There is neither a clouding of consciousness, as in delirium, nor an impairment of intellectual ability, as in dementia.

1. Alcohol-Induced Persisting Amnestic Disorder

This disorder, also called **Korsakoff's syndrome**, results from chronic abuse of alcohol combined with thiamine (vitamin B) deficiency. Deterioration of the brain and nervous system can be identified. Poor alcoholics are likely to spend their limited money on alcohol rather than food. It is thought that a deficiency of thiamine is primarily responsible for the deterioration of the brain. However, massive alcohol consumption can also destroy brain tissue. The brain damage is likely chronic and irreversible.

Along with the typical symptoms of amnestic syndrome, the person is likely to experience **delirium tremens.** He may visibly shake, break out in a cold sweat, become terrified, and have awful hallucinations, such as being attacked by animals or having bugs crawl all over him. He may experience illusions like perceiving wrinkles in sheets as snakes, or the closing of a door as a gunshot. One alcoholic patient, who was typically very docile when undergoing hospital detoxifications, became violently resistant when aides attempted to get him on an elevator upon admission. Although scarcely weighing 100 pounds and in a state of nutritional emaciation, three aides were required. Later, he explained to me that he had been having a hallucinatory dream in which he read his obituary in a newspaper. He had died in an elevator crash.

There may be blackouts, in which the person may lose consciousness, cannot account for blocks of time, and not remember what happened. For example, the person may awaken in a strange place, be unaware of how he got there, nor recall the location of his vehicle.

CATEGORY III. MENTAL DISORDERS DUE TO A GENERAL MEDICAL CONDITION

This is a newly created category in DSM—IV. It includes people who have *mental* symptoms that are judged to be the direct physiological consequence of a general medical condition. The prior category, Delirium, Dementia, and Amnestic and Other Cognitive Disorders, contained disorders which were the result of a general medical condition and had primarily *cognitive* symptoms. The symptoms in

Figure 4-6. Composer George Gershwin became irritable and depressed in the year prior to his death from an undiagnosed brain tumor. (Corbis-Bettmann.)

this category are more typical of traditional mental disorders in that they may be affective and behavioral, as well as cognitive in nature.

Mental disorders due to a general medical condition may be diagnosed if there is a temporal association, or a coincidence in time, in which a mental disorder and a general medical condition begin. For example, a healthy, active man who has become paralyzed in a car accident may become acutely depressed. Because he had no prior history of depression, and the disorder began at the onset of his paralysis, a causal link can be inferred.

Another example cited in DSM—IV is that of a mental disorder that appears months before the detection of the underlying pathological process. An anxious or depressed mood may be evident before the choreiform writhing movements of Huntington's disease appear. Seemingly unexplained depression and a significant unintended weight loss might imply the presence of an undiagnosed general medical condition such as cancer (DSM—IV, 1994, p. 166-167). Hopefully, the inclusion of this category will encourage psychologists to refer patients to physicians if the presenting mental disorder suggests an underlying medical condition.

CATEGORY IV. SUBSTANCE-RELATED DISORDERS

Substance-related disorders are those that involve the taking of drugs or alcohol, the side effects of medication, or toxin exposure. America is a substance-oriented society. Substance usage permeates our lifestyle so extensively that it is difficult to appreciate its full impact. We use substances for medicinal and recreational purposes. We use them to start and end our days. They are used to stimulate and relax. They are used as social lubricants. Our food contains them, and we use them to gain and lose weight. We are continually bombarded by media efforts to convince us that we need them. How many of us can claim to use no form of drug, alcohol, caffeine or nicotine?

Since substance use is so common and pervasive, it is generally regarded as normal. In many social situations it is not only accepted but expected. But at what point does substance use become serious enough to be considered a mental disorder? The philosophy of moderation seems relevant. In general, substance-related disorders are diagnosed when usage is pathological, or in excess of what most reasonable people would consider normal.

The use of the term addiction has been avoided in the *Diagnostic Manuals* because of its ambiguity. Instead, "This diagnostic class deals with symptoms and maladaptive behavioral changes associated with more or less regular use of psychoactive substances that affect the central nervous system. These behavioral changes would be viewed as extremely undesirable in almost all cultures." (DSM—III-R, 1987, p. 165.) This emphasis is maintained in DSM—IV. Emphasis is placed upon impaired occupational, social, or academic functioning that results from substance use. I once worked with an Army psychiatrist who demonstrated this philosophy prior to its inclusion in the DSM. When an officer expressed concern that he suspected one of his men was drinking excessively, the psychiatrist would ask, "Is the soldier doing his job?" If the response were affirmative, he would respond, "There is no problem. You've got the wrong Army. This is the U.S. Army. We make noise and break things. You want the *Salvation Army*. They save souls."

This category is divided into two groups: substance use disorders (*substance dependence* and *substance abuse*), terms which indicate the severity of the condition; and *substance-induced disorders*, which describe symptoms caused by the use of the substance.

A. Substance Use Disorders

1. Substance Dependence

This diagnosis requires significant impairment of functioning or distress as demonstrated by three or more of the following in a twelve month period:

- Tolerance—increased amount of the substance is required for intoxication or desired state, or the effect is diminished with continued use of the same amount of the substance.
- Withdrawal—physiological and cognitive symptoms when substance dosage is reduced or stopped. Withdrawal varies with substance and is typically the opposite of the intoxicated state (Alcohol is used to reduce stress and to feel euphoric. Alcohol withdrawal is characterized by anxiety and physical discomfort.).
- Substance is taken in larger amounts over a longer period than intended.
- Has been unsuccessful in efforts to stop using the substance.
- Devotes a great deal of time to use of the substance.
- Gives up important activities in favor of substance use.
- Continues substance use despite knowing that it causes or exacerbates physical or psychological problems (continued drinking despite realization of ulcer irritation) (DSM—IV, 1994, pp. 1-81).

2. Substance Abuse

This is basically a residual category that is reserved for people who do not meet the criteria for substance dependence, although they do have a substance-related problem. By definition the criteria do not include tolerance, withdrawal, or a pattern of compulsive use. Examples include an executive who drinks heavily, drives while intoxicated, but still functions well, and a college student who binges on cocaine every few weekends, but still gets passing grades. If a person continues a pattern of abuse, dependance will likely follow.

According to DSM—IV, the following substances can produce both substance dependence and abuse: alcohol, amphetamine (speed), cannabis (marijuana), cocaine, hallucinogen (LSD), inhalant (glue, gasoline, paint thinners, and other volatile compounds containing esters, ketones, and glycols), opioid (heroin), phencyclidine (angel dust), and sedative-, hypnotic-, or anxiolytic-related drugs (prescription anti-anxiety and sleeping medications). Polysubstance dependence describes a person who has repeatedly used at least three groups of substances during the last twelve months (DSM—IV, 1994, pp.

Figure 4-7. The youthful grins of Mickey Mantle and Billy Martin betray their penchant for mischief. (AP/Wide World Photos.)

175-272).

DSM—III described only cocaine abuse. DSM—III-R and DSM—IV additionally include cocaine dependence. Cocaine's ability to impair function can be documented through the ruin of the careers of athletes, musicians, performers, or perhaps someone you know. Tolerance is demonstrated by the craving for the drug in its purer form- "crack." Cocaine either caused or contributed to the deaths of Boston Celtics first round draft choice Len Bias, muscians Jerry Garcia and Andy Gibb, Atlanta Falcons cornerback David Croudip, and entertainer John Belushi. Belushi was a star of *Saturday Night Live, Animal House,* and *The Blues Brothers.* In *The Short Life and Fast Times of John Belushi*, Robert Woodward makes some observations about Belushi. He writes, "Giving or selling drugs to John was a kind of game, like feeding popcorn to seals at the zoo. Give him a little and he would perform and be crazy; a little more and he'd stay up all night, outdancing, out-doing, outlasting everyone around him." (Woodward, 1984.)

New York Yankee legends Mickey Mantle and Billy Martin were famous for their play on the field and notorious for their actions off. They contributed to Yankee success despite their abuse of alcohol. Retrospectively, Mantle attributes his premature retirement from baseball at age 37 to alcohol. "God gave me a great body to play with, and I didn't take care of it."

Mantle and Martin were particularly prone to drink heavily when on the road.

> One night in Detroit after quite a few drinks, we went back to our hotel room, and Billy said, "Let's climb out on the ledge and see what's going on in the other rooms," We happened to be staying on the 22nd floor. He climbed out the window, and I was right behind him. Well, the stunt got old pretty fast because nobody's lights were on—and I'm afraid of heights. But the ledge was so narrow that we couldn't turn around, so we had to crawl all the way around the building to get back to our room. (Mantle, 1994, p. 74.)

Billy Martin was killed in an alcohol related pick-up truck accident on Christmas Day of 1989. Mantle sought treatment in 1994 at the Betty Ford Center and counseled kids about drug, alcohol, and smokeless tobacco abuse. He died following an heroic battle with liver cancer in August, 1995.

B. Substance-Induced Disorders

This category describes symptoms caused by the use of a substance. **Substance intoxication** is a reversible (temporary) substance-specific syndrome due to recent ingestion of a substance. Maladaptive behavioral changes result, such as impaired mood, judgement, coordination, and functioning ability (drunk, stoned, or high) (DSM—IV, 1994, pp. 183-184). Absent from the manual's description of intoxication is the mention of any feelings of pleasure or euphoria, disinhibition or perceived wit, insight, and ability. British Prime Minister Sir Winston Churchill piloted his nation through World War II. Though inadequate to repel attacking Nazi war planes, Churchill said of his heroic Royal Air Force, "Never have so many owed so much to so few." He was notorious for his extremes of mood, often aroused by alcohol. When criticized by a woman for being drunk, his response was, "Madam, you're ugly. Tomorrow morning, however, I shall be sober ..." (Evans & Frothingham, 1992, p. 15).

Substance withdrawal is a substance-specific syndrome due to stopping or reducing heavy and prolonged substance abuse. The person experiences significant distress or impaired function.

CATEGORY V. SCHIZOPHRENIA AND OTHER PSYCHOTIC DISORDERS

This category includes disorders characterized by psychotic features. People with these disorders are likely to have delusions, hallucinations, illusions, disorganized speech, impaired affect, faulty logic and cognition, and impaired function. Specific symptoms define the disorders. This category combines three separate categories from DSM—III-R.

A. Schizophrenia

Schizophrenia is a very serious type of psychosis. It is among the foremost challenges faced by the mental health profession today. The chance that any individual will be diagnosed schizophrenic at some point in his life is about one in a hundred.

Schizophrenia, formerly called dementia praecox, has puzzled mankind for thousands of years. Because of the vague ways it had been defined in DSM—II (1968), the label had been used to describe the most severely impaired chronic patients who were in locked wards of mental hospitals, as well as "anyone who wanders in the hospital door looking befuddled . . ." (Haley, 1965).

To demonstrate this, David L. Rosenhan (1973) enlisted eighteen normal people to seek admission in twelve mental hospitals on the East and West coasts. The patients presented at the hospitals complaining of hearing voices. The voices were unclear, but seemed to say "empty," "hollow," and "thud." Otherwise, the pseudopatients acted normally. All were admitted and, with the exception of one, received a diagnosis of schizophrenia. Furthermore, it was often other patients that realized the pseudopatients were not schizophrenic and were "checking up" on the hospital. Length of hospitalization ranged from seven to fifty-two days, with an average of nineteen. Psychiatry was harshly criticized for its inability to distinguish normal people from schizophrenics. Diagnostic rigor and precision were dramatically improved in *Diagnostic Manuals III, III-R,* and *IV.*

Often, people assume that schizophrenics have "split personalities." This is a misconception. The prefix "schiz" does mean split, but it refers to a split with reality, a key feature of psychosis. It also refers to an affective split. The person is often emotionally withdrawn and avoids relationships with others. He may laugh wildly in a sad situation or sob in a happy one. The term "split personality" more appropriately describes someone with a dissociative identity disorder, which we will cover later in this chapter.

Many schizophrenics hallucinate. They may see things that do not exist. The size, shape, and brightness of things they really do see may continually change. They may hear sounds that do not exist and answer aloud to imagined voices. They may experience tactile hallucinations, such as feeling nonexistent fingers wrapped around their throats. They may also have delusions, which are false beliefs. Some of these might include persecution ("I'm being followed by the FBI"), jealousy ("Everyone is trying to get my money"), scrutiny ("The football players in the huddle are talking about me"), or grandeur ("I can control the weather"). They may believe that others can hear their thoughts, or that others are capa-

Figure 4-8. A person with schizophrenia plugs ears attempting to stifle an auditory hallucination. (Photograph by Jim Rooney.)

ble of either putting thoughts into their minds or taking them out.

Delusions may be bizarre, or nonbizarre. A bizarre delusion is one which is patently absurd, clearly implausible, and does not derive from ordinary life experiences. "I am Igmar from Konan. Evil forces are jamming my cosmic wave communication system. They emanate from Atlantis in the Sargasso Sea, ruled by Hillary Saddam. Help me find Superman so I can get my waves back."

Although the distinction between bizarre and nonbizarre delusions may not be completely clear, nonbizarre delusions could possibly have a basis in fact. After having been fired from a series of jobs and rejected by various lovers, it is delusional, but not bizarre for the person to think, "People do not like me and wish me ill, so police follow me to tell others how to avoid me." This distinction is very important for discriminating disorders in this category.

A schizophrenic's logic may be disturbed. A schizophrenic may reason, "It rained last Thursday. It's raining today. Therefore, today is Thursday." His language is often characterized by a "poverty of content" and may seem to ramble endlessly without point or conclusion. He may confabulate, or confuse fact with fantasy in his conversation. When experiencing a mental block, verbal nonsense is spoken. His speech may be echolalic, repeating almost verbatim what has just been said, without indication of meaning.

The schizophrenic may create neologisms, or new words. The words seldom mean anything to anyone but the individual. He may use words that sound like they have meaning. He may use proper sentence structure, grammar, and voice inflection. However, the key word is often a neologism. The use of neologisms is reminiscent of a comedian performing double talk.

The neologism may express a concept that he otherwise could not express. It may be a type of linguistic shorthand in which the schizophrenic attempts to express the content of a whole paragraph in

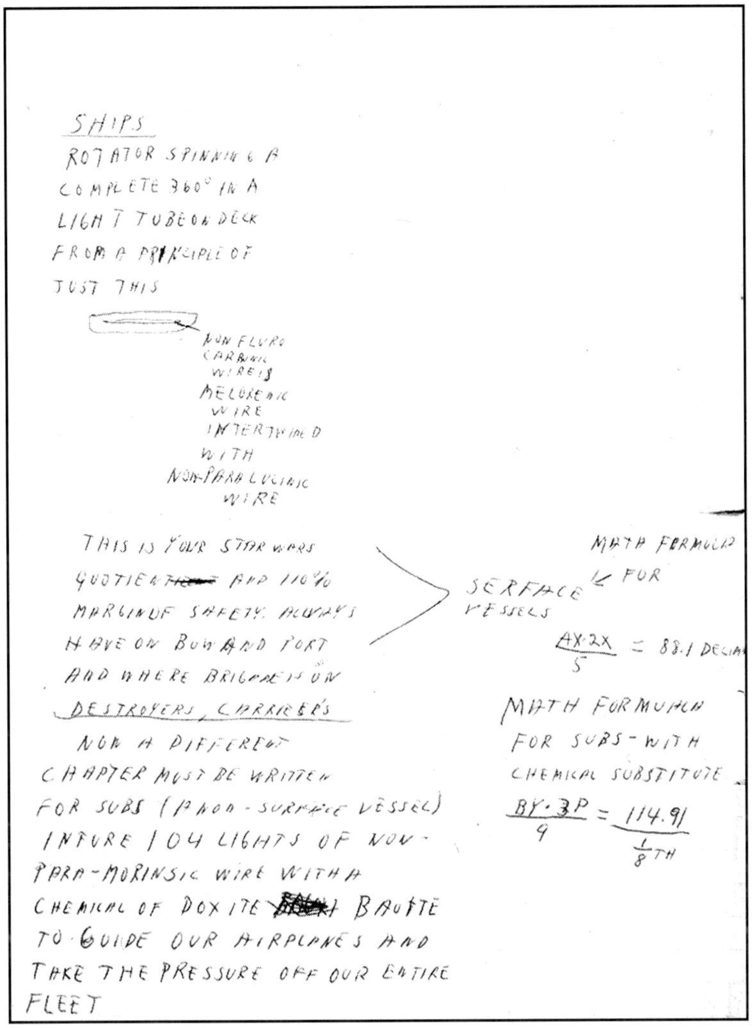

SHIPS
ROTATOR SPINNING A
COMPLETE 360° IN A
LIGHT TUBE ON DECK
FROM A PRINCIPLE OF
JUST THIS

NON FLURO
CARBON
WIRES
MELOREAIC
WIRE
INTERTWINED
WITH
NON-PARA LUCINIC
WIRE

THIS IS YOUR STAR WARS
QUOTIENT AND 110%
MARGIN OF SAFETY. ALWAYS
HAVE ON BOW AND PORT
AND WHERE BRIGADES ON
DESTROYERS, CARRIERS
NOW A DIFFERENT
CHAPTER MUST BE WRITTEN
FOR SUBS (PHON-SURFACE VESSEL)
INFURE 104 LIGHTS OF NON-
PARA-MORINSIC WIRE WITH A
CHEMICAL OF DOXITE BAUTTE
TO GUIDE OUR AIRPLANES AND
TAKE THE PRESSURE OFF OUR ENTIRE
FLEET

MATH FORMULA
FOR
SERFACE
VESSELS

$$\frac{AX \cdot 2X}{5} = 88.1 \text{ DECIM}$$

MATH FORMULA
FOR SUBS - WITH
CHEMICAL SUBSTITUTE

$$\frac{BY \cdot 3P}{9} = \frac{114.91}{\frac{1}{8}TH}$$

Figure 4-9. The pressured rumination of a paranoid schizophrenic in a locked ward. Is this plan feasible?

one word. Lehmann (1967, pp. 627-628) describes the meaning that a neologism had for one patient:

A schizophrenic woman who had been hospitalized for several years kept repeating, in an otherwise quite rational conversation, the word "polamolalittersjitterstittersleelitla." The psychiatrist asked her to spell it out, and she then proceeded to explain to him the meaning of the various components, which she insisted were to be used as one word. "Polamolalitters" was intended to recall the disease poliomyelitis, since the patient wanted to indicate that she was suffering from a serious disease affecting her nervous system; the component "litters" stood for untidiness or messiness, the way she felt inside; "jitterstitters" reflected her inner nervousness and lack of ease; "leelitla" was a reference to the French *le lit là* (that bed there), meaning that she was both dependent on and feeling handicapped by her illness.

The appearance of the schizophrenic may be quite slovenly. He may not wash, shave, change his clothes, or attend to personal hygiene. His manners may be crude. A significant segment of the homeless population likely satisfy diagnostic criteria for schizophrenia.

The purpose of the preceding discussion was to describe some general symptoms of schizophrenia. Since the diagnosis of schizophrenia has been controversial in the past, great pains were taken in DSM—III, —III-R, and —IV to improve the criteria set for it. In order to diagnose schizophrenia in

DSM—IV, the patient must "test positive" in each of six areas. These areas are:

1. Two or more of the following must persist for a significant portion of a one month period: delusions, hallucinations, disorganized or catatonic behavior, incoherence, illogical thinking, flattening of mood, or environmental withdrawal. Only one symptom is required if the delusions are bizarre or the hallucinations are auditory (If you build it . . . he will come).
2. Social/occupational impairment. The patient's ability to function occupationally, socially, and interpersonally has markedly deteriorated.
3. Duration: continuous signs of the disturbance must persist for at least six months.
4. Mood disorder exclusion: In some ways, the symptoms of schizophrenia overlap the symptoms of mood disorders, which will be described later. To diagnose schizophrenia, mood disorders must be ruled out. Therefore, there is no major depressive, manic, or mixed episodes in schizophrenia.
5. Substance/general medical condition exclusion: It cannot be demonstrated that the disturbance is the result of a substance or a general medical condition.
6. A previously diagnosed autistic patient must additionally display delusions or hallucinations for a month (DSM—IV, 1994, pp. 285-286). Presence of hallucinations are often inferred in nonverbal autistic children, as they poke fingers in ears to stop voices, or swat at perceived insects.

Subtypes of schizophrenia include:

- **Paranoid type** (preoccupation with delusions or frequent auditory hallucinations without disorganized speech or catatonic behavior).
- **Disorganized type** (prominant disorganized speech and behavior with inappropriate mood).
- **Catatonic type** (stupors characterized by the assumption of bizzare body postures, excessive purposeless motor behavior, or catalepsy (frozen posture which can be manipulated by another), also called "waxy flexibility.")

Schizophreniform disorder is diagnosed if the schizophrenic syndrome has persisted more than one month, but less than six. Brief psychotic disorder describes an episode of at least one day, but less than a month, and often follows unexpected traumas or disasters such as tornadoes and earthquakes.

B. Delusional Disorder

The essential feature of this disorder is the presence of one or more nonbizarre delusions that persists for at least one month. The person has never met the diagnostic criteria for schizophrenia. His ability to function is not markedly impaired, and his behavior is not obviously bizarre or odd (DSM—IV, 1994, pp. 296-301).

Although the intent of this category may have been to provide a residual category for people who do not meet all of the criteria for paranoid schizophrenia, it is a very useful category and probably underdiagnosed. The prediction of dangerous or violent behavior is very difficult. However, people with this disorder are among those who represent a great potential for danger and harm to themselves or others.

Paranoid schizophrenics may have bizarre delusions of extreme persecution, such as "All of the cosmic forces are conspiring to kill me, so I must destroy the universe!" This is a patently absurd, bizarre delusion. Destruction of the universe is an improbable event, and one that is logistically difficult to execute. The paranoid schizophrenic is likely to be so disorganized and debilitated that he could neither logically form nor execute a plan that would cause harm to others.

By definition, people with delusional disorder have delusions that are nonbizarre. It is not totally irrational to believe that your boss is out to get you if you have just been fired. Typically, paranoid people are very rigid and are governed by their religious, moral, or ethical principles and philosophies. A paranoid person is likely to perceive being fired as very bad and feel extremely guilty. It is unlikely that he would attribute his dismissal to poor performance. He would likely reason that an evil person fired him, and that the evil person must be killed so that he could not fire other virtuous people. Because his ability to function is not appreciably impaired, he is capable of planning and executing a violent act. Such people are termed "overcontrolled" paranoids. Their hostility and anger accumulates to a "boiling point," at which they are likely to commit extreme acts of violence *from* a sense of conscience. There is typically a single violent act. Upon completion, the perpetrator often feels a sense of relief that justice has been served.

John T. Miller had a history of arrests spanning twenty years for failure to pay child support. In 1992 he entered the Schuyler County Department of Social Services Support Collection Unit in Watkins Glen, New York. He shot four workers to death. He did not flee. He remained in the building and appeared relieved. With weapon in hand, he was confronted by police. He dropped the gun and stood motionless. "Basically, he said he killed everyone that he had come to kill," said Sheriff Michael Maloney (Kates, 1992, p. 9A). Similar cases of mass murder, unfortunately all too common, are committed in post offices by disgruntled employees. Mass murderers are unlike serial killers, who kill repeatedly over a prolonged period of time, are sexually motivated, and experience no guilt or remorse.

Predicting dangerousness is difficult. The best single variable predictor of a violent act is a violent past. If at age twenty you have never struck another person in anger, I bet you won't. Having committed a previous violent act does not mean the person will commit another, but the probability is greater.

Making threats is another predictor of violent behavior. Most paranoid people who commit acts of violence have threatened their targets and told family and confidants of their intent. J.M. MacDonald (1963, 1967) studied the post-release behavior of patients who were hospitalized because they had made threats to kill. Three of seventy-seven committed murder, and four committed suicide. Ten percent of those who threatened killed others or themselves. Thus, only a small percentage of threats are carried out. However almost always, threats proceed a violent act committed by one who is paranoid.

The probability that someone will perform a violent act is greater if the person clearly identifies who or what he feels is threatening him. "They are out to get me" represents a vague target. "The FBI is out to get me" is more specific. "Agent Jones of the FBI is out to get me" is the most specific.

James Oliver Huberty killed twenty-one people and wounded nineteen others in a McDonald's restaurant in San Ysidro, California in 1984. Huberty was upset about being fired from his job as a security guard. The Associated Press reported that Huberty's wife said, "He constantly played with his weapons collection. He kept guns in every corner of the bedroom. He was always mad at somebody. Before he left he said 'I'm going hunting humans.'" I have visited the site of the crime. The restaurant has been torn down. A monument remains.

In May of 1988, Lori Dann, upset over being fired from a babysitting job, fatally shot one child and wounded six others. Prior to this she had made numerous death threats and sent poisoned food and drink to twenty-one people. Prosecutors were investigating her in three states. Although her behavior was outrageous, it was not surprising.

J. D. Salinger's classic 1951 novel, *The Catcher in the Rye*, tells the story of Holden Caulfield, an idealistic teenager who endeavors to improve an imperfect world. He envisions himself as the "catcher" who stands on the edge of a cliff at the end of a field of rye. Should an innocent child fall from the field toward a world of hypocrisy, he will catch and rescue him. This theme appeals to paranoid minds.

In 1991 Robert Bardo was sentenced to life in prison without parole for the murder of Rebecca Schaffer, star of television situation comedy *My Sister Sam*. He fell in love with her for her innocence, and had the erotomanic delusion that she would love him too. He sent her a letter and she responded with one with a peace symbol and heart signed "Love, Rebecca." He became incensed when she appeared in a love scene with an actor in another film. Bardo then perceived her as just another

"Hollywood whore." He obtained her address through the Department of Motor Vehicles, stalked her relentlessly, and killed her. He had been reading *The Catcher In The Rye* (Tharp, 1992, pp. 28-30). At least twenty-one states have passed anti-stalking laws.

Mark David Chapman killed John Lennon of the Beatles on December 8, 1980. He idolized Lennon, played his music on his guitar, and signed into motel rooms under his name. He became disenchanted with Lennon because of perceived hypocrisy. Following a failed suicide attempt in Hawaii (he was discovered by a jogger as he tried to asphyxiate himself in his automobile), he returned to New York with the intent of killing Lennon. He retraced the steps of Holden Caulfield through New York, even asking people in Central Park, "Where do the ducks go in Winter?" as Holden did. He stalked Lennon and shot him to death outside the Dakota apartments where Lennon lived. Shortly after the murder, he was asked why he killed Lennon. "The reason I killed John Lennon was to gain prominence to promote the reading of J.D. Salinger's, *The Catcher In The Rye*," was his reply (*Frontline*, The Man Who Shot John Lennon, WGBH, Boston).

A memorial service was held for Lennon in front of his apartment. Standing in the crowd was another man who possessed a wrinkled copy of *The Catcher In The Rye*. Three months later John W. Hinckley, Jr. attempted to assassinate President Ronald Reagan. Reagan and his aide, James Brady, were wounded. Federal legislation bearing Brady's name now restricts illegal hand guns. Hinckley had the erotomatic delusion that movie actress Jodie Foster would love him if she only knew him. Shooting the president would attract her attention, he reasoned. Although judged to be not guilty by reason of insanity, Hinckley had the presence of mind to select more damaging hollow-headed bullets, was able to locate the president, penetrate presidential security, and fire quickly with great accuracy. It is unlikely that someone actively psychotic could have done this. Congress passed the Insanity Defense Reform Act in 1984 because of critism following the Hinckley decision.

C. Shared Psychotic Disorder

Formerly called induced psychotic disorder, this intriguing condition is diagnosed when an individual becomes deluded in the same way or in a similar way as someone close to him. The primary case, or the inducer, is likely to have delusional disorder. The delusion is likely to be of grandiosity (God speaks to me. I interpret his words. You must come to know him through me.). Such a delusion may seem bizarre, it is not; it is pragmatic and self-serving. To compare oneself to God is a compelling metaphor. Followers do not appear for one who perceives himself as a plumber. The inducee is likely to be a relative, or have a close relationship with the primary case, and be vulnerable and dependent. Prior to the development of this condition, the inducee was not delusional. The delusion may come to be shared by a group, which can become quite large. People do not typically present for treatment for this disorder. They do not perceive their beliefs as delusional.

Your initial reaction may be that this disorder is not likely to occur, or that anyone who develops it must be incredibly gullible or naive. However, a nonbizzare paranoid or grandeur delusion can be very compelling. In one case, a bright young woman with dependent personality started dating a man. At first she was "a little suspicious" of his belief that he was being followed. He explained that years ago he was involved in a bad business deal and that although his former associates had done nothing to harm him, they had threatened him. She moved in with him, apparently not very concerned with his preoccupation with weapons, survival paraphernalia, security devices, and threats of violence against specific people. Eventually she realized that he was paranoid and attempted to leave him. He consequently perceived her as part of the conspiracy against him and threatened to kill her if she left. She stayed because she was afraid of him. While she lived with him, however, she began to share some of his delusions. Ultimately, she willingly hung meat to dry in the kitchen so that they would have food if they had to flee. He eventually did flee to a wilderness area and committed suicide.

Charles Manson, mastermind of the 1969 murder of actress Sharon Tate and six others in California, had the paranoid delusion that an inevitable race war, "Helter Skelter," must happen. His followers were similarly deluded and, upon his instruction, committed the murders that were to begin the war. Lynette Fromme, called "Squeaky" because of noises made during sex, was one of the most loyal members of the "Manson Family." She is now serving a life sentence for her 1975 attempted assassination of President Ford. She escaped from prison in 1987 for two days upon hearing a false rumor that Manson was suffering from testicular cancer. Sandra Good also maintains her loyalty. "Charles Manson is the most enlightened human being I have ever known," is her steadfast belief. Although forbidden to see him, she lives near Corcoran Prison where Manson resides (Kramer, 1993, pp. 52-53).

During the 1970s, Reverend Jim Jones founded the Peoples Temple in San Francisco. He developed a loyal following. His followers came to believe that he was literally, and not metaphorically, God. Complaints were made by some members to authorities that he was maltreating his followers. When authorities began investigating Jones, he and his followers fled to form Jonestown, his religious colony carved from the jungle of Guyana in South America. Reports of further abuse reached the United States.

> Jim Jones did everything he could to perpetuate the myth that he was God: fraudulent psychic-healing demonstrations; searching members' garbage for information to "reveal"; drugging his followers to make it appear as though he were actually raising the dead.

United States Congressman Leo Ryan led an expedition to investigate Jonestown. Ryan offered safe passage to those who wanted to return to the United States. Only a few chose to leave. Jones ordered him to be killed. Following Ryan's murder, Jones feared the inevitable recourse of the American government. (Are you only paranoid if someone is *not* out to get you?) Jones ordered his followers to drink cyanide-laced Flavor-Aid. Nine-hundred thirteen people, including Jones, died in the largest recorded mass suicide-murder in November 1978. Many willingly drank the poison, others were compelled to by Jones' "Angels," a euphemism for his personal thugs. Jones never drank the poison, had millions of dollars in foreign bank accounts, and likely planned to flee. He was probably murdered by one of his guards or mistresses who perceived Jones' ruse, albeit too late (Harrary, 1992, p. 67 ff).

On February 28, 1993, the Bureau of Alcohol, Tobacco, and Firearms raided the Waco, Texas compound of the Branch Davidian sect, led by charismatic, diabolical, David Koresh. Incredibly underestimating Koresh's tactical capabilities, which included .50-caliber sharp-shooting rifles and M-60 machine guns, four federal agents were killed and sixteen wounded. A seige that would last 51 days began.

Law enforcement tactics and strategy differ according to the situation. A hostage-barricade situation occurs when unwilling participants are held in a restricted or confined area by a hostage taker or takers. A potential for mass suicide-murder exists if a group of likeminded people willingly remain together in some form of a sanctuary and resist police attempts to "rescue" them. What distinguishes the two situations is that in a hostage-barricade situation, hostages have no identity with their captors, resist them to their capabilities, will escape if possible, and willingly leave if given the opportunity. In a mass suicide-murder scenario, failure of people to leave when provided an opportunity indicates allegiance to the group and its leadership. For example, in the Jonestown case, Congressman Ryan offered safe passage from Jonestown for inducees. When few left, the potential for mass suicide-murder increased.

Parallels between Jonestown and Waco are obvious. Each was characterized by a group of likeminded people who were secluded and controlled by charismatic, paranoid leaders. The leaders were primarily interested in obtaining the money of the inducees, and the young women for their purposes. For example, Koresh preached from the 45th Psalm where it is written that the king's head is anointed with the "oil of gladness." Koresh's analysis of the oil refers to vaginal secretions which during intercourse with his 19 "wives" anoint the head of their king's penis (Beck, et.al., 1993, p. 56). Each group was in an untenable position. Jones had killed Congressman Ryan; Koresh had killed agents of the Department of Alcohol, Tobacco, and Firearms. Each would face loss of power and lengthy confine-

Figure 4-10. Branch Davidian Compound prior to apocalypse. Was the cult members' delusion of government persecution bizarre? (© Bob Daemmrich/Sygma.)

ment, if not execution, if apprehended. Each vowed never to be taken alive. To complete the metaphor, Christ dies in the end for his followers. So must they. Koresh called his compound "Ranch Apocalypse."

As my professor in graduate school, forensic psychologist Murray Myron taught this distinction between a hostage-barricade and a potential mass suicide-murder situation. Ironically, ABC News reported on April 20, 1993, that he had advised the FBI that Koresh was not suicidal and wanted to go on preaching his mission. FBI Director William Session said, ". . . the time had come for him to submit himself to the law. Enough is enough."

On April 19, 1993 FBI forces rammed the compound with a combat engineer vehicle. An inferno resulted, engulfing the compound in flames, and it was quickly consumed. Eighty-six people, many of them children, and Koresh, died. His prophesy of apocalypse was complete. Two years later, symbolically on the same day, came the bombing of the Federal Building in Oklahoma City. FBI tactics have been tempered since, as evidenced by a successfully resolved standoff with the Freemen in Montana in 1996.

CATEGORY VI. MOOD DISORDERS

The essential feature of this group of disorders is a disturbance of mood that is not due to any general medical condition or other mental disorder. These disorders can take a variety of forms, depending upon the moods demonstrated, their severity, and their duration. They may or may not include psychotic features. DSM—IV has expanded the mechanism for diagnosing mood disorders such that virtually any extreme variation of mood could be described. We will concentrate on mood disorders that are most common and receive the most attention.

A. *Bipolar Disorders*

Just as the North Pole is on the opposite end of the earth from the South Pole, bipolar disorder describes people whose moods are variant, volatile and extreme. Bipolar disorder was called manic-depression prior to 1980, and is still used. Mania describes how people feel when they are extremely "high" emotionally; depression depicts how they feel when they are extremely "low."

A manic episode is diagnosed when a person demonstrates a "distinct period of abnormally and persistently elevated, expansive, or irritable mood that persists for at least one week" (DSM—IV, 1994, p. 332) and may last for months. Manic people seem to have unlimited energy. They are infectiously enthusiastic, bubbly, inspired, and euphoric. They can work for days on end with very little sleep. They have fantastic, although often irrational, goals and expectations for the future, and perceive no task as too large, difficult, or complex. Ideas continually race through their minds. They cannot sit still. They often have incredible self-confidence and can be very charming, persuasive, and charismatic. They approach strangers without inhibition. They often become impulsively involved in highly speculative business endeavors, which often lead to failure and painful consequences. Psychotic features, such as delusions of grandeur and hallucinations, may be present in extreme manic states. Judgement may also suffer. In the 1993 movie *Mr. Jones,* Richard Gere portrays a man who, when in a controlled state of mania, is charming and magnetic. At other times, his mania is extreme and he becomes psychotic. Precariously standing on ledges of high buildings, he entertains grandeur delusions of flight.

A major depressive episode is diagnosed when a person has had a depressed mood for at least two weeks. Depressed people are sad, listless, lethargic, and apathetic. They are melancholic, or anhedonic, meaning they do not derive pleasure from things that once made them, or make other people, happy. They have feelings of inadequacy and extremely poor self-esteem. Speech may be slow and monotone. The person is chronically exhausted, yet has difficulty sleeping. Expectations for the future are bleak. She feels hopeless.

Depression is the inverse of mania. It is usually accompanied by a slowing down of the person's physiological processes. The person will lose weight due to loss of appetite. As he becomes less active, muscles and joints will become sore more readily. He may become constipated. Psychotic features may be present. Depression is much more serious than the "down in the dumps" or "blue" feelings that we all have occasionally. Depression often follows loss. Anything which one values, cherishes, and loses, may serve as a trigger for depression.

Bipolar I disorder describes a person who has had one or more manic episode, and has likely also had one or more depressive episode. This is used to describe a person who over an extended period of time is predominately manic. For example, a woman had gone into depression for a two month period following the birth of her child almost twenty years ago. Since that time she has had numerous extreme manic episodes. The depressive phase has not recurred.

Bipolar II disorder describes a person who has had one or more major depressive episode, with periods of mania insufficient to meet diagnostic criteria for a manic episode. The person is predominately depressed over time.

Bipolar disorder, mixed, describes a person who meets the criteria for a manic and major depressive episode simultaneously. Moodswings occur abruptly, with rapid alternation of manic and depressive symptoms. Clinically, such volatile affect is indicated by a rapid-cycling specifier.

Long periods of remission may separate the manic and depressive phases. People who invest wildly and spend foolishly when manic may attempt or commit suicide when they begin to enter a depressive phase. They soon realize that they are financially destroyed and that they face the prospect of months of depression. It may seem strange, but severely depressed people often lack the initiative to attempt suicide. They sometimes discover it when entering a manic phase.

A seasonal pattern specifier is used to describe fluctuations of mood that correspond to seasonal changes. Many mammals hibernate. In the northern hemisphere, duration and depth of hibernation increases with latitude. Humans do not hibernate, but mood may be affected by seasonal changes. As day length decreases significantly in November, a depressive episode may begin. Winter time fatigue, Winter weight gain, increased sleep, and decreased social activity accompany the condition. In Fairbanks, Alaska, where there is only three hours and forty-two minutes of available daylight at Winter solstice, 9.2% of subjects studied met diagnostic criteria for seasonal affective disorder. Only 1.4% met the criteria in Sarasota, Florida (Booker & Hellekson, 1992, p. 1176). To quote the Eagles' song, *Desperado*, "Don't your feet get cold in the Winter time. The sky won't snow, and the sun won't shine. It's hard to tell the nighttime from the day." This depression persists through the Winter, and lifts with daylight increases in March and April.

Controlled mania, without psychotic features, is common in high achievers. Golfer Bert Yancey's professional career spanned more than three decades. He won over $1,000,000 during his career. In 1975, he was diagnosed as manic-depressive. David Kindred of the Washington Post wrote:

> In the winter of 1974, Yancey was floating on a high. He knew it, he says today, and as all manic-depressives would, he loved it. The high is intoxicating. It is a feeling the manic-depressive craves just as the alcoholic thirsts for the bottle's deliverance from life's pain.

He didn't know what to make of it in 1960, but Yancey recognized the symptoms of his illness.

> "I couldn't sleep. I went for three nights and four days without sleeping. When you're high your mind just works and works constantly. That's when you're creative. You really get charged up."

> "What happens," Yancey said, trying to explain the catalyst of his manic highs, "is that when you succeed, believe it or not, you become depressed. For me, anyway, you become depressed because your body feels now it has to succeed again, and again. . . . so my body was saying, 'Man, I'm tired. I'm tired of this. I'm depressed because we can't keep up this pace.' So a manic episode follows." (Kindred, 1978.)

Since then, Yancey had a series of serious manic episodes. He was hospitalized and believed that the Mafia was infiltrating the hospital to kill the patients with poison gas. He began taking Tegretol in 1984 and the manic episodes stopped. Also gone were the hand tremors, which he had experienced when he was taking lithium, another drug used to treat bipolar disorder. The tremors had impaired his fine muscle coordination; as a result, his golf game suffered. In 1986 Yancey attempted a comeback. He won $500 in the Tallahassee Open, his first paycheck since 1975 (Dougherty, 1987).

His golf game improved. Between 1988 and 1993 he made over $400,000 on the Senior PGA tour. He publicly advocated that people with bipolar disorder seek treatment, offering himself as an example. In August of 1994, Yancey died of a heart attack on the practice range of Park Meadows Golf Course, anticipating playing in the Franklin Quest Championship (*Golfer*, 1994, C1 ff).

Ronald Fieve, expert on mood disorders, feels that some of history's most productive and creative people have been victims of bipolar disorder. Ernest Hemingway's mood swings made national headlines. He spent great amounts of time writing. When he wasn't writing, he was hunting, fishing, or fighting—anything to keep active. He referred to his depressive episodes as his "black-ass days." He eventually killed himself during such an episode. Abraham Lincoln suffered numerous episodes of depression. During one such episode his friends had to keep razors and knives away from him for fear he would kill himself. Fieve also surmises that Theodore Roosevelt and Winston Churchill had bipolar disorder (Fieve, 1975, pp. 116-145).

Bipolar disorder afflicts about two percent of the American population. Many people are diagnosed and treated for the disorder. Others struggle through their lives plagued by their recurring extreme mood swings; neither recognizing nor seeking treatment for their condition. The manic stockbroker who must occasionally be absent from the exchange because of recurring bouts of depression, or the homemaker, who cannot find the energy to get out of bed one week, and then buys new curtains, rugs, and appliances the following, represent cases of ambulatory, undiagnosed bipolar disorder.

B. Dysthymia

Depression may be the "common cold" of mental disorders. About fifteen to twenty percent of the general population experience dysthymia in their lifetime, and five to eight percent of all adults experience dysthymia each year (DSM—IV, 1994, p. 339-349). The symptoms are very similar to those of major depressive disorder. In general, dysthymia is thought to be less severe. However, two years of depressed mood are required for a diagnosis of dysthymia; only two weeks are required for a major depressive disorder. Also, psychotic features can be present in a major depressive disorder, but by definition, are generally excluded from dysthymia. In explanation of his chronic melancholy, a person with dysthymia may say, "I don't really want to feel like this. It's just the way I am."

Although people with dysthymia are still capable of functioning and are not psychotic, they are still victims of a serious disorder. Often, suicide attempts are made with full appreciation of the consequences. This is unlike a person with psychotic depression who may commit suicide because "voices" told him to do so. Life with dysthymia is extremely painful. Dysthymics may see the future as hopeless and perceive death as their only alternative.

A conservative estimate is that fifty-thousand Americans commit suicide annually. Following a suicide, friends and family members often cry, "We didn't know he was going to do it!" However, there are many reasonably evident indicators of suicide. About eighty percent of suicides are committed by people who are depressed. Contrary to common adage, "He tried it once, he didn't want to die," more than fifty percent of completed suicides are preceded by prior attempts. Also, contrary to common belief that, "those who talk about suicide never do it," about eighty percent of completed suicides have expressed suicidal intent, or made threats. About four of five of completed suicides are men, who likely are in their early forties and have recently experienced a significant loss such as divorce or bankruptcy. Although they die less frequently from suicide, women attempt three times more often. Men are likely to shoot, jump, or hang themselves; methods which have a high probability of death. Women, slit wrists, take pills, or use gas; methods which disfigure less, and give them time to change their mind. Better than fifty percent of completed suicides are committed when under the influence of a substance. Death results in only about two percent of attempted suicides (Garland and Zigler, 1993, p. 170).

Although a person may have been depressed for a long time, there may be indications of impending suicide. "Closure" behaviors prepare a person for death by attending to personal affairs. An individual may give away prized possessions, pay bad debts, make amends with friends and relatives, make a will, order finances, or confess to a spouse a long distant sexual indiscretion. Suicidal people may "cut ties to life." They become socially withdrawn, and no longer participate in family, occupational, or recreational activities. Isolation is compatible with suicide. Uncharacteristic joy in a person who has been seriously depressed (the "smiling depressant") can indicate that he has finalized his decision and formulated his plan to commit suicide. Although someone may threaten suicide to gain leverage in an interpersonal relationship, no threat of suicide should ever be dismissed.

Dysthymia often follows a loss that an individual has experienced. The types of losses that can be serious enough to trigger this disorder are many and varied. The loss of a loved one, job, or health are some of the more common events that precede it. Women, who give birth to healthy babies sometimes

Figure 4-11. *On the Contrary*: Kay Sage, 1952. A visual representation of the existentialist void of depression. (*Collection of the Walker Art Center, Minneapolis.*)

become depressed. The baby that had been inside the mother for nine months is now living in the external environment. The mother may feel a sense of loss. When people do things that they believe are wrong and in violation of their personal moral codes, they often feel extremely guilty and become depressed. Their self-esteem has been lost (Mowrer and Veszelovky, 1980).

I have been involved in a number of cases in which women with no past histories of mental disorder became acutely depressed following an abortion. Some attempted suicide. Some of these women never ruled out having the abortion because of possible guilt. Guilt can be a major factor in dysthymia, major depression, and suicide (Smrtic, 1979).

There is reason for cautious optimism regarding the course of depression that results following loss. Regardless of the type of loss, people typically adjust. Two years from now, the source of present depression will likely not be the most serious problem one faces. New ones may replace it. Depression following a severe loss such as divorce is often characterized by negative personal attributions and a hopeless attitude that things will not get better. However, time often heals "wounds."

"In this sad world of ours, sorrow comes to all, and it often comes with bitter agony. Perfect relief is not possible, except with time. You cannot now believe that you will ever feel better. But this is not true. You are sure to be happy again. Knowing this, truly believing it, will make you less miserable now. I have had enough experience to make this statement."

—Abraham Lincoln

CATEGORY VII. ANXIETY DISORDERS

Anxiety is not necessarily bad. It alerts us to potential danger in the environment. It incites us to make adjustments in life. It motivates us to study for exams and write term papers. This category contains conditions in which anxiety has increased above an acceptable level, has become a source of discomfort and distress, and inhibits the ability to function. From this category we will describe panic disorder, agoraphobia, specific phobia, obsessive-compulsive disorder, generalized anxiety disorder, and posttraumatic stress disorder.

A. *Panic disorder*

Panic disorder is characterized by recurrent, unexpected panic attacks. These attacks occur abruptly and peak within ten minutes. The person may believe he is dying. Symptoms include nausea, dizziness, heart palpitations, profuse sweating, trembling, and sensations of smothering, numbness or tingling. The attack will subside with time. However, once a person has had a panic attack, he may anticipate future ones. Anticipatory anxiety and perception of impending catastrophe impair functioning ability.

Panic attacks are often cued by an incorrect attribution of physiological distress or arousal. After climbing a flight of stairs, a person may perceive accelerated heart rate as signaling an impending heart attack. The person hyperventilates and becomes dizzy. The anxiety is interpreted as discomfort that accompanies a heart attack. Sweating, trembling, and shortness of breath further convince the person that she is dying. When the attack subsides, the person believes she has survived a close brush with death, rather than acknowledge that she was not having a heart attack. Anticipatory anxiety persists as she believes she may not be so fortunate next time.

B. *Specific Phobia*

Phobias are acute fears that are experienced when specific situations or objects are encountered. Acute fear refers to fear that is extremely intense and sudden in onset. The phobic may realize that his fear is excessive, but has little control over it. Phobias often result from unpleasant experiences with particular stimuli. We tend to fear things that we feel are potential sources of danger. If never had man been harmed by animals, heights, or water, it would be unreasonable to fear them. However, occasionally, dogs bite, bridges collapse, and people drown. I have never heard of anyone who was afraid of his mittens; mittens are our friends, and pose no threat to our survival.

Phobics avoid those things or situations that they perceive as potentially harmful, and tend to overestimate the probability of potential danger or harm. The *Diagnostic Manual* describes the fear as "excessive or unreasonable." Such a judgement implies that the clinician has had a similar experience, and fear is unjustified. Prior to DSM—IV, these phobias were called "simple" phobias, an apparent misnomer. In the Spring of 1987, a New York State Thruway bridge collapsed into the rain-swollen Schoharie Creek. I spoke with a woman who felt the bridge shake as she crossed it. It disintegrated seconds later. She watched as cars plunged into the torrent. She is afraid of bridges. Is her fear "excessive or unreasonable?" Phobics seek treatment when their ability to function has become impaired.

The list of possible phobias is virtually endless. Franklin Delano Roosevelt, in his first inaugural address of 1933 said, "The only thing we have to fear is fear itself," implying that Americans are phobophobiacs, or people who fear fear. To avoid listing a plethora of phobias, four subtypes are described.

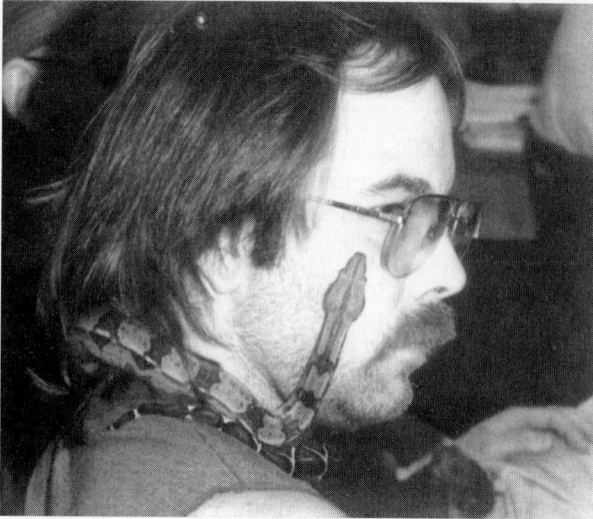

Figure 4-12: Obviously this person is without ophidiophobia: a specific phobia of snakes. (Photograph by Jim Rooney.)

- **Animal Type:** The fear is cued by animals or insects. I had never been afraid of bees. However, after a sting which resulted in a severe allergic reaction which required hospitalization, my "respect" for bees has increased.

- **Natural Environment Type:** Fear is cued by objects or events in the natural environment, such as storms, heights, or water.

- **Blood-Injection-Injury Type**: This phobia is cued by either experiencing or seeing some form of injury, witnessing blood, or receiving an injection. I was once the Operations Officer in an Army Drill Sergeant Battalion. Basic trainees would delight, could they see their stern, compassionless mentors whimper and moan at the prospect of an injection, then twist and faint when the inevitable occurred.

- **Situational Type:** This type is cued by specific situations such as public transportation, bridges, elevators, flying, driving, or enclosed places (DSM—IV, 1994, p. 406).

John Madden, former Oakland Raiders coach and National Football League analyst, is notorious for his nostalgic desire for football as it was once played. "Three things we don't need are Astroturf, indoor stadiums, and the wave." Football was meant to be played outside, where you know it's cold, "when you spit, and it freezes before it hits the ground." Madden has been claustrophobic since childhood. While coaching, he suffered unavoidable plane flights. He no longer travels by plane, preferring his specially outfitted bus, the "Madden-mobile" (Madden, 1984, pp. 34-35.).

C. Social Phobia

Social phobias are those in which the individual becomes intensely anxious in situations where he perceives he may be the object of scrutiny, ridicule, or humiliation. This type of phobia includes fear of giving a speech before a group, eating in a restaurant, and urinating in a public lavatory. Such phobias may limit the career of talented people whose ability to function professionally is impaired. Singer Carly Simon had gone fifteen years, and Barbara Streisand twenty-eight years, between concert performances because of stage fright.

D. Agoraphobia

More people seek treatment for agoraphobia than any other phobia. Literally, agoraphobia means fear of the outdoors or marketplace. The individual becomes extremely anxious in situations from which escape might be difficult or when help is not available in an emergency. Agoraphobiacs often become reclusive and seldom leave their homes. Home is the only place in which they feel relatively secure. Agoraphobia is often accompanied by panic attacks.

An obese man had been subjected to ridicule and humiliation continually throughout adolescence and early adulthood. He seldom left the house, anticipating perceived inevitable ridicule. "If I go out there, they'll make fun of me. Besides, Mom's bringing home groceries and I told her that I'd open the door." With much cajoling, his therapist convinced him to walk alone to a neighborhood store. While en route, he fell down and was unable to get up. A crowd of children encircled and taunted him. He became more reclusive.

E. Obsessive-Compulsive Disorder

An individual is obsessed when preoccupied with unwanted ideas, thoughts, or impulses which constantly pervade consciousness. An individual is compelled when he feels an irresistible urge to act, regardless of whether his actions are excessive or unreasonable. The goal of the compulsion is to prevent or reduce anxiety or distress, not to provide pleasure or gratification. If at all, the reduction of anxiety is temporary. An individual may compulsively tap a desk or count aloud tiles in a wall while involved in face to face interaction. The ritual continues despite embarrassment and humiliation. The person would become extremely anxious if situational factors prevent the performance of rituals. To receive this diagnosis, the person must be preoccupied with his obsessions or compulsions for more than one hour a day, feel distressed, and demonstrate impaired ability to function.

Obsessions and compulsions are typically symbolically related to a conflict an individual is experiencing, or a perceived personal defect. One common obsession is an extreme concern with health and cleanliness. Cleanliness rituals may represent a symbolic undoing of perceived personal impurity. One nurse was so obsessed with the possibility of getting the flu that she would perform a fifteen-minute ritual of sanitizing the office after each patient left. Any object the patient had touched would be wiped clean. She sprayed disinfectant around the room and on the chair in which the patient had been sitting. The doctor fired the nurse because her compulsions prevented her from running the office efficiently. Being healthy and clean are desirable. However, such concern is objectively unreasonable and excessive. Other obsessions center around money, power, or checking that everything is in order before leaving the house. One patient was very concerned that the light in the refrigerator would not go out when he closed the door.

F. Generalized Anxiety Disorder

The essential feature of this disorder is excessive anxiety, apprehension and worry, which occurs more days than not for a period of at least six months. The anxiety and worry are also accompanied by physical and cognitive symptoms. The focus of the apprehension is not confined to features of another Axis I disorder, like fear of weight gain in a person with Anorexia. The person experiences distress and the ability to function is impaired.

We all know what it is like to be anxious. It is often an appropriate response to an environmental demand. Anxiety often motivates us to solve problems. Once our problems have been solved, our anxiety typically dissipates. Feelings of anxiety normally diminish after taking an exam, paying a bill, or ending a relationship. For people with anxiety disorders, the anxiety does not diminish when problems are solved. Their anxiety is chronic and exhausting.

Unlike phobics, who are very certain of the stimuli and situations that make them anxious, people with anxiety disorders experience vague, nebulous, unfocused, and free-floating anxiety. Although they express concern over the health of family members and over work, family problems, and finances, their concern is exaggerated and disproportionate. They may sense impending doom. They feel that something bad is bound to happen, but don't know why, when, or how. One elderly woman was intensely apprehensive that her heat would be shut off even though she had never missed a payment and had no outstanding bill. When told by her son that her fear was excessive and he would never allow her heat to be shut off, she reminded him of his failure to pay a bill some years ago and recounted the story of an elderly Ohio couple who froze when their power was turned off. Often the anxiety is about things over which the person has no control, such as the possibility of an earthquake or nuclear destruction.

To receive this diagnosis, an adult must demonstrate three of the following physical and cognitive symptoms: 1) restlessness, 2) fatigue, 3) difficulty concentrating or mental lapses, 4) irritability, 5) muscle tension, or 6) sleep disturbances (DSM—IV, 1994, pp. 432-436). Years ago patients with anxiety disorder would graphically describe to me their nausea and how their "guts felt twisted." At the time I did not know the sensation, but since then I have experienced it. You may know the feeling. Imagine it persisting for months. It is very exhausting. Those of you who do not know the feeling have something to look forward to.

G. Post-Traumatic Stress Disorder

Post-traumatic stress disorder was an innovation of DSM—III in 1980. Its inclusion was strongly advocated by the Vietnam veteran's lobby. During the past two decades, the category has been accorded legitimacy. It is also increasingly being used to describe victims of catastrophe, disaster, violent or sexual assault, or being held captive as a hostage. Its general diagnostic criteria are that the person:

- has experienced, witnessed, or was confronted with an event or events that involved actual or threatened death, serious injury, or a threat to the physical integrity of self or others. The event is outside the realm of usual human experience and caused the person intense fear, helplessness, or horror.

- has flashbacks, in which the event is recreated through frequent distressful recollections, recurring dreams, or sensations. The flashbacks may be triggered by an external stimulus, such as a low flying plane, and involve the vivid reexperiencing of visions, feelings, smells, tastes and sounds of the traumatic experience.

- has three or more of the following symptoms:
  – attempts to avoid thoughts, feelings, people, activities, or places associated with the trauma.
  – is emotionally numb and lacks capability or desire to have affectionate relationships. ("I swore I would never again let anyone matter to me, so I couldn't ever hurt that much again," said a veteran remembering the combat death of his best friend.)
  – is unable to recall important aspects of the trauma.
  – has a sense of foreshortened future (does not expect to have career, marriage or children).

- has two or more of the following symptoms:
  – Difficulty sleeping.
  – Irritability and outbursts of anger.
  – Difficulty concentrating ("zoning out").
  – Hypervigilance (perpetual preparedness, e.g., having children perform guard duty at night).
  – Exaggerated startle response (shell shock). This involves an exaggerated physiological response to any startling stimulus reminiscent of the traumatic event, e.g., a car backfiring.

- Has had this disturbance for at least one month.

War has always been horrifying. Each is unique in its potential for producing trauma. There are many reasons why an estimated 470,000 Vietnam veterans suffer psychological disorders related to the war; sixty-six thousand specifically have post-traumatic stress disorder (Roberts, 1988, p. 788), and, as reported by CNN in January of 1992, 250,000 veterans are homeless. The war was fought without immediate danger to the security of the United States. The economy was good, and the World Series was played every October. The draft discriminatly conscripted only young males who were faced with the dilemma of either fighting in a heinous war or evading, and facing legal and moral consequences.

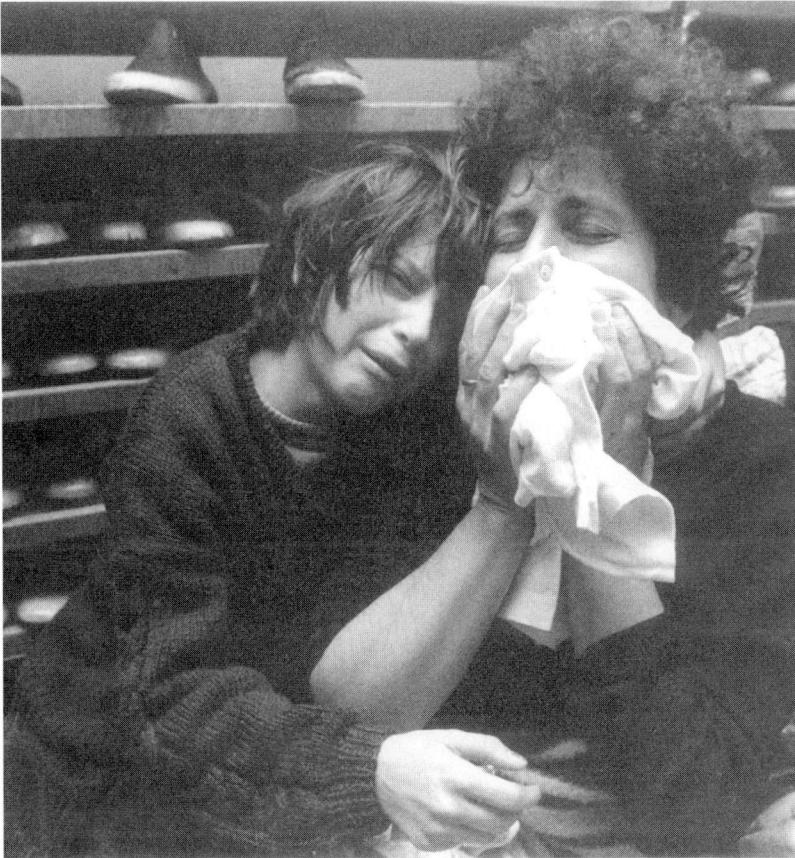

Figure 4-13.
16-year-old Samra Kapatoanovic was killed by a mortar shell as she played outside her Moslem family's shoe factory refuge, Sarajevo, Bosnia and Herzegovina, 1992. Her mother and sister clutch her blouse. (Reuters/Corbis-Bettmann.)

The average age of the combat soldier was nineteen years.

As it continued, the Vietnam War became less popular. The nation and families were divided. It was fought without a definite military mission and without a declaration of war. Veterans returned home two days after being in combat with little time to put the experience into perspective. They were often ridiculed and taunted, or worse, ignored. Guilt, remorse, anger, and regret are strong emotions for the Vietnam veteran. Popular motion pictures like *Apocalypse Now, Coming Home, Platoon, The Deer Hunter, Full Metal Jacket,* and perhaps most poignantly and graphically, *Jacob's Ladder*, describe the trauma of the war.

In 1984, a monument was built in Washington to commemorate the lives of the 58,175 men and 8 women who were killed in the Vietnam War. I visited it and was powerfully moved. Others wept, said prayers, or stood in silence. Two young men pointed to a name on the monument and left flowers for a father they barely remember. Others walked the path quickly, barely looking. For them, the monument merely provided a short cut to the rest room.

The diagnostic criteria for post-traumatic stress disorder were made more stringent in DSM—IV. Apparently the disorder was being overdiagnosed such that people with job losses, custody battles, and divorces were receiving the diagnosis. These events are surely distressful, but not traumatic. Also, military clinicians, who have a dual role of supporting the military mission and treating their patients, may have employed too low a threshold for diagnosing stress related disorders (Camp, 1993, pp. 1000-1009). Furthermore, some veterans malingered to obtain benefits. Ironically, many legitimate sufferers have failed to present because of pride, or perceived weakness or stigma.

About ten percent of the 1990-91 Persian Gulf War veterans show signs of at least "mild" post-traumatic stress disorder, and three percent are at risk for serious combat related problems (Elias, 1992, C.). While the Gulf War was certainly briefer, tactically more technological, and had a clear military objective, it involved other risk factors. Those most likely to be affected were: troops in the immediate danger zone; troops outside the zone who were at risk for entering it; Reservists who were activated for the war; soldiers responsible for spouses, parents or children; and soldiers who had other major upheavals in their lives (Hobfoll, et.al, 1991, p. 849). As an Army Reservist, I was activated for the Gulf War. Although I did not serve in the danger zone, I shared the other risk factors and have empathy with those who are affected.

CATEGORY VIII. SOMATOFORM DISORDERS

This group of disorders is used to describe people who have symptoms that suggest the existence of a general medical condition, even though thorough medical examination fails to reveal any adequate explanation. "Soma" means body; these people perceive there is something wrong with them. The precise nature of the reported symptoms varies among the disorders in the category. They may include some type of loss of physical function, as in paralysis or blindness, an abnormal body function, or a variety of pains and discomforts. Some people with these disorders have uncontrollable episodes of vomiting, hiccupping, or defecation. A woman may, on rare occasions, develop a false pregnancy, complete with morning sickness, cessation of menses, and enlargement of the abdomen. People with these disorders are chronic "doctor shoppers," a source of anguish for medical practitioners, and disproportionally consume medical resources and services.

People with a somatoform disorder must be distinguished from malingerers, or fakers. This is very difficult in many cases. Malingerers will often fake physical symptoms to collect insurance money, get discharged from the military, or even gain admittance to a mental hospital. Their "performances" are often compelling. They must also be distinguished from those with a factitious disorder, which will be covered later, in which symptoms are voluntarily produced. People with somatoform disorders actually believe they are physically afflicted. Their condition causes them distress or impaired function.

A. *Somatization Disorder*

A diagnosis of *somatization disorder* is made when a person has a history of numerous physical symptoms without apparent medical causes over a period of several years. Since people present with this condition in adolescence or early adulthood, and after age thirty such symptoms can be understood as part of the aging process (which some of us may find discomforting), the diagnosis must be made before the age of thirty. Somatization disorder is diagnosed when the clinician believes the patient experiences the presenting symptoms despite inadequate medical explanation.

To receive this diagnosis, a patient must have a minimum of eight items from the following symptom groups:

- **Four pain symptoms**—head, abdomen, joints, back, extremities, chest, rectum, urination.
- **Two gastrointestinal symptoms**—nausea, bloating, vomiting, diarrhea, intolerance of different foods.
- **One sexual symptom**—sexual indifference, erectile or ejaculation dysfunction, abnormal menstruation.
- **One pseudoneurological symptom** (a symptom or deficit that suggests a neurological condition) —paralysis or weakness, difficulty swallowing, loss of touch or pain sensation, blindness, deafness, or seizures (DSM—IV, 1994, pp. 449-450).

B. Conversion Disorder

This disorder was called conversion hysteria prior to DSM—III. *Hysteria* is the Greek word for uterus. The ancient Greeks felt that conversion hysteria was strictly a female disorder that resulted from abnormal movements of the woman's uterus (Nemiah, 1967, p. 871). This belief persisted into the middle period, when demonic forces were believed to make the uterus stray. A priest implored:

> . . . I conjure thee, O womb, in the name of the Holy Trinity to come back to the place from which thou shouldst neither move nor turn away . . . and to return, without anger, to the place where the Lord has put thee originally (Zilboorg and Henry, 1941, quoted in Zimbardo, 1992, p. 621).

Feminists argued strongly against retaining "hysteria" in DSM—III because of its derogatory connotation. They were offended by the supposition that women could be predisposed to this condition because of a "wandering uterus." They also argued that the disorder occurs in both sexes. The name was therefore changed to conversion disorder.

A major distinction between somatization and conversion disorder is that in conversion disorder the clinician has some reason to believe that the symptoms are related to some type of psychological conflict or need. Also, in conversion disorder, patients typically voice one major complaint, which involves a loss of, or abnormal, physical function.

The diagnostic manual claims not to endorse any theoretical model, and therefore, provides an "atheoretical" description for this disorder. However, because Sigmund Freud provided such a compelling explanation and description of the disorder, I will present it.

In the late 1890s he proposed that conversion hysteria resulted when a person was subjected to severe physical or sexual trauma and failed to either resist or react to the violation. Because the person did not react to the trauma, the psychological energy that should have been used to repel the attack remained in the person's system, and was then "converted" into a physical symptom (Freud, 1962). Conversion symptoms typically bear a symbolic relationship to the specific conflict or trauma. Prior to symptom formation, the person is highly anxious. Upon the "conversion," there is a reduction in anxiety and the attitude is one of relative indifference.

Although the patient is judged not to be malingering, or have a factitious disorder, symptom formation does provide the individual an advantage, or *gain*. In *primary gain,* the symptom allows the person to avoid an unpleasant conflict or situation. By becoming blind, a witness to a violent crime may not have to testify. A reluctant soldier with a paralyzed hand cannot be expected to fire his weapon in combat. A college student who loses his voice may be excused from giving his speech in class. In *secondary gain*, the symptom invites sympathy or attention from associates. A paralyzed dominant hand solicits help in household chores. I have known a small number of people with carpal tunnel syndrome, a condition assumed to result from inflammation of hand and wrist ligaments caused by extensive typing or other repetitive manual work. Most disliked their job.

There is no conclusive evidence that these people voluntarily control their symptoms. People with conversion deafness do not flinch when a loud unexpected noise is made. For all intents and purposes, they are deaf. However, the symptoms often follow the individual's conceptualization of the condition, rather than a valid anatomical explanation. For example, in hand paralysis, or "glove anesthesia," the pain or numbness horizontally crosses the wrist, unlike a neurological paralysis. Sometimes further medical evaluation does discover medical explanations for the symptoms at a later point, often years.

Although this disorder is uncommon, it typically follows Freud's description. In one case, a young woman had been subjected to extreme physical and sexual abuse throughout her childhood. She eventually married a man who treated her well. She became pregnant, and was more apprehensive than normal in anticipating her first child. She gave birth to a healthy baby. She was extremely anxious. On the

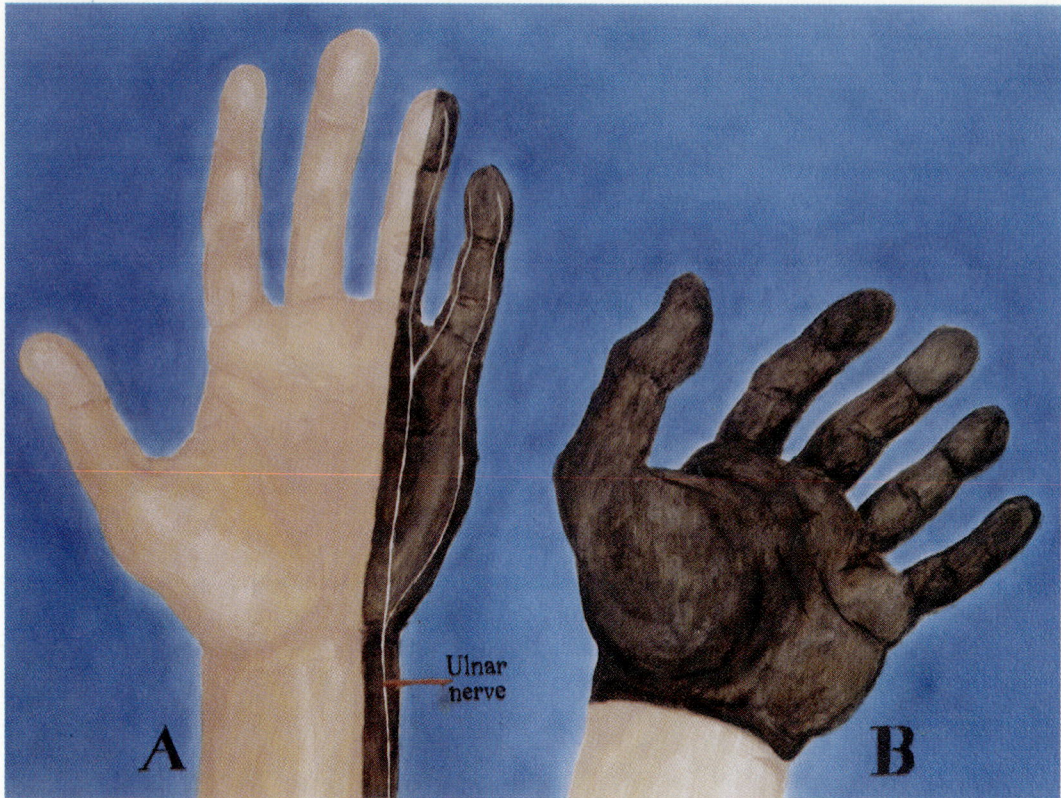

Figure 4-14. A. Nerve damage. B. Glove Anesthesia. (Illustration by Jim Rooney.)

way home from the hospital, she told her husband, "Don't ever let me do anything to hurt our baby!" Shortly thereafter paralysis started in her right, dominant hand and spread down her side. As the paralysis worsened, her anxiety diminished; she was relatively indifferent to her condition. That she could not hurt her baby because of paralysis demonstrated primary gain. That her husband sympathetically assumed household chores evidenced secondary gain. Thorough neurological tests revealed no general medical condition. Seldom do cases fit a description or satisfy a theory so clearly.

R. Peter Mogielnicki has observed parents who came to an emergency room at a hospital with complaints of blindness, paralysis of arms, nausea, and shortness of breath. In some cases it was found that the parents had strong urges to abuse their children prior to the onset of the symptoms. One man developed paralysis in the arm with which he used to beat his child. Mogielnicki urged that hospital staff question all patients who present in emergency rooms with conversion symptoms about possible abuse (Mogielnicki et al., 1977).

C. Hypochondriasis

Marcel Proust made the following appropriate comments about hypochondriasis:

> For each ailment that doctors cure with medications (as I am told they do occasionally succeed in doing) they produce ten others in healthy individuals by inoculating them with that pathogenic agent a thousand times more virulent than all the microbes—the idea that they are ill. (Barsky and Klerman, 1983.)

The essential feature of hypochondriasis is a fearful preoccupation that a person has a serious disease or illness. The adage, "A little knowledge can be a dangerous thing," is appropriate in describing hypocondriacs. They are often chronic "doctor shoppers" who are obsessed with medical literature, programming, and paraphernalia. Their medicine cabinets can be quite impressive. While they may know some of the primary symptoms of a serious disease or illness and perceive that they have them, they either do not know enough about the disease or fail to appreciate they do not have it. Their fear persists despite medical assurance there is nothing wrong with them. When told by a doctor they have nothing to fear, they do not believe him, and seek alternative opinions. They often willingly and regularly endure expensive and painful, multiple invasive diagnostic procedures. They often have "gridiron abdomens" from scars caused by exploratory surgeries. Such passion distinguishes the hypochondriac from the malingerer. They are very concerned with their condition, unlike the relative indifference of somatization and conversion disorders.

It is very difficult to live with hypochondriacs because of their excessive concern with themselves. They may force their family to make dramatic concessions to accomodate their perceived conditions. If a person perceives an impending heart attack, he may compel the family to move to a lesser desirable location without stairs.

Hypochondriacs are usually concerned with one disease or illness at a time; such as heart or respiratory disease, cancer, AIDS, cirrhosis of the liver in an alcoholic, or Alzheimer's dementia in an elderly person. While their concerns are exaggerated, they are not delusional. They do not perceive their digestive pains as caused by insects, or fingers wrapped around their throat as sources of their respiratory distress.

Hypochondriacs disproportionally consume medical resources or services. In one case, a hypochondriac's medical bills for a year totaled $250,000. Why is this allowed to happen? There are many reasons. Patients seldom present for hypochondriasis and will see a number of different physicians. Although hypochondriasis is diagnosed after excluding a general medical condition, serious diseases in early stages may be undiagnosable. Ultimately, every hypochondtriac is right once. If physicians are to err, they would rather treat a misdiagnosis than fail to treat an existing one, and risk seeing an obtiuary saying, "I told you I was sick." Treating hypochondriacs can be lucrative.

CATEGORY IX. FACTITIOUS DISORDERS

Factitious means not natural, spontaneous, or genuine. The laugh of a student, who feels compelled to laugh at his professor's corny jokes, is factitious. Munchausen syndrome is often used synonymously with factitious disorder. Hieronymus Karl Fredrich Von Munchausen was a German cavalry officer who gained fame for his extensive travels and exaggerated tales of his exploits during the late eighteenth century. Thus, Munchausen syndrome connotes a facetious and disparaging reference to people who voluntarily fabricate symptoms to present for professional attention. Physical and/or psychological symptoms may be produced.

Because factitious means unreal might imply that this disorder is not serious. It is. The symptoms are real. Physical damage often results. Permanent damage and death sometimes result as well. Deliberate self-harm syndrome describes self-inflicted injuries without the intent to die. Depressed people who wish to commit suicide perceive death as their solution. Thus, maximum intent suicides employ methods that are quick and certain, such as a gunshot to the head. People with factitious disorders will likely employ methods of lower lethality which will likely produce long-term, or permanent pain and discomfort. The only apparent motive for such self-destructive behavior appears to be the desire to assume the role of the hospitalized patient. People with factitious disorders are often referred to as "hospital hoboes." They have extensive knowledge of medical and hospital procedures, present frequently, and seldom pay their bills. They are unlike malingerers, who may desire hospitalization to avoid an unpleasant circumstance such as a jail term.

Factitious disorders always imply psychopathology (DSM—IV, 1994, p. 471). Such people have weak "ties to life," and poor presentment of future. The types of things they do to themselves demonstrate their lack of self-regard.

In one case, an adolescent girl sat at the kitchen table. She was drinking heavily and taking drugs. She crushed cigarette butts on her arms and methodically cut herself with a paring knife, dunking bread into her wounds. She seemed to be experimenting with death. When she regained consciousness in the hospital, she seemed somewhat pleased that she was there. However, she indicated that death would have been acceptable.

Other examples of people with factitious disorders include those who gorge on sweets despite diabetes, take hallucinogens to produce psychotic symptoms, or eat peanuts despite severe hemorrhoids. They may drink caustic solvents or cleansers, such as a patient who swallowed a time-release Draino capsule.

A. *Factitious Disorder By Proxy*

Included for the first time in Criteria Sets and Axes Provided for Further Study in DSM—IV is factitious disorder by proxy. A proxy is a person authorized to act for another. The condition is characterized by the intentional production of physical and/or psychological symptoms in another person who is under the individual's care. The perpetrator is likely a mother who produces symptoms in her child to satisify her own needs. Also characteristic of this disorder is the repeated presentation of the child by the caretaker for medical evaluation and care. Upon questioning by the hospital staff, the perpetrator vehemently denies any knowledge about the cause of the child's condition. There is quick resolution of symptoms when the child and perpetrator are separated in the hospital and often, evidence of abuse emerges.

Sleep apnea is a breathing related sleep disorder in which a person spontaneously stops breathing for a duration of typically twenty to forty seconds. It is assumed to be associated with sudden infant death syndrome, in which children inexplicably stop breathing while sleeping.

A symbiotic parenting relationship exists when a parent, likely a mother, has a child to satisfy her own unfulfilled needs for love and attention. The mother tends to act toward the child as a peer or playmate, and has a vested interest in keeping the child dependent upon her. Psychoanalytical literature describes this mother as the "smothering" type.

Clinically it is difficult to distinguish children who are brought to the hospital with sleep apnea from a factitious disorder by proxy, in which the mother has temporarily suffocated the child with a pillow, or pinched the nostrils ("near miss cot death" syndrome).

In factitious disorder by proxy, the mother may have presented the child previously for a similar complaint at this hospital, or others. She will frantically exclaim, "Save my baby! She stopped breathing. I have no idea why." The child will have no further apneic episodes once removed from the mother's care, and pinch marks will often appear on the child's nose a couple of days later.

This condition was placed in *Criteria Sets and Axes Provided for Further Study* because of insufficient data to justify its inclusion as a mental disorder. Because this behaviour is so heinous, the public and medical profession are reluctant to believe it exists. Mothers are supposed to love their children. In a study of thirty-two children in which factitious disorder by proxy was suspected as a cause of apnea; three children died, one was severely brain damaged from abuse, and five siblings were dead (Light and Sheridan, 1990, pp. 162-168).

In 1987, Marybeth Tinning was convicted on a single count of murder in the death of her daughter, Tami Lynne. She is also suspected of killing her eight other children during the period from 1972 to 1985 in Schenectady County, New York. Tami Lynne had been suffocated with duct tape across her mouth. Apparently, Tinning suffocated the other children with a pillow, shrewdly applying pressure equally across the face, thereby preventing surface hemorrhages. In Joyce Egginton's *From Cradle to Grave: The Short Lives and Strange Deaths of Marybeth Tinning's Nine Children*, Dr. Michael M. Baden, director of the New York State Police's forensic sciences unit, was quoted:

> . . . the causes of death as attributed were incorrect. It didn't make sense for all those deaths to be natural. Except for rare occasions, natural deaths don't occur suddenly and unexpectedly, and if there is more than one in a family, you have to be very suspicious (p. 200).

In describing Marybeth, her mother-in-law said, "She was craving for love and having babies fulfilled that need in her" (p. 71), and a former friend said, "She was an unwanted child who never grew up" (p. 331). How could such an atrocity go undetected? "Every funeral was a party for her with hardly a tear shed. After three or four of them, I gave up going" (p. 52) said a relative, and "What could I do? I couldn't prove anything. I didn't see anything. I had no evidence, but I knew," (p. 79) pleaded a neighbor.

Three babies who Marybeth confessed to killing were crying when she suffocated them. She was very sensitive to loud noise, as her father spoke very loudly because of hearing loss. While in prison, she had a violent reaction to a fellow prisoner singing gospel music in a loud but true voice. With annoyance, and a forefinger drawn across her mouth, she said to a guard, "Duct tape. That's what we need." (p. 351). Tinning represents the epitome of the "smothering mother" taken beyond the metaphor.

Among other fabricated illnesses are: causing fever by injection of contaminated material into a child's vein; causing vomiting by giving an emetic such as ipecac or antifreeze; and simulating failure to thrive by the mother secretly sucking stomach contents from her hospitalized child through a nasogastric tube (Meadow, 1989, p. 249). I suspect this condition will be included as a mental disorder in the next diagnostic manual.

CATEGORY X. DISSOCIATIVE DISORDERS

To dissociate means to separate. In dissociative disorders, in some way, an aspect of consciousness is separated from awareness. Normal conscious process is altered. There "is a disruption in the usually integrated functions of consciousness, memory, identity, or perception of the environment. The disturbance may be sudden, gradual, transient, or chronic" (DSM—IV, 1994, p. 477).

Freud considered the dissociative disorders as types of hysteria, as they share many significant features. Recall conversion disorder, which Freud called conversion hysteria. It involved a loss of physical function which followed trauma. Intense anxiety diminished following symptom formation. The symptom, although judged not to be voluntarily produced, provided the individual gain. In dissociative disorders, the altered state of consciousness archetypically follows trauma. The symptoms provide a means for dealing with anxiety, which remits with symptom formation. The gain is typically obvious, which makes the distinction between dissociative disorder and malingering difficult in forensic situations. We will describe two of the five types of dissociative disorders.

A. Dissociative Amnesia

Dissociative amnesia was formerly called psychogenic amnesia, indicating the cause of the memory loss as psychological. According to DSM—IV, the predominant disturbance is one or more episode of inability to recall important personal information of a traumatic or stressful nature that is too extensive to be explained by forgetfulness. Also explained are amnesias that result from general medical conditions, substances, or somatoform disorders (p. 478-481). I surmise that amnesia resulting from loaning close friends money is also excluded. To avoid deference to psychoanalytic theory, other aspects of Freud's description are absent.

Understandably, this disorder often coexists with post-traumatic stress disorder. Failure to remember a traumatic combat experience provides the soldier an opportunity to avoid unpleasant conflict and anxiety. In Freudian terms, the repression of the trauma, or its relegation to the unconscious mind, provides the individual gain. His inability to remember that period of time is a way in which he can avoid the painful memories of war. In one case, a Vietnam veteran had an amnesic block for a specific time period during which he was in intense combat in the bush. A decade later, a therapist was treating him for other presenting problems. While under hypnosis, he had a vivid recollection of throwing a grenade into a trench, blowing a baby from it. He became haunted with guilt after regaining awareness of the event. Therapeutically this raises an interesting question. Should a "sleeping dog" be aroused, or left to lie?

In April of 1989, a woman was savagely beaten and sexually assaulted by a group of antisocial miscreants while jogging in New York's Central Park. She was left for dead. Fifteen months later, the "Central Park Jogger," wounded, scarred, yet amazingly resilient, testified in court, in front of three defendants, about the attack. Although of questionable relevance, she was asked about and revealed intimate details of her previous sex life. She described her childhood, employment, and how it was that she was running in the park the night of her attack. When asked if she had any memory of the assault, she said "No, I do not. I remember waking up in the hospital on a Friday evening late in May and a very good friend of mine was in the hospital room . . ." (quoted. in Sullivan, 1990, p. C). Surely the assault was traumatic. The amnesia provided primary gains in that she could not testify against her attackers and risk retribution, or recall the horror of the event. National sympathy evidenced secondary gain.

B. Dissociative Identity Disorder

Dissociative identity disorder was called multiple personality prior to DSM—IV. This condition is very controversial, and opinions on it vary greatly. Some experts rigidly believe in its reality. Others doubt its existence, and call it the UFO of psychiatry; something everyone talks about but no one has seen. The condition probably exists, but is likely overdiagnosed.

Because of the controversy over the description of this condition, the *Diagnostic Manual* briefly and succinctly describes it as the presence of two or more distinct identities or personality states which recurrently take control of the person's behavior. There is an inability to recall important personal information that is too extensive to be explained by forgetting. General medical conditions, substances, factitious disorder, and malingering are ruled out (DSM—IV, 1994, p. 487).

Before describing the dissention regarding this condition, let us assume it exists. Freud considered multiple personality a type of dissociative hysteria. As you might expect, dissociation, trauma, and gain are integral elements of the condition. In true dissociative identity disorder, the personality which is typically in conscious control is called the *executive*. The episodic personality is called the *alter ego*. There is a "split personality," unlike schizophrenia, in which there is a split with reality. If truly a dissociative state, the executive should not be aware of the alter ego, although the alter may be aware of the executive. The structure and content of the personalities should be consistent over time, and the boundries between them clear, distinct, and stable. The shifts in personality should occur spontaneously, and not upon cue.

Such was the case of Chris Sizemore, described by Drs.Thigpen and Cleckley in the book, *The Three Faces of Eve*. Eve White, Eve Black, and Jane were distinct personalities that emerged following a traumatic childhood. Seventy to ninety-five percent with the condition have suffered physical and sexual abuse in childhood (Coons and Milstein, 1984, p. 839). The alternate personalities are typically foils. If one is good, the other is bad. Eve White was good; Eve Black evil. The evil alter ego does what the good executive is prohibited by conscience from doing, thus providing gain. In some cases, the alters and executive have different brain wave patterns, allergies, dominant hands, and in women, multiple menstrual cycles.

Although at one time very rare, there has been a sharp rise in reported cases of dissociative identity disorder in the United States in recent years. Some believe that greater awareness and sensitivity of domestic violence and abuse has encouraged victims to present. Others believe the condition is over-diagnosed in highly suggestible people with motive to falsely present. Melody Gavigan, then thirty-nine, a computer specialist from Long Beach, California suffered from chronic depression. Her counselor repeatedly suggested her depression resulted from incest during her childhood. Although at first she had no recollection, the therapist kept prodding. "I was so distressed and needed help so desperately, I latched on to what he was offering me . . . I accepted his answers" (quoted in Jaroff, 1993, p. 52). Ultimately she recalled allegedly repressed memories of lurid rape and sodomy. She confronted her father with accusations and severed her relationship with him, forming an incest survivor's group. After studying college psychology, she realized the recollections were false. She begged her father's forgiveness. Responding to this case, Johns Hopkins University Psychiatrist Paul McHugh said, "If penis envy made us look dumb, this will make us look totally gullible."

In November of 1990, Mark A. Peterson of Oshkosh, Wisconsin, stood trial for sexually assaulting a woman who allegedly had forty-six personalities. After meeting Sarah, Peterson realized she demonstrated abrupt changes in personality. Sarah had described one such personality; the promiscuous Jennifer. Cannily, Peterson called for a date asking for Jennifer. They had sex in Peterson's car.

Sarah charged Peterson with rape. Prior to the trial, four of Sarah's personalities were sworn in. Others would emerge during the trial, often upon cue. Although Peterson was convicted, the judge overturned the verdict because Sarah was not examined prior to the trial. Under Wisconsin law it is a crime to have sex with a person known to suffer from a mental illness. Apparently, it was felt that Peterson should not be expected to make an accurate "backseat" clinical diagnosis, when the experts cannot agree upon the condition.

One reason for renaming this condition dissociative identity disorder was because of the obvious financial, legal, or forensic gain that might result from successful insanity pleas based upon multiple personality. A malingerer may feign multiple personality to avoid criminal prosecution for acts he has committed. In July of 1978 Lemuel Smith confessed to his psychiatrist that he had committed three murders in the Albany, New York area because he was driven by the spirit of a nonexistent brother who Smith felt had died before his own birth. The jury did not believe him. He was convicted and sentenced to life in prison.

Since that time Smith was convicted of murdering a female corrections officer, which, under New York State Law is a capital offense. Execution had not been practiced in New York state for decades despite legislative attempts that came close to overriding gubernatorial vetoes. Because of the heinous nature of his crimes, Smith was often referred to as the "poster boy" for capital punishment in the state, should it be resumed. In 1986, the state Court of Appeals said the death penalty could not be carried out against him, perhaps sparing him from the conservative political trend of the mid-1990s.

Smith is considered one of New York State's two most violent prisoners. I know a man who spent hundreds of hours guarding him, although he did not know of Smith's multiple personality plea. He said at times in the midst of placid deep sleep, Smith's teeth would grit. His fists would clench, and his muscles tighten. A horrifying grimace would come over his face as he grunted ominously. "It's like there is two people inside of him," he said.

In October of 1979, Kenneth Bianchi pleaded guilty and was sentenced to eight life terms for the "Hillside Strangler" rape-murders that terrorized Los Angeles two years earlier. Bianchi had skillfully used multiple personality as a defense in his insanity plea. Three expert clinicians interviewed him for sixty-five hours. The expert testimony was mixed. However, some excellent police work and forensic analysis by Dr. Martin Orne exposed Bianchi as a malingerer. There was no corroboration for the alter ego called Steve. The alter often appeared upon cue, and the executive was aware of the alter. Densely, Bianchi had chosen Steven Walker as the alter ego, which was also the real name of the person whose

Figure 4-15. *Left:* Kenneth Bianchi (AP photograph), The Hillside Strangler, whose malingering was ferreted out by Dr. Martin Orne (*right*) (UPI photograph).

credentials he had stolen to fake being a psychologist. A classic psychopath, Bianchi pleaded guilty to avoid execution. He also provided testimony against his cousin, Angelo Buono, an accomplice in ten of the murders (APA Monitor, 1984).

Another reason for questioning the validity of this condition is that it is culture-bound. It is seldom diagnosed outside the United States. Just as we may find curious the Asian disorder Koro, an episode of sudden, intense anxiety which results from the belief that the penis will recede into the body and possibly cause death from internal strangulation, foreigners perceive the notion of having more than one personality preposterous. Surely there are many aspects to our personalities. Right now you are a student. During the course of the day, you may be a parent, worker, friend, lover, athlete, or gardener. All of these are aspects of your personality; not separate ones. We are intrigued with this condition. It is the subject of numerous books, films, and talk shows. Because we look for it, we find it. Foreigners find it amusing that murder can be excused based upon this diagnosis.

During work group debate on this condition, it was suggested that primary clinical emphasis should be placed on treating the *delusion* of more than one personality; not the personalities. The debate will continue.

CATEGORY XI. SEXUAL AND GENDER IDENTITY DISORDERS

To speak with opinion about sex, politics, or religion invites argument. Since what constitutes sexual pathology is subjective and controversial, this category was very cautiously and compassionately composed, for the most part. Because of wide variation in sexual preference and appetite, there was a general reluctance to define any form of desired pleasurable sexual behavior between consenting adults as pathological.

The category is divided into three sections: *sexual dysfunctions*, in which there is disturbance in sexual desire, arousal, or capability; *paraphilias*, which involve unusual objects, activities, or situations as the primary or exclusive source of sexual arousal; and, *gender identity disorders,* in which there is strong and persistent cross gender identification, and discomfort with one's natural sex.

A. Sexual Dysfunction

Sexual dysfunction is diagnosed when the individual lacks the desire or ability to satisfactorily function sexually. The dysfunction is a source of individual and interpersonal distress. People seek treatment to relieve distress, improve function, and satisfy their partners. General medical conditions, such as diabetes, vascular disease, or nervous system injury, and substances, such as alcohol, must be ruled out.

In *female sexual arousal disorder* there is a persistent or recurrent inability to maintain an adequate lubrication-swelling response during sexual intercourse. The condition was previously called frigidity, in contradiction of feminine characteristics like nurturance and warmth, perhaps exacerbating anxiety. In *female orgasmic disorder*, there is delay in, or absence of, orgasm following a normal sexual excitement phase. It is judged that the orgasmic capacity is less than what would be expected for a woman of her age, sexual experience, and adequacy of sexual stimulation (DSM—IV, 1994, p. 506).

In *male erectile disorder* there is a persistent or recurrent inability to attain or maintain an adequate erection which adversely affects sexual behavior. This condition was called impotence, in contradiction of masculine characteristics like strength and efficacy. Again, anxiety about being able to have intercourse further compounds the problem. In *premature ejaculation*, orgasm and ejaculation occur with minimal sexual stimulation and prior to the desired time. In *male orgasmic disorder* there is an absence of orgasm following a normal sexual excitement phase (DSM—IV, 1994, pp. 507-511).

B. Paraphilias

This subclass refers to disorders in which the abnormality (para) stems from whatever it is that the person is attracted to (phila). The stimulus is typically strongly preferred or the exclusive source of sexual stimulation. Bizarre, unusual, and socially condemned stimuli are generally necessary for the individual's sexual excitement. The following are considered paraphilias:

- *Exhibitionism* is the urge to or act of exposing one's genitals to an unsuspecting stranger. The individual may masturbate while exposing himself, and there is typically no attempt at further sexual activity with the stranger. The exhibitionist's thrill is in the reaction of the witness. He wishes to see shock, rage, and surprise. Seldom do they present for treatment, as this is their primary means for sexual arousal. In one case, an exhibitionist exposed himself to a woman. Instead of reacting with shock, she approached him and asked to examine him further. Petrified, he ran. He sought treatment following this encounter. Apparently, such behavior has some public appeal, as many rock musicians disrobe, flash, or fondle themselves while on stage. Madonna seems to enjoy the audience reaction to her exposure and self-manipulation. Actor Paul Reubens, of Pee Wee Herman fame, plead no contest in 1991 to indecent exposure charges after being observed masturbating during theater showings of *Nancy Nurse* and *Turn Up The Heat.*

- *Frotteurism*, from the French "frotter" (to rub), is the persistent urge to touch or rub against a nonconsenting person. It is the touching and not the coercive nature of the act that is sexually stimulating. During the act, the frotteur fantasizes an exclusive romantic relationship with the victim. Ideally, he would like to accomplish orgasm before being detected. The acts typically occur in elevators, busy sidewalks, or crowds. Medical professionals, such as gynecologists or dentists, are sometimes accused of fondling and rubbing their patients beyond what is required by circumstance, yet short of attempting intercourse. Frotteurism was depicted in the film, *The Hand*

That Rocks The Cradle. John D. Lancie portrayed an obstetrician who molested his patients.

• *Fetishism* is a disorder in which nonliving objects are required for sexual excitation or gratification. Typical stimuli include articles of underwear, shoes, boots, or life-size inflatable dolls. Often, the stimuli have mental association with the person's initial, or superlative, sexual experience. Sexual dysfunction may occur in the absence of the stimuli. Fetishism may occur within consenting adult relationships. Treatment is typically not sought, as the partner views the practice at least tolerable, if not desirable.

• *Pedophilia* involves a preoccupation with prepubescent children as sexual objects. In mild form, the pedophiliac merely fantasizes about a child while masturbating. More commonly, intercourse, fellatio, and penetration with foreign objects occur. Such acts are violations of the penal code. In prior editions of the *Diagnostic Manual,* pedophilia had been very compassionately described. DSM—III-R (1987) stated, "Isolated sexual acts with children do not necessarily warrant the diagnosis of pedophilia. Such acts may be precipitated by marital discord, recent loss, or intense loneliness" (p. 285). Mike Tyson was convicted of raping one adult female, but isolated sex acts with children did not warrant a diagnosis of pedophilia. I could not comprehend this. This language has been removed from DSM—IV. Furthermore, ruses employed by pedophiliacs are described, such as the "educational" value of the experience, or convincing the child that he/she is provoking the act, or will enjoy it (DSM—IV, 1994, pp. 527-528). In incestual relationships, a father may inveigle his daughter into sex by explaining that, "Mom has been working hard and is tired. You're becoming a woman and it is time for you to help in family responsibilities."

Gene Able of Emery University in Atlanta studied five-hundred seventy one sex offenders who had committed sixty-seven thousand cases of child sexual abuse. The offender is almost always a male, and begins molesting before age fifteen. He molests an average of one-hundred seventeen youngsters, most of whom do not report the offense. The victim is likely to be someone he knows.

Pedophiliacs gravitate to situations where children are available. They have common interests and hobbies with children such as frequenting movie theaters and video arcades. They often select children who are abused or neglected, as they are more vulnerable. The pedophile was likely abused himself, is *overly* active in activities with children, and has few adult friends (McCormack and Selvaggio, 1989, p. 39).

Millions of adults participate in activities that benefit children. Unfortunately, pedophiles represent a subset of adults who participate in such activities for nefarious reasons. "Boy lovers" love to work where boys are. ABC PrimeTime News reported on December 3, 1992 that the Roman Catholic Church had spent four-hundred million dollars in settlements for sexual abuse committed by priests. The Associated Press reported in 1993 that the Boy Scouts of America dismissed about one-thousand eight hundred scoutmasters suspected of molesting boys between 1971 and 1991. The North American Man/Boy Love Association is a group which advocates adult sex with children. Its motto is "sex by year eight, or else you're too late" (quoted in de Young, 1984, p. 72). The NAMBLA Bulletin advises how to entice a child into sex, "Leave a pornographic magazine someplace where he is sure to find it" (quoted in Leo, 1993, p. 37). Michael Jackson repeatedly grabbed his crotch during his ten minute half-time show in the 1993 Super Bowl. Shortly thereafter he fled the country when accused of child molestation.

• *Sexual masochism* involves people who experience sexual gratification when bound, beaten, humiliated, or otherwise made to suffer. The acts are real and not simulated. Blindfolding, paddling, whipping, and electric shocks are often involved. Death sometimes results. The disorder

Figure 4-16. Degradation Ceremony. Drill sergeant and cadre savor their control over a recalcitrant trainee. (Photograph by Jim Rooney.)

was included despite protest from feminists who argued the diagnosis would most likely apply to women. Masochistic themes involving the degradation of women are common in "punk" and "heavy metal" music and videos. Infibulation, the ornamental pinning and piercing of the body, is increasingly more common in men and women. Do parents and young people appreciate the masochistic underpinnings of these things?

• *Sexual sadism* is diagnosed when an individual derives sexual gratification from the infliction of psychological and physical pain and suffering on his partner or victim. In some cases, the sadist participates in sexual behavior with a consenting partner, who is likely masochistic. Although real acts that cause suffering occur, the motive is sexual gratification, not the permanent damage or death of the partner.

Necrophilic sadism involves a preoccupation with death, as well as pain and suffering. Legend has it that Necrophilia was a nursing mother with a bra of leather and spikes. As she pulled her infant closer to nurse, the child was pierced by the spikes. To obtain love required pain. The necrophilic sadist is aroused by knowing the victim is in pain; climax occurs with the death of the victim. The sadistic connotation in the names of contemporary rock groups Metallica, Porno For Pyros, Alice in Chains, and Nine Inch Nails is obvious.

Serial killers are typically necrophilic sadists with antisocial personality disorders. They are sexually motivated and kill a series of victims over a prolonged period of time. They lack guilt or remorse for their crimes. They are unlike mass killers, who are often overcontrolled paranoids motivated by a perception of righteousness. They kill a number of people at one time. Included in the profile of serial killers, developed by the Federal Bureau of Investigation's Behavioral Science Unit, is a history of childhood physical and sexual abuse. They typically wet the bed past the age of toilet training (enuresis), which likely indicates childhood anxiety, inability to control impulses, and voluntary attempts to discourage sexual abuse. They are often pyromaniacs. David Berkowitz, alias "Son of Sam", was a prolific fire setter. They are intrigued with sadistic Nazi and punk paraphernalia. They are animal mutilators.

Freud described sado-masochism as the organism's capacity to experience any intense stimulus as sexually pleasurable. In some sado-masochistic relationships, each partner demonstrates both roles. In March of 1988, Robert Chambers pleaded guilty to a charge of manslaughter in the death of his girlfriend, concluding the case of the "preppie murderer." Allegedly they were involved in "rough sex" possibly including erotic strangulation resulting in her death. The victim's mother organized a petition signed by fifty-thousand people urging denial of Chamber's parole. He has been denied parole twice.

• *Transvestic Fetishism* occurs when a heterosexual male becomes sexually aroused and gratified when he dresses as a female. He is not repulsed by his genitals, and is comfortable with gender. Women are not diagnosed as transvestites because dressing as males, such as wearing pants, is culturally approved. While subtle cross-sex dressing in a woman, such as wearing her lover's shirt, may enhance her perceived femininity, overt cross-sex dressing seldom occurs in heterosexual females.

Transvestites are often married. Thirty-six percent of wives knew of their husbands' cross-sex dressing before marriage and seventy-three percent were aware within five years. Over sixty percent of wives saw their mates as having positive qualities when dressed as women. Women with high self-esteem perceive their husbands' cross dressing as a sexual "turn on." In such cases, tranvestites seldom present for treatment as the practice is mutually satisfactory. Should the wife disapprove and the man be forced "out" to satisfy his desire, distress increases (Weinberg and Bullough, 1988, p. 264). Some transvestites try to keep their preference secret; others flaunt it and flagrantly shop for women's apparel.

C. Transsexualism

Most of us have speculated about what it would be like to be a member of the opposite sex. It was probably just a passing thought. In transsexualism, a type of gender identity disorder, there is a persistent discomfort with one's anatomical sex that originated in childhood. Sometimes evident as early as age three, the child insists he/she is the other sex, and has an intense desire to participate in sterotypical games and pasttimes of that sex. Transsexuals are repulsed by their own primary and secondary sex characteristics, and desire those of the other sex. They feel they are "men trapped in women's bodies," or vice versa. There is a persistent desire to become and live as a member of the other sex. Previously transsexualism was included in the disorders of infancy, childhood, or adolescence because of its early origin.

The culmination of transsexualism is a sex change operation. Before a person has sex change surgery, he is counselled about the ramifications of such a drastic decision. Often, they are discouraged from having it, and a waiting period is enforced. Males take female hormones that stimulate fatty tissue development, and have their facial and body hair removed. Females take male hormones that stimulate hair growth and lower their voices, and then may exercise to develop their muscles. Finally, the genitals are operated upon.

During the 1970s, Dr. Richard Raskin, also a Lieutenant Commander in the United States Naval Reserve, was a competitive amateur tennis player. He had sex change surgery. She described the incredible pain of the operation. Yet, she was steadfast in her conviction. After the operation, in the recovery room, she reflected, "At that moment I realized that I would rather have died in the attempt than live any longer in a nightmare of duality" (Richards, 1983, p. 283). After a period of obscurity, Raskin created great controversy when she emerged as Renee Richards and attempted to play professional tennis as a woman. After much debate, she was allowed to join the Woman's Tennis Association. She was the woman's singles champion in the La Jolla tennis tournament in 1976.

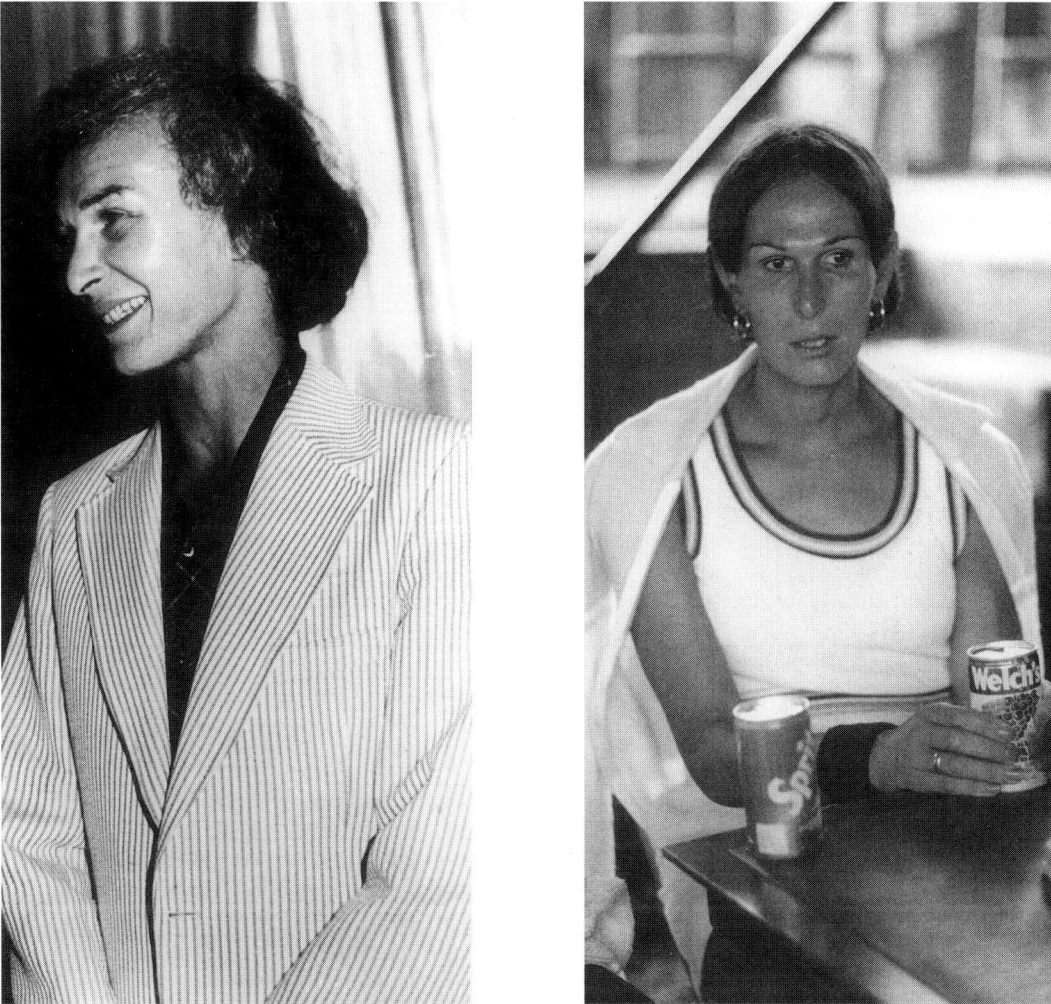

Figure 4-17. *Left*: Dr. Richard Raskin in 1974, prior to his sex-change operation (AP/Wide World Photos). *Right*: Renee Richards (Corbis-Bettman).

Mellon, et al., (1989) reported the case of a twenty-six year old transsexual with schizophrenia. He requested a sex change operation, but was turned down because of his psychotic condition. The patient surgically removed his own genitals by a progressive strangulation technique with slow daily tightening of a constricting string. Final removal took place with the use of cocaine as a local anesthetic. Furthermore, he continued to create a facsimile of a vagina that was so compelling that it was misperceived by a physician. He was willing to accept further surgical help, but was prepared to continue by himself.

CATEGORY XII. EATING DISORDERS

This is a newly created category in DSM—IV. Previously it was included as a disorder of infancy, childhood, or adolescence, as onset is typically prior to adulthood. The two specific diagnoses are anorexia nervosa and bulimia nervosa.

A. Anorexia Nervosa

Anorexia nervosa, sometimes called the "starvation disease," is a disorder in which the individual systematically reduces her intake of food because of an intense fear of becoming obese. In a world where starvation poses a threat for millions, we have a disorder in which starvation is self-imposed. The disorder is diagnosed when the individual's weight is fifteen percent below what is considered normal for someone of that sex, age, and height. Typically, Metropolitan Life Insurance tables are used. Also, she must miss three consecutive menstrual cycles, which indicates starvation. The disorder usually begins during adolescence, with mean onset at age fourteen, or, occasionally during early adulthood. It occurs ninety five percent of the time in females, although there are indications it is occurring more often in males. Although few mental disorders are fatal, this one is. Studies report mortality rates as high as eighteen percent. Between half and one percent of young females satisfy the full criteria set for anorexia nervosa. Many others are subthreshold for the disorder (DSM—IV, 1994, pp. 539-545).

Two subtypes are described. In the restricting type, weight is lost by failure to eat. In the binge-eating/purging type, the person engages in binge-eating or purging behavior (attempts to prevent nutrition through self-induced vomiting, excessive exercise, laxatives, diuretics and enemas).

People with this disorder often have compulsive personalities. They are often very concerned with being on good terms with their parents. Many are envied by their peers, who perceive them as likely "Miss America" contestants. During early onset, they are generally very attractive and meticulous about their grooming and appearance. They are usually good students and popular as well. They are sought as friends. Superficially, they appear very well adjusted.

However, further analysis often reveals pathological conditions and motives for the self-imposed starvation. Marcus and Wiener (1989, pp. 346-354) provided six psychopathological patterns common in anorexia. In self-punishment, the person perceives herself as bad, and therefore does not deserve to eat. I believe that many anorexics experience extreme feelings of guilt and a strong need for self-punishment. What better punishment is there than a painful, self-imposed starvation? In one case a young woman had an extreme need for parental approval. Despite her father's protest, she married a man whom her father said would leave her. Shortly after the wedding, he did. She began to starve herself. She felt as if she had disgraced her family and was no longer worthy of food. Achievement and the need for approval are high in anorexics. Guilt results from failed expectations. Avis Rumney's *Dying To Please*, and Steven Levenkron's *The Best Little Girl in the World* are books that describe the high levels of achievement imposed by parents, and the internalization of these standards by the girls.

In the negativistic pattern, refusal to eat is an attempt to control and punish the parents, whom she perceives, often with justification, have mistreated her. The attention centering pattern is characterized by playing with the food on the plate, inviting attention, sympathy, and encouragement from the parents. In the distracting pattern, the victim's condition is employed to provide parents a common cause to stop fighting and remain together. The childlike pattern, or "Peter Pan" syndrome, involves a desire to avoid adult responsibility and, because of immature physical appearance, discourage sexual advances. Although isolated cases were reported in Europe in the late 1800s, the disorder increased dramatically when western culture began to equate thinness with physical attractiveness during the 1960s. Emaciation is perceived as desirable and appealing in the attractiveness pattern.

Anorexics seem to fail to appreciate or recognize the damage that they are causing. To do so, might serve as a deterrent. At first, self-induced vomiting is aesthetically repulsive and difficult. First attempts are facilitated with expectorants, such as ipecac or projectiles, like a twig. Eventually vomiting can be willed, and ultimately, stomach contents involuntarily spill from a distended digestive tract when bending over. Menstruation ceases in women. Teeth, once braced and capped, now decay from gastric juices and become black and "moth eaten." As taste buds are destroyed, the taste of vomit is less repugnant. Victims feel chronically cold with body temperatures dipping to ninety-six degrees, and pulses of less than forty per minute. Unsightly body hair grows as bodies attempt to conserve heat. Skin dries and

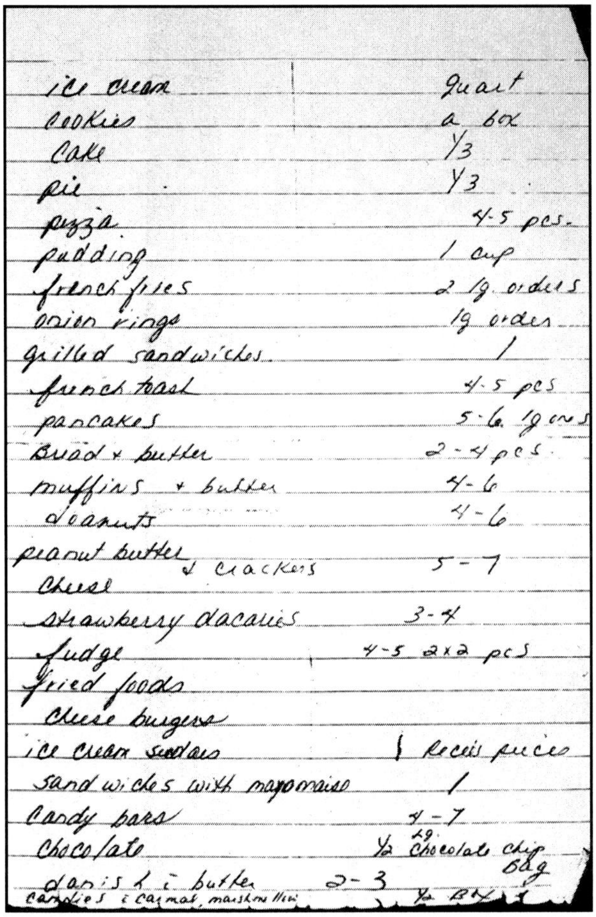

ice cream	quart
cookies	a box
cake	1/3
pie	1/3
pizza	4-5 pcs.
pudding	1 cup
french fries	2 lg orders
onion rings	lg order
grilled sandwiches	1
french toast	4-5 pcs
pancakes	5-6 lg ones
bread + butter	2-4 pcs
muffins + butter	4-6
donuts	4-6
peanut butter & crackers	5-7
cheese	
strawberry dacaries	3-4
fudge	4-5 2x2 pcs
fried foods	
cheese burgers	
ice cream sodas	several pieces
sandwiches with mayonnaise	1
candy bars	4-7
chocolate	1/2 chocolate chip 6 lg
danish i butter	2-3
candies i caynal, maishmellow	

Figure 4-18. Shopping list for a weekend bulimic binge.

cracks and lacks lustre. Because of estrogen and calcium deficiencies, the female skeletal system becomes vulnerable to osteoporosis (Rigotti et al., 1984, and Kaplan and Woodside, 1987, p. 645-653). Singer Karen Carpenter died from anorexia nervosa. For other famous dancers, athletes, and actresses, it is a continual battle.

B. Bulimia Nervosa

The other subcategory is *bulimia nervosa*. Bulimics have the same obsessive fear of being fat as anorexics, but eat much more than them. During a binge-eating/purging episode, a bulimic may consume thirty-thousand calories (the equivalent of seventy Big Macs). They may eat until full, vomit, and then resume eating. An episode may last hours. Other compensatory behaviors include the misuse of laxatives and diuretics, fasting, enemas, or excessive exercise. Two episodes a week for three months are required for the diagnosis. Despite purging, their nutrition is sufficient to maintain normal weight. About sixty percent of bulimics have been sexually/physically abused (Bower, 1993, p. 366, and Shure, 1989, p. C).

When anorexics are under social scrutiny, they will take hours to nibble at a small amount of food. Peas are eaten singly with a fork. They welcome those periods when nobody is home since there is no pressure to eat. Bulimics also want to be alone, but rather to binge and purge without criticism. Despite some differences in these eating disorders, there are also many similarities. Fifty percent of those diagnosed as anorexic also binge and purge (Polivy and Herman, 1985). Likely, anorexia and bulimia represent extreme ends of a spectrum of eating disorders that defy clear-cut distinction (Anderson, 1983). Thus, DSM—IV lists six examples of eating disorders not otherwise specified, such as continued menstruation despite meeting criteria for anorexia, or binge-eating without compensatory behavior.

CATEGORY XIII. SLEEP DISORDERS

Sleep, when restful, sufficient, and voluntary, rejuvenates the mind and body for involvement in life. When eventful, of poor quality, in extreme, or involuntary, distress and impaired functioning result. Sleep disorders was an innovation in DSM—III-R. Disorders of sleep were judged to be of sufficient prevalence and severity to warrant a separate category.

Primary sleep disorders are those that are not the result of a general medical condition, a substance,

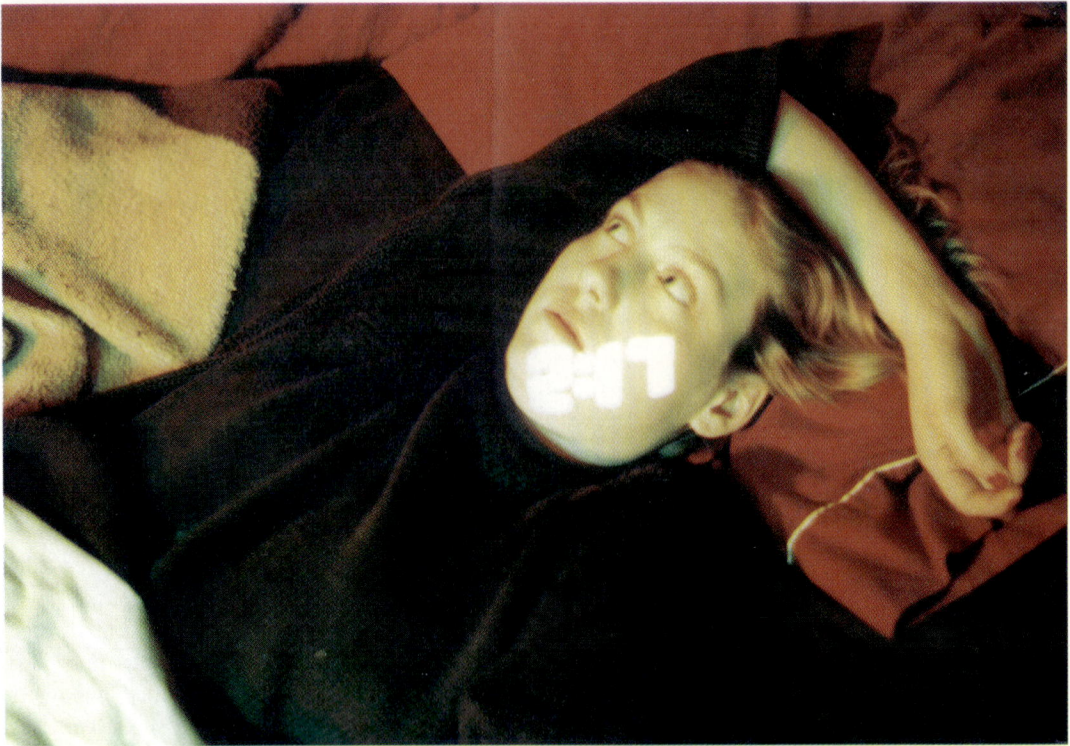

Figure 4-19. Insomniac's nightmare. (Photograph by Jim Rooney.)

or another mental disorder. They are presumed to arise from individual abnormalities in sleep-wake generating or timing mechanisms, and are complicated by conditioning factors (DSM—IV, 1994, p. 551). Dyssomnias and parasomnias are primary sleep disorders.

A. Dyssomnias

These disorders are characterized by a disturbance in the amount, quality, or timing of sleep. There are four types of dyssomnias: primary insomnia, primary hypersomnia, narcolepsy, and breathing-related sleep disorder.

Primary insomnia is diagnosed when the person has difficulty initiating or maintaining sleep, or sleeps for a seemingly adequate amount of time but is unrested. Daytime fatigue follows. The disturbance must last a month, be a source of distress, and affect the ability to function. Although most people have difficulty falling asleep on occasion, it is difficult to appreciate the frustration and exhaustion of insomnia. Of the living, insomniacs most closely approximate comprehension of eternity. Insomnia often coexists with depression. A depressed person struggles, exhausted, through the day, longing for nightime, anticipating sleep. However, sleep does not come and eyes are glued to the ceiling throughout the night. Another day of exacerbated weariness follows.

Primary hypersomnia is diagnosed when a person is excessively sleepy during the day despite an adequate amount of nocturnal sleep. Transition from the sleep to wake state is longer than normal. Unintentional sleep episodes often occur during meetings or lectures, despite efforts to resist. Such episodes are likely to be negatively interpreted by teachers or supervisors as signifying boredom, rudeness, or malaise. Embarassment causes distress and function may suffer. The risk of accidental injury from falling asleep while driving or operating machinery is ever present.

Narcolepsy is characterized by irresistable attacks of refreshing sleep that occur daily for at least three months. Cataplexy (brief episodes of loss of muscle tone, in which individuals drop objects, buckle at the knees, or fall to the ground), occurs in seventy percent of individuals with this disorder. The episodes are often triggered by a strong emotional stimulus such as anger, shock, or surprise. Many with this condition experience intense dreamlike hallucinations and temporary paralyses before and after episodes of sleep. People with primary hypersomnia generally report satisfactory nocturnal sleep and may be chronically sleepy throughout the day. Their daytime sleep is not refreshing. People with narcolepsy report less satisfactory nocturnal sleep, although their daytime sleep is restorative. The urge to sleep is more compelling in narcolepsy (DSM—IV, 1994, pp. 562-567).

Breathing-related sleep disorder occurs when ventilation ceases during sleep, resulting in distress, insomnia, and excessive day-time sleepiness. Apneic episodes typically are of twenty to forty seconds duration, but may last several minutes, escalating probability of brain damage or death. The individual may or may not realize he has stopped breathing. If the individual is not distressed, family members often are. An apneic episode may begin when snoring ceases. A conditioned spouse or family member awakens, sees the individual is turning blue, and attempts to resuscitate him. They may rest comfortably only when the individual snores, as they know he is well.

The condition occurs in between one and ten percent of the adult population, and is most common in middle aged, overweight males. Snoring is caused by breathing through a partially obstructed airway. The tongue, tonsils, adenoids, or uvula (the fleshy verticle conical attachment suspended from the soft palate above the back of the tongue), are common sources of obstruction. Apneas may occur without obstruction in the elderly and may result from cardiac or neurological conditions (DSM—IV, 1994, pp. 567-573).

B. Parasomnias

Parasomnias are diagnosed when an abnormal behavioral or physiological events are associated with sleep. Two examples of parasomnias are sleepwalking and nightmare disorder. Sleepwalking disorder consists of complex motor behaviors initiated during sleep. The individual may rise from bed and walk about. The face is blank, and the individual is relatively unresponsive to others. The episode is not remembered upon awakening. In nightmare disorder, the individual is repeatedly awakened by extremely frightening dreams involving threats of survival, security, or self-esteem. The dreams may involve past actual traumas. This disorder often coexists with depression, insomnia and posttraumatic stress disorder (DSM—IV, 1994, pp. 579-591). Frequent nightmares are associated with psychotic symptomtology (Berquier and Ashton, 1992, p. 246).

CATEGORY XIV. IMPULSE-CONTROL DISORDERS NOT ELSEWHERE CLASSIFIED

Compulsivity is a personality trait that is an integral element of many of the disorders that we have described. It is significant in obsessive compulsive disorder, eating disorders, substance use disorders and the paraphilias. People with impulse-control disorders fail to resist an impulse to perform some act that is harmful to themselves or others. They experience great tension and arousal when planning the act and have a feeling of euphoric release (sometimes sexual) when the act is being committed. We will describe three disorders in this category.

A. *Kleptomania*

A kleptomaniac is a person who cannot resist the impulse to steal. Career criminals shoplift for the value of the stolen goods. In 1993, The Schenectady Gazette reported that Sherry Kaye, alias "Shrimp Lady," was arrested following discovery by police of $404,000 inside a new Cadillac she used to travel the country. Upon investigation, it was learned that the money was obtained by returning shoplifted canned goods, mostly shrimp and meat, from grocery stores for cash refunds. Such is a calculated scheme to steal. Kleptomaniacs steal for thrill. The goods stolen may be hidden, hoarded, given away, or even surreptitiously returned to the store. The stolen articles are usually not particularly needed or desired. When apprehended by police, kleptomaniacs are likely to have sufficient money with which to pay for the goods, and to have a closet full of items that are similar to these at home. Sophisticated security systems in stores only add to the intrigue.

Kleptomaniacs are often middle and upper class teenage females who steal cosmetics, jewelry, clothing, and audio entertainment. They are typically not very concerned with the legal consequences of getting caught, nor are they worried about being a source of humiliation for their families. Edwin S. Porter depicted his perceptive profile of this disorder in his 1905 film, *The Kleptomaniac*. The film portrays a New York socialite who is taken to Macy's by horsedrawn carriage. She is one of the store's best customers. She experiences great pleasure when stealing and eventually gets caught.

B. *Pyromania*

The pyromaniac often cannot resist the impulse to set fires. He is extremely fascinated by fire, and achieves an intense state of excitement while watching it. The disorder is more common among men, and often the person is unconcerned with the damage done or the threat to life that his acts represent. Pyromaniacs are sometimes injured or killed in their own fires because of their compulsive behavior. One pyromaniac told me how he used gasoline, which is highly volatile, to light his fire. He was in the room when he struck a match and an implosion ensued. He ran to the door, but was unable to open it because the fire kept it sucked shut. I asked him if he had learned anything from the experience. He replied, "Yeah. Make sure you're outside the room if you use gas." Donald Sutherland skillfully portrayed the role of a pyromaniac in the film Backdraft. His captivation with fire was so compelling that he could not conceal it, even during his parole hearing.

Pyromaniacs often regularly watch fires and become especially titillated while watching the fires they have set. They have the reputation of being the first on the scene. Arson detectives gain clues by watching the reactions of people at the fire.

A distinction must be made between the pyromaniac, who sets fires for thrill, and the career criminal who sets fires for economic reasons. Because the pyromaniac is so compulsive, he does not exercise much caution to avoid being discovered. He may even purposely leave clues. By comparison, "torches" are extremely careful. They are criminals who engage in arson for money. They take their work seriously and study the best way to set the fire and minimize the chance that people will be hurt, inviting more intense police investigation.

Pyromaniacs are often members of fire departments. When one is discovered in the fire department, the public reaction is one of surprise. It shouldn't be. Pyromaniacs naturally gravitate toward an agency whose purpose is to deal with fire. They overly enjoy the trucks, badges, uniforms, communications equipment, literature, and other trappings of the profession. They are so aroused by the fire that they will violate fundamental safety procedures, thus endangering themselves and others. Should a firefighter report one off-duty fire, he becomes suspect. Pyromaniacs often move to a new area when they are suspect. Some keep scrapbooks of fires they have set. What is the pyromaniac's favorite first toy? A fire truck, of course.

Figure 4-20. "The Big One." Exhilarated gamblers plan their coup. (Photograph by Jim Rooney.)

Pyromania often coexists with other forms of criminal behavior. Serial killer David Berkowitz, alias "Son of Sam," set more than 2,000 fires and made 337 false alarms in New York City between 1974 to 1977. The calls were made to the police and he identified himself as the "Phantom of the Bronx" (Wooden, 1985, p. 26).

C. Pathological Gambling

Normal people may gamble, however they do so only occasionally. They may wager on the Kentucky Derby or the World Series, but not on the second race at Pimlico or on a spring training game. Such is not the case with the pathological gambler. His life revolves around gambling. He does not meet important social or occupational obligations because of it. He remembers the isolated "big score" and selectively forgets the multitude of losses. He would rather lose than not bet. The worst day at the track is better than the best day off. The pathological gambler often commits crimes to finance his gambling or to pay back loan sharks, who are not known for their patience or compassion.

In the long run, according to gambler Wilson Mizner, "Gambling is the sure way of getting nothing for something." Some gamblers excel in a type of gambling, such as casino blackjack. They are experts at probability, disciplined, and can remember which cards have been played. Most gamblers concede an edge of five percent of their wager to the house as fair compensation for the opportunity to gamble. "Vigorish," a term used by gambling proprietors, is a euphemism for the advantage enjoyed by the house. Regardless of talent, vigorish will destory most gamblers over time. Pathological gamblers often lack comprehension of the aforementioned, and impulsively bet large amounts on outcomes of incredibly low probability.

State governments derive exorbitant profits from legalized lotteries. New York State spends $15,000,000 annually pushing Lotto sales. Tasteless themes, like "A Dollar and a Dream," are directed to entice those who can least afford to gamble. New Yorkers spend more than 1.6 billion per year on lottery tickets. More than half goes to the state, considerably in excess of reasonable vigorish (Sifakis, 1990, p. 206).

Art Schlichter was once a promising National Football League quarterback for the Indianapolis Colts. While in high school, he won $200 on a horse race. His gambling compulsion began. He was suspended by the league for gambling in 1985 and filed for bankruptcy in March of 1988. Despite the salary he had earned, he reported debts of about one million dollars. As of 1989, he was working as a salesmen in a sporting goods store; daily resisting the impulse to gamble. In 1989 Pete Rose was banished from baseball for illegal wagering. He served a prison term for tax crimes; not reporting money gained from signing autographs and used to finance his gambling. Despite his heroics on the field, it is dubious that he will be elected to the Hall of Fame. Michael Jordan, arguably the best basketball player in history, allegedly lost large amounts of money betting on his golf game. His attempt to play professional baseball was less than inspiring. Wisely, he returned to his best game.

Figure 4-21. "Mommy." Homesickness is a source of adjustment disorders in college freshmen. (Photograph by Jim Rooney.)

CATEGORY XV. ADJUSTMENT DISORDER

Adjustment disorders describe maladaptive reactions to psychosocial and environmental problems that occur within three months of the onset of the stressor. Typically, the symptoms remit, often without treatment, within six months following the termination or resolution of the stressor. Adjustment disorders involve impaired occupational and social function, or marked distress, in the form of anxious or depressed mood, in "excess" of normal and expected reactions to the stressor. The specific psychosocial and environmental problem(s) would be listed on Axis IV. This clinical judgement must be carefully made, as determining what a "normal" reaction to a stressor is, ultimately requires the clinician having experienced it. Comparatively, drapetomania was a 19th century term used to describe slaves who could not adjust to slavery and attempted to run away. Slaves and slave owners look at the world through different eyes.

These disorders produce severe distress. However, compared with other disorders, they are of briefer duration and have lesser long term impact. Adjustment disorders are subthreshold to depression and posttraumatic stress disorder. Metaphorically, adjustment disorders can be likened to a first degree burn caused by sunburn (painful, short term, with complete healing); depression to a second degree burn causing blisters (very painful, will heal with time, and perhaps leave scars); and posttraumatic stress disorder to a third degree burn which chars flesh (extremely painful, of long duration, and permanent damage).

Adjustment disorders are likely to occur at predictable points of life. Stress often results when one leaves a comfortable station in life and embarks upon the unknown. Adjustment disorders are likely to occur when going to school for the first time, leaving home, attending college, changing jobs, getting married, becoming a parent, and reaching retirement. The saying "Man hath no fear like that of the unknown" is particularly relevant. Some people can tolerate and cope with uncertainty better than others. Some actively seek the unknown. Others find it a source of confusion, danger, and fear. They are prone to developing adjustment disorders.

Often this diagnosis is used in forensic settings. Young entrepreneurs involved in drug trafficking often believe they will not get caught, let alone be sentenced to prison. However, they often are. Although "street tough," they are no match for hardened criminals serving lengthy sentences who spend their days lifting weights. Sexual or physical assaults against such inmates often necessitate their removal from the general population to protective custody or a forensic hospital.

We have now described the major diagnostic categories of DSM—IV. Perhaps as you read this chapter, you wondered why it was necessary to describe the disorders in such detail. Students need a knowledge of the various mental disorders to appreciate and understand abnormal psychology. Most major courses of study which require abnormal psychology want their students to know diagnostic procedures, criteria, and terminology. Just as "you can't tell the players without a score card at a ball game," you can't fully appreciate the perspectives approach to abnormal psychology without knowing the mental disorders. Two case studies follow. They stress the experiential aspects of the disorders, so that you might speculate about, and try to understand, what having the disorders is like.

References

APA *Monitor* (Washington, D.C., American Psychological Association, April, 1984).

A Decade of Loss (1993, January 18). *Newsweek*, 22-23.

Adler, T. (1989, July). Cocaine Babies Face Behavior Deficits. *American Psychological Monitor*, 14.

Anderson, A. (1983) Anorexia and Bulimia: A Spectrum of Eating Disorders. *Journal of Adolescent Health Care*, 4:15-21.

Arnold Jr, H. (1984, April 20) Penicillin and Early Syphilis. *JAMA,* 25I(15).

Asimov, I. (1972). I Remember, I Remember. In Hamachek, D. (Ed), *Human Dynamics in Psychology and Education. Massachusetts*: Allyn and Bacon.

Barsky, A. and Klerman, G. (1983, March) Overview: Hypochondriasis, Bodily Complaints, and Somatic Styles. *The American Journal of Psychiatry*, 140:3.

Beck, M., et.al (1993, March 15). The Messiah of Waco. *Newsweek*, pp. 56+.

Berquier, A. and Ashton, R. (1992). Characteristics of the Frequent Nightmare Sufferer. *Journal of Abnormal Psychology,* 101 (2), 246-250.

Booker, J.M., PhD and Hellekson, C.J., MD. (1992). Prevalence of Seasonal Affective Disorder in Alaska. *American Journal of Psychiatry* 149:9, September, 1176-1182.

Bower, B. (1993). Tracing Bulemic Roots to Early Sexual Abuse. *Science News,* 143, 366.

Boxing Should Be Banned in Civilized Countries--Round 2. (1984). *JAMA*, vol. 251, no. 20, 2696-2697.

Browne, A. and Finkelhor, D. (1986) Impact of Sexual Abuse: A Review of the Research. *Psychological Bulletin*, 99(1).

Camp M.D., N. (1993). The Vietnam War and the Ethics of Combat Psychiatry. *American Journal of Psychiatry*, 150:7, 100-1009.

Campbell, S. (1994, October 30). Aikman Should Take a Bye. *Albany Times Union*, D1.

Carson, R.C. and Butcher, J.N. (1992). *Abnormal Psychology and Modern Life* (9th ed.). New York:HarperCollins Publishers Inc.

Casson, I., et al. (1984, May 25) Brain Damage in Modern Boxers. *JAMA*, 251(20).

Coons, P. and Milstein, V. (1984). Rape and Post-Traumatic Stress in *Multiple Personality. Psychological Reports*, 55, 839-845.

de Young, M. (1984). Ethics and the "Lunatic Fringe": The Case of Pedophile Organizations. *Human Organization*, 43(1), 72-74.

Diagnostic and Statistical Manual of Mental Disorders (1987) (3rd ed. Rev.). Washington, D.C.: American Psychiatric Association.

Diagnostic and Statistical Manual of Mental Disorders (1994) (4th ed.). Washington, D.C.: American Psychiatric Association.

Dorris, M. (1990, June 25). A Desperate Crack Legacy. *Newsweek*, 8.

Dougherty, P., (1987, May 12) The Ultimate Comeback. *Rochester Democrat and Chronicle*.

Egginton, J. (1989). *From Cradle to Grave: The Short Lives and Strange Deaths of Marybeth Tinning's Nine Children*. New York: W. Morrow and Company, Inc.

Elias, M. (1992, June 22). Many Desert Storm Vets Suffering Effects of War. *Utica Observer Dispatch*, C.

Evans III, W. and Frothingham, A. (1992). *Well-Done Roasts*. New York:St. Martin's Press.

Farrell, B. (1994, June 5). Syphilis Resurgence Continues in State. *Observer-Dispatch* [Utica, New York], 4A.

Feighner, J., et al. (1984, April) A Double-Blind Study of Bupropion and Placebo in Depression. *The American Journal of Psychiatry*, 141(4).

Fieve, R. (1975) Moodswing: *The Third Revolution in Psychiatry*. New York: William Morrow and Company.

Freeman, D.H. (1994, October 30). Heading Toward Retirement? *Observer-Dispatch* [Utica, New York], C2.

Freud, S. (1962) On the Psychical Mechanism of Hysterical Phenomena, A Lecture. In (1983) *The Standard Edition of the Complete Works of Sigmund Freud*. (Vol. III) London:The Hogarth Press.

Garland, A. and Zigler, E. (1993). Adolescent Suicide Prevention: Current Research and Social Policy Implications. *American Psychologist*, 48(2), 169-179.

Golfer Bert Yancey Dies at Tourney. (1994, August 27). *Observer Dispatch* [Utica, New York], sec. C, p. 1+.

Haley, J. (1965). The Art of Being Schizophrenic. *Voices*, Vol. 1.

Haney, D.Q. (1992, August 30). Down Syndrome: 3-Test Combo Can Help. The Associated Press. In *Observer Dispatch* [Utica, New York], E:3.

Harrary, K. (1992, March/April). Jonestown 13 Years Later—Why We Should Still Be Afraid. *Psychology Today*, pp. 67+.

Hobfoll, S, et.al (1991, August). War-Related Stress: Addressing the Stress of War and Other Traumatic Events. *American Psychologist*, 46:8, 848-855.

Jaroff, L. (1993, November 29). Lies of the Mind. *Time,* 52+.

Kaplan, A., and Woodside, D.B. (1987). Biological Aspects of Anorexia Nervosa and Bulimia Nervosa. *Journal of Consulting and Clinical Psychology*, 55(5), 645-653.

Kaplan, H.I. and Sadock, B.J. (Ed.).(1985) *Comprehensive Textbook of Psychiatry/IV*, Vol. 2, 4th ed., Chapter 2. Baltimore: The Williams and Wilkens Company.

Karasu, T.B., et.al. Treatments of Psychiatric Disorders. (Vols. 1-4). *American Psychiatric Association:Washington*, D.C..

Kates, W. (1992, October 16). Watkins Glen Gunman Kills 4, Self. Utica, *New York Observer-Dispatch*, sec. A, p. 9.

Kindred, D. (1978, March 27) Golfer Bert Yancey's Long Struggle. *The Daily Press* [Utica, New York].

Kramer, M. (1993, March). The Manson Family Album: Tracing the Bloodlines. *Crime Beat*, pp. 48+.

Lehmann, H.E. (1967). Schizophrenia I: Introduction and History. In Freedman and Kaplan (eds). *Comprehensive Textbook of Psychiatry*. Baltimore: The Williams and Wilkens Company.

Leo, J. (1993, October 11). Pedophiles in the Schools. *U.S. News & World Report*, 37.

Light, M. and Sheridan, M. (1990). Munchausen Syndrome by Proxy and Apnea (MBPA). *Clinical Pediatrics*, 29 (3), 162-168.

MacDonald, J.M. (1963). The Threat to Kill. *American Journal of Psychiatry*, 120, 125-130.

_____ (1967). Homicidal Threats. *American Journal of Psychiatry*, 124, 475-482.

Madden, J. (1984). *Hey Wait a Minute, I Wrote a Book*. New York:Villard Books.

Manning, A. (1989, February 1). All In The Family: Genetics Research Unlocking Mysteries of Hereditary Illnesses. Gannett News Service. In *Observer Dispatch* [Utica, New York], C:3.

Mantle, M. and Lieber, J. (1994, April 18). Time In A Bottle. *Sports Illustrated*, 66-77.

Marcus, D. and Wiener, M. (1989, July). Anorexia Nervosa Reconceptualized From a Psychosocial Transactional Perspective. *American Joural of Orthopsychiatry,* 59(3), 346-354.

McCormack, A. and Selvaggio, M. (1989). Screening for Pedophiles in Youth-Oriented Community Agencies. Social Casework: *The Journal of Contemporary Social Work*, 70, 37-42.

Meadow, R. (1989). Munchausen Syndrome By Proxy. *BMJ*, 299, 248-250.

Mellon, C, et.al. (1989, February). Autocastration and Autopenectomy in a Patient with Transsexualism and Schizophrenia. *The Journal of Sex Research*, 26(1), 125-130.

Mogielnicki, R.P., et al. (1977). Impending Child Abuse. *JAMA*, 237:11.

Mowrer, O.H. and Veszelovky, A.V. (1980, Winter). There May Indeed Be a "Right Way": Response to James D. Smrtic. *Psychotherapy: Theory, Research, and Practice,* 17:4.

Mulder and Dale. (1967). Brain Syndrome Associated With Infection. In Freedman and Kaplan (eds). *Comprehensive Textbook of Psychiatry*. Baltimore: The Williams and Wilkens Company.

Nemiah, J.C. (1967). Obsessive-Compulsive Reaction. In Freedman and Kaplan (eds). *Comprehensive Textbook of Psychiatry*. Baltimore: The Williams and Wilkens Company.

Polivy, J. and Herman, C.P. (1985, February). Dieting and Binging. *American Psychologist*, 40:2.

Raeburn, P. (1994, October 21). Test for Down Syndrome is Safe. *Observer Dispatch* (Utica, New York), A 11.

Reilly, R. (1993, November 15). Quest for Perfection. *Sports Illustrated*, 79(20), p. 80-84.

Richards, R. with Ames, J. (1983). *The Renee Richards Story: Second Serve*. New York: Stein and Day.

Rigotti MD, N.A., et al. (1984, December 20) Osteoporosis in Women With Anorexia Nervosa. *The New England Journal of Medicine*, 31:25.

Roberts, L. (1988, August 12). Study Raises Estimate of Vietnam War Stress. *Science,* 241, 788.

Rosenhan, D. (1973). On Being Sane in Insane Places. In S. O. Lilienfeld, *Seeing Both Sides*, 20-29. Pacific Grove:Brooks/Cole.

Ross, R.J., et al. (1983, January 14). Boxers: Computed Tomography, EEG, and Neurological Evaluation. *JAMA*, 249:2.

Shure, J. (1989). Sexual Abuse Linked to Eating Disorders. *The Renfrew Perspective*, Summer, C+.

Sifakis, C. (1990) *Encyclopedia of Gambling*. New York: Facts on File, Inc.

Smrtic, J.D. (1979, Summer). Time to Remove Our Theoretical Blinders: Integrity Therapy May Be the Right Way. *Psychotherapy: Theory, Research, and Practice*, 16:2.

Sullivan, R. (1990, July 17). Jogger Testifies 12 Minutes, Giving Scant Details. *New York Times,* A, C.

Tharp, M. (1992, February 17). In the Mind of a Stalker. *U.S. News & World Report*, pp. 28-30.

The Boxing Champ Who Declined To Fight: Muhammad Ali. (Fall 1990) *Life,* 13(12), 47.

Tony Brown's Journal. (1994, October 24). With Tony Brown and Peter Buxtun. PTB, WNET, New York.

Treffert, D.A. (1988, May). The Idiot Savant: A Review of the Syndrome. *American Journal of Psychiatry*, 145(5), 563.

Weinberg, T. and Bullough, V. (1988). Alienation, Self-Image, and the Importance of Support Groups for the Wives of Transvestites. *The Journal of Sex Research*, 24, 262-268.

Wooden, W. (1985, January). The Flames of Youth: Arson is Epidemic—and Spreading Like Wildfire. *Psychology Today*, 22-28.

Woodward, B. (1984, June 24). The Short Life and Fast Times of John Belushi. *The Times Union* (Albany, New York).

Wright, R.R., et.al (Ed.). (1976) *The Mentally Retarded Child.*New York: McGraw-Hill Inc.

Zimbardo, P. (1992). *Psychology and Life* (13th ed.). New York: Harper Collins Publishers

Figure 4-22. Oscar Levant. (Illustration by Jim Rooney.)

READING 4A

A PORTRAIT OF NEUROSIS

Oscar Levant

Since DSM—III (1980), neurosis has not been an official diagnostic term. However, the concept of neurosis remains a useful tool in helping to understand certain types of mental disorders. Neurosis refers to behavior and personality that is not as severely impaired and debilitated as in psychosis, a portrait of which follows this selection. Neurosis and psychosis were discussed earlier in Chapter 3. The purpose of this selection is to enable the reader to understand that, although neurotics have difficulty coping, and their lives are painful, they are still able to maintain their social and occupational duties. Such will not be the circumstance in case study 2, A Portrait of Psychosis.*

Dramatist S.N. Berman once observed that if Oscar Levant "did not exist," he "could not be imagined." He was a truly gifted pianist, actor, composer, and radio and television personality who was known for his cutting, caustic wit. I can recall seeing Levant on the Steve Allen and Jack Parr television shows; forefathers of Johnny Carson and David Letterman. I remember a disheveled looking, humorous piano player who continually smoked cigarettes. Despite his talent, he was extremely neurotic. Throughout his life he behaved in a bizarre manner and spent the last ten years of his life as a recluse. He once said, "There is a thin line between genius and insanity. I have erased that line." Levant demonstrated the symptoms of a variety of disorders we have dealt with in this chapter. As you read this first person account of what it is like to be neurotic, look for specific symptoms of the disorders we have described.

Instant unconsciousness had been my greatest passion for ten years. During the most acute phases of my mental depression, which lasted many years, my most unabated obsession was instant unconsciousness. For a short interval I was administered eighteen electrical shock treatments, which had dire results. However, they had one incalculable pleasure—each shock treatment was preceded by an intravenous injection of sodium pentothal. Afterward I was hooked on intravenous injections of pentobarbital (Nembutal), which had an even more luxurious and longer lasting unconsciousness. This addiction was discontinued—it was short lived. I not only ran out of doctors, but out of veins. During these comatose seizures, the only exercise I got was stumbling, tripping and falling into comas. My deterioration was bottomless. At one time I was in a state of apathy and then later lapsed into a deep depression. During the deep depression period, where I became zombie-like, I would get nostalgic for the good old apathy days. Incidentally, "apathy" and "deep depression" are precise terms in psychiatric terminology.

I would endlessly complain at the prospect of consciousness. Once I told June, "You ought to hit me on the head." But after I'd said it I was frightened because I'd made such a remark, and the barbiturate dose she gave me didn't work, due to my fear. Yet it's true: I had an insatiable craving for unconsciousness. It was my only surcease. I rated the drug Demerol over sex as the ultimate pleasure at one time. Now I don't have access to either. Speaking of Demerol and just for the record, it has been many years since I've been administered this deleterious narcotic.The other

From *Memoirs of an Amnesiac* by Oscar Levant (1965, The Putnam Berkely Group, Inc.) Reprinted with permission of June Levant.

day I was walking upstairs and I was breathing heavily. "You know, walking upstairs is just as bad as sex," I complained. "I get the same reaction from both. Terrible chest pains."

The horrors of my subconscious had left me with a fanatical disbelief in myself, which displays sound judgment. I was an inert, happy-go-lucky derelict who could have been created by Gogol.

* * *

Rituals have taken the place of religion for me. These superstitions started the second time I appeared on *Information Please* in the late 30's. (The first time I appeared I didn't even know what the show was all about.) I had a cup of coffee in a drugstore in Radio City before the program and left a dime tip. This began the whole pattern. From then on, every time I was to appear on that show, no matter how late I was, I dropped into that drugstore, sat on the same stool, ordered a cup of coffee and left a dime. Often I didn't even drink the coffee. I never changed my clothes till I had a bad show. From this simple beginning, my program of rituals has become as complex as the Canadian Air Force exercises.

Today my rituals are more elaborate and they increase with my anxieties as the years go by. At times I have to perform some of these rites in front of my wife, and she sneers. This deflates me and I beg for her tolerance; I can't give up either my rituals or my wife. When guests are there I try to perform them covertly, or if the compulsion is strong, I perform them flagrantly, but I am deeply embarrassed. The rites give me something—not necessarily peace of mind, but a kind of puerile comfort and security.

In 1952 I had a heart attack. After I refused to go to the hospital, the doctor told me that I should undress and get to bed. I did, but I insisted on performing all my undressing rituals, even with the heart attack.

I usually perform them when I dress or undress, when I go to bed, and when I open a pack of cigarettes. Everything that is pleasurable, I give a pagan benediction.

A few years ago someone suggested that I read Spinoza. The first chapter in this particular volume was about superstitions and rituals. Here was my faith! Spinoza said rituals are all based on fear. My faith destroyed, I put down the book. My rituals are automatic, mechanical and absolutely necessary, and I perform them without thinking. But when I occasionally forget one, I feel a temporary euphoria, but it is evanescent. A sixth sense (I lack the other five) tells me that I am in serious difficulties.

When I button my shirt, for example, I always button the lowest button first. When I take off my shirt, I do it from the top down. When I turn on water faucets the first time, I tap each faucet with both hands eight times before I draw the water. After I've finished, I tap each of them again eight times. I also recite a silent prayer. It goes: Good luck, bad luck, good luck, Romain Gary, Christopher Isherwood and Krishna Menon. I also tap my clothes.

There's no symbolism involved in the count of eight. I started out with smaller numbers but—due to inflation and increased anxiety—it's now eight. I skipped seven. I don't like the number seven.

I stir my coffee four times one way with a teaspoon . . . then pause a moment . . . then two times more. I recently added two more stirs but discarded them because they took too long. The coffee got cold.

My napkin has to be on the left side before I put it down. If the cream pitcher has a crack, I have it removed. I don't allow any cracks at the table; I demand an absolutely pristine, unadulterated topography.

When I play the piano—a form of tactile therapy—I always play a few bars of the Fourth Etude of Chopin, Opus 12, and as I finish playing I always add a few bars of the same, a few bars of the Eighth Etude, and then the coda of the prelude from the Prelude and Fugue in C minor of Bach's "Well-Tempered Clavichord." Then I go back to Etude 4, Etude 8, and then a little bit of Etude 4 again. I finish every practice period that way. I guess that's because I'm the fourth child. This has been with me for many years.

George Gershwin used to practice the First Etude of Cramer in C major. When I resumed concert playing after Gershwin died, I adopted that and also always wore the specially inscribed wristwatch he once gave me. Then I suddenly gave up the Cramer Etude. Fortunately I have given up anything associated with George. It was too obsessive.

A girl I liked before I was married once gave me a pair of gloves. Before a concert, I'd touch the gloves; I don't remember how many times in those days – the economy was different then. Later my wife gave me some gloves and I discarded the first pair.

I used to drive to Edgemont Hospital in Hollywood for shock treatments in 1956. Every time I passed a funeral parlor I would be sure that there was no cigarette in my hand. I would also stop breathing until the traffic lights changed and the car moved on. If anyone in the car spoke, I would become very disturbed physiologically. One of the funeral parlors has now been replaced, but I still observe my obeisance. I never look.

I have many bottles of the pills I take. Some are tranquilizers. I gave up vitamin pills, although my doctor and wife insist that I take them. I never was convinced of the efficacy of vitamins. They were introduced publicly, incidentally, by the St. Louis Cardinals when they were called the Gashouse Gang. They presented vitamins to the public—public relations they call it—but in my lexicon it was chutzpah!

Yet there is a certain method in my method, to uncoin a phrase. The sequence remains fixed. I take certain pills first, second, third and so forth. Then I arrange them in a precise order on the table. That's fixed, too. It's like finger painting by a monkey.

All my medicine bottles must be placed with their backs toward me, including the Sweeta; I never look at the fronts of the bottles. I also have a collection of old medicine bottles which nobody is allowed to touch although I'd like to get rid of them. If they're touched my day is ruined. They symbolize unfortunate experiences.

When I go into the bathroom, I put the index fingers of both hands on the slit of the door and silently count to eight. I repeat this once more. On my exit, I also do this twice. I always keep the toilet seat covered at all times. If anything is one quarter of an inch out of place in my bathroom, I lapse into a deep funk. I raise hell. Pandemonium breaks out.

I cannot stand an open door. Every closet door has to be closed.

When I'm taking off my trousers or pajama pants, the count is eight. But when I lie down on my bed, I lean my head to one side on my pillow and silently count to five twice. I have rigid rules about my pillows—which side they're on.

It takes a long time for me to open a package of cigarettes. It calls for the count of one to five twice over, and I take the tinfoil off during the latter half of the second count. If June talks during this ritual, I'm not allowed to rebuke her anymore because she'd beat the hell out of me, but I throw the pack away and wait until she leaves the room before I start opening another. Mine is always the most mangled pack of cigarettes around. The tinfoil must go into the silent butler and the paper into the wastebasket. But I allow very few things in my wastebasket. If it is anything of evil, sinister or possible catastrophic design, I put it in my wife's wastebasket.

* * *

When I'm in the hospital or if I'm not doing well in my career, I'm more relaxed about this ritualistic straitjacket. If I have nothing impending I relax, but as my engagements increase I get worse. I'm like a ballplayer on a streak.

In the middle and late 50's I was in hospitals constantly. I was committed every time I drew a breath or took an extra twelve pills—which never affected me much because I'm not suicidal.

Recently we were watching the *Eleventh Hour* on television. As the advice and behavior of the psychiatrist team became more and more appalling my wife shouted, "You're quacks, both of you!"

Last year in the book review section of *The New York Times* there was an irate article by a psychoanalyst who did not approve of commitments, which he felt were often the worst possible of terrors and punishment. I read it and thought it was completely justified and was inflamed; my wife had committed me so many times. I took the article to her.

"Just read this!" I demanded.

She read it and shrugged. "You don't know what I've been through," she replied.

Ethel Merman once said to me, "Oscar, your wife sure loves you."

"She's pretty noncommittal about showing it," I grumbled.

June yawned. "I guess I'll have to throw myself in front of a streetcar to prove it, Ethel."

"There are no streetcars anymore," I pointed out in my usual literal fashion.

Ethel replied, "They go uphill in San Francisco." I've been pondering that one.

Florence, the best maid we ever had, used to come on Wednesdays. I always dreaded that day because my wife would have Florence dust the table in my bedroom where I keep my newspapers and magazines. They each have to be in just the right position. The most sanctified object on that table was my latest copy of the London *Observer*. One day Florence touched it while she was dusting. I exploded. She sat on a chair and cried. Then I apologized; I'm always dreadfully contrite at a time like this. I got down on my knees and begged her to forgive me. But she left and never came back.

I complained to one psychoanalyst about my wife—not about anything irrational, but that she touched magazines or other objects that were quite holy to me. I told him I'd get into a cold sweat and a kind of paralysis and absolute congealed hysterics when this happened.

The doctor said, "You can't blame your wife for behaving normally."

I tried to use this as an antidote, but it doesn't work.

I find most forms of exercise repugnant and aimless; walking without an objective, dull and pointless. Also fatiguing. Psychologically it is important to know this although few may consider my views on the matter significant. It was better and more meaningful when I used to go shopping with my wife, when we had an objective, going from one store to another or going to a friend's house. Then the walking took on briskness and purpose. It's the difference between practicing at the piano in your room and playing a concert. There is no tension in your room. The audience that you have to overcome (overwhelm is the better word) isn't there. Even playing in a room full of people, which I haven't done for a long time, creates tension and therefore makes the playing more important. No matter how much you practice, I discovered years ago when I was concertizing, you are never in shape until after five or six concerts in front of the public.

I bought a bicycle in the spring of 1958. I rode up to Pamela and James Mason's, and he was so excited about it that he was envious. He took his daughter Portland's tricycle and got on it and we both rode through the streets of Beverly Hills.

I finally gave up riding it. It was too strenuous, what with the traffic in Beverly Hills and the Tanner buses with the tourists. Every time I left my house the bus would stop and the driver would point his finger and give a lecture about me. I'd run in terror.

Recently I've had a yen for gefullte fish. There are two makes: one is taboo in my home — it's called Mother's (an unfortunate commercial title); the other is Manischewitz. My wife bought some, but it was put on top of a couple of cans of sardines. When I was in my prime, I was an egomaniac and didn't allow my wife to buy the best sardines—the King Oscars—which bear my name. I felt there should be only one king in the house. But I finally compromised and let her buy Oscar Mayer products. Yet this jar of gefullte fish was on top of the sardines I wanted and I suddenly saw that it was Mother's. So I didn't have sardines for three months.

I finally got up the courage to order my wife to throw out the jar of gefullte fish. A couple of days after it disappeared she told me that it had been Manischewitz all the time. I have neurotic eyes. (Sometimes I have neurotic ears, too.) But I still didn't have sardines for three months because I was afraid that if I touched them, I'd get contaminated by my neurosis. It's quite volatile.

Food confuses me. An unscrupulous doctor who used to prey on my weakness, using extortionist rates, was once giving me shots and placebos and a few pills. My taste buds were dulled, as they are now, too. Suddenly I could only eat chili con carne. I'd eat it about 12:30 at night. I had always loathed chili con carne before.

I like tart things. One midnight recently I told one of my daughters to bring me some salad with sardines and herring on it. She was aghast, but that's my Ovaltine before I go to bed.

My food obsessions change. The other night my daughter Lorna reminisced about the time I regressed to complete infantilism. We were having dinner and tapioca pudding was served. A wild glint came into my eyes and in the presence of my wife and children I shrieked at the top of my voice, "I love this more than anything in the world!" I had to be withdrawn from tapioca pudding slowly. It was one of the few times I wasn't committed to achieve withdrawal. I just had a teaspoonful less every night. The last time it was served to me it looked like soap shavings. At the table I sometimes discourse on the cynicism of the blintz, particularly our homemade variety, or the bottled anger and rapelike aggressiveness of Coca-Cola.

About a year before my tapioca kick, I had a passion for chocolate—especially chocolate mousse and chocolate parfait. Whenever I was in New York, I'd sit in a completely reclining position at Le Pavillon and watch the waiters serve chocolate mousse. It became a hobby. I had so many chocolate stains on my suit that when the waiter would come with mine I'd say, "Just serve it on my lapel."

* * *

One time in the 40's I was taking my usual train trip to California from New York. During the stopover in Chicago I was restive and suddenly took a plane. My untrammeled fears about flying and the fact that it was Yom Kippur provided an opportunity to broaden the spectrum of my superstition rituals. I created a new ritual which I retained until recently. I "read" punctuation marks, including parentheses, exclamation points, commas—even accents on French words and dollar signs. I mutely say all of them in my mind. On this trip I repeated phrases ten times, in case I missed a word or forgot a comma. (When the late President Kennedy was revealed as a speed reader, it took me three hours to read the article about it.) This includes Walter Winchell, with the three-dot form of journalism. Actually there are four, but I consider the first one a period, then I do the three dots. This form of journalese is characteristic of many of the trenchant modern American writers. (The style is trenchant but the content is as phony as whipped cream in a chain drugstore.) It's quite tedious and limits my reading time. And I know it's all a conspiracy to deny me pleasure. I love reading.

* * *

In New York in the old days, my shirts had to be put in backwards in the drawers. At that time I always smoked the cigarette of my sponsor. In those days it was Lucky Strike and they had a bad habit of putting the packs carelessly into cartons. Some cartons had them upside down. I would never touch those. Lux Soap disturbed me a lot . . . L.U.X. They had "Lucky Lager" which always makes me squirm. Olympia Beer must be pretty distressed – they use a horseshoe. I shudder at the hard-pressed situation where they have to appeal to the public with "Lucky" or a horseshoe. That's pretty inane and unimaginative. I have great contempt for that. Both words are taboo with me. When the Lucky Lager commercial is on, I don't smoke until the commercial is over—or with Olympia Beer, either. I never smoke a cigarette when there is a commercial with an umbrella in a closed room. As a matter of fact, an open umbrella any place is taboo. I desist from smoking.

Speaking of superstitions, Truman Capote and I finally met recently. I'd read an interview with Capote in the *Paris Review* several years before and knew that he was as superstitious as I.

He said he never allowed three cigarette butts in an ashtray. Since then, in my bedroom—the high altar of my rituals and the place where I'm most tyrannical—I've cut mine down to one butt per ashtray.

* * *

Until 1958, if one of my friends was sick, I'd cut him off and not see him again. I viewed it as a personal affront to me. Also when someone once asked, "Do you remember me?" I replied giddily and with some joy, "Fortunately I'm suffering from amnesia."

When I'm in the mood, I vary the reply to this question. A woman once tricked me by asking, "Do you remember when you and I were in the earthquake?"

I dismissed her beautifully. "Every moment

is an earthquake to me," I replied.

And to another woman who squirmed up to me at a party with the classic query, I answered, "No," and when she told me her name, added, "I make it a point never to remember you." Then I added guiltily, "Because I see you so seldom."

I have acrophobia. It's not only the fear that I'll jump off high places, it's that if I do . . . well, I hate mingling with strangers.

I won't get dressed unless my wife urges me to. And I'm indifferent to my appearance. Years ago Stanley Marcus, of the Neiman-Marcus Department Store in Dallas, Texas, introduced himself to me. "We're supposed to look alike," he said. We both stared at each other in mutual horror.

When I was young, I looked like Al Capone but I lacked his compassion. Once my composer friend David Raksin told me that he was taking his three-year-old son to the San Diego Zoo to see the gorilla. I told him to bring the child to my house and save the trip.

Apparently I enjoy self-chastisement. When I used to speak of the lunatic fringe, I didn't know I was going to head it.

People often ask me why I moved to the West Coast from New York. I like to explain that it was because the eastern waves aren't big enough for surfing. "Besides," I used to cry, "how can I go back to New York when my daughter is the chief pompom girl at Beverly High?"

I understand that President Kennedy once considered me to head the physical fitness program. It was politics. I could have delivered the mental illness vote in a solid bloc. Instead, he chose Stan Musial, who has the Polish bloc.

I get glimmers of my real character from time to time. Once a Beverly Hills cop stopped me when I was trying to enter my own house, and was going to arrest me because I looked so furtive.

"Do I look like a criminal?" I asked indignantly.

"You sure do," he replied.

I took him into the house and had my wife identify me.

At one time I was a pretty good driver, except I refused to back up my car and I never knew how to get into a parking place.

Once I was going over the speed limit and a cop stopped me and gave me a ticket and told me what mileage I was doing. I said, "But I was humming the last movement of the Beethoven Seventh Symphony," and I sang it to him, in its furious tempo. Then I said, "You can't possibly hum the last movement of Beethoven's Seventh Symphony and go slow." He agreed. I didn't get a ticket.

A psychiatrist once diagnosed my troubles as "an abdication of will." I wake up, and the feeling of terror is so knife-edged . . . just the idea of waking up and facing a day of inertia and fear makes me long for a return to the unconscious. That's one reason why I address sleep with such great reverence; I can escape fear and melancholia.

Once you're in a mental hospital, you might as well make up your mind to look after yourself and recognize my axiom: The patient is never right.

A few years ago when I was suffering from a nutritional deficiency and had anorexia they were feeding me pureed food, catering to my womb-like regression. I hit upon a brilliant idea to supplement my nutrition.

"Why not give me Metrecal?" I asked the doctor. He was impressed by my ingenuity. That's how much they get accustomed to routine. But the Metrecal disagreed with me.

As for the axiom, I recall being given a sleeping medicine called Somnos, a form of chloral hydrate with alcohol in it. One night in the hospital my Somnos dose tasted weak, flaccid, and apparently watered and it proved inefficacious that night. I told the head nurse that the dose was inadequate. She protested that it was the regular dose. I raised hell. The next morning my doctor bawled me out for questioning the word of the nurse. He practically accused me of being irreligious, his faith in the staff was so prodigious. Later one of the nurses admitted that I had been right. What had happened was that the bottle was nearly empty, it was a Saturday night, and they had forgotten to renew the order.

On the psychiatric floor at Mount Sinai Hospital, which I've been in and out of from 1956 to 1962, the regime is strict and confining, particularly for the deeply depressed and catatonic patients. I don't believe that confining a deeply depressed patient in a solitary cell helps anyone —except the hospital administration. The attendants are nearly always Irish Catholic, for some reason. I once commented that you needed a permit from Pope John to get two Bufferin there. The meals come on the typical hospital schedule. I told Dorothy Parker that dinner was at quarter to five P.M. "That makes for a nice long evening," she replied.

I used to have an excellent memory, but when I was giving piano recitals "With Comment" (that was how it was billed), one of my remarks was that I was writing, a book to be called *Memoirs of a Man Suffering from Amnesia.* I did indeed suffer from amnesia after my shock treatments. One time when I was home either recuperating or just treading water—I can't remember which—I was watching a television picture of an old English film starring Sir Ralph Richardson.

June entered the room and asked, "What are you watching?"

I explained that it was an absorbing story in which Richardson played the role of a man who had an attack of amnesia—and I was anxious to see how it came out.

June sighed, "You saw that movie last week," she said.

I'm so guilt-ridden that when I watch *The Defenders* on television and the jury shuffles in and the judge says, "Have you reached a verdict?" I start to panic. When the foreman stands up and says, "Yes, Your Honor," and the judge adds, "Will the defendant please rise?" I always stand up. And get hysterically happy when the jury finds me guilty.

Years ago there was a play called *The Amazing Dr. Clitterhouse* which was later made into a movie with Edward G. Robinson. At the end of the second act the judge orders the protagonist to stand, and announces, "You are guilty," and the man falls down.

When I got up for a smoke after that second-act curtain, I fell right down. It was complete neurotic association. Actually, about four attorneys general in different administrations could sue me for monopoly of guilt.

During the summer of 52, I again went east to play at the Lewisohn Stadium in New York.

Before the concert all the strength left my body. It was unbearable neurotic hysteria which included a psychogenic paralysis. During the performance I lost my coordination. I managed to finish the concert but after that ordeal I declared a hiatus.

In 1953 I spent most of my time in bed in a dazed, drugged loneliness, days and nights fading into one another without meaning.

Ahead—although I didn't know it then— was nearly a decade of addictions and withdrawals, of commitments and subtle revolts of my subconscious which would manifest themselves in anguish.

It all blends into a phantasmagoria, a gray blur in which people and events emerge now and again and then recede. I remember hospital beds, a parade of doctors, homosexual male nurses, friends and fellow patients coming and going. Above all, I remember the never-ending desire for those drugs which would give me instant oblivion, the wild and neurotic quest for unconsciousness. Woven through the warp and woof of this fabric of terror and pain were threads of manic elation, deep depression and fantasy.

In trying to recollect those years, incidents fade into one another and perspective vanishes. The details and chronology are not easily recalled.

Figure 4-23. Joan. (Illustration by Shane Hainey.)

READING 4B

A PORTRAIT OF PSYCHOSIS

Norman Cameron

Norman Cameron was associated with the Institute of Human Resources at Yale University. He had extensive experience in the practice of psychoanalysis, or Freudian psychotherapy. Of all of his patients, I feel that the case of Joan R., a woman with schizophrenia, is the most compelling. Although Cameron's psychoanalytic bias is evident in his presentation of Joan, the constellation of symptoms characteristic of schizophrenia is vividly described. As you read about Joan's psychosis, try to make distinctions between her and Oscar Levant, whose neurosis was previously described.

**A Schizophrenic Reaction
In An Adolescent Girl**

Joan R., a Kansas City high school girl, was admitted to a psychiatric clinic after she had attempted suicide by drinking iodine. We shall begin with her childhood. She had suffered the loss through death of two important mother figures, one when she was two years old, the other when she was fourteen. These are critical ages in personality development, ages when a mother figure plays her most significant roles. Joan's mother had been ill for some time before her death, so that the little girl lacked the ego support which should have been available to her for the structuring of her early personality. At fourteen, when an adolescent normally lives through in altered form the oedipal conflicts of early childhood, Joan's foster mother died, and Joan was again left with no one to help her build her adolescent personality. To further complicate matters for Joan, her foster mother was her father's sister, a domineering widow with a daughter of her own. It will be simplest if we present briefly the patient's life history.

As we have said, Joan was two years old when her mother died. Her father's sister moved at once into the home, taking Joan's mother's place, and bringing with her Peggy, an eight-year-old daughter. We shall see how Joan tried to repeat what her foster mother had done as soon as death left her place vacant. Peggy's mother was an anxious, probably superstitious woman who encouraged Joan to be over-dependent. The two girls apparently hated each other. When Peggy's mother died, Joan was fourteen and Peggy a grown woman of twenty. The household now consisted of Joan, Peggy and Joan's father, a scholar with little psychological understanding.

To her father's surprise Joan showed no sorrow over the death of her foster mother. Instead, she tried at once to take her place in the home, just as her foster mother had immediately taken her own mother's place. She became self-assertive, arrogant and demanding. The home, she said, was now hers, and Peggy could henceforth obey her orders. Joan's father spent the next two years trying unsuccessfully to keep the peace between these two girls, rivals for control of the home.

Without a mother figure and without a stable personality of her own, Joan soon got out of control. She continued for the time being to be affectionate to her father, but she also behaved toward him as a nagging wife rather than as a young adolescent daughter. She openly criticized his appearance and his ways, even in front of guests. She demanded that he give her more attention and more money. She reminded her father that her foster mother, her father's sister, had been afraid of the house, often saying that there was a curse upon it. She protested violently against his going out in the evening and leaving the latchkey under the mat, where strangers might find it. As we shall see Joan was already beginning to develop delusional fears in relation to this evening situation. Toward Peggy, her grownup cousin, she remained relentlessly hostile. Once during a quarrel over the radio she bit Peggy severely, giving her a wound that took two weeks to heal. From other evidence it is clear that Joan's emotional problems, with which no one helped her, were precipitating a general personality disorganization.

When Joan was sixteen her cousin married. This removed her rival from the home; but it also left Joan, in a state of emotional turmoil, alone in the house with her father. Her attitude toward him abruptly changed. She no longer gave or accepted tokens of affection. The hate that she had visited upon her cousin she now directed toward her father. She behaved insolently toward him, accusing him even before visitors of mistreating her. These accusations, which completely mystified her father, were actually the product of delusional experiences that she was having, experiences in which weird primary process fears and wishes had escaped repression and were mingling with preconscious and conscious organization. What these were we shall soon see. Whenever Joan had frightening dreams she would make her father join her in bed, as her aunt had always done, but later she would rail against him for having done this and accuse him of mistreatment. He was greatly disconcerted by all this contradiction and confusion; but he did not know what to do about it. He thought she would outgrow it. One night he came home late to find his daughter thrashing about the room with a cane – killing snakes, she said. She used to keep her light on all night long because she was having "frightening dreams," which were probably delusional and hallucinatory experiences rather than dreams.

As might be expected, after the aunt's death, when Joan was fourteen, her school work grew poorer and poorer. She seemed bored, inattentive and irritable. By the time she was fifteen and a half she needed a tutor to keep her from being dropped from school. Eventually even this help was not enough. When she was sixteen, Joan was dropped from school, and her father was told to consult a psychiatrist. The psychiatrist recommended immediate treatment, but his recommendation was not followed. Joan simply stayed at home.[1]

Joan showed a corresponding decline in her social relationships. Undoubtedly because of her personality defects, and because she was over dependent upon her foster mother, Joan had never reached an adequate level of social skill. She frightened and repelled the neighborhood children with her temper tantrums and uncompromising demands. As an adolescent she was far too much involved in the rivalry with her cousin for domination of the home, in her own revived edipal conflicts and her preoccupations with frightening experiences to be able to interact normally with her peers, the boys and girls around her.

The climax came when Joan was sixteen, a year before she came to the hospital. She bought a new dress for a high school dance, but when her escort arrived she refused at first to see him. After considerable persuasion she finally consented to go with him; half an hour later she returned home without her escort. Perhaps she knew that her father had arranged to have her escorted when he found that nobody had invited her to the dance. At any rate this was her last social engagement. Following Joan's withdrawal from school, her father arranged little parties for her, "to help her get well," but she would shut herself in her room until the guests left the house. The best he could do about the situation was to engage a housekeeper.

During the months between leaving school and entering the hospital Joan was living in a nightmare. She was afraid to sleep at night because of all that seemed to be going on. During the day she lay around the house, preoccupied, worn out and doing next to nothing. Her behavior became obviously strange, reflecting the hopeless confusion of her thinking. For example, her father gave her forty dollars to buy some clothes, and she spent it all on history books which she never read. On another occasion she went out and spent twelve dollars on cosmetics, but a few days later she destroyed the lot. She got up early one morning, collected all the playing cards in the house and burned them, saying that they were sinful. She began talking about religion, the church, sin, charity and the hereafter. She gave the housekeeper five dollars because she had to be charitable "to get to heaven."

Joan said that all her troubles came from masturbation. At fifteen she concluded without telling anyone that this was driving her crazy. Her conclusion increased her already intolerable guilt, anxiety and confusion, and contributed to her belief that she would burn in hell for her sins, and that her hands were diseased. "I have leprosy!" she said at the hospital, "look at my hands. But that's not punishment enough for all my evil. Faust, yes, he gave himself to the devil. That's what I've done. Don't touch me! You'll be sorry, you'll get leprosy too![2]"

The girl's unconscious material, which ultimately emerged and overwhelmed her, seems to have appeared first as anxiety dreams and frightening nighttime fantasies – of snakes, assault, strangers in the house and murder. "I used to read stories and things," she said, "and then I'd go to bed and lie awake and think about them. I'd be scared silly to be in the room by myself. That house is so spooky." The last statement repeats what her foster mother had always said. When Joan closed her eyes and tried to sleep, she would have horrible visions, and see faces that seemed to grow enormous.[3] She thought men were walking on the roofs, which were flat and connected with one another, and that they were climbing in the window. Eventually a man across the street seemed to control the house; and she began hearing voices. Finally a man's voice dominated, telling her to do whatever she was told.

Joan now used weird delusions to reconstruct the reality that she had lost in her steady regression and disorganizations, delusions which would help explain her previously unconscious fantasies, now fully conscious. Her home, she told herself, was now the headquarters of a dope ring. Her father had been murdered and an impostor put in his place. "My father wouldn't treat me the way this man has treated me," she said. "My father and I were friends. This man will get into bed with me. I've been love-starved

and forsaken; and I thought someone was bringing in opium." The similarity of this tale to the common dope ring mystery story is obvious, and its appeal is probably to the same unconscious needs.

In her fantasies, which Joan considered real, people seemed to beat her and tie her up. They seemed able to read her mind, to control her by reading her thoughts. She tried to keep back her thoughts; but the effort hurt the back of her head.[4]

Joan began having horrible dreams and fantasies of killing her father and other people, of cutting them up and chewing their flesh, of being God, and of being murdered as a sacrifice.[5] She felt at times that she was someone else, that her body was changing, that she might be going to have a baby, that she had a brain tumor and was going crazy.

In the hospital, where people listened to her when she spoke, some of her sadomasochistic fantasies became obvious. Joan said that her suicidal attempt was an act of self punishment. She was going to hell for her sins, she thought, and the quicker she got there the better. "I thought it would make me suffer. If I hadn't become so hardened it would have hurt terribly." At times she was sure she would be executed for her crimes, which seemed real to her, or that she would get life imprisonment. She wished that she would "get black smallpox or something." She said, "I got hipped on the subject of Christianity. I thought I should torture myself. . . . I try to figure out ways of torturing people. It seems I have been in so much pain; and I want other people to have the same thing."

Joan had many outbursts of rage. One night a nurse found her trembling and wringing her hands. "I think I'm pushing people's eyes in. I'm dreadfully wicked. . . . It's those awful thoughts that go through my head." Once in the daytime she cried to a group of patients, "If I had the strength of Christ I would kill every one of you! Yes, I would kill you all because a more horrid doom awaits you than death." There is a sign of confusion between herself and the others in this histrionic statement. Another day Joan became angry and struck an inoffensive depressed patient. "That's nothing in comparison with what

I'm going to do," she cried, "I'm going to chop off your heads, every one of you. You'd better go home and chop off your families' heads. . . . You're not going to keep me here and make me bear children!" In the more permissive atmosphere of the hospital, Joan was giving vent to the violent aggression that she had felt for years at home.[6] After expressing it, she excused herself on the grounds that she would be saving the patients from something worse by killing them.

There were grandiose delusions also. Joan said that she felt she had a powerful influence over people and was responsible for everything that happened. She thought that she might get superhuman ideas, "such as how Christ turned water into wine – I had to find out how it was done." As God, she thought, she must suffer to help others; and because of her sins she ought to kill herself. But the attempt failed. "So," she said, "I came to the conclusion that I would have to forget. As time goes on, I'll forget all my troubles, my experiences and so forth." This was just what Joan seemed to be achieving. She expressed, in well-organized secondary process speech, the disintegration which she was experiencing, and to which she was resigned.

Years before, when her foster mother died, Joan had begun a struggle at home with a tangled personal situation involving real persons, her father, her cousin and herself. For such a struggle, with no one around to understand her, Joan's personality organization was unprepared. As time went on, this shared social community was gradually replaced by the even greater complexities of Joan's delusional pseudocommunity, with its mixture of real and imagined persons, of fact and reconstructed delusion. Now she seemed to be making a final retreat. She was withdrawing into an autistic community which consisted mainly of fantasized persons and action with the background of her own private fantasies.[7]

There were two definite catatonic episodes. One day, while telling her therapist that she liked dreamy states, Joan slipped into a stupor. Her eyes closed, her eyeballs rolled upward, and her limbs went limp. Her eyelids resisted opening, however, and her jaws and limbs grew stiffer as they were manipulated. When she was left alone she soon recovered. Another day Joan was lying on her side on her bed, just before lunch, when there was a sudden loud clap of thunder close by. Joan instantly became so rigid that the nurses could pick her up and place her in a sitting position with no more change in her posture than if she had been a statue. Then the lunch trays arrived, and an experienced nurse began coaxing her gently and spoon-feeding her. After about ten minutes of this, the girl suddenly got up, rubbed her eyes as though she had just awakened, and ate her lunch with the others as if nothing had happened.

Therapy was unsuccessful with Joan. She slept well at night without medication, in spite of occasional disturbing dreams. In the daytime she spent most of her time daydreaming. She became less and less communicative, her talk developed more and more disorganization. She was frequently observed talking excitedly to herself. Sometimes she smiled and laughed as though she were hallucinating. Often she stood straight against the wall with her hands high above her head; but she would give no explanation of this posturing. Her father decided to place Joan in a state hospital near her home. Her prognosis for social recovery was poor.

Notes

[1] Bower, E. M., Shellhamer, T. A., and Daily, J. M., "School characteristics of male adolescents who later became schizophrenic," *Amer. J. Orthopsychiat.*, 1961, 30, 712-739.

[2] Compare this with the neurotic compulsive reaction to soiled hands, as in the case of Sally J., who washed and scrubbed her hands when she had evil thoughts.

[3] Such changes in size have been reported by normal adults who have studied their visions when falling asleep. Cf. Silberer, H., "Report on a method of eliciting and observing certain symbolic hallucination-phenomena," in Rapaport, D. (Ed.), *Organization and Pathology of Thought.* New York: Columbia Univ. Press, 1951; Isakower, O., "A contribution to the pathopsychology of phenomena associated with falling asleep," *Internat. J. Psychoanal.*, 1938, *19*, 331-345.

[4] When adults anticipate a small child's actions, it must seem to the child that they know his thoughts. Such childhood experiences are probably the origins of this common form of schizophrenic delusion.

[5]Cannibalistic dreams are not rare among neurotic persons. Such dreams and the fantasies of this patient probably revive early childhood feeding fantasies which, in the adult, take on a more definite form.

[6]There is a recent discussion of sadomasochism in relation to aggression in Gero, G., "Sadism, masochism and aggression," *Psychoanal. Quart.,* 1962, *31*, 31-42.

[7]For a comparison of *pseudocommunity* and *autistic community,* see Cameron, N., and Magaret, A., *Behavior Pathology.* Boston: Houghton Mifflin, 1951, Chapters 13 and 14.

The Caduceus. A winged staff with serpents twined around it, carried by the Greek god Hermes. It is a symbol of the medical profession. (Illustration and photograph by Jim Rooney.)

Chapter 5

THE ILLNESS PERSPECTIVE

How much is known about the brain and the nervous system; how little is known. Neuroscience is capable of measuring specific neurotransmitter levels and mapping behavioral correlates of particular brain structures. "Minimal brain dysfunction," too subtle to detect, is assumed to produce significant pathology. In other cases, extensive brain injury has minimal impact. In 1848, Phineas P. Gage received serious brain damage in a railroad demolition accident. A premature blast shot a three-foot long, one and one quarter inch diameter tamping iron through Gage's skull; entering near the jaw, and exiting the

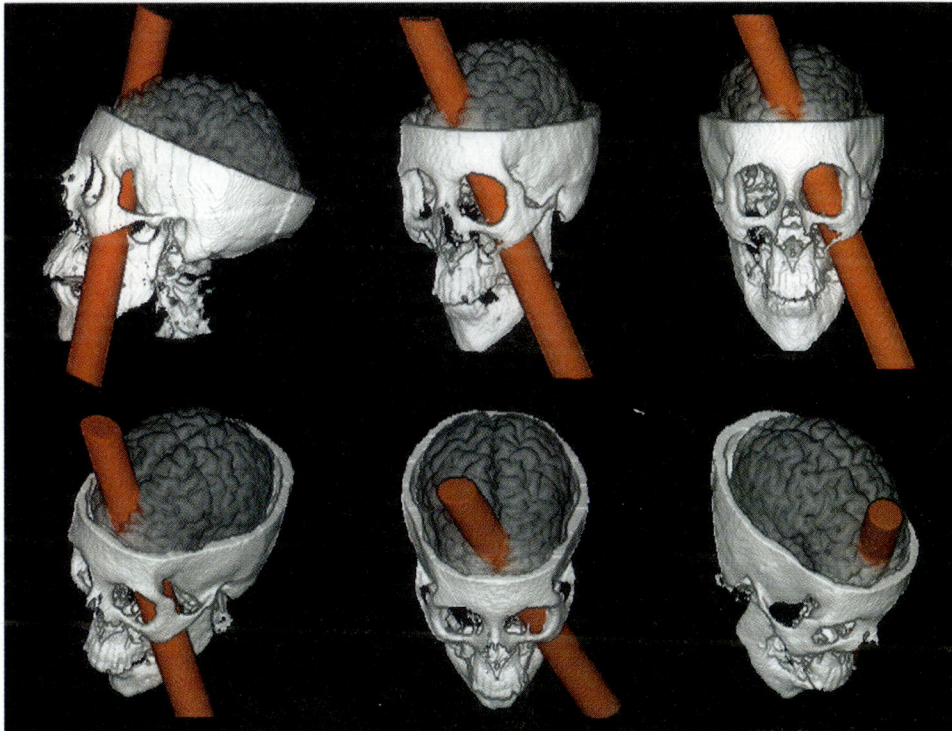

Figure 5-1. Six computerized images demonstrate the likely path taken by a tamping iron through the frontal lobes of Phineas P. Gage, from H. Damasio, T. Grabowski, R. Frank, A.M. Galaburda, and A.R. Damasio: The Return of Phineas Gage: Clues about the brain from the skull of a famous patient. *Science*, 264: 1102-1105, 1994. Reproduced with permission of Dr. Hanna Damasio.

top of his head. He spoke within a few minutes and ultimately regained good physical health. His personality became more volatile, and he complained of a "queer feeling" which he could not explain (Harlow, 1868). In February, 1993, Hippocrates magazine reported that Arthur Ekvall was shot with an arrow by his former lover. It entered the back of his neck, and protruded from his forehead. He later testified against his assailant.

The first of six major perspectives we will cover is the illness perspective. It is also often called the neuroscience perspective because it deals with how the human brain and nervous system are related to abnormal behavior. It is the oldest of the perspectives. It is probably the most popular and influential, and the one with which the layman is most familiar. It employs a medical model for the understanding and treatment of mental disorders. Its practitioners are psychiatrists and neurologists. The treatments of the perspective are typically chemical in nature (drugs), surgical (psychosurgery), or electrical (electroconvulsive therapy).

Although the most significant advances in neuroscience have been made in the past few decades, medical treatments for mental disorders have been employed for thousands of years. Electroconvulsive therapy has been used as a treatment for depression since the 1930s. It involves passing an electrical current through the patient's brain, the magnitude of which produces a convulsion. However, thousands of years ago the technique of applying an electric eel, capable of producing a shock of six hundred volts, to the skull of the patient was practiced by the ancient Greeks, Romans, and Egyptians. Electric fish were used to expel devils from the human body in Ethiopia during the sixteenth century (Torry, 1972, pp. 69-70).

American psychiatry began using the major tranquilizers in the treatment of psychosis during the 1950s. Reserpine (Sandril) is a tranquilizer derived from the rauwolfia, or snakeroot plant. It has been used as an antidote for cardiac acceleration caused by snakebites and as a tranquilizer for centuries in India and by "primitive" West African shamans (Torrey, 1972).

Psychosurgery, which involves surgical operations performed on the brain, remains a controversial issue. However, it is not new, either. The technique of trepanning was used in ancient Peru to treat what would today be called epilepsy. Trepanning involved drilling holes in the patient's skull to allow evil spirits to escape. The hole was sometimes as large as a quarter, and patients sometimes survived the ordeal. Throughout history, shamans have demonstrated therapeutic expertise within their cultures. Shamans are both religious and medical authorities. Tribal members have tremendous confidence in their ability to heal. They often use music, drum beating, drugs, smoking, and alcohol to create the proper therapeutic atmosphere. Medical treatment for mental disorders is thousands of years old.

The medical model involves a reapplication of the terms and concepts of physical medicine to the behavioral realm. In physical medicine, when a person is in a state of health, his body functions normally and he feels well. However, this state of health can be disrupted. For example, a person may have a heart attack and suffer heart damage. The person is in poor health. Measurable damage has been done to the heart. Symptoms such as discomfort, loss of strength, shortness of breath, and poor circulation may result. He must be hospitalized. Medical treatments, such as drugs and surgery, may be employed in the attempt to restore his physical health.

The same basic logic and methodology is employed by the illness perspective in the treatment of mental disorders. When the structure and function of the brain and body are normal, the person's behavior is normal, and he is "mentally healt He feels well and is satisfied with his behavior. However, "mental health" can also be disrupted. Should neurological pathology occur, behavioral, affective, and cognitive symptoms are likely to result, and the person can be diagnosed with "mental illness." Medical interventions will then be employed, in clinical settings, to treat the condition. If successful, the symptoms should remit, with the person returning to his premorbid state of "mental health." Thus, concepts such as health, illness, symptoms, treatment, and hospitalization are common to physical medicine and the illness perspective.

People understand the concept of physical illness and its need for medical treatment. Abnormal behavior is more abstract. Therefore, physicians have tried to enhance the public's understanding of it by explaining, "It is as if the person is mentally ill." As the metaphor has become more common, it has lost its "as if" quality. Mental illness and the illness perspective were thus created.

Six articles will be presented to illustrate the illness perspective. The first, "Should Some People Be Labeled Mentally Ill?" by Albert Ellis, investigates the utility of conceptualizing abnormal behavior as illness. The second, "Divided Selves" by Tony Dajer, presents evidence for viral and genetic causes of schizophrenia. The third, "To Catch a Killer Gene" by Susan Katz Miller, describes a horrible genetic disorder and recent astonishing discoveries about it. Fourth is "Psychosurgery: Damaging the Brain to Save the Mind", by Joann Ellison Rogers. It tells the story of a troubled young man named Matthew and a valiant effort to help him. The fifth article of the chapter, "The Blood of Madness" by Mary Long, describes a controversial treatment for schizophrenia. Finally, "Electroshock: Fifty Years Later", by Russ Rymer, describes the advantages and disadvantages of electroshock therapy.

References

Harlow, J.M. (1868). Recovery from the passage of an iron bar through the head. *Publication of the Massachusetts Medical Society, 2,* 327.

Torrey M.D., E.F. (1972). What Western Psychotherapists Can Learn From Witchdoctors. *American Journal of Orthopsychiatry, 42*(l).

_____ (1972). *The Mind Game: Witchdoctors and Psychiatrists.* New York: Bantam.

Figure 5-2. Albert Ellis. Proponent of calling abnormal behavior "mental illness" and originator of Rational-Emotive Therapy. (Photograph courtesy of Dr. Ellis.)

SHOULD SOME PEOPLE BE LABELED MENTALLY ILL?

Albert Ellis

Does mental illness exist? Opinion is divided. The debate began in 1960 with the publication of The Myth of Mental Illness, by psychiatrist Thomas Szasz, his own profession's most tenacious critic. Szasz has never committed anyone, given electric shock, or even prescribed drugs to his patients. He claims mental illness is a myth, a bad metaphor. During the Inquisition, the devil was blamed for bizzare behavior. Today it is attributed to schizophrenia, without further understanding. Most "mental illness" is primary, without known cause. Illnesses have causes. Instead, he argues, psychopathology is better understood as "problems in living." This does not minimize their severity and recognizes that people bear responsibility for the cause, course, and solution of their problems. He argues that psychiatrists are "travel agents disguised as mechanics." They can counsel and guide, but not fix defective brains.

David P. Ausubel wrote Personality Disorder is Disease *in 1961. He argued that mental and physical illness are each characterized by subjective judgements of pain and discomfort by patient and physician. The pain of mental and physical illness is real. Since general medical conditions have been discovered as causes for Huntington's disease, neurosyphilis, and Down Syndrome, they may also be found in other primary disorders. There are treatments that work for both types of illness; illness results when the treatments are given to well people. Although the specifics may be unknown, it is inherently logical that there is something wrong with one in a florid state of psychosis.*

Although the issue is not fully resolved, mental illness is the prevailing metaphor for understanding abnormal behavior. We have come to consider virtually any abnormal behavior or condition that causes us distress as mental illness. We consider alcoholics, substance abusers, pathological gamblers, and habitually violent felons as ill.

Of greater relevance is the utility of the practice of calling abnormal behavior mental illness. Is it beneficial or detrimental to the ailing individual and his society? The issue is complex; for every advantage there is a disadvantage. Dr. Albert Ellis examines the value of the concept of mental illness from a variety of perspectives in the following article. It was originally published in 1967, so some of the language and terminology is dated. Many articles have been written on the subject since. I feel this one is still the best.

The question considered is whether it is proper to label some people mentally ill in view of the social discriminations, self-denigration, interference with treatment, impeding of social progress, and unscientific close-mindedness which may ensue when this kind of labeling is employed. It is shown that it is not the labeling process itself which is necessarily harmful, but that if such terms as "mental illness" are operationally defined and if the individuals so described are not negatively evaluated as persons, it may be possible to employ these terms scientifically and usefully.

Albert Ellis: Should People Be Labeled Mentally Ill? *Journal of Consulting Psychology*, 31, 435-446.Copyright © 1967 by the American Psychological Association. Reprinted with permission.

For the last two decades there has been increasing objection by a number of psychologists and sociologists (as well as an even greater number of nonprofessional writers) to labeling certain people as "mentally ill" or "emotionally sick." Thus, Szasz (1961, 1966) has vigorously alleged that the concept of mental illness "now functions merely as a convenient myth." Mowrer (1960) has contended that behavior disorders are manifestations of personal irresponsibility and sin rather than of disease. Whitaker and Malone (1953), as well as many other experiential and existential psychotherapists, have held that emotional disturbance is a rather meaningless term because practically all therapists are just about as sick as their patients. Keniston (1966) and a number of sociological writers have insisted that individual psychodynamics are not nearly as important as has commonly been assumed in the creation of human alienation and insecurity, but that our technological society itself lays the groundwork for the growing estrangement of young people and, to one degree or another, makes us all emotionally aberrant.

The question of whether some individuals are especially "mentally ill" and should be clearly labeled so is of profound importance, since it affects decision making in the areas of hospitalization, imprisonment, psychotherapy in the community, vocational training and placement, educational advancement, and many other aspects of modern life. Siegel (1966) has recently reported that high school students who are hospitalized for emotional disturbance or who undertake psychotherapy without hospitalization, are frequently held to be poor risks for higher education and are consequently refused admittance to college. Obviously, labeling a person "mentally ill" has more than theoretical import.

To my knowledge, no dispassionate discussion of both sides of this question has yet been published. I shall, therefore, try to list the main disadvantages and advantages of labeling certain people "mentally ill," so that psychologists in general and psychotherapists in particular may be better able to see and cope with this problem. The main issues that have recently been raised in connection with diagnosing individuals as "emotionally sick" involve (*a*) social discrimination

against the "mentally ill," (*b*) self-denigration by disturbed people, (*c*) moral responsibility and "mental illness," (*d*) prophylaxis and treatment of aberrant individuals, (*e*) social progress and emotional disturbance, and (*f*) scientific attitude and advancement in regard to labeling people "mentally ill."

Social Discrimination against the "Mentally Ill"

There are several discriminatory practices which seem to be inevitably connected with labeling an individual as neurotic, psychotic, or emotionally disturbed. When so diagnosed, either officially or semiofficially, he is often discriminated against in some practical ways–is refused jobs, kept out of schools, rejected as a love or marriage partner, etc. This discrimination is entirely unjust in many cases, since the sick individual is not given a chance to prove that he can succeed vocationally, educationally, or otherwise. In some instances, a person who behaves unconventionally or idiosyncratically may be adjudged psychotic and may be forcibly hospitalized. Consequently, his—and everyone else's—freedom of speech may be restricted by his incarceration or threat thereof. Siebert(1967) has noted in this connection:

The thing that has pained me for so long is that, while Americans will go to extreme lengths to protect a person's right to speak, there is really very little freedom in this country to express all of one's thoughts. I talked to many, many people in mental hospitals who were placed there because they revealed some personal thoughts to a relative or to a psychiatrist. Few citizens realize how easy it is to lock up a person who has "undesirable" thoughts [p. 11].

Practically all psychological labels today are inexact. What is more, they keep changing from diagnostician to diagnostician and from decade to decade. Thus, most of the patients whom Freud called neurotic would today be designated as borderline psychotic or schizophrenic reaction. Yet, once a person is psychiatrically labeled, he is treated as if that label were indubitably correct and as if it accurately describes his behavior. His remaining inside or outside of a mental institution, being employed or unemployed, or remaining married or unmarried may depend on the particular kind of labeling done by a given psychologist or psychiatrist who is in a certain mood at a special time and place.

Labeling some people as emotionally disturbed tends to set up a caste system, with consequent social discriminations. In most communities of our society, so-called healthy individuals are socially favored over the "mentally sick." But in some groups—Bohemian, hippie, criminal, or drug-taking groups—the reverse may be true, and the sick individual may be considered "in" and may be favored over the "square."

As an escapee from a New York mental hospital points out (Anonymous, 1966), individuals who commit clearly illegal acts, such as trespassing on others' property and refusing to support their wives, may be discriminated against once they are judged to be "mentally ill" by not being held morally responsible for their acts and not being given a stipulated prison term for committing these acts, but, instead, being indefinitely committed to a mental institution. These individuals are thus deprived of their moral (or immoral) choices and of being held accountable for such choices.

Our psychiatric terminology itself, as Davidson (1958) and Menninger (1965) indicate, is highly pejorative. Referring to people with behavior problems by such designations as "anal character," "sadistic," "castrating," "infantile," "psychopathic," and "schizophrenic" hardly helps their states of mind and adds grave doubts to the attitudes of life insurance companies, social clubs, officer groups, and other organizations about their eligibility. Nor, as Menninger (1965) points out,

is the patient, or ex-patient, the only sufferer from this situation. An entire family can be hurt by the diagnostic label attached to one of its members, because of the various implications such labels have in the minds of the various groups of people with whom that family comes in contact [p. 45].

With the very best intentions, then, psychologists and psychiatrists who are instrumental in labeling individuals as "mentally ill" may unwittingly subject these individuals to a variety of social and legal discriminations and may seri-ously interfere with their civil and their human rights. And not all psychiatric intentions are the very best! Redlich and Freedman (1966), while favoring involuntary commitment of psychotics in many instances, admit that

"Certainly, commitments in many cases are entirely rational acts; however, in some cases there is evidence that psychiatrists and other involved persons are motivated, in part, by counter-aggression toward very provocative patients [p. 780]."

So, quite apart from the contention of groups helping ex-mental patients (during the last two decades) that many Americans have been and still are being railroaded by their relatives into institutions when they are not truly disturbed, there seems to be considerable evidence that commitment procedures leave much to be desired and that various discriminatory mistakes are made in this connection.

There is, however, another side to the story. Some individuals in our society, whatever we choose to call them, are clearly unfit to live unattended in the community—as even Szasz (1966) admits. Many of them should, perhaps, best be placed in regular prisons, even though today that solution is hardly ideal! Others, such as those who have committed no crimes but are obviously on the brink of harming themselves and/or other people, can hardly be incarcerated in jail, nor can they even properly be given determinate sentences in a mental hospital. If their behavior is sufficiently aberrant, they may well have to be placed in some kind of protective custody for an indeterminate period, and what better place do we have for this kind of treatment than a mental institution?

The main point here is that labeling an individual as "mentally ill," and thereby being enabled to send him for therapy either in a suitable institution or as an involuntary patient in his own community, frequently subjects him to unfair legal and social discrimination. Nonetheless, many other people, and sometimes this individual himself, may be unfairly discriminated against if this kind of procedure is not in some way followed. Take, for example, the case of a suicidal individual. Morgenstern (1966) states:

Since suicide is not only irrational—it punishes oneself for rage directed at others—but is also irrevocable, the psychiatrist and society have the human obligation to force reconsideration. All of us are at times tempted to do the irrational and the irrevocable, and I would doubt that, having been stopped, we were ungrateful [p. 4].

The seriously disturbed person, in other words, may well be unfairly discriminating against himself, even to the point of irrevocably harming himself in some major ways. Is it not, therefore, fair under these conditions to judge him ill and forcibly restrain him from his self-sabotaging, even at the expense of possibly discriminating against him in other ways?

Granted that this question may have no utterly agreed-upon, clear-cut answer, here is another that warrants asking: Assuming that legal and social discriminations may accrue to the individual who is labeled "mentally ill," is it not sometimes necessary to discriminate against him in this manner in order to prevent him from needlessly harming others? Mrs. Hyman Brett (1966), in a letter to the *New York Times* following its publication of Szasz' article, "Mental Illness is a Myth" (1966), puts this question in more detail:

What about the freedom and the liberties of the relatives of the mentally ill person who consistently refuses care? At the same time that we refuse to tamper with the mentally ill person's freedom are we not tampering with theirs? By returning the mentally ill member to his family we are chaining his relations to a life of dread, despondency and frustration. When we allow the neurotic or psychotic the freedom to reject care we are allowing him at the same time another very special freedom: the freedom to drive his family over the border line into the realm of mental illness, too. For though his condition may not be a danger to society, it is a very grave and definite threat to the emotional stability of the members of his family [p. 4].

Mrs. Brett may exaggerate here, since family members of a "mentally ill" individual may, at least to some extent, choose whether or not to be unduly influenced by his illness. Her general point, however, seems to have some validity. For in giving a highly disturbed person his full civil rights, we may easily infringe upon those of others whom he may incessantly annoy, frustrate, maim, and even kill, his behavior ranging from

playing his radio very loudly all night to mowing down some of his neighbors with a machine gun. Just as the protection of the civil rights of Jews or Negroes does not extend to their rights to libel, injure, or slay non-Jews and non-Negroes, so may the civil rights of highly idiosyncratic individuals have to be curtailed when they infringe upon the similar rights of not-so-idiosyncratic others.

Self-Denigration by Disturbed People

Perhaps the most pernicious aspect of a person's being labeled "mentally ill" is that he not only tends to be denigrated by other members of his social group, including even the professionals who diagnose him, but also that he almost always accepts their estimations of himself and makes them his own. This is exceptionally unfair and pernicious; even if he can unmistakably be shown to be disturbed, he is obviously not entirely responsible for being so, but has been born and/or reared to be sick and is not to be condemned for his state of being.

It is true that an individual, unless he is in a state of complete breakdown, is somewhat responsible for his acts, since he performed or caused them and usually has some degree of choice in doing or not doing them. Not every psychotic murders, and under the old McNaughten rule there was some justification for our courts holding certain disturbed people responsible for their crimes, as long as it could be shown that they were aware of what they were doing when they committed these crimes and that they had some choice in their commission. There is no reason, however, why even thieves and murderers have to be condemned in toto or held to be worthless persons for their misdeeds. They are, like all of us, intrinsically fallible humans and to demand that they (or we) be infallible is unrealistic. They, moreover, are much different from and greater than their performances, and although we can legitimately measure and evaluate an individual's *products,* there is no way—as Hartman (1959, 1962) has shown—of accurately assessing his *self.* Finally, when we do assess a person as a whole for his performances, we inevitably make it impossible for him to have self-respect; for as soon as he does something wrong, which, being fallible, he soon must, we label *him* as bad and, thereby, strongly imply that as a bad *person* he has no other choice than to keep doing wrong acts again and again (Ellis, 1962).

This is what frequently happens when we pejoratively label an individual "mentally ill." Instead of indicating to him that some of his *behavior* is inefficient or mistaken, we insist that *he* is psychotic or sick, whereupon he logically concludes that he is probably unable to do anything efficiently or right, gives in to his illness, and keeps perpetuating ineffectual behavior that he actually has the ability to change or stop. To the degree that he feels denigrated by the label of "mental illness," he is likely to feel hopeless about acting in anything but a sick manner and likely to continue to act in a negative manner that is congruent with this label. Self-deprecation, as practically all psychologists and professionals agree, is one of the main causes of disturbed behavior. Labeling an individual as emotionally ill or schizophrenic often tends to exacerbate this cause.

It must be admitted, on the other hand, that people in our society are predisposed to condemn themselves in toto when they perceive that their performances are wrong or ineffective and that one of the best ways to help them to ameliorate or stop their self-denigration is to show them that they are basically immature or sick. They then are likely to conclude either that they are not truly responsible for their misdeeds or that even though they are responsible, they are not to be blamed or condemned. It is perhaps a sad commentary on our society that the only individuals who are not consigned to everlasting Hell for their sins are little children and sick adults, but the fact is that we do largely exonerate "mentally ill" people for their misdeeds and forgive them their sins. Until society's attitudes in this respect significantly change, labeling a person "ill" has distinct advantages (as well as disadvantages) in minimizing his self-denigration.

Moral Responsibility and "Mental Illness"

Mowrer (1960) and Szasz (1961, 1966) have persuasively argued that if we cavalierly and indiscriminately label an individual "mentally ill," we are thereby glossing over the fact that he is still responsible for a good deal of his behavior, that it is quite possible for him to change his performances for the better, and that (in Mowrer's terms) he is not likely to improve his condition until he fully acknowledges his sins and actively sets about making reparations and correcting them. By focusing on the illness of certain individuals, these writers would contend, we give them rationalizations for being the way they are and fail to teach them how to modify their self-destructive and immoral deeds.

Ellis (1962), Glasser (1965), Morgenstern (1966), and various other psychotherapists have recently emphasized the point that people are personally responsible for the social consequences of their behavior and that unless they admit that they can largely control their own destinies, in spite of the strong parental and societal conditioning factors that existed during their childhood, they are not likely to change their ineffectual behavior. As Morgenstern (1966) points out, labeling a person as "mentally ill" and involuntarily committing him to a mental institution frequently "reinforces the immature wish to avoid this responsibility, by blaming the illness for failure to achieve desired goals [p. 4]."

As usual, however, there is another side to the story. Ausubel (1961) heartily concurs with Mowrer that "personality disorders . . . can be most fruitfully conceptualized as products of moral conflict, confusion, and aberration [p. 70]," but he seriously questions the notion that these disorders are basically a reflection of sin; he demonstrates that most immoral behavior is committed by individuals who would never be designated as ill or disturbed and that many people who display disordered behavior are not particularly sinful or guilty. Moreover, Ausubel points out that not all "mentally sick" persons are truly responsible for their behavior:

It is just as unreasonable to hold an individual responsible for symptoms of behavior disorder as to deem him accountable for symptoms of physical illness. He is no more culpable for his inability to cope with sociopsychological stress than he would be for his inability to resist the spread of infectious organisms. In those instances where warranted guilt feelings do contribute to personality disorder, the patient is accountable for the misdeeds underlying his guilt, but is hardly responsible for the symptoms brought on by the guilt feelings or for unlawful acts committed during his illness. . . . Lastly, even if it were true that all personality disorder is a reflection of sin and that people are accountable for their behavioral symptoms, it would still be unnecessary to deny that these symptoms are manifestations of disease. Illness is no less real because the victim happens to be culpable for his illness. A glutton with hypertensive heart disease undoubtedly aggravates his condition by overeating and is culpable in part for the often fatal symptoms of his disease, but what reasonable person would claim that for this reason he is not really ill (pp. 71-72)?

Prophylaxis and Treatment of Aberrant Individuals

In several important ways labeling an individual as "mentally ill" may interfere with the treatment of any behavior problem he may display and may hinder the prevention of emotional disorder. For example:

1. Calling a person "mentally sick" frequently enhances his feelings of shame about his "illness," so that he defensively refuses to admit that he has serious behavior problems and therefore does not seek help with these problems.

2. A person who is set apart as being emotionally aberrant may become so resentful of this kind of segregation that he may refuse to acknowledge his "persecutors" efforts to help him and may get into hostile encounters with them and others that only serve to increase his living handicaps.

3. In many instances, the "mentally ill" individual is forcibly incarcerated in an institution where he is kept from doing many things he enjoys and where his condition may become aggravated rather than improved.

4. Labeling a person as psychotic may easily imply, to himself and those who may be able to help him, that he is hopeless and that little can be done to get him to change his behavior. As Menninger (1965) indicates, psychological treatment today is carried out by many people in addition to psychologists and psychiatrists, and the cooperation of family members is often urgently needed. "Schizophrenia" and "mental illness" are such impressive labels that they induce many people to feel that only highly trained professionals, if indeed anyone, can work with sick people and to ignore the fact that less trained individuals can often be specifically shown how to help troubled humans.

5. By being encouraged to label other people as sick, many of us fail to consider adequately our own problem areas. If we are not seen as being totally ill, we easily assume that we have few or no shortcomings; when we can easily label others as neurotic or psychotic we tend to assume that we are not in the least in such a class. By an all-or-none labeling technique, we tend to gloss over our own correctable deficiencies.

6. Labeling individuals as "mentally ill" often bars them from various social, vocational, and educational situations where they would best learn how to help themselves. It sometimes interferes with adequate research into treatment, while focusing on more precise research into diagnosing or labeling. It consumes psychological and psychiatric manpower which might better go into treatment.

7. If people have close relatives who are labeled psychotic, they sometimes become so afraid of going insane themselves that they actually bring on symptoms of disturbance and begin to define themselves as "mentally ill."

On the other side of the ledger, if we have a clear-cut concept of "mental disease" and if we unequivocally refer to certain kinds of behavior as neurotic or psychotic, many benefits in preventing and treating "emotional disturbance" are likely to accrue. For instance:

1. If needlessly self-defeating and overly hostile behavior does exist and is to be fought and minimized, the individual who exhibits it has to acknowledge (*a*) that it exists and (*b*) that he is to some degree responsible for its existence and, hence, can change it. This is what we really mean when we say that an individual is "mentally ill"—that he has symptoms of mental malfunctioning or illness. More operationally stated, he thinks, emotes, and acts irrationally and can usually uncondemningly acknowledge and change his acts. If this, with-out any moralistic overtones, is the definition of "mental illness," then it can distinctly help the afflicted individual to accept himself while he is ill and to work at changing for the better.

2. When an individual fully accepts the fact that he is emotionally disturbed, he often starts to improve (Redlich & Freedman, 1966).

Why? Because (*a*) to some extent he knows why he is behaving ineffectively; (*b*) he can begin to define in more detail exactly what his sickness consists of and what he is doing to cause and maintain it; (*c*) he may accept his symptoms with more equanimity and tend to be less guilty about creating them; (*d*) he may be much more inclined to seek professional help, just as he would if he were physically ill.

3.   By accepting the concept of "mental illness," a person can often accept and help others who are neurotic or psychotic. I have seen many parents with highly disturbed children who, after learning that their child's peculiar behavior is the result of a deep-seated disturbance which is biologically as well as environmentally rooted, became enormously less guilty and were able to sympathetically accept their child and do their best to help him ameliorate his symptoms.

4.   There is an essential honesty about the full acceptance of states of "emotional illness" that is itself often curative. In the last analysis, almost all neurosis and psychosis consists of some fundamental self-dishonesty (Glasser, 1965; London, 1964; Mowrer, 1960, 1964) or some self-deceptive defense that one raises against one's perfectionistic and grand-iose leanings (A. Freud, 1948; S. Freud, 1963). When, therefore, one fully faces the fact that one is "mentally ill," that this is not a pleasant way to be, and that one is partially responsible for being so, one becomes at that very point more honest with oneself and begins to get a little better.

5.   Accepting the fact that he is emotionally sick may give an individual an incentive to improve his lot. Most confirmed homosexuals in our society utterly refuse to admit that their homosexuality is a symptom of disturbance (Benson, 1965; Wicker, 1966[1]). They mightily inveigh against clinicians such as Adler (1917), Bieber et al. (1962), and Ellis (1965a), who insist that they are sick. As a result, relatively few mixed homosexuals come for psychotherapy, and of those who do come only a handful work to change their basic personality structure and to become heterosexually interested and capable. At the same time, many phobiacs admit their disturbance, come for therapy, and are significantly helped (Red-lich & Freedman, 1966; Wolpe,

1958). This is not to say that all those who accept the idea of their being "mentally ill" work hard at becoming better. Far from it! But their chances are often improved, compared to those who insist that they are no more disturbed than is anyone else.

6.   Psychotherapists are often more effective when they face the fact that their patients are "mentally ill." When they look upon these patients as merely having behavior problems, they work moderately hard with them and often become disillusioned at the poor results obtained. When they acknowledge that their patients often have basic, deep-seated emotional disorders, they know they are in for a long hard pull, work with greater vigor, expect many setbacks and limited successes, and take a realistic rather than an over-optimistic or over-pessimistic therapeutic view.

7.   Whether we like it or not, it sometimes seems to be necessary for some individuals to be adjudged "mentally ill" and even to be forcibly incarcerated, if they are to be treated effectively. A dramatic case in point is the recent one of the Texas resident, Charles Whitman, who killed 16 innocent bystanders shortly after he had gone for one interview with a psychiatrist and failed to return for further treatment, although he was found to be potentially homicidal. Redlich and Freedman (1966) remark:

As therapeutic interventions increase in intensity and scope, we more frequently encounter the question of a person impulsively leaving treatment when there appears to be a good chance that he could further improve his status and diminish his self-destructive behavior. Without some element of restraint, such a person might not have received therapeutic help at all. Nonetheless, it is probably best, both for society and for therapy of the patient, that coercion be restricted to the minimum necessary for the protection of life [p. 782].

Redlich and Freedman note how difficult it often is, as in the case of James Forrestal, Secretary of the Navy, who committed suicide while under psychiatric observation in a naval hospital, to adequately supervise persons of high position and eminence who are seriously disturbed. While their book was going through the press, Hotchner's (1966) *Papa Hemingway* appeared. According to Hotchner, Hemingway, because of his literary genius, was treated with unusual leniency by psychiatrists at the Mayo Clinic, and the day after he returned home from the Clinic he shot and killed himself. There is little doubt in Hotchner's mind that Hemingway might have lived for many more years if he had been honestly adjudged "mentally ill" and had been involuntarily treated.

8.   If the facts of "mental illness" are forthrightly faced and it is recognized that numerous individuals in our population are predisposed, for biosocial reasons, to be severely disturbed, educational prophylaxis will tend to be stressed. For if none of us is truly sick, just because all humans have some problems of adjustment, it seems futile to teach people the principles of mental hygiene, methods of sound thinking about themselves, and ways of coping with reality. But if it is accepted that all of us are a bit "touched" and that some of us are more so, greater efforts toward prevention of "mental illness" may become the rule.

9.   If the concept of emotional disturbance is admitted, proper surveillance of predisposed individuals can be instituted for preventive, protective, and curative reasons. Thus, if a child or adolescent is known to have tendencies toward severe illness, he can be specifically watched to see when these are breaking out. He can be kept out of situations where he may inflict damage on others, can at times be placed in protective custody to safeguard himself and others, and can be regularly treated to minimize his sick tendencies. In this respect, I recall a patient who was referred to me by a psychologist almost 20 years ago because, although he was only moderately disturbed, his twin brother had just been institutionalized with a diagnosis of paranoid schizophrenia. I saw this patient steadily for a couple of years and since that time have been seeing him a few times a year. I believe that it is largely as a result of my treating him and seeing him through a number of incipient crises during these years that he has been helped to remain only moderately ineffective and never to be in danger of a serious break, although in my opinion he is clearly a borderline schizophrenic. Similarly, other incipient psychotics can, if recognized early enough, be helped to remain perennially incipient and prevented from overtly breaking down.

Social Progress and Emotional Disturbance

If we label people who display various adjustment problems or idiosyncratic ways of living as "mentally ill," we may impede social progress in various ways. Many of the world's great statesmen, innovators, and creative artists have been "crackpots" who might well have been diagnosed as neurotic or psychotic and whose contributions to the world could have been (and in some cases actually were) sadly curtailed because of such labels. Thus, Dorothea Dix, who helped reform our mental hospital procedures, was opposed because she was deemed a "screwball," and Richard Wagner had difficulty getting some of his works performed because he was considered a "madman." In our own way, highly qualified people may not be elected to public office because of their unconventional and "crackpotty" views. Diplomats may not take with sufficient seriousness the statements of the Hitlers of the world because these leaders are seen as maniacs. Notable inventions may go unused because their inventors are considered "crazy."

Actually, an individual's aberrant or peculiar characteristics may have distinct advantages as well as disadvantages. Rank (1945, 1958) held that what is normally called neurosis is a creative process that may lead to beneficial and exciting aesthetic productions, and several other writers have noted the creative aspects of some psychotic states, but once an idiosyncratic individual in our society is labeled "mentally ill," it is assumed that his illness is wholly pernicious and that it must quickly be interrupted and abolished.

The very concept of illness or disease, as applied to emotional malfunctioning, may be socially retrogressive, since it limits thinking in this area. As Albee (1966), Rieff (1966), and several other students of mental health have recently shown, the medical or disease model of human disorder is restrictive and misleading, in that it implies that the afflicted individual has a specific handicap caused by a concrete organism or event and that his troubles can fairly easily be diagnosed and cured, as is the case in many physical disorders. Actually, what has been called "mental illness" appears to have multifarious causative factors and appears to be interrelated with the individual's entire existence and his global philosophy of life. It is therefore best understood and attacked on a philosophical, sociological, and psychological level rather than a narrow medical level, and those who practice psychotherapy (in itself a bad word because of its medical origins and implications) would aid their patients (another medical term!) in particular and the art of mental healing (!!) in general if they forgot about the illness or disease aspects of ineffectual behavior and focused in a more global way on the causes and amelioration of such behavior.

Viewing disorganized thought, emotion, and action as "mental illness" may again limit social and psychotherapeutic progress by supporting the concomitant view that only psychiatrists and other physicians are truly equipped to treat the emotionally disturbed, when, actually, some of the best theoreticians and practitioners in the field have been psychologists, social workers, marriage counselors, clergymen, and various other kinds of non-medical workers. Social progress is at present probably being seriously hampered in the field of mental health by professional opposition to non-professionals, such as intelligent housewives and college students, who have been found to be quite helpful with sick individuals but who have often been kept from doing very much in this respect because their patients are designated as being "mentally ill" (Ellis, 1966).

As usual, much can be said in opposition to the view that diagnosing people as "emotionally sick" tends to hinder social and therapeutic progress. First, there is no good evidence to support Rank's (1945, 1958) view that neurosis is a creative process and that it should be cherished if artists and their public are to continue to make great progress. Nor is there any reason to believe that many of the outstanding innovators of the past and present would not be ignored and opposed by their contemporaries even if the latter could not call them "mentally ill" or "crazy."

As for the concept of "mental disease" aiding social reaction and blocking therapeutic progress, Menninger (1965) points out that modern medicine is not atomistic but holistic and that good physicians see disease in a broad, almost nonmedical (in the old sense of the term) way. He quotes Virchow, "Disease is nothing but life under altered conditions," and Engel, "Disease corresponds to failures or disturbances in the growth, development, functions, and adjustments

of the organism as a whole or of any of its systems," (Menninger, 1965, p. 460) to show that the medical model of "mental illness" that Albee (1966) so severely criticizes is no longer typical of modern psychiatrists.

Ausubel (1961, p. 70) contends that to label personality disorder as disease not only would not hinder social and therapeutic progress but that the Szasz-Mowrer view of the "myth of mental illness" would "turn back the psychiatric clock twenty-five hundred years." The most significant and perhaps the only real advance registered by mankind in evolving a rational and humane method of handling behavioral aberrations has been in substituting a concept of disease for the demonological and retributional doctrines regarding their nature and etiology that flourished until comparatively recent times. Conceptualized as illness, the symptoms of personality disorders can be interpreted in the light of underlying stresses and resistances, both genetic and environmental, and can be evaluated in relation to specifiable quantitative and qualitative norms of appropriately adaptive behavior, both cross-culturally and within a particular cultural context. It would behoove us, therefore, before we abandon the concept of mental illness and return to the medieval doctrine of unexpiated sin or adopt Szasz' ambiguous criterion of difficulty in ethical choice and responsibility, to subject the foregoing proposition to careful and detailed study.

Ausubel (1961, p. 69) also points out that labeling individuals with aberrant behavior "mentally ill" does not preclude nonmedical personnel from helping these individuals, since "an impressively large number of recognized diseases are legally treated today by both medical *and* non-medical specialists (e.g., diseases of the mouth, face, jaws, teeth, eyes, and feet)." Consequently, even if we maintain the concept of "mental illness," we can justifiably allow and encourage all kinds of professionals and nonprofessionals to treat the ill.

Scientific Advancement and the Label of "Mental Illness"

There would seem to be several impediments to the use of the scientific method and to the advancement of science when we label individuals "mentally ill." For one thing, this kind of labeling leads to over-categorization and higher-order abstracting, which obscures scientific thought and leads to countless human misunderstandings. (Korzybski, 1933, 1951). To say that an individual is bad because his *behavior* is poor is to fabricate a sadly over generalized and invariably false description of him, as it is most unlikely that *all* his behavior—past, present, and future—was, is, or will be poor. Similarly, to label a person as a genius is to describe loosely and inaccurately, because it is likely that (at most!) he displays certain aspects of genius in only some of his productions—even if his name is Leonardo da Vinci; it is most probable that in many or most of the other aspects of his life, for example, his playing pingpong, making love, and cooking a soufflé, he is far from displaying many aspects of genius (Ellis, 1965b).

This kind of over generalizing distorts reality and causes the unrealistic (and often unfair) condemnation or deification of a human as a whole for relatively isolated parts or aspects of his functioning. Just as an individual's good deeds do not prove that he, on the whole, is a genius, so his bizarre or dysfunctional acts fail to show that he is totally "mentally ill" or incompetent. Designating him in this manner may, therefore, lead to misapprehension and misunderstanding of his sick and healthy behavior.

Labels of all kinds promote close-mindedness rather than open-minded, experimental, scientific attitudes. Calling an individual "mentally ill" tends to put him in a niche, from whence his removal may never be considered. It encourages us to diagnose an individual's condition and then to forget about it because it has been neatly categorized, to rigidify our thinking in the field of mental health itself, and to help us forget that the patient's "illness" is more of a hypothesis than a well-established fact.

Szasz (1961) has contended that the concept of "mental illness" is antithetical to science because it is demonological in nature, in that it follows the lines of religious myths in general and the belief in witchcraft in particular and because it uses a reified abstraction, "a deformity of personality," to account causally for disordered behavior and human disharmony. Many

other writers, such as Ellis (1950) and LaPiere (1960), have held that the Freudian Terms, in which most forms of emotional disturbance are put today (e.g., "weak ego" and "punishing superego"), are reifications that have no actual substance behind them and are hence mythical and misleading entities. The entire field of "mental health" appears to be replete with these kinds of myths.

While some of these objections to the diagnosis of "mental disease" are important (and others seem to be trivial), there is much to be said in favor of the notion that categorizations of this sort are, when carefully made, reasonably accurate and quite helpful to the cause of scientific advancement. Arguments in this connection include the following:

1.   Although it is inaccurate to state that the individual in our culture who is usually labeled "mentally ill" is a much different kind of person from the healthy individual, or that he exhibits entirely aberrant behavior, or that he is a bad or lower kind of person because he sometimes behaves oddly, the fact remains that there is almost always some significant difference between the actions of this ill individual and those of another who is well. What is more, the existing difference is one that can usually (if not always) be detected by a trained observer, is fairly consistently evident, and leads to definite behavior of a self-defeating or antisocial nature. If the individual with aberrant behavior is not in any way to be labeled "mentally ill," neurotic, psychotic, or something similar, the peculiarity, undesirability, and improvability of his behavior is likely to be overlooked, some segment of reality will thereby be denied, and the essence of science—observation and classification—will be rejected.

2.   There is considerable and ever-increasing scientific evidence to show that although the term "mental illness" itself is vague, the major characteristics which are subsumed under its rubric, such as compulsion, over suspiciousness, phobia, depression, and intense rage, do exist and have observable ideational and physiological correlates. Thus, feelings of depression are usually accompanied by the individual's belief that "When I do the wrong thing, I am no good and

will probably always remain worthless," and "If significant people in my life do not approve of me, I can't approve of myself." These feelings are, in addition, frequently accompanied by fatigue, poor appetite, insensitivity to stimulation, ineffective performance, etc. Objectively, therefore, some individuals can be described as being consistently depressed and in that sense, at least, may be thought of as being "mentally ill."

3. Some kind of general factor of emotional distress appears to exist in certain individuals, since they are observed to display various major symptoms (e.g., hostility, anxiety, and depression), while other individuals are practically symptom free. Thousands of years of observation would seem to attest to the existence of this general factor, as many of the descriptions of peculiar people in past centuries are amazingly similar to modern clinical descriptions. Recently, moreover, a great deal of evidence has accumulated which tends to show that people who display severe behavior problems are to some degree biologically different from others (Chess, Thomas, & Birch, 1965; Greenfield & Lewis, 1965; Redlich & Freedman, 1966) and that they can be reliably selected from the general population (Joint Commission on Mental Illness and Health, 1961). To ignore this evidence of "mental illness" would seem to be highly unrealistic; to acknowledge it would be to accept people as they truly are.

4. Although all self-defeating human behavior may well have the elements of social learning and may be best understood, as Szasz contends, by being studied in a sociological context and in the light of social deviance, the fact remains that the individual himself contributes significantly to what he accepts or rejects from his culture and, at times, may therefore be justifiably deemed sick or disordered. Anyone of us, as Messer (1966) observes, may be neurotically influenced by dramatic television commercials which convince us that we have acid indigestion when we experience abdominal discomfort. Few of us would conclude, however, that the discomfort represents a demon tearing away the lining of our stomachs and that unless the pain stops we must cut ourselves open to get at this demon. Those few, who gratuitously add their own dis-

torted perceptions and thoughts to their socially imbibed neurotic ideas, may justifiably be diagnosed as psychotic, even though some of their notions (e.g., that demons could exist) are partially derived from their cultures.

5. Although we may concede Szasz' (1961) points that what we usually call "mental illness" is largely an expression of man's struggle with the problems of how he should live and that human relations are inherently fraught with difficulties, Ausubel (1961) demonstrates that,

there is no valid reason why a particular symptom cannot both reflect a problem in living and constitute a manifestation of disease .... Some individuals, either because of the magnitude of the stress involved, or because of genetically or environmentally induced susceptibility to ordinary degrees of stress, respond to the problems of living with behavior that is either seriously distorted or sufficiently unadaptive to prevent normal interpersonal relations and vocational functioning. The latter outcome—gross deviation from a designated range of desirable behavior variability—conforms to the generally understood meaning of mental illness [p. 71].

Discussion

It would appear that there are important disadvantages as well as advantages in labeling people "mentally ill." Many of the disadvantages result from our tendency to include in the terms "mental illness," "neurosis," and "psychosis" not only a description of the fact that the afflicted individual behaves self-defeatingly and inappropriate to his social group, but also the evaluative element that he is bad, inferior, or worthless for so behaving. If this evaluative element were not gratuitously added, the term "mental illness," even though an abstraction that is not too precise, might have descriptive, diagnostic, and therapeutic usefulness. It is a kind of shorthand term which can be used to describe the usual and fairly consistent state of a person who keeps driving himself to act ineffectually and bizarrely.

Thus, instead of saying, "He is mentally ill," we could say, "He is a human being who at the present time is behaving in a self-defeating and/or needlessly antisocial manner and who will most probably continue to do so in the future, and, although he is partially creating or causing (and in this sense is responsible for) his aberrant behavior, he is still not to be condemned for creating it but is to be helped to overcome it." This second statement is more precise, accurate, and helpful than the first one, but it is often impractical to spell it out in this detail. It is, therefore, legitimate to use the first statement, "He is mentally ill," as long as we clearly understand that it means the longer version.

A good solution, then, to the problem of labeling an individual "mentally ill" is to change the evaluative attitude which gives the term "mental illness" a pejorative tone and to educate all of us, including professionals, to accept "emotionally sick" human beings without condemnation, punishment, or needless restriction. This, to some degree, has already occurred, since the attitude that most of us take toward disturbed people today is much less negative than that taken by most people a century or more ago; much, however, remains to be accomplished in this respect.

Meanwhile, what is to be done? For psychologists, psychiatrists, psychiatric social workers, and other professionals, the following conclusions are in order:

1.   The term "mental illness," or some similar label, is likely to be around for some time, even though continuing efforts can be made to change current psychological usage.

2.   An individual who is "mentally ill" may be more operationally defined as a person who, with some consistency, behaves in dysfunctional ways in *certain aspects* of his life, but who is rarely *totally* "disturbed" or uncontrolled.

3.   It is highly dangerous to evaluate a "mentally ill" person as you would evaluate his acts or performances. If he is sufficiently psychotic, he may not even be responsible for his acts. If he is less disturbed, he may be responsible but not justifiably condemnable for his deeds, since they are only a part or an aspect of him, and to excoriate him in toto for these deeds is to make an unwarranted and usually harmful overgeneralization about him.

4.   Although most "mentally ill" individuals perform bizarre and unconventional acts, not all people who perform such acts are sick or ill. Neurosis or psychosis exists not because of an individual's deeds, but because of the overly anxious, compulsive, rigid, or unrealistic manner in which he keeps performing them.

5.   Most "mentally ill" individuals are variable from day to day and changeable from one period of their lives to another. The fact that they act inappropriately today does not mean that their behavior was equally dysfunctional yesterday nor that it will be so tomorrow. Such people usually have considerable capacities for growth and can change radically for the better (as well as for the worse).

6.   People, no matter how "mentally ill" they may be, are always human. We owe them the same kind of general respect that we owe to all human beings, namely, giving them the rights to survive, to be as happy as possible in their handicapped conditions, to be helped to function as well as possible and to develop their potentials, and to be protected from needlessly harming themselves and others.

If these approaches to individuals with severe emotional problems are kept solidly in the forefront of our consciousness and are actualized in our relationships with them, the question of whether to label them as "mentally ill" may well become academic.

Notes

[1].R. Wicker. Statement made on the Larry Glick Show, radio station WMEX, Boston, January 8, 1966.

Figure 5-3. *Left*: **E. Fuller Torrey** examines brain scans for evidence of viral damage. *Right*: **Irving Gottesman**, a proponent of genetic explanations in schizophrenia. (Photographs courtesy of Max Aguilera-Hellweg.)

READING 5B

DIVIDED SELVES

Tony Dajer

Research in neuroscience is growing at a tremendous rate. Sophisticated technological advancements allow us to conduct research today that would have been impossible thirty years ago. The illness perspective is deeply involved in studying the biological aspects of schizophrenia. Genetics, infection, neurotransmitter imbalance, and structural abnormality of the brain are viewed as some of the most potentially fruitful areas of neuroscientific research.

Another compelling issue is that of the complex and delicate interaction of hereditary (nature) and environmental (nurture) factors that yield schizophrenia. Paul Meehl (1962) argued in his specific etiology theory that "schizophrenia, while its content is learned, is fundamentally a neurologic disease of genetic origin." Rosenthal (1970) elaborated on this notion in the diathesis-stress model. A diathesis is a hereditary predisposition for schizophrenia which is triggered by stressors; illness, the use of substances, or negative life events.

E. Fuller Torrey advocated the abolishment of psychiatry in his 1974 book, The Death of Psychiatry. *Ironically, recently he has lamented the plight of the homeless mentally ill (Torrey, 1988). A man of varied interests, he has also written about a group of bandits who operated in the Nine Mile Swamp, south of Utica, New York (Torrey, 1992). He is also a staunch advocate of the viral theory of schizophrenia.*

In the following article, Torrey debates Irving Gottesman, a proponent of the genetic theory. A variety of other possible factors become involved in the course of the debate. The article implies that neuroscience will ultimately be the key that unlocks the secret of schizophrenia.

Fuller Torrey has one goal in life: to prove Irving Gottesman wrong. Gottesman, for his part, is just as determined to nail Torrey. And either would be delighted to see the other win. Torrey, 55, senior psychiatrist at St. Elizabeths Hospital in Washington, D.C., is a world expert on the viral theory of schizophrenia. Gottesman, 61, Commonwealth Professor of Psychology at the University of Virginia, is one of the best science sleuths around. The question at hand: whether the baffling illness of schizophrenia springs primarily from an infection or is caused by defective genes. To settle the issue, the friendly arch-rivals have embarked on an unusual venture designed to leave one of them in the dust. "Irving," says Torrey, "is a lively and honest researcher with whom I can disagree with pleasure." The whole enterprise hinges on a medical quirk. Schizophrenia is a common disease, affecting over a million people in this country alone. Given such large numbers it's possible to find occasional cases of people with schizophrenia who have an identical twin, a sibling who shares their exact genetic heritage. About half the time the twin is also schizophrenic, but the rest of the time the twin is normal (though some display borderline schizophrenic traits that label them as slightly eccentric). These "discordant" twin pairs—one ill, one well—constitute a potentially powerful means to tease out schizophrenia's secrets.

Despite the mental devastation it creates, schizophrenia leaves maddeningly few traces. You can't point to a definite cause like a virus or a bacterium or a defective gene, as you can with many other brain diseases. Nor can you see glaring damage like holes or scars when you autopsy a schizophrenic's brain. And although researchers have tried scanning the brains of hundreds of schizophrenics and healthy volunteers, they've been unsure if the differences they saw were due to schizophrenia or to individual brain variation.

That's why twins are so inordinately useful for this kind of study. If you could compare a schizophrenic with his or her genetically identical yet normal twin, any differences would very likely be due to the disease process. It would be like superimposing, in the same person, the cardboard cutout for disease on the one for health. If you found discrepancies between the two, you could conclude that that's where schizophrenia probably lurks and search for its cause.

That, in short, was Torrey's reasoning. So in 1986, after seeking out Gottesman's involvement as a "respected counterpoint to my own bias," he assembled a sample of willing twins and a network of psychologists, geneticists, virologists, biochemists, statisticians, and brain scanners to launch an unprecedented assault on the roots of madness.

The first descriptions of what a modern psychiatrist would call schizophrenia were written in 1809, but it wasn't until a century later that Eugene Bleuler, a Swiss psychiatrist, gave the disease a name. Schizophrenia literally means "split mind", but popular myth notwithstanding, it has nothing to do with multiple personalities. Bleuler was referring to an odd ungluing of the mind, to the kind of striking dissociation of reason and emotion that makes patients laugh during funerals or imbue a mundane object or gesture with some spectacularly inappropriate significance. Schizophrenics, who are typically diagnosed when they are adolescents or young adults, become prey to fantastic hallucinations and hear voices conversing in their head. They may develop paranoid or grandiose delusions—a fear that the CIA can control or read their thoughts,

for example, or the conviction that their destiny is to fulfill some exalted messianic mission. Yet they can also become intensely withdrawn, apparently unfeeling, or overcome by an apathetic stupor. So profoundly does schizophrenia unhinge the mind that many victims never make their way back to reality.

Torrey vividly remembers his first encounter with the illness. He was 19 and a premed student at the time. "It was the summer before Rhoda, my seventeen-year-old sister, was supposed to start college," he recounts. "She began having delusions that the British redcoats were attacking America. My mother told me she would discuss the Revolutionary War at dinner, the kind of stuff you learn in history class. At first my mother thought Rhoda was kidding. But then one day she found her lying on the front lawn talking to imaginary voices about the British attacks. When I got home from college, my sister looked physically, neurologically sick to me. In just weeks she'd gone from normalcy—the sister I'd grown up with—to full-blown psychosis."

By the end of medical school Torrey had decided to specialize in psychiatry. After completing his residency at Stanford Medical School and doing a stint at the National Institute of Mental Health, he was put in charge of a ward at St. Elizabeths. There the young psychiatrist quickly found himself immersed in the mystery of his patients' insanity.

A major influence on him at the time was the physician and virologist Carleton Gajdusek. In 1972 Gajdusek jolted the medical world with his discovery that so-called slow viruses could linger in the brain for 20 years or more before causing symptoms. The classic disease of this kind was kuru, which started as clumsiness and ended in mind-obliterating dementia and which afflicted only men in the New Guinea highlands who ate the brains of the deceased during their funeral rituals. To contract kuru, Gajdusek found, you had to consume the brain of someone already infected. Gajdusek (who won the 1976 Nobel Prize for medicine) proved his point by injecting infected brain tissue into chimpanzees: not only did they get the disease but their damaged brains developed the same peculiar Swiss-cheese appearance as those of human kuru victims. When New Guinea highlanders stopped eating brains," Torrey says, "they stopped getting kuru."

As a psychiatrist, though, Torrey was swimming against the tide of his profession by even considering biological explanations for mental illness. The rise of psychoanalysis at the turn of the century—and a paucity of biological findings—had given psychological explanations like upbringing and bad parenting a stranglehold on the debate over the causes of schizophrenia.

"When I met Gajdusek," he recalls, "the first thing he did was blast me: You psychiatrists have gotten so hung-up on Freud, you've forgotten how to be scientists! And he was right; we had stopped treating schizophrenia like a physical, measurable disease." Goaded by Gajdusek, Torrey began acting like a microbiologist. He asked permission from patients to perform spinal taps and analyze their cerebrospinal fluid, the fluid that bathes the brain and spinal cord, to look for the footprints of viral infection. He didn't find much, but back then, no one did. (Gadjusek tried injecting chimps with brain tissue taken from autopsied schizophrenics, but the experiment failed to work.) "When I look back," says Torrey, "I shudder to think how primitive our methods were. In the 1970s viral research was barely in its infancy."

In the meantime, however, the advocates of a biological explanation were getting reinforcements from a very different quarter. Although it was known that schizophrenia can run in families, the blame had usually been ascribed to nurture (the home environment) rather than to nature (the patient's genes). But in the late 1960s and early 1970s studies began to show that genes far outweighed upbringing as a risk factor for schizophrenia. Children of schizophrenics adopted by normal families, for example, had the same risk of developing the illness as children raised by schizophrenic parents. What's more, an identical twin of a schizophrenic was four times as likely to develop the illness as a nonidentical twin.

One of the young researchers who was helping kick the door open for biology was Gottesman. In 1971 he had joined a pioneering team of Danish geneticists that was studying the children of identical twins who were discordant (one ill, one well) for schizophrenia. After following the families for 18 years, Gottesman confirmed the startling finding that the risk of schizophrenia in the children of either twin was exactly the same: 17 percent. That meant that even if "schizogenes" were not activated in one generation, they could be passed on to the next and then make mischief.

But while studies like these showed that schizophrenia had to have a genetic component, they left a thorny question in their wake: If schizophrenia were due only to genes, why didn't 100 percent of the identical twins—not the observed 50 percent—share the disease? "The most likely explanation," ventures Gottesman, "is that the right combination of genes—probably four or five—plus some as yet undefined environmental stressors must be thrown together to trigger schizophrenia. But before we can figure out what activates the genes in the twins who become ill, we must first find the genes themselves. The trick now is to hunt those genes down to their chromosomes and map them"—a trick that he hopes some of Torrey's twins will help him pull off.

While Gottesman was making a name for himself studying Danish twins, Torrey continued to collect schizophrenics' cerebrospinal fluid and blood in pursuit of a "schizovirus." It was a monumental wild-goose chase, but a number of clues sustained him in his belief.

For example, viral infections of the temporal lobes—notably herpes simplex type I, the common cold-sore virus—can produce hallucinations and bizarre behavior bearing an uncanny resemblance to schizophrenia. In fact, physicians often mistake the one for the other. Moreover, unlike any other mental illness, schizophrenia is more common among those born in winter, when viral infections abound. In a Scandinavian study of children with a strong family history of schizophrenia, an increase of 70 percent in the rate of schizophrenia was found among those whose mothers had contracted influenza during the second trimester of pregnancy.

Yet despite such circumstantial evidence, Torrey's cerebrospinal-fluid and blood analyses failed to turn up solid viral suspects. And even if his schizovirus existed, those tests couldn't tell him where in the brain it might be doing its work. To identify the virus he would have to locate its base of operations.

A possible approach turned up in the 1980s with the introduction of a brain scanning technique called magnetic resonance imaging (MRI). Compared with existing technologies such as CT scans, the new tool produced dazzling brain pictures with an astonishing amount of anatomical detail. Even so, it wasn't initially all that helpful for schizophrenia. It found variations in schizophrenics' brains – but they were subtle and not peculiar enough to schizophrenia to distinguish it from other brain diseases or even from normal variation. Studies showed, for example, that the ventricles, a pair of fluid filled structures that curve around the brain's inner pith like ram's horns, were often unusually large in schizophrenics. But enlarged ventricles were also seen in Alzheimer's and Parkinson's patients, and even in normal old people.

By 1986 it was clear to Torrey that only identical twins who were discordant for schizophrenia could show up the small discrepancies he needed to flush out his prey. Through the National Alliance for the Mentally Ill, he gathered twins that fit the bill. So far he has found 30 pairs of clearly discordant twins—and, for comparison, 30 more pairs who are either both schizophrenic, both normal, or somewhere in between (one schizophrenic twin and one ostensibly normal twin with schizophrenic tendencies).

The studies haven't been easy to do, however. MRI scans are obtained by submitting the brain to strong magnetic fields and then measuring the signals from the different tissues inside it. Taking these images requires patients to lie without moving a muscle inside a dark, clanking, tubelike chamber, a process that terrifies even normal patients who have a touch of claustrophobia. For patients whose grip on reality is already fragile, the procedure required immense courage. With one schizophrenic twin, Torrey recalls, "I had to promise to buy her a skirt and blouse if she went through the whole thing. I held her hand the whole time. She was very brave." Altogether, 15 pairs of discordant twins were examined for Torrey's initial MRI study.

The results, published in March 1990 in the *New England Journal of Medicine* caused quite a stir. Like earlier MRI studies, this one showed that the schizophrenic twins had enlarged ventricles, but it also revealed a striking change in a crucial brain structure called the hippocampus. The hippocampus (the name derives from the Greek for "sea horse", which it's said to resemble) clings to the inner surface of the temporal lobes, which are behind the temples, on either side of the brain. The hippocampus is apparently where input from the senses is hammered into new memories and where the components of old memories are reassembled for recall. And lo and behold, in Torrey's schizophrenics, the hippocampus, especially the left half of the hippocampus, was noticeably smaller than in the normal twins. Indeed, his scanning team thinks that the ventricles may become enlarged in schizophrenics because of a loss of surrounding tissue, including shrinkage of the hippocampus.

That evidence seemed to tie in nicely with autopsy studies begun in the mid 1980s that showed signs of cell loss and disarray in the left hippocampus and its anatomic neighbors in the limbic system. The limbic system controls our emotional response—another function thrown out of whack by schizophrenia. And it fit with another finding: that schizophrenics did poorly on certain memory tests, suggesting that impaired memory was perhaps a component of schizophrenia.

Classically, schizophrenia was considered a disease of the frontal lobes, the seat of abstract, higher thought. (This idea had unfortunate repercussions: in the 1940s, it served as the rationale for the frontal lobotomies that were performed on thousands of schizophrenics.) But the left hippocampus, linchpin of memory, is part of the left temporal lobe. Could schizophrenia be a problem of the left temporal lobe instead?

Another newer school of thought implicated the entire left side of the brain – the hemisphere that generates language and thus defines the interpretation of words and symbols. One thing that makes the world so terrifying for schizophrenics is the destruction of those defining limits. Thus a misplaced coffee cup can become imbued with peculiar meaning; a stranger's gesture can signal the arrival of the redcoats or the CIA. The result is a paralyzing paranoia.

Torrey, for his part, suspected that the temporal lobe was to blame. But for him the hallmark of schizophrenia is hearing voices. "No other symptom," he argues, "is as specific to schizophrenia: 75 percent of all patients hear voices—voices that command you to kill yourself, voices from outer space, two voices carrying on a conversation, even the voice of God. To us scientists, they seem to be saying, Pay attention, there may be a big clue here."

The temporal lobe, it turns out, is home not only to the hippocampus and other limbic structures but to the nerve fibers that carry input from the ears. If an infection caused the limbic-system damage seen in the autopsy studies, Torrey argues, then maybe it could damage these fibers as well, and one might hear voices. "Autopsies showing cell disarray in these areas," he says, "appear to fit with what we've found on our MRIs."

Still, good as the MRIs have been at locating abnormalities in the brain, they could say nothing about when the damage occurred. That's the question Stefan Bracha, a psychiatrist at the University of Arkansas Medical School in Little Rock, set out to answer. One of schizophrenia's peculiarities is its predictable age of onset: 18 for men, 23 for women, on average. Does that mean that young adults are more susceptible than other age groups to certain viruses or genetic malfunctions? Or is schizophrenia a delayed reaction to damage that occurred years before? (Kuru, recall, took up to 20 years to manifest itself in New Guinea highlanders who had eaten infected brains.)

Pathological studies of schizophrenic brains have never shown signs of the scarring one would expect from viral infections. However, in the special case of damage caused to a fetus in its mother's womb, the brain doesn't form scar tissue. Instead it ends up with just the kind of cell disorganization described in the autopsies. At the very least, then, these autopsy findings were consistent with the idea that the damage had occurred prenatally. Adding weight to the notion was the Scandinavian study suggesting that influenza infection in the second trimester of pregnancy—months four, five, and six—boosted the risk of schizophrenia.

Bracha knew that the time-tested way of looking for evidence of prenatal infection was dermatoglyphics, the study of fingerprints and finger structure. "But it was old technology, so no one else wanted to do it," he recalls wryly. He also knew that the second trimester of pregnancy is a time of major brain-cell reorganization. If a virus hits at that particular time, it might also affect the hands, which are simultaneously undergoing finishing touches.

Unlikely as it sounds, it is possible for a virus to infect one identical twin fetus and not the other. So Bracha examined 24 pairs of Torrey's twins for the odd fingerprint whirls and stunted digits that are the "fossilized" evidence, as he puts it, of infections inside the womb. His study, published in November 1991, found that schizophrenics had four times as many abnormalities as their healthy twins, who showed Bracha what the schizophrenics' hands "should have looked like."

These divergent fingerprints suggested that the seeds of schizophrenia are indeed sown very early in life. In the same vein, Torrey has recently completed another study, which uses family interviews and school records to show that the twins start diverging before the age of five. By putting a ceiling on the time of infection, he can focus his search on agents that act in infancy or before.

Meanwhile, back in the geneticists' camp, Gottesman is aware that Torrey has stacked the deck a bit by focusing on clearly discordant twin pairs. This group most likely has a low genetic predisposition to schizophrenia, requiring a big environmental jolt to make the twins so different. But Torrey, remember, has also recruited less clear-cut pairs, where one twin is schizophrenic and the other, apparently healthy one is only mildly schizoid. From Gottesman's point of view, these twins may prove the most useful of all.

"In these pairs, the healthy twin has some, but not all, of the symptoms of schizophrenia," he says. "So we assume they carry some predisposing genes for the disease, even if they're not fully turned on. Moreover, these healthy twins often display subtle physical signs like abnormal eye tracking or easy distractibility. If we're lucky, these abnormalities may lead us to DNA 'markers,' which are like visible flags inherited along with the actual disease genes. Then we can look for each marker to see if it turns up consistently among families of schizophrenics. If the markers and genes are truly linked—that is, are situated close by on the same stretch of DNA—we may be able to track down some of the genes we think are involved."

In practice, this approach works well for single-gene diseases such as Huntington's chorea. But when four or five genes are involved, as is thought to be the case with schizophrenia, the task explodes into mind-numbing complexity. Yet if the genes can be found, the rewards will be enormous; researchers will be able to tell very quickly what proteins they make and, eventually, what the proteins do (or fail to do) to cause schizophrenia.

While Gottesman pursues the genes that make the schizophrenic brain malfunction, Torrey is beginning to look at how and where it malfunctions. The procedures he and his colleagues are using can literally see the brain in action. Cerebral blood flow studies and PET (positron emission tomography) scans offer a color-coded glimpse into the brain's workings as eerie as MRI's sharp dissection of its living anatomy. For the cerebral blood flow studies, xenon gas is inhaled into the lungs to make the patient's blood briefly radioactive; the harder the cells in a particular brain region work, the more blood flow they get and the more detectable radiation they emit. PET uses radioactive glucose or oxygen to similarly light up areas of "hot" metabolic activity in the brain.

Initially Torrey was reluctant to subject his twins to PET scans. "The scans are tough. I take all the tests the patients do and I found this one uncomfortable. They have to lie in a ring of sensors with their heads pinned by a form-fitting mask and IV lines in their arms. And besides, you're asking to read the thoughts of someone who's already paranoid about his thoughts being read." What changed his mind was a study by Susan Resnick, another of his extended network of researchers, at the University of Pennsylvania. PET scans of seven schizophrenics and their normal twins showed a consistent difference in the basal ganglia, acorn-size cell clusters lying beneath the ventricles at the brain's center. The ganglia are action integrators – if you're a catch-

er, they help you get the mitt between the fastball and your groin – but in seven out of seven schizophrenics (in contrast to their well twins) the basal ganglia mysteriously "lit up" even when they were resting.

Using such scans, Torrey's Washington team made another intriguing discovery. When they challenged twins to sort playing cards by suit, number, or color, they found that the schizophrenics not only did worse than the normals but also failed to activate a region–technically known as the dorsolateral prefrontal cortex, or DLPFC—within the frontal lobe. This region, says Daniel Weinberger, a psychiatrist collaborating with Torrey, is critical to performing complicated tasks and thinking well-ordered thoughts: "It's highly evolved and serves perhaps more than anything else as a hallmark of the human brain." What's more, this year, by comparing the blood-flow scans with MRI data, the team showed that poor DLPFC activation correlated with small hippocampus size. For the first time in the history of schizophrenia research, a functional deficit in one brain area was linked to an anatomical defect in another.

That seems to imply, says Torrey, that schizophrenia is not simply a disorder of particular areas in the brain, but a breakdown—most likely on the brain's left side—in the connections between them. And it so happens that the DLPFC, the hippocampus, the emotion-regulating limbic system, and the basal ganglia are all part of what's known as the brain's dopamine network. Dopamine is a neurotransmitter, and almost all the drugs for treating schizophrenia's symptoms are known to block dopamine receptors. In the dopamine network, too little activity in one area could lead to overactivity in another. A DLPFC that's too quiet, Weinberger speculates, "may disinhibit the limbic system and lead to the florid, inappropriate emotionality seen in many schizophrenics." In other words, if the Speaker of the House falls asleep, over-emotional congressmen may soon get out of control.

Of course, that still doesn't settle the question that launched Torrey and Gottesman's original bet: Are genes or a virus the main actor in schizophrenia? Although there's evidence for both, neither researcher is ready to call it a draw.

The point is, says Gottesman, to what degree is each important? Could schizophrenia occur without a viral insult? Could there even be nongenetic cases?

"We must each push our theory as far as it will go," Gottesman insists. "If we don't try our darndest to prove the other wrong, we'll never prove anything right. Is schizophrenia nine-tenths genetic, or one-twentieth? That's what we need to find out?"

References

Meehl, P. (1962). Schizotaxia, Schizotypy, Schizophrenia. *The American Psychologist*, 17(12), 827-837.

Rosenthal, D., (1970). *Genetic Theory and Abnormal Behavior*. New York: McGraw-Hill.

Torrey, E.F. (1988). *Nowhere to Go: The Tragic Odyssey of The Homeless Mentally Ill*, 1st. ed. New York: Harper & Row.

_____(1992). *Frontier justice: The rise and fall of the Loomis gang*. Utica, New York: North Country Books.

Figure 5-4. Nancy Wexler shares a moment of joy with a child from her Venezuelan "distant family." (Photograph by Nick Kelsh, copyright © 1993 The Walt Disney Co. Reprinted with permission of *Discover* magazine.)

READING 5C

TO CATCH A KILLER GENE

Susan Katz Miller

As described in Chapter 4, Huntington's disease is a progressive, degenerative dementia that is ultimately fatal. Memory becomes impaired and mental functioning deteriorates. The victim loses motor control and is afflicted with involuntary jerking and twitching. Death is slow and certain.

Tremendous advances have been made in the study of the disease. In DSM--I (1968) the condition was considered a psychosis with degenerative disease of the central nervous system. It was then learned to be a genetic disorder caused by the inheritance of a dominant gene.

The following article relates the courageous story of Nancy Wexler, who inspired research that located the gene on chromosome 4 more than a decade ago. Continued intensive research recently revealed the specific location of the gene, which may herald its ultimate eradication.

In the upper reaches of Manhattan's west side, in her office overlooking the Hudson River at Columbia University College of Physicians and Surgeons, psychologist Nancy Wexler is explaining how she came to be at the centre of the search for the gene that causes Huntington's disease. "It was literally an accident of fate," she sighs. In high school, she learnt that all three of her mother's brothers had died from the relentless and fatal neurodegenerative disease. The family was under the delusion that the disease affected only males until her mother was diagnosed as having Huntington's in 1968, and Wexler and her sisters learned that they each had a 50 percent risk of inheriting the genetic disorder.

But her father, Milton Wexler, was not one to give in to bad news. "He's a tenacious guy. And at the time we were very optimistic," says his daughter. That same year, Milton Wexler set up the Hereditary Disease Foundation to fund the search for a cure. Nancy's mother, a fruit-fly geneticist, died of the disease in 1978. "We thought if we started right away, maybe we would figure out a cure in time for my mother. Then we thought maybe it would be in time for my sister and me," says Wexler. "Now in a way,

I feel like I have such a huge family of thousands of people at risk of Huntington's all around the world. We're hoping we will find a cure in time for all of them."

Last month, after more than a decade of conflicting signals, sudden reversals, and countless nights and weekends in the lab with success always just out of reach, a unique collaborative research team organized by the Wexlers came a step closer to finding a cure when they identified the genetic mutation that causes Huntington's disease. The researchers found a stretch of DNA where the nucleotide triplet C-A-G repeats like a sort of genetic stutter. Those people without the disease appear to have between 11 and 34 copies of the triplet. Those with the disease have anywhere between 42 and 86 triplet repeats, according to the preliminary research.

It was in 1872 that New York physician George Huntington first described the disease that bears his name. Though found throughout the world, it is most common in Caucasian populations. In the US, the prevalence of the disease is about 10 cases per 100,000 people—about 30,000 people in all. There are another 150,000 who, like Wexler and her sister, had a parent with

Susan Katz Miller: To Catch a Killer Gene, from *New Scientist*, April 24, 1993, 37-41. Reprinted with permission of *New Scientist*.

the disease and are waiting to discover whether they will develop it. Typically, the first symptoms appear in middle age as tics or coordination problems. Over ten to twenty years, the symptoms progress to violent uncontrolled movement, and finally death. Although the disease impairs thinking and disturbs the emotions, patients remain keenly aware of who they are, of family and friends, and of their own physical and cognitive decline.

In the 1970s, the Wexlers' foundation concentrated on funding research on therapies for Huntington's disease. So little was known about the disease that experimental drugs were never very promising, but searching for the genetic mutation that causes the disease looked daunting. At that time, scientists could trace a gene to a specific chromosome only if they knew which protein caused the disease and could trace the faulty DNA sequence from the protein. They then had to use a clone of the gene sequence itself to find the location, a technique known as functional cloning. The idea of "positional cloning", mapping a gene for an unknown protein, remained theoretical.

Then, in 1981, Nancy Wexler learned that Americo Negrette, a Venezuelan physician and biochemist, had found an extended family at Lake Maracaibo, in the remote northwestern part of his country, with the highest incidence of Huntington's disease in the world. This huge family was to serve as the key to many of the advances in the search for the Huntington's gene.

Each March, Wexler has taken a research team to Lake Maracaibo, tracing the gene through more than 11,000 descendants of one woman with the mutation who lived in the 19th century. Back in New York, Wexler sent blood samples from the Venezuelan Huntington's patients to James Gusella at Massachusetts General Hospital. In 1981 Gusella had just started experimenting with using bacteriophage probes to identify segments of DNA which vary between individuals—known as restriction fragment length polymorphisms (RFLPs—pronounced "riflips")—and which could act as markers to genetic mutations that cause disease. The more frequently the RFLP marker and a disease are inherited together, the more likely it is

that the defective gene lies nearby on the same chromosome. Using the Venezuelan DNA, Gusella confirmed that he had found a RFLP marker that allowed him to map the Huntington's gene to the short arm of chromosome 4. The finding, published in *Nature* in 1983, was the first time a disease gene had been mapped to a specific chromosome based purely on the inheritance pattern of the disease and genetic markers.

Everyone assumed that discovering the identity of the gene and its exact location on the chromosome would quickly follow. The human genome is about a meter of DNA containing 3 billion pairs of bases or nucleotides. About 2 percent of the genome consists of stretches of DNA which encode genes. Instead of scouring billions of bases on all the chromosomes to trace a sequence of bases that could represent the Huntington's gene, the researchers had only to search a relatively short piece of chromosome 4 containing about 5 million base pairs.

But in the decade that followed researchers had to watch in sheer frustration and jealousy as the genes for other diseases seemed to pop out of the genome with relative ease. The gene for Duchenne muscular dystrophy was mapped to a particular chromosome and then identified in 1986, cystic fibrosis in 1989, Wilms' tumour in 1990 and Fragile X syndrome in 1991. In none of these examples was the protein for which the gene encodes known, and researchers used positional cloning to find the mutation without knowing its effect. In many cases, the discovery of the gene has been followed by identification of the protein it codes for deeper understanding of the disease, better diagnostic testing and new hope for treatments.

Despite the difficulty of the search for the Huntington's gene or perhaps because of it, some of the best and brightest minds in medical genetics and genome mapping were drawn to the project. And most of them signed on with the Huntington's Collaborative Research Group, set up by Wexler and the Hereditary Disease Foundation soon after Gusella mapped the gene in 1983. In the end, the group included six teams. One was led by Gusella, and the others were headed by Francis Collins of the University of Michigan in Ann Arbor, who was on the teams that identified the cystic fibrosis and neurofibromatoses genes and who is the incoming director of the US National Center for Human Genome Research; Peter Harper of the University of Wales College of Medicine; David Housman of the Massachusetts Institute of Technology; Hans Lehrach of the Imperial Cancer Research Fund in London; and John Wasmuth at the University of California at Irvine.

To an unprecedented degree, the collaborators agreed to share data during the search, and credit for the ultimate discovery of the gene. The group agreed that the author of the paper would be given as the Huntington's Disease Collaborative Research Group—which avoided invidious decisions about who should be listed first and last. "The collaboration has been very unique in the length of time and the number of people it involves," says Lehrach,

Wasmuth for one appreciated the moral support of the other scientists in the group when the search was taking so long. "Some of my friends give me trouble about the fact that we've been working very hard for eight or nine years on Huntington's and in the meantime all of these other genes have been found. But people like Housman and Collins have been finding those other genes. So obviously the problem is not with the caliber of the researchers," Wasmuth said just weeks before the find was announced. "But without Nancy Wexler, the collaboration would have fallen apart many times over the past six years."

Through the foundation, Wexler provided supplementary funding to the various labs, organized meetings of the collaborators in appealing locations—there was an annual trip to Florida in May—and kept the group organized. This intimate involvement of someone who is, herself, at risk from the disease has also personalized the search for many of the researchers, helping them to keep going during the long search for the Huntington's gene.

Subtle mutation

In part, the difficulty stemmed from the relative subtlety of the mutation. Many other disease genes have been more obvious due to gross structural rearrangements in the chromosome, such as a translocation or large deletion. "With Duchenne muscular dystrophy, they looked down at the chromosome and saw a defect the size of the Grand Canyon," says Wexler, with evident jealousy. With Fragile X syndrome, a weak spot on the chromosome caused a breakpoint. In contrast, Huntington's researchers had to whittle away slowly at the area in which the gene was located by finding new markers. "One of the reasons it has taken so long is that when we started out nine years ago, we didn't have all these markers. Everyone had to fashion their own," says Wexler.

To narrow the search, the team needed to find recombinants—Huntington's patients who had inherited a chromosome 4 carrying not only the disease defect but a stretch of DNA from the short arm of a normal chromosome 4. This kind of inheritance (which occurs because the chromosomes of reproductive cells occasionally "swap" segments of DNA) is especially informative: it tells researchers that the disease gene must lie outside the region that has been swapped. Unfortunately the Huntington's gene was in a region where these cross-overs of chromosomal material are rare. The search for new recombinants kept Wexler bringing back blood samples from Venezuela, year after year.

As the years passed, the researchers developed a series of markers on the short arm of chromosome 4 that drove them farther and farther towards the tip of the arm. But the closer they got to the tip, the stranger the genetics became. Finally, they ended up with four people who appeared to have Huntington's disease but who also seemed to have an entirely normal set of markers on the short arm of chromosome four. Perhaps, the scientists reasoned, the gene was on the very tip of the chromosome, beyond the farthest marker.

Then in 1990, Gillian Bates in Lehrach's laboratory cloned the region near the tip from the DNA of one of the Venezuelan patients and found that it looked just like the region near the tip of most chromosomes, with lots of repeating sequences and very little DNA that looked like it coded for genes. At the same time, results began coming in from another form of genetic analysis called linkage disequilibrium, which allows researchers to compare the patterns of markers in different Huntington's families. The results of the linkage studies helped to convince the researchers that the gene was probably not at the very tip, but in the lowest half of the 5 million base-pair region. "Half the data said he went that-ta way, and half the data said he went thatta way, and everyone started feeling very dismayed," recalls Wexler.

Blind alley

It had begun to dawn on the researchers that they had spent years chasing some sort of phantom gene along the chromosome. In the end, most decided to go back and search the lower part of the region, a length of about 2.2 million base pairs, for the gene. The race to the end of the chromosome, says Lehrarch, "cost us a lot of time".

In the absence of many recombinants, researchers were left with a large region to scour for candidate genes, pulling up each one in turn and trying to determine whether it differed between people carrying the disease and normal people. If it did, geneticists had to determine whether the difference was one of the many harmless DNA variations that occur throughout the genome, or whether it was a mutation altering some protein in a way that could cause Huntington's disease. Once again, the Huntington's researchers were particularly unlucky because this region happens to be rich in genes. There may be as many as a hundred genes in the region, and the gene hunters knew they might have to evaluate all of them before finding the right one.

Excluding innocent genes

It takes a team of four people working full time for at least a month, and perhaps a few months if the gene is large, to tentatively rule out a candidate gene. By February, at least 50 candidate genes had been pulled out of the region and characterized to some extent, though only a handful had been tentatively ruled out as the Huntington's gene. Each gene had to be scrutinized for mutations, either by direct sequencing—working out the exact sequence in which the base pairs are laid out along the chromosome—and comparison with the same gene in a person who has not inherited Huntington's disease, or through various short-cut methods that are less precise. "All the methods we have now are unwieldy," says Richard Myers, who was also searching for the gene at the University of California, San Francisco. "Direct sequencing will be the best, but it is still too expensive and time consuming."

Part of the strategy, therefore, was determining which genes should be given priority for evaluation. After the discovery that repeating triplets of nucleotides cause other genetic diseases, including Fragile X syndrome, myotonic dystrophy and spinobulbar muscular atrophy, the team was naturally drawn to the idea of genetic stutters in the Huntington's region. But these trinucleotide stutters are not uncommon. Lehrach's group set about systematically evaluating each of the 25 or so such repeats found in the 2.2 million base pair region, a strategy he says was deliberately conservative. "We gambled once and lost in believing the recombinants that pointed to the tip," he said. "In a sense I didn't feel like making another bad guess."

In contrast, Gusella's team decided to gamble on a much smaller portion of the region, the segment of 500,000 bases that seemed to be common to many different families with the disease, based on an analysis of the patterns of markers in the region. "It was too frustrating, at that point, to work in more than one place," says Gusella.

"That's why these gene hunters are so heroic, because they've endured all this," said Wexler earlier this year when it looked, at last, as if the gene hunters were closing in on their prey. "And the amazing thing about it is that they are still enormously energetic and enthusiastic." The gene hunters believe some of the credit should go to Wexler. "Nancy has leveraged a lot of work going into Huntington's," Lehrach explains. "And the collaboration has made for a much more efficient exchange of ideas and information."

Despite the benefits of sharing ideas and information, and the motivations and incentives provided by Wexler's foundation, not every research team signed on with the collaborative group. Myers and David Cox conducted their own search for the gene at the University of California, San Francisco. "I have not remained independent because I want to be a hero," Myers said just before the discovery was announced. "I just felt that it was the best way to do my science. I think that it's good that there's some competition. And the competition is not unfriendly, most of the time."

Michael Hayden of the University of British Columbia, who runs a large Huntington's disease programme including genetic testing, was also searching for the gene. He had about ten people in his laboratory working on the project. "We're tiny," he admitted. "We're the David up against Goliath."

Early this year, the tension created by the imminent discovery of the gene after so many years became almost unbearable. By February, Gusella's laboratory had found five genes in the region they were looking at, and had already ruled out two of them when they began to realize that one of the others, which they had dubbed IT15, for "interesting transcript number 15", might be the holy grail.

Nerve-racking rumours

More than once, a rumour went out that one laboratory had found the gene, plunging rival researchers into depression. Myers called the competition "kind of nerve-racking. It's exciting, because we need to find the gene. But it's also scary because there's a little bit of a sociological element of winner takes all." Of course, all the researchers insisted that the most important thing was to find the gene, not who found it. But Wasmuth added, "I really hope it's the collaborative group that finds the gene. Nancy deserves it."

At the end of February, three days before she left for this year's trip to Venezuela, Wexler received a phone call from Gusella with the news that the team in his laboratory, led by Marcy MacDonald, were sure they had found the gene. The quarry turned out to be an unusually long gene with the Huntington's mutation "expanded like an accordion", according to Gusella, at the very beginning of the gene. The gene codes for an unknown protein which the collaborative group has dubbed huntingtin. The team would be submitting a paper describing

their discovery to the weekly journal *Cell* the next day. He swore Wexler to secrecy. When she hung up the phone, she sat quietly gazing out her window at the Hudson River. "I was totally stunned," she says. "As if I had fallen and had the breath knocked out of me. I had been having nightmares that there wasn't any gene, or that the gene was on another chromosome."

The news of the gene's discovery was scheduled to be released to the public on Thursday 18 March. A week before, the collaborative group learnt that Hayden had a paper coming out in *Nature*, one day ahead of its *Cell* paper, describing a "strong candidate" for the Huntington's gene. Neither team had seen the other's paper, but a series of phone calls established that the two genes were different. Hayden's team had found a DNA variation in two people with the disease, but the mutation did not appear in 238 other families with the disease. In response to Hayden's paper, *Cell* decided to move the press embargo date for release of the collaborative paper forward to the Tuesday, leapfrogging the release of the *Nature* paper. In the end, the two papers were released simultaneously.

By the Saturday before the gene's discovery was announced, Hayden had conceded that the collaborative group had found the Huntington's gene. One member of the collaborative group describes Hayden's finding as "interesting but irrelevant" and says that publishing such a speculative paper in *Nature* was "really pushing it". Hayden says it was most probably "a cruel hoax": a mutation that happened to be found in these two families but was unrelated to the disease.

Many researchers believe that the era of such lengthy and arduous searches is nearing an end, as the Human Genome Project begins to make headway in cataloguing every marker, and eventually every nucleotide, on the human chromosomes. "This search would have been a heck of a lot easier if the Human Genome Project had been completed. It would have been a matter of just sitting down at a computer," says Collins. "When the project is complete, what has been a ten year process will instead take months or even weeks."

More questions than answers

The next step for researchers will be to

understand the normal function of huntingtin in the body, and how the mutation disrupts this function. They will try introducing the mutation into a mouse to develop the first animal model for the disease. "The sequence of the large protein does not give any clues as to what the protein does in cells, or how the alteration causes the death of cells," said Gusella at the press conference to announce the gene's discovery. Wasmuth said that the discovery of the gene had "raised a lot more questions than it answers". Does the mutation exert its effect at the messenger RNA or the protein level? Does it, as some researchers suspect, cause the protein to disappear too quickly, or hang around too long? Or to be expressed at the wrong time? If the protein is expressed throughout the body, why are brain cells killed selectively by the mutation? But with the gene at last pinned down, says Wasmuth, "We have the tool now to address these questions and answer them."

With the discovery of the gene, at least one mystery surrounding Huntington's disease seems well on its way to being solved. While most Huntington's patients are diagnosed in their thirties or forties, some come down with symptoms as children, and a few do not have symptoms until they are in their eighties. Researchers now believe that there is a rough correlation between the number of triplet repeats and the age of onset of the disease, though they caution that this correlation should not be used yet to predict the age of onset in individual patients. MacDonald's team found the longest segment of repeats, estimated at 86, in a Venezuelan child who began having symptoms of Huntington's disease at the age of two. In early onset cases, the disease appears to be more severe, and is more likely to be inherited from the father than the mother. In those rare cases where a child inherits the gene from both parents, the longer of the two segments seems to determine the age of onset.

The most immediate impact of the gene's discovery on families affected by Huntington's disease will be easier testing for people who want to know if they have inherited the disease. Wexler sees this as a mixed blessing. Since shortly after Gusella found the first marker for Huntington's, researchers have been able to do "presymptomatic" testing in Huntington's families with a fair degree of accuracy, provided the individual comes from a large enough family. Testing based on markers requires blood samples from several family members, the more the better, in order to establish the inheritance patterns correctly. The process takes up to a year. The test is "fraught with dangers in terms of accuracy", says Wexler. What genetic counsellors delicately call a "non-paternity" in a previous generation, in other words an assumed father who was not the biological father of an offspring, can yield an incorrect result.

A test which identifies the genes should overcome these technical problems. However, "the problem is that the dangers are as great or even greater in the psychological realm", says Wexler. The current waiting period of a year leaves plenty of time to prepare for bad news. "If you get the answer in a couple of weeks you can be stunned." The psychological issues are not frivolous: in the US, the suicide rate among people with Huntington's disease is seven times the norm.

Of course, for families affected by Huntington's, the ultimate goal has never been identifying the gene but finding an effective therapy or cure. A few days after the triumphant press conference last month, Wexler flew to Venezuela to complete her annual research, and to celebrate the good news at a massive party with the Venezuelans that she has come to see as part of her extended Huntington's family. "I don't think people really feel that there will be a treatment or a cure tomorrow," she says. "But at least now it's more possible that something good will happen."

Postscript

Nancy Wexler will not discuss her decision regarding her own test. She considers it a private issue. She is concerned that people who test positive could be discriminated against when seeking health insurance or employment. "Is the chance of release from (the risk of) Huntington's," Dr. Wexler asks, "worth the risk of losing joy?"

Reference

Turkington, C. (1994, January). Wexler wins Lasker award for her work on Huntington's. *APA Monitor,* Science Directorate, 20-21.

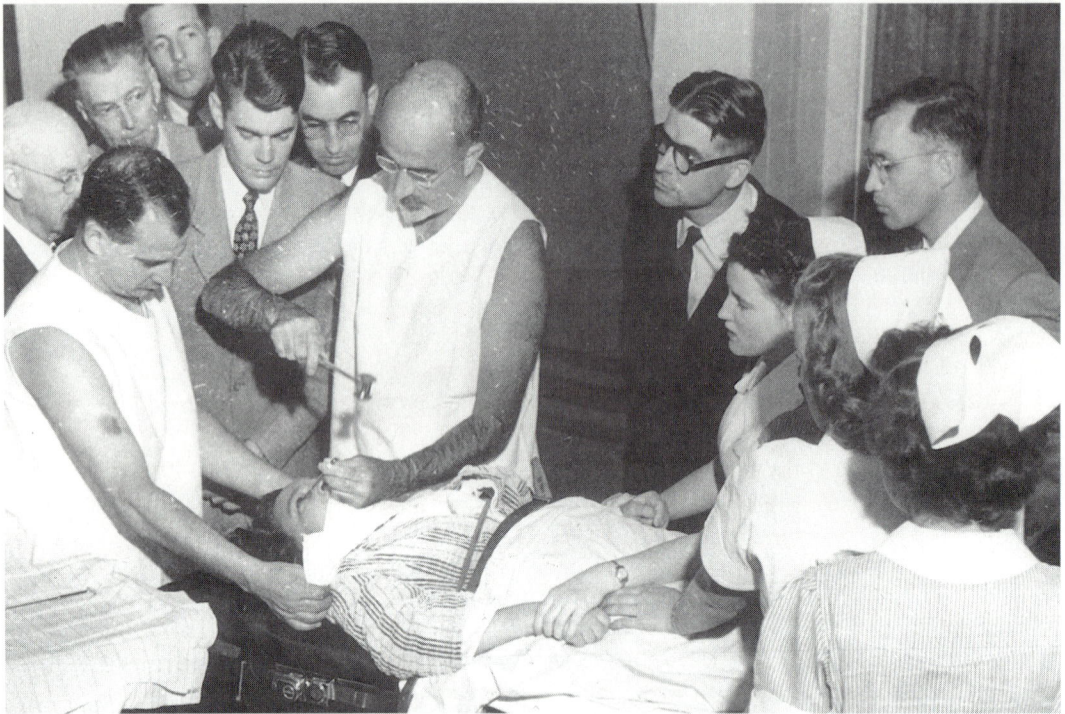

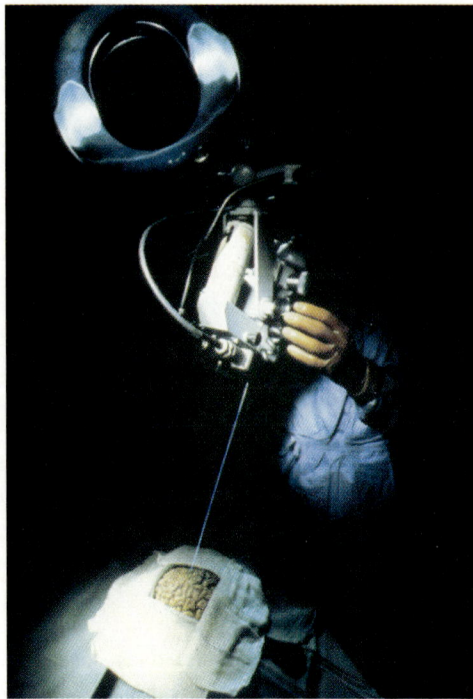

Figure 5-5. *Upper*: Walter Freeman performing an ice-pick lobotomy in 1949. (Photograph courtesy of UPI/Bettman.) *Lower:* Kinder and gentler psychosurgery of today. (Photograph copyright © by Alexander Tsiaras, Stock, Boston.) Laser surgery can be directed at extremely small areas of the brain.

READING 5D

PSYCHOSURGERY:
DAMAGING THE BRAIN TO SAVE THE MIND

Joann Ellison Rodgers

Psychosurgery refers to the surgical or electrical alteration of the human brain. Six decades after its introduction, it remains controversial. This procedure is the logical extreme of the illness perspective. According to early psychosurgeon O.J. Andy, "All abnormal behavior results from structurally abnormal brain tissue. Now, psychiatric techniques are in most instances futile·in dealing with these abnormalities. In fact, adequate therapy can be obtained only by techniques, such as surgery, which deal directly with the structurally abnormal brain tissue" (Restak, 1976).

Portuguese neurologist Egas Moniz performed the first prefrontal leucotomy (lobotomy) in 1937. B. V. J., his first patient, had been hospitalized for five years because of violent psychosis and attempted suicide. A week later "she left the hospital and now after six months she remains in entirely normal condition" (Moniz, 1937). Moniz won a Nobel Prize for the lobotomy. Unfortunately, he was shot in the spine by one of his patients, apparently unappreciative of his award winning treatment.

In 1952, Time magazine reported that neurologist Walter Freeman had performed thousands of lobotomies, more than two hundred in a single week. He developed a ten minute procedure. The patient was rendered unconscious with three electric jolts. Gold plated, ice pick-like leucotomes were inserted under each eyelid, hammered through the eyesocket, and into the brain. Carefully manipulating the ice picks, Freeman severed the connection between thalamus and frontal lobes. Freeman reported "good results" in forty-five percent of his patients, although forty-three of 617 died in one study (Noonan, 1989, p. 203).

Critics argue that although our understanding of the brain is improving, it is overly optimistic to link specific brain parts with behaviorial, cognitive, and affective functions. They argue that psychosurgery has been used in the past to deal with society's dissidents and undesirables. Psychosurgery critic Peter Breggin has stated, "It surpasses outright killing as a method of control" (Stavro, 1980).

Psychosurgery is generally viewed as an experimental procedure, as it has not demonstrated sufficient clinical efficacy to be considered a treatment. In 1973 the Department of Health, Education, and Welfare (renamed the Department of Health and Human Services) published a code of regulations governing experimentation with human subjects. These regulations state that no experimentation should be conducted with human subjects unless the possible benefits to the subject are greater than the possible risk. This cannot really be determined beforehand. Also, the psychosurgeon must legally inform the subject about the procedure and obtain his consent. Can the mind of a sick brain make this decision?

Gross excess and abuse of psychosurgery is in the past. Today, psychosurgery is practiced much less frequently and more discriminately. It employs a vastly improved technology, destroys much less tissue, is more humane, and is performed with specific therapeutic objective. It is still typically chosen as a procedure of last resort. The following article illustrates the present practice of psychosurgery.

Joann Ellison Rodgers: Psychosurgery: Damaging the Brain to Save the Mind, *Psychology Today*, March/April 1992, 35-39, 78, 84, 86. Copyright © 1992 Joann Ellison Rodgers. Reprinted with permission of Elaine Markson Agency, Inc.

Philosophers tell us that the horizon of knowledge is always out of reach. How far out of reach is the practical question and the source of all dilemmas having to do with treating the sick. Do doctors wait until they really *know*—or know more—before they try this treatment or that? If they wait, will it mean more suffering for a patient? Is suffering tolerable if there are means of relieving it? Are some risks ever worth taking? Are some ever not?

The treatment dilemma posed by psychosurgery—surgery to treat psychiatric disorders—is this: Experts know something about mental illness and about operations that can help some patients; but they don't know enough to completely assure patients, families, each other, or the rest of us that surgery is the best, or proper, course. That it is ever worth the risk.

Perhaps they can *never* know enough. Driving the demand for and use of psychosurgery is the belief—some call it the pretension—that the human brain can understand and repair its own mind. And more, that scientists come to understand the mind and brain better by studying it the way they study it now—anatomically, biochemically, and empirically, by analyzing and observing its parts and the things it does.

Publicly, the subject of psychiatric brain surgery hasn't been discussed since 1978, when the National Commission for the Protection of Human subjects of Biomedical and Behavioral Research issued a report saying that psychosurgery had a deservedly bad reputation for wretched excess. But the report also documented successes, declared that psychosurgery was not the unmitigated horror its critics had labeled it, and decreed that—with strict regulations and safeguards—psychosurgery was acceptable for certain cases and that more research and good record-keeping were needed.

As a result, perhaps, psychosurgery—albeit under new names, more refined and more selective than the lobotomies that psychiatrists and neurosurgeons abandoned more than 30 years ago—is still very much around. Actually, it never completely went away.

Although the number of procedures have plunged since the heyday of psychosurgery (50,000 estimated in the United States alone between 1939 and 1960), there are still at least 200 to 300 openly declared psychosurgeries labeled as such each year being performed by a few dozen surgeons here and abroad. Reports are trickling in of more operations being done in South America and the developing world. And if we count the operations that affect the "psyche" but disclaim changes in mood and behavior as primary goals, the total is certainly in the thousands and growing.

Psychosurgery has now greatly evolved. Surgeons no longer destroy large amounts of brain tissue in futile efforts to "cure" schizophrenia and neurosis. Instead, they take pinpoint aim at millimeter-long clusters of cells to stop suicidal depression, disable obsessive-compulsive disorders, cripple anxiety, and smother the uncontrollable rage and aggression that keep sick people in locked wards. They go after destructive behavior that accompanies organic diseases of the body and brain.

The great promise of psychosurgery is not without critics. For some, the abuses of the past remain open sores on the national conscience. Some see it as Frankenstein-style science. Others dismiss the whole idea as plain goofy—based on oversimplified views of human behavior and emotional chaos. And certain religious groups, such as the Scientologists, brand psychosurgery and all physical treatment of mental illness as assassination attempts on the mind.

Practically nothing has been written to update the general public in the last 10 years about the new operations, their availability, and any ongoing problems they pose. While psychosurgery's past excesses have been forever characterized by Ken Kesey's Randle McMurphy in One Flew over the Cuckoo's Nest, the conventional wisdom of that era is now vulnerable to new knowledge and rising demands for help from the mentally ill and their advocates. Moreover, today, as in the past, the need to balance treatment with protection from abuse is especially important for the ill who are homeless, poor, female, children, imprisoned, and minorities: They were historically the guinea pigs of psychosurgery and could become so again. On the other hand, they could become beneficiaries of a therapy that still has promises to keep.

They could be Matthew.

I must tell you that I am very afraid of this man. Even under guard he is unpredictable, very scary. He is like a feral animal, a cat. He raises his arms and dives into people. He could kill.

—Matthew's neurosurgeon, 1990

The story of Matthew frames much of the reasonable and unreasonable debate over the need for psychosurgery and its potential abuse. Matthew has a social history of violent behavior and a medical history that makes modern psychosurgery a last—and long delayed—hope. The following excerpts from a letter written on January 4, 1990, to Matthew's lawyer from a neurologist describe the cold, clinical details:

Dear Mr.—

Matthew is a 24 year old, right-handed man who has had severe and uncontrollable seizures since age 11. The cause of the seizures is encephalitis, which is an infection (presumed viral) of the brain. This infection produced scarring which resulted in spontaneously recurrent abnormal electrical discharges. When the electrical discharges build up to a certain level he will have seizures. During his seizures, he will have an aura [warning] of an unpleasant emotion, he will become confused, he will yell, grimace, turn his [head] side to side and will run about.

I have personally observed several of these episodes. He appears very frightening to others during the episodes. On one occasion we had a laboratory technician hide behind the door for many minutes after Matthew slammed into the door during a seizure. If someone is in his path, he will stare at them, then run into them or push them violently out of the way.

We monitored him in our critical care neurology unit with videoelectroencephalography recordings in June of 1986. During that time we could observe his typical range episodes, and correlate them with abnormal electrical activity in the brain. His seizures have occurred as often as 10 times a day.

On October 5, 1987, Matthew had surgery on the right side of his brain, and on November 24, 1987, on the left side of his brain in a struc-

ture called the amygdala. This is a structure that is often involved in seizures and in manifestations of violent behavior. Unfortunately, the procedure was of no lasting benefit to Matthew. I believe that Matthew has sufficient brain injury that he cannot control his outbursts of aggression. Some of these are explicitly because of seizures [and] completely beyond his control. Others are not related to seizures, but occur because he has brain damage, delusional thinking, and lacks the normal inhibitory behavior that people must exert in society.

Regrettably, this is likely to be a continuing condition with Matthew.

It is sometimes difficult to tell whether violence is part of a seizure, or whether it is acting out of "bad temper." In Matthew's case, I think all these are [beyond his control].

Matthew's medical situation is unfortunate. We have been unable to manage this satisfactorily with medications and with surgery. I would hope that the court and authorities would view his problems as a medical rather than a criminal issue.

Sincerely...

Matthew is slight in build, with boyishly silky, slightly long, dark wavy hair; he sports a neatly trimmed beard. On an early June evening in 1990, he has permission for a special visit with his parents and a guest—special because authorities at the high-security hospital for the criminally insane are strict about the number of visits to each inmate per week. Matthew has spent almost a year here, and 16 more years in schools and hospitals for young people with severe neurological and psychiatric disease. Since the beginning of the summer, the internal review board of a prestigious medical center has been considering his parents' request for neurosurgery to get him out.

We had to put our belongings in a metal locker behind the guard's desk, keeping only a small tape recorder, and passed through an airport-style metal detector. Armed guards escorted us through two sets of locked doors, along a corridor into a room with brown Formica furniture upholstered in bright blue vinyl. Matthew sits in one of the chairs, facing us, wearing khakis, clean white socks, slip-on Keds, a hospital shirt tucked neatly into his beltless pants, and sunglasses. A burly security guard stays for the visit, too—protection against Matthew's unpredictable and violent rages.

Matthew: (Shaking hands.) How do you do ma'am. How about a soundcheck? Sure. (Leaning forward, singing into the tape recorder.) "I just called to say I loooove you, I just called to say how much I care."

Visitor: I want to ask you about your feelings, Matthew, about getting a brain operation.

Matthew: Yes. I want to leave here. With violent seizures, I have been put here. They don't really know about them and they think it's just me being bad and acting out. When I was in [a state mental hospital] this lady named Fran told me I was a bad case, and making it up. Yes ma'am, she said it, but I'm not.

Visitor: If doctors said to you, "Matthew there's a chance this could help," you would do this, have an operation on your brain?"

Matthew: Yes. (Turning to look at the guard talking loudly on the wall phone.) Can you wait until he is off the phone? I am having trouble concentrating. I'm sorry for the interruption. Please excuse me for saying to wait.

Visitor: When you have your violent seizures, do you remember anything?

Matthew: No, wait, wait, yes. Sometimes. Yeah. Like I was telling my father last night. I don't know how I do it. But—put your fingers over your ear (we all cup our hands over our ears) and for about a second, I hear a muffling sound. You can hear air coming.

Visitor. You mean like putting a seashell over your ear?

Matthew: Yes, yes, yes, exactly, exactly. After that, I get a ringing sound in both ears. One time with a violent seizure, I was in the shower room up at ward 8 and I went into one of the showers, and I went in there and I was hearing the ringing sound. And what happened was this man Rudolph—

Visitor: [Rudolph] works in the hospital?

Matthew: Yeah, and he walked in and I hit him, I forget where, I hit him and he grabbed me and I think we were fighting. (Matthew clenches his fists and works them back and forth to indi-

cate a fight.) And he threw me in seclusion and it's just that I think some of this problem is 50-50, you know, part violent seizures, and they [the attendants] just ... just (a long pause).

Visitor: They don't know what to do?

Matthew: They don't know if it's a seizure or if like once when I was on [ward] 3, I just want my way. Wanting your way, what I mean by that is, on 3, here I am, and I was mad and when I get mad, first I'm mad, then I'm madder, then madder and madder and so forth. [But] on 8 I wasn't about to blow my top or get mad.

Matthew's mother: Or get out of control?

Matthew: (Smiling and with a chuckle.) Yes, thank you, out of control. What happened was, they said, "Matt, how long would you like to be in your room?" [I guess all the] seclusion rooms were taken or something, I'm not sure. So they put me in my room and I was lying down like this (he leans over in the chair onto his side) and suddenly I went into a seizure like that (he snaps his fingers) and with no ringing in the ear or anything.

Visitor: Sometimes you have a warning and can remember and sometimes you can't.

Matthew: Yes ma'am. And what happened was I was lying on my bed and I guess I got scared or something else bad and I grabbed the pillow and put it over my face and I started to scream and after that, well, I forgot what happened but nothing positive. I went to a screened window in the room and I was banging on that, and screaming, not from the seizure but just screaming and a lady walked in and said, "Matthew, if you don't stop it I'll take your cigarettes away from you." And so I'm in this seizure.

Matthew's father: No, you said you were not in the seizure. That you are finished with the seizure. Did this happen after the seizure? Can you tell when the seizure is over? That's what you told us before. Your mind is fuzzy and you don't always know what's going on.

Matthew's mother: Can you feel when it's over?

Matthew: Sometimes I can. Sometimes I'm not really conscious. This one I'm talking about was one where I was still in seizure. I will say that when I went to the [screened-in] window, I was banging with my hand, and banged on the two beds and what happened is that I had a feeling like one time that I was looking through this window on 3 and so I (long pause) ... I couldn't control what I was doing, but my mind was telling me what to do. Like I—if I was in seizure now I'd look at this wall (he points to a wall next to us) and say let's do that and I would go to the wall and kick it or whatever and that's what it was like at the screened window and I saw that and I thought of things.

Visitor: What things?

Matthew: (Glancing quickly at his parents.) My mother and father know about this. About God. What it is is that I had a feeling that this happened before, that I did that before and, well, what it was then was there was this other window and this man would always tell me to look out the window. He said, "Matt, look what's out there," and I'd say "what, what," and once he said to me, "Matt look out there, look at that," and I said, "No, no I'm not going to look out there because it will happen again."

Visitor: What happened then that you did not want to happen again?

Matthew: I'm not about for that to happen again. What it was, I had this feeling that the person said to me, "You'll see out the window, you'll see what happens when you die." And so I, um, I just had the feeling I was supposed to do this and do that and I was in the seizure but for some reason I, well, like what I said about the wall.

Matthew's mother: Is this the thing where you believed God was out there, out of heaven, and it was your fault that God wasn't in heaven anymore and that's why so many terrible things were happening to you and everyone else and—

Matthew: Yes. Also, I had a feeling I was supposed to bang the window and beds and I was there and I hit the window like this (he demonstrates with his arm) and [a] male staff [member] was called and he said, "Matt, calm down now," and they put me in bed and next thing I knew, they shut the door and took my clothes off.

Visitor: If you could leave here, what would you like to do?

Matthew: You mean a job?

Visitor: Anything.

Matthew: I would like to go home with my parents and see my sisters-in-law, my brothers, and my neighbors. And my grandmother. Whenever I get to two months without acting out, I act out or get a bad seizure and then I have to start over and I can't go home. But I like the things my father and I used to do. We went to [a] park and walked around a lot. I'd like to live in a group with other people, and the Epilepsy Foundation has places and that's where I'd like to go after I'm out of here, yes ma'am.

Matthew's father: After he got encephalitis, everything left. Matthew didn't remember knowing how to count, or say the alphabet, or even how to walk for a long time. Now he can do some things. Matt, you're a survivor. Don't forget that.

Matthew's mother: What mommy says. Say it. You don't belong here.

Matthew: I will get out if I can stay calm, cool, and collected. (Lots of laughter.)

The hour is over. Matthew shakes hands. The guard asks another to escort the visitors out so he can take Matthew back to his ward. Matthew is smiling in the hall. He extends his arms out wide and says something to the visitor in Polish. His father translates: "He says he loves you, and will you marry him?"

* * * *

Matthew's parents live in a middleclass neighborhood in a medium-size, mid-Atlantic city. His father, retired after a nearly fatal heart attack several years ago, worked in a maritime-industry plant as an engineer. His mother, robust and sad, is a full-time homemaker. Their super-clean brick row house is pleasantly furnished and crowded with memorabilia of their children; but their memories are overwhelmed by the details of Matthew's sickness, which began with a viral illness during a vacation at the beach when he was 10.

Matthew's mother: The first really awful time was after his initial illness, after we thought he might really get completely well. I'll never forget it. Matt came out of the bedroom shrieking that his hands were growing, that he had to go to the bathroom but the "poopie" was all over and was attached to him by strings, and begging us to cut them. We thought that he was having a nightmare. So his daddy went to lay down with him and soon he fell asleep.

Then at 8 A.M. we heard Matthew [again]. We heard him running. He was only a little boy. It was his first grand mal seizure and it led him delusional, hallucinating, and robot-like walking into walls. He stopped breathing [so] we headed for the hospital. That's when his hospitalizations became multiple and the specialists diagnosed him as having brain damage from a viral infection. That's what they think, though they never really know. And the seizures began in earnest, one after the other, sometimes hundreds a day and violent.

Matthew's father: We had to make sure he was restrained on the number of occasions that he was hospitalized. He would bite his mother's ear. And he would make these inhuman noises. If he ever got a hold of you, he'd grab you like a vice.

Matthew's mother: It's a helplessness you feel every day of Matthew's life. Among other things, it took more than a year for doctors at [the medical center] to finally witness one of the animal rages we were living with and fearing every day. You know. Like when you stop having a toothache when you go to the dentist. He wouldn't have them when we went to the hospital or for a check-up, and it got to the point where no one believed us. We were accused of being hysterical, of exaggerating, of not wanting to care for Matthew.

Matthew's father: One day we went to the seizure clinic for blood tests of his drug levels and we were in the courtyard to smoke and he began to attack me with animal noises, and he burst through the security guards and raced through the seizure clinic. Two doctors grabbed him. He growled and fought. He ripped their clothes. They really got an eyeful. He was well over 18 by then. When this happened, the doctor said to bring him into the intensive care unit to monitor him. Like always, it came from nowhere, out of the blue. They strapped him down and he just tore the cloth strips off. He made huge screams. He flipped his hospital bed upside down and shrieked and shrieked. His mother went into the room to try and calm him. She took her life in her hands.

Matthew's mother: Well, now he is in a hospital for the criminally insane, but he is not a criminal really, and whether or not he is psychotic is open to question. We know the things he does are bad. But his brain is damaged, and no one can predict when he'll get his attacks. Sometimes he gets depressed and obsessed with anything he hears, sees, or talks about for long periods of time.

Matthew's father: I visit him every day they let me, every day.

Matthew's mother: I feel guilty about not going to see him very much. I'm worried about it. If we tell him to get his okay for us to come, then he'll drive himself and us nuts asking about it. And then he might get upset while you're there. The Epilepsy Foundation has a group home. If he got better, they might be able to take him there. I know that. In the institution, I worry about men taking advantage of him. And I worry about what will happen to Matt when we go. His brothers will take care of him. They're very close, but it hurts and it's tough. God it's tough. What is especially heartbreaking is that his anger is not bad, not wrong. Matt knows what he has lost.

* * * * *

Less clear is what he might gain from surgery. But on November 20, 1990, two days before Thanksgiving, Matthew, his family, and his doctors get the chance to find out.

Since the 1940s and '50s, neurosurgeons have removed areas of the amygdala and the temporal lobe to stop violent behavior, with variable success. In 1987, surgeons operated on both the right and left amygdala in Matthew, whose temporal-lobe epilepsy apparently damaged circuits involved in the hypothalamus. Located under the thalamus, the hypothalamus receives input from most other parts of the brain and regulates many body activities as well as the hormone-producing pituitary gland, at the base of the brain. Along with the pituitary, the hypothalamus is one of the major routes carrying signals of psychological stress—good and bad—to the heart, lungs, bladder, and other internal organs. The damage to Matthew's hypothalamus left him with an unpredictable, assaultive, dangerous, hair-trigger temper. He also suffers from obsessive thoughts and behavior.

The amygdalotomies unfortunately did not work. After three years, dozens of rage seizures, and a violent assault on a nurse, surgeons will try again to kill—by cutting out a small part of Matthew's abnormal brain—about a square centimeter of it. He'll have a cingulotomy: an operation designed to dampen motivation, to calm. It is also performed for cancer pain that even narcotics can't help. "I did one on a bone-cancer patient," said the surgeon. "Before the operation he cried in agony all day. After, he was completely relaxed. He read most of the time. He had no more suffering. He had no more emotions, either, nor was he capable of any real mental work. It was drastic. Like a lobotomy. Matthew's will not be that drastic."

Drastic or not, there is nothing left to try. "This kid's brain is totally out of control," says a child neurologist who consulted on Matthew's condition. "When the amygdalotomies failed, his own neurologist wept. He said he didn't know how to face the family. He cried, really cried. There's nothing left now but high-security institutionalization and sedation to the point of near coma. The new surgery is a chance. It's a Hobson's choice for us all," the neurologist added. "Even if it stops the violent rages, we don't know if it will stop the obsessive behavior."

* * * * *

7:15 A.M. In the wide corridor of the medical center's basement neuroradiology suite, Matthew waits on a gurney, held securely in four point restraints. With him are his mother, older brother Jim, and a guard from the state mental hospital. In anticipation of his cingulotomy, he had been transferred from the high-security, prison-style hospital; there is hope that if the surgery succeeds, the halfway house, sheltered workshop training, and independence await. Matthew is nervous but cheerful, wrapped in pastel gowns, his feet and legs in vented stockings, IV line taped securely to his right arm. "I'm not getting my hopes too high this time," his mother says, her eyes on Matthew. "I am," his father says. Matthew is quiet.

Matthew's surgeon walks by in a three-piece suit he'll soon exchange for pale green scrubs. He stops for a minute to talk, holding on all the while to his briefcase. He pats Matthew's foot. "I'll see you soon," he says.

Matthew's family will see neither their son nor the surgeon for the next nine hours.

* * * * *

Operating suite 2 really is a suite. The largest of the rooms is the operating room itself; unlike conventional ORs, it houses a modern CT scanner, with its hollow scooped bed and donut-shaped scanning apparatus. Five freestanding monitors are on site as well, to track drugs and vital signs. Behind the scanner, Vincent Lerie, a radiation technician, and Gerry Beveringen, a scrub nurse, set up three sterile tables for equipment.

Most prominent alongside the usual scissors, knives, sutures, gauze pads, needles, and tubes are the Radio Frequency Lesion Generator and the stereotactic halo. This circular frame holds the patient's head in a fixed position and guarantees millimeter-precise positioning of the brain probe and needle tip that the Lesion Generator will heat to 75 degrees Centigrade. Over the next few hours, Lerie will switch it on 10 separate times to destroy 10 tiny pieces of brain tissue in Matthew's cingulate gyrus, deep in the temporal lobes beneath his cerebral cortex.

The cingulum itself is part of the limbic system (or "primitive" emotional brain) that carries signal-making nerve fibers around the system—including the signals that trigger Matthew's rage-producing seizures. The heated needle will create dead space to act as "firebreaks" in Matthew's brain and hopefully stop transmission of these rage-triggering signals. The stereotactic equipment eliminates the risk of "blind" freehand reaches into the limbic system by automatically lining up points on the computer to make a topographic map of Matthew's brain.

The CT roadmaps guide the surgical probes safely past areas of the cerebral cortex that control sensory and motor functions (including smell and sight, and arm and leg movement) and safely away from the thalamus that is the main relay station taking messages to the higher centers of the cortex.

To compare this cingulotomy to old prefrontal lobotomies is like comparing a Civil War conscript's musket fire to the launch of a Tomahawk missile. The lesions to be made in Matthew's cingulum are anatomically "miles" from the frontal lobe, but the changes—the calming, flattening—they produce will be somewhat similar. That's because the neural fiber pathways work in parallel and bundle together in various spots deep in the brain. Thousands of psychosurgeries, along with modern technology have brought less of the knife and enough of the desired effect, without the mutilating damage of frontal lobotomy.

Space is crowded in the suite, especially with plans for a half-dozen or more onlookers: radiologists, students, physician assistants. A glass-walled anteroom faces the OR and contains four computer monitors and other equipment. All of it will be used to display and interpret scanner information and pinpoint targets for the team that has planned this sortie into Matthew's limbic system like a military operation.

An adjacent small room holds the computer that operates the scanner, and connecting the areas is a small corridor and cul-de-sac enclosing a "light wall" to read the pictures made of the scans. It also houses a 30-cup, ever-filled coffeepot.

7:50 A.M. Toby Eagle, the nurse anesthetist, and Steve Derrer, the anesthesiologist, bring Matthew in and transfer him to the CT scanner bed where he will stay, anesthetized, throughout the operation. They gently explain the tubes.

"Matt, I'm going to give you some medicine through the tube," Derrer says. "It'll feel hot for a second," adds Eagle. Matthew whimpers for an instant and then is quiet. Eagle puts a nose and mouth mask quickly over his face. "Just a little oxygen," she fibs to him. It's really nitrous oxide, and in just moments, he is asleep. Derrer has injected a cocktail of drugs through the tube—Pentothal, fentanyl, flourane. "Have a good rest, Matt," Eagle says gently. He can't hear her.

7:56 A.M. Eagle passes a breathing tube into Matthew's throat, adds more line. The front part of his hair is shaved from his forehead to about halfway back. They leave the rest, including beard and sideburns. "He cares a lot about his hair," says Gerry. "Most young guys do." Matthew's eyes are taped shut now and the supporting part of the stereotactic frame is placed under his head and shoulders, clamped to the bed that supports him and screwed into his skull with four white screws at the temples.

8:35 A.M. Vince clears everyone out of the room so he can turn on the CT scanner, which hums. The surgeon, Sumio Uematsu, along with the radiologists, neurologists, and technicians, are crammed into the CT monitor room on and off for most of this first hour. At about 9 A.M., Uematsu looks at reconstructed scans that highlight an important landmark: the telltale butterfly-shaped structure of the corpus callosum. From there, it's only about two centimeters back to the cingulum—the target. He also locates, among the varied shades of white, gray, and black, the cerebral artery he must avoid.

More than 35 scans are done. "It's got to be right, perfect, absolutely right. We need to check and recheck, check and recheck," says Uematsu. He keeps saying this aloud, yet to himself, almost like a prayer or a mantra.

9:30 A.M. A neurologist who has cared for Matthew for many years arrives with a copy of a medical journal article written by Tom Ballantine, a Massachusetts neurosurgeon who has done more than 600 cingulotomies for chronic pain. In it are detailed photographs of the sites in the brain where Ballantine recommends placing lesions.

Still holding the article, he gazes at Matthew's draped form through the glass. He does not go into the operating room even when this first round of scanning is completed at l0:15. Instead, he leaves the suite to see Matthew's family. He will come and go often during the day.

10:16 A.M. Physician's assistant Debbie Mandelblatt places a white stretch cap on Matthew's skull, and over the cap a clear, stretchable plastic—not unlike thick Saran wrap—and fastens it down like a sausage casing. The wrap holds the scalp skin taut and sterile and isolates the slits the surgeon will cut in it to reach the skull and brain. "We'll make two burr holes, or entries," Uematsu tells onlookers. "The right side first." Two hours and l5 minutes into this operation, the first real surgery is about to happen.

Five separate times the surgical team validates the settings on a mockup before the coordinates are locked down on the stereotactic frame. Now the electrode probe is positioned on every plane: It can be moved in any direction and the target will always be in the center of the probe.

10:30 A.M. Uematsu makes a one-inch cut in the Saran wrap and skull cap, then slices the skin and underlayers of the scalp. He uses a retractor to hold the skin back and stitches it in place. It's quiet in the room as Uematsu picks up a hand drill, and drills the burr hole, beginning slowly and building to a vigorous circular motion with the handle. He drills and drills into the skull. With suction and irrigation, pieces of bone and tissue gush out on the table under Matthew's head, but very little blood. He sleeps peacefully.

10:45 A.M. Drilling stops. Uematsu uses currettes (tiny, sharp, curved knives) to clean out the hole. The top half of the stereotactic frame is fastened over the hole. There is a faint smell of burning as he electrically seals the covering of the brain, or dura. Now it's time to set the electrode needle into the brain. The necessary apparatus, already locked into the right place, is lifted from the mockup frame and placed over the bottom half of the device affixed to Matthew's skull. The surgeon will not need to make any judgments about where to put it. The probe will go through the holder and stop automatically at the target area.

He selects the right-size probe from the stainless-steel tray held by Gerry Beveringen, and sets it aside. The frame is ready, the coordinates have been checked a dozen times.

"No," he says. "We'll scan again." Another cross check. He will inject air into the brain, take more scans and make sure the frame's positioned for exactly the right spot. "Then," Uematsu says, "if we are, I put the needle in."

Vince clears the OR for the scans.

11:30 A.M. It has taken 45 minutes and two injections of air to learn that the black dots of air highlighted in the scanning images are right on target. "Better than textbook, better than perfect," Uematsu exclaims for the first of many times this day. "Now. Now we're ready to go."

The probe is in place, the needle tip resting on the target. Gerry wheels over the Frequency

Lesion Generator, irreverently referred to as the "cooking machine." It is the only gallows humor of the day. But it is accurate.

The electrode is hooked up to the source of current. Gerry squirts a clear gel on a tinfoil-covered rigid plate and inserts it under Matthew's back. Then he runs a wire with an alligator clamp to the retractor handles and hooks it up. "Grounding Matthew" he says to no one in particular. "Grounded."

"In case something breaks," Uematsu explains.

11:43 A.M. "Set for seventy-five degrees for ninety seconds," Uematsu orders Gerry. The dials are set.

"Okay," Uematsu says, "cook." He forces a smile. No one returns it.

Through the same hole, Uematsu positions the probe four more times in the same plane to create four other tiny lesions around this first central lesion. Some at 90 seconds, some at 45 seconds. All at 75 degrees Centigrade. "Cook," he orders. "Cook," again. "Cook." "Cook." The lesions are less than an eighth of an inch apart, all on the right side. That's Matthew's right, his right hemisphere, his right cingulum. It's close to noon.

The right side is pronounced finished, and a new set of scans is taken to confirm the lesions. "There," says Uematsu quietly pointing to a perfect circle of black blots. "All there. Perfect. Better than the textbook. Now, ready to do the left side."

12:15 P.M. "Do you know how we learned how long to cook?" Uematsu asks as he makes the second burr hole. "Egg whites. We picked egg whites in 1967, in our first studies, to see how long and how hot to go through egg whites and create a hole of the right diameter that would not close up."

Over the next two hours, five more lesions are placed in the cingulum on the left side of Matthew's brain. The air target studies are again done to verify the placement, then they "cook", the heated tip cutting the brain. Then more scans make sure the lesions are sufficient and in place.

3:40 P.M. Steve Derrer has awakened Matthew and escorted him to the recovery room. Uematsu and others have talked to Matthew's family. "Perfect." Uematsu announces. "Better than the textbook." But they all must wait now, to see if the "textbook" surgery was not just successful in its execution, but also in its goal.

Matthew's neurologist is nervous. There's much that can still go wrong, he says. Brain damage or return of the seizures that might have found an alternative pathway for the abnormal electrical signals [could occur].

6 P.M. Matthew wakes fully and talks a "blue streak," but then unexpectedly lapses into a stupor. He apparently is unable to talk, move his limbs or arms. An angry, upset neurologist says. "It's not looking good." They take Matthew back to the OR for an emergency scan. Everything looks okay. The doctors hope the problem is temporary from swelling that will subside. Matthew's parents are with him all night.

Wednesday, November 28. 11 A.M, eighth floor of the neuroscience wing: Matthew is propped up in bed in room 811, eating seedless red grapes from a plastic bag, half watching a television set suspended from the corner of the ceiling above his bed. His mother is all smiles, his father grinning.

"God, we are happy today," his mother says. "I knew it all the time. He's doing just great." Matthew has no pain, not even a headache, but he is still somewhat stunned and slow to react. Full recovery from the surgery is still days or more away, although he will return to Spring Grove Hospital on Sunday if all goes as planned. After six months without rages, they'll know if the cingulotomy has brought success—peace and the chance for a better life.

This morning, little more than a week after his operation. Matthew remembers names and faces slowly, but he does remember. His arms and legs and toes work. He can talk. "Rodgers," he says after his mother's prompt of a visitor's first name. "Writing a book," he says. A moment later there's a smile, which broadens when his father says quietly, "Perfect. So far, perfect. Better than the textbook."

Over Memorial Day weekend, 1991, six months after Matthew's surgery, his parents are still careful not to trumpet their hope. But all the signs remain positive. Over the holiday, Matthew is spending most of his time on a home visit with

his family, and weekend leave from the hospital is now regularly scheduled. Matthew's social worker has begun the process of enrolling him in a special course at the hospital that teaches independent living skills—cooking fundamentals, washing clothes—because paperwork is under way to place him in a community-based group home.

"There have been no rages since his operation," Matt's mother says. "He's still having seizures, but no rage episodes at all. And he seems to have much, much better control of his anger. It doesn't escalate into chaos. He takes the time to calm down when he becomes angry. We think we have a success here, but the doctors—and we—still don't know how long it will last.

The absence of experience is a lingering reminder of the ongoing ignorance surrounding the new psychosurgery—and of the continuing political, medical, and social isolation of patients like Matthew and of his family. There is still a giant wall of timidity surrounding surgical treatment of psychiatric and behavioral disorders that turns away heads and minds. Even in the wake of success, the doctors don't want to go public with their endeavor. Lost in the silence most of all is that there are newer psychosurgical treatments for mental illness that need cheering on. So far, the cheerleaders are mostly the families of patients. And even their cheers are muted, reflecting the cautions and concerns of the medical profession.

"Matt's still scared." his mother says. "We are, too. That suddenly something will happen. When Matt comes on visits, he gets angry with me at times because he senses that I'm still wary of being alone with him. I'm still remembering those rages, his physical strength: how he could hurt others and himself. It hurts Matt now to think that I'm leery of him, that I'm afraid to be alone around him."

Confidence that the scars made in his brain can keep control of his mind will take time to build. Meanwhile, the family cautiously moves ahead.

Epilogue: The week before Christmas, 1991, I talked at length with Matthew's father, the cockeyed optimist who always believed that his son deserved another, surgical chance for a life free of rages.

"Everything," he told me, "is looking good. The best news is that Matthew is now living in a low-security area [of the state hospital] and has great freedom. We're working hard to get him into a group home next, and since he's been free of rages for more than a year now, we think this will work out."

"What will Matt do for Christmas?"

"He'll be home with us and the family. It's gonna be a great Christmas."

As we spoke, I sensed some reserve in the father who has seen too much to be sanguine and too little to be cynical. And yet, there was a future to hope for, to plan and to execute for Matthew and his family. A future of relative tranquillity and contentment, this Christmas and next.

Reference

Moniz, E. (1937, May). Prefrontal Leucotomy in the Treatment of Mental Disorders. In *American Journal of Psychiatry* 151:6, June 1994 Sesquicentennial Supplement.

Noonan, D. (1989). *Neuro: Life on the Frontlines of Brain Surgery and Neurological Medicine*. New York: Simon and Schuster.

Restak, R. (1976). The Promise and Peril of Psychosurgery. *Saturday Review.*

Stavro, B. (1980, January/February). Psychosurgery Resurgent. *Politics Today.*

Figure 5-6. Dr. Herbert Wagemaker, biological psychiatrist. (Illustration by Jim Rooney.)

READING 5E

THE BLOOD OF MADNESS

Mary Long

In explanation of the assassination of John F. Kennedy in November of 1963, the Warren Commission stated "one bullet pierced J.F.K's back and neck, then John Connolly's chest, wrist and hand, and ended up on the Governor's stretcher virtually pristine" (Grunwald, 1991, p. 44). This has become known as the dubious "magic bullet" theory. Within the illness perspective there have been numerous magic bullets; treatments which suddenly burst onto the scene, offer great promise, but upon further experimentation, prove ineffective.

In 1969, neurologist Oliver Sacks used the "miracle drug" L-Dopa on a group of chronic patients who had been frozen in sleeping sickness for decades. They made remarkable, albeit, temporary recoveries. Collateral effects of the treatment were so severe that some opted to stop treatment and return to silence. The role of Sacks was played by Robin Williams in Awakenings.

The notion that blood impurities were a factor in schizophrenia was investigated by Louisiana physician Robert G. Heath. Non-psychotic prisoners were injected with "taraxein", a substance obtained from the blood serum of schizophrenics. "All subjects developed symptoms which have been described for schizophrenia" (Heath, et. al., 1958.)

In 1972, Dr. Robert Cade, Director of Renal Medicine at the University of Florida, and inventor of Gatorade, began doing research with dialysis in the treatment of schizophrenia. He reasoned that dialysis cleansed the blood of substances associated with the disorder. He was joined in this research by his close friend, Dr. Herb Wagemaker, now a biological psychiatrist in Jacksonville, Florida. Their research produced much controversy. Was it a significant advance in the treatment of a dreaded disorder? Or was it another stray magic bullet? Mary Long's The Blood of Madness *examines the issue. The postscript provides an update.*

By the time she was 20, Linda Cook had already seen 45 psychiatrists. Tormented by an unrelenting madness, she found conventional therapy of little or no value. When she tried to tell people how she felt, they changed shape in front of her eyes. The Devil ceaselessly shrieked advice, generally suggesting violence; singing hymns in her church choir, Linda would dream of murder.

In desperation, she committed herself to a state mental institution but soon ran away. For months thereafter, she drove around the South, "made up like the witches in MacBeth," boiling over with chaotic chatter and wrecking one car after another.

In 1972, when she was 29, Linda developed high blood pressure. Her mother took her to Shands Hospital at the University of Florida in Gainesville. There, they consulted renal specialist Robert Cade.

After he had treated her high blood pressure, Cade told Linda he wanted to look into her schizophrenia. With ready access to kidney dialysis

Mary Long: The Blood of Madness. *Science Digest,* August, 1983. Reprinted with permission of Herbert Wagemaker, MD.

machines, he had considered using them to help schizophrenics.

Concluding that she had very little to lose, Linda agreed. One large needle was stuck into her wrist, another into her groin. She watched as her blood shot into the tubing, thick and straight as a red cable. For six hours, the blood was cycled through the dialysis machine, an artificial kidney that filters out impurities before returning the blood to the body. At the end of the session, she hobbled out of the laboratory, left the hospital and hitch-hiked home.

For five days, Linda did not hallucinate. Gradually, her mind cleared and her speech became coherent. For the first time in years, she could concentrate. Within 13 weeks, after being dialyzed once a week, she was free of all the symptoms of schizophrenia. Miraculously, her affliction seemed to have been cured.

Linda remains well to this day. She can continue without dialysis for a period of up to five months before her symptoms begin to creep back.

Robert Cade feels he has found an answer to the anguish of schizophrenia in some patients. The vast majority of the medical community vehemently—and perhaps rightly—disagree.

Cade's Basic Principles

The principles behind Cade's theory are quite simple. Studies have long indicated that schizophrenia runs in families, evidently passing from afflicted parent to child. The problem thus seems to be in the genes. "The most likely result of such a genetic abnormality would be an enzyme defect," Cade says. "Such a defect in turn could cause an accumulation of a particular substance within the blood, which, if it were toxic, could cause schizophrenia. And if that substance were toxic and in the bloodstream, it seemed to me that I could remove it with dialysis. I can remove all kinds of things from the blood with that machine."

Schizophrenia, once known as dementia praecox, is a catastrophic disorder that usually strikes during late adolescence. Almost everything about its cause and treatment is fraught with uncertainty. There are, however, certain consistent symptoms: hallucinations, faulty contact with reality, bizarre—often violent—behavior and withdrawal from other people. Some experts believe that the disorder, if it is indeed a single disorder, is the result of disastrous interpersonal relationships in childhood. Others consider it a biochemical disturbance. The prevailing view at the moment is that it is a combination of the two. Only one thing is certain: No one is certain that he knows for certain.

For three years, Linda was Cade's only schizophrenic patient. Then another young woman—who carefully scheduled her first appointment around her regular visit to an exorcist—was put on the machine. She improved even more readily than Linda. Then a young man joined the group and made progress. Soon, Gainesville professor of psychiatry Herbert Wagemaker was referring his other severely afflicted schizophrenic patients to Cade. Most of them improved as well. By 1978, Cade reported that 16 of 25 patients he had treated at Shands had either completely recovered or shown marked improvement.

Despite such results, most researchers are not impressed with Cade's figures. And for compelling reasons. Since the time Cade first reported his findings, the National Institute of Mental Health (NIMH) has funded four independent studies of schizophrenia and dialysis. Only one—conducted by Wagemaker himself—has been reported to reproduce Cade's results. It is important to understand what scientists mean by the word "reported." A finding can be reported without the detail necessary for another scientist to try to replicate the result. That can only be found when the study is published. When one scientist says to another "Publish," he is, in effect, saying "Put up, or shut up."

The other three investigators were traditional controlled, double-blind, cross-over studies. Over a period of weeks, schizophrenic patients received both real and sham dialysis treatments. Neither the patients nor the researchers knew which was which. The system was designed to rule out the possibility that the patients were improving not because of filtering of the blood but, rather, because of a positive psychological reaction to treatment by a powerful and complicated machine.

In two of these studies—at the NIMH itself and at the University of Maryland School of Medicine—researchers came up empty. (The third, in progress at the University of Washington School of Medicine, reports equally disappointing preliminary findings.) With few exceptions, the patients showed no improvement whatsoever. As families of schizophrenics continued to deluge Cade with hopeful phone calls, fellow medical specialists began dismissing him as a charlatan, out to exploit human misery for his own gain.

The controversy shows no signs of abating. And Cade shows no signs of wavering. To be sure, many of his reasons for believing in his theory seem sound. Chemicals from the blood of dialyzed patients were analyzed by Roberta Palmour of the University of California, Berkeley, and Psychiatrist Frank Ervin of UCLA. In a number of cases, an abnormal beta endorphin was found. Four studies in the United States and Germany, however, failed to replicate the finding.

Cade had suspected for some time that such a chemical might be his toxin. Beta endorphins are hormones, produced by the pituitary gland, that are taken up by the cells of the brain, where they can influence behavior. For instance, a rat whose brain is injected with large quantities of beta endorphin becomes catatonic, its body so stiff it can be laid like a tiny bridge across the space between two bricks. As the endorphin wears off, the rat grows first lethargic, then frantic. Catatonia is often an aspect of schizophrenia, and Cade's recovering patients often become frantically hyperactive, and some begin to convulse.

A normal human beta endorphin has 31 amino acids: the one in the fifth position is methionine. But in some of the baths studied by Palmour and Ervin, the fifth was leucine. Present in relatively high concentrations in the first baths, it declined in the course of treatment.

Cade speculates that the body can't properly metabolize the abnormal amino acid; its concentration thus builds steadily until, eventually, it causes schizophrenia. None of the published NIMH-funded studies checked the baths of their patients; instead they looked at spinal fluid and found no anomalies in the beta endorphins.

The doctors who conducted those studies maintain that Cade's results are nothing more than good examples of the placebo effect at work. "With dialysis, you bring the patient into the hospital for an experiment, and a number of things change for that patient," says psychiatrist Charles Schultz, formerly of the NIMH and now at the Medical College of Virginia. "They can get therapy more often; they feel very special because they are in an important and interesting project. These are very withdrawn people, and a great deal of time, care and enthusiasm is given to them."

Psychiatrist William Carpenter and psychologist Thomas Hanlon, who participated in the NIMH-sponsored work at the University of Maryland School of Medicine, note that some of the improvement the subjects evidenced might have been due simply to the discontinuation of antipsychotic drugs, which often have strong and unpleasant side effects.

Psychiatrist Robert Waters, who worked with Dr. Rex Gentry on the University of Washington study, offers an intriguing explanation as to why some patients might have found dialysis beneficial. "Blood is a powerful symbol," he says. "When the families of these patients come in and look at the tubing on the machine, it has a potent effect on their emotions. The literature is considerable on the psychological influence on a normal person hooked up to a dialysis machine; you can imagine what happens with people who are not psychologically normal. Some of my patients have believed that their blood was being siphoned from them and returned flushed with poisons or that it was extracted and sold."

A more positive delusion, based on the belief that dialysis is good, could presumably have a powerful—and constructive—effect. Cade himself does not deny this possibility. "We unquestionably have a placebo effect with dialysis," he concedes. He is now conducting experiments at Shands to determine just how great a role the phenomenon plays in his studies.

Observing Improvement

Such psychological variables notwithstanding, Cade remains convinced that dialysis works for some schizophrenics. Of the NIMH findings, he says, "They dialyze for eight weeks and the patients don't appear to be getting well, so they think, 'forget it.' But we've had a number of patients who, after fourteen or sixteen weeks, looked only a little better and were certainly still sick. We continued to dialyze them, and at thirty-two weeks, lo and behold, they were observably improved."

If dialysis begins removing toxins from the blood after the first treatment, why should recovery take so long? Cade believes the answer lies in the fact that blood chemistry is only part of the schizophrenic puzzle. In order to get well, patients must also get over the destructive effects of previous treatments. "The behavior—the survival techniques—learned on a psychiatric ward are quite different from those taught in schools or skyscrapers or polite society. They've learned that if someone looks at them twice, they should scream bloody murder. How long will it take them to unlearn this behavior?"

While Cade's dialysis research is earning him sharp—even hostile—criticism, it is by no means the first time he has sparked such controversy. Pioneering the use of Imuran, an immunosuppressant, to treat rheumatoid arthritis and lupus, he drew both rage and ridicule from colleagues. Nevertheless, points out internist Gerald Stein at the University of Florida, the drug is now widely used for arthritis that is not responsive to standard treatments.

Cade's real problem may be that he doesn't fit the mold of the conventional medical specialist. To more territorial practitioners, his comparatively free-wheeling approach to problem-solving sometimes seems like irresponsible poaching on other disciplines. One psychiatrist, for example, scornfully refers to Cade as a "renegade nephrologist."

Even worse, from the point of view of the purely research-oriented, may be Cade's unabashed, commercial pragmatism. A prolific inventor, he is the man who developed Gatorade—named after the University of Florida Gators—the first of the glucose-electrolyte fluid-replacement drinks. Since then, he has gone on to produce medical equipment, light alcoholic drinks and a football helmet with an internal hydraulic network designed to reduce head injuries. "He walked around wearing the helmet,"

Stein reports, "having people hit him on the head with baseball bats."

It is not yet certain whether Cade's dialysis experiments will work out as well as his earlier reports indicated. If they indeed prove successful, the most likely explanation will be that he has found a particular group of schizophrenics who respond especially well to this type of therapy. In the opinion of Dr. William Carpenter, who worked on the University of Maryland study, "Schizophrenia is a single label that is applied to what may well be multiple illnesses, which may have any number of different forms and causes. Although our study does not exclude the possibility that a hemodialysis-responsive subgroup exists, there is little evidence that such is the case." Cade is beginning to put schizophrenics into two distinct classes: those who respond to dialysis alone and those who respond to dialysis supplemented by drug treatment. Curiously, women appear to be more responsive to dialysis alone than men are.

Supplemental Funds

Experimentally verifying such findings will be a long and expensive process and money is in short supply. Currently, Cade pays for the dialyses of Linda Cook and his five other schizophrenic patients out of his own pocket. His most consistent source of supplemental funds is a University of Florida sorority that sponsors a dance to raise money for his work.

Though few other people seem willing to finance—or in some cases even acknowledge—Cade's studies, he is not utterly alone in experimenting with the dialysis-schizophrenia link. Research now under way in Italy is doing much to buttress the Gainesville experiments. Though the Italian study has not been placebo-controlled, the research group has been dialyzing as many as 25 patients at a time for over three years, with an impressive improvement rate. These researchers, too, believe they are dealing with a specific group of people who are "dialysis responders."

Cade is under no illusions as to the need for extensive study and corroboration of his findings. He, like others, takes a skeptical attitude toward his results and is willing to see them scrutinized.

"In everything," he says, "I want to be able

to ask a question and, if I want, do studies that answer that question. The attempt to deprive me of my right to ask a question and seek its answer is what has bothered me most."

Linda, who is today active as the head of the Linda S. Cook Foundation for Behavioral Research, adds this: "I do not believe dialysis is an end in itself. Rather, it's just one tool to be used until a better answer can be found. I believe that the treatment is totally legitimate. I even feel that the studies that show the treatment doesn't work have as much validity as our studies. It's just as important to find out why it didn't work as it is to find out why it did."

References

Grunwald, L. (1991, December). Why We Still Care. *Life*, 35+.

Heath R.G., et. al (1958, April). Behavioral Changes in Non-Psychotic Volunteers Following the Administration of Taraxein, the Substance Obtained From Serum of Schizophrenic Patients. *American Journal of Psychiatry*, 114, 917-920.

Postscript

I interviewed Doctors Cade and Wagemaker via telephone conference call in January of 1994. They are still using dialysis with schizophrenia and are even more convinced it is not a stray magic bullet. They related case after case of successful treatment; people who were incapacitated by schizophrenia and are now living productive lives. Carol North, diagnosed with schizophrenia in early adulthood, was treated with dialysis and recovered. She is now a physician. Her story is told in her book Walk of Silence.

Their current treatment regimen consists not only of monthly dialysis, but includes dietary restriction and antipsychotic medication. Analysis of freeze-dried residue from the urine of dialyzed schizophrenics revealed high levels of casein and gluten. These substances are implicated in schizophrenia. Thus, sources of casein, like dairy products, and gluten, wheat and other grains, are restricted. Dr. Wagemaker is very much impressed with the new antipsychotic medication clozapine, which not only blocks dopamine, as other neuroleptics do, but also serotonin. In combination, these treatments comprise a powerful arsenal against schizophrenia.

Cade and Wagemaker feel that other researchers have failed to duplicate their results because of faulty procedure and methodology. The major critical studies were done on groups of only seven and fifteen patients; too small to derive valid results. William Carpenter, participant in the National Institute of Mental Health study at the University of Maryland, would not share his data with Cade and Wagemaker. Clinicians often misdiagnose bipolar disorder as schizophrenia. To support this, Dr. Wagemaker gave one hundred bipolar patients, previously misdiagnosed as schizophrenic, lithium. Sixty went on to "do very well; work, and lead normal lives." Some patients do not respond until a year, yet cases were counted as failures" in only a few months. Critics claim that successes were not really schizophrenic.

Cade and Wagemaker are frustrated that some of their work goes unpublished and grants are not funded. "I'm sorry," I told them. "What can you do?" lamented Wagemaker. Ultimately, to determine whether the treatment is a "magic bullet," requires the opportunity to fire the gun.

"You sly son of a bitch, Chief!" exclaims McMurphy.

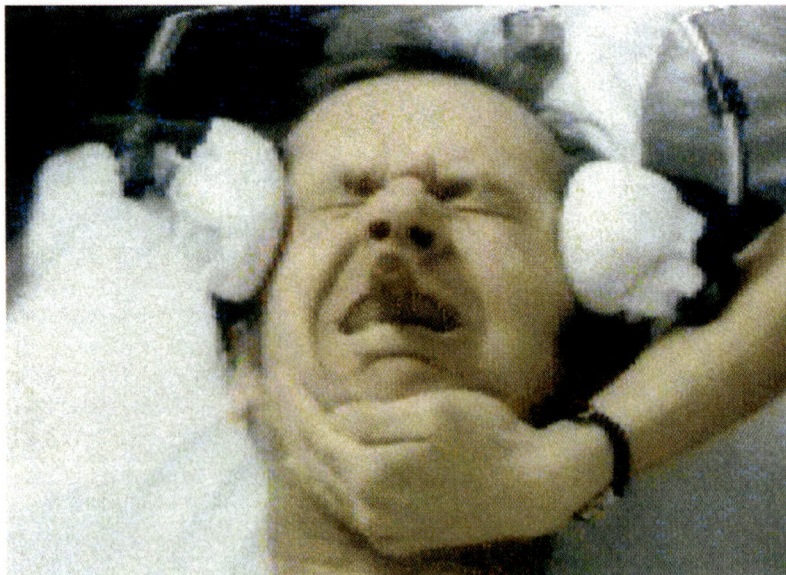

Moments later, electroshock is administered.

Figure 5-7. From the movie *One Flew Over the Cuckoo's Nest*. (Copyright © 1983 by The Saul Zaentz Company. All rights reserved.)

READING 5F

ELECTROSHOCK: FIFTY YEARS LATER

Russ Rymer

Ken Kesey's 1962 masterpiece, One Flew Over the Cuckoo's Nest, *tells the story of Randle Patrick McMurphy, an inmate who tired of weeding peas at a penal farm and feigned madness to be moved to a perceived malleable mental institution. He befriends giant Chief Bromden, whose tribe was ravaged by alcoholism when salmon fishing was ruined by a hydroelectric dam. He pretends to be deaf and mute to avoid the fate of his tribespeople. As McMurphy challenges the authority of the institution, the staff exacts stronger control measures.*

"Sentenced" to electroshock therapy, the pair anxiously waits in the hall. McMurphy, played by Jack Nicholson in the 1975 award winning movie, offers the Chief a piece of gum. Solemnly, the Chief utters "Ummmm, Juicy Fruit." They bond. McMurphy enters the treatment room. Electrodes are attached and the shock delivered. McMurphy writhes in violent pain. Although this segment lasted only a few seconds, it left the public with an indelible, adverse image of electroshock therapy.

What is the present status of electroconvulsive therapy? How is it performed differently today? What are its strengths and weaknesses? What is it used to treat? What are its collateral effects? The following article, Electroshock: Fifty Years Later, *answers these questions.*

The two are certainly strangers and veritably neighbors, their homes separated by a few golden miles of rolling California countryside and the mile-long span of the Golden Gate Bridge. They come from similar backgrounds—he from a prosperous East Coast family, she from one of prominence in the West. They are alumni of the same institution: Napa State Hospital for the Mentally Ill. But on the central issue of their lives, they could not be further apart. Leonard Roy Frank and Susan Hale are divided by the thing they have most in common: their experience with electroshock therapy, the practice of passing electrical current through a patient's brain to relieve symptoms of mental illness. The treatment saved her life, she says. But it very nearly ruined the rest of his.

Considering that electroshock therapy has only been used for half a century, Susan Hale's familiarity with it is almost dynastic. She had her first treatment 30 years ago, soon after leaving the University of California at Berkeley, and her most recent one last month. A heavy woman with a blunt manner and a sharp intelligence, she lives in the Canal District of San Rafael, a brackish alley of relative poverty in one of the richest counties in the nation. Ten blocks from the town's main street, familiar to moviegoers as the real-life backdrop for the film *American Graffiti*, her tiny subsidized apartment is decorated with photos of her patrician past, and vivid oils of flowers she painted while in an asylum. It seems to be Hale's lot in life to know wealth, security, health, and sanity by proximity, as the birthright she never quite received.

Hale was troubled from her earliest days. She first attempted suicide at the age of five, swallowing two bottles of aspirin when her parents left her at boarding school. "I was manic-depressive," she says. "But usually, I was manic." It was for mania that she saw her first psychiatrist, and received her first shock treatments, when she was 21. "They didn't really work," she recalls. "I left the hospital still feeling pretty much the same. They call it manic. I call it high."

In her early 30s, she suffered a breakdown, left her job as an executive receptionist, and began her slide into a precarious life on the wrong side of the tracks and, often, the wrong side of the law. One night in 1975, she ran amok in her Canal District neighborhood, rampaging through the streets in a red nightgown and tearing a local bar to pieces with a steel knife sharpener. She was detained by the police; the adventure earned her a stay in Napa State Hospital.

"It's a dangerous place," she says. "I prefer it in jail."

But the bottom didn't entirely fall out until ten years later. She remembers the morning. "I'd been to a great party the night before," she says. "The next day I was so depressed I couldn't get out of bed, couldn't wash my hair, couldn't eat, couldn't do anything. I was immobilized. Something in the chemistry of my body had gone haywire. It lasted for two years. I tried everything, every drug known to man, tried therapy, tried taking walks. Nothing worked."

She tried suicide, too—four times. When it was clear that the drug therapies were having no effect and that her life was in danger, her psychiatrist sent her to a colleague, James Mickle, the only doctor in Marin County who still does electroshock, or, as psychiatrists prefer to call it, electroconvulsive therapy—ECT for short.

"Doctor Mickle said that he could save me," Hale says, "and he did."

He booked her into Ross Hospital for a series of six shock treatments. They worked dramatically, lifting the veil that had enshrouded her. In two weeks, she was back home again, her spirits freed.

Hale seemed the model patient for electroshock, waking up easily immediately after each treatment and suffering none of the side effects, such as memory loss, that others report. The depression returned a year later and again

several months after that. Each time it was alleviated with a series of shocks. Finally Mickle put her on a regimen of maintenance ECT—one session each month—that has kept her beyond the grasp of the disease that disfigured her life.

Many of the years that Hale lost to manic depression are lost to Leonard Frank completely; he simply can't recall them. He passes the standard memory test of his generation—he remembers where he was when John Kennedy was shot. But remembering Kennedy's presidency is another matter. Frank is not a victim of mental illness. He is a victim of the cure.

In 1962, Frank was a recent arrival in San Francisco, a young graduate of the Wharton School of Business. He had left his real estate job, grown a beard, and was spending his time studying philosophy and religion. He had, in short, dropped out.

His family was concerned enough to call in a psychiatrist, who found in Frank's long hair and lack of ambition ample evidence of schizophrenia. Armed with that diagnosis, they had Frank involuntarily committed to a series of mental hospitals, including Napa State. He was given 50 insulin treatments, where comas are induced with injections of insulin, and 35 ECT treatments. When he was released, after nine months of incarceration, he moved into an apartment on San Francisco's Webster Street, wondering who he was, and more importantly, who he had been. "I was a brain-damaged person," he says. "I had lost all memory of the two years before the shocks, and pieces of my life going back as far as ten years. In terms of experience and education, I was a twelfth-grader. But I'd also lost the ability to concentrate, to learn, and to remember what I learned."

He lives in the apartment still. Over the decades it has become a shrine to his effort to rebuild his life. Bookshelves line the walls to the ceiling, packed two deep with the texts he bought to help him recapture his education, and with rows of loose-leaf notebooks. Taking down one of the notebooks, he opens it to a closely lined page covered with neatly handwritten words. The words are arranged in columns, and the columns fill page after page, volume after volume. The later pages are typed, the single words evolving

days were positioned to "ride" the patient—restraining her during her 30 to 90 seconds of neural and muscular mayhem—but two. Two orderlies and, between them, the woman on the gurney, over whom the conversation flutters like chatter over a dinner table. "I know," the other responds, as she sticks three electrodes to the patient's abdomen. It wasn't the technique I minded so much. It was the brutality of it, the inhumanity." She checks the catheters in the back of the woman's right hand "Thank God it's not like that anymore."

"Oh, basically it's not any different," the first orderly says. "But the patient has a much easier time of it."

The patient, in this case, lifts her left arm up to her face and, with anxious fingers, squeezes the bridge of her nose.

"We're ready," the orderly says, and he taps against the wall the familiar tattoo—"Shave and a haircut"—with his latex knuckles.

The answer comes back through the wallboard: "Two bits," and soon Glen Peterson appears in the doorway and walks to the patient's side. He is a tall, mild-looking man in a blue suit and sandals, a stethoscope draped around his neck. He looks her over quickly. The wires from her abdomen are connected to a heart monitor mounted on the wall, which emits a reassuringly regular pinging. The electrodes on her head are connected to another machine, a box the size of a toaster oven, one side of which measures and records brain waves. The other side of the same box is marked ECT, and has wires leading to a pair of hand-sized wands with round metal pads on the end.

The orderly rubs conductive jelly on the patient's temple as Peterson empties a large syringe into her catheter, the first of two injections that will anesthetize the woman and keep her immobile, making her seizure an internal event with few outward dramatics and no chance of broken bones. This is the major modification in "modified ECT."

"Just relax," Peterson says in a hypnotist's honeyed voice as he listens to her heart through the stethoscope. "You'll start feeling dizzy." Her jaw begins shaking, an effect of the anesthesia, and soon her head lolls. The orderly inserts a rubber disk in her mouth to insure that there is no damage to her tongue and teeth; the black end of the disk protrudes from between her lips like the nozzle of a hose.

Peterson gives her the follow-up shot, then lifts her leg and tests her reflexes with a rubber mallet. There is no response.

"This woman had her first mental illness in her twenties," he says. "She's in her sixties now. Her liver and spleen are damaged, so as a result it's not safe for her to have certain drugs. This treatment is the only recourse she has left. Today we'll give her, oh, probably more than a hundred joules, roughly a hundred watts of power for one second."

He steps to the front of the gurney; taking an ECT wand in each hand, he holds one to the woman's right temple and the other to the top of her head. This placement represents another frequent modification in the new ECT—called unilateral because it concentrates the current in one half of the brain, it supposedly causes less memory damage (and according to some doctors, is less effective), than the bilateral method, in which an electrode is placed on each temple.

With his thumb, Peterson presses a trigger on the right wand and a dull thud resonates through the room, the hollow sound of a dropped book. For as long as it takes Peterson to put away the wands, there is no reaction from the shape on the gurney. Then her arms break out in goose bumps, and her seizure begins. Her head seems to strain against the bed, and her face flushes intensely. The orderly holds an oxygen mask over her mouth, pumping her with air from a large plastic bottle. Her feet begin a frenzied, jiggling dance. The heart monitor's beeping races irregular and wild.

After 70 seconds, timed carefully by a nurse with a stopwatch, the episode is over. The strain goes out of the unconscious body and the panic goes out of her pulse. The neck relaxes, and soon she is snoring noisily. Peterson pulls an EEG readout from the machine, a running chart of the patient's brain waves, and tears off a two-inch section showing the four sawtooth jolts of the shock itself and the irregular exuberant swings of the seizure. He jots the patient's name on it, and as she is wheeled out to make way for another, he leaves for the adjacent room, the provisional office he inhabits three mornings a week, the mornings he gives up the talking cure for the electrical one.

"Most of my patients are referrals," he says, dropping the scrap of EEG paper on his desk. "There aren't a lot of doctors who do this anymore. I'd say maybe fifteen or twenty in the Bay Area, out of a couple thousand psychiatrists. There's a stigma. There's a lot of bad press."

"Even though there's no objective test to show there's any memory loss from this technique, the protesters are still out there calling us Nazis and brain burners. They can always find some doctor willing to come up to the state capital and ignite a Brillo pad with an electric spark or cook an egg or something. As if that had anything to do with it."

Critics, unimpressed with the reformed reputation of the new ECT, do not see Leonard Frank as a relic of the psychiatric Pleistocene; rather, they view his experience as a dramatic example of what can happen with even the most refined of modern techniques. "How do I know these techniques aren't new?" Peter Breggin asks. "Because I was giving modified ECT at Harvard in 1963, and it's the same old thing. It's as dangerous as it ever was." Breggin is perhaps the foremost among ECT's critics, a psychiatrist who takes time out from his Bethesda, Maryland, practice to speak against shock at conventions and on talk shows and to testify against it in court. "ECT is inherently damaging to the brain," Breggin says, "for a very simple reason. The combination of electricity and seizures is bad for the brain."

While shock doctors maintain that Breggin's accounts of the effects of shock therapy are misleading and anecdotal, they have a harder time refuting his observation that there is no solid theoretical explanation for ECT's effectiveness. "We don't know exactly how it works," Richard Weiner says. "But we know a lot. We know that ECT causes biochemical changes in the brain." Research on the matter is so tentative that doctors are free to subscribe at will to any of a handful of competing notions: that neurotransmitters such as norepinephrine are affected, or

that the seizures change the way the brain receives chemicals that regulate perception of pleasure and pain. "I have the only really good mainstream theory," says Max Fink, good-naturedly discounting the efforts of friends and colleagues. "The seizure causes the brain to produce a hormone which regulates the levels of other bodily hormones essential to our well-being. It's a magic substance, somewhat similar to insulin for diabetics. We haven't found this hormone yet, but I've made up a name for it. I call it 'antidepressant.'"

Critics have a simpler explanation. "It's so uncomplicated, it's embarrassing," says Breggin. "ECT causes organic brain syndrome. It's in DSM-III. Look it up." DSM-III, the diagnostic bible of the American Psychiatric Association, describes organic brain syndrome as any generalized disorder of the brain. One common feature of brain damage is a temporary delirium, feeling of well-being, and feeling of release from physical or mental ailments. Another feature is temporary or permanent amnesia.

"All ECT does," John Friedberg concurs, "is produce brain damage, which some people like." Friedberg, a neurologist in Berkeley, California, has been an outspoken critic of ECT ever since he first witnessed it while in medical school in the late 1960s. "I'm a libertarian," he says. "If you want brain damage, it's your prerogative. It's what people get with alcohol, or drugs. But there's no more effective way than ECT. It's more effective than a car wreck, or getting hit with a blunt instrument. It's more effective than anything except possibly a good case of herpes simplex encephalitis with massive hemorrhaging."

Ironically, many early users of shock therapy would have agreed with Friedberg. "I think disturbance of memory is probably an integral part of the recovery process," Abraham Myerson reported of his experience with ECT in 1942. "It may be true that these people have, for the time being at any rate, more intelligence than they can handle and that the reduction of intelligence is an important factor in the curative process." Others conjectured that ECT was somehow able to cause selective brain damage, killing only those neurons that were diseased or problematic.

Their modern colleagues would disagree—

vehemently. "The possibility of brain damage is absolutely refuted," Glen Peterson says, "by brain scans, by neuropsychological studies, by autopsies, by animal studies, and by analysis of cerebrospinal fluid and blood chemicals. There are certain chemicals that leak from damaged nerve cells that aren't detected in ECT patients."

Other doctors, while admitting that the evidence against brain damage is inconclusive, feel the burden of proof should be on the other side. "I can't prove there's no brain damage," says Max Fink. "I can't prove there are no other sentient beings in the universe, either. But scientists have been trying for thirty years to find both, and so far they haven't come up with a thing."

Nor are donors convinced by tales of permanent memory loss. "There may be some spotty losses of the time during the treatment, and sometimes of a period before the treatment," Weiner says. "And there is absolutely no evidence that the ability to learn new things and then recall them is impaired. Where there is anecdotal evidence, it is not borne out by controlled studies."

The anecdotal evidence runs both ways. There is Norman Endler, a psychologist living in Toronto, who was repelled by electroshock when he witnessed it as a student in the 1950s, but who decided to undergo a series of treatments to help his depression in 1976. His book about his recovery, *Holiday of Darkness*, tells of his total lack of permanent side effects. And then there is Marilyn Rice, who underwent a series of eight bilateral treatments during her stay at the Psychiatric Institutes of Washington, D.C., in 1973. She lost one complete year, parts of the previous two decades, and the "vast edifice" of her vocational knowledge. As a result, she also lost her high-level job as an economist with the Commerce Department.

There are, doctors admit, a lot of people who think they have memory problems following ECT. Proving the provenance of such problems can be difficult, since presumably they may have been caused by the patient's mental instability, not by the cure. It's normal, doctors point out, for a person who has had shock to be more sensitive to the least sign of memory trouble, elevating the importance of normal, everyday lapses.

Such uncertainties do not dissuade Marilyn Rice. She has joined with 224 other former shock patients in the Committee for Truth in Psychiatry, which lobbies for strong informed consent laws. Recently it has been fighting the efforts of psychiatrists to have the FDA change its classification of shock machines. Currently, the machines are listed as Class III, a category including devices like pacemakers that can be lethal if they misfunction, and others deemed experimental or dangerous. "We aren't trying to ban ECT," Rice says. "I know what it means to have a breakdown—every organ and gland in your body is either overworking or not working, your heart is pounding, every nerve is sending the wrong signals. For a state of physical suffering of nervous origin, ECT relaxes the mind. It's like a cocktail multiplied by a million. The trouble is, nobody has told the truth about this. There is always permanent memory loss. It's something the patient has to know before giving consent."

Consent, however, can be a tricky business in psychiatry. Patients who refuse shock are faced with the specter of being evicted from expensive private hospitals when their several months of insurance run out, only to languish in state institutions. A series of ten electroshock treatments can run $12,000 or more, but the expense may be reimbursed by insurance plans that will not pick up the tab for lengthier alternatives such as counseling or extended hospital rest. Patients are often on drugs during the time they must make decisions about electroshock. They are further faced with a psychiatric Catch-22: Those who reject treatment are denying their illness and showing a pathological resistance, and thus need the treatment more. According to some patients, who recall lying about the benefits of the technique just to escape it, "Thanks, I feel better" may be, for some, the modern way of saying, *"Non una seconda. Mortifere."*

Linda Andre knows these issues by heart; she claims to have been coerced into a series of 15 shock treatments with veiled threats, while on drugs, and without any accounting of its dangers. Citing the consent issue and others, she has filed a $110 million suit against New York Hospital, her doctor, and the manufacturers of the ECT machines.

Last fall, at the annual conference of the

National Association for Rights Protection and Advocacy, she addressed a group of psychiatric support workers and ex-patients. Among those listening to Andre and others in the gilded basement of the Portland, Oregon, Marriott were Peter Breggin and Leonard Roy Frank.

"A set amount of shock has a very different effect on different brains," Andre said. "When I was released in 1984, I was told that my memory deficit would cure itself in about six weeks. I went home. I didn't recognize my roommate, or where my clothes had come from. People called up and said 'Hi,' but I didn't know who they were. Did I have a college education? I read articles I'd written in magazines and didn't know what they were about. After six weeks had passed it began to dawn on me that this wasn't going to get any better.

"It's possible to build a new sense of self after shock, but it's hard, and you have to do it alone. My friends and I had nothing in common anymore. We didn't have a shared history, because I didn't know the history. I was ashamed. I can't think like I used to, can't remember new ideas easily. There's no way I couldn't feel inferior to the person I used to be."

"Do you know what they called me in grade school?" she said. "'The Brain.' Isn't that ironic?"

After her speech, Andre left the hotel to take in the sights. She had been excited about the chance to get a glimpse of Oregon, until friends told her she'd been to Oregon before.

Andre's lawsuit may make hers the most celebrated case of ECT during the next couple of years. Mary Rose's is more typical for its quiet obscurity. The ex-teacher from eastern Pennsylvania has no pulpit, and wants no audience. Mary Rose is not her real name, and she talks about her experience only with her privacy guaranteed by the anonymity of a phone line.

"I don't believe I'd be alive today, except for ECT," she says. Her suicidal depression was alleviated with two series—25 treatments in all—of electroshock. She regained her sanity, but lost 10 years and believes she lost some thinking ability as well. She has no memory of her sickness, and no memory of her first marriage, either. But she'd do it all again.

"It's pretty hard to accept the memory loss," she says. "My husband teases me all the time, tells me what a great first date we had. I can't read well now. I can't tell you much about current events. It's hard to get me into an intelligent conversation. But I function. I didn't lose my creativity. I can tell you when I got pregnant, and I can tell you about my new son, how wonderful he is. I have new friends, and my old friends accept me. And I have my family. I've lost a lot of my life. But I'm alive.

"Before anybody takes ECT," she says, "it should be the last resort, and they should be made aware of what can happen. But if the pain is that bad, it's an option. For me, it was worth trying, and I'd do it again, but I wouldn't do it lightly. If you're out the window and standing on the ledge, come back in and try shock."

A week after the Portland conference Leonard Frank is back in San Francisco, attending to his correspondence, spending his morning before the computer he has bought to help him index his ideas and catalogue his thoughts. Ten miles to the north Susan Hale is coping as best she can with the latest tragedy of a life that has been spent in harm's way. Jeff, her companion of three years, has been found dead in the back seat of his car; dead after a long illness, a victim of the alcoholism he was never able to shake. His parents send Hale a photograph of him, and she puts it on the table. Unlike the last crisis, she will have to face this one without him.

Across the bay in Oakland, in the basement of Providence Hospital, Glen Peterson hears the knock on the wall. "Shave and a haircut," it calls. And he answers, "Two bits."

This patient, like the last, is female and elderly. "She's chronically mentally ill," he says as he hustles through the post-op ward, past the gurneys of reviving surgery patients, and into the ECT room. "Two weeks ago she was violent, kicking, hallucinating. Now she's calm. She feeds herself. Today's her last treatment."

The woman is especially reliant on ECT because she has neuroleptic malignancy syndrome—a rare, sometimes fatal reaction to antipsychotic drugs—that has caused her feet and hands to shrivel and curl. Standing beside her gurney, Peterson holds one of her little fists and asks her, "Can you tell us what caused your hands to shrivel up?" She ignores him and he repeats himself more loudly. "Do you remember what I told you about why your hands shriveled up?"

"No," she says in a shy, tiny voice.

"Do you remember?" he persists, trying to elicit even a modicum of conversation, as her head, with the electrodes perched above each eyebrow, rolls back and forth on the pillow. "Do you remember? Do you remember?"

Anesthesia is injected, and soon it takes hold. Peterson lifts her left leg, with a blue terrycloth sock on the foot, and taps her knee occasionally with the mallet until it ceases to respond.

He moves to the front of the gurney and places the electric wands gently against her head.

The goosebumps start and the face strains. Roseate clouds of blood blossom and fade under the exposed skin of her abdomen. The sound of her electronically monitored heartbeat fills the room and the post-op ward, where other patients awaken groggily from their various misfortunes, and it fills the vacant office where the scraps of EEG paper, tiny messages of desperation and hope, the tattered evidence of *grand mal* seizures intentionally induced, litter the desktop like so many fallen leaves. The sound of her heartbeat gallops frantically for a while, and in a while, it quiets down.

Postscript

In 1977 ABC News presented Madness and Medicine, *a documentary which portrayed grim conditions and coarse treatments in American mental hospitals. Segments were filmed at Napa State Hospital. Leonard Frank, Ted Chabasinsky, and Marilyn Rice were interviewed. The film fueled sentiment to close mental hospitals. This issue will be covered more thoroughly in Chapter 10,* The Social Perspective.

At One With the Universe. (Photograph by Jim Rooney.)

Chapter 6

THE HOLISTIC PERSPECTIVE

The most recent perspective to emerge in American mental health is the holistic. Its theoretical underpinnings are not new. Holistic is derived from the Greek word *holos* and entails treating the whole body, instead of its parts, in a total environment. Oriental Taoists, Native American healers, and Shamans throughout the world have employed methods today considered holistic. Modern technology has provided a means to improve techniques and conduct research on their effectiveness.

Some consider this perspective an offshoot of the illness perspective, as it is concerned with general medical conditions and their relationships to abnormal behavior. The illness perspective, however, is more concerned with "body" explanations and treatments of the disorders. During the 1600s, French philosopher Rene' Descartes presented a dualistic view of man, divided into "mind" and "body" components. The mind controlled cognition and affect; the body executed the mind's plan. Defects in body could be treated without inclusion of mind. This philosophy contributed to the separation of psychology and medicine. Present-day metaphor, likening the mind to a computer and the body to a machine, only reinforces this distinction.

The holistic perspective, on the other hand, is concerned with the interaction of mind and body. This approach perceives the mind and body as so integrated and interrelated that efforts to distinguish the two are unnecessary and misguided.

Thus, the human being is best understood as a **fluid, yet static, integrated, interdependent, reciprocal, and complementary organism.** It is fluid, in that it can adapt to environmental demands, such as extremes in temperature; static, in that it regulates internal states, such as body temperature at a constant level; integrated, as all organ systems are connected; interdependent, as the lungs require the nourishment of blood pumped by the heart, and the heart, the oxygen procured by the lungs; reciprocal, in that change in one system affects others; and complementary, as the bladder stores the urine produced by the kidneys.

The origin of Western holism can perhaps be traced to Gestalt psychology. The Gestalt school was a group of German psychologists who studied perception during the early part of the century. Gestalt is a German word which translates "a ghost-like image that lingers." Think of the most joyous day of your life. What is instantly recalled is the Gestalt. It is a physical, psychological, or symbolic configuration or pattern so unified as a whole that its properties cannot be derived from its parts.

One of the basic premises of Gestalt psychology is that perceptually the whole is greater than the sum of its parts. An individual voice may sing beautifully. When voices combine, harmony is created. While most of us cannot recognize in which key a melody is played, we can recognize it played in any key. We can comprehend the National Anthem whether played solemnly by the United States Army Band, matchlessly sung by Whitney Houston during the Super Bowl as the Gulf War raged, or dese-

Figure 6-1.
Michael Andretti
(AP/Wide World Photos)

crated by Roseann Arnold. We think in patterns or wholes.

Not only is the whole greater than the sum of its parts, but it is also dependent on each. In 1992, Michael Andretti led the Indianapolis 500 by four laps with just ten to go. All elements of man and machine were operating optimally, when his car stopped dead because of a broken fuel pump. Defects in seemingly insignificant parts can render the organism, whether mechanical or human, dysfunctional. The cause of a specific problem may be quite removed from its overt symptoms. A pinched nerve can produce extreme pain in a distant part of the body.

Canadian Hans Selye has been a pioneer in furthering our holistic understanding of man. He initiated the study of stress and its ability to cause illness. While studying endocrinology, he noticed that only certain symptoms were specific to a particular disease. Most symptoms can indicate a variety of diseases. Medicine should concentrate not only on specific diseases, he argued, but on the "syndrome of just being sick," which is common to virtually all diseases. Psychological, social, and biological factors must all be considered in order to fully understand the patient's condition (Malmo, 1986, pp. 92-93). During a period of medical specialization, such global concern is often lacking.

Stress Research: Issues for the Eighties was published in 1983, a year after Selye's death. Selye had been ill while writing the book, and commented on the first page, ". . . I do not consider my work on stress to be finished—far from it! I know very well that I shall never see the end of this study. . . . I think I can safely say, without exaggerating the vitality of this work, that it will go on forever, as long as biology and medicine exist, alongside the study of psychology and sociology." This is the essence of holism.

Thus, holistic practitioners are sensitive to all aspects of a patient's existence. They attempt to convey to the patient how biological, psychological, and sociological factors can interact to produce illness, and that its cause may not be directly related to its symptoms. People are more resilient under stress when they are healthy. They are less susceptible to disease. Holistic practitioners teach people how to live healthy lives.

Where the primary emphasis of the illness perspective is on the treatment of existing disorders, the holistic perspective is more concerned with three levels of their prevention: primary, preventing the development of disorders; secondary, early intervention to deter exacerbation; and tertiary, which attempts to limit or minimize damage.

Holistic practitioners employ a variety of therapies and interventions. Among them are stress management, diet, exercise, goals and values clarification, biofeedback (developing an awareness of an ability to control internal bodily functions), and psychoneuroimmunology. All of these have received scientific scrutiny and have demonstrated some degree of empirical validity. Others include chiropractic, homepathy, acupuncture, dance and music therapy, rolfing (deep massage and manipulation), and meditation.

Five articles have been selected to portray the holistic perspective. The first, *Psychoneuroimmunology: The Interface Between Behavior, Brain, and Immunity* by Steven F. Maier, Linda R. Watkins, and Monika Fleshner, describes recent advances in this fascinating new field. The second article, *The Mastery of Stress*, is an edited chapter from *The Stress of My Life* by Hans Selye. It is a concise description of what he learned in fifty years of stress research. The third article, *Influence of Aerobic Exercise on Depression* by I. Lisa McCann and David S. Holmes, is a testimony for the psychological benefits of exercise. The fourth article, *Diet for a Small Madman: Food Chemicals and Behavior* by Christopher Norwood, examines the role of diet in attention-deficit/hyperactivity disorder. The fifth article, *The Pace of Life* by Robert V. Levine, explores the link between Type *A* personality and heart disease.

Reference

Robert B. Malmo, "Obituary for Hans Hugo Selye." *American Psychologist*, Volume 41, Number 1, January 1986.

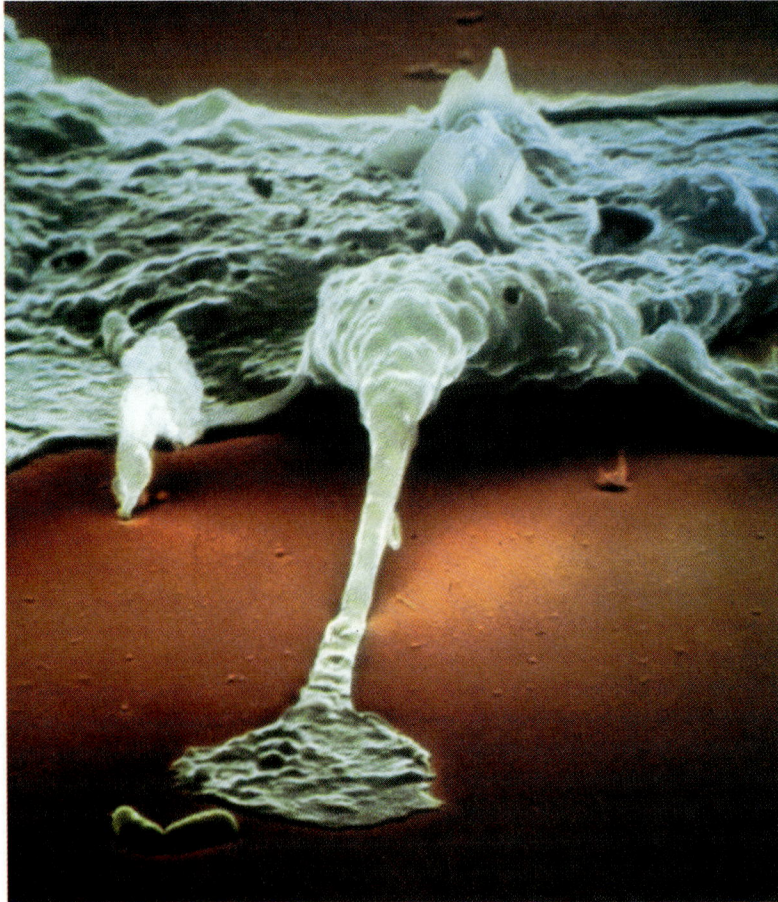

Figure 6-2. Phagocyte Stalking Bacteria. (Image produced by Lennart Nilsson, originally published in *National Geographic*, June, 1986, Vol. 169, no. 6. Photograph © Boehringer Ingelheim Pharmaceuticals, Inc. All rights reserved.)

READING 6A

PSYCHONEUROIMMUNOLOGY: THE INTERFACE BETWEEN BEHAVIOR, BRAIN, AND IMMUNITY

Steven F. Maier, Linda R. Watkins, and Monika Fleshner

In 1981, The Journal of the American Medical Association *reported the case of a young Philippine-American woman who was diagnosed with systemic lupus-erythematosus, a disease in which the body's immune system attacks healthy organs. She was recommended an aggressive therapeutic regimen to reverse her immune system's assault. She refused treatment and returned to her remote native village. Her shaman removed a curse that had been placed on her by a former lover. In three weeks she returned to the United States completely cured. Her physicians were astonished (Hall and Goldstein, 1986).*

*Hans Selye, previously described as a proponent of the holistic approach, is credited with the theory of how the body adapts to stress in the three phases of the **general adaptation syndrome**. In the first phase, the alarm reaction, the body has recognized a real or perceived demand upon it. The autonomic nervous system controls involuntary processes, like cardiovascular function, respiration, digestion, and neurotransmitter levels. Simplistically, it is subdivided into two branches. The parasympathetic branch operates during periods of emotional calm and its purpose is to conserve resources to be used in an emergency. The sympathetic branch operates under stress. It prepares us for "fight or flight" by mobilizing the body's resources as quickly and efficiently as possible.*

Once the alarm has triggered the activation of the sympathetic system, and accomodations are made, the phase of resistance begins. The entire organism has been stimulated to optimally deal with the stress. Relative comfort results; we have gained our "second wind." Healthier individuals can tolerate more severe and protracted stress. Metaphorically, they have "thick" phases of resistance.

The third phase is exhaustion. If the defenses of the body are inadequate or if the stress is too great or chronic, the weakest point in the system becomes vulnerable. Damage may result. It may be minor or fatal. A poorly conditioned jogger may experience a muscle cramp or heart failure.

A psychosomatic disorder occurs when a general medical condition is caused, contributed to, or exacerbated by stress. The mechanism, or explanation, of how stress causes illness is known in many cases. People with chronic high blood pressure who experience extreme stress may suffer brain hemorrhaging, or stroke. Excessive secretion of gastric juices in a vulnerable stomach may produce ulcer.

Can stress adversely affect the body's immune system making it more susceptible to serious illnesses, such as cancer? To demonstrate this, it must be shown that the organism is indeed integrated;

Steven F. Maier, Linda R. Watkins, and Monika Fleshner: "Psychoneuroimmunology: The Interface Between Behavior, Brain and Immunity, American Psychologist, December 1994, Vol. 49, no. 12, 1004-1017, #0003-066X/94. Copyright © 1994 by the American Psychological Association. Reprinted with permission of the authors.

the brain, nervous system, immune system, and affected organ are all connected. If the mind can make us ill, can it also heal? Can psychology affect the course of a serious illness? The following article, Psychoneuroimmunology: The Interface Between Behavior, Brain and Immunity, *shows indeed, that the organism is integrated and reciprocal, and that although the mechanism by which stress may influence the course of disease is not fully understood, it is surely plausible.*

The purpose of this article is to provide psychologists with an overview of the new field of psychoneuroimmunology (PNI), which has developed over the past 10 to 15 years. A detailed review is not possible here; various aspects of PNI have recently been given extensive review (Ader & Cohen 1993; Ader, Felten, & Cohen 1991; Cohen & Williamson, 1991; Kemeny, Solomon, Morley, & Bennett, 1993; Plotnikoff, Murgo, Faith, & Wybran, 1991). Neither is the purpose to review our own work in this area. Instead, our goals are to provide (a) a sketch of the basic core facts that led to the coalescence of a new discipline, (b) some indication of the possible functional significance, of the basic aspects of organization that have been discovered, (c) a feel for some of the exciting possibilities provided by PNI, and (d) some cautions to note. We will concentrate on the "whys" rather than provide a list of studies. For example, in our discussion of stress and immunity we will not provide extensive documentation that stress can alter immune function—that is well-known and has often been reviewed. The "hows" (what type of stressor, which hormone is the critical mediator, etc.) have also been reviewed elsewhere. Instead, we will attempt to rationalize why it is that stress alters immunity and why this might be adaptive and functional, or might have been adaptive in evolution, rather than simply being a curiosity. These are the questions that psychologists typically ask when they are presented with work in this area. Discussions such as these often will be, of necessity, quite speculative. However, it is our belief that the psychologist will be as captivated by this field as we are only if some of these evolutionary–functional possibilities are elaborated, so that the connections between behavior and immunity come to make intuitive sense.

PNI is the study of interactions between behavior, the nervous system, and the immune system. It grew from the realization that the immune system does not operate autonomously, as had often been supposed. The typical view, held as recently as 10 years ago, was that the immune system was a closed system. It was thought to be driven by challenges from foreign substances (antigens) and regulated by soluble products produced and released by immune cells (lymphokines or cytokines, more generally). These products serve both to communicate between immune cells both locally and at distant sites and to control the progress of the immune response. Although antigens do initiate immune responses and cytokines do regulate immune processes, a wide array of recent research demonstrates that there are bidirectional communication pathways between the immune system and central nervous system (CNS), with each providing important regulatory control over the other.

As will be noted, immune function can require global alterations involving the entire organism (e.g., a shift in energy balance) as well as the more usually considered local processes (e.g., selective rapid multiplication of T cells in a lymph node in response to a detected antigen). Only the CNS can orchestrate such widespread outcomes in a coordinated fashion. Thus the CNS must be able to exert control over some aspects of the immune response. Conversely, in order to accomplish this function, the CNS must receive information about events in the body (e.g., an infectious agent has penetrated the skin) and the status of immune processes. Indeed, the immune system serves as a diffuse sensory organ to provide the brain with a variety of input. Thus the immune system controls neural function, and the CNS controls the immune system. Of course, the existence of neural–immune interactions permits behavioral–psychological events to enter the matrix; if neural processes regulate immune processes, then there is a pathway by which psychological factors could impact immunity. Conversely, if immune processes alter neural function, then they can also potentially impact on behavior, emotion, and thought. PNI, then, is the study of these complex interactions between neural, immune, and behavioral processes.

The multidisciplinary nature of PNI makes this review somewhat complex. We ask the reader to bear with us, for we believe that this field is of great potential significance for psychologists. A brief preface might help orient readers and keep them aware of why specific topics are included and presented in the order that they are. We begin with a brief description of the immune system, as many readers may not be familiar with its organization, and without some understanding, it is not possible to see how interactions between behavioral and immunological processes might be adaptive. (Readers familiar with basic immunology can easily skip this section.) We next describe why it is that the immune system is now thought to be under neural regulation. After establishing the basis for thinking that there is a communication pathway between the CNS and the immune system, we briefly review what is known about psychological modulation of immune function. We then consider the other direction in the bidirectional pathway between the immune system and the CNS and review connections from the immune system to the CNS and immune modulation of behavior. The final section focuses on the functional significance or the reasons why—why would it be reasonable for stress, for example, to impact on immunity and why the observed pattern of behavioral changes that occur during immune challenge are both logical and adaptive. This section delves into the evolution of immunity, the costs of immunity (any biological process has costs as well as benefits), and issues of energy balance to attempt to come up with a rational set of reasons. The point of view that we develop is speculative, frankly, but it makes sense to us. We end with some conclusions and the hope that we have convinced the readers that this field is on to something.

The Immune System

The purpose of this section is to provide the necessary basics to understanding interactions between behavior and immune function. The major thought is that the specific immune response to an invading pathogen (virus, bacteria, etc.) is a process that extends over many days and requires complex coordination between many different types of cells that have to interact with each other in very circumscribed ways. It is a dynamic process over time, not a discrete or punctate response.

The immune system is so-called from the Latin term *immunis*, meaning "exempt," and is the body's defense against invading pathogenic microorganisms and tumors, as well as being an important component of tissue repair processes after injury. It is divided into *innate* (or nonspecific) and *specific* acquired immunity. Innate immunity refers to one's resistance to pathogens, which is present from birth and which operates in a nonspecific way without regard to the exact nature of the pathogen (e.g., whether it is a pneumococcus bacterium, a polio virus, or some other). There are a wide variety of innate immune defenses. Some are anatomical (e.g., the skin prevents the entry of many pathogens and its acidity limits bacterial growth), some are physiological (e.g., mucus contains substances that can destroy bacterial cell walls), and some are phagocytic (e.g., macrophages can engulf and destroy microorganisms that they contact). Perhaps the most important innate defenses are provided by the inflammatory and acute phase responses, which will be described later.

Specific immunity is acquired, rather than innate. It involves two separate but related processes—recognition of foreign, "nonself" substances called *antigens* (derived from "antibody generator") and destruction (removal of antigen). T and B lymphocytes are critical to these processes. T cells arise from progenitor cells in the bone marrow and migrate to the thymus where they mature. After maturation, the T cells circulate through the blood and lymph and often reside in secondary immune organs, such as the spleen, and lymph nodes. Each T cell has an exquisitely selective receptor on its surface that can recognize and bind only a single antigen. A given T cell has many receptor sites, but they are all specific for a same single antigen.

T cells cannot recognize antigens by themselves. Instead, the antigen must be presented to T cells in a processed form. Antigen processing and presentation is most often accomplished by immune cells called *macrophages.* Macrophages engulf and digest the antigens. They then excrete chunks of the digested antigen, and these antigen fragments bind onto the exterior surface of the macrophages. It is this processed macrophage-bound form of antigen with which the T cells interact. Thus the macrophages bearing the antigen must contact those few T cells that happen to have the receptor for that antigen. Because there are on the order of 10^{15} different T-cell receptors in humans and each T cell has only one type of receptor, it follows that there cannot be very many T cells with a receptor for any particular antigen. Obviously, to be able to defend oneself against foreign invasion, one needs to quickly create many T cells with a receptor for the antigen that has now invaded the body, so that the antigen can be attacked effectively.

T cells circulate in an inactive form, so the first task is to activate the T cells with the appropriate receptor. To do this, the macrophages release a cytokine called *interleukin-1* (interleukin refers to chemicals that are used to communicate between leukocytes or white blood cells), which activate T cells. There are several different types of T cells. One, the T helper, becomes activated and secretes other cytokines that control the progress of the immune response. For example, the activated T helper cell releases interleukin-2, which promotes multiplication and maturation of T cells that are specialized to fight the antigen that began the process. The cytokines released by the T helper cells also help cytotoxic T cells to multiply, if they are specialized for killing the invading pathogen (i.e., have the appropriate receptor), whether it is an antigen-bearing microbe or antigen-infected cell. Thus the effector of this type of immune defense, called *cellular immunity,* because the killing is being done by a cell, is the activated cytotoxic T cell with a receptor that can detect and bind the antigen. Note that this whole process takes several days, inasmuch as it extends from detecting an invader to creating an army of cells to fight it. Finally, memory T cells develop that have a very long life span and can rapidly recognize the antigen if it is encountered again.

B cells mature in the bone marrow. They also have specific receptors on their surface, but they have a different structure than the T-cell receptor and are called *antibody molecules.* When a B cell encounters the antigen that can bind its receptor (membrane-bound antibody), it begins to divide, and its progeny differentiate into memory B cells and plasma cells. This process is aided by a large number of different cytokines secreted by activated T helper cells. This is a complex multiday process that is orchestrated by interleukins secreted by T helper cells. The T helper cells release different interleukins in a very specific sequence across days, which control the maturation of memory and plasma B cells. The plasma cells develop a new form of its surface receptor that does not remain membrane bound but rather is secreted as a soluble receptor into the circulation. These antigen-specific receptors released from plasma cells are called *antibodies.* The antibody will bind the antigen wherever it comes into contact with it and functions as the effector of this form of immunity, called *humoral immunity.* The process of binding the antigen by antibody is sometimes sufficient to eliminate it. In addition, the bound antigen-antibody complex can activate a blood system called *complement,* which can destroy the antigen. The process of generating antibody takes roughly five or more days. If the antigen is encountered again in the future, the antigen-specific memory cells can produce a much more rapid and potent reaction.

In sum, innate immune mechanisms operate as a first line of defense against invading pathogens. However, the nonspecific nature of the processes allows some pathogens to escape. Specific immunity enables the development of defense responses to a staggering number of potential antigens. Unfortunately, the specificity of the mechanisms involved requires that the response will be slow and delayed, because receptor specificity means that there cannot be many lymphocytes with receptors for any particular antigen. This means that lymphocytes specific to the antigen have to multiply greatly before a defensive response can occur, and the biology of cell proliferation is such that it requires several days. Fortunately, the memory processes built into the specific immune response allow a further encounter with the antigen to be dealt with much more rapidly. This is where the specific response is most effective.

Connections from the Central Nervous System to the Immune System

The purpose of the following discussion is to provide the basics of how it is that we know that the brain regulates the immune system. Two conditions would have to be demonstrated. First, the brain would have to make physical contact with the immune system in some way. Second, alterations in the activity or integrity of these connections would have to affect the course of immune responses to antigens. The first question one might ask concerns how the brain is able to connect with and control other peripheral processes. The brain has two ways to control peripheral organs and processes. One is through the peripheral nervous system. The autonomic nervous system, composed of sympathetic and parasympathetic branches, innervates visceral organs such as the stomach and the heart. Research conducted during the past dozen years (e.g., D.L. Felten, Ackerman, Wiegand, & Felten, 1987) demonstrated that the sympathetic nervous system innervates immune organs such as the thymus, bone marrow, spleen, and, even, lymph nodes. Sympathetic nerve terminals release the catecholamine, norepinephrine, and immune organs and cells contain catecholamine receptors. Furthermore, the terminals of sympathetic nerves in these immune organs make contacts with lymphocytes themselves, and these contacts have the ultrastructural features of synaptic contacts (S.Y. Felten & Felten, 1991). Thus the brain is physically connected to the immune system. The other way in which the brain can communicate to peripheral organs is by releasing factors that cause endocrine glands to secrete hormones into the circulation, thereby enabling the hormones to reach the various organs and bind to hormone receptors on the organs. An example that will be of particular relevance later in this article concerns hormones produced by stress. Many of the bodily effects of stress are produced by steroid hormones called glucocorticoids, which are released from the outer portion (cortex) of the adrenal glands. Indeed, the presence of stress is often defined by the existence of high levels of these hormones in the blood. The sequence of events is that both physical and purely psychological stressors lead cells in the paraventricular nucleus of the hypothalamus to synthesize and release a substance called corticotropin releasing hormone into the portal blood system at the base of the brain. This hormone then reaches the anterior lobe of the pituitary gland where it leads to the synthesis and release of adrenocorticotrophic hormone into the blood. This pituitary hormone ultimately arrives at the adrenal gland where it causes release of the glucocorticolds. The concept is that the brain released something that led to hormones being released into the general circulation. T and B cells have receptors for many of these hormones, including the stress hormones just noted (Plaut, 1987). Activation of the sympathetic nervous system by stressors also leads to the release of catecholamines (i.e., norepinephrine and epinephrine) from the inner portion (medulla) of the adrenal gland into the blood; lymphocytes have catecholamine receptors as well. It is important to appreciate that immune cell function is altered by the action of these hormones and transmitters at receptors on the lymphocytes.

In sum, the anatomical arrangements are such that the brain could control immune cells and organs in the same ways it controls other peripheral structures. However, the fact that the brain can does not mean that it does. Is there evidence that the brain does participate in controlling normal immune responses? If the brain participates in the regulation of the immune system, then brain lesions and stimulation at some brain site(s) ought to modulate some aspect(s) of immune responses. The hypothalamus plays a key role in integrating neural control of visceral processes in general, and so it is not surprising that lesions of the hypothalamus alter the course of a variety of immune processes. This is true for in vivo measures of immune function such as antibody production and rejection of tissue transplants (Macris, Schiavi, Camerino, & Stein, 1970) and in vitro measures such as stimulated lymphocyte proliferation (Roszman, Cross, Brooks, & Markesbery, 1985). Moreover, lesions in other regions can also alter immune function (Nance, Rayson, & Carr, 1987). Conversely, electrical stimulation of hypothalamic regions has been reported to augment several immune parameters (Korneva, 1967). With regard to the autonomic nervous system, chemical destruction with 6-hydroxydopamine can impair some aspects of immune function (Livnat, Felten, Carlson, Bellinger, & Felten, 1985). The point is that destruction or stimulation of neural pathways that are connected to the immune system do, in fact, alter the function of the immune system, and so the connection between the CNS is of real significance, not merely an anatomic curiosity. Similarly, blocking the hormone receptors on lymphocytes alters the course of immunity (Blalock, Smith, & Meyer 1985).

Psychological Modulation of Immunity

The interactions between the CNS and immunity summarized above suggest that psychological events should be capable of altering immunity, because such events both alter and are expressed in neural activity and neural events make contact with the immune system. Research concerning psychological modulation of immunity has centered on two topics—classical conditioning of immunity and the impact of stress.

Classical Conditioning.   Processes under the control of the CNS are generally modifiable by associative processes. Modern interest in the conditioning of immune responses stems from a study by Ader and Cohen (1975) in which a taste paired with an immunosuppressive drug in a Pavlovian manner acquired the ability to suppress antibody responses to an antigen. A large amount of subsequent research (see Ader & Cohen, 1993, for a review) has confirmed the generality of this finding across conditioned stimuli, immunomodulatory unconditioned stimuli, and immune measures. The initial studies used animal subjects, but conditioned modulation of immunity has also been demonstrated in humans (Smith & McDaniels, 1983). Furthermore, both immune suppression and enhancement of the immune response can be conditioned as well (Solvason, Ghanta, & Hiramoto, 1988).

Two questions are at the heart of current research concerning conditioned immunomodu-

lation. One concerns the mechanisms involved: Are the immune changes "directly" conditioned or is something else conditioned (e.g., fear, anxiety, aversion, glucocorticoid release) that is then responsible for the immune alterations? The second involves the potential practical implications of conditioned immunomodulation. Could conditioned immune responses occur in real-life settings and influence disease processes, and could conditioning procedures be used in clinical settings?

Indeed, there is promise of clinical application. In a classic study, Ader and Cohen (1982) explored the development of systemic lupus-erythematosus-like autoimmune disease in genetically prone mice. The onset of lupus symptoms can be retarded and survival prolonged by immuno-suppressive drugs such as cyclophosphamide. A neutral stimulus (saccharine flavored water) was paired with cyclophosphamide in a Pavlovian manner. That is, rats were allowed to drink the solution and then were immediately injected with cyclophosphamide. Weekly treatments with cyclophosphamide are required to delay the onset of lupus symptoms; administration of cyclophosphamide every other week has no measurable effect. However, Ader and Cohen (1982) found that the saccharine solution could be substituted for cyclophosphamide every other week and delay the onset of the autoimmune disorder, but only if it had been paired with cyclophosphamide (also see Klosterhalfen & Klosterhalfen, 1983). Moreover, reexposure to the saccharin cue after the cyclophosphamide treatment was discontinued prolonged survival (Ader, 1985). Because cyclophosphamide is quite toxic, as are many chemotherapeutic agents, this sort of use of conditioned immune change may be of considerable benefit. In more recent work (Grochowitz et al., 1991) it has also been suggested that conditioned immunosuppression can delay rejection of tissue transplants, suggesting a use in organ transplantation.

In more general terms, conditioned immunosuppression might be expected to occur whenever an organism repeatedly encounters an immunosuppressive agent in a particular environment. Chemotherapy for cancer is a particularly important example. Chemotherapeutic drugs are chosen for their ability to inhibit the cell division of rapidly replicating cells, among which are cancer cells. However, these agents also inhibit the replication of other rapidly dividing cells such as immune cells. Thus chemotherapeutic agents are immunosuppressive. Indeed, cyclophosphamide is an often used drug for cancer chemotherapy. The repeated chemotherapy is typically done in the same room in the same hospital setting, and so conditioned immunosuppression might be expected to develop. Consistent with this argument, Bovjberg et at. (1990) found that women who had undergone a number of chemotherapeutic treatments for ovarian cancer displayed immunosuppression after simply being brought to the hospital prior to chemotherapy. This learned immune change could easily exacerbate the unconditioned effects of the drugs on the immune system, further compromising the ability of the patients to fight the cancer. The psychologist of learning could suggest many procedures that should reduce the conditioning (e.g., giving the chemotherapy in different environmental contexts, rather than always in the same context). Such work is currently under way.

Stress and Immunity. Much of the current interest in PNI stems from the possibility that exposure to environmental stressors might interfere with the immune response, thereby providing a potential link between stress and physical disease. Because stressors activate both the sympathetic nervous system and the hypothalamo-pituitary-adrenal axis (see Stanford & Salmon, 1993, for a recent comprehensive review), it is not surprising that stressors can impact on immunity. This is because, as noted earlier, plasma catecholamines released by sympathetic terminals and the adrenal medulla, as well as hormones released by the pituitary and the adrenal cortex, participate in the regulation of the immune response.

Indeed, numerous studies conducted over the past 30 or so years have demonstrated that a wide variety of stressors can alter many aspects of the immune response (see Solomon, 1969, for an excellent early example). In animals, acute exposure to electric shocks (Keller, Weiss, Schleifer, Miller, & Stein, 1983), social defeat (Fleshner,

Laudenslager, Simons, & Maier, 1989; review by Bohus & Koolhaas, 1991), maternal separation (Coe, Rosenberg, & Levine, 1988; Laudenslager, Held, Boccia, Reite, & Cohen, 1990), rotation (Esterling & Rabin, 1987)), the odor of a stressed conspecific [member of same species](Zalcman, Richter, & Anisman, 1989), immersion in cold water (Jiang, Morrow-Tesch, Better, Levy, & Black, 1990), restraint (Bonneau, Sheridan, Feng, & Glaser, 1991a, 1991b), handling (Moynihan et al., 1990), intraperitoneal injection of saline (Moynihan, Koota, Brenner, Cohen, & Ader, 1989), and loud noise (Monjan & Collector, 1977) have all been shown to suppress some aspect of immunity. Chronic stressors such as crowding (Rabin, Lyte, Epstein, & Cagglula, 1987) have also been examined. Immune measures have ranged from effectors of cellular immunity, such as the development of cytotoxic T cells to an antigen, to effectors of humoral immunity, such as the development of antibody to an antigen, to nonspecific measures, such as mitogenic stimulation of lymphocyte proliferation. The function of specific cell types, such as macrophages, has also been examined after exposure to a stressor (Zwilling et al., 1990), as has the secretion of soluble mediators such as the interleukins and the development of surface receptors for them (Weiss, Sundar, Becker, & Cierpial, 1989). Stressors have also been shown to alter the migration pattern of immune cells between and into compartments of the immune system such as spleen, thymus, and lymph nodes (Fleshner, Watkins, Bellgrau, Laudenslager, & Maier, 1992). Indeed, it is difficult to think of an aspect of immunity that has not been found to be altered by some stressor.

One question that psychologists often ask when presented with work such as this concerns whether the influence of stress on immunity merely reflects a simple physical impact of painful or arousing events or whether the interaction between stress and immunity embodies some of the more subtle aspects of psychological modulation of stress effects that can be observed in other areas of stress research. The answer is that the impact of stress on immunity cannot be explained in simple physical terms. As an example we chose some experiments from our own research. If several male rats are allowed to live together in a large enclosure, one will become dominant, that is, the alpha male. If a stranger is introduced into the environment, the alpha male will attack the intruder. The intruder begins by engaging in defensive aggression but invariably gives up and adopts species-typical defeat postures. Intruders never beat residents. Being placed into the established territory of the other rat, even for a brief period of time, severely inhibits the production of antibody to antigen administered before the intruder is introduced into the territory (Fleshner, Laudenslager, Simons, & Maier, 1989). This effect is all the more impressive when it is recognized that antibody is not measured until one to three weeks later. However, the important point is that it can be determined whether the inhibition of antibody is produced by the physical aspects of attack, such as being bitten or pushed, or the psychological factor of being defeated. This is because adopting and maintaining defeat postures tend to inhibit the attacks from the alpha male. That is, the two are negatively correlated. Thus one can ask whether it is engaging in submissive behaviors or being bitten and assaulted that is correlated with the reduction in antibody formation. It was the adoption of submissive behaviors—the correlation between time spent in defeat posture and antibody was −.80. Indeed, there were a small number of animals who did not submit at all and received numerous bites. Antibody in these animals was unaffected.

On the human level, acute stressors, such as final examinations (Dorian et al., 1982), battle task vigilance (Palmblad et al., 1976), and sleep deprivation (Palmblad, Petrini, Wasserman, & Akerstedt, 1979), have been shown to impact on immune parameters. More chronic conditions, such as divorce (Kiecolt-Glaser, Fisher, et al., 1987), bereavement (Schleifer, Keller, Camerino, Thornton, & Stein, 1983), and Alzheimer caregiving (Kiecolt-Glaser, Glaser, et al., 1987), also alter measures of immunity. The literature demonstrating these links has been the subject of numerous recent reviews (Ader &, Cohen, 1993; Cohen & Williamson, 1991; Weiner, 1991) and will not be reviewed here yet again. However, it should be emphasized that the study of the psychological modulation of immunity has only

scratched the surface of the relationships that probably exist. Obviously, psychological factors cannot directly contact white blood cells and are capable of altering immunity because they modulate autonomic function and the release of peripheral hormones that modulate immunity. Thus any psychological event that alters these neural and hormonal factors is capable of modulating immunity. As an example, mood states such as depression are associated with dysregulation of the pituitary-adrenal system (Holsboer, Von Bardeleben, Gerken, Stalla, & Muller, 1984), and depressed individuals often have chronically elevated levels of glucocorticoids in blood (Carrol, 1978). As would therefore be expected, immune system dysfunction has often been reported to exist in depressed populations (Irwin, Daniels, Bloom, Smith, & Weiner, 1987; Schleifer et al., 1984). Emotions such as anger and anxiety might also be expected ultimately to impact on immunity (Fleshner et al., 1993). Indeed, thoughts ought to be capable of altering immunity. Thinking about or encountering a learned signal for an aversive or unpleasant event can activate autonomic outflow and the release of hormones and so are capable of impacting on immunity. For example, presentation of a previously neutral stimulus (a light, a tone, etc.) that has come to signal an aversive event can suppress a number of aspects of immunity (Lysle, Cunnick, Kucinski, Fowler, & Rabin, 1990).

This line of reasoning suggests more than the fact that emotions and thoughts impact on immunity. It further suggests that these effects will be subtle and selective. Stressors are not generic events that have identical peripheral outcomes. Different stressors produce different mixes of autonomic activation and hormones (Mason, 1971). For example, one stressor might lead to intense autonomic activation and consequent plasma catecholamine release but relatively little activation of the pituitary and adrenal glands and their hormones. Another might produce the opposite pattern. In addition, the time course of these changes will differ for different stressors, emotions, and thoughts. Moreover, personality, coping processes, and the like modulate the autonomic and hormonal consequences of exposure to stressors (Ursin & Olff, 1993). They too will then modulate the immune consequences of stressors (e.g., Mormede, Dantzer, Michaud, Kelly, & LeMoal, 1988). For example, the impact of final examinations depends on the student's level of loneliness (Kiecolt-Glaser et al., 1984), and the effects of divorce depend on the degree of prior attachment to the partner (Kiecolt-Glaser, Fisher, et al., 1987). This sort of modulation by psychological variables is not restricted to the effects of stress. For example, we noted earlier that repeated chemotherapeutic treatments result in conditioned immunosuppression to cues that regularly precede chemotherapy. However, this conditioning may be restricted to patients who are high in state anxiety, as measured in the hospital environment (Fredrikson, Furst, Lekander, Rotstein. & Blomgren, 1993). Thus different stressors and other psychological events that do impact on immunity may do so in different ways, producing different outcomes.

Yet another complexity stems from the fact that the specific immune response involves a complex cascade of events that extends over many days. The peripheral products of stress play numerous roles in regulating this cascade, and so the effects of stress will of necessity be variable. There will be conditions under which stressors interfere with immunity, have no effect, or even enhance immune measures (e.g., Croiset, Heijneri, Veldhuis, deWied, & Ballieux, 1987, Lysle, Cunnick, & Rabin, 1990; Lysle, Lyte, Fowler, & Rabin, 1987; Rinner, Schauenstein, Mangge, & Porta, 1992). The effects observed will depend on the precise blend, duration, and timing of hormones and sympathetic activation produced by the stressor. For example, Fleshner et al., 1992, and Zalcman, Minkiewicz-Janda, Richter, and Anisman, 1988, have found that a stressor will interfere with the production of antibody to an antigen (measured 1-3 weeks after antigen administration) only if stress occurs within narrow time ranges relative to antigen exposure. In addition, different aspects of the immune response are differently affected by autonomic function and hormones, and so the effects of a particular stressor on immunity might be quite selective, impacting on one kind of immunity but not on another. It is quite possible for a stressor to alter antibody generation, for example, but not

alter T-cell proliferation (Maier & Laudenslager, 1988). Research exploring these sorts of interactions is in its infancy. However, efforts in these directions will doubtlessly uncover a rich matrix of psychological influence.

This discussion also leads to a caution. Not infrequently investigators have drawn sweeping conclusions such as "stress suppresses immune function" from studies that have measured but one aspect of immunity at one point in time. This is akin to measuring a single aspect of neural function (e.g., the release of a single transmitter in a single nucleus) and making claims about what "stress does to the brain." Furthermore, these measures have often been nonspecific and assess some intermediate aspect of the immune response (e.g., production of interleukins, proliferation of cells in response to mitogens) rather than an effector endpoint that detects and clears antigen, recognizes and destroys tumors or virally infected cells, and so forth. The immune system contains a high degree of redundancy, and so the fact that an event might alter an intermediate product or step does not provide convincing information about whether the event in question would impact on a normal endpoint of the immune response (e.g., the production of antibody). Indeed, there are instances in which a condition influences one but not the other (Cunnick, Lysle, Armfield, & Rabin, 1991; Sheridan et al., 1991). It will take a considerable amount of research to distill the truly general principles from the specifics.

Implications for Disease. The popular press is replete with conclusions concerning stress-induced immunomodulation as the mechanism mediating between stress and disease. There is no question that stress can alter immunity and that stress can alter disease, but there is actually very little work directed at determining whether the effect on immunity is causal to the effect on disease. This is an issue because stressors can modulate many factors other than immunity that can impact on disease directly without intervention by the immune system. Some of these factors are biological. For example, numerous experiments have shown that exposure to a stressor can accelerate the growth of implanted tumors (Sklar &

Anisman, 1981). The natural assumption has been that this is because the stressor impacted on immune processes involved in tumor control. However, stressors also alter blood flow, levels of hormones such as prolactin, body temperature, and so forth, all of which can directly affect the rate of growth of a tumor. In addition, human studies allow mediation by behavioral variables. Most chronic stressors (e.g., bereavement) doubtlessly change behavior patterns (e.g., eating, sleeping, drug intake, interaction with others), which can modulate the course of a tumor.

Clearly, careful analytic work is required to tie the impact of a stressor on disease to mediation by immunity. Fortunately, there are a small number of studies that do just that. An elegant example is provided by a series of studies conducted by Ben-Eliyahu, Yirmiya, Liebeskind, Taylor, and Gale, 1991. They worked with a tumor cell that is known to be very sensitive to regulation by natural killer (NK) cells. (NK cells are a type of lymphocyte that does not have to be activated for it to be able to destroy cells and responds in a relatively nonspecific way to a variety of tumor–and virally infected cells.) This gave them the advantage of knowing which aspect of immunity to measure. They implanted these tumor cells in rats and found that a stressor would exaggerate tumor growth and metastasis if it was given within 24 hours of tumor implantation. The stressor also reduced the ability of NK cells to kill tumor cells as measured directly in an assay. The question was then whether the effect on NK cells mediated the effect on tumor growth. Ben-Eliyahu et al. approached this question in two ways. First, they blocked the effect of the stressor on NK cells using a pharmacological agent that had no direct effect on the tumor. However, the agent blocked the effect of the stressor on the tumor. They then used an antibody directed against NK cells to produce the same change in NK activity that the stressor had produced, but without administering the stressor. This enhanced tumor growth. Thus the change in NK cells was both necessary and sufficient to produce the facilitation of tumor development. The same sort of conclusion can be drawn from work by Bonneau et al. (1991a, 1991b) using the herpes simplex virus. More work of this sort will

be needed before we can make confident assertions about links to disease. Nevertheless, it is clear that stress can alter immunity and that this can exert major effects on disease. The next few years of research will determine the role of these links in human disease and will explore whether psychological interventions are capable of modifying the course of disease. A particularly promising study of this sort was reported by Fawzy et al. (1990). They found that cancer patients who received psychiatric group intervention showed an increase in NK cell activity, compared with untreated control participants. Furthermore, this change was correlated with changes in anxiety. Much more work like this is needed and is under way.

Connections from the Immune System to the Central Nervous System

Thus far we have been concerned with the influence of the CNS and psychological processes on immune function. We now turn to the other direction of influence in the bidirectional interactions between behavior and immunity—the impact of immune responses on brain and behavior. We begin with the immune-to-CNS link. The immune response occurs outside the nervous system in the periphery in response to peripheral antigen. For the brain to participate in the regulation of this response it must therefore receive information that an immune response is in fact occurring. Moreover, the generation of a specific immune response is a complex affair extending over a number of days and involving the interaction of many different cell types and mediators. Thus it might even be necessary for the CNS to receive detailed information about the course of the response. As would be expected, both the electrical and chemical activity of the brain do change as immune responses occur. For example, Besedovsky, Sorkin, Felix, and Haas (1977) found hypothalamic neural activity to increase at the time of peak B-cell proliferation to an administered antigen. Similarly, neurotransmitters in the hypothalamus, such as norepinephrine, also show profound changes at this time (Carlson, Felten, Livnat, & Felten, 1987). The antigen used in these experiments was a harmless protein, not an agent that produces illness or disease. Thus it was not illness or disease that altered neural activity; rather, the activity of the brain changed with the progress and course of an immune response per se.

How could this occur? After all, the cells of the immune system, such as T cells, B cells, and the like, have only limited access to the brain, because of the blood-brain barrier. This is a key question that has generated considerable excitement recently. Much of the focus has been on the soluble proteins released by immune cells, the cytokines, during the course of the immune response. These have always been thought of as messengers between cells of the immune system, but they may also converse with the nervous system. Space does not permit a discussion of the many cytokines; thus only one, interleukin-1 (IL-1), will be used as an example.

IL-1 is synthesized and secreted by a number of different cells. However, activated macrophages are the major source of IL-1 during the specific immune response. Macrophages are activated either by engulfing antigen or by a number of chemical signals that bind to surface receptors on the macrophage. Activation of macrophages with virus or bacterial endotoxin produces a release of IL-1 and a subsequent alteration in the electrical activity of the brain (Saphier, 1992), as well as metabolism of the neurotransmitters norepinephrine, serotonin, and dopamine in a number of discrete brain regions (Dunn, Powell, & Small, 1989). These CNS changes to virus and endotoxin are known to be produced by IL-1, because an antagonist to the IL-1 receptor blocks them and the peripheral or central administration of IL-1 produces them (Dunn, 1993). Thus IL-1 and other cytokines may well be the communicators between the immune system and the brain, with potent effects on neural activity.

However, an interesting question remains. IL-1 and other cytokines are large lipophobic proteins and are therefore unlikely to readily cross the blood-brain barrier. Several possibilities have been proposed with regard to how cytokines could then alter neural activity. One is that there is an active transport mechanism to carry IL-1 across the barrier (Banks, Kastin, & Durham, 1989). Another is that IL-1 is able to cross the vascular endothelium in regions of the brain

where the barrier is weak or absent, such as in the organum vasculosum lateralis terminals (Katsuura, Arimura, Koves, & Gottchall, 1990). A final possibility is that IL-1 can stimulate peripheral nerves, such as the vagus, that send afferent input to the brain (Watkins et al., 1994). This suggests that the immune system may truly act as a sensory organ conveying information to the brain.

Immune Modulation of Behavior

The focus in PNI has been on psychological modulation of immunity. However, there are recent suggestions that events in the immune system can also modify behavior. Behavior, thoughts, and emotions vary across time in ways that often seem unpredictable. At the very least, psychological processes sometimes change, even though events in the external environment seem to have been constant. Internal events are doubtlessly responsible for some of these dynamics, and events in the immune system may well be a previously unsuspected part of this matrix.

The first hint of an immune-to-behavior causal link was provided by studies indicating that there is an increase in autonomic nervous system activity and the levels of pituitary-adrenal stress hormones in blood at various stages of an immune response to an antigen (Besedovsky, Sorkin, Keller, & Muller, 1975). That is, the occurrence of an immune response leads to the peripheral physiological equivalent of a stress response. In addition, the pituitary-adrenal response is activated by the same mechanisms that activate their response to stressors. The paraventricular nucleus of the hypothalamus is induced to release corticotrophin releasing factor into the portal blood; that is, the immune response communicates with the brain in order to release the peripheral stress hormones. The communication link is provided by IL-1 and perhaps other cytokines released by immune cells during the immune response (Berkenbosch, VanOers, Del Rey, Tilders, & Besedovskv, 1987). It is important to recognize that in these studies an immune response was elicited by administration of a harmless protein, not a pathogen. Thus it is the immune response itself that produced what appeared to be a stress response.

The foregoing description might suggest that behavioral manifestations of stress will appear at some stages of the immune response. Animal experiments support this contention. Animals exposed to fear or anxiety arousing stimuli engage in a well-characterized set of behaviors including reductions in the following: activity, tendencies to explore novel objects, social interaction, food and water intake, and willingness to engage in sexual behavior. The administration of IL-1 or of substances that stimulate immune cells, such as macrophages, to release IL-1 produce all of these behavioral changes (Dantzer, Bluthé, Kent, & Goodall, 1993).

The behavioral effects of immune products are not limited to stress and stress-related behaviors. For example, we have recently begun to study potential relationships between immune processes and pain. The CNS contains circuitry that, when activated, enhances the pain that results from a painful stimulus, above and beyond that which the stimulus normally produces (see Coderre, Katz, Vaccarino, & Melzack, 1993, for a review). These mechanisms in the brain and spinal cord are especially important because they are thought to be involved in the production of chronic pain pathologies that create so much human misery. All of the studies of these neural mechanisms had activated them through direct electrical or chemical stimulation of the neurons involved. We wished to determine whether there were naturally occurring environmental events that would activate these neural hyperalgesia circuits. We reasoned backwards and asked whether there were circumstances under which it would be adaptive to experience exaggerated pain from a painful stimulus. It seemed to us that illness or injury might be such a condition. During these times it might be useful to be especially attentive to sites of pain. Pain could serve to guide recuperative behaviors, such as licking the site of injury (Bolles & Fanselow, 1980), and lead to the conservation of energy during illness (see below). We conducted a series of experiments in which rats were made ill by administering agents that induce illness, and in all cases a long-lasting hyperalgesic response to pain stimuli was induced (Wiertelak et al., 1994). This does not by itself implicate the immune system. However, in

further studies we demonstrated that the hyperalgesia occurred because the illness-inducing agents stimulated macrophages to release IL-1 (Maier, Wiertelak, Martin, & Watkins, 1993) and that IL-1 did activate the hyperalgesia circuitry in the brain and spinal cord (Watkins et al., 1994). Note that injury as well as pathogenic agents will produce the release of cytokines such as IL-1 (see below).

We are unaware of comparable human studies. However, it would be intriguing to determine whether mood, emotional reactivity, pain, attention, and other processes might be affected by the status of the immune system, even when the immune system is merely responding to harmless as well as pathogenic agents that we all encounter in our daily experience. This could account for some of the seemingly unmotivated mood swings that we all experience.

Functional Significance–Inflammation and the Acute Phase Response

We next turn to a consideration of some of the "whys." Why would it be useful for stressors and other behavioral events to impact on immunity, and why should immune responding alter behavior? In particular, how could it be adaptive to interfere with the immune response? Is this simply pathophysiological or does stress-induced immunosuppression play a physiological role? Another way to inquire into this issue is to wonder why stress hormones are immunosuppressive. Conversely, why should immune responding produce what looks like a stress response?

Until now we have focused on the specific immune response. However, specific immunity is a more recent evolutionary development than innate immunity; it evolved from processes present in innate immunity. Indeed, specific immunity is present only in vertebrates (Reinisch & Litman, 1989). The stress response is far older in evolutionary time. Innate immune defenses are also quite old. For example, phagocytic cells that engulf and destroy particles are present in the sponges, the most primitive multicellular organism known. Thus an understanding of the physiological role of stress-induced immune changes might be illuminated by considering innate immunity and the role of stress.

Inflammation and the acute phase response (see Baumann & Gauldie, 1994, for a review) are particularly important aspects of innate immunity. These are innate or nonspecific because the cells involved do not respond only to a specific antigen or molecule but act on a broad range of substances. There is no antigen-driven multiplication of cells specific for an antigen.

Inflammation. Inflammation is a local response to tissue injury, microbial invasion or infection, and irritants. The purpose of the inflammatory response is to limit damage caused by injury to a local site. In the case of a pathogen, inflammation limits its spread and kills and removes the pathogen through phagocytosis, primarily by macrophages and neutrophils called to the site. In addition, inflammation involves the initiation of repair processes designed to fix any tissue damage. This involves proliferation of connective tissue, production of collagen and elastins, and so forth. The time course of these responses is on the order of hours—inflammatory responses can be observed within 1 to 2 hours after infection, and the acute phase response (see below) occurs 8 to 12 hours after local infection. Recall that the specific immune response requires days to generate effectors that can kill antigen. Thus inflammation and the acute phase response are the first line of defense against agents that have penetrated anatomic and physiological barriers.

Assume that a microbe enters the body or that tissue injury occurs. This activates a number of systems that ultimately lead a variety of cells to migrate to and enter the injured or affected area. The macrophage is perhaps the most important cell. Chemical signals that macrophages resident in the area receive from the initiating events in inflammation and signals that macrophages newly arrived in the area receive from resident macrophages activate the macrophages to produce a variety of products. Some are enzymes that help destroy pathogens and cellular debris produced by injury, and others regulate the activity of a number of other cells. Macrophages can also engulf and destroy microbes. An important point is that many macrophage products act back on the macrophage itself in a positive feedback fashion. For example, IL-1 released from macrophages stimulates IL-6 released from fibroblasts and macrophages themselves, which stimulates further IL-1 release. IL-1 can even induce itself, upregulating IL-1 gene transcription (Schindler, Bhezzi, & Dinarello, 1991). This is noted here because many macrophage products are highly dangerous and can kill healthy tissue as well as pathogens; proteases and lysosomal enzymes are examples. The message is that the inflammatory response has to be limited in some way because of the positive feedback properties involved.

The Acute Phase Response. The inflammatory process is localized at the site of injury or infection. It can trigger a general or systemic response, the acute phase response, that both supports the local reaction and fights infections that are no longer localized and have become systemic. Some of the support involves delivering more needed building blocks, such as amino acids, to the site of inflammation. Other aspects of the support involve the delivery of additional mediators, and still other aspects entail more global metabolic changes that facilitate the cellular processes of destruction of pathogen and repair of tissue, at the same time limiting pathogen growth. IL-1, IL-6, and tumor necrosis factor (TNF) produced by macrophages at the site are critical triggers of this acute phase response (Baumann & Gauldie, 1994). These products stimulate further cytokine release from local endothelial cells and fibroblasts, and when they accumulate in sufficient quantity they enter the circulation and orchestrate the elements of the acute phase response.

The acute phase response involves numerous processes. Leukocytes are produced in bone marrow and then enter the circulation and can migrate to the local site. In addition, a number of enzymatic reactions cause reductions in plasma iron and zinc, both of which are required for the growth of certain pathogens. Acute phase proteins are synthesized and released by the liver. These are a group of about 30 plasma proteins that play diverse roles, such as scavenging and removing cellular debris, promoting destruction of bacteria by activation of complement, for example. Importantly, fever is produced.

Fever is a phylogenetically old mechanism and is highly adaptive. Numerous experiments have demonstrated that reducing fever by various means decreases survival after infection. The increased body temperature produced by fever accelerates a number of enzymatic reactions at the site of inflammation that operate suboptimally under normal circumstances because they can be damaging to healthy tissue, slows replication of microbes, and enhances the rate of proliferation of immune cells. It is important to understand that fever is not just an increase in body temperature. Rather, the set point for temperature is increased in hypothalamic temperature control centers by IL-1 action at the brain (Rothwell, 1992). Thus mechanisms to increase temperature are engaged that decrease temperature loss (e.g., peripheral vasoconstriction and huddling) and increase temperature production (e.g., muscular activity involved in shivering).

Energy Demand and Balance. All of this creates a tremendous energy demand. For example, it is estimated that each degree increase of body temperature requires from a 7% to a 13% increase in caloric energy production or metabolism, depending on the species and circumstances. Furthermore, the production of acute phase proteins and all of the cellular proliferation, production of cytokines, collagens, proteases, and so forth, require a large supply of amino acid building blocks. An energy demand of this magnitude requires changes that range from metabolism to behavior; this can only be coordinated by the CNS.

The cytokines, such as IL-1, IL-6, and TNF, may again be key coordinating elements, both peripherally and through their ability to communicate with the CNS. At the cellular level, IL-1 promotes the breakdown of muscle protein into amino acids (Baracos, Rodemann, Dinarello, & Goldberg, 1983), a process that is responsible for the muscle soreness experienced during infection. IL-1 also increases the availability of glucose for metabolism by peripheral tissues and the release of fatty acids from fat stores for similar use.

Recall that IL-1 and other cytokines produce a set of behavioral changes that are similar to those seen after stress: decreases in activity, exploration, social interaction, and food and water intake. Hyperalgesia was also discussed. All of these are also considered to be part of the acute phase response. Somnolence and increased slow wave sleep can be added to this set of changes. An examination of the list suggests that all of the behaviors are designed to reduce unnecessary energy expenditure, so that available energy stores can be used to fight infection or injury. Reductions in food and water intake might not make sense in this context, but consider that organisms in which these systems evolved must forage to find food and water and that digestion is energy intensive. Indeed, IL-1 and TNF slow digestion. Hyperalgesia should operate to reduce activity and direct behaviors such as licking to the site of inflammation. Increased sleep, particularly slow wave sleep, should reduce the brain's glucose demand, the brain being the body's major user of glucose.

In short, the intense energy demands of inflammation and the acute phase response may require a shift in the organism's entire energy balance, and this can only be accomplished by involving the CNS, so that the array of changes from metabolism to behavior can be orchestrated. This is another important reason why immune products must be able to communicate with the CNS. Again, IL-1, TNF, and IL-6 are key elements of the communication (Kent et at., 1992). Clearly, the suggestion is that the behavioral consequences of IL-1 and immune responding may function as behavioral energy conservation and may have evolved for that purpose.

Glucocorticoids. The level of adrenal glucocorticoids in blood rises sharply during inflammation and is considered part of the acute phase response. Again, cytokines released by macrophages and other cells are the mediators of the increased glucocorticoid synthesis and release from the adrenal cortex (Baumann & Gauldie, 1994). Similar to the sequence of events described above during the specific immune response, the cytokines appear to lead to a glucocorticoid response by acting at the hypothalamus, thus initiating a full hypothalamo-pituitary-adrenal response.

It is important to understand that the peripheral physiological action of glucocorticoids is to mobilize energy (Sapolsky, 1992). Glucocorticoids promote breakdown of muscle protein into amino acids, facilitate the conversion of amino acids and liver glycogen to glucose, antagonize the action of insulin (insulin stimulates glucose uptake into fat and muscle and suppresses liver glucose production), and enhance fat mobilization. In sum, glucocorticolds potentiate glucose increases while further breaking down protein. Here glucocorticoids and IL-1 operate in concert.

These actions produce the energy demanded by inflammation and the acute phase response. A final regulatory factor is required. Recall that a number of potentially destructive substances are released during inflammation and that there are positive feedback loops inherent in the biochemistry. Something must limit this process; an argument can be made that it is glucocorticoids. Glucocorticoids do inhibit or oppose a large number of the key mediators of inflammation. It should be obvious that IL-1, IL-6, and TNF are the key orchestrators of inflammation and the acute phase response, and glucocorticoids inhibit their synthesis at the genetic level (see Barnes & Adcock, 1993, for a review). In addition, glucocorticoids can interfere with the synthesis of receptors for these cytokines, thereby interfering with both the substances and the ability of cells to respond to them. Most or all of the other mediators of inflammation that were omitted from this review for simplicity are also inhibited by glucocorticoids (Barnes & Adcock). The conclusion is that glucocorticoids exert a strong counter regulatory effect on inflammatory processes. Consistent with this conclusion, numerous experiments have demonstrated that removal of the adrenal potentiates inflammation after infection and can lead to septic shock (Barnes & Adcock).

Indeed, one might wonder how inflammation and the acute phase response ever proceed, given that glucocorticoids do rise. Obviously, the issue is one of balance between stimulatory and inhibitory forces. Glucocorticoids restrain; they do not prevent. In addition, glucocorticoids do not rise until a number of hours have passed and many of the early events have already taken place. The cytokines that stimulate glucocorticoids through an action at the brain have to accu-mulate in sufficient quantity to enter the circulation and ultimately alter neural activity. Finally, many of the actions of glucocorticoids are genomic and therefore require substantial periods of time to occur.

The Stress Response. We are now in a position to speculate about why stress impacts on immunity. The first question should be "What is a stress response, really?" It is really a fight-flight response, a set of changes that mobilize the organism for energy production. That is, it involves, a shunting of energy toward muscular exertion and high levels of brain energy use (Sapolsky, 1992). As in the innate immune response, energy stores are mobilized but motor function is enhanced with increases in cardiac output due to increases in heart rate and contractile force and dilation of muscle arterioles, increasing blood supply to exercising muscles. In addition, the sensory side is enhanced—vigilance is induced, pupils are dilated for better distance vision, and so forth.

Although both the innate immune and fight-flight responses require energy mobilization, the energy must go to different places, and the behavioral requirements are completely different for the two responses. In fact, they are roughly opposite. During a fight-flight emergency it would not be useful for energy to be used to produce inflammation and the acute phase response; energy needs to go to the muscles and brain. It would not be adaptive to maintain fever, reduced activity, huddling, shivering, and somnolence. Hyperalgesia would not be adaptive, inasmuch as the organism would be likely to direct attention to sites of injury rather than engage in defense. Analgesia would be desirable, and that is what stress produces (Kelly, 1986). In short, except for the fact that both produce energy mobilization, inflammation and the stress response generally have opposite effects.

What this means is that during a fight-flight emergency it would be adaptive to produce energy and to inhibit inflammation and the acute phase response, should there be injury or infection during the encounter. Moreover, if the encounter is extended with periods of respite during which inflammation develops, it would be adaptive to reduce the innate immune response if the encounter starts again. There is something that does this—glucocorticoids. Therefore, during a fight-flight emergency it would be useful to produce glucocorticoids quickly, rather than several hours after the initiating event. This would produce energy and inhibit the inflammatory response before it can develop, should there be injury. This is exactly what stressors do. Thus, when considering the innate response, there is a clear argument for an adaptive function of stress-induced immunosuppression.

It is possible to continue this line of argument by speculating about evolutionary considerations. The innate immune response is very old in evolutionary terms, probably older than the fight-flight response. Macrophages are extremely primitive cells. After all, defense against pathogens and tissue damage repair is required by even simple organisms. However, fight-flight can come into play only in an organism that has the sensory capacity to detect predators or other dangers, the motor capacity to make organized movements directed away from the danger or to damage the predator, and the integrative abilities to relate the two. Perhaps the fight-flight response evolved out of the inflammatory-response-acute-phase response machinery. Evolution works by using old parts for new purposes; organisms already had a system to defend against damage and infection. Energy was still needed, but it had to go to a different place, muscle and brain. A mechanism existed to produce energy and to reduce the energy demand made by inflammation and the acute phase response by inhibiting them, thereby allowing the energy to go to another area of demand such as muscle. All that was required was to move the glucocorticoid response forward in time. So, perhaps all that was needed was to initiate the hypothalamo-pituitary-adrenal response from a new source. Remember that macrophage-produced cytokines initiate the pituitary-adrenal response by acting at the hypothalamus. So, in the stress response it is initiated by neural input, rather than by peripheral cytokines.

You might also note that stressors, or events that elicit fight-flight, can bear a close resemblance to physical damage or events that produce physical damage. This concept goes back at least to Selye (1936), who viewed inflammation as a prototypical stressor. Interestingly IL-1 and receptors for IL-1 are located in brain (Breder, Dinarello, & Saper, 1988; Takao, Tracey, Mitchell, & DeSouza, 1990). Perhaps physically challenging fight-flight stimuli activate the hypothalamo-pituitary-adrenal axis by activating brain IL-1. It is interesting to note that physical restraint activates messenger RNA for IL-1 in brain (Minami et al., 1991). Physical stressors might even be able to activate elements of the inflammatory response directly, thereby providing a pathway to brain. Perhaps more psychological stressors then evolved other pathways to activate the hypothalamo-pituitary-adrenal axis.

A final consideration is that the specific immune response evolved out of and uses many of the components of the innate immune system. Thus, stress-induced modulation of specific immunity might be a remnant of its effects on innate immunity. In fact, thinking of innate immunity and specific immunity as separate processes may be as misleading as thinking of cellular and humoral immunity as separate.

Conclusions

The major theme of this article is that the immune system and brain form a bidirectional interacting set of processes, each regulating the other. Psychological processes can influence this network and in turn be modulated by it. We hope that we have provided some insight into the adaptive reasons why these links might exist and be sensible. These links provide great promise in terms of understanding health and disease, but as reviewed, a great deal of work needs to be done before strong conclusions are warranted. The issues involved are too important to allow sweeping conclusions at the present stage of knowledge.

It is our feeling that the next few years will be an exciting time in PNI research. Because PNI is a new field, the existing knowledge is, of necessity, first-order knowledge. Classical conditioning can modify immune processes, stress can alter immunity, and immune products can feed back and modulate behavior. However, the complexities, breadth, and richness of the interactions have yet to be elucidated. In addition, the details of the mechanisms involved are largely un-known. In the next few years, work of increasing sophistication at the behavioral, neural, and immunological levels should be accomplished.

PNI is one of the new emerging interdisciplinary fields being driven by the growing realization that systems cannot be understood in isolation. Simply studying immunology at the level of immune cells, neuroscience at the level of neurons, and psychology at the level of behavior cannot capture the complex interactions between levels. Living organisms are not composed of disconnected systems or processes. It is our conviction that progress waits at the interfaces between systems and levels. Comprehension of health and disease in particular awaits such analyses.

References

Ader, R. (1985). Conditioned immunopharmacologic effects in animals: Implications for a conditioning model of pharmacotherapy. In L. White, B. Tursky, & G. Schwartz (Eds.), *Placebo: Theory, research, and mechanisms* (pp. 306-323). New York: Guilford.

Ader, R., & Cohen, N. (1975). Behaviorally conditioned immunosuppression. *Psychosomatic Medicine, 37*, 333-340.

Ader, R., & Cohen, N. (1982). Behaviorally conditioned immunosuppression and murine systemic lupus erythematosus. *Science, 215*, 1534-1536.

Ader, R., & Cohen, N. (1993). Psychoneuroimmunology: Conditioning and stress. *Annual Review of Psychology, 44*, 53-85.

Ader, R., Felten, D.L., & Cohen, N. (1991). *Psychoneuroimmunology* (2nd ed.). New York: Academic Press.

Banks, W.A., Kastin, A.J., & Durham, D.A. (1989). Bidirectional transport of interleukin-1 alpha across the blood-brain barrier. *Brain Research Bulletin, 23*, 433-437.

Baracos, V.E., Rodemann, H.P., Dinarello, C.A., & Goldberg, A.L. (1983). Stimulation of muscle protein degradation and prostaglandin E2 release by leukocytic pyrogen (interleukin-1): A mechanism for the increased degradation of muscle proteins during fever. *New England Journal of Medicine, 308*, 553-558.

Barnes, P.I., & Adcock, I. (1993). Anti-inflammatory actions of steroids: Molecular mechanism. *Trends in Pharmacological Sciences, 14*, 436-441.

Baumann, H., & Gauldie, J. (1994). The acute phase response. *Immunology Today, 15*, 74-8 1.

Ben-Eliyahu, S., Yirmiya, R., Liebeskind, J.C., Taylor, A.N., & Gale, R.P. (1991). Stress increases metastatic spread of a mammary tumor in rats: Evidence for mediation by the immune system. *Brain, Behavior, and Immunity, 5*, 193-205.

Berkenbosch, F., VanOers, J., Del Rey, A., Tilders, F., & Besedovsky, H. (1987). Corticotropin-releasing factor-producing neurons in the rat activated by interleukin-1. *Science, 238*, 524-526.

Besedovsky, H.O., Sorkin, E., Felix, D., & Haas, H. (1977). Hypothalamic changes during the immune response. *European Journal of Immunology, 7*, 323-330.

Besedovsky, H.O., Sorkin, E., Keller, M., & Muller, J. (1975). Changes in blood hormone levels during immune response. *Proceedings of the Society for Experimental Biology and Medicine, 150*, 466-470.

Blalock, J.E., Smith, E.M., & Meyer, W.J. (1985). The pituitary-adrenocortical axis and the immune system. *Clinics in Endocrinology & Metabolism, 14*, 1021-1038.

Bohus, B., & Koolhaas, J.M. (1991). Psychoimmunology of social factors in rodents and other subprimate vertebrates. In R. Ader, D.L. Felden, & N. Cohen, (Eds.). *Psychoneuroimmunolgy* (2nd ed., pp. 807-831). New York: Academic Press.

Bolles, R.C., & Fanselow, M.S. (1980). A preceptual-defensive-recuperative model of fear and pain. *Behavioral and Brain Sciences, 3*, 291-323.

Bonneau, R.H., Sheridan, J.F., Feng, N., & Glaser, R. (199la). Stress-induced suppression of herpes simplex virus (HSV)-specific cytotoxic T lymphocyte and natural killer cell activity and enhancement of acute pathogenesis following local HSV infection. *Brain, Behavior. and Immunity, 5*, 170-192.

Bonneau, R.H., Sheridan, J.F., Feng, N., & Glaser, R. (199lb). Stress-induced effects on cell mediated innate and adaptive memory components of the murine immune response to herpes simplex virus infection. *Brain,*

Behavior, and Immunity, 5, 274-295.

Bovjberg, D.H., Redd, W.H., Maier, L.A., Holland, J.C., Lesko, L.M., Niedzwiecki, D., Rubin, S.E., & Hakes, T.B. (1990). Anticipatory immune suppression in women receiving cyclic chemotherapy for ovarian cancer. *Journal of Consulting and Clinical Psychology, 58,* 153-157.

Breder, C.D., Dinarello, C.A., & Saper, C.B. (1988). Interleukin-1 immunoreactive innervation of the human hypothalamus. *Science, 240,* 321-324.

Carlson, S. L., Felten, D.L., Livnat, S., & Felten, S.Y. (1987). Alterations of monoamines in specific central autonomic nuclei following immunization in mice. *Brain, Behavior, and Immunity, 1,* 52-64.

Carrol, B.J. (1978). Neuroendocrine function in psychiatric disorder. In M.A. Lipton, A. DiMaschio, & K.F. Killam (Eds.), *Psychopharmacology: A generation of progress* (pp. 487-497). New York: Raven Press.

Coderre, T.J., Katz, J., Vaccarino, A.L., & Melzack, R. (1993). *Contribution of central neuroplasticity to pathological pain: Review of clinical and experimental evidence. Pain, 52,* 259-285.

Coe, C.L., Rosenberg, L.T, & Levine, S. (1988). Effect of maternal separation on the complement system and antibody response in infant primates. *International Journal of Neuroscience, 40,* 289-302.

Cohen, S., & Williamson, G.M. (1991). Stress and infectious disease in humans. *Psychological Bulletin, 109,* 5-24.

Croiset, G., Heijnen, C.J., Veldhuis, H.D., deWied, D., & Ballieux, R.E. (I 987). Modulation of the immune response by emotional stress. *Life Sciences, 40,* 775-782.

Cunnick, J.E., Lysie, D.T, Armfield, A., & Rabin, B.S. (1991). Stressor-induced changes in mitogenic activity are not associated with decreased IL-2 production or changes in lymphocyte subsets. *Clinical Immunology & Immunopathology, 60,* 419-429.

Dantzer, R., Bluthé, R.M., Kent, S., & Goodall, G. (1993). Behavioral effects of cytokines: An insight into mechanisms of sickness behavior. In E.B. DeSouza (Ed.), *Neurobiology of cytokines* (pp. 130-151). San Diego: Academic Press.

Dorian, B.J., Garfinkel, P., Brown, G., Shore, A., Gladman, D., & Keystone, E. (1982). Aberrations in lymphocyte subpopulations and function during psychological stress. *Clinical and Experimental Immunology, 50,* 132-139.

Dunn, A.J. (1993). Infection as a stressor: A cytokine mediated activation of the hypothalamo-pituitary-adrenal area. In *Corticotropin releasing factor* (Ciba Foundation Symposium 172, pp. 226-243). West Sussex, England: Wiley.

Dunn, A.J., Powell, M.L., & Small, P.A., Jr. (1989). Virus infection as a stressor: Influenza virus elevates concentrations of corticosterone and brain concentrations of MHPG and tryptophan. *Physiology & Behavior, 45,* 591-594.

Esterling, B., & Rabin, B.S. (1987). Stress-induced alteration of T-lymphocyte subsets and humoral immunity in mice. *Behavioral Neuroscience, 101,* 115-119.

Fawzy, I.F., Kemeny, M.E., Fawzy, N.W., Elashoff, R., Morton, D., Cousins, N., & Fahey, J.L. (1990). A structured psychiatric intervention for cancer patients: II. Changes over time in immunological measures. *Archives of General Psychiatry, 47,* 313-319.

Felten, D.L., Ackerman, K.D., Wiegand, S.J., & Felten, S.Y. (1987). Noradrenergic sympathetic innervation of the spleen: I. Nerve fibers associate with lymphocytes and macrophages in specific compartments of the splenic white pulp. *Journal of Neuroscience Research, 18,* 28-36.

Felten, S.Y., & Felten, D.L. (1991). Innervation of lymphoid tissue. In R. Ader, D.L. Felten, & N. Cohen (Eds.), *Psychoneuroimmunology* (2nd ed., pp. 27-7 1). San Diego: Academic Press.

Fleshner, M., Brohm, M.M., Laudenslager, M.L., Watkins, L.R., & Maier, S.F. (1993). Modulation of *in vivo* antibody response by a benzodiazepine inverse agonist (DMCM) administered centrally or peripherally. *Physiology and Behavior, 54,* 1149-1154.

Fleshner, M., Laudensiager, M.L., Simons, L., & Maier, S.F. (1989). Reduced serum antibodies associated with social defeat in rats. *Physiological Behavior, 45,* 1183-1187.

Fleshner, M., Watkins, L.R., Beilgrau, D., Laudenslager, M.L., & Maier, S.F. (1992). Specific changes in lymphocyte subpopulations: A mechanism for stress-induced immunomodulation. *Neuroimmunology, 41,* 131-142.

Fredrikson, M., Furst, C.J., Lekander, M., Rotstein, S., Blomgren, H. (1993). Trait anxiety and anticipatory immune reactions in women receiving adjuvant chemotherapy for breast cancer. *Brain, Behavior, and Immunity, 7,* 79-90.

Grochowitz, P.M., Schedlowski, M., Husband, A.J., King, M.G., Hibberd, A.D., & Bowen, K.M. (1991). Behavioral conditioning prolongs heart allograft survival in rats. *Brain, Behavior, and Immunity, 5,* 349-356.

Holsboer, F, Von Bardeleben, U., Gerken, A., Stalla, G.K., & Muller, O.A. (1984). Blunted corticotropin and normal cortisol response to human corticotropin releasing factor in depression. *New England Journal of Medicine, 311*, 1127-1137.

Irwin, M., Daniels, M., Bloom, E., Smith, T.L., & Weiner, H. (1987). Life events. depressive symptoms, and immune function. *American Journal of Psychiatry, 144*, 437.

Jiang. C.G., Morrow-Tesch, J.L., Beller, D.S., Levy, E.M., & Black, P.H. (1990). Immunosuppression in mice induced by cold water stress. *Brain, Behavior, and Immunity, 4*, 278-291.

Katsuura, G., Arimura, A., Koves, K., & Gottchall, P.E. (1990). Involvement of organum vasculosum of lamina terminalis and preoptic area in interleukin-1 beta induced ACTH release. *American Journal of Physiology (Endocrinology and Metabolism), 258*, E163-E171.

Keller, S.E., Weiss, J.M., Schleifer, S.J., Miller, N.E., & Stein, M. (1983). Stress-induced suppression of immunity in adrenalectomized rats. *Science, 221*, 1301-1304.

Kelly, D.D. (I 986). Stress-induced analgesia. *Annals of the New York Academy of Sciences, 467.*

Kemeny, M.E., Solomon, G.F., Morley, J.E., & Bennett, R.L. (1993). Psychoneuroimmunology. In C.B. Nemeroff (Ed.), *A comprehensive textbook of neuroendocrinology* (pp. 563-592). Boca Raton, FL: CRC Press.

Kent, S., Bluthé, R.M., Dantzer, R., Hardwick, A.J., Kelley, K.W., Rothwell, N.J., & Vannice, J.L. (1992). Different receptor mechanisms mediate the pyrogenic and behavioral effect of interleukin-1. *Proceedings of the National Academy of Sciences, 89*, 9117-9120.

Kiecolt-Glaser, J.K., Fisher, L.D., Ogrocki, P., Stout, J.C., Speicher, C.E., & Glaser, R. (1987). Marital quality, marital disruption, and immune function. *Psychosomatic Medicine, 49*, 13-25.

Kiecolt-Glaser, J.K., Garner, W., Speicher, C., Penn, G.M., Holliday, J., & Glaser, R. (1984). Psychosocial modifiers of immunocompetence in medical students. *Psychosomatic Medicine, 46*, 7-17.

Kiecolt-Glaser, J.K., Glaser, R., Shuttleworth, E.C., Dyer, C.S., Ogrocki, P., & Speicher, C.E. (1987). Chronic stress and immunity in family caregivers of Alzheimer's disease victims. *Psyhcosomatic Medicine, 49*, 523-533.

Klosterhalfen, W., & Klosterhalfen, S. (1983). Pavlovian conditioning of immunosuppression modifies adjuvant arthritis in rats. *Behavioral Neuroscience, 97*, 663-666.

Korneva, E.A. (1967). The effect of stimulating different mesencephalic structures on protective immune response patterns. *Sechenov, Physiological Journal of the USSR, 53*, 42-50.

Laudenslager, M.L., Held, P.E., Boccia, M., Reite, M.L., & Cohen, J.J. (1990). Behavioral and immunological consequences of brief mother-infant separation. *Developmental Psychobiology, 23*, 247-264.

Livnat, S., Felten, S.Y., Carlson, S.K., Bellinger, D.L., & Felten, D.L. (1985). Involvement of peripheral and central catecholamine systems in neural-immune interactions. *Journal of Neuroimmunology, 10*, 5-13.

Lysie, D.T, Cunnick, J.E., Kucinski, B.J., Fowler, H., & Rabin, B.S. (1990). Characterization of immune alterations produced by a conditioned aversive stimulus. *Psychobiology, 18*, 220-226.

Lysie, D.T, Cunnick, J.E., & Rabin, B.S. (1990). Stressor-induced alteration of lymphocyte proliferation in mice: Evidence for enhancement of mitogen responsiveness. *Brain, Behavior, and Immunology, 4*, 269-277.

Lysie, D.T., Lyte, M., Fowler, H., & Rabin, B.S. (1987). Shock-induced modulation of lymphocyte reactivity: Suppression, habituation, and recovery. *Life Sciences, 41*, 1805-1814.

Macris, N.T, Schiavi, R.C., Camerino, M.S., & Stein, J. (1970). Effect of hypothalamic lesions on immune processes in the guinea pig. *American Journal of Physiology, 219*, 1205.

Maier, S.F., & Laudenslager, M.L. (1988). Commentary: Inescapable shock, shock controllability, and mitogen stimulated lymphocyte proliferation. *Brain, Behavior, and Immunity, 2*, 87-91.

Maier, S.F., Wiertelak, E.P., Martin, D., & Watkins, L.R. (1993). Interleukin-1 mediates the behavioral hyperalgesia produced by lithium chloride and endotoxin. *Brain Research, 623*, 321-326.

Mason, J.W. (197 1). A re-evaluation of the concept of "non-specificity" in stress theory. *Journal of Psychiatric Research, 8*, 123-140.

Minami, M., Kuraishi, Y., Yamaguchi, T, Nakai, S., Hirai, Y., & Satoh, M. (1991). Immobilization stress induces interleukin-1 beta mRNA in the rat hypothalamus. *Neuroscience Letters, 123*, 254-256.

Monjan, A.A., & Collector, M.I. (1977). Stress-induced modulation of the immune response. *Science, 196*, 307-308.

Mormede, P., Dantzer, R., Michaud, B., Kelly, K., & LeMoal, M. (1988). Influence of stressor predictability and behavioral control on lymphocyte reactivity, antibody responses, and neuroendocrine activation in rats. *Physiology & Behavior, 43*, 577-583.

Moynihan, J., Brenner, G., Koota, D., Breneman, S., Cohen, N., & Ader, R. (1990). The effects of handling on antibody production, mitogen responses, spleen cell number, and lymphocyte subpopulations. *Life Sciences, 46*, 1937-1944.

Moynihan, J., Koota, D., Brenner, G., Cohen, N., & Ader, R. (1989). Repeated intraperitoneal injections of saline attenuate the antibody response to a subsequent intraperitoneal injection of antigen. *Brain, Behavior, and Immunity, 3*, 90-96.

Nance, D.M., Rayson, D., & Carr, I. (1987). The effects of lesions in the lateral septal and hippocampal areas on the humoral immune response of adult female rats. *Brain, Behavior, and Immunity, 1*, 292-300.

Palmblad, J., Cantell, K., Strander, H., Froberg, J., Karlsson, C., Gronstrom, M., & Unger, P. (1976). Stressor exposure and immunological competence in man: Interferon producing capacity and phagocytosis. *Journal of Psychosomatic Research, 20*, 193-203.

Paimblad, J., Petrini, G., Wasserman, J., & Akerstedt, T. (1979). Lymphocyte and granulocyte reactions during sleep deprivation. *Psychosomatic Medicine, 41*, 273-285.

Plaut, M. (1987). Lymphocyte hormone receptors. *Annual Review of Immunology, 5*, 621-669.

Plotnikoff, N., Murgo, A., Faith, R., & Wybran, J. (1991). *Stress and immunity*. Boca Raton, FL: CRC Press.

Rabin, B.S., Lyte, M., Epstein, L.H., & Caggiula, A.R. (1987). Alteration of immune competency by number of mice housed per cage. *Annals of the New York Academy of Sciences, 469*, 492-500.

Reinisch, C.I., & Litman, G.W. (1989). Evolutionary immunobiology. *Immunology Today, 10*, 278-293.

Rinner, I., Schauenstein, K., Mangge, H., & Porta, S. (1992). Opposite effects of mild and severe stress on in vitro activation of rat peripheral blood lymphocytes. *Brain, Behavior, and Immunity, 6*, 130-140.

Roszman, T.L., Cross, R.J., Brooks, W.H., & Markesbery, W.R. (1985). Neuroimmunomodulation: Effects of neural lesionson cellular immunity. In R. Guillemin, M. Cohn, & T. Meinechuk (Eds.), *Neural modulation of immunity* (pp. 95-111). New York: Raven Press.

Rothwell, N.J. (1992). Metabolic responses to interlueukin-1. In N.J. Rothwell & R.D. Dantzer (Eds.), *Interleukin-1 in the brain* (pp. 115-135). Oxford, England: Pergamon Press.

Saphier, D. (1992). Electrophysiological studies of the effects of interleukin-1 and a-interferon on the EEG and pituitary-adrenocortical activity. In J.J. Rothweil & R.D. Dantzer (Eds.), *Interleukin-1 in the brain* (pp. 51-75). Oxford, England: Pergamon Press.

Sapolsky, R.M. (1992). *Stress: The aging brain and the mechanisms of neuron death*. Cambridge, MA: MIT Press.

Schindler, R., Bhezzi, P., & Dinarello, C.A. (1991). IL-1 induces IL-1 IV; IFN suppresses IL-1 but not LPS-induced transcription of IL-1. *Journal of Immunology, 144*, 2216-2222.

Schleifer, S.J., Keller, S.E., Camerino, M., Thornton, J.C., & Stein, M. (1983). Suppression of lymphocyte stimulation following bereavement. *Journal of the American Medical Association, 250*, 374.

Schleifer, S.J., Keller, S.E., Meyerson, A.T., Raskin, M.J., Davis, K.L., & Stein, M. (1984). Lymphocyte function in major depressive disorder, *Archives of General Psychiatry, 41*, 484.

Selye, H. (1936). A syndrome produced by diverse noxious agents. *Nature, 38*, 32-36.

Sheridan, J.F., Feng, N., Bonneau, R.H., Allen, C.M., Huneycutt, B.S., & Glaser, R. (1991). Restraint stress differentially affects antiviral cellular and humoral immune responses in mice. *Journal of Neuroimmunology, 31*, 245-255.

Sklar, L.S., & Anisman, H. (1981). Stress and cancer. *Psychological Bulletin, 89*, 369-406.

Smith, G.R., & McDaniels, S.M. (1983). Psychologically mediated effect on the delayed hypersensitivity reaction to tuberculin in humans. *Psychosomatic Medicine, 45*, 65-70.

Solomon, G. (1969). Stress and antibody response in rats. *Archives of Allergy, 35*, 97-104.

Solvason, H.B., Ghanta, V.K., & Hiramoto, R.N. (1988). Conditioned augmentation of natural killer cell activity: Independence from nociceptive effects and dependence on interferon-beta. *Journal of Immunology, 140*, 661-665.

Stanford, S.C., & Salmon, P. (1993). *Stress: From synapse to syndrome*. London: Academic Press,

Takao, T., Tracey, D.E., Mitchell, W.M., & DeSouza, E.B. (1990). Interleukin-1 receptors in mouse brain: Characterization and neuronal localization. *Endocrinology, 127*, 3070-3078.

Ursin, H., & Oiff, M. (1993). The stress response. In S.C. Stanford & P. Salmon (Eds.), *Stress: From synapse to syndrome* (pp. 4-24). London: Academic Press.

Watkins, L.R., Wiertelak, E.P., Goehier. L., Mooney-Heiberger, K., Martinez, J., Fumess, L., & Maier, S.F. (1994). Neurocircuitry of illness-induced hyperalgesia. *Brain Research, 639*, 283-299.

Weiner, H. (1991). The dynamics of the organism: Implications of recent biological thought for psychosomatic theory and research. In R. Ader, D.L. Felten, & N. Cohen (Eds.), *Psychoneuroimmunology II* (pp. 955-1013). New York: Academic Press.

Weiss, J.M., Sundar, S.K., Becker, K.J., & Cierpial, M.A. (1989). Behavioral and neural influences on cellular immune responses: Effects of stress and interleukin-1. *Journal of Clinical Psychiatry, 50*, 43-53.

Wiertelak, E.P., Smith, K.B., Fumess, L., Mayr, T., Maier, S.F., & Watkins, L.R. (1994). Acute and conditioned hyperalgesic responses to illness. *Pain, 56*, 227-235.

Zalcman, S., Minkiewicz-Janda, A., Richter, M., & Anisman, H. (1988). Critical periods associated with stressor effects on antibody titers and on the plaque-forming cell response to sheep red blood cells. *Brain, Behavior, and Immunity*, 2, 254-266.

Zalcman, S., Richter, M., & Anisman, H. (1989). Alterations of immune functioning following exposure to stressor-related cues. *Brain, Behavior, and Immunity, 3*, 99-109.

Zwilling, B.S., Brown, D., Christner, R., Faris, M., & Hilberger, M., McPeek, M., Epps, C.V., & Hartlaub, B.A. (1990). Differential effect of restraint stress on MHC class II expression by murine peritoneal macrophages. *Brain, Behavior, and Immunity, 4*, 330-338.

Additional Reference

Hall, N.R. and Goldstein, A.L. (1986, March/April). Thinking Well: The Chemical Links Between Emotions and Health. *Science*.

Figure 6-3. Dr. Hans Selye, October 25, 1950, Director, University of Montreal's Institute for Experimental Medicine and Surgery. (UPI/Bettman.)

THE MASTERY OF STRESS

Hans Selye

The work of Hans Selye has been described previously in this chapter. His career spanned fifty years; ten at McGill University and forty at the University of Montreal. He spoke eight languages and would moderate heated discussions about his research in the native tongue of the participants. He published more than 1,600 scientific articles, over forty monographs and surveys, and numerous books.

The Stress of My Life: A Scientist's Memoirs, was published in 1979. It was a compilation of many of his previous works. In Chapter 9, The Mastery of Stress, *Selye reflects on his research, career, and life. He succinctly summarizes what he learned that has been of greatest value to him, and of potential significance for us .*

The term "stress" has been used so loosely and applied to so many areas that it is perhaps easiest to understand what stress is *not*. Contrary to widespread public opinion, stress is not synonymous with nervous depression, tension, fatigue or discouragement. The only way to characterize stress is to call it a nonspecific response of the body to any demand. Under given circumstances, stress may cause exhaustion, a nervous breakdown, a cardiac accident, asthma or muscular fatigue. Still, these disturbances are not stress, but rather its diverse effects upon certain individuals.

You *should not and cannot avoid stress*, because to eliminate it completely would mean to destroy life itself. If you make no more demands upon your body, you are dead. Whatever we do—run up a flight of stairs, play tennis, worry or fight starvation—demands are made upon us. A lash of the whip and a passionate kiss can be equally stressful! Although one causes distress and the other eustress, both make certain common demands, necessitating adaptation to a change in our normal resting equilibrium. Even while we sleep, the heart must continue to beat, we must move the muscles that help the lungs to breathe, we continue to digest last night's meal, and even the brain does not cease to function as we dream. Consequently, it would be quite unthinkable that anyone could, or would even want to, avoid stress. However, the more we learn about conditioning and about the ways to deal with the stress of life, the more we can enjoy eustress, which is the spice of our existence. It gives us the only outlet we have to express our talents and energies, to pursue happiness.

Every one of us must learn to recognize what for him is "overstress" (hyperstress), when he has exceeded the limits of his adaptability; or "understress" (hypostress), when he suffers from lack of self-realization (physical immobility, boredom, sensory deprivation). Being overwrought is just as bad as being frustrated by the inability to express ourselves and find free outlets for our innate muscular or mental energy.

The way I see it, the stress of life has four basic variations, although in their most characteristic nonspecific manifestations they all depend upon the same central phenomenon. This might be illustrated as follows:

From *The Stress of My Life, A Scientist's Memoirs*, 2nd. edition, 1979, by Hans Selye. Reprinted with permission of Van Nostrand Reinhold.

```
          Overstress
         (hyperstress)
              |
Good stress ——STRESS—— Bad stress
 (eustress)    |        (distress)
          Understress
          (hypostress)
```

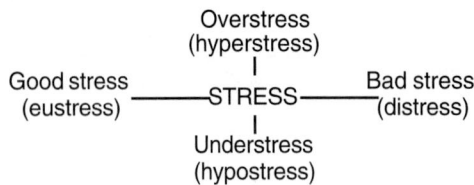

Our goal, then, is to strike a balance between the equally destructive forces of hypo- and hyperstress, to find as much eustress as possible and minimize distress.

In the course of human history a multitude of recommendations have been made to find peace and happiness. The most popular among these included a rigid enforcement of the country's laws, a rigorous adherence to the commands and teachings of some purportedly infallible leader (sage, prophet or divinity), and the promotion of progress in science, technology or politics. Yet history has continued to demonstrate the fragility of all these guidelines.

With the ease of communications today, we are constantly bombarded by new methods of "coping with life." Journalists, sociologists and psychologists tell us that, as the population grows and the pace of life quickens, the world is becoming an increasingly frustrating place. Whether this is truer now than in the past, we would certainly all like to rid our lives of the bad effects of stress and enjoy as much eustress as possible. To meet this longing, new techniques spring up daily, all claiming to "reduce stress." Among these, some are worth taking seriously, others are nothing but fads. Because the field of stress research is so vast, I cannot claim to be an expert on every technique that attempts to provide means to reduce distress, but I do have some opinions based on our own research, and on self-observation.

It is usually not enough to say, "Relax and refrain from strenuous activities." Some people find sufficient diversion in leisure activities to keep their own stress level at a desirable point. But many of us have an irresistible drive to seek stress, in the form of challenge, competition and the like, even when we are supposed to be playing. It is a common experience for a person under pressure to get the feeling of merely wasting time when indulging in leisure activities. Not everyone knows how to play or how to enjoy the passive experiences of music, spectator sports or reading. When the pent-up energy of highly motivated people has no outlet for the type of work that they consider eustressful play, they turn to drugs, violence and other destructive activities. But there are alternatives, some good, some not so good.

Smoking, alcohol, tranquilizers and eating all help to relieve distress in those who suffer from nervous excitation. The trouble here is that these remedies tend to become problems themselves through their habit-forming properties.

The most diverse kinds of therapy are used to decrease the effects of distress. These include exercise, psychotherapy, physiotherapy, acupuncture and moxibustion, chiropractic, electroshock, sauna, hot and cold baths, balneotherapy, shortwave therapy—the list goes on and on!

In recent years, some of the Eastern methods of stress reduction have become very popular. Ginseng or eleutherococcus (extracted from Asiatic plants and long used in Eastern medicine) has received a great deal of attention. There are many clinical and a few experimental observations that suggest these preparations might exert a nonspecific antistress effect. Meanwhile, the results obtained in our own labs have been inconclusive.

Other procedures of Eastern origin that have taken hold, especially in North America, include Zen Buddhism, Hare Krishna, Yoga and—most popular of all—Transcendental Meditation (TM) and its variant, the "relaxation response." I am often associated with the TM movement having frequently lectured on stress both to TM teachers and to potential students. TM purports to relieve the bad effects of stress, and what I have tried to do is merely explain what stress *is*. However, a misconception has grown that I am an expert in TM: I have tried to clarify this by admitting that I have never taken a course in TM. I am not a meditator and I have never conducted research on the effects of this technique.

I have spoken with Maharishi about the underlying principles and have written introductions and epilogues to several books on the subject, again limiting my remarks to the explanation of stress in the medical sense of the word without claiming to be an expert on the effects of the method. I would like to take the course if I ever have the time, because I have met many practitioners who attest to its usefulness. Of course, I would like to understand the underlying biological mechanisms through which it exerts its curative actions; but if something is proven to be helpful by experience, that's good enough for me. After all, no one knows how aspirin really works, yet it has helped relieve pain in millions of people and no physician considers it unethical to employ this drug.

A modified version of this technique is advocated by Dr. Herbert Benson of Harvard, who calls his variant the "relaxation response." Like TM, this is a mental technique of deep relaxation which helps you clarify your thoughts. Benson's method differs from TM in that it demysticizes the ceremonies behind meditating; he refuses to attach any importance to ceremonies, mantras and the like, and he comes up with a system that can be learned by anyone without the costly instruction involved in TM.

These schools of thought, and others like Jacobson's "progressive relaxation technique," claim results that are quite impressive. Like those previously mentioned, the latter appears to produce some measurable objective physiological changes in the body, opposite to those considered to be characteristic of excessive stress. Most of these techniques simply help us withdraw from our everyday preoccupations through physical and mental relaxation (whether or not accompanied by prayers, rituals and ceremonies). In any event, the subjective feeling of relaxation produced is claimed to be more complete than that of a good night's sleep. If this is true I support them, but I think we need more evidence before we can objectively choose among these techniques. In my opinion, we cannot deny the value of such procedures simply because we do not know enough about them. After all, there is no logical relationship between religion and music or certain ceremonies either, yet all religions have (often quite independently of each other) developed rituals which include music, ceremonies and wearing certain vestments, all of which may largely help through subconscious mechanisms that are not explicable in modern scientific terms.

I mentioned earlier the differences between eustress, distress, hyperstress and hypostress. All of these have certain characteristics in common and are ramifications of the general stress concept. Hyperstress may be due to an excess of eustress (for we cannot tolerate excessively prolonged ecstasy or orgies) or to an excess of distress (for we cannot long withstand intensely unpleasant things). The various types of relaxation techniques seem to be able to combat hyperstress of either sort.

Relaxation therapy could not have any value in combating hypostress. In fact, exaggerating the time spent daily on TM or other methods has been said to cause disturbances similar to those of sensory deprivation (a form of hypostress). But in the rat race of modern life, hyperstress is the greater problem. Therefore, it seems to me, these techniques can be very useful to many people.

Most of these methods teach us—some more effectively than others—how to deal with "the cruel world." To my mind, however, our goal should not be merely to master techniques for shutting out the reality but to devise a better lifestyle. That is why my principal object is to perfect the behavioral code of altruistic egoism, which is in harmony with the laws of Nature.

We have tranquilizers that can reduce anxiety and tension, and we know of a variety of specific drugs that combat stress-induced high blood pressure, peptic ulcers, headaches and many other disturbances usually caused by stress in predisposed individuals; but all of these drugs are of limited efficiency and have some undesirable side-effects. Perhaps, eventually, pharmacology will give us a perfect remedy in the form of some totally innocuous pill or elixir which will protect the body and mind against all the bad effects of stress. Perhaps. Meanwhile, anybody can find help by following a code of behavior which is based on natural laws. This has already been tried by many people wishing to establish a state of emotional equilibrium and well-being in the face of adversity. . . .

Once we really understand stress, each of us will be his own best physician, for no one can appreciate our mental needs better than we ourselves. Everyone must learn to measure the stress level at which he personally functions best and then not go either above or below that. By careful self-observation we can gradually develop an instinctive feeling telling us that we are running above or below the stress level that corresponds to our own nature. In practice, no refined chemical tests can do more for us. I know when I have just "had enough of it," and then I stop, I don't need any complex scientific machinery for this.

Judging what is best for us personally is a matter of training through experience, which everybody has to acquire for himself. But in this task we can be greatly aided by a thorough knowledge of the basic natural laws that have been clarified through research on stress. You must learn to balance the pleasures and stimulation of social engagements, trips and successful work against your requirements for peace, solitude and serenity. Everybody will arrive at this aim in a somewhat different manner, always characteristic of his own individuality. Some understand their inner needs through meditation and silence: others may only find their own stress level through danger signs such as insomnia, irritability, indigestion, headaches or depression. First of all, we must learn to analyze and be honest with ourselves. Then, step by step, an intelligent person will usually succeed in developing his own techniques, limiting his unnecessary telephone calls, his participation in social life, committee meetings, civic activities, etc., which he has blindly undertaken because "they were expected of him." This will leave much more time to do other things at which he is really good and which may be more useful both to himself and to society. Don't accept social obligations that people try to impose upon you if you dislike them. "Worthy causes" are not natural obligations and will only bore you, so disregard them. Do what you like and respect, without worrying about criticism, scandal or even all the money that you lose by deviating from generally accepted standards.

If you read the daily papers or watch news programs on television that do not interest you, just give that up and turn your attention to other things that you find more edifying. Don't allow the verbal terrorism of others to give you guilt feelings. Instead, save your energy for activities that are really meaningful.

"Even if you have the misfortune of having badly chosen your wife, at least choose your occupation wisely, because you will spend much more time with it than with her." I do not remember the author of this advice but, in any event, I fully agree with him—and by "occupation" I don't mean only your job, but whatever you decide to do throughout each day.

You must satisfy yourself first of all. Pleasure will come only from what you have done to earn it. As much as possible, try to awaken the creativity that may lie buried in your subconscious mind. Whatever steps you must take to exteriorize your talents, the accomplishment of this is the basic prerequisite for your development and satisfaction. It really doesn't matter whether you are a scientist, gardener, poet, musician, athlete or even a beachcomber: the essential thing is that you unfold your personality as far as you can, and thereby achieve happiness.

You should try very honestly to establish what you consider a noble aim in life, a goal worthy of your efforts, a pursuit which gives you maximal satisfaction. This is not always easy. You must be extremely sincere with yourself; you have to remember to choose only what *you* really want to do, not what your parents, friends, neighbors, teachers or preachers have virtually brainwashed you to do. To establish this is of the utmost importance because it helps you avoid some of the major frustrations in life, which are the principal sources of distress.

After that you must fight hard to attain your goal, but always stay within the limits of your capacity to withstand stress. We must learn how to face life gracefully from what we have established about the actions of syntoxic and catatoxic hormones. We need to know how to accept defeat when it is not worthwhile to win, or when the goal we have set for ourselves turns out to be unattainable; but we must also fight stubbornly until death if under given conditions, without defense, death would be inevitable anyway.

Each time you are the victim of some family disagreement or a disappointing experience at work, examine carefully whether it is really worth your while to defend your point of view. If not, just ignore the friction or, if necessary, cut your ties with the offender; if the goal is important, fight with all your strength. After the combat is over, whether you win or lose, return to solitude, breathe calmly, relax your muscles and empty your mind and body of all the aftermaths of the struggle, gradually returning to your normal pace of life. I once summarized these thoughts in a jingle that first appeared in *The Stress of Life*. It has now been reprinted on cards for distribution to student groups, tourists and other visitors to our Institute:

> "Fight for your highest
> Attainable aim
> But do not put up
> Resistance in vain."

Fifty years of research in laboratories and clinics have convinced me that the physiological mechanisms of adaptation to the stress of life are essentially the same on the cellular and molecular level as they are with regard to interpersonal and international relationships.

To my mind, the general syndrome of adaptation to the demands of life, which I have already outlined, is at the root of the great tensions characteristic of our time that manifest themselves in the relations between individuals and nations. Perhaps humanity's greatest problem today is determining how to face interpersonal and international stress situations as well as those created by changes in our inanimate environment.

Frustration and indecision are the most harmful psychogenic stressors, because neither uninhibited successful work nor even final and hopeless defeat (which can be solved by resignation to fate) is as demanding as the friction from unresolved contradictory efforts. We must learn to cope with the problems and demands which confront us daily in the twentieth century. That is why I have spent so much time and energy on efforts to apply the results of laboratory and clinical research to the formulation of natural directives for everyday behavior.

I start with the principle that man needs more natural ideals than those that guide his conduct at present. Consequently, I feel that the rules we must follow have to be based on the laws of Nature. We are part of Nature and therefore cannot disregard her laws with impunity. The beauty of this code is its perfect compatibility with any religion, political system or philosophy; yet, at the same time, it is quite independent of these.

My skepticism about the applicability of the "golden rules"[*] led me to the formulation of my code of behavior, which I labeled altruistic egoism.

In naming my code of behavior, I wished to distinguish between egoism which is, according to *Webster's New World Dictionary*, "the doctrine that self-interest is the proper goal of all human actions" and egotism—"constant, excessive reference to oneself, self-conceit, selfishness." The possible confusion is understandable: I myself failed to make the proper distinction in *Stress Without Distress*. As explained by *Webster's*: "Egotism and egoism are sometimes used interchangeably, but egotism is generally considered the more [derogatory] term."

The concept of altruistic egoism appears paradoxical because it is difficult to conceive of someone who is both an altruist and an egoist at the same time. Yet the underlying idea is very simple: you can be *effectively* selfish, giving free expression to your particular talents, and still maintain peace of mind. Altruistic egoism lets us give vent to our natural human egoistic tendencies without producing guilt feelings—for who would condemn him whose egoism expresses itself in the insatiable desire to be useful to others and thereby earn their love?

To fully understand the enormous biological force that can be derived from such a philosophy, it helps to remember what we have learned from Claude Bernard on the importance of the fixity of the *milieu intérieur*—that is, everything comprised within our skin surface, the totality of our person. If someone is exposed to cold, he shivers to produce heat and reestablish the fixity of the *milieu intérieur*— that is his "homeostasis." When a person is given an inherently poisonous substance, he will try to destroy and get rid of it by means of catatoxic responses. If he overreacts to unimportant irritants, he will have to produce syntoxic hormones to diminish the excessive and

---

*Love thy neighbor as thyself," and "Do unto others as you wish them to do unto you."

useless defense reactions that are actually the immediate cause of his suffering. In both cases he will have to maintain the *status quo*, the internal equilibrium, in order to assure his own well-being.

To illustrate the practical applicability of altruistic egoism, take the following example:

Twenty-four passengers arrive at a little airport. All of them need to get to the same hotel, but there are only six taxis. One of three things can happen. The most aggressive egoists could run for the taxis and jump into them, leaving the other eighteen stranded and bitter with resentment. The pure altruist could yield precedence to all others and remain behind waiting indefinitely for a new taxi to arrive. The third possibility is that one person, overcoming his shyness, takes the initiative to suggest that, since there are only six taxis, the passengers should split up into six groups of four persons and everyone will get a ride. The twenty-four passengers do not act this way by either pure altruism or egoism but by altruistic egoism, because what is good for any one of them is also good for all others.

The passenger who proposed the generally satisfactory solution was an altruistic egoist, yet his conduct was in perfect agreement with the Biblical teaching, because he did unto others what he wanted them to do unto him. Instead of creating resentment, he earned gratitude and friendly feelings. In daily life you will encounter many situations where an altruistic-egoistic solution is much more difficult to find, yet it is the only acceptable one. . . .

At first the concept of altruistic egoism strikes some people as a repulsive bargain, in conflict with many religious ideals and based on the most selfish of needs. The impression is often left that my code is just another way of saying, "I'll scratch your back if you'll scratch mine." That is not at all what I wish to convey. My code has no strings attached. I offer figuratively to "scratch your back" without asking for anything in return. The value of this system rests purely on the statistical probability that if you have been unconditionally useful to many, in the long run some of the recipients of your goodwill will want to help you out. I try to be useful to people, convinced that, even if I never ask for reciprocity,

some will eventually turn around and help me, trusting that in the future I might help them out again. And even if no one does, I have lost nothing.

Executives of large enterprises, generals, movie stars, and multimillionaires can all be very successful in their own fields and yet complete failures as regards their personal happiness. From my point of view, such a person should not be envied, because real success depends not only upon public acclaim but much more upon an inner satisfaction and a sense of fulfillment. It is also possible for someone to achieve success as an altruist by being useful to others while neglecting himself. Even if such attitudes are admirable in a sense, they cannot be considered as fulfilling the characteristics of complete success.

To adjust to the world you must establish an equilibrium with it. You must be able to say, "My ideal is to stay at my natural level of accomplishment and behave as appropriately as I can." This is the way I try to stay in balance with my surroundings, both animate and inanimate. I need not have feelings of guilt and shame nor any inferiority complexes about my behavior, because I know I can do no more. . .

Everyone must decide for himself just what his aims in life should be, and I leave it up to philosophers, theologians and others to debate the ultimate purpose of man's existence. I see my own goal as the development and application of the code of behavior and motivation that I find best for myself. Because of the public acceptance I have met in explaining altruistic egoism, I continue to believe that it is a sound set of guidelines by which to live, and therefore feel it my "duty" to teach the code to those who want to listen. However, this is not a duty in the usual sense of the word, for it is not an obligation imposed upon me by someone else, it is one that makes me happy. As Nietzsche said:

> I slept and I dreamed that life is pleasure;
> I woke and I saw that it is duty;
> I worked and I realized that duty is pleasure.

The basic principles of altruistic egoism can be summarized by two simple words: *be necessary!* The trouble is that the scientific justification of the code cannot be explained in so few words; you have to live it to understand it completely. It has always been most frustrating to me when interviewers from the media have asked me to sum it up in a few sentences. . . .

It is only fair to say that many people apply my code to their own existence before ever having heard anyone speak about it or even realizing that this is what they do. Science has shown that people do many things well before they know why they do them. When we are hungry, we eat; when our muscles become sluggish from sitting too long in the same position, we move about to relax them. It is not necessary to understand the biochemistry of digestion or muscular contraction in order to act properly under such conditions. But understanding the mechanism helps to strengthen our faith and enables us to improve our performance. If a slot machine gets stuck, it is sometimes enough to give it a kick, but it is safer to call a mechanic who can repair it on the basis of his understanding.

Altruistic egoism has always been my unconscious guideline, although it took me a lifetime to formulate my concept of motivation in scientific terms and to illustrate it with examples of laws regulating tissue reactions in biology and particularly in medicine. I first tried to analyze my code scientifically because of a deep desire to help my children overcome the difficulty of readjusting their motivation in our age of changing value systems, permissiveness, student unrest and continual strikes.

Unfortunately, a code of behavior, unless followed instinctively or taught at an early age, is not easily accepted. In all honesty I must admit that I have not been uniformly successful with my efforts to help adults who already have deeply ingrained codes of their own. Although I have not always achieved my goal with those in my immediate surroundings, I seem to have succeeded much better with scientists and laymen who have read my writings or listened to my lectures. As the old saying goes, no one is a prophet in his own country.

Even if I cannot explain stress within the space limits of an autobiography, I can try to summarize the code in a few easily remembered points. When I wrote the first edition of *The Stress of Life* I was very proud to have converted thirty long years of research into a mere 300 pages: but when I took it to my publisher he informed me that the material was too long. "Well, perhaps it isn't worth publishing," I suggested. "No, no," he replied, "this is good, but you have to make a summary for people to read. We have to publish the whole book, because if your peers don't have the factual material on which to accept it, nobody will listen to you." Undaunted, I returned to my office and turned out a ten-page summary. The editor looked at this and said, "Well, doctor, this is a little better, but you still have to cut it down." I didn't see how I could possibly describe the stress concept in fewer words, but he insisted on a summary of the summary. It was then that I thought up my jingle about not putting up resistance in vain.

Now I can do even better, if pressed, to condense the thoughts behind altruistic egoism. As I said, the entire philosophy boils down to two words: *be necessary!* But if asked to pick out the basic points for a "recipe against distress," I would reiterate:

Stress cannot be avoided. It is the body's response to any demand, and without making demands on any of our capacities, we would be dead. Our goal should be to live in the manner that gives us the most eustress (which is pleasant) and the least distress (which is detrimental).

We must each of us find our own stress level, and live neither more nor less intensely than Nature has intended.

We must have a goal, a "port of destination" that we ourselves, and not only society, consider worthy of our efforts.

We cannot avoid being egoists, because all living creatures are made to look out for themselves and for their own species first. This does not imply that we should be reckless egoists, caring nothing about the interests of others, for that would be unacceptable, not only on moral grounds, but because it is disadvantageous. We could not live in constant fear of retaliation from those we have wounded, nor could we tolerate the traumatic guilt complexes resulting from such behavior.

We must be altruists, not only because our creeds and education command us to do so, but

because altruism has great value in terms of biological survival. Man is a social being who
depends upon his environment; often he can earn
the indispensable support of his surroundings
only by offering his support in return. However,
absolute altruism is contrary to man's nature, and
would only encourage parasitic behavior where
each person would rely solely on the assistance of
others. It is possible to marry these two apparently contradictory concepts through the code of
"altruistic egoism," in which each member of
society works for his own good but adjusts his
aims to be maximally useful to others, thereby
assuring his own security.

Bringing our own modern concepts to the
ancient wisdom of the Bible, we can learn to
"*earn* thy neighbors love," each of us finding a
way to protect our own interests by *being necessary and useful* to our fellow-men.

Even those who accept the value of my code
as a means of facing the adversities inflicted by
psychological reactions often doubt that it can be
applied to extreme situations—for instance, coping with incurable disease or advanced age. Yet
from my own experience, I believe that altruistic
egoism can be just as useful in dealing with life's
worst crises as in handling everyday problems.

When I was fifty years old, I began to develop an osteoarthritis, a deformation of the hip joint
that was so painful that even large doses of strong
painkillers had little effect. Eventually I could
move about only with the help of two crutches
and was confined to a wheelchair. Needless to
say, I was greatly disturbed at the prospect of
having to give up all my activities.

My surgeon, Dr. F. E. Stinchfield, recommended an operation which at the time was very
dangerous: he would expose and remove all the
bony irregularities, covering the joint surface
with a metallic cap. Afraid of becoming nothing
more than a burden to my family and myself, I
agreed to the surgery.

As a result of the operation I developed a
severely bleeding stress ulcer, much to the merriment of all the interns and residents of the hospital who came to see Selye suffering from "Selye's
ulcer." Nevertheless, I continued to perform a
daily regimen of exercises to maintain the motil-

ity of the painful artificial hip. Eventually I
recovered and was able to return to my routine,
proud to have licked the disease.

The operation had been performed in New
York, and I had spent a long time recuperating
there. I was full of restless energy and anxious to
get right back to work. As soon as I landed at
Montreal's Dorval airport, I phoned the institute
to announce that I was back and on my way to the
university. Upon my arrival I found two of my
assistants waiting on the ground floor to help me
into the elevator with my crutches. I flatly
refused their aid, protesting that I had been taught
in the hospital how to climb stairs on crutches
and needed to practice. I went up four flights
under my own steam, much to the terror of the
escorts who insisted on following me. When I
finally reached the institute I greeted everyone
with a radiant smile of triumph!

That same day I wanted to spend some time
in the sun, as I try to do whenever possible.
During the summer the sun comes in at such a
straight angle from above that I had to lie on the
window sill to get its rays. This didn't bother me,
even with my artificial hip, but everyone around
me worried that my handicap would make it more
likely than ever that I would finally fall off the
seventh-floor ledge.

The staff was relieved when I eventually
eased myself down from the window. But a few
minutes later I informed them that, these barriers
crossed, I now wanted to see if I could drive
using only my good left leg. After quite a struggle to get into the car with my crutches and ride
around the parking area, I looked up to the seventh floor to find the entire staff leaning out of
the windows, nervously watching my performance. Although I had managed to circle around
the courtyard, my circles were a little uncertain
and square. The second time everything went
perfectly, and I continued to drive myself to and
from the university throughout my time on
crutches.

I was really desperate when, a few years
later, it became apparent that an osteoarthritis had
attacked my other hip too. Still determined not to
become an invalid, I once more agreed to undergo surgery. This time a somewhat improved technique was used: the head of my hipbone was

completely sawed off along with the socket from my pelvis. The surgeon replaced them with plastic objects, permanently inserted in my bones like fillings in a tooth. I went through the prolonged painful exercise period a second time, calling upon all my motivation to get me through the difficult time. Finally I was ready to get back to work, able to move about unaided. By now, the technique of this operation has improved so much that those who have undergone it in recent years will no longer be able to understand how difficult it was to face similar situations when the procedure was just in its developing stage.

Several years went by with few problems until, once again, I found myself needing surgery. This turned out to be a much more dangerous situation. An egg-shaped tumor had developed under the skin of my thigh, and it was diagnosed as a histiocytic reticulosarcoma, one of the most vicious cancers known to man. I had it removed immediately by a Montreal surgeon, Dr. J. E. Tabah, and his team. After the operation they severely irradiated the surrounding area with a cobalt bomb. I insisted on knowing my chances for a lasting recovery. Dr. Tabah spoke frankly, admitting that this type of cancer spreads rapidly and almost always kills within a year, except in the extremely rare cases when, purely by chance, the surgeon succeeds in removing all the cancer cells.

I refused to retreat from life in desperation and, although I knew it would take tremendous self-discipline, I was determined to continue living and working without worrying about the end. It's difficult to live normally when you are treated like a man condemned to die, so I told no one outside my immediate family about my predicament. In a sense, I refused to believe in my fate; I suppressed any thoughts of my presumably imminent death, and apparently even my closest friends and associates failed to notice any difference in my behavior. I rewrote my will, including several suggestions for the continuation of my work by my colleagues; and having taken care of that business, I promptly forced myself to disregard the whole calamity.

I immersed myself in my work, summoning all my strength to get on with living and avoid brooding. A year went by, then two, and it turned out that I was that fortunate exception. Now, years after the discovery of my cancer, I know the danger, though slight, still exists. My artificial hips could break down, my cancer could regain its vitality. In any case, I shall eventually die of old age. But nothing could ever deprive me of those years during which my code has allowed me to enjoy a life so full of pleasure and satisfaction. I may say that, apart from a few bad moments, I have lived happily through my seventy-one years.

I can never be sure if I handled my troubles in the best possible way; certainly my approach would not work for everyone. Sometimes the prolonged distress of knowing that you or someone you love will inevitably die causes irreparable damage. Perhaps it is best to leave the incurable patient and his family blissfully ignorant. But in my case, I derive a great deal of satisfaction from knowing that even when I believed I was going to die I still lived up to my highest ideals.

I recently had another chance to act as a human guinea pig and put my code to the test. I had to undergo an emergency prostatectomy, requiring three days of pretreatment in the hospital. However, I had committed myself to a lecture before an important audience at one of Montreal's largest hotels and, as the sponsors had gone to a lot of trouble publicizing my address, I did not have the heart to call it off, even though the event fell on the third day of the pretreatment. I convinced my physicians to give me a four-hour leave from the hospital, allowing me to attend the scheduled cocktail party and dinner and present my address without disturbing the plans. The doctors warned me that I would not be able to lecture anyway, under such conditions, but I argued that I could.

Aided by altruistic egoism, I took up the challenge and reacted quite calmly and syntoxically. During the dinner, several of the guests asked me the meaning of the small wristband I had hoped to hide from view, but I answered that I would tell them only after the address. I spoke for over an hour in the same leisurely manner as usual. Being perfectly resigned to the inevitable events of the next day, I did not get excited or worried, because I did not want to "fight in vain."

The lecture was very well received, and after considerable applause and a standing ovation, the chairman gave me a gift and expressed his gratitude. Before the crowd dispersed I held up my hands and asked them to remain for one last remark. I then explained that the wristband was my identification as a resident patient at Hôtel Dieu Hospital, and that the following morning my surgeon, Dr. Jean Charbonneau, would be performing a major operation on me. In fact, I told them a car was waiting to take me back for some final preoperative treatment that same night. Because I was so relaxed myself, I had not wanted to make the audience feel ill at ease, but now that it was all over, I wished to tell them what was in store for me to illustrate the practicality of my code.

The applause was perhaps the warmest I have ever received: some of the women even had tears in their eyes as I quickly walked through the crowd to my car. And, you see, this really, was not a major sacrifice for me, as I enjoyed every minute of it. As I have often said, "It is not what happens to you, but the way you take it." It gave me such satisfaction to know that, even under these difficult conditions, I knew how to take it. The operation went well, and I am now pleased as punch to be able to discuss it in retrospect, having managed once more to meet the stress of life, deriving only eustress and not distress.

My philosophy keeps me from fearing any other catastrophes which might spoil the enjoyment of my remaining years. During this time I shall pursue at my stress level the goals that I consider worthwhile and which correspond to *my* nature, without making any compromises to the prejudices of society and the behavior that is expected of me.

Figure 6-4. Runners approach finish line of the Boilermaker Road Race. Held annually in Utica, New York, it attracts thousands. (Photograph by Jim Rooney.)

READING 6C

INFLUENCE OF AEROBIC EXERCISE ON DEPRESSION

I. Lisa McCann and David S. Holmes

The autonomic nervous system was discussed earlier in this chapter. The sympathetic branch operates during periods of stress and emergency. Its purpose is to mobilize the body's resources as efficiently as possible to meet the demands of the stressor. Neurotransmitters serotonin and norepinephrine are released into the system. Serotonin increases blood pressure and norepinephrine heightens emotional arousal and constricts the blood vessels, enabling more efficient flow. Heartbeat and respiration increase. As digestion slows, blood is diverted to the brain and the skeletal muscles. Beta-endorphin and enkephalin suppress pain, facilitating persistence in the emergency situation and later, a calming effect, which promotes rest and healing. Vigorous physical exercise also triggers the sympathetic nervous system.

It is firmly established that serotonin and norepinephrine are depleted in people with depression. Fluoxetine (Prozac) increases the availability of serotonin, and electroconvulsive therapy is assumed to increase levels of both. Minor tranquilizers, such as diazepam (Valium) and alprazolam (Xanax), are anti-anxiety drugs. They facilitate the binding of neurotransmitter GABA to $GABA_A$ receptor sites which inhibit anxiety (Kolat, 1995, p. 434-435).

Many people who exercise regularly claim that their spirits are lifted and that they feel more alert and invigorated after exercising. They also claim to be less anxious. It can be argued that the body is miraculously designed to inoculate us naturally against depression and anxiety. Can exercise have a therapeutic effect on mood, thus decreasing the need for drugs or electrochock? The following article by researchers I. Lisa McCann and David S. Holmes investigates this issue.

There is currently a substantial amount of interest in the use of strenuous aerobic exercise for reducing depression. The interest in the effects of exercise on depression appears to have been stimulated initially by the "feeling good" phenomenon associated with exercise (Cooper, 1968). That is, although the exercise may be demanding, grueling, and exhausting, many normal persons report that they feel good after completing the exercise. There are at least two ways in which running could influence depression. First, it has been suggested that some endogenous depressions are associated with low levels of norepinephrine in the central nervous system (Collis & Shepherd, 1980; Garvey, 1980; Maas, 1975, 1979; Schildkraut, 1965) and that strenuous aerobic exercise may facilitate the production of that neurotransmitter substance (Cronan & Howley, 1974; Howley, 1976) and thereby relieve depression. Second, it is possible that the psychosocial effects that are associated with running (e.g., achievement of goals, camaraderie, distraction) serve to relieve depression.

Unfortunately, the existing research concern-

Lisa McCann and David S. Holmes: Influence of Aerobic Exercise On Depression, *Journal of Personality and Social Psychology*, Vol. 46, 1984, 1142-1147. Copyright © 1984 by the American Psychological Association. Reprinted with permission of the authors.

ing the influence of exercise on reductions in depression is very limited and is plagued with methodological problems. Indeed, other than numerous case studies (e.g., Blue, 1979; Kavanagh, Shephard, Tuck, & Qureshi, 1977), there appear to be only two published experiments on the topic, and both lack necessary controls (Brown, Ramirez, & Taub, 1979; Greist, Klein, Eischens, & Faris, 1978).[1]

In the Greist et al. (1978) experiment, depressed persons were assigned to either a running therapy condition, a long-term psychotherapy condition, or a time-limited psychotherapy condition, and depression was assessed at the beginning and at the end of the treatment period. Inspection of the data indicated that the subjects in the running therapy condition evidenced reductions in depression that were as great as those evidenced by subjects in the two psychotherapy conditions, and therefore the authors concluded that running has been effective for reducing depression. Unfortunately, the experiment did not include either a placebo treatment condition or a no-treatment condition. The absence of the no-treatment condition is particularly serious because depressions are subject to fluctuations or "spontaneous remissions," and in the absence of the no-treatment condition, there is no base against which to compare the changes in patients who were given treatment. Furthermore, it is very important to recognize that no statistical tests were reported, and thus there is no indication of the reliability of the findings. Clearly, no conclusions can be drawn from this investigation.

In the Brown et al. (1979) experiment, depression was assessed in 26 subjects who elected to jog five times per week, 65 subjects who elected to jog three times per week, and 10 subjects who elected not to jog. The results indicated that the subjects who jogged showed reliably greater declines in depression than did the subjects who did not jog. However, because the assignment of subjects to conditions was not random and because there is a strong possibility that the demand characteristics influenced the subjects' reports, conclusions concerning the impact of jogging on depression cannot be drawn from this investigation.

In considering the previous research, a comment might be made about one other investigation (Morgan, Roberts, Brand & Feinerman, 1970), the results of which are sometimes misinterpreted. In that investigation, "subjects were given the option of participating" in one of four exercise programs, whereas another group of subjects "who could not participate in the exercise program because of scheduling conflicts" served as control subjects (Morgan et al., 1970, p. 215). That quasi-experimental design (subjects were not randomly assigned) did not reveal greater decreases in depression among exercising subjects than nonexercising subjects. The authors pointed out, however, that the subjects were generally within the "normal range" of depression and that "subjects scoring within the normal range on a psychological variable would not be expected to change following the administration of a treatment" (Morgan et al., 1970, p. 216). The investigators then examined the depression scores of the 11 most depressed subjects from the total group of subjects and found that there was a reliable decline in depression from the pretest to the posttest. It is important to note, however, that exercising subjects were not compared with nonexercising subjects, and thus no conclusions concerning the effects of exercise can be drawn. The decline in depression may have been due to spontaneous remission, which is often noted with depression.

The present investigation was conducted to provide a controlled experimental test of the hypothesized relationship between strenuous aerobic exercise and decreases in depression. In this investigation, depressed subjects participated in either an aerobic exercise treatment condition, a placebo treatment (relaxation training) condition, or a no-treatment condition. Relaxation training was selected as a placebo treatment because it is a well-known technique for dealing with stress-related problems, and thus it has credibility as a treatment, but it is the antithesis of exercise and is not actually used for the treatment of depression. Depression was assessed with self-report measures twice before the treatment period, once during the treatment period, and once after the treatment period.

METHOD

Subjects

Approximately 250 undergraduate women who were enrolled in a general psychology course at the University of Kansas completed the Beck Depression Inventory (Beck, Ward, Mendelson, Mock, & Erbaugh, 1961). From among those women, approximately 60 who had scores above 11 (the cutoff point for mild depression) were contacted by telephone and invited to participate in an experiment that would satisfy the research participation requirement for their psychology course. Forty-seven subjects agreed to participate, and each one was then randomly assigned to either the aerobic exercise condition (N = 16), the placebo condition (N = 15), or the no-treatment condition (N = 16). Over the course of the experiment, 1 subject withdrew from the aerobic exercise condition, 1 withdrew from the placebo condition, and 2 withdrew from the no-treatment condition, and therefore the analyses were based on 43 subjects. The overall initial mean depression score for these subjects was 15.35.

Procedure

Pretreatment. Subjects in each condition were asked to come to an initial meeting to learn more about the experiment and have their aerobic capacity measured. In these meetings, subjects were first told that the experiment involved helping women deal more effectively with the stress in their lives. They were then told that it is common for undergraduate students to experience stress, including feelings of unhappiness, irritability, fatigue, and other troubling feelings. They were then told that the test they had taken indicated that they might be experiencing some of those feelings. Caution was taken not to talk specifically about depression and not to imply that the subjects were in any way abnormal. Rather, the experiment was focused on stress management.

When the general introduction was finished, the subjects were asked to complete the depression inventory again, and then the procedures specific to the conditions to which they had been assigned were explained to them (see Conditions section).

Next the subjects in all of the conditions participated in a 12-min walk-run test of aerobic capacity (Cooper, 1968). In this test, subjects were asked to run (or walk if it became necessary) as far as possible during a 12-min period. The test was conducted on a 1/8 mile (201 m) indoor track with a synthetic surface, and the distance a subject covered was the measure of her aerobic capacity.[2]

Midtreatment. After 5 weeks, all of the subjects completed the depression inventory again.

Posttreatment. Five weeks after the midtreatment assessment, all of the subjects again completed the depression inventory, participated in another 12-min walk-run test of aerobic capacity, and provided another 24-hr urine sample.

Conditions

Aerobic exercise. Subjects in the aerobic exercise condition were told that previous research had indicated that strenuous exercise was effective for helping persons overcome stress, and they were then enrolled in a rhythmical aerobics class offered by the Department of Health, Physical Education, and Recreation. This class met for 1 hr twice per week and was focused on the development of aerobic capacity through strenuous dancing, jogging, and running. In addition to class participation, subjects in the aerobics class were required to participate in exercise outside of class at least to the point of achieving a total (including class exercise) of 30 aerobic points per week (Cooper, 1968).

Placebo. Subjects in the placebo condition were told that previous research had indicated that relaxation exercises and very mild physical exercise were effective for helping persons overcome stress. They were then given verbal and written instructions for the use of progressive muscle relaxation and were instructed to practice this 15-20 min a day 4 days per week. In addition, the subjects were instructed to begin their relaxation sessions by taking a leisurely walk of at least 5-min duration.

No treatment. Subjects in the no-treatment condition were told that because there was no room in the exercise classes or the relaxation training group, their treatment would have to be temporarily postponed.

Expectancies

At the end of the initial meeting at which the procedures were explained to the subjects, the subjects in the aerobic exercise and placebo conditions were asked to respond to a three-item questionnaire that was designed to measure their expectations for the success of the treatment in which they were to participate. Specifically, using 11-point Likert scales, the subjects responded to the following items:

1. "Rate the degree of progress you feel you will make in managing stress more effectively."

2. "To what extent does the training you will receive seem as though it should help?"

3. How would you rate the probability of the training helping you to manage the stress you typically feel?"

RESULTS

The mean screening, pretreatment, midtreatment, and posttreatment depression scores of subjects in the aerobic exercise, placebo, and no-treatment conditions are presented in Figure 1.

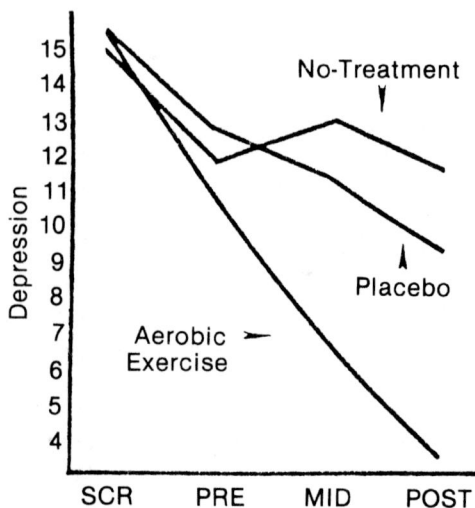

Figure 6-5. Mean screening (SCR), pretreatment (PRE), midtreatment (MID), and posttreatment (POST) depression scores for subjects in the aerobic exercise, placebo, and no-treatment conditions.

Screening and Pretreatment Levels of Depression

An analysis of variance (ANOVA) conducted on the depression scores obtained from subjects when they were being screened for participation in the experiment did not reveal a reliable difference among the conditions, $F(2, 40) = .04$. Similarly, an ANOVA conducted on the pretreatment depression scores that were obtained from subjects just prior to the beginning of their treatments did not reveal a reliable difference among the conditions, $F(2, 40) = .58$. From these results it is clear that there were no initial differences in depression scores among the conditions.

Pretreatment Reductions in Depression

A comparison of the screening and pretreatment depression scores would indicate whether the subjects showed changes in depression independent of the treatments. Findings from such a comparison would be important for determining whether a no-treatment condition is essential in studying the effects of treatments on depression. A 3×2 (Conditions × Trials) ANOVA with repeated measures that was conducted on the depression scores revealed only a reliable trials effect, $F(1, 40) = 26.65, p < .001$ (screening $M = 15.35$, pretreatment $M = 11.74$). This finding clearly indicates that subjects did show reliable and substantial reductions in their depression that were independent of any specific treatment, and it raises serious questions about the interpretations of previous results that did not include data from a no-treatment condition (Griest et al., 1978).

Influence of Treatments on Aerobic Capacity

To determine whether the treatments had differential effects on subjects' aerobic capacity, the posttreatment 12-min walk-run scores of the subjects in the three conditions were compared with an analysis of covariance in which the subjects' pretreatment 12-min walk-run scores were the covariate.[3] This analysis revealed a reliable treatment effect, $F(2,27) = 10.98, p < .001$. Subsequent paired comparisons indicated that the subjects in the aerobic exercise condition had reliably higher scores than did subjects in either the placebo condition, $t(27) = 3.50, p = .002$, or the no-treatment condition, $t(27) = 4.23, p < .001$, and that there was not a reliable difference between scores of the latter two conditions, $t(27) = 0.56$. (For these and all subsequent paired comparisons following an overall ANOVA, the error term and degrees of freedom were obtained from the ANOVA.) The subjects in the aerobic exercise condition evidenced a 10% improvement in aerobic capacity, an improvement that is comparable to those reported by other investigators working with similar programs (e.g., Jasnoski & Holmes, 1981; Jasnoski, Holmes, Solomon, & Aguiar, 1981). From these findings it is clear that the subjects in the aerobic exercise condition evidenced reliably greater improvements in aerobic capacity than did subjects in the other conditions, and thus it can be concluded that the aerobic exercise treatment was effective in improving physical fitness.

Expectancies of Treatment Effectiveness

Before examining the effects of the treatment on subjects' depression, it was necessary to determine whether the subjects in the aerobic exercise and placebo conditions had comparable expectations for the success of the treatments. To test that, a 2×3 (Conditions $\times$ Expectancy Items) ANOVA with repeated measures (items) was conducted on the responses of the subjects in the two conditions to the three items that measured expectancies for treatment success. That analysis did not reveal a reliable conditions effect, $F(1,26) = 1.30$, or a reliable Conditions $\times$ Expectancy Items interaction effect, $F(1,52) = 1.04$. From these results it can be concluded that the subjects in the two treatment conditions did not evince an overall difference in expectancies and made comparable responses to each of the three expectancy items.

Influence of Treatments on Depression Scores

Having determined that the aerobic exercise was effective for improving physical fitness of subjects in the aerobic exercise condition, and having determined that the subjects in the aerobic exercise and placebo treatment conditions had comparable expectancies concerning the psychological effects of their respective treatments, we could then determine the effects of the treatments on depression. To test the effects of the treatments on the depression scores, a 3×2 (Conditions $\times$ Trials) analysis of covariance was conducted in which the covariate was the pretreatment depression scores. This analysis revealed a reliable trials effect that reflected an overall decrease in depression between the midtreatment and posttreatment points, $F(1, 40) = 9.62, p = .003$, and it revealed a reliable conditions effect, $F(2,39) = 6.04, p = .005$. Subsequent paired comparisons indicated that subjects in the aerobic exercise condition had reliably lower depression scores than did subjects in either the placebo condition, $t(39) = 2.02$, $p = .05$, of the no-treatment condition, $t(39) = 3.44, p = .001$ and that there was not a reliable difference between scores in the latter two conditions, $t(39) = 1.42$. From these results it is clear that subjects in the aerobic exercise condition evidenced reliably greater decreases in depression than did subjects in the placebo or no-treatment condition. The absence of a reliable Conditions $\times$ Trials interaction effect indicates that the effect of the treatment was achieved within the first 5 weeks of treatment and that the second 5 weeks of treatment did not add substantially to the effect (see Figure 1).

DISCUSSION

The results of this investigation provide clear evidence that participation in a program of strenuous aerobic exercise was effective for reducing depression. Specifically, subjects in the aerobic exercise condition showed greater reductions in depression than did subjects in the placebo treatment condition and subjects in the no-treatment condition. These findings have a variety of interesting and potentially important practical and theoretical implications regarding the association of decreases in depression with participation in an exercise program.

Although these findings provide controlled evidence for a relationship between exercise and reductions in depression, it is important to recognize that they do not provide evidence concerning the process by which the exercise influenced the depression. That is, from these findings it cannot be determined whether the effects of exercise on depression were mediated by increases in norephinephrine, psychosocial factors, or some other process or processes.

The results of this investigation also documented a reduction in depression that was independent of the treatment, thus demonstrating the necessity of a no-treatment control condition in research on depression. This decrease in depression independent of treatment raises questions concerning the interpretation of the results of previous investigations that did not use a no-treatment condition (Greist et al., 1978). In the clinical literature, such reductions are often referred to as "spontaneous remissions," but that is probably somewhat of a misnomer. Rather, the reductions are probably due to regressions to the mean in the measurements, changing situational circumstances, and the normal fluctuations in symptomatology. Independent of the process, however, these findings highlighted the effect of and the need for controls.

NOTES:

[1]The research by Greist has been reported in a number of articles with different titles and various combinations of authors (e.g., Greist, Klein, Eischens, Faris, Gurman, & Morgan, 1979). It is important that the reader recognize that the articles constitute repeated presentations of the same data and not replications.

[2]At the end of the session the subjects were provided with detailed verbal and written instructions regarding the collection because we had planned to examine the effects of the treatments on MHPG (the major metabolite of central nervous system norepinephrine). Unfortunately, during the preservation process, the MHPG in the urine was accidentally destroyed, and therefore the analyses could not be conducted.

[3]When examining changes in aerobic capacity and changes in depression, analyses of covariance were used to eliminate the possible influence of the law of initial values (Lacey, 1956; Wilder, 1962). That was done although there were no reliable differences among the conditions because it has been demonstrated that even unreliable initial differences can contribute to or obscure subsequent differences (Kinsman & Staudenmayer, 1978).

REFERENCES

Beck, A.T., Ward, C.H., Mendelson, M., Mock, J., & Erbaugh, J. (1961). An inventory for measuring depression. *Archives of General Psychiatry, 4*, 561-571.

Blue, F.R. (1979). Aerobic exercise as a treatment for moderate depression. *Perceptual and Motor Skills, 48*, 228.

Brown, R.S., Ramirez, D., & Taub, I. (1979). The prescription of exercise for depression. *The Physician and Sportsmedicine, 1978*, 35-45.

Collis, M.O., & Shepherd, J.T. (1980). Antidepressant drug action and presynaptic a-receptors. *Mayo Clinical Procedures, 55*, 567-571.

Cooper, K.C. (1968). *Aerobics*. New York: Bantam Books.

Cronan, T.L., & Howley, E.T. (1974). The effect of training on epinephrine and norepinephrine excretion. *Medicine and Science in Sports, 5*, 122-125.

Garvey, M.J. (1980). Biochemistry and treatment strategies for depression. *Journal of Family Practice, 11*, 215.

Greist, J., Klein, M., Eischens, R., & Faris, J. (1978). Antidepressant running: Running as a treatment for non-psychotic depression. *Behavioral Medicine, 5*, 19-24.

Greist, J., Klein, M., Eischens, R., Faris, J., Gurman, A., & Morgan, W. (1979). Running as treatment for depression. *Comprehensive Psychiatry, 20*, 41-54.

Howley, E.T. (1976). The effects of different intensities of exercise on the excretion of epinephrine and norepinephrine. *Medicine and Science in Sports, 8*, 219-222.

Jasnoski, M., & Holmes, D.S. (1981). Influence of initial aerobic fitness, aerobic training, and changes in aerobic fitness on personality functioning. *Journal of Psychosomatic Research, 25*, 553-556.

Jasnoski, M., Holmes, D., Solomon, S., & Aguiar, C. (1981). Exercise, changes in aerobic capacity, and changes in self-perceptions: An experimental investigation. *Journal of Research in Personality, 15*, 460-466.

Kavanagh, T., Shepherd, R.I., Tuck, J.A., & Qureshi, S. (1977). Depression following myocardial infarction: The effect of distance running. *Annals of the New York Academy of Science, 301*, 1029-1046.

Kinsman, R., & Staudenmayer, H. (1978). Baseline levels in muscle relaxation training. *Biofeedback and Self-Regulation, 3*, 97-104.

Lacey, J. (1956). The evaluation of autonomic responses: Toward a general solution. *Annals of the New York Academy of Science, 67*, 123-164.

Maas, I.W. (1975). Biogenic amines and depression. *Archives of General Psychiatry, 32*, 1357-1361.

Maas, J.W. (1979). Biochemistry of the affective disorders. *Hospital Practice, 14*, 113-120.

Morgan, W.P., Roberts, J.A., Brand, F.R., & Feinerman, A.D. (1970). Psychological effect of chronic physical activity. *Medicine and Science in Sports, 2*, 213-217.

Schildkraut, J.J. (1965). The catecholamine hypothesis of affective disorders: A review of supporting evidence. *American Journal of Psychiatry, 122*, 509-522.

Wilder, J. (1962). Basimetric approach (law of initial values) to biological rhythms. *Annals of the New York Academy of Science, 98*, 1121-1220.

Postscript

This article was published in 1984. Since then, Doyne, et.al (1987), Rape (1987), Ossip-Klein, et al (1989), and Dua and Hargreaves (1992) have also demonstrated the antidepressant effect of exercise.

For the purposes of depression/anxiety management, enhanced self-esteem, and cardiovascular fitness that many of us desire, there is reasonable consensus that exercise should be done three times per week, for a minimum of thirty minutes, at sixty percent of maximum exertion ("flirting" with the threshold of discomfort during the workout). In April of 1995 the Associated Press reported the results of twenty-six years of data taken on more than 17,000 Harvard alumni who graduated between 1924 and 1954. Only those who exercised vigorously (fast walking, jogging, or swimming laps) lived longer, although moderate exercisers enjoyed benefits of improved quality of life, lower blood pressure and reduced risk of diabetes.

Unfortunate events, beyond our control, happen at inopportune times in the lives of reasonable people. Through exercise we can become more resilient to stress by increasing the "thickness" of our phase of resistance. A convenient measure of resistance and life stress is the resting pulse rate. Low resting pulse indicates an efficient cardiovascular system and desirable stress level. High resting pulse likely indicates a less efficient system and distress. Normal pulse rate is about 72 per minute. Casual monitoring of resting pulse can provide one with valuable information. Seeing it decrease over time provides reinforcement for exercise and indicates that "on course" life corrections were wise. Increases serve as a negative reinforcer for exercise and may indicate need for on course corrections.

References

Doyne, E., et.al (1987). Running Versus Weight Lifting in the Treatment of Depression. *Journal of Consulting and Clinical Psycholoqg*, 748-754.

Kolat, J.W. (1995). *Biological Psychology.* New York: Brooks/Cole Publishing Company.

Race, R. (1987).Running and Depression. *Perceptual and Motor Skills*, 64, 1303-1310.

Ossip-Klein, et.al (1989). Effects of Running or Weight Lifting on Self-Concept in Clinically Depressed Women. *Journal of Consulting and Clinical Psychology*, 57(1), 158-161.

Dua, J. and Hargreaves, L. (1992). Effect of Aerobic Exercise on Negative Affect, Positive Affect, Stress, and Depression. *Perceptual and Motor Skills, 75*, 355-361.

Figure 6-6. Junk Food Junkie. (Photograph by Jim Rooney.)

READING 6D

DIET FOR A SMALL MADMAN:
FOOD CHEMICALS AND BEHAVIOR

Christopher Norwood

Let thy food be thy medicine and thy medicine be thy food.
—Hippocrates

Your body can process and metabolize only what you provide it. Logically, it can do its best if properly nourished. We consume a variety of chemicals and substances. Not many of us can claim that we use no alcohol, caffeine, or tobacco. We often use a variety of medications. The American diet is also a source of chemicals. Read the ingredient labels on the packages in your pantry. It can be frightening.

Attention-deficit/hyperactivity disorder, in which a child is unable to maintain attention, and exhibits excessive, purposeless motor activity, was described in Chapter 3. Hyperactive children have traditionally been treated with stimulants, such as methylphenidate (Ritalin), which paradoxically have a calming effect on them. In 1974, San Francisco allergist Ben Feingold published Why Your Child Is Hyperactive. *He strongly argued that the treatment of hyperactivity should not involve drugs. The basis of his argument was that there were already too many additives in the typical diets of children. He suggested that these children could be effectively treated by purging these chemicals from their diets.*

The diet has been the subject of much controversy since. Advocates of it demonstrate a nearly religious zeal. The Feingold Association of the United States (Box 6550, Alexandria, VA 22306) is an organization whose purposes are to support their members in implementing the Feingold Program and to generate awareness of the role of foods and synthetic additives in behavior, learning and health problems. Critics argue that improvements result merely from placebo effect. Not surprisingly, much criticism comes from the very food companies who manufacture chemical-laced products. In 1978, Dan White killed San Francisco officials George Moscone and Harvey Milk. His defense argued he should not be held fully culpable because his diet contained too much sugar. In what became known as the "Twinkie Defense," White was convicted of manslaughter, not murder. Both sides were critical of the decision.

Misdiagnosing poorly behaved children as hyperactive, maintaining compliance with the diet, and employing the term to assuage parents' feelings of inadequacy, all contribute to research difficulty.

In 1982 the National Institutes of Health held a conference in order to reach a consensus on "Defined Diets and Hyperactivity." It could conclude only that defined diets couldn't hurt and should be tried if parents believed in them. Weiss (1982) reported that ten percent of hyperactive children are helped by the diet, but that is of significance. Kaplan et.al, in Pediatrics, *January 1989, reported that,*

> *Our research...demonstrates a larger potential impact of diet than previously reported. These results suggest that pediatricians and other practitioners might consider dietary modifications worth trying, particularly in younger children.*

Christopher Norwood: Diet For a Small Madman: Food Chemicals and Behavior, *New York Magazine*, August 8, 1987, 46-52. Reprinted with permission of the author.

Many teachers are intuitively aware of hyperactivity spikes on Halloween. I have received abundant unsolicited testimonials from students who claim the diet has benefitted someone they know. Although published in 1977, the following article by Christopher Norwood illuminates many salient issues in the stalemate.

Among the mysteries of childhood is a crushing disorder known as hyperkinesis or hyperactivity, which snatches away normal behavioral control from its young victims. They break into frantic motion—motion that ranges from the merely annoying to the dangerous. They live in a bizarre world where their conscious minds struggle toward normalcy, but their bodies seem to have assumed an angry, restless life of their own. Hyperactive children often lash out wildly at themselves and others; they will assault siblings, set fires, or compulsively bang their heads against a wall. In a diary account of just ten minutes from "an ordinary day" in the life of her nine-year-old hyperactive son, a Tennessee mother describes the child's attempt to do homework. It comes at the close of an afternoon already marked by the boy's having set two fires, kicked a woman neighbor, and smashed his few remaining toys to dust. "Child bangs door, slumps in chair, snaps point of pencil, jumps on furniture, scratches paper, plays with toes, knocks over lamp, constant wiggles, loud noises," reads the entry. "Mother gives up."

Millions of dollars in research effort have failed to disclose the cause—or causes—of these abrupt shifts in behavior. And, in the absence of a cure, medicine has adopted the common if dubious, practice of controlling these children with drugs. The products used to medicate these children are derived mainly from amphetamines, which are known in the vernacular as "speed." These "pediatric" amphetamines do not in any way alleviate the basic disorder. They act, instead, as a kind of pharmaceutical straitjacket to keep children still—so still that some schools in New York City, and presumably elsewhere, now have cots for those drugged pupils who habitually fall asleep. Current sales figures suggest that not fewer than 500,000, and probably closer to 1 million American children, the bulk under ten years of age, are now tethered to a daily regimen of psychotropic (behavior-altering)

medications. They represent an ominous leap toward mass behavior control and a situation that demands attention.

[In 1973], Dr. Benjamin F. Feingold, a 77-year-old California physician, began to pay attention. After 50 years in medicine, the first half spent as a pediatrician and the second as an allergist, he had retired as head of the allergy department at the Kaiser-Permanente Medical Center in San Francisco. During his long combined career, certain incidents had convinced him that some food additives, predominantly the synthetic flavors and colors, can trigger the bizarre behavior associated with hyperkinesis. In the early 1970s, employing his new leisure to translate this conviction into a treatment program, he launched four hyperactive children on a special "elimination diet." Unlike diets which direct exactly when and what a patient may eat, this plan allows the patient to eat any food desired—except certain forbidden items. Feingold's elimination plan forbade all foods containing synthetic colors or flavors. A boy named Michael Keyser, who was then seven, typified the first group of children. He had been cranky from birth, a fighter from the time he could walk, and since age three and a half, had lived on an array of potent prescription drugs intended to restrain his outbursts. Four years later, and still adhering to Feingold's elimination plan, he needs no drugs, has been shifted to a normal classroom from one for "troubled" children, and is described by his mother as "an entirely different child. He's lovable, has a real sense of humor, and most of all, he likes himself."

Proceeding from these early successes to treat hundreds of hyperactive children, Feingold found that up to half of them returned to normal or near normal behavior when separated from the synthetic colors and flavors. His work received what could be termed its formal debut in a paper presented at the 1973 annual convention of the American Medical Association. Considering its implications for the treatment of a major, debilitating disorder, it was received with odd indifference. Initially no leading medical journal would publish Feingold's research. And those federal agencies assigned to protect food, health, and children carefully ignored the portentous shadow he had cast over the retail food industry; two years passed before the Food and Drug Administration so much as encouraged other researchers to simply investigate his findings. None of this surprised Feingold. "People," he observes congenially, "tend to think you're a little nuts when you first tell them a food additive can make a child violent. It takes a while to sink in."

Here is a complaint about additives radically different in its dimensions from the usual. Unlike others, which have focused on a single additive at a time, it sweeps through the whole field of food protection like a swarm of avenging locusts, raising questions that promise to be more complex than any yet encountered. The average American now annually swallows more than five pounds of synthetic additives in the form of some 4,000 different chemicals. It is a chemical indulgence unmatched elsewhere in the world; moreover, it has usually been assumed that any price to be paid would surface in a tangible physical form— such as malignant cells or diseased livers. Feingold raised the novel possibility that this indulgence has been accompanied by the creation of a distinct class of behavior-disturbed children. Once considered a rare disorder, hyperactivity has within the past decade become what is often said to be the fastest-growing childhood affliction in the United States.

Feingold points out that the apparent emergence of hyperactivity as a modern plague has paralleled an explosion in the usage of the very chemicals he bans. The manufacture of synthetic food dyes, for example, almost doubled between 1960 and 1970. This doubling reflected the use of new marketing techniques which saw foods as diverse as cereal, lunch meat, and baby preparations tinted almost neon in the competition for the customer's eye. Various official and semiofficial estimates for the number of hyperactive children, meanwhile, mounted steadily. As is often the case with behavior disorders, firm figures are simply not to be had, but it has been claimed that as many as 2 million to 5 million children have now

been sentenced to hyperkinesis.

All told, Feingold's research was as simple in clinical application as it was complex in social consequence. On the one hand, it proffered a hope for remission for thousands, perhaps millions, of desperate children. On the other hand, by condemning the American food industry as being mad in a literal sense not even the sternest critic had yet thought to suggest, Feingold's work demanded that a stunning spectrum of America's institutions be examined. Would, for instance, food additives take a place beside hard drugs as a cause for the blank, compulsive fury of juveniles? Should the multibillion-dollar retail food industry be junked and retooled? The overwhelming nature of the Feingold thesis was a thing that, in itself, made it hard to consider, much less accept. Moreover, it was hard to evaluate because of the especially elusive nature of hyperkinesis. The disorder is probably the most baffling major syndrome in the pediatric showcase, and it is impossible to discuss research into its cause and cure without taking due account of its caprice.

Despite intensive research and all the tools of modern physiology—the EEG's and the blood counts, the microscopes and urinalyses—no one has been able to decipher what has gone wrong inside the bodies of these children. They are otherwise quite healthy. And, although the disorder has been observed in both children of genius I.Q. and those too retarded to speak, as a group, hyperactive children appear to have above-average intelligence. Some people suggest that the misfortune that overtakes them could be a biochemical imbalance; others think it could be some kind of "minimal" brain injury that manages to affect behavior without harming intelligence. No evidence favors either theory; however, loose talk about brain damage has given these children the stigma of such labels as "minimally brain damaged" or "minimal brain dysfunction."

The disorder does not even have a discernible pattern. It sometimes lasts for months, other times for years, and seems occasionally not to be outgrown at all. It marches indiscriminately across racial and social barriers. It does appear to affect boys about six times as often as girls. This circumstance has been taken as a signal of genetic involvement but could also mean nothing more than the nursery-rhyme wisdom that boys, being made of puppy-dog tails, generally have more trouble growing up. Another curiosity is that many, but not all, hyperactive children display sensorimotor deficits. These difficulties in fine and gross motor control, in balance and eye focus, can render such school-related tasks as holding a pencil cruel obstacles.

It is not even clear that hyperactivity has made the giant leaps in incidence often reported. As with most behavior disorders, the lack of a diagnostic test and identifying physical symptoms means that it exists mainly in the eye of the beholder. The beholding of hyperactivity has ranged from the less than 2 percent of school-children proposed a few years ago by the federal Office of Education to the 25 percent or more now claimed by some school districts. Skeptical observers, however, suggest the term has lost its true medical meaning to become a catchword for any annoying or frantic behavior on the part of the young; and, in pediatrics, hyperactivity has garnered something of the reputation of "a diagnostic garbage pail." A recent book by Peter Schrag and Diane Divoky sternly titled *The Myth of the Hyperactive Child* further proposes that some groups, particularly the drug industry, which has been engaged in its own frantic campaign to establish psychotropic medications as the modern solution to troublesome children have a real stake in inflating the incidence of the disorder.

There is just no certain way of mediating between the view that hyperkinesis is rampant and the view that it is rampantly overstated. These children's individual distress, however, is cause for concern, whatever their aggregate number may be. The natural remission of the disorder often comes too late to retrieve lost chances for the child to learn, to mature, and even to become a social being. There are, of course, persons who surmount the ravages of a hyperactive childhood. The inventor Thomas Alva Edison is an engaging example of one who matured to use the restless intelligence often associated with the condition. But when Edison was removed from school—a routine occurrence for these children—his mother determined to teach him herself. More commonly, the fate of the hyperactive child seems to parallel the fate of the abused child. They are thought to form a disproportionate number of dropouts and the criminal young. The difference is that they have been flogged into a maligned self-image by their own bodies.

The suspicion that food additives can play a major role in the dismal tale of hyperkinesis had formed very slowly in Dr. Feingold's mind. The first clue surfaced in 1965 in the rather odd shape of a 40-year-old woman who appeared at Kaiser-Permanente suffering from what he retrospectively refers to as "a very fortunate case of giant hives." Feingold advised her to eliminate two groups of substances from her diet. The first included synthetic colors and flavors, and the second, all foods and medicines containing the salicylate radical. (The salicylate radical is a certain grouping of atoms found in aspirin, tea, one vegetable–cucumber–and several fruits, among them apples, tomatoes, oranges, and peaches.) For reasons not entirely understood, the salicylate radical and the synthetic colors and flavors all can act as culprits in the outbreak of hives and other rashes. Banning them has become a routine procedure.

At the time, however, a ban on all three together was a rather new tactic. It quickly conquered the hives, but it also brought Feingold an excited phone call from the chief of psychiatry at Kaiser. He briskly inquired what the allergy department had "done to that woman." It seemed that soon after her hives subsided, so had the angry, hostile behavior for which she was in therapy. Feingold, with the skepticism native to the scientist, dismissed as coincidence this first suggestion of a link between additives and behavior. Two years passed before the continuing reports of odd behavior changes associated with this elimination diet finally inspired him to investigate a specific link to hyperkinesis. There was logic in the thought that substances that seemed to unhinge an occasional adult might have an especially savage effect on the young.

Acting at first on the clue furnished by the serendipitous case of hives, he banned salicylates and synthetic colors and flavors alike in treating hyperkinesis. This diet has since come to be known as the K-P (Kaiser-Permanente) or Feingold regimen. But experience revealed that most children could tolerate the reintroduction of salicylates into their stomachs and livers—a tolerance that pointed to the colors and flavors as the primary *provocateurs* in behavior disturbances. Experience also revealed that the effectiveness of the diet steadily diminishes the older the child. Teenagers, for example, tend not to respond, or their improvement is spotty. To Feingold, this is a sign that they may have sustained some form of permanent damage.

Age also tends to govern the length of time required for a child who does basically respond to the diet to clear his system of chemical intruders and retrieve control over his physical self. A Washington, D.C., pediatrician with some 40 children on the diet describes watching some younger ones, those under five, "entirely change their personality in 48 hours." Older children may need a month to get going and an even longer period to overcome the psychological devastation imposed by their former, "bad" self. Accompanying sensorimotor deficits also tend to fade, again to an extent that depends on the age and condition of the child. A year and a half ago, an eleven-year-old named David Hathaway testified on this point at hearings held before the health subcommittee of the Senate Labor and Public Welfare Committee. He said that, for him, the major benefit of the diet was the increased hand coordination. For the first time in his life, he could build model airplanes.

In medicine, of course, the observations of a single physician are not considered proof of anything. It seemed that after Feingold's initial presentation of his work, the diet was destined for outright oblivion or, at most, semi-quack status. It garnered brief media attention and the expected clucking in *Prevention*, a magazine that serves as the *National Enquirer* of the American digestive tract ("Are you listening, FDA? Is anybody listening?"). But none of the half dozen or so federal agencies that could have sponsored the long, expensive process of controlled studies that do count as proof in science were interested in Feingold. Among these agencies are the National Institutes of Mental Health, and of Child Health and Human Development. The Institute of Mental Health alone has sponsored more than $1 million in studies lauding the use of drugs in hyperkinesis.

At age 73, however, Feingold was a remarkably formidable opponent. He was endowed with abundant charm, upright posture, and lively brown eyes. He was driven by a conviction that food technology is scarring thousands of the young. And he was determined to force the Department of Health, Education, and Welfare "to begin to help these parents understand that they have some alternative to drugging their children." The result was that he launched a one-man campaign which saw him crisscrossing the country, giving interviews, guiding parents groups, and lecturing. He wrote a book called *Why Your Child Is Hyperactive*, a chatty, anecdotal account of the discovery of the diet that includes additive-free recipes supplied by his wife, Helene, a retired ballerina. But above all, Feingold treated hundreds of hyperactive children without charge. Whatever conventional medicine might say about him, the parents of these youngsters were willing to attempt almost anything to aid a child whom conventional medicine could only drug or ignore. Packing special lunches, baking homemade cookies, and reforming their food habits, they presented Feingold with an endless stream of success stories to, in turn, present to officials at HEW. (Not incidentally, these parents also found it easier than expected to wean their children from the candy-coated glories of an American childhood. Those children who respond to the K-P regimen feel so much better that they tend to police their own food. One satisfied six-year-old observed that his body "wasn't angry anymore.")

Within the medical profession, this combination of public pressure and parental testimony earned Feingold the suspicion that falls on any doctor who moves beyond the circumspect world of medical journals in order to prove a point; yet it seemed to be what was required to move the federal government to subject the diet to open, scientific research. In response to Feingold's lengthening backlog of success stories, the National Institute of Education finally allotted $59,896 to Dr. Keith Conners of the University of Pittsburgh for a brief controlled study on fifteen children. In early 1975, Conners, an occasional drug-company consultant who had frankly thought the diet would be quickly disproved, reported back some positive results. These emerged, he says, "much to my own surprise."

Meanwhile, the Food Research Institute at the University of Wisconsin, in pursuit of Feingold's hunch that salicylates affect only a few children, commenced to evaluate the result of forbidding additives alone. For two months, the Research Institute supplied all food for an experimental diet entirely free of synthetic colors and flavors and for a control diet containing these additives to the families of two groups of boys. In the first group were 36 hyperactive boys between the ages of six and twelve; in the second, ten boys between three and five. The behavior of the older children was rated by three groups—their parents, teachers, and trained observers. (In keeping with the protocol for "blind" studies, none of the families or observers knew when the diets were switched or even the purpose of the experiment.) The result with the older children was that 11 percent of them were judged by all observers to have improved behavior while on the additive-restricted diet. The younger children were judged only by their parents. All the mothers and more than half of the participating fathers cited a behavior improvement during the time on the diet free of synthetic colors and flavors.

But perhaps the most impressive support for Feingold has not come from university research or from believing parents or even from six-year-olds who talk about their bodies "being quiet." Perhaps it has come from children too hopeless to even speak for themselves. These are children who suffer the double blow of hyperactive behavior and known neurological damage—retarded, mongoloid, and brain-injured children. They are not children who, in Dr. Feingold's phrase, "will ever be smart, but they may lead productive lives outside institutions if their behavior straightened out." Scattered reports suggest that the diet's effect on them is dazzling. For example, the Brant Sanatorium, an Ontario, Canada, home for retarded and handicapped children, tried the K-P diet on a profoundly retarded and endlessly violent eight-year-old boy and on a ten-year-old girl with a congenital condition known as meningomyelocele, which leaves the spinal cord exposed. The girl stopped the self-abusive tantrums during which she'd scratch herself until

she bled; the boy, according to a staff report, for the first time was able "to form relationships with Staff members . . . and is able to express affection. "Writing a decade ago in *Science* magazine, Walter Modell, a now retired member of the pharmacology department at the Cornell Medical College, proposed that the great potential for mass drug disasters no longer lay with the occasional prescription drug—thalidomide is an example—that somehow outwits testing procedures; it had shifted to substances which were not tested at all because "they are not always defined as drugs and are used in industry and agriculture—pesticides, herbicides, gasoline additives, and so on." Now, ten years later, it is still not commonly understood that everyday chemicals affect the mind, as well as the body, as do drugs. In this sense, food additives may retrospectively stand as a kind of missing link in the perception of environmentally induced behavior problems.

Even Feingold found it difficult at first to conceive that a sensitivity or "allergy to additives might manifest itself in the form of a behavior problem, rather than as a rash, hives, or other physical symptom." He eventually decided that the situation lost all mystery with the recognition that food additives, ingested through the stomach and coursing through the bloodstream, could be considered just drugs in another form. Genetic predisposition would explain why these additive-drugs affect some children and leave others unscathed. Human physiology, after all, is so diverse that a body burden of lead that kills one child won't bother the next, that aspirin plunges an occasional victim into shock, and that penicillin is fatal to about one in a thousand persons. "What it amounts to," Feingold now insists, "is that these children are being drugged already."

There is, at present, no way to prove this notion of genetic susceptibility and druglike response. But much research and circumstance do suggest that a child somehow under assault from an environmental intruder will appear to be hyperactive. Lead-poisoned children, for example, have long been observed to have a high rate of hyperactivity. Monkey infants nursed on milk containing levels of the industrial chemical PCB only notches above that frequently found in human breast milk also tend to be hyperactive.

John Ott, while director of the Environmental Health and Light Research Institute in Sarasota, and Dr. Lewis Mayron, a nuclear-medicine specialist, demonstrated that constant exposure to low-level electromagnetic radiation from such sources as television and fluorescent lighting can contribute to the distress of some children. The New York Institute of Child Development, Inc., a nonprofit center in Manhattan that attempts to take a biochemical, physiological approach to troubled children, is a particularly rich source of revealing incidents. Over the years, analysis of factors ranging from glucose tolerance to diet to trace-metal levels has yielded children who regained their composure when separated from items as diverse as cow's milk and copper.

An encounter with two eight-year-olds graphically underscores the often odd relations between physiology and behavior. One child was a sunny, blond boy whom the staff had nick-named "Adorable Arthur" in honor of how really good he was when good. Still, for all his charm, Arthur had occasional fits which saw him smash anything, human or object, within reach. Detective work correlating his appetite to his rages revealed that his parents had not understood apples were included among the salicylate foods forbidden to this child.

Yet, for the other angry eight-year-old, apples were a fortunate fruit. He was suffering from an excess copper ingestion—an excess perhaps taken in with his drinking water. A daily half cup of homemade apple sauce (an overprocessed commercial brand would not have worked) served as a natural chelating agent to draw out the offending chemical. "No matter how long you work in this field," comments William Mullineaux, the institute's clinical director from 1973 to 1975, "you are still astonished by what some of the most common things will do to a child whose system can't handle them."

Meanwhile, it is hard to suggest what should—or even can—be done about the situation with food additives. On the one hand, it may seem only obvious that chemicals that can condemn some children to misery should not be sold from every supermarket in the land. On the other hand, it is unlikely that a public accustomed from birth to Count Chocula cereal, to 48 flavors, and

to beautifying its food with suspected carcinogens would give up these indulgences for an undisturbed group of children. There are not, for instance, enough vanilla beans produced in all the world to supply even the American demand for vanilla ice cream from natural sources.

Current law, in any case, requires that additives be tested and banned individually. At present, it is not known whether the children who respond to the diet are sensitive to just one, to some, or to all of the dozens of synthetic dyes and the several hundred synthetic flavorings now in use. Testing this number of additives could turn into a scientific scavenger hunt that would last for decades. As an interim measure, Feingold suggests that a special mark or symbol be stamped on all foods containing no synthetic colors or flavors. This mark is intended as a shopping aide to families on the diet and as an antidote to the laxity in labeling which allows even foods such as butter and oranges to be colored without the consumer's knowing.

Before leaving office, former FDA Commissioner Alexander Schmidt said that his agency has neither objection to this symbol nor power to enforce its use. A special HEW panel formed to evaluate the whole question of additives and behavior reported back, in the fashion typical of bureaucratic panels, that it can reach no conclusions about the K-P diet except that "further investigation" should take place. Dr. Bernard Weiss, a behavioral toxicologist at the University of Rochester, is currently trying to work around the problems of testing the diet for the vague symptoms of hyperactivity by monitoring its potential impact on many and specific kinds of behavior—on, for example, the tendency of children to have nightmares or sleepless nights, bite their nails, and throw tantrums. Somewhat similarly, a private pediatrician well experienced in using the diet observes that he no longer recommends it only for "the classic, aggressive hyperactive child." He also uses it on children who are just cranky and unhappy for no real reason—children whose parents I know are nice people successfully raising other kids. It often does wonders for them too."

And there matters rest. Quite possibly the evidence that we *really* have gone too far has surfaced only to reveal that there is little room for retreat. Quite probably Americans will concede a certain number of children who scratch themselves until they bleed and smash their own heads, who assault siblings and rage through playgrounds, as the price for what they have come to regard as food. "Drugged" into a shadow of madness and drugged again into submission, they are the creation of a society that has lost control of its own chemistry.

Reference

Weiss, B. (1982). Food Additives and Environmental Chemicals as Sources of Childhood Behavior Disorders. *Journal of the American Academy of Child Psychiatry,* 21, 144-152.

Take this test before reading the following article:

TYPE A–B PERSONALITY TEST

Instructions: You will be shown a number of adjectives. Use these words to describe yourself by indicating, on a scale of 1 to 7, how true of you these various characteristics are. Please give your own opinion of yourself. If you are not sure, put down the number that comes closest to what you think best describes you. Do not leave any blank spaces if you can avoid it.

1	2	3	4	5	6	7
Never or almost never true	Usually not true	Sometimes but infrequently true	Occasionally true	Often true	Usually true	Always or almost always true

1. Energetic	____	14. Unrealisitic	____	27. Excitable	____
2. Idealistic		15. *Relaxed*	____	28. Snobbish	____
3. *Quiet*		16. Headstrong	____	29. *Mild*	____
4. Outspoken		17. Tense	____	30. Loud	____
5. Self-confident		18. Unstable	____	31. Individualistic	____
6. Cooperative		19. Enthusiastic	____	32. Stingy	____
7. *Peaceable*		20. Irritable	____	33. *Easy-going*	____
8. Aggressive		21. *Informal*	____	34. Talkative	____
9. Quick		22. Ambitious	____	35. Outgoing	____
10. Helpful		23. Dominant	____	36. Original	____
11. *Calm*		24. Assertive	____	37. *Cautious*	____
12. Forceful		25. Sly	____	38. Strong	____
13. Enterprising		26. Argumentative	____		

Scoring key:

Type A items: 1, 4, 5, 8, 9, 12, 13, 16, 17, 19, 20, 22, 23, 24, 26, 27, 30, 31, 34, 35, 38
Type B items: 3, 7, 11, 15, 21, 29, 33, 37 (in italics)

1st.: Type B items must be converted by subtracting each response from 8. i.e. 7 = 1, 6 = 2, etc.

2nd.: The total Type A score is obtained by adding the 21 Type A items to the 7 transformed Type B items.

Type A-B Scale:

28	112	196
Extreme Type B	Mean	Extreme Type A

Figure 6-7

READING 6E

THE PACE OF LIFE

Robert V. Levine

An upholsterer noticed an unusual wear pattern on the seats of chairs in the reception room of San Francisco cardiologists Meyer Friedman and Ray H. Rosenman. Patients had been waiting on the "edge of their seats." Type A Behavior and Your Heart *was published in 1974. In the book's preface, Friedman and Rosenman made a bold statement:*

> *In the absence of Type A Behavior Pattern, coronary heart disease almost never occurs before seventy years of age, regardless of the fatty foods eaten, the cigarettes smoked, or the lack of exercise. But when this behavior pattern is present, coronary heart disease can easily erupt in one's thirties or forties.*

> *"Type A Behavior Pattern is an action-emotion complex that can be observed in any person who is aggressively involved in a chronic, incessant struggle to achieve more and more in less and less time, and if required to do so, against the opposing efforts of other things or other persons" (67). Type A individuals have excessive competitive drive, and a chronic sense of time urgency (hurry sickness). They walk, talk, and eat rapidly, and manifest polyphasic thought and action (eating, talking on the phone, or even reading while driving). Their conversations gravitate to issues of self-interest. Clenched fists, gritting of teeth, tense stomach, and other indications of sympathetic response are prominent. The dominant mood is anger with seethed hostility (67-85).*

> *Research during the past twenty years has shown that hostility and impatience are particularly dangerous components of Type A personality. Levenkron, et al (1983) showed that subjects trained to control hostility and impatience demonstrated lower self-reported stress reactions and fatty acid reactivity (192). As reported in the* American Heart Journal *in 1994, Friedman updated the list of characteristics. Time urgency and hostility were given particular emphasis.*

> *Does Type A behavior predict heart disease? The following article empirically investigates this question.*

When I was teaching in Brazil some years ago, I noticed that students there were more casual than those in the United States about arriving late for class. I was puzzled by their tardiness, since their classroom work revealed them to be serious students who were intent on learning the subject. I soon found, however, that they were likely to be late not only in arriving for class but also in leaving it afterward. Whatever the reason for the students' lateness, they were not trying to minimize their time in the classroom.

In my classes in the United States I do not need to wear a watch to know when the session is over. My students gather their books at two minutes before the hour and show signs of severe anxiety if I do not dismiss them on time. At the end of a class in Brazil, on the other hand, some students would slowly drift out, others would

Robert Levine: The Pace of Life, *American Scientist*, Vol. 78, September-October, 1990, 450, 452-459. Reprinted with permission of the author.

stay for a while to ask questions, and some would stay and chat for a very long time. Having just spent two hours lecturing on statistics in broken Portuguese, I could not attribute their lingering to my superb teaching style. Apparently, staying late was just as routine as arriving late. As I observed my students over the course of a year, I came to realize that this casual approach to punctuality was a sign of some fundamental differences between Anglo-American and Brazilian attitudes toward the pace of life.

My experience in Brazil inspired an ongoing research program whose aim is to devise ways of measuring the tempo of a culture and to assess peoples' attitudes toward time. Every traveler has observed that the pace of life varies in different parts of the world, and even from place to place within a single country, but it is not obvious how to quantify these differences. We could question individuals about their concern with time and about the course of their days, but this method yields subjective descriptions that do not allow for systematic comparisons between groups. Without a suitable basis for comparison, it becomes difficult to gauge the meaning of "fast" or "slow."

In the past few years my colleagues and I have attempted to develop reliable, standardized measures of the pace of life. Our measurement techniques are based on simple observations that require no equipment more elaborate than a stopwatch. Much of the field work has been done by students in the course of their travels on summer vacation or during breaks between semesters.

Pace and Culture

There is value in describing and appreciating another culture's sense of time. We might, for example, begin to understand the source of some of the difficulties we experience when we are exposed to another culture. Adjusting to an alien pace of life may present almost as many difficulties as learning a foreign language. This was revealed most dramatically in an investigation into the roots of culture shock among Peace Corps volunteers returning from overseas assignments. James Spradley of Macalester College and Mark Phillips of the University of Washington found that two of the three greatest adjustment

difficulties were the "general pace of life" and the "punctuality of the people." Only the "language spoken" proved to be a more stressful change. The temporal aspects of life may even be thought of as a silent language. As the American anthropologist Edward Hall has noted, these informal patterns of time "are seldom, if ever, made explicit. They exist in the air around us. They are either familiar and comfortable, or unfamiliar and wrong."

Misinterpreting this silent language may lead to serious difficulties in communication. In 1985, for example, a group of Shiite Muslim terrorists hijacked a TWA jetliner, holding 40 Americans hostage with the demand that Israel release 764 Lebanese Shiite prisoners being held in Israeli prisons. The terrorists handed the hostages over to Shiite Muslim leaders who assured the American negotiators that nothing would happen to the hostages if all demands were met. At one point during the delicate negotiations one of the leaders of the Shiite militia Amal said that the hostages would be returned to the hijackers in two days if there were no movement toward meeting their demands. The American negotiators knew that neither they nor the Israelis would be able to forge a settlement in such a short time. By setting a limit of two days, the Shiites made a compromise unlikely and elevated the crisis to a very dangerous level. But when the Shiite leader realized how his statement was being interpreted, he quickly backed off: "We said a couple of days but we were not necessarily specifying 48 hours" (United Press International June 23, 1985). Forty lives were put in jeopardy by a misinterpretation of the word *day*.

A society's pace of life may have consequences for the health of the inhabitants as well. This idea has been widely publicized in the wake of the observation that individuals with a constant sense of time urgency described as type-*A* behavior, may be more susceptible to heart disease than individuals who have a more relaxed attitude toward time.

With these considerations in mind my colleagues and I have carried out a series of studies across and within cultures over the past 15 years. Our results indicate that differences in the pace of life exist not only between the Northern and

Southern hemisphere but also between the Eastern and Western worlds; indeed, important differences can be perceived between the regions of a single country.

The Pace of World Cities

In collaboration with Kathy Bartlett of California State University, Fresno, I have attempted to extend and refine our understanding of cross-cultural differences in the perception of time. Rather than focus on some single dimension such as punctuality, we used several objective measures that assessed the more general issue of the pace at which people live their lives. We collected our data from six countries: Japan, Taiwan, Indonesia, Italy, England and the United States. The selection of these countries allowed for comparisons between Eastern and Western cultures with varying degrees of economic development. In each country we collected data from the largest city and from one medium-size city (the populations ranged from 415,000 to 615,000).

We examined three indicators of tempo in each city. First, we measured the accuracy of a sample of outdoor bank clocks in the main downtown area. Fifteen clocks were checked and their times compared to that reported by the telephone company; deviations from the "correct time" were measured to the nearest minute.

Second, we measured the average walking speed of randomly chosen pedestrians over a distance of 100 feet. The measurements were made on clear summer days during business hours in at least two locations on main downtown streets. We avoided crowded or congested areas, so that the pedestrians could potentially walk at their own preferred maximum speed. In order to control for the effects of socializing, only pedestrians walking alone were timed. Subjects with obvious physical handicaps, and those who appeared to be window-shopping, were excluded from the survey.

Third, as an indicator of working pace, we measured the speed with which postal clerks fulfilled a standard request for stamps. In each city we presented clerks some paper money (the nearest equivalent of a five-dollar bill) and a note in the native language requesting a common denomination of stamp. We then measured the elapsed time between the passing of the note and the completion of the request.

Our results revealed a number of significant differences between the six countries. The Japanese cities rated the highest on all three measures: They had the most accurate bank clocks, the pedestrians there walked the fastest, and their postal clerks were the quickest to fulfill our request. In contrast, the Indonesian cities had the least accurate public clocks and the slowest pedestrians. The distinction of having the slowest postal clerks went to the Italian cities, where buying a stamp took nearly twice as long as it did in Japan.

There were also a number of differences between the large and the medium-size cities within each country. In particular, we found that people in the larger cities walked faster than those in the smaller communities. The difference was greatest in the least-developed countries in our sample, namely Indonesia and Taiwan. This may reflect the persistence of a traditional village life style among people in the smaller cities of those countries. (It would be interesting to investigate the pace of life in rural areas and small towns, but a different set of measures would be needed; there are few bank clocks in farming villages.)

What impressed us most about these findings was the high correlation between the three pace-of-life measures for each city. The accuracy of the bank clocks is strongly correlated with walking speed; the correlation coefficient, r, is .82. (An r value of 1 indicates perfect correlation.) There is also a strong correlation between clock accuracy and the speed of the postal clerks ($r = .71$). Finally, walking speed is positively correlated with postal-clerk speed ($r = .56$). The high correlation between these distinct measures supports the notion that a city has a definable overall pace, which manifests itself in the behavior of the inhabitants. It appears reasonable, then, to speak of a characteristic pace of life for a particular area and to distinguish between cultures on the basis of this characteristic.

The Pace of U. S. Cities

Intrigued by our findings that various world

cities have a particular pace of life, we decided to take a closer look at the cities of the United States. Are Californians really more laid-back than people in other parts of the country? Do New Yorkers live up to their reputation of living in the fast lane? What we learned confirmed many of our general preconceptions, but we also found some surprises.

Our methods were similar to those we employed in our studies of world cities. We examined nine cities in each of four regions of the United States: the Northeast, Midwest, South and West. Within each region, we studied three large metropolitan areas (population greater than 1,800,000), three medium-size cities (population between 850,000 and 1,300,000) and three smaller cities (population between 350,000 and 550,000).

Within each city we measured four indicators of the pace of life. First, we determined the walking speed of pedestrians over a distance of 60 feet. The speeds were measured during business hours on a clear summer day along a main downtown street. We applied the same restrictions on the selection of subjects and locations as in our international study.

Second, in order to gauge the speed of working life, we measured how long it took bank clerks to complete a simple request: We asked a teller in each of at least eight downtown banks to make change for two $20 bills or to give us two $20 bills for change.

Our third indicator of pace was talking speed. We asked postal clerks to explain the difference between regular mail, certified mail and insured mail; we recorded their responses and calculated their speaking rate by dividing the total number of syllables by the total time of their response.

Fourth, as a measure of the population's concern with time, we counted the proportion of men and women in downtown areas during business hours who were wearing a wristwatch.

Each of these measures considered individually has certain quirks. The number of people wearing a watch, for example, reflects not only a society's preoccupation with time but also its sense of fashion and perhaps its level of affluence. Basing measurements on interactions with postal clerks and bank tellers puts undue emphasis on these rather specialized subpopulations; furthermore, the performance of the clerks and tellers depends on their skill and knowledge as well as on their general tendency to hurry or tarry. To compensate for these distortions we combined the scores from the four sets of measurements, creating an overall index of the pace of life in each city. First we normalized the scores, so that they all extended over the same range (an operation that has the effect of assigning equal weight to all four factors); then we added the normalized values.

In general, our results confirmed the widespread impression that the Northeastern United States is fast-paced, whereas the West Coast is a little more relaxed. We found that people in the Northeast walk faster, make change faster, talk faster and are more likely to wear a watch than people elsewhere. In fact, seven of the nine fastest cities are in the Northeast. Boston, Buffalo and New York are the fastest overall; a big surprise was that New York does not lead the list. (Manhattan residents might be excused a couple of steps, however, in order to watch the local events; during an interval of an hour and a half, our observer on one New York street corner reported an improvised concert, an attempted purse-snatching, and a capsized mugger.)

The slowest pace is on the West Coast, and the slowest city overall is Los Angeles. The residents of that city scored 24th out of 36 in walking speed, next to last in speech rate and far behind everyone else in the speed of the bank tellers. The Los Angelenos' only concession to the clock was to wear one: the city was 13th highest in the proportion of the population wearing a watch.

Pace and Consequences

These temporal measures serve not only to inform us of differences between peoples, but they may also be used to examine relations between the pace of life and other traits of a population. One trait that has long been suspected of being associated with the pace of life is psychological and physical health. Of particular note is the reported association between a fast-paced life and a high incidence of heart disease.

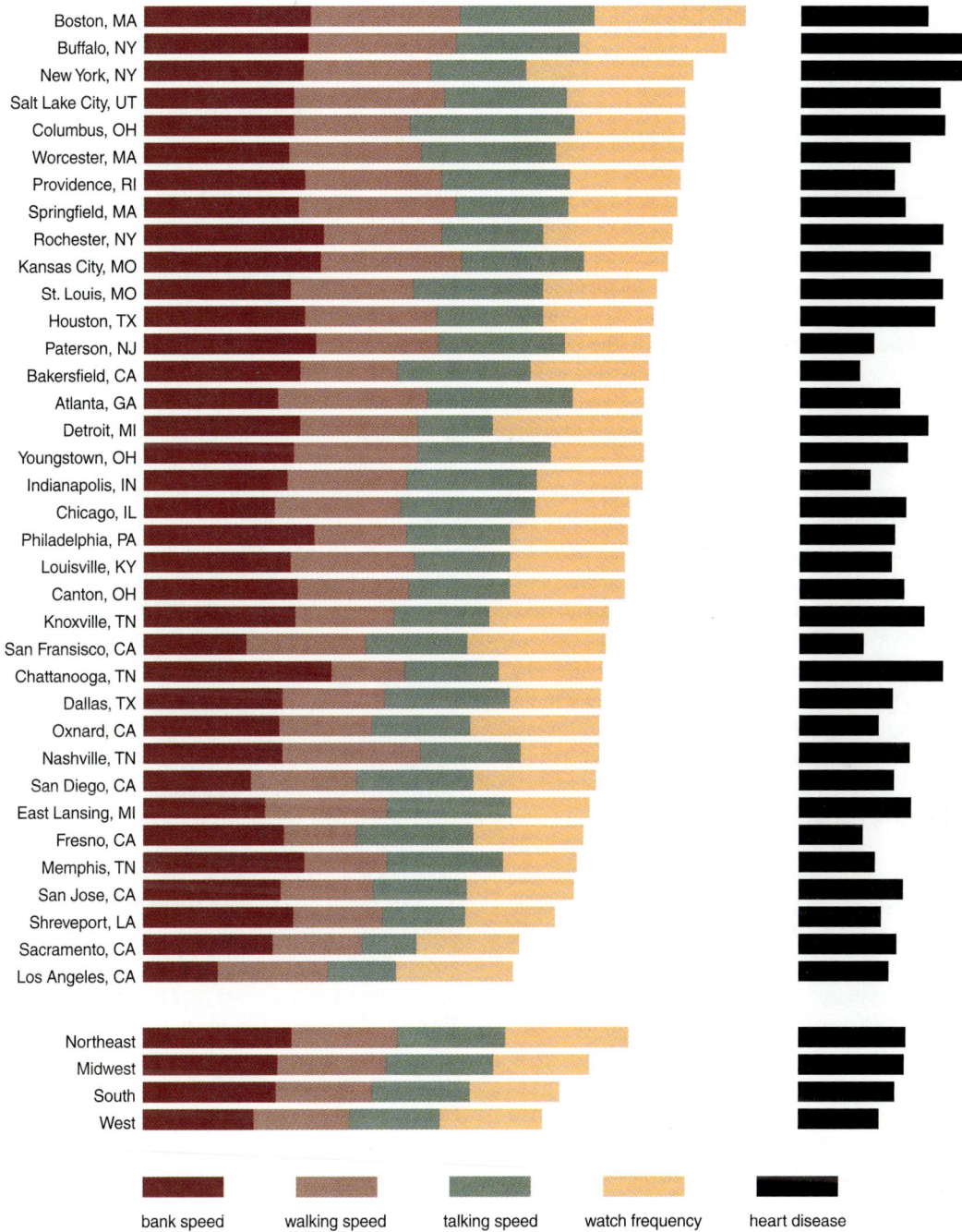

Figure 6-8. American cities were ranked on four pace-of-life measures: the speed at which bank tellers were able to fulfill a request for change, the walking speed of downtown pedestrians, the talking speed of postal clearks, and the proportion of people wearing wristwatches. In each case a longer bar corresponds to a faster pace. There is significant and positive correlation between the overall pace of life for a city and the incidence of heart disease in that city. Data from nine cities in each of the four regions of the U.S. were pooled to express the average pace of life for each region.

In 1959 Meyer Friedman and Ray Rosenman reported that men who exhibit a behavior pattern characterized by a sense of time urgency, hostility and competitiveness are **seven** times more likely than others to have evidence of heart disease and are more than **twice** as likely to have a heart attack. People who exhibit this behavior pattern, which Friedman and Rosenman called type *A*, tend to walk quickly, eat quickly, do two things at once, and take pride in always being on time. The study seemed to support suspicions that behavior patterns can affect the incidence and course of a disease.

Since that first report, however, the association between type-*A* behavior and heart disease has become increasingly controversial. A number of authors have not been able to reproduce the results found by Friedman and Rosenman. The nature of our own studies suggested that we might be able to shed some light on this issue by investigating the relationship between the pace of life and the incidence of heart disease for particular populations. We were especially struck by the similarities between type-*A* behavior and those traits that we measured as indicators of a fast pace of life. Our research provides a unique perspective on the question since most studies linking heart disease with a sense of time urgency have focused on individuals, not on geographic areas.

We began with the hypothesis that the faster a city's overall pace of life, the higher will be its rate of death from heart disease. To test the hypothesis we compared the overall pace of life measured in our 36 American cities with the death rate in each city from ischemic heart disease (a decreased flow of blood to the heart). The death rates were those reported by the Department of Health and Human Services for the year 1981. Since age is positively correlated with the incidence of heart disease, we statistically adjusted the death rates for the median age of each city's population. In this way we hoped to isolate the effects of social factors on heart disease.

Briefly, our results reveal a significant correlation between the pace of life and the rate of death from ischemic heart disease. The magnitude of the correlation ($r = .50$) is higher than that usually found between heart disease and measures of type-*A* behavior in individuals. In other words, our data suggest that the **pace** of a person's environment is at least as good a predictor of heart disease as his or her score on a type-*A* personality test. This was true whether we corrected for age or not.

Why are people in fast environments more prone to heart disease? In large part, we suspect that fast environments attract fast-moving, type-*A* people. The psychologist Timothy Smith and his colleagues at the University of Utah have shown that type *A* individuals both seek and create time-urgent environments. The fastest cities in our study may represent both the dreams and the creations of people who live under a sense of urgency.

The development of a fast-paced city could be explained by the following scenario. First, type-*A* people are attracted to fast-paced cities. In turn, the greater proportion of type-*A* residents serves to maintain and further promote a fast-paced way of life. Meanwhile, slower, type-*B* individuals tend to migrate away from fast-paced cities to environments more compatible with their temperament. Smith's research suggests that the temporal expectations of fast-paced cities demand time-urgent behavior in all people—type *A*'s and type *B*'s alike. The result is that type-*B* individuals act more like type *A*'s, and type *A*'s strive to accelerate the pace still more.

The precise mechanism linking time-urgent behavior to heart disease is not known. Nevertheless, some recent statistics from the Department of Health and Human Services hint at one possibility: the incidence of cigarette smoking follows the same regional pattern as that of ischemic heart disease and the pace of life. That is, the rates for cigarette smoking and ischemic heart disease are highest where the pace of life is fastest: the Northeastern United States. The Northeast is followed by the Midwest, the South and then the West on all three variables.

Cigarette smoking has been identified as the single most important preventable cause of heart disease. It is also well documented that cigarette smoking is often related to psychological stress. These correlations suggest but do not confirm, the possibility that a causal relation exists between these variables. One possibility is that stressful, time-pressured environments lead to unhealthy behaviors such as cigarette smoking and poor eating habits, which in turn increase the risk of heart disease. Our model of the fast-paced "type-*A* city" may provide a basis for examining this hypothesis.

Closer examinations of modern life offer an interesting perspective on our way of living, but a caveat is also in order here. Although we have come to view the choice between rushing and leisurely activity as a trade-off between accomplishment and peace of mind, we should note that time pressure is not always stressful; it may also be challenging and energizing. The optimal pressure seems to depend on the characteristics of the task and the personality of the individual. Similarly, what we have characterized as a type-*A* environment will affect different people in different ways. What may be most important is fitting people to their environment. Although a type-*A* setting may be stressful to a type-*B* individual, a type-*A* person may experience more distress in a type-*B* environment. Given that heart disease remains the single largest cause of death in the United States, the search for a healthy person-environment fit takes on great importance.

Bibliography

Amato, P. R. 1983. The effects of urbanization on interpersonal behavior. *Journal of Cross-Cultural Psychology* 14:153-367.

Booth-Kewley, S., and H. Friedman. 1987. Psychological predictors of heart disease: A quantitative review. *Psychological Bulletin* 101: 343-362.

Bornstein, M. H. 1979. The pace of life: Revisited. *International Journal of Psychology* 14:83-90.

Chernoff, Herman. 1973. The use of faces to represent points in k-dimensional space graphically. *Journal of the American Statistical Association* 68:361-368.

Cohen, J. B., S. L. Syme, C. D. Jenkins, A. Kagan, and S. J. Zyzanski. 1975. The cultural context of Type A behavior and the risk of CHD. *American Journal of Epidemiology* 102:434.

Freedman, J., and D. Edwards. 1988. Time pressure, task performance, and enjoyment. In J. E. McGrath (ed.), *The Social Psychology of Time: New Perspectives* (pp. 113-133). Newbury Park, CA: Sage.

Friedman, A. P., and R. H. Rosenman. 1974. *Type A Behavior and Your Heart.* New York: Alfred A. Knopf.

Hall, E. T. 1959. *The Silent Language.* New York: Doubleday.

Lauer, R. H. 1981. *Temporal Man: The Meaning and Uses of Social Time.* New York: Praeger.

Levendron, J., et. al. 1983. Modifying the Type A Coronary-Prone Behavior Pattern. *Journal of Consulting and Clinical Psychology,* 51(2), 192-204.

Levine, R. 1988. The pace of life across cultures. In J. E. McGrath (ed.), *The Social Psychology of Time: New Perspectives* (pp. 39-62). Newbury Park, CA: Sage.

Levine, R., and K. Bartlett. 1984. Pace of life, punctuality and coronary heart disease in six countries. *Journal of Cross-Cultural Psychology* 15:233-255.

Levine, R., K. Lynch, K. and M. Lucia. 1989. The type A city: Coronary heart disease and the pace of life. *Journal of Behavioral Medicine* 12:509-524.

Levine, R., L. West and H. Reis. 1980. Perceptions of time and punctuality in the United States and Brazil. *Journal of Personality and Social Psychology* 38:541-550.

Marmot M. G., and S. L. Syme. 1976. Acculturation and coronary heart disease in Japanese-Americans. *American Journal of Epidemiology* 104:225-247.

Matthews, K. 1988. Coronary heart disease and Type A behaviors: Update on an alternative to the Booth-Kewley and Friedman (1987) quantitative review. *Psychological Bulletin* 104:373-380.

McGrath, J. E. 1989. The place of time in social psychology: Some steps toward a social psychological theory of time. Paper presented at the Seventh Conference of the International Society for the Study of Time, July, 1989, Glacier Park, Montana.

Reid, D. D. 1975. International studies in epidemiology. *American Journal of Epidemiology* 102:469-476.

Smith, T., and N. Anderson. 1986. Models of personality and disease: An interactional approach to Type A behavior and cardiovascular risk. *Journal of Personality & Social Psychology* 50:1166-1173.

Spradley, J. P., and M. Phillips. 1972. Culture and stress: A quantitative analysis. *American Anthropologist* 74:518-529.

Werner, C. M., I. Altman and D. Oxley. 1985. Temporal aspects of homes: A transactional perspective. In I. Altman and C. M. Werner (eds.), *Home Environments: Human Behavior and Environment. Advances in Theory and Research.* (Volume 8, pp. 1-32). New York: Plenum.

Wright, L. 1988. The type A behavior pattern and coronary artery disease. *American Psychologist* 43:2-14.

The Psychoanalytic School, Clark University, Worcester, Massachusetts, 1908. *Top row, from left to right*: A.A. Brill, Ernest Jones (Freud's biographer), and Sandor Ferenczi. *Bottom row, from left to right*: Sigmund Freud, G. Stanley Hall (then president of Clark University), and Carl Jung. (The Bettman Archive.)

Chapter 7

THE PSYCHOANALYTIC PERSPECTIVE

Sigmund Freud, founder of the psychoanalytic perspective and its primary spokesman until his death in 1939, stands alone as the most significant contributor to clinical psychology and psychiatry. The beginnings of psychoanalysis can be traced to the 1890s when Freud, a neurologist in Vienna, Austria, became convinced that hysterical neurosis was caused by strictly psychological factors. During the nineteenth century, the somatic school, forerunner of the contemporary illness perspective, prevailed in the Vienna medical establishment. Psychoanalysis was perceived as a revolt against established medical practice and Victorian morality. Freud was considered a radical. He chose the lot of an outsider rather than compromise his beliefs.

Freud learned hypnosis from mentors Charcot, Bernheim, and Breuer, and employed the technique on his patients. He observed that while hypnotized, his patients could recall information from their past that they could not recall in their normal, conscious, waking state. This observation led him to postulate the existence of the unconscious mind, which he felt harbored the roots of psychopathology. Freud felt that if he could bring the deep-rooted, unconscious conflicts to the conscious level, they could finally be dealt with appropriately and laid to rest. He employed the technique of catharsis, or abreaction, in his therapy. The therapist uses this technique to help his patient psychologically relive the traumatic experience and release previously repressed rage ("austoben") and sorrow ("ausweinen"). He observed that his patients' neurotic symptoms often improved following this process. Freud eventually became disenchanted with hypnosis, and began using free association (saying the first thing that comes to mind) and dream interpretation to unlock the mysteries of the unconscious.

Freudian theory is strong in its contention that adult psychopathology is rooted in unresolved sexual conflict from childhood. The conflict is likely the result of abusive parental or caretaker treatment. In 1896, Freud presented the "seduction theory." Seduction, euphemistically employed, described sexual assaults perpetrated upon children by the very caretakers entrusted with their welfare. Although Freud anticipated approval from his colleagues, the medical society was indignant with the insinuation that such maltreatment existed in conservative, self-righteous, Victorian Vienna. We will examine this issue more thoroughly later in this chapter.

Beginning in 1884 Freud began experimenting with cocaine. After successfully treating a stomach disorder of one patient with this "magical" drug, he wrote his fiance,

> If it goes well I will write an essay on it and I expect it will win its place in therapeutics, by the side of morphium and superior to it. I have other hopes and intentions

about it. I take very small doses of it regularly against depression and against indigestion, and with the most brilliant success. I hope it will be able to abolish the most intractable vomiting, even when this is due to severe pain; in short it is only now that I feel I am a doctor, since I have helped one patient and hope to help more. If things go on in this way we need have no concern about being able to come together and to stay in Vienna (in Byck, 1974, p. 7).

His enthusiasm escalated. He urged his friends and colleages to use cocaine in their medical practices and for their own edification. He authored a series of articles, which were ultimately collectively published in 1963 as the Cocaine Papers. Again, approval from his colleages was not forthcoming. His work was attacked. In 1885, Louis Lewin criticized Freud's contention that cocaine was harmless, and A. Erlenmeyer called cocaine the "third scourge" of the human race (in Byck, 1974, Chronology). Nevertheless, the use of cocaine increased. Coca-Cola has not been "The Real Thing" since cocaine was removed in 1903.

Freud was a Jew, and he was deeply troubled by the discrimination suffered by them. Later in life, he reflected on entering the University of Vienna in 1873. "I experienced some appreciable disappointments. Above all, I found that I was expected to feel myself inferior and an alien because I was a Jew." He indignantly refused to accept this status. Freud's atheism alienated him from Jews as well (in Gay, 1989, xv). He once commented that Jews were allowed to make a living only as long as they were "willing to step into the gutter to let a Christian pass."

His colleagues spurned his work. The presentation of the seduction theory met with an "icy reception." The chairman of the conference commented, "It sounds like a scientific fairy tale." Freud's classic "Studies on Hysteria" is considered to be the formal starting point of psychoanalysis. It sold only 626 copies in its first thirteen years (a fact I keep in mind while writing this book). Carl Jung and Alfred Adler, two of Freud's staunchest disciples, eventually parted with him to develop their own psychoanalytic theories. Freud smoked about twenty cigars a day, developed cancer of the mouth and jaw, and underwent a series of painful operations.

In 1933 the Nazis declared war on psychoanalysis and ordered Freud's books burnt in the streets of Berlin. Despite his anguish, Freud was able to sarcastically, yet humorously note, "What progress we are making. In the Middle Ages they would have burned me; nowadays they are content with burning my books" (Schultz, 1960, pp. 264-267). Upon the invasion of Austria in 1938, Freud's friends tried in vain to persuade him to leave. Searching for valuables, Nazi S.A. men invaded Freud's home. Freud sneered at them and they left. They were not usually that easily deterred. His sisters were sent to concentration camps and gassed. Freud reluctantly fled to London in 1938. He died there in 1939 (Appignanesi, 1979, pp. 165-168). In bitter irony, the full appreciation and impact of his work was never known by him.

The impact of psychoanalysis extends beyond psychology. It has had significant impact on Western society. Theorists and therapists who claim to reject Freud often use theories and techniques suspiciously reminiscent of his. Few modern figures have been quoted, or misquoted, more than Freud. Controversial theories often encounter resistance. Psychoanalysis was ultimately the first comprehensive theory of psychopathology and its treatment. Despite efforts by various factions to discredit Freud and his theories, they remain a vital force in clinical psychology and psychiatry. While there may be "little new under the sun," Freud was an original thinker.

The first selection to be presented is entitled *Altered States: Peeling Away the Layers of Multiple Personality* by Frank W. Putnam. It examines the legitamacy of dissociative identity disorder. The second, *Posttraumatic Stress Disorder and the Treatment of Sexual Abuse*, by Sylvia B. Patten, et.al., provides a model for the treatment of trauma-related pathology. *Lies of the Mind*, by Leon Jaroff, follows third. It investigates the validity of repressed memories in abuse victims. Fourth, *The Psychodynamics of Suicide*, by Herbert Hendin, offers psychoanalytic insights regarding suicidal motivation. Fifth is *Lecture XXVIII, Analytic Therapy,* by Sigmund Freud. It is the last of his lectures to his students of psychoanalysis in 1917. The chapter concludes with *Erik Erikson's Eight Ages of Man*, by David Elkind, a description of a model which complements and extends Freudian theory.

References

Appignanesi, R. (1979). *Freud For Beginners.* New York: Pantheon Books.
Byck, R. (1974). *Cocaine Papers by Sigmund Freud.* New York: Meridian.
Gay, P. (1989). *The Freud Reader.* New York: W.W. Norton & Company
Schultz, D.P. (1960). *A History of Modern Psychology.* New York: Academic Press, Inc.

Figure 7-1. Frederic March in the movie version of *Dr. Jekyll and Mr. Hyde* by Robert Louis Stevenson. The movie provides a prototype for multiple personality. (Paramount, 1932. Photograph courtesy of Wisconsin Center for Film and Theatre Research.)

READING 7A

ALTERED STATES:
PEELING AWAY THE LAYERS
OF MULTIPLE PERSONALITY

Frank W. Putnam

In 1895, Freud and his mentor/colleague Joseph Breuer published Studies On Hysteria. *It is considered the formal beginning of psychoanalysis and is comprised of five case histories; the first of which is Miss Anna O., one of Breuer's patients during the early 1880s. "Hysterics suffer mainly from reminiscences" of traumatic events, they claimed. An "energetic reaction" from the victim was absent at the time of the trauma. Thus, the psychic energy associated with the recollection is relegated to the unconscious, and causes pathology because it has not been catharted. Often, hysteria is associated with a "double con- science" and a tendency to dissociation. Treatment lies in allowing the "strangulated affect" a means of escape through speech; a "talking cure" (Breuer and Freud, 1893, pp. 7-17). Anna O. called this process "chimney sweeping" (Monte, 1995, p. 41). Thus, multiple personality was considered a type of dissociative hysteria by Freud.*

Reread the sections on conversion disorder presented in Chapter 4, Category VIII, and dissocia- tive identity disorder, Category X. Recall that hysteria was eliminated as a diagnostic term in 1980. Multiple personality was changed to dissociative identity disorder in DSM-IV (1994) because of poten- tial forensic, financial, or relationship gain and because the disorder is culture-bound. However, the debate regarding the legitimacy of this condition continues.

Theoretically, a true multiple personality should be characterized by:

- *Distinctly different personality states or identities.*
- *Alter ego(s) may be aware of the executive personality, but executive personality should not be aware of the alter(s).*
- *Spontaneous switches.*
- *A history of trauma.*
- *Alter(s) are foils of the executive.*
- *There is evidence of primary\secondary gain, but it is insufficient to constitute malingering.*
- *A reduction of anxiety upon symptom formation.*
- *A general medical condition is ruled out.*

The following article, published in 1992, was written by Frank W. Putnam, a child psychiatrist and chief of the Unit on Dissociative Disorders, Laboratory of Developmental Psychology, at the National Institute of Mental Health. Blended with the case of Anna O. is a presentation of what has recently been learned about the condition. Does Anna O. represent a classic case of multiple personality as described by Breuer and Freud more than a century ago? Does multiple personality exist, or is skepticism justified?

References

Breuer, J. and Freud, S. (1955). *The Complete Psychological Works of Sigmund Freud, vol. II, Studies on Hysteria.* London: The Hogarth Press.

Monte, C. (1995). *Beneath the Mask: An Introduction to Theories of Personality*, 5th ed., New York: Harcourt Brace College Publishers.

To psychiatry she is known as Anna O. With a quick grasp of ideas, intelligence, energy, tenacity and persistence to the point of obstinacy, she was regarded as a practical, eminently rational young woman. Although much given to day-dreaming—her "private theater"—she enjoyed excellent mental and physical health throughout her childhood and adolescence. But at the age of twenty-one Anna O. fell ill in an astonishing fashion. Her condition was thought to have been precipitated by the protracted illness of her father, whom she was devotedly nursing. Certainly that conjecture made sense, for it was in December 1880, five months after her father had taken ill, that Anna displayed her first symptoms: blurred vision and intermittent paralysis of her right arm and both legs.

Shortly thereafter other sensory and motor aberrations appeared. Anna began to have trouble speaking and was revolted by the sight of food. Her behavior became increasingly, uncontrollably erratic—so much so that she complained of having two selves—one real, and the other an evil variation. As desperate as she was perplexed, she consulted the Viennese physician and physiologist Josef Breuer. Breuer was a friend of the young Sigmund Freud's, who was just then completing his medical studies. Years later, in 1895, the two men would make the case history of Anna O. the centerpiece of their collaborative volume *Studies on Hysteria*. The cathartic treatments described in that book mark the beginnings of psychoanalysis.

Upon meeting with Anna, Breuer perceived that the young woman did indeed inhabit two distinct states of consciousness, which alternated and became increasingly differentiated over time. In one state she was her normal self, albeit depressed and anxious; in the other, Anna's physical symptoms became more pronounced, and she hallucinated and turned abusive.

Breuer probed his patient, asking her to relate the details of her experience and occasionally to submit to hypnosis. It became clear that Anna's two conscious states existed side by side, often separated from each other by an amnesic barrier: while she was in one state, she had no memory of her behavior in the other. Changes between states, called switches by modern psychiatrists, were extremely rapid. They took place spontaneously or in response to an emotionally charged stimulus—an orange, for instance, Anna's principal source of nourishment while she was nursing her father.

Some of the differences between Anna's two states were baffling. When she felt her best she spoke in French and Italian as well as in her native German. In her second state she usually spoke only in English, although she could understand German. At other times in that second state, however, she was mute or spoke in garbled mixtures of four or five languages. Now and then Anna seemed to have a foot in each of her personas: she might have terrifying hallucinations of black snakes, yet at the same time part of her would recognize that she was only seeing the ribbons in her hair. In those moments of dual awareness, Breuer wrote, Anna noted the presence of a detached "clear-sighted and calm observer sitting in the corner of her brain and looking on at all the mad business."

Today Anna's condition would be called by its clinical name, multiple-personality disorder. MPD is characterized by the existence of two or more markedly contrasting "alter personalities" that exchange executive control over a person's behavior. The syndrome is perhaps the most extreme of the dissociative disorders—psychiatric conditions characterized by profound disturbances in memory and identity. In MPD dissociation, a normal coping mechanism has gone awry in the face of overwhelming trauma. Alter personalities have been known to show significant differences in heart rate, respiration, brain wave patterns and many other measures. About a third of the psychotherapists who treat MPD victims report that a given medication can have different effects—ranging from sedation to activation—depending on which personality is being displayed by the patient. Another typical scenario is that one personality gets drunk and another experiences the hangover. In some cases of MPD different allergic responses have been reported, a finding that has inspired a good deal of inconclusive investigation.

Perhaps understandably, in view of such an unusual cluster of symptoms, the conventional view of MPD has long been one of fragmentation: the victim was seen as having been shattered into several or many separate, dysfunctional and somehow lesser individuals. But research in the past decade suggests an apter image, one that conveys the idea of a layering, of different ways of being that are embedded within a whole. Much of that new approach derives from the work of the psychologist Charles T. Tart of the University of California at Davis, who introduced the term *discrete states of consciousness* to describe unique, recurrent psychological and physiological patterns. Recent studies by other workers suggest that shortly after birth, a baby's behavior is organized into a series of such discrete states. The transitions between states in fact, closely resemble the personality switches observed in MPD victims. During normal development those transitions smooth out, and most people more or less succeed in consolidating an integrated sense of self. MPD is the most drastic example of what can take place when that process is explosively derailed. The layers of the self are peeled away and exposed, affording a singularly revealing window on the state of being.

The idea that one person can experience a number of separate, distinctive mental states has a long history in Western thought. The concept was central to the development of hypnosis, for instance, and it reverberates through the phenomena of sleep, dreaming, meditation, catatonia, panic disorder, mind-altering drugs, manic-depressive illness and, of course, MPD itself. The earliest recorded explanations of MPD, popular throughout most of the nineteenth century, centered on the supernatural. The patient was assumed to be possessed by evil spirits or, perhaps, to be the victim of some form of reincarnation gone horribly wrong.

From about 1880 until the 1920s the disorder was increasingly viewed as a physiological malfunction. A powerful influence on diagnosticians was the discovery that certain functions of the brain—such as speech and hearing—are localized in either the right or the left cerebral hemisphere. MPD was widely thought to be the result of some short-circuiting between the two sides of the brain. That line of thinking is still being pursued by some investigators, though definitive results have been elusive.

From the 1920s until about 1970 interest in MPD declined precipitously. During much of that time a reactionary, skeptical atmosphere prevailed, as many investigators wondered whether the syndrome was nothing more than a fad or a fraud. But in the past two decades the pendulum has swung back, and MPD is now widely recognized as a legitimate form of mental illness. Many detailed cases were recorded in the 1970s and 1980s, notably that of Sybil which became the basis of a popular television film.

With the renewal of interest has come diagnostic progress. Similarities noted in various case histories pointed overwhelmingly to childhood trauma as the root cause of MPD. Severe, repeated sexual abuse, generally incestuous, was seen to be the most pervasive trauma associated with the disorder. That may help explain why a great majority of reported MPD sufferers have been female; most of them (by a ratio of roughly five to one) were victims of sex crimes as children.

There is a striking quality of extreme, often bizarre sadism reported by many MPD victims. Torture with matches, steam irons, razor blades or glass is not uncommon. Confinement—even live burial—is a recurring theme in an alarming number of instances. A range of other traumas, particularly ones involving the violent death of a loved one, have also precipitated MPD. I have encountered a number of such cases among children and adolescents from war-torn regions including Cambodia and Lebanon. In each instance the victim had witnessed the massacre of family members by some military faction. One girl said she had seen her parents blown to bits in a mine field; her anguished response was to try to piece their bodies back together.

In the face of such ghoulish circumstances, the dissociative response can be commensurately extreme. Some children create a system of imaginary companions—dwarfs, genies, angels, animals, superheroes. Those companions may at first be experienced as distinct from the child's true self, only later to become internalized as alter personalities—or they may be internalized from the start. In any event each dissociated state acquires a specific sense of self, a set of behaviors and biographical details that are elaborated over time as the child repeatedly escapes from traumatic reality. When those alter personalities begin to trade off control of the person's behavior, MPD has taken hold.

A personality switch in a victim of MPD is usually signaled by a blink or an upward roll of the eyes. Sometimes the eyelids flutter rapidly, and the face often twitches or grimaces. The person may display bodily twitches, shudders, abrupt changes in posture or even convulsions, which have been mistaken for epileptic seizures. But often the person has learned to disguise or veil such switching behavior. Women frequently turn their heads away, momentarily shield their faces with their hands or allow their hair to fall over their faces. An alter may even time its emergence so that it takes hold while the therapist treating the MPD victim is looking away or is otherwise distracted. Once a new personality has emerged, the patient may engage in behaviors therapists refer to as grounding—touching the face, pressing the temples, touching the chair, scanning the room, shifting posture restlessly. Grounding is thought to be part of an orientation process for an alter that suddenly finds itself in a new situation. There are at least four variations of switching in MPD. Rapid switches, similar to the startle response in normal people, can take place in fractions of a second. In the second kind of switching, the patient passes through an unstable intermediate stage that includes features of both the old and the emerging state. During such transitions the patient may have the sense of dual awareness that Anna O. described. The same form of transition is sometimes seen in bipolar illness, as the victim switches from mania to depression. Intriguingly, the switch from depression to mania can be either rapid or slow, passing along the way through several stable mood states.

In the third form of switching MPD patients pass through another kind of intermediate phase, which can be described as a trance or a void. One alter personality fades away into an unresponsive blankness that can last several minutes before the next alter comes to the fore. Finally, in the fourth kind of switching the MPD patient falls asleep for several hours, until a new personality emerges. Clinicians have also noted an intervening period of sleep in some bipolar patients during the switch from mania to depression.

I do not think anyone really knows what ultimately constitutes an alter personality. For example, there is some disagreement about the distinction between an alter with a fully developed sense of self and a so-called personality fragment, which typically displays a limited range of such emotions as anger and joy. I must stress that whatever an alter personality is, it is *not* a separate person. Rather, all of the alters represent differentiated aspects of a single whole. The therapist who treats a victim of MPD must apply that idea with some sensitivity in the treatment, because the alters themselves may protest their submergence into a larger personality, insisting on their own uniqueness. And certainly, a nonspecialist might be tempted to agree with them, given their apparent autonomy of mind and body.

It is always dangerous to generalize in science. Nevertheless, certain broad categories of alter personalities exist in most MPD patients. Every victim, for instance, has at least one host personality, which dominates the body most of the time and generally becomes identified as the "patient," at least at the start of medical or psychological treatment. Typically the host is depressed, anxious, rigid, frigid, compulsively good, conscience-stricken and masochistic and suffers any number of physical symptoms, most often headaches. Host personalities usually feel overwhelmed by life, at the mercy of forces far beyond their control. In many cases a host either is unaware of the alter personalities or, in the face of all evidence to the contrary, strongly denies their existence. The host personality is almost never the patient's original personality—the identity that developed between birth and the experience of trauma. That self usually lies dormant and emerges only after extensive psychotherapy.

Virtually every MPD patient manifests a number of child and infant personalities. Those alters are usually frozen in time, prisoners of some trauma that took place at their particular age. If they are young enough they may be nonverbal, and if they are frightened or abused they may curl up into the fetal position, writhe on the floor or throw themselves against walls. On the other hand, a child or infant personality may serve as a counterbalance, with a sunny, trusting Pollyanna outlook, and may even idealize the person who has abused them.

It is also common for MPD patients to have persecutor personalities, internal saboteurs that often attempt to maim or kill the host or some of the other personalities—a characteristic that reinforces their highly developed self-perception of being separate from the other alters. The enormous anger locked up in persecutors drains much of the energy and strength an MPD patient needs to survive and improve. In addition to persecutor personalities there are sometimes suicidal personalities, bent on killing themselves alone.

Were those violent or self-destructive personalities given free rein, MPD victims would have radically abbreviated life expectancies. The disorder is distinctive however, for its internal system of checks and balances: most MPD patients have an array of protector or helper personalities to offset their darker side. In women, such guardians are frequently male; indeed, cross-gender personalities show up in at least half of MPD cases. The personalities dress their parts and may be sexually active with either heterosexual or homosexual orientations, leading, as one might expect, to much confusion.

There are numerous other kinds of alter personality, some more common than others: obsessive-compulsive; substance abuser; autistic or handicapped; or analgesic (in which feeling pain is denied). Some MPD patients even have impostor personalities that mimic the other alters, and nearly all such patients have promiscuous personalities that act on forbidden impulses. A common scenario among women patients is for a promiscuous alter to pick up a strange man, stage an often masochistic tryst and then vanish, leaving the frightened, probably sexually frigid host to contend with the aroused and no doubt equally perplexed stranger. Prostitute alters are fairly widespread in women, serving to handle sexuality for the personality system as well as provide a source of income.

The striking differences between the many alter personalities extend far beyond behavior and emotional attitude. MPD patients seem to undergo a complete metamorphosis as they pass from one alter to another. The physical transformations can be dramatic. Facial lines may turn from vertical wrinkles to horizontal lines; the jaw may shift from an overbite to an underbite. Posture, body language and motor skills often change radically. Petite women often have male protector personalities that are exceptionally powerful physically, and many MPD patients have alters with special artistic or athletic talents—observations that raise some intriguing questions about human potential. On the other end of the spectrum, it is not unusual to encounter an alter personality suffering from a severe physical disability, say, blindness, deafness or muteness, that is psychogenic.

A pervasive effect of MPD—an effect also observed in other discrete states of consciousness, when the patient is drunk or under hypnosis, perhaps—is known to clinicians as state-dependent learning and memory retrieval. Information or behavior learned in one discrete state is most readily remembered in that same state. In the classic state-dependent learning experiment the subject is taught different information, lists of words, for example, in two of his distinct mental states. Thus word list A is taught while the person is sober, and list B is taught while he is intoxicated. Later the person is asked to remember words from each list while sober and then again while intoxicated. Typically in the sober state the subject recalls words from list A more accurately than those from list B, but vice versa while intoxicated. A less controlled example of the same principle is the stuff of situation comedy: the newly sobered drunk must get drunk again to remember where he left his car keys during a preceding binge.

Neuropsychologists often divide memory functions into two basic systems, the explicit and the implicit, which each appear to be mediated by a different brain system. The explicit memory system stores facts and information, together with the context in which the information was acquired. If your first acquaintance with the distributor in your car took place when it failed one dark night on a lonely highway, you will probably recall that experience in any future discussions about distributors in automobiles. The knowledge available from implicit memory, on the other hand, is generally retrieved with no recall of the external circumstances in which it was acquired. When you multiply numbers, you probably do not remember the specific events that led to your learning the multiplication tables. Although people are often unaware that implicit information exists, it can exert a powerful influence on conscious behavior

Different discrete states of consciousness show the effects of state dependency, according to whether the information is tapped by explicit or implicit memory. For drug- and alcohol-induced states, state-dependent effects are greatest for explicit information. In contrast, MPD patients, for reasons not yet clear, show much greater state-dependency for implicit information. Although information is always more accessible in a state at least similar to the one in which it was acquired, recall across different states is asymmetrical: thus for an MPD victim such as Anna O., alter personality A may have more awareness of alter B than B has of A. That property, directional awareness, or its opposite, directional amnesia, has been recognized in MPD patients since the turn of the century.

One important recent contribution to the understanding of discrete mental states has come from the study of normal newborn infants. Some of the most extensive work in the area was reported by the child psychiatrist Peter H. Wolff of Boston Children's Hospital in his book *The Development of Behavioral States and the Expression of Emotions in Early Infancy.*

In his studies Wolff classified the infants' various discrete states according to heart rate, motor activity, facial expression and vocalization. An infant in what Wolff calls state I (regular,

quiet sleep), for example, is at rest, with pliant muscle tone and little motor activity except for occasional involuntary twitches and bursts of rhythmic mouthing. The baby's eyes are closed and relatively still, its skin (in Caucasians) is pale or light pink and its face is relaxed and symmetrical. Infants in state I breathe regularly and rarely make a sound.

Quiet sleep contrasts sharply with state V, which Wolff describes simply as "crying" (state II is restless sleep; state III is alert inactivity; and state IV Wolff calls "fussy"). In state V infants fluctuate between the extremes of whimpering and screaming. Their faces become flushed and contorted; their muscles turn rigid; their limbs usually become extended; and their movements become diffuse. An infant that has been startled or injured can switch from state I to state V in just a few seconds. In contrast, a transition from the agitation of state V to the calm of state I may require a more substantial period of soothing parental interventions such as feeding or rocking. Nevertheless, Wolff points out, any behavioral state in normal infants is active for only a limited time. Even if a crying baby is left alone, it will eventually cycle back to quiet sleep.

Wolff's studies are instructive because they show that even among newborns—virtually blank ledgers, unscarred by psychological stress—complex behavior is made up of perhaps as many as half a dozen sequences and cycles of discrete states. Thus what we consider a person, even at the most fundamental level, is not a static, monotonous entity. Rather the person is fluid, layered and ever changing in response to outside stimuli. As the child matures, additional discrete behavioral states—more complex sequences with branching patterns and side loops—are created by life experiences. Switches take place when one state is disrupted and gives way to a new one in which the infant's psychological and physiological regime is reorganized.

Although the switches between states are generally imperceptible in a normal, fully integrated adult, there are exceptions. A familiar example is the emergency startle response evoked by sudden danger—say, a near collision while driving an automobile. Often the imperiled person describes an electrifying rush of adrenaline through the body, associated with a stiffening jerk and hyperalertness. Whatever the train of thought or the conversation at the moment of the emergency, it is instantly suspended, as the person concentrates on avoiding the hazard at hand. The ability in such cases to change rapidly from one state of being to another can obviously be a lifesaver.

It is the adaptive value of being able to switch behavioral states that seems to underlie the phenomenon of dissociation. Up to a point, the dissociative process is considered a normal defense against stressful or traumatic experiences: one seeks refuge in a more hospitable state of consciousness. A benign, commonplace example of the strategy is daydreaming on the job.

But when a trauma is severe, the same tactic can be taken to extremes, and it becomes classified as a dissociative disorder. MPD can manifest itself some time after a trauma that takes place during the crucial developmental period, when children are integrating their behavioral states. When a vulnerable, impressionable young life becomes a sentence of unrelenting trauma, pain or abuse, new, aberrant discrete states are created and evoked. The sense of self changes, and with it memory, intellect and even the body's regulatory physiology. The whole of a person becomes differentiated into two, three or as many as twenty parts. The layers of the self become increasingly distinct and autonomous. The passage between them, normally as seamless as the movements of a fine symphony, is now so jarring, so violent in some instances, that it seems—albeit incorrectly—as if one person has become several or many different people.

Because some symptoms of MPD are so startling, it is easy to be misled into thinking the disorder is unique. Variations in physiological functions among the alters, for instance, are often mistakenly pointed to as proof that alter personalities are as different as separate people. In fact, a number of other psychiatric disorders, such as manic-depressive illness, manifest marked physiological changes from one discrete state to another. And some normal, healthy people can manifest the same effects through meditation or hypnosis.

The clinical literature and lore are also filled with accounts of MPD patients in whom different personalities react differently, both psychologically and physiologically, to the same stimulus. But state-dependent responses to the same stimulus are not an exclusive province of MPD either. As Wolff's infant studies have shown, that tendency may be innate in human beings. An example familiar to any parent is a baby's changing susceptibility to being awakened by handling at different points in the sleep cycle. In state I sleep infants can be picked up, changed, dressed, undressed or moved with relative impunity; in state II they are awakened by the slightest touch. Only in state II sleep will they smile in response to a high-pitched voice or a bird whistle.

One cannot overstress the importance of drawing parallels between normal infants and victims of MPD. The understanding that MPD is an extreme outgrowth of seeds planted almost at the start of life, when discrete behavioral states take form, is crucial to treating the disorder. We all are born with the potential for multiple personalities, and as such we must never regard MPD victims as many-headed freaks of nature. At the same time, one must never forget that each patient is unique. Consequently, there is no single intervention, no panacea for MPD. Many patients and therapists have looked to medication for relief, but unfortunately no magic pill exists. Through hypnosis, the analysis of dreams, and other means, the life of each victim must be plumbed for its traumas, dissociations and other biographical vagaries and then be reconstructed. Abreaction, the cathartic discharge of suppressed, unconscious, emotionally laden memories, controlled by the therapist, has proved useful in many cases. With painstaking slowness the pieces fit together.

Even with appropriate treatment, many MPD patients never achieve a fully integrated sense of self. Even when fusion does take place, much work is left to be done. New defenses to the stresses of life have to be erected, and important relationships must be renegotiated. The discovery of new, hidden layers of alters is a constant possibility. The patient may always be tempted to return to the divided state and may even mourn the loss of the alter selves. Vigilance is essential.

Sometimes, even when treatment fails, life goes on. Anna O. was never cured by Josef Breuer, who abruptly released her from his care in 1882. (Breuer reportedly acted at the insistence of his wife, who thought he had become too involved in the case.) Anna was hospitalized several times thereafter, but by 1888 she had resumed an active life. Now it is known that her real name was Bertha Pappenheim and that she went on to become a pioneering social worker and a staunch crusader against the sexual abuse of women. Although there is no record that she, in contrast to so many other victims of MPD, was abused in childhood, her heroic career suggests a passionate, deeply personal interest in the subject. She was renowned for her fearless forays into the brothels of Europe, Russia and the Near East to free women trapped in prostitution and white slavery. She even wrote a play titled *Women's Rights,* featuring sadistic men who sexually exploit women.

All the while she carried on a full and rich second life as a member of the artistic and cultural bourgeois of Vienna. She collected lace, china and glassware, wrote short stories, fairy tales and travel accounts, and edited ancient Jewish religious works into modern forms. A friend remarked that many of Pappenheim's acquaintances could not understand her "double life" as a radical social reformer and as a member of an elite artistic circle.

In 1936 Bertha Pappenheim died of cancer. It is said she left two wills, each written in a different hand.

Postscript

As mentioned in the article, Bertha Pappenheim became a crusader against the abuse of women. She established a high quality girls' school. When Hitler overtook Europe, the school was to be turned into a whorehouse with the current students as prostitutes. All poisoned themselves to avoid this fate (Simons and Comer, 1992, p.20).

Reference

Simons, J. and Comer, R. (1992). *Instructor's Manual to accompany Comer: Abnormal Psychology.* New York: W.H. Freeman and Company.

Figure 7-2. Shattered Innocence. (Photograph by Jim Rooney.)

READING 7B

POSTTRAUMATIC STRESS DISORDER AND THE TREATMENT OF SEXUAL ABUSE

Sylvia B. Patten, Yvonne K. Gatz, Berlin Jones, Deborah L. Thomas

The criteria set for posttraumatic stress disorder was presented in Chapter 4, Category VII. Severe pathology results from events that involved actual or threatened death, or a threat to the physical integrity of the individual. The reaction was one of intense fear, helplessness, or horror. Children may also demonstrate disorganized or agitated behavior.

After Studies in Hysteria *(1895), Freud published* The Seduction Theory *in 1896. He alleged that his patients had been subjected to sexual abuse, largely perpetrated by their fathers. Professional and social pressure were placed on Freud to recant this theory. As mentioned previously, Freud was considered a radical and an outsider for a variety of reasons. In 1897, Freud wrote his confidant, Wilhelm Fliess, that he was reconsidering the seduction theory. His reasons were rationally and logically based in his theory:*

- *If his theory was correct, then his cathartic treatment should result in cure; often it didn't.*
- *He found it difficult to believe "that perverted acts against children were so general."*
- *He realized that it was impossible to distinguish "between truth and emotionally charged fiction" in the self-reports of his patients.*
- *Themes of trauma were absent from the delusions and hallucinations of his psychotic patients (Meissner, 1985, p. 349).*

However, Freud's critics argued that his retraction was more due to political pressure rather than theoretical rationale.

The extent to which he disclaimed The Seduction Theory *is debatable. After the retraction, in his classic essay,* Sexuality in the Neuroses *(1905), he reflected on his work with his neurotic patients and concluded, "Unless these sexual traumas of the childhood were taken into account it was impossible either to understand the way in which they were determined or to prevent their recurrence. In this way the unique significance of sexual experiences in the etiology of the psychoneuroses seemed to be established beyond a doubt; and this fact remains to this day one of the cornerstones of my theory." Later in the essay he states. "... among the determinants of the onset of the illness, analysis invariably shows that it is the sexual component of the traumatic experience—a component that is never lacking—which has produced the pathogenic result." In his essay,* Infantile Sexuality *(1905), he predicted the types of pathology likely to occur in the victims of sexual abuse. "It is an instructive fact that under the influence of seduction children can become polymorphously perverse, and can be led into all possible kinds of sexual irregularities" (Freud, 1953).*

Sylvia B. Patten, Yvonne K. Gatz, Berlin Jones and Deborah L. Thomas: Posttraumatic Stress Disorder and the Treatment of Sexual Abuse, *Social Work*, 34 (3), May 1989, 197-203. Copyright © 1989, National Association of Social Workers. Inc.

In 1984, Jeffrey Moussaieff Masson wrote The Assault on Truth: Freud's Suppression of the Seduction Theory. *It was the catalyst for the continuing debate among scholars regarding this topic. Recently, Masson defended Freud saying, "One hundred years later we are back where we started. Freud was a lone, unique voice in the wilderness crying out . . . terrible things were happening to women. He was the only one. We have got to stop it. He was silenced." (PBS, 1995).*

This article describes the historical development of posttraumatic stress disorder as a diagnostic entity and indicts sexual abuse as a cause. Psychoanalytic implications for its explanation, description, and treatment are provided. The article demonstrates a cogent, theoretically sound model for helping victims of sexual abuse.

References

Divided Memories, Part 1, Frontline. (1995) Documentary Consortium of Public Television Stations: Public Broadcasting System.

Freud, S. (1953). *The Standard Edition of the Complete Psychological Works of Sigmund Freud,* VII. London: The Hogarth Press.

Meissner, W. in Kaplan, H.I. and Sadock, B.J., (eds.) (1985). *Comprehensive Textbook of Psychiatry/IV,* 1 (4th ed.). Baltimore: Williams & Wilkins.

When a mental health treatment center in a southern city began to offer treatment to sexually abused children in 1984, the social work clinicians assumed that the center would receive about three referrals each month. In the first month, the center received 15 referrals, and by the sixth month sexual abuse accounted for 40 percent of the caseload. The treating clinicians had difficulty determining diagnoses because of the perplexing variety of symptomatology presented by their young patients. Presenting in one session as withdrawn, subdued, and mute, in a following session a patient might be overreactive, overresponsive, and hyperactive. Sometimes bizarre behaviors or patterns of behavior had psychotic elements. Scattered, unable to concentrate one week, the next week a patient might be able to engage in activity with forcefulness and attention to purpose. Anxiety reactions, phobias, and depression all were present over time, interspersed with symptom-free periods during which the child presented normally. More and more often the staff began to identify posttraumatic stress disorder as the most appropriate diagnosis to account for this range of symptomatology.

Historical Overview

The hypothesis of sexual trauma as a precursor or causative factor in mental illness has had a long battle for acceptance. When Freud postulated sexual abuse as the cause of hysteria in 1896, the Vienna Psychoanalytical Society refused to publish a summary of the presentation (Masson, 1984; Strachey, 1953). Freud eventually turned to the Oedipal theory, which postulated that such sexual experiences and desires on the part of the child are fantasy. When Freud's friend and colleague, Ferenczi, asserted in 1932 that similar trauma was the result of sexual abuse, his work was dismissed as the ravings of a failing scientific mind (Masson, 1984). Ferenczi's (1949) work remains one of the most eloquent statements about sexual abuse. He recognized such dynamics as the validity of the trauma, the introjection of guilt by the child, the projection of guilt by parent on the child, the pseudomaturity and early maturity of the victim, multiple personality as an outcome, and the child's loss of senses because of an inability to accept the truth. When Masson (1984) reviewed these events, he promptly was dismissed from his position as provisional projects director at the Freud Archives (Crewdson, 1988; Malcolm, 1985).

The concept of posttraumatic stress disorder seems to have formed in the midnineteenth century when Charles Dickens wrote of his experience and slow emotional recovery after a railway accident (Forster,1969). Nervous disorders attributed to spinal shock from such accidents became an important issue when compensation for injury laws were introduced in Prussia in 1871 (Trimble, 1985). Psychological trauma was recognized again when World War I veterans were classified as suffering from "war neuroses" with underlying predisposing personality defects (Kardiner, 1941). World War II veterans were said to suffer from "exhaustion," and by the Korean War, veterans officially were diagnosed as having "gross stress reactions" by the newly published *Diagnostic and Statistical Manual* (DSM-I) of the American Psychiatric Association (APA) (1952). DSM-II (APA, 1968) recognized only the more general "adult adjustment reaction." After the Vietnam War and persistence by therapists such as Figley (1985b), who recognized the effects of catastrophe and trauma, the psychiatric community again categorized posttraumatic stress disorder specifically in DSM-III (APA, 1980) and DSM-III-R (APA, 1987).

Despite the availability of the diagnosis, current medical thinking often leans toward broader diagnostic categories. Posttraumatic stress disorder symptoms sometimes are diagnosed as adjustment disorder, major depression, or closed head injury (Lyons, 1987). The extensive use of the diagnosis of borderline personality is interesting in the light of estimates of as many as 35 percent of borderline patients who have experienced incestuous sexual abuse (Herman, 1988; Nielsen, 1983; van der Kolk, 1986; Wilson, 1988). Coons (1986) found that patients who suffered from multiple personality disorder almost invariably had been physically or sexually abused. A study of female inpatients in a psychiatric setting found a 75-percent rate of physical or sexual abuse, and the researchers recommended a posttraumatic stress disorder diagnosis as an initial approach to treatment (Bryer, Nelson, Miller, & Krol, 1987). Indeed, Ellenson (1986) found that perceptual disturbances, sometimes dismissed as psychotic, may serve as diagnostic indicators of posttraumatic stress disorder and hidden histories of sexual abuse.

Process of Recovery from Sexual Trauma

The process of recovery from sexual trauma is similar to recovery from other psychological stress. Horowitz (1976) advocated trauma as a primary cause of severe malfunctioning and developed a cognitive model based on the Freudian "urge to completion" concept. Freud advised that "hysterics suffer mainly from reminiscences" (Horowitz, 1976, p.83), which Horowitz (1976) attributed to the fact that they "cannot remember and they cannot 'not' remember" (p. 83). Horowitz categorized as denial such symptoms of inability to remember as emotional constriction, numbness, inability to evaluate stimuli, forgetting, and selective amnesia. Symptoms of "cannot not remember" are categorized as intrusion and include such symptoms as flashbacks, hypervigilence, nightfears, and inability to concentrate. Horowitz labeled the initial period after shock as "outcry" and said that the victim alternates between denial and intrusion until, through cognitive completion, the event is resolved as part of conscious experience.

Horowitz also categorized symptoms of both denial and intrusion under each bodily system and made treatment recommendations. If a client experiences numbness as a symptom of denial in the emotional system, treatment recommendations include encouraging catharsis, supplying appropriate objects, and encouraging emotional relationships. If an individual experiences intrusion symptoms in the emotional system—such as attacks or "pangs" of fear, rage, shame, or sorrow—treatment recommendations include support; suppression (for example, with medication); desensitization; and biofeedback. Horowitz asserted that both intrusion and denial phases help individuals to function until the trauma is resolved.

The models of the posttraumatic stress disorder process developed by Figley (1985a) and others recognize a more comprehensive approach to the experience. Recovery from trauma occurs when a victim is transformed into a survivor who is able to integrate the catastrophe into his or her life history and use it as a source of strength. Figley divided the process into five stages: (1) the catastrophe, which lasts until the victim feels safe; (2) relief and confusion; (3) avoidance, which reduces anxiety and is used as needed by the victim; (4) reconsideration, which involves an ability to confront the trauma; and (5) adjustment. These models recognize such personality factors as coping styles, life assumptions, and previous traumas or emotional problems.

Factors of the trauma itself influence recovery—such as the length of the trauma, exposure to the grotesque, and the passive or active role of the victim (Green, Wilson, & Lindy, 1985). Age of the sexually assaulted victim also would be a factor. Much of the research on sexual assault and its treatment can be subsumed into these models (Burgess, Groth, Holmstrom, & Sgroi, 1978; Burgess & Holstrom, 1974). The nature and role of the environment can be a positive or negative factor in the recovery process. A model developed by Anderson (1987) expands the scope of the process by recognizing institutionalized presocialization factors (such as the principle of "honor thy parents" as it affects incest situations) and by recommending such nonclinical interventions in the process as political action, public education, and community organization.

Additional clinical data need to be gathered about the time lapse between the abuse and the development of symptoms; such data would help to identify differences between chronic and acute posttraumatic stress disorder. [In 1976, 26 school children and their bus driver were kidnapped at gunpoint and forced into a buried truck trailer near Chowchilla, California. Sixteen hours later they were rescued.—Ed.] Terr (1983) found differences in early and late symptoms of the kidnapped children of Chowchilla, who all experienced some degree of posttraumatic stress disorder. Previous vulnerability and posttrauma family problems were found to affect the severity of the symptoms.

Traumatic Effects of Sexual Abuse

As the recovery process takes place, certain traumatic effects often emerge. Finkelhor and Browne (1986) best integrated the themes and content of therapy of the sexually abused individual. Developed to apply to child sexual abuse, the model appears to address adult treatment issues as well. Finkelhor and Browne identified the dynamics, psychological impact, and behavioral manifestations of each of the categories to assist clinicians in moderating symptoms by addressing the underlying area of concern. Traumatic effects

of sexual abuse are divided into four categories: (1) traumatic sexualization, (2) stigmatization, (3) betrayal, and (4) powerlessness.

Traumatic Sexualization

Traumatic sexualization refers to a process in which an individual's sexuality, including both sexual feelings and attitudes, is shaped in a developmentally inappropriate and interpersonally dysfunctional fashion. This process can result in a premature eroticization of the abused child, who then relates to others in a flagrantly erotic manner. Conversely, traumatic sexualization can result in the persistent intertwining of sexuality and arousal with the sense of shame and guilt often associated with the traumatic event. In the adult, such sexual dysfunctions as sexual avoidance syndromes and anorgasmia can be found. Problems can range from negatively charged sexuality to inappropriately compulsive eroticism. A related concept is Ochberg's negative intimacy, a component of posttraumatic stress that the victim must confront therapeutically to resolve feelings of disgust and degradation (Frank, 1988). Negative intimacy is the intrusion of the undesired sexual experience, which invades personal space and provokes associations of disgust and even self-loathing. What normally should be desirable (intimacy) becomes repulsive.

Stigmatization

Stigmatization refers to the negative connotations (badness, shame, guilt) that are communicated to the abused individual and often are subsequently incorporated into his or her self-image. Sgroi (1982) calls this category the "damaged goods" syndrome.

Betrayal

Betrayal for abused children refers to the dynamics in which the children discover that someone on whom they are dependent has harmed them or failed to protect them. For adults, betrayal issues tend to relate to a sense of a "just world," wherein victimization does not come to people who do not "deserve" it. Such victims often blame themselves and see their environment as having betrayed them. Janoff-Bulman (1985) found that this issue affects victims' belief in personal invulnerability, perception of the world as meaningful, and perception of self as positive.

Powerlessness

Powerlessness is the feeling engendered when a victim's will, desires, and sense of efficacy have been overcome or are contravened continually. Issues of powerlessness are particularly crucial for adolescents, who normally are struggling developmentally with issues of dependency and identity, and for children, who are vulnerable in any case. In incest situations, abusers often emphasize the victim's helplessness as a control technique. For male victims, powerlessness often is the crucial issue because their victim status undermines male identity as strong and aggressive.

Affective Stages of the Recovery Process

As the individual goes through the posttraumatic stress disorder resolution process and deals with the traumatic effects, predictable affective responses usually occur. Agosta and McHughes (1987) have labeled these responses as denial, catharsis, guilt, loss of control, anger and rage, and integration and acceptance. Clinicians who work with sexually abused victims should be prepared to recognize these stages and be supportive as clients deal with such feelings. Clients' feelings of being overwhelmed with each new emotion may trigger periods of denial. Clinician acceptance and facilitation of these affective states can speed the resolution process.

Integrative Model of Sexual Trauma Recovery Process

A synthesis of process, therapy content, and affective stages provides a working view of recovery from sexual trauma. In evaluating the client, clinicians should recognize the individual's personality, coping mechanisms, past experiences, past victimizations, and perception of the event. The nature of the trauma also must be understood— including the type of assault (such as date rape, incest, and so on); the nature of the assault (for example, length of time and resulting physical injuries); and the passive or resisting role of the victim. The client's environment includes the support system, institutional interventions, family and peer reactions, and the like. The victim of the sexual trauma must deal with issues of traumatic sexualization, stigmatization, betrayal, and powerlessness within his or her environment and with his or her characteristics. The client accomplishes this resolution by alternating between an intrusive-repetitive state and a denial-numbing state while experiencing a succession of emotional responses.

The intrusive and denial stages have both negative and positive aspects. Too much intrusive-repetitive phenomena is overwhelming, but controlled and limited intrusion leads to the positive, necessary processing of the trauma. The denial-numbing of complete avoidance can lead to blocking and an inability to progress through recovery, but periodic respites from processing are a necessary part of the resolution cycle. Need for respite after the outcry experience is a culturally accepted response to trauma. Soothing and reassurance are normal human responses to an individual in such a situation. The authors propose relabeling the intrusive and denial stages of Horowitz by calling this positive resolution an experience of processing and respite.

Assessment of each client's pace in the sexual trauma recovery process is crucial to successful treatment. The occurrence of trigger symptoms (such as flashbacks or nightmares) usually indicates that more processing is necessary. Other examples of ongoing processing include cognitive reframing of the event, ventilation of feelings, and growing ability to discuss the trauma. A client who is avoiding processing should be evaluated to see if he or she is experiencing a needed respite period. If the social worker believes that respite is becoming denial, the social worker then should assist the client in returning to the processing mode. Also important is determining which symptoms of intrusion-processing or denial-respite relate to which issues of treatment. An intrusive nightmare might relate to a betrayal issue such as parental protection or to another content area. A treatment chart can be used to analyze the treatment needs of each client (Figure 7-3). The plan of therapy is to move from symptomatology of each category to the treatment goals within that category. The treatment planning

Stages	Treatment Issues			
	Traumatic sexualization	Stigmatization	Betrayal	Powerlessness
Processing (intrusive-repetitive)	From symptomatology: To treatment goals:	From symptomatology: To treatment goals:	From symptomatology: To treatment goals:	From symptomatology: To treatment goals:
Respite (denial-numbing)	From symptomatology: To treatment goals:	From symptomatology: To treatment goals:	From symptomatology: To treatment goals:	From symptomatology: To treatment goals:

Figure 7-3. Sample Treatment Chart for Sexual Trauma Recovery.

chart can help clinicians to organize and formulate goals for each client. The following case material illustrates this methodology.

Susan

Susan was a 4-year-old girl who was kidnapped from her home in the middle of the night by an unknown assailant, sexually assaulted, and left abandoned by the side of a road. The assailant entered the home easily because the doors had been left unlocked, and the parents and 7-year-old brother did not awaken during the kidnapping. After the assault and abandonment, the child was found weeping under some bushes beside a house in a residential neighborhood. Police were called, the parents were located, and the child was returned to her home.

Various intrusive-processing symptoms were identified by the social worker as needing intervention. In the area of traumatic sexualization, the child was overwhelmed by images and memories of the attack and was prone to impulsive

verbalization about the event, often at inappropriate times and places. One treatment goal was for the parents to provide Susan with opportunity for ventilation without inappropriately suppressing the child's need to process the event. The social worker and the parents also identified important caretakers who needed to understand the process to handle the child's verbalization appropriately. For example, Susan's nursery school teacher was given information concerning the event so that she would not dismiss Susan's experiences as fantasy. A second intervention in this area was play therapy to give Susan an opportunity to act out the attack to diminish her anxiety.

In the area of stigmatization, the social worker was concerned that Susan's parents and others might feel that the child was "damaged goods." Both parents were given much opportunity to ventilate their feelings in this area. In addition, the social worker assisted the parents in identifying appropriate family members to advise of the event. A treatment goal was to identify family members who would be of assistance to Susan's recovery rather than who would undermine the process or who would demand nurturing by the already overwhelmed parents. An emotionally dependent grandmother therefore was not advised of the event because she would have required much emotional support from the parents, who were not able to give it.

Susan clearly demonstrated that she felt betrayal over her parents' inability to protect her. When she was returned home, she demanded of her mother, "Why didn't you come when I called you?" She did not meet her parents' outstretched arms with a loving reaction because she was angered by her parents' inability to be available when she needed their protection. Her previous life experience had been one of adequate parental protection and aid in times of trouble. In the next few weeks and months, the mother noted Susan's increased testing of well-established rules regarding structure and play activities. The social worker saw this testing as a projection of underlying feelings of anger and hostility that Susan directed toward her parents for letting her down. Three treatment goals were established in this area. First, the child needed continued reassurance of her parents' love and reestablished protection. Second, the parents addressed their guilt regarding their failure to secure the home. The social worker provided support for the parents' past and future adequacies and strengths. Third, the parents needed to continue appropriate limit-setting with Susan, as they had before the traumatic incident. The social worker encouraged the parents to avoid letting guilt undermine their performing a necessary parental role for their child. The social worker also helped the parents to understand that because of Susan's age, she might find it difficult to express her anger directly.

In the area of powerlessness, the family felt helpless when the police were unable to apprehend the perpetrator. The social worker supported a ritualized checking of the house each night as a method of symbolically regaining control of the environment. As each door and window was locked, Susan felt some empowerment to control her own environment, and the parents could symbolize their renewed protection of her.

This case is an example of the benefit of early therapeutic involvement to prevent lasting trauma. The family's ability to assist the child through intrusive processing stages was immediate, and Susan exhibited few examples of denial-respite. In this instance, the influence of the social worker on the child's family to facilitate a helping and nurturing environment greatly contributed to an early resolution of the child's trauma.

Margaret

An inpatient in psychiatric treatment, Margaret was 11 years old and had been sexually abused during her latency years. Her mother appeared to have condoned sexual abuse of the daughter by the landlord because she often was in the residence when the abuse took place. A state investigation resulted in criminal charges against the abuser, and Margaret was placed with her father. She became increasingly unmanageable and was placed in shelter homes from which she also ran away. Inpatient admission was sought because she was dangerous to herself on these occasions.

In the area of traumatic sexualization, Margaret demonstrated intrusive symptomatology such as sexual acting-out and risking sexual assault during episodes of running away. A treatment goal was to turn this intrusive behavior into processing by decreasing the anxiety that led to her run-away behavior, helping her choose age-appropriate sexuality, and validating her experiences as being traumatic. Margaret's denial symptomatology in this area was her inability to discuss her abuse and the pseudomaturity she demonstrated over sexual matters. Treatment goals were to give her control over the rate of disclosure and to reinforce her appropriate behavior as it appeared.

In the area of stigmatization, Margaret demonstrated intrusive symptoms of self-blame. She believed that she was a bad person and at fault for her abuse. Treatment goals included helping her move from blaming herself as "bad" to viewing her behavior as inappropriate because such a view would provide her with a cognitive defense. Current research in victimology indicates a beneficial effect in the persistent tendency of victims to find reasons to blame their behavior at the time of the trauma (Davis &

Smith, 1987; Janoff-Bulman, 1985). If a victim believes that his or her behavior is partially at fault, modifications of behavior can lead to a sense of protection and of regaining control over the environment. Margaret verbalized anger over her previous inability to seek help, help that she now saw as having been available had she only asked earlier. Margaret needed assistance to see that her previous isolation, lack of information about the availability of assistance, and fear of her abuser had been valid obstacles that prevented her from helping herself. New knowledge, however, could protect her from further abuse. Denial symptoms in this area included Margaret's sense of isolation from other children and the emotional limitations she forced on herself. Treatment goals were to build her self-esteem and to work on recovering appropriate family and peer relationships. Unfortunately, control of all aspects of the recovery environment is not possible, and Margaret returned to the hospital from one visit home with an analogy from her father of herself as the "bad apple" spoiling the barrel.

Betrayal issues figured largely in the intrusive model. Margaret had nightmares, including one in which she was sleeping in her bed when her mattress would disappear and she would fall on knives. Providing a secure hospital environment was a short-term treatment goal, and the rebuilding of trust was a long-term goal for this maternally betrayed child. Denial symptoms included Margaret's inability to express anger toward her mother on a conscious level and her denial of needing others. A major treatment goal was to assist Margaret to recognize her own needs without assuming that no one would be available to meet them.

Powerlessness also was a major intrusive pattern for Margaret. Some staff members saw her running away behavior as attempts to control her environment, in contrast to times in the past when she was physically powerless and assaulted. Fight-flight responses that Margaret previously could not act on she now used intrusively when she became anxious. The social worker began a process of empowerment to assist Margaret in gaining control over her behavior (Taubman, 1984). New abilities and coping mechanisms were emphasized to help Margaret realize her

ability to make better decisions about her behavior (Adams-Tucker, 1985). However, Margaret's continued denial in this area was leading to apathy on her part and to repeated victimization as she let herself continue at risk. She continued to be at high risk for self-harm (Sanford, 1987)

Role of the Social Worker

In utilizing the recovery model to treat posttraumatic stress disorder, social workers should begin by identifying symptoms as in either the processing or respite category and by identifying the appropriate treatment issue to which the symptoms relate. Social workers can outline symptoms as they appear at intake or as they manifest during the course of treatment. In working with young children, social workers often will need to include family members' symptoms as they relate to symptoms of the patient. Likewise, treatment goals of young patients likely will incorporate parent or caregiver input and support (Figley, 1988). Social workers' role will be to move the patient from intrusion into processing and from denial into respite when such facilitation appears needed. Facilitating the alternation between processing and respite is the function of therapy. Social workers should model the appropriate environment by validating the trauma as real, accepting the emotional stages of the resolution process, and providing the necessary therapeutic supports while the patient works out his or her recovery.

Evaluating the Recovery Process

Social workers can evaluate from a posttraumatic stress disorder perspective the clinical progress of sexually abused clients through several approaches. Because anxiety can be the predominant emotional response during intrusive phases, periodic assessments of client perception of the degree of anxiety experienced will be helpful. *The Clinician's Guide to Assessing Generalized Anxiety Disorder Symptomatology or the Clinical Anxiety Score* (Thyer, 1987) and the *Cognitive-Somatic Anxiety Questionnaire* (Schwartz, Davidson, & Goleman, 1987) are suggested instruments. *The Generalized Contentment Scale* (Hudson, 1982) is helpful in determining the levels of depression often seen during the denial stage.

Because subsequent sexual dysfunction often is a symptom of sexual trauma, another scale of assistance is the Index of Sexual Satisfaction (Corcoran & Fischer, 1987; Hudson, 1982). The Waring Intimacy Questionnaire can be helpful if marital intimacy issues are a factor, particularly in evaluating sexuality, identity, and affection (Fredman & Sherman, 1987).

Horowitz, Wilber, and Alvarez (1979) have developed an instrument (Impact of Event Scale) that specifically assesses the effect of traumatic events and that recognizes both intrusion and avoidance stages. The instrument is sensitive to change and is recommended for monitoring client progress in treatment (Corcoran & Fischer, 1987). Several clinical measurement instruments have been tested specifically with rape victims and have norms for this population (Beck, Ward, Mendelsohn, Mock, & Erbaugh, 1961; Spielberger, Gorsuch, & Lushene, 1968; Veronen & Kilpatrick, 1980).

Related instruments for children in therapy include the Birleson (1981) Depression Self-Rating Scale for Children; the Kazdin, French, Unis, Esveldt-Dawson, and Sherick (1983) Hopelessness Scale for Children; and the Lipsitt (1958) Self-Concept Scale for Children, in which low self-concept scores correlate with high anxiety in the Children's Manifest Anxiety Scale (Corcoran & Fischer, 1987).

The self-evaluation aspect is one of the assets of the treatment chart's use in treatment. Once the client is aware of recurring treatment themes and the alteration of the processing-respite stages, self-assessment can be ongoing. Periodic updates of the chart can be made with the client's identifying continued areas of difficulty and areas in which treatment goals have been reached.

Conclusion

The sexual trauma recovery process model provides a way to view patients with histories of sexual trauma. Posttraumatic stress disorder literature enriches understanding of these cases and expands treatment options. The recovery process model emphasizes that recovery from sexual abuse is a normal and valuable aspect of human resiliency. The treatment chart provides a tool to organize symptoms and treatment goals so that social workers and clinicians can facilitate recovery for clients who have been victims of sexual trauma.

References

Adams-Tucker, C. (1985). Defense mechanisms used by sexually abused children. *Children Today, 14,* 9-34.

Agosta, C. A., & McHughes, M. L. (1987). Sexual assault victims: The trauma and the healing. In T. Williams (Ed.), *Posttraumatic stress disorders: A handbook for clinicians* (pp. 239-251). Cincinnati, OH: Disabled American Veterans.

American Psychiatric Association. (1952). *Diagnostic and statistical manual of mental disorders.* Washington, DC: Author.

American Psychiatric Association. (1968). *Diagnostic and statistical manual of mental disorders, Second edition.* Washington, DC: Author.

American Psychiatric Association. (1980). *Diagnostic and statistical manual of mental disorders, Third edition.* Washington, DC: Author.

American Psychiatric Association. (1987). *Diagnostic and statistical manual of mental disorders, Third edition, Revised.* Washington, DC: Author.

Anderson, W. A. (1987, March). *Posttraumatic stress as a unifying exemplar: Teaching a model of social responsibility.* Paper presented at the Annual Program Meeting of the Council on Social Work Education, St. Louis, MO.

Beck, A., Ward, C., Mendelsohn, M., Mock, J., & Erbaugh, J. (1961). An inventory for measuring depression. *Archives of General Psychiatry, 4,* 561571.

Birleson, P. (1981). The validity of depression disorders in childhood and the development of a self-rating scale: A research report. *Journal of Child Psychology and Psychiatry, 22,* 73-88.

Bryer, J. B., Nelson, B. A., Miller, J. B., & Krol, P. A. (1987). Childhood sexual and physical abuse as a factor in adult psychiatric illness. *American Journal of Psychiatry, 144,* 1426-1430.

Burgess, A. W., Groth, A. N., Holmstrom, L. L., & Sgroi, S. M. (1978). *Sexual assault of children and adolescent* Lexington, MA: D. C. Heath.

Burgess, A. W., & Holmstrom, L. L. (1974). Rape trauma syndrome. *American Journal of Psychiatry, 131,* 891-896.

Coons, P. M. (1986). Child abuse and multiple personality disorder: Review of the literature and suggestions for treatment. *Child Abuse and Neglect, 10,* 455-462.

Corcoran, K., & Fischer, J. (1987). *Measures for clinical practice: A source book* New York: Free Press.

Crewdson, J. (1988). *By silence betrayed: Sexual abuse of children in America.* Boston: Little, Brown.

Davis, R. C., & Smith, B. (1987). Crosstalk: Let's be careful out there. *Psychology Today, 21,* 10.

Ellenson, G. S. (1986). Disturbances of perception in adult female incest survivors. *Social Casework, 67,* 149159.

Ferenczi, S. (1949). Confusion of tongues between adults and the child: The language of friendliness and the language of passion. *International Journal of Psycho Analysis, 30,* 225-230.

Figley, C. R. (1985a). From victim to survivor: Social responsibility in the wake of catastrophe. In C. R. Figley (Ed.), *Trauma and its wake: The study and treatment of posttraumatic stress disorder* (pp. 70-87). New York: Brunner/Mazel.

Figley, C. R. (Ed.). (1985b). *Trauma and its wake: The study and treatment of post-traumatic stress disorder.* New York: Brunner/Mazel.

Figley, C. R. (1988). Post-traumatic family therapy. In F. Ochberg (Ed.), *Post-traumatic therapy and victims of violence* (pp. 83-109). New York: Brunner/Mazel.

Finkelhor, D., & Browne, A. (1986). Initial and long-term effects: A conceptual framework. In D. Finkelhor, S. Araji, L. Baron, A. Browne, S. D. Peters, & G. E. Wyatt (Eds.), *A sourcebook on child sexual abuse* (pp. 186-187). Beverly Hills, CA: Sage.

Forster, J. (1969). *The Life of Charles Dickens* (Vol. 2). London, England: J. M. Dent & Sons.

Frank, A. (1988). Post-traumatic therapy and victims of violence. In F. Ochberg (Ed.), *Post-traumatic therapy and victims of violence* (pp. 3-19). New York: Brunner/ Mazel.

Fredman, N., & Sherman, R. (1987). *Handbook of measurement for marriage and family therapy.* New York: Brunner/ Mazel.

Green, B. L., Wilson, J. P., & Lindy, J. D. (1985). Conceptualizing post-traumatic stress disorder: A psychological framework. In C. R. Figley (Ed.), *Trauma and its wake: The study and treatment of post-traumatic stress disorder (pp.* 53-69). New York: Brunner/Mazel.

Herman, J. (1988). Father-daughter incest. In F. Ochberg (Ed.), *Post-traumatic therapy and victims of violence* (pp. 190-191). New York: Brunner/Mazel.

Horowitz, M. J. (1976). *Stress-response syndromes.* New York: Jason Aronson.

Horowitz, M. J., Wilber, N., & Alvarez, W. (1979). Impact of event scale: A measure of subjective stress. *Psychological Medicine, 41,* 209-218.

Hudson, W. W. (1982). *The clinical measurement package: A field manual.* Chicago: Dorsey.

Janoff-Bulman, R. (1985). The aftermath of victimization: Rebuilding shattered assumptions. In C. R. Figley (Ed.), *Trauma and its wake: The study and treatment of post-traumatic stress disorder* (pp. 15-35). New York: Brunner/ Mazel.

Kardiner, A. (1941). *The traumatic neuroses of war.* New York: Hoeben.

Kazdin, A., French, N. H., Unis, A. S., Esveldt-Dawson, K., & Sherick, R. B. (1983). Hopelessness, depression, and suicide intent among psychiatrically disturbed children. *Journal of Consulting and Clinical Psychology, 51,* 504-510.

Lipsitt, L. P. (1958). A self-concept scale for children and its relationship to the children's form of the Manifest Anxiety Scale. *Child Development, 29,* 463-472.

Lyons, J. (1987). Post-traumatic stress disorder in children and adolescents: A review of the literature. *Developmental and Behavioral Pediatrics, 8,* 349-356.

Malcolm, J. (1985). *In the Freud archives.* New York: Vintage.

Masson, J. (1984). *The assault on truth: Freud's suppression of the seduction theory.* New York: Farrar, Straus, & Giroux.

Nielsen, G. (1983). *Borderline and acting-out adolescents: A developmental approach.* New York: Human Sciences Press.

Sanford, L. (1987, Summer). Pervasive fears in victims of sexual abuse: A clinician's observations. *Preventing*

Sexual Abuse, 2, 1-3.

Schwartz, E., Davidson, R., & Goleman, E. (1987). Cognitive-somatic anxiety questionnaire. In K. Corcoran & J. Fischer(Eds.), *Measures for clinical practice. A sourcebook(pp.* 128-129). New York: Free Press.

Sgroi, S. M. (1982). *Handbook of clinical intervention in child sexual abuse.* Lexington MA: D. C. Heath.

Spielberger, C., Gorsuch, R., & Lushene, R. (1968). *The state-trait anxiety inventory.* Palo Alto, CA: Consulting Psychologists.

Strachey, J. (Ed.). (1953). The aetiology of hysteria. In *The standard edition of the complete psychological work of Sigmund Freud* (pp. 191-221). London, England: Hogarth and the Institute of Psycho-Analysis.

Taubman, S. (1984). Incest in context. *Social Work* 29, 35-40.

Terr, L. (1983). Chowchilla revisited: The effects of psychic trauma four years after a school-bus kidnapping. *American Psychiatric Journal,* 140, 1543-1550.

Thyer, B. (1987). *Treating anxiety disorders: A guide for human service professionals.* Newbury Park, CA: Sage.

Trimble, M (1985). Post-traumatic stress disorder: History of a concept. In C. R. Figley (Ed.), *Trauma and its wake: The study and treatment of post-traumatic stress disorder* (pp. 5-14). New York: Brunner/Mazel.

van der Kolk, B. (1986). *Psychological trauma.* Washington, DC: American Psychiatric Press.

Veronen, L., & Kilpatrick, D. (1980). Self-reported fears of rape victims: A preliminary investigation. *Behavior Modification,* 4, 383-396.

Wilson, J. (1988). Understanding the Vietnam veteran. In F. Ochberg (Ed.), *Post-traumatic therapy and victims of violence* (pp. 246-251). New York: Brunner/Mazel.

Figure 7-4. Shadow of a Doubt. (Photograph by Jim Rooney.)

LIES OF THE MIND

Leon Jaroff

Believe the Survivor. You must believe that your client was sexually abused, even if she sometimes doubts it herself. Doubting is part of the process of coming to terms with abuse. Your client needs to stay steady in the belief that she was abused....

No one fantasizes abuse. Neither children nor women make up stories that they were abused because they were attracted to their fathers or other adults.

— from *The Courage to Heal*, by Bass and Davis, 1988, p. 347.

The March, 1993, newsletter of the American Psychology Society published a letter by 17 psychologists from 12 research institutions contending that no data support the existence of a "false memory syndrome" and branded the term an invention of the False Memory Syndrome Foundation.

"I don't care if it's true. . . . What actually happened is irrelevant," said Dr. Douglas Sawin, in reference to allegations of sexual abuse. Patient welfare is of primary importance (PBS, 1995).

Hypnosis is a valid technique to enhance memory. The bus driver of the Chowchilla child kidnapping could not recall information about the vehicle which overtook the bus. However, under hypnosis, he recalled the numbers and letters in the license plate, resulting in the arrest and conviction of the kidnappers (People vs. Schoenfeld, 1980).

or

"Suggestion is a potent disrupter of truth," (child cognitive psychologist, Jean Piaget).

The Courage to Heal *is "a very dangerous book" by unqualified therapists. It is part of a "sex abuse industry," (Dr. Harold Lief, specialist in sex research and therapy, quoted in Taylor, 1992).*

The childhood sexual molestations of Freud's patients "were Freud's own reconstructions, tenuously inferred from somatic symptoms on the basis of preconceived theory, . . ." from a letter sent to me by Allen Esterson, of Southwark College, London, and author of Seductive Mirage: an Exploration of the Work of Sigmund Freud.

The sexual abuse of children is an emotionally charged topic. Our society feels compassion for vulnerable children who suffer in silence. However, false allegations impugn the reputation and destroy the lives of those denigrated. As recognized by Freud one hundred years ago, ascertaining objective truth in such instances is a tenuous endeavor. The following article presents arguments regarding the validity of recollections of sexual abuse which occured years earlier.

References

Bass, E. and Davis, L. (1988). *The Courage To Heal: A Guide for Women Survivors of Child Sexual Abuse.* New York: Harper & Row.

Divided Memories, Part 1, (1995). Frontline. Documentary Consortium of Public Television Stations: Public Broadcasting System.

Taylor, B. (1992, May 16). What if Sexual Abuse Memories are Wrong? *Toronto Star* (Toronto, Canada), G1+

Suffering from a prolonged bout of depression and desperate for help, Melody Gavigan, 39, a computer specialist from Long Beach, California, checked herself into a local psychiatric hospital. As Gavigan recalls the experience, her problems were just beginning. During five weeks of treatment there, a family and marriage counselor repeatedly suggested that her depression stemmed from incest during her childhood. While at first Gavigan had no recollection of any abuse, the therapist kept prodding. "I was so distressed and needed help so desperately, I latched on to what he was offering me," she says. "I accepted his answers."

When asked for details, she wrote page after page of what she believed were emerging repressed memories. She told about running into the yard after being raped in the bathroom. She incorporated into another lurid rape scene an actual girlhood incident, in which she had dislocated a shoulder. She went on to recall being molested by her father when she was only a year old—as her diapers were being changed—and sodomized by him at five. Following what she says was the therapist's advice, Gavigan confronted her father with her accusations, severed her relationship with him, moved away and formed an incest survivors' group.

But she remained uneasy. Signing up for a college psychology course, she examined her newfound memories more carefully and concluded that they were false. Now Gavigan has begged her father's forgiveness and filed a lawsuit against the psychiatric hospital for the pain that she and her family suffered.

Gavigan is just one victim of a troubling psychological phenomenon that is harming patients, devastating families, influencing new legislation, taking up courtroom time, stirring fierce controversy among experts and intensifying a backlash against all mental-health practitioners: the "recovery"—usually while in therapy—of repressed memories of childhood sexual abuse, satanic rituals and other bizarre incidents.

"If penis envy made us look dumb, this will make us look totally gullible," says psychiatrist Paul McHugh, chairman of the psychiatry department at Johns Hopkins University. "This is the biggest story in psychiatry in a decade. It is a disaster for orthodox psychotherapists who are doing good work."

No one questions that childhood sexual abuse is widespread and underreported. The subject, rarely mentioned and then only in hushed tones until the 1980s, has become the stuff of talk shows, movies and feature articles. Indeed, many, perhaps millions of Americans have jarring and humiliating memories of abuse, recollections that, painful as they are, have stayed with them through the years.

But can memories of repeated incest and other bizarre incidents be so repressed that the victim is totally unaware of them until they emerge during therapy or as the result of a triggering sight, smell or sound?

Across the U.S. in the past several years, literally thousands of people—mostly women in their 20s, 30s and 40s—have been coming forward with accusations that they were sexually abused as children, usually by members of their own family, at home or, in many cases, at hidden sites where weird rituals were practiced. Says McHugh, "It's reached epidemic proportions."

Unlike the countless adults who have lived for years with painful memories of actual childhood sexual abuse, most individuals with "recovered memory" initially have no specific recollection of incest or molestation. At worst, they have only a vague feeling that something may have happened. Others, simply seeking help to alleviate depression, eating disorders, marital difficulties or other common problems are informed by unsophisticated therapists or pop-psychology books that their symptoms suggest childhood sexual abuse, all memories of which have been repressed.

In the course of the therapy, many of these troubled souls conjure up exquisitely detailed recollections of sexual abuse by family members. Encouraged by their therapists to reach deeper into the recesses of their memories—often using techniques such as visualization and hypnosis—some go on to describe events that sorely strain credulity, particularly tales of their forced childhood participation in satanic rituals involving animal and infant sacrifices, as well as sexual acts.

In many cases the therapists conclude, and eventually convince the patients through suggestion, that the repressed memories of childhood abuse have caused them to "dissociate." As a result, they appear to develop multiple-personality disorder, the strange and, until recently, rare condition brought to wide public attention by the 1973 book, *Sybil,* which describes the condition of a woman who develops several strikingly different but interchangeable personas.

Legislatures in nearly half the states have responded to the widespread public acceptance of recovered memories by applying a strange twist to venerable statute-of-limitations laws. In general, the new legislation allows alleged victims of child abuse to sue the accused perpetrators within three to six years after the repressed memories emerge. This means that with little more than the recollection of the accuser, a parent or other relative can be hauled into court decades after the supposed crime.

Taking advantage of the newly enacted legislation, some of the supposed victims have successfully brought civil and even criminal actions against members of their own families. Juries have awarded them damages, and in a few cases the accused parent has been sentenced to jail—based entirely on the recovered memory of his adult offspring.

To many critics of the recovered-memory movement, the accusations and convictions are reminiscent of the 17th century Salem witchcraft trials, in which elderly women and an occasional man were condemned to death, often on the basis of a single unsubstantiated charge that they had demonstrated witchlike behavior.

"Recovered-memory therapy will come to be recognized as the quackery of the 20th century," predicts Richard Ofshe, a social psychologist at the University of California, Berkeley. And in the process, Emory University psychiatry professor George Ganaway fears, it may "trigger a backlash against [legitimate charges of] child abuse. As these stories are discredited, society may end up throwing the baby out with the bath water—and the hard-earned credibility of the child-abuse-survivor movement will go down the drain."

The backlash has already begun. In Texas this summer, a woman patient won a settlement from two therapists and a psychiatric hospital after suing them for therapeutic negligence and fraud. She claimed that four years of recovered false memories had made her a "walking zombie." It was the first of what some reputable therapists fear will be many such rulings that will ultimately give their profession a black eye.

An increasing number of recovered-memory accusers have recanted, and some have reunited with their families and joined them in suing the therapists and clinics they claim led them astray. Many of them are among the more than 7,000 individuals and families who have sought assistance from the False Memory Syndrome Foundation, a Philadelphia-based organization that has taken the lead in publicizing the wrongdoings and in helping the victims of recovered-memory therapy. Pamela Freyd, who cofounded FMSF in 1992, has yet to be reconciled with her accuser daughter.

Growing controversy and concern in the mental-health community has led the American Psychological Association to appoint a false-memory working group to investigate the phenomenon. At a meeting of the American Psychiatric Association last May, the issue of false memories was addressed in three sessions and heatedly debated by experts on both sides. The American Medical Association's house of delegates also indicated its discomfort with such memory-enhancement techniques as guided imagery, hypnosis and body massage, all of which heighten suggestibility and are widely employed by recovered-memory therapists. Use of these practices in eliciting accounts of childhood sexual abuse, the AMA delegates concluded, was "fraught with problems of potential misapplication."

"I wish I could say the debate just involves a few kooks," says Stephen Ceci, a Cornell University developmental psychologist who is a member of the American Psychological Association's work group. "It's much broader than that, happening among the cream of the crop of psychiatrists and clinical psychologists." The battle could not have come at a worse time, says Ceci; some professionals are currently pushing for increased coverage of mental health in the President's proposed national health plan. "It's not a good time for us to be airing our dirty laundry."

Still, the opposing camps are doing just that, arguing bitterly about repressed memories. Critics of recovered-memory therapy insist that there is no scientific evidence for the reality of repression and that many, if not most, of the recovered-memory claims are false. Advocates have no doubts, citing studies on amnesia and clinical experience showing that repression is commonplace. Given that psychology is an inexact science, any resolution of the issue seems distant, at best.

Judie Alpert, a professor of applied psychology at New York University, refutes the critics of recovered-memory therapy. "There is absolutely no question that some people have repressed some memories of early abuse that are just too painful to remember," she says. "In their 20s and 30s some event triggers early memories, and slowly they return. The event has been so overwhelming that the little girl who is being abused can't tolerate to be there in the moment, so she leaves her body, dissociates, as if she is up on a bookshelf looking down on the little girl who is being abused. Over time, she pushes it deep down because she can't integrate the experience."

Christine Courtois, also in the APA work group and a clinical director at the Psychiatric Institute in Washington, charges that criticism of the recovered-memory phenomenon is part of a backlash against society's tardy recognition of widespread sexual abuse. The "wholesale degradation of psychotherapy by some critics," she

says, represents "displaced rage" at therapists for bringing the issue to public attention.

That kind of reasoning does not sit well with Margaret Singer, a retired professor from the University of California, Berkeley, and an expert on cults and influence techniques. She has interviewed 50 people who once believed they had recovered repressed memories of incest or ritual abuse but now think they were mistaken. All 50, Singer emphasizes, were in therapy when they "recovered" terrifying memories of abuse. "These people are reporting to me that their therapists were far more sure than they were that their parents had molested them."

Singer insists that trauma does not cause people to repress memories, although bits and pieces of experience can be lost through amnesia. In fact, she says, trauma has just the opposite effect: people can't forget it. As an example, she cites the cases of Vietnam veterans who suffer flash-backs and posttraumatic stress disorder.

Psychologist Ofshe is particularly disdainful of the concept of what he calls "robust" repression: the instantaneous submergence of any memory of sexual abuse. Recovered-memory therapists, he says, "have invented a mechanism that supposedly causes a child's awareness of sexual assault to be driven entirely from consciousness." According to these therapists, Ofshe explains, "there is no limit to the number of traumatic events that can be repressed, and no limit to the length of time over which the series of events can occur" Belief in robust repression, he concludes, "can be found only on the lunatic fringes of science and the mental health professions."

"Repression definitions are so loose and varied, so abundant, so shifting that it is like trying to shoot a moving target," says Elizabeth Loftus, professor of psychology and law at the University of Washington and an authority on cognitive processes, long-term memory and eyewitness testimony. "If repression is the avoidance in your conscious awareness of unpleasant experiences that come back to you, yes, I believe in repression. But if it is a blocking out of an endless stream of traumas that occur over and over that leave a person with absolutely no awareness that these things happen, that make them behave in destructive ways and re-emerge decades later in some reliable form, I don't see any evidence for it. It flies in the face of everything we know about memory."

If such recovered memories are indeed false, where do they originate? From two sources, critics say: the popular culture and misguided or inept therapy. Sensational tales about recovered memories of incest have been grist for celebrity-magazine cover stories. And repressed-memory incest and satanic-ritual-abuse victims have been featured prominently on Geraldo, Oprah, Sally Jessy Raphaël and other daytime TV talk shows.

In bookstores, pop-psychology sections are filled with dozens of self-help survivor titles. By far the most controversial and best selling (more than 700,000 copies) of these books is *The Courage to Heal* by Ellen Bass and Laura Davis. In their 1988 publication, considered the bible of the recovered-memory movement, they include such dogma as "If you think you were abused and your life shows the symptoms, then you were," and "If you don't remember your abuse, you are not alone. Many women don't have memories . . . this doesn't mean they weren't abused" Like many of the authors of these self-help books, neither Davis nor Bass has any academic training in psychology, although Davis claims to be an incest survivor. Yet many therapists urge their patients to read *Courage* and other similar volumes.

Many of these books contain laundry lists of symptoms of repressed-memory victims. They inform their readers that even though they have no memory of the acts, they may have been victims of childhood sexual or ritual abuse if they experience some of the following conditions: depression, anxiety, loss of appetite or eating disorders, sexual problems and difficulty with intimacy. The all-inclusive nature of that list, critics say, suggests that among the entire U.S. population, only the rare individual has managed to escape childhood sexual abuse. That doesn't seem to surprise therapist E. Sue Blume. In her book *Secret Survivors,* she writes, "It is not unlikely that *more than half of all women* are survivors of childhood sexual trauma"

Almost any night, in any major American city, adult incest and ritual-abuse survivor meetings are held in church basements and community rooms. Churches and other institutions also offer counseling for dissociative disorders and satanic-ritual-abuse victims.

Private psychiatric hospitals, which advertise in medical journals and airline magazines, are profiting as well. "We can help you remember and heal," promises one ad for ASCA Treatment centers in Compton, California. "Remembering incest and childhood abuse is the first step to healing."

The thriving recovered-memory industry dismays psychiatrist Ganaway. "In some cases," he says, the hospitals and clinics "are memory mills with an almost assembly-line mentality," he says. "A patient comes in with no memories but leaves with memories of childhood incest or ritual abuse." Yet even some well-trained family and marriage counselors, psychologists and psychiatrists seem too quick to tie their patients' problems to repressed memories of incest and ritual abuse. "That makes psychotherapy very easy at first," explains Johns Hopkins' McHugh. "Therapists and patients can say, 'We found the secret.' The fact that the patients and families steadily become more confused, incoherent and chaotic is then believed to be an expression of the original incest." What is really happening, he says, is that "conflicts are being generated by false memories. We have found something to make therapy easy."

Some patients now leave their therapist's office convinced that they suffer from multiple-personality disorder, which is said to stem from repressed memories of early childhood trauma, including physical and sexual abuse. Until the publication of *Sybil,* MPD was apparently rare; around the world, only a few hundred cases had been documented over the previous three centuries. Since then, however, many thousands of supposed cases of MPD have been identified in the U.S. alone—most of them incorrectly, say critics, by therapists who are looking for an easy solution in their search for evidence of childhood sexual abuse or who too easily accept the likelihood of the disorder. One problem, says Ganaway, is that once these patients have been diagnosed with MPD, they are convinced that they have it, tend to exhibit what they think are the symptoms and often reinterpret their entire life histories accordingly.

Those charges infuriate Dr. Richard Kluft, a

Philadelphia psychiatrist, who works extensively with MPD patients. "It's an absolute lie that MPD is a rare psychiatric disorder," he says. He attributes the sharp rise in reported MPD cases to the rise of feminism and the resulting willingness of people "to speak out more openly on issues of exploitation and abuse."

Another doctor who believes that MPD is fairly common is Bennett Braun, medical director of the dissociative-disorders program at Rush-Presbyterian-St. Luke's Medical Center in Chicago. Braun says the number of cases of MPD has risen not for faddish reasons but because therapists have become better at recognizing the symptoms.

In his 12-bed unit at Rush North Shore Medical Center in Skokie, a branch of Rush-Presbyterian-St. Luke's Medical Center, Braun treats MPD cases, some of whom think that they are victims of satanic-ritual abuse. When he first began to hear the satanic stories in 1985, Braun says, he was incredulous. Now, having heard similar tales from many people from different states and countries and having treated more than 200 of them, he declares, "Yes, there is satanic-ritual abuse "

If some of the recovered memories of familial childhood abuse sound fanciful, the recollections of satanic-ritual abuse are downright bizarre. These tales have proliferated since the publication in 1980 of *Michelle Remembers,* a book about a belatedly aware satanic-ritual victim. They describe a massive secret conspiracy to abuse children sexually in order to brainwash them into worshiping Satan. Victims recall being raped by their parents and then by members of a cult who drink blood and sacrifice fetuses. More often than not the abusers are pillars of their communities—the mayor, police chief or school superintendent—who come out at night and join their parents in terrifying ceremonies.

But could such satanic rituals be that commonplace, let alone exist at all? In 1990, a group of researchers at the State University of New York at Buffalo conducted a nationwide sample of clinical psychologists, asking them if they had encountered claims of ritual abuse. Some 800 of the psychologists, about a third of the sample, had treated at least one case.

Yet, law-enforcement authorities report that not one shred of reliable evidence has turned up to support these claims—no documented marks of torture, no bones of sacrificed adults, infants or fetuses and no reputable eyewitnesses. Lorraine Stanek, a Connecticut rehabilitation counselor for trauma survivors, also stresses the lack of evidence. "If you look at the alleged number of deaths that would be accounted for," she says, "there should be bodies in all our backyards." Still, incest-survivor groups are inundated with these claims. Monarch Resources, a California referral service for survivors, is said to receive more than 5,000 calls annually from people who believe they have been victims of satanic abuse. Alleged ritual abuse is also involved in about 16% of the calls to Philadelphia's False Memory Syndrome Foundation.

Braun demonstrated his belief in satanic rituals during a 1991 trial, when he testified in behalf of two daughters seeking damages from their 76-year-old mother. Recovering childhood memories, they had accused her of abusing them in bloody and murderous ceremonies. Both claimed that they had developed MPD as a result. After Braun told of treating similar cases, the jury found in favor of the two daughters.

Now, however, the tables have turned. Braun and the Chicago medical center are being sued for negligence by a female patient who had two years of in-patient treatment for supposed MPD "recovered" memories of involvement in satanic rituals with her father, mother and relatives. The rituals supposedly included torture, murder and cannibalism of large groups of people—as many as 50 on an average weekend. In addition, before growing doubts led the woman to terminate Braun's treatment in 1992, she had been made to believe she had 300 "alters" or personas, possibly setting a new MPD record. According to her lawyer, she is not currently undergoing any treatment and is doing well.

The ultimate victim of repressed memory may be the psychotherapeutic profession itself. "Therapists are terrified," says MPD specialist Kluft. "Many are feeling very hamstrung because they fear any time they ask a question, it can result in a lawsuit." Instead of seeing a patient "as a person in pain and in need of help," Kluft complains, "the therapist is looking at a potential litigant. Some people have discontinued treating trauma patients."

S. Scott Mayers, a psychotherapist in Venice, California, is hardly terrified. But he is cautious. "What I do to ensure that I don't inflict my agenda or opinion," he says, "is go with the patients' presentation and stay with it, using their own words, their own scenarios. I'm so cautious because we are all very suggestive."

Recovered-memory therapists might do well to heed those guidelines before they cause irreparable damage to their profession. For, as the public begins to recognize that people have been falsely accused by recovered-memory patients, says psychiatrist McHugh, it "opens us up to skepticism and dismay about our capacity to do things. This is a bubble that is going to burst. We will end up having to recreate the trust this country puts in psychotherapy."

Postscript

Dr. Steven Ceci, mentioned in the article, and skeptical of the validity of recovered-memories, told me of legal efforts to block the publication of his book *Jeopardy in the Courtroom*. The book describes his research demonstrating how easily childrens' memories can be distorted. The controversy continues. The inside cover pages of the October, 1996, edition of the *American Psychologist*, flagship journal of the American Psychological Association, contain two advertisements: one about a book that questions validy of recovered-memories, the other instructs therapists where and how to establish practices to treat them.

Figure 7-5. The Near Death Experience may provide symbolic rebirth for a suicidal person. Detail from *Ascension to the Empyreum* by Hieronymous Bosch. Accademia, Venice, Italy. Copyright © 1990 Archivi Alinari. (Alinari/Art Resource, NY.)

READING 7D

THE PSYCHODYNAMICS OF SUICIDE

Herbert Hendin

The Interpretation of Dreams *was published in 1900. Freud considered it his most valuable work. He claimed dreams were the "royal road to the unconscious." Freud's view was that dreams contained content that had been repressed from conscious awareness by the defensive activities of the ego. The manifest content of the dream is its fairly obvious and superficial meaning. It is what is consciously recalled upon awakening of the dream and is simply the end result of the unconscious mental activity (dream work) that takes place during sleep. Freud was more concerned with the dream's latent content, which was transformed into the manifest content by the dream work. Through associative exploration Freud tried to reveal the latent content, which held core meaning (Kaplan & Sadock, 1985, p. 350). Have important decisions in your life been guided by dream work?*

Critics claim that dreams are highly subjective and cannot be scrutinized empirically. Indeed, interpretation of the same dream by different therapists are often dissimilar. J. Alan Hobson has studied brain activity during sleep at Harvard Medical School. He commented,

> *Dreams are like a Rorschach inkblot . . . They are ambiguous stimuli which can be interpreted in any way a therapist is predisposed to. But their meaning is in the eye of the beholder— not in the dream itself (quoted in Goleman, 1984, B2).*

It is estimated that fifty thousand Americans commit suicide annually. The actual number may be much higher. We don't know how many deaths classified as accidental are really suicides. It is likely that many single vehicle, high speed fatalities are suicides and not accidents.

But what motivates a person to take his own life? What thoughts race through his mind? What are his attitudes about death? In the following article, Herbert Hendin offers some insights into the motives of suicidal individuals. His theoretical orientation is psychoanalytic and he used analytic techniques such as hypnosis and dream interpretation to gather his data.

I hope that as you read the article you will appreciate Dr. Hendin's modest air. He developed an ingenious way of interviewing patients who have come as close to death as possible and still survived. Try to envision the difficulty of such interviews for patient and therapist. Contemplate his interpretations of his patients' suicidal motives. Are they merely subjective interpretations of ambiguous mental events, or has Hendin adroitly distinguished signal from noise? Although thirty years old, the article is a classic demonstration of analytic interpretation.

References
Goleman, D. (1984, July 30). A new Awakening. *Miami News* (Miami, Fla.), B1 & B2.
Kaplan, H.I. and Sadock, B.J., (eds.) (1985). *Comprehensive Textbook of Psychiatry,* IV, 1 (4th ed.). Baltimore: Williams & Wilkins.

Herbert Hendin: The Psychodynamics of Suicide. *Journal of Nervous and Mental Disease,* Vol. 136, no. 3, March 1963, p. 142. Reproduced by permission of Williams & Wilkins, A Waverly Company.

What the suicidal patient wishes to get away from in life is only part of his story. His observed attitudes toward death, dying and afterlife are equally revealing about him and his motivation for suicide. This paper will indicate some psychodynamic patterns of suicide based on differing attitudes toward death on the part of suicidal patients. The case illustrations are taken from patients seen by the writer in New York City at Bellevue Hospital, the New York State Psychiatric Institute and St. Luke's Hospital, as well as from patients observed in three Scandinavian countries.

Background of the Problem

The first important psychological insight in the literature about suicide came from Freud. He was not working directly with the problem of suicide and in his work described only one patient who actually made a suicide attempt. What he did see, however, and in good number, were depressed patients. Freud observed in "Mourning and Melancholia" (1916) that the self-hatred seen in depression originated in anger toward a love object turned back by the individual on himself. Freud reasoned that suicide was the ultimate form of this phenomenon and that there would be no suicide without the earlier repressed desire to kill someone else. The concept that suicide can be a kind of inverted murder was extremely important, although unfortunately it became overworked by some in an effort to explain all suicide.

Freud made his observations on depression years before he had concluded that anger or aggression could be non-erotic in origin. At the time he wrote "Mourning and Melancholia," all aggression had to have, in Freud's view, a sexual origin, so that the paper is filled with complicated and undemonstrable discussion of what amounts to retroflexed anger. Ten years later Freud expressed surprise at his having overlooked the "universality of nonerotic aggression". He never rewrote his earlier work so the extraneous libidinal explanations for the existence of anger remain unaltered. This, however, should not lead one to overlook the basic psychological truth contained in the 1916 paper, namely, that anger can become self-directed, can lead to depression and can be a motivating force in suicide.

The current view of depression has also been revised over the years. The significance of both dependency and expiation in depression was made clear by Sandor Rado. The idea that retroflexed anger and self-punishment can have atonement or expiation as goals, the individual hoping thus to win back love and affection, does not appear in "Mourning and Melancholia," and was primarily Rado's contribution. And just as retroflexed anger can at times be the motivating force in suicidal patients, so, too, can suicide be an act of expiation.

Despite the help that a knowledge of the psychology of depression gives to the understanding of suicide, it is far from the whole picture. A great number of suicidal patients do not manifest the clinical features or classical psychodynamics associated with depression. Most important to keep in mind, however, is the fact that many depressed patients are just not suicidal. This alone would emphasize that the psychodynamics of depression are not sufficient to explain suicide, and thus the study of depressed patients cannot be used as a substitute for directly studying suicidal patients. In investigating suicidal patients one often sees patients who appear to view their death as internalized murder, while others' suicide attempts are acts of expiation, but there is, in addition, a broad range of other attitudes toward death and meanings of the act of suicide.

How To Study The Problem

In first working with the problem of suicide at Bellevue, 100 consecutive admissions of attempted suicides to the hospital were interviewed. They were seen as often as was felt necessary to get a full psychodynamic picture of each case. Patients who had made suicide attempts were later taken into therapy, criteria for selection being as varied a sampling of suicidal motivations and situations as possible. As many as 15 patients who had made suicide attempts were in therapy at one period during this investigation. Currently at St. Luke's Hospital, in addition to the intensive interviewing of the suicidal patients, the writer has also been working with hypnosis, in an attempt to get at the psychodynamics of individual patients and what their motivations for suicide are. In all these approaches, however, as well as in cross-cultural work that the writer has been doing with suicidal patients in Scandinavia, all patients seen have attempted suicide and, obviously, survived. The question often raised—are those who attempted suicide and survived a comparable group in terms of personality and motivation to those who actually died?—bears on any evaluation of the psychodynamics of suicide.

Long ago it proved helpful to rate or evaluate suicidal patients on a scale of one to three with regard to their suicidal intent (1—the patients with minimal intent; 2—with moderate intent; and 3—with maximal suicidal intent). The following two cases illustrate types of patients in the maximal intent group. One was a girl who jumped under a subway train, had two cars pass over her and still lived. This was possible in the particular subway, since there was sufficient room between the wheels and under the train, but this was not known by the girl at the time. A second patient had made a suicide pact with his homosexual partner. They made their attempt in their hotel room on a Saturday night, knowing they would probably not be discovered by the chambermaid until Monday morning. They each took 50 barbiturates of 1/10th gram strength. When found and admitted to the hospital on Monday, they were both comatose and remained so for several days. The initial hospital opinion was that neither would survive. As it turned out, one died and the other lived. The one who lived, however, was placed in the group of those with maximal intent.

It seems reasonable to include the girl under the train and the homosexual man in this group and to assume that in working with them one is working with a situation as close to that resulting in actual suicide as one needs to get. When suicidal patients are divided into intent groups, the group with maximal intent has an age and sex distribution statistically comparable to that of actual suicides, and is quite different from that found when one takes all attempted suicides together.

A great deal about suicide can also be learned from the study of patients in the lower intent groups. When, for example, suicide is an act of self-punishment, for one patient only death will be sufficient atonement, while for another the self-damage done in a suicide attempt may suffice. The study of both types, however, throws a light on the psychology of self-punishment and its relation to suicide.

While distinguishing between a patient who is very serious about suicide and one who is not serious at all is not very difficult, the situation is a little more complicated with patients who are in the intermediate group. Patients who have survived taking as many as 25 sleeping pills may say they only wished to sleep and yet admit that they did have the thought that it might be nice never to wake up. They can appear themselves to be unsure whether they wanted to die. One is impressed that there are mixed feelings about the wish to die in most suicidal patients. Menninger, in particular, has stressed and illustrated some of the variations seen in patient's conscious and unconscious wishes with regard to dying. Tolstoy describes in *Anna Karenina* the heroine's last feelings and sensations after jumping in front of a train: she feels that she has perhaps made a mistake and struggles unsuccessfully to get up before the train hits her. Tolstoy's sensitive intuition in this regard seems very much borne out by what is learned from actual suicidal patients. One suspects that if a man jumping from a tall building could be interviewed while still in the air three floors down from the top, his feelings about dying would often be already different from what they had been a few seconds before. A recently interviewed patient said she had wished to change her mind right before jumping from a building, but that since she had committed herself in a letter to this action, she was unable to back out.

Hypnosis can be useful in evaluating a patient's suicidal intent as well as his motivation. It is of most obvious use in reconstructing and recovering amnesias connected with suicide attempts. Patients who were under the influence of alcohol at the time and are vague as to the details of the attempt can often recall under hypnosis far more than otherwise. Similarly, one patient who had shot himself with a shotgun and survived was amnestic for all that happened in the minutes prior to pulling the trigger. Under hypnosis his thoughts and feelings during that period as well as the details of his attempt could be recovered.

The most important use of hypnosis as a

research tool in studying suicide, however, comes from another direction. As will be more evident in the section below on the psychodynamics of suicide, the dreams of these patients immediately before or after their suicide attempts often deal directly with their death or suicide and are of very great value in getting a psychodynamic picture of the patient. This seems natural enough, for when patients are interviewed soon after their attempts, the dynamics are close to consciousness and apt to be revealed in their dreams. When months have elapsed, these dynamics may be so repressed that a patient may have to be seen in therapy for a long time before the material becomes similarly accessible. Thus, generally it is advisable to see patients within the first days after their attempted suicide. When patients have not been obliging enough to remember dreams during the period of their suicide attempts, hypnosis can be of value. The writer has hypnotized such patients and had them go back in their thoughts to the time of their attempt and to the mood of that time. It was then suggested to them that they would have a dream while under hypnosis, such as they might have had the night they made their suicide attempt, and which would throw some light on their reasons for wanting to kill themselves. While such a technique is productive with only about a third of suicidal patients, from the research standpoint invaluable material can be so learned. In discussing the psychodynamics of suicide some of this material will be considered.

The Psychodynamics Of Suicide

The details, method and circumstances of the suicide attempt often give the first important clue as to the psychodynamics of the particular patient, and they must be carefully established. Often the suicide attempt is a kind of psychological drama and the very way in which it is made is extremely revealing. One woman jumped from a window with a picture of her son in her brassiere and a message on the back of the picture saying, "Timmy knows I love him." Years before, at the time of her divorce, this woman actually had given away her young son to be raised by his paternal grandparents. While she still saw him up to the time of the attempt, she appeared to be tor-

tured by her difficulties in love relationships and her inability to love her son. The picture and message were an attempt to deny the true state of affairs and yet gave the first clue that put one on the right track.

Another older man who made an attempt with barbiturates arranged his attempt so he might be found by his son before succumbing. The man had been separated from his wife for a year, after 25 years of marriage, and despite the details of the attempt the relationship with his wife first appeared to be the crucial factor. Only when, after three days in the hospital, he reported a dream in which his son fed him poison was it possible for me to reverse my thinking: it became obvious it was the patient's relationship with his son which was the major determinant in this case.

The choice of method involved may very often reveal a good deal about the organization and integration of the personality. Disorganized or multiple suicidal methods, or those carried out in a chaotic manner and lasting over several days, are generally chosen by disorganized, schizoid patients.

It may seem surprising that, in many studies of suicide in the literature, the attitudes of suicidal patients toward death, dying and afterlife have been neglected. In a large measure, this can be attributed to anxiety and inhibition of psychiatrists in relation to suicidal patients. It is reflected right down to the resident on the ward who will ask a patient after ten minutes' acquaintance if he has had homosexual experiences or what he does with regard to masturbation, but will not ask a suicidal patient about his attitude toward death, about what he thinks happens after death, about what he thought of after he turned on the gas and what he might have dreamt of while he was unconscious. These last four questions can elicit invaluable material bearing on the understanding of suicidal patients and their motivation.

The following are some of the varying psychodynamic constellations with regard to death and suicide that have been observed in suicidal patients:

Death as retaliatory abandonment: A homosexual college boy of 18 who was failing in school was seen following a serious suicide attempt with 60 barbiturate pills which he barely survived. During a hypnotic interview it was suggested to the patient that he would have a dream such as he might have had the night of his suicidal attempt. His dream was a simple one. He was working for the United Nations and had an office that occupied the entire first floor of the UN building in New York. A friend of his was applying for a position and the patient was interviewing him and reviewing his qualifications. He told his friend that he did not qualify and could not have the job. During his waking associations to the dream he revealed his preoccupation with this friend. It appeared that he "had a crush on," but had never tried to become involved sexually with the friend although the friend may have become alarmed at the intensity of the patient's feelings. The friend had been quite obviously backing out of the relationship and several months prior to the attempt had more or less broken off with the patient.

What does the patient accomplish in the dream and by the suicide attempt? He gains an illusory control over the situation that involves rejection. In the dream, if there is any rejecting to be done, he is going to do it; by committing suicide, he is the one who leaves or does the rejecting. The conception that death involves an act of having, i.e., an abandonment, is known to derive from childhood. Children's reactions to death most frequently center around its being a violent act inflicted on the dead person or as his having "left" voluntarily. Children who lose or are separated from their mothers invariably react as though the mothers had chosen to leave them. The continuation of this psychological equation is seen in adult life among patients with extreme fears of dying which are usually emotionally linked with the most primitive abandonment fears from childhood .

That this patient also experienced a *feeling of omnipotent mastery through death* is strongly suggested by the important UN position and large office in his dreams. Suicide attempts and the idea of suicide seem to give an illusory feeling of mastery over a situation through the control one has over whether one lives or dies. Another patient who had been a chemistry major in college had struggled through school with a cyanide capsule in his desk, consoling himself with the thought that if he could not manage his work he could always take the cyanide. On graduation he threw it out and never made a suicide attempt. A female patient who eventually did make a very serious suicide attempt had, in the years prior to her attempt, kept a toy pistol in her drawer and had comforted herself through an unhappy love affair with the fantasy that if things got too bad she could always kill herself.

Death as retroflexed murder: A woman of 44 had made a serious suicide attempt with sleeping pills about a year after the breakup of her marriage. Her husband had been unfaithful during their twenty years' marriage and she had alternately managed to deny this to herself or to reassure herself by saying that these affairs were unimportant to him. The last such relationship, however, had gone on for almost two years and, while her husband evidently still did not want to leave her, she precipitated a crisis by barging in on him in the other woman's apartment. He had then begun to live with this woman. About six months later she herself became involved rather unsatisfactorily with a younger man. Her stated attitude immediately following her suicide attempt was that both her children and her husband would be better off with her dead. The children were a boy of 19 and a girl of 15 and she said that they would be better off in a new home. There had been an earlier attempt ten days before: she had gone out to a lake with the intention of drowning herself, "changed her mind" and came home and took fifteen sleeping pills instead. She woke up by herself a day and a half later and the next time took twice that dose. While under the influence of the first pills she had the following dream: she saw a cap belonging to her husband's father floating on the sea and realized that he had drowned. Her husband's father had been a sea captain whom she saw as very much like her husband—extremely domineering, critical and difficult to get along with. At first she saw the dream in terms of her own martyred role, but eventually she related it to her desire to strike back at her husband. She spoke vindictively of the problems with the children that her death would cause him. It soon became evident that her suicide attempt came out of her anger at her husband and was an ineffective attempt at revenge. She was the kind of woman who could do little that was effective with her anger or self-assertion and could not even fight for her children. Her situation illustrates the classical one described by Freud in which the suicide is basically an inverted homicide.

Death as a reunion: One patient made three suicide attempts, scattered over a period of some 20 to 25 years. When seen for the first time, following her third suicide attempt, she was 47 years old. Each attempt had been more serious than the one before; she had been extremely fortunate to survive the last one, with gas. An unfortunate or unhappy love affair was time-related to all three attempts. After two months of treatment following the last attempt, during which the same love affair as had preceded it was continuing unsuccessfully, the patient became acutely suicidal and required admission to the hospital. That night she had the following dream: "I was living in an apartment in Baltimore that I lived in 25 years ago. There were a lot of people around telling me to put on a beautiful wedding dress that was hanging on the wall, and I would not put it on."

Her association was to the apartment in Baltimore where her first romantic liaison had lasted for two years, until one night her lover told her he was going to marry another girl. She thereupon made a suicide attempt. Everything in the dream was the same as it had been in her room at the time of that first attempt. In the wedding ceremonies of her two unhappy marriages she had never worn a wedding dress although she had always wanted to. She felt she had lost the really great love of her life with the end of this first relationship. What impressed her most in the dream was that the wedding dress "looked more like a shroud than like a wedding dress." Union with this first love was to be achieved, apparently, only through her death. This patient recalled that she had had this same dream recurrently before each suicide attempt, an interesting detail.

She was, in her dream, refusing to put on the dress, while struggling, in reality, against suicide. Death was the unpleasant price she must pay for the gratification of her desires for love and affection. For other patients with similar but more masochistic psychodynamics, the act of dying

itself can be conceived as pleasurably incorporated into the reunion fantasy. Most frequently the emphasis is not put on the dying but on the gratification to follow; the feeling tone in the reunion dreams of such patients is pleasant. In the overwhelming majority the gratification is of an extremely dependent variety, either directly with parental figures or with wives, husbands or siblings operating as substitute parental figures.

While usually such fantasies are unconscious and have to be elicited from dreams, they can also be conscious. One patient, who was seen following a suicide attempt which eventually proved to be fatal, spent the entire year after his wife's death preoccupied with fantasies about her and with mental pictures of being reunited with her in death.

Death as rebirth: A young woman in her twenties had jumped under a train and lost a leg; this suicide attempt was precipitated by one of the unhappy and impossible love relationships with which her life had been filled. Several years earlier she had been intensely involved with a married Negro man. A few years before that she had been involved with a Communist under investigation by the FBI, who was at that time trying to use his relationship with her to get into the United States. This patient was both extremely bright and well-educated. When she was 13 years old, her father had deserted the family and she had never seen or heard from him again. She had some fascination with death and dying all through adolescence and always remembered by heart death scenes in novels. Under hypnosis and with the suggestion to have a dream about her suicide attempt, she produced the following: She was in a long, narrow tunnel and could see a light at the end of it. She walked toward the light and when she got there, saw a man and woman standing over a manger. In her associations to the dream, the tunnel suggested to her the subway from which she jumped and the way in which the train came out of the tunnel and into the lighted platform area. Coming out of the darkness of the tunnel into light brought to her mind the process of birth. The man and woman she saw as her mother and father. The child in the manger was both the Christ-child and herself. One can see how much she accomplishes in her death fantasy.

She is reborn, is a boy, is reunited with her father and is, in addition, omnipotent. It is not hard to imagine that for a patient with such fantasies, dying has a very strong appeal.

Death as self-punishment: A lawyer in his thirties had made a moderately serious suicide attempt stemming from his lack of success in a legal career. It was impossible to hypnotize him during his stay in the hospital following his suicide attempt; he exemplifies one of the difficulties involved if one were tempted to use hypnosis as a routine matter for the evaluation of all psychiatric patients. He was later quite easy to hypnotize when he returned for a second try after hospital discharge, and it became evident that he feared being hypnotized while in the hospital when he was still actively preoccupied with suicide because he felt that if he revealed material related to the suicide attempt, he would not be discharged. His dreams under hypnosis were of the most elemental kind, involving his running to catch a boat and just missing it. His associations revealed that "missing the boat" symbolized the view he took of his entire career. His legal ambitions were very great and he could make no compromise with his grandiose success fantasies. The aggression connected with this grandiosity interfered with his actual performance. This constellation is frequently observed in male patients with extremely high and rigid standards for themselves. What they see as their failure causes an enormous degree of self-hatred, and their suicide can be a self-inflicted punishment for having failed. A high percentage of the male patients in this group have demonstrated a paranoid personality structure in the years prior to their becoming depressed or suicidal. A typical example is one stock-broker of 55 who had been depressed to the extent that he was unable to work for several years prior to the suicide attempt which occasioned his being seen by the writer. Before that he had a career spanning thirty years, but changed positions every two or three years. In each he had been the victim, he said, of mistreatment, personal favoritism or corruption. Eventually a combination of these factors and the emotional breakdown of his daughter proved too great for his paranoid defenses, and what was probably always a latent depression made itself evident. He then began blaming himself and his unworthiness for his work failures and bemoaning his misfortune with his daughter. In the course of several months' therapy he became paranoid toward the writer; at the same time, his depression lifted sufficiently so that he could resume work. When his paranoid defenses were activated in relation to his psychiatrist, his depressive symptomatology lessened and he became able to function.

These sorts of suicidal self-punishment reactions with women over failure at work have not been observed, however. A suicidal self-punishment reaction that is often seen in women was illustrated by the case mentioned earlier of the woman who felt herself unable to love her child. When a woman is unable to love her child and this is accompanied by the expectation that she should feel what she is not feeling—strong self-hatred with a consequent need for self-punishment can be the result.

A variation of the view of suicide as a self-punishment seen in patients of both sexes may be illustrated by the following patient. He was a thirty-year-old man from a relatively stable rural family. He was the sixth of eight children and stated that he had felt "superfluous" since childhood. All the other siblings were married and he felt that they were leading responsible lives, and that he was the black sheep of the family. Since the age of 18 he had been a moderately severe alcoholic. He had made an impossible marriage in which he also had felt "superfluous" and which quickly led to divorce. His employment had been mainly as a seaman, but his explosive temper and frequent fights aboard ship had made it impossible for him to continue in this capacity and he was depressed over this. He reported the following dream immediately prior to an impulsive suicide attempt in which he jumped in front of a moving car. "An atom bomb was falling." . . . "I was in hell and about to be burned. My brother was above, saying that I should be burned." The patient said he would end up in hell if he did not lead "a more Christian life." Eight months earlier he had begun attending church in an effort to force himself to live differently, but without success. His mother was extremely religious and opposed to drinking, smoking or any amusement for its own sake. He had never been close to her, but had taken over her religious beliefs, although he felt unable to live up to them. The brother in the dream was the family member the patient had felt most close to although the relationship has been characterized by fights and reconciliations until the time of his brother's death three years earlier.

The patient had made several impulsive suicide attempts during the previous eight years, including one where he jumped in front of a moving jeep and had been severely injured. Suicide was for him an act of atonement, and death a punishment he felt he deserved for his explosiveness, his anger toward his siblings and the world and for the asocial existence he was leading.

Among the most disturbed male and female suicidal patients seen in the mental hospital, feelings of being worthless and no good predominate, and self-punishment is a prominent feature. The original motivation may be centered around failure, guilt over aggression or attempted expiation, but the self-punishment can become dissociated from these goals and become almost an end in itself. Such patients can then become preoccupied with delusional feelings of guilt, sin and unworthiness.

The patient who sees himself as already dead: One man who jumped in front of a train had lost one leg almost to the hip, and an arm. Some months after the attempt he related a dream in which he was shopping for a coffin and the coffin-maker told him that his coffin was a little over half-finished. Considering that he had lost two limbs in his suicide attempt, the dream seemed a fairly obvious current picture of himself. His associations and elaborations to the dream indicated that he felt that only his physical death was half completed. He considered that he had died emotionally or affectively several years before making any suicide attempt.

One very withdrawn suicidal girl of 18 seen by the writer had a recurrent nightmare in which she saw dry ice coming closer and closer to her and threatening to envelop her, until she woke in panic. She was tormented by her inability to feel for people and she not only felt dead but her physical and motor appearance suggested a kind of walking death. Her dry ice image was a self-image—a self that was seen as permanently frozen, dangerous to others and self-destructive.

These patients were representative of an entire group who are preoccupied with feeling already dead, generally not in a delusional sense but in the sense of being emotionally dead. Strong feelings of detachment, repressed aggression and dampened affectivity are often perceived by the patients as a kind of emotional dying or death. Clinically, they will often appear apathetic rather than depressed, and their suicide attempts do not usually change this mood. Despite the overt apathy, such deadness is experienced by the suicidal patients as extremely torturous and they seem to see suicide both as a release from suffering and as merely carrying out an event which has already happened.

Summary

This article attempts to demonstrate some of the psychodynamic patterns seen in suicidal patients based on different fantasies and attitudes toward death. Seven such patterns are outlined and illustrated: death as abandonment, death as omnipotent mastery, death as retroflexed murder, death as a reunion, death as rebirth, death as self-punishment or atonement, death as a process that in an emotional sense has already taken place.

The death fantasy of the suicidal individual is not simply helpful in revealing his motivation for suicide but is also intriguingly a part of his entire attitude towards life as well as death. The individual who expects his suicide and death to continue a punishment which he deserves is quite different from the individual who hopes for the gratification of dependent desires in a protected reunion with a maternal figure. They reveal quite different character structures and not different suicidal psychodynamics. Death fantasies thus come to serve as a natural aid in distinguishing the various motivations seen in suicide.

Figure 7-6. Sigmund Freud (1856-1939) in 1922. (The Bettman Archives.)

LECTURE XXVIII: ANALYTIC THERAPY

Sigmund Freud

Whether we realize it or not, Freudian psychoanalysis has had a great impact upon Western culture. Many Freudian terms have become part of contemporary language. If you have ever viewed an object as a "phallic symbol"; said someone was "repressing" a traumatic experience; referred to a self-centered person as on an "ego trip", or made a "Freudian slip" in your speech; you have used Freudian terminology.

Although millions of people have strong opinions about Freud and his theories, many have never read any of his original works. When introducing Freud's work in class, I am surprised that many students already have formed definite opinions, mostly dubious. Much of what people know of Freud was learned through secondary sources, table conversations, or media talk shows. Therefore, I feel it is important to include some of Freud's original work in this book.

It is not uncommon to hear "Freud said 'this,'" from one person, and "Freud said 'that'" from another. Freud wrote and spoke in German. His work was translated primarily by European scholars. The First American Edition of the Collected Papers of Sigmund Freud was published in 1959. According to editor Ernest Jones, M.D.,

> *It is unfortunate that the English-speaking public should for years have had access only to what may be called the superstructure of his work, the application of his psychoanalytic method to the study of dreams, sexuality, totemism, and so on, while the basis of it all remained buried in a foreign tongue (Ed. Preface).*

Furthermore, there is loss in translation. For example, the names of the structures of personality, critical to the understanding of Freud's theories, were translated into Latin, not English. "Es" in German was translated to the Latin "id." In German, "es" means "it," and connotes "a thing" inside which compels to immediate, instinctive, hedonistic gratification. "Ich" in German was translated to "ego." "Ich" means "I" and connotes self. "Überich", translated "superego," is roughly synonymous with "conscience." However, in German Überich translates as "an entity that hovers over the self," conveying a more sinister and punitive image. Comprehension and appreciation of Freud would be enhanced by a contemporary translation in American English.

Textbook authors often take extreme license in interpreting Freud. I have seen numbers of pages in Introductory Psychology texts without a citation of Freud, inviting author embellishment. The assumption that what Freud meant is "common knowledge" tempts distortion.

Between 1915 and 1917 Freud delivered a series of 28 lectures on psychoanalysis to the medical students at the University of Vienna. The following selection, "Lecture XXVIII, Analytic Therapy," is the last of this series of lectures, and represents the culmination of two year's work with his students. James Strachey, translator of this lecture, commented in his introduction to The Complete Lectures on Psychoanalysis *that "... there is no rival to the analysis of the process of psychoanalytic therapy given in the last lecture of all."*

In the lecture Freud describes the basic theory of psychoanalysis. He points out how transference, or the patient's perception of the analyst as the reincarnation of significant people from his past, can be used to help the patient's ego gain control over the libido, or sexual instinct, so that the underlying causes of the patient's condition can be resolved. He also rebuts criticisms of psychoanalysis.

Psychoanalytic scholar Robert R. Holt offered beneficial guidance when reading Freud. Some of his main points are:

- *Beware of statements of Freud that are lifted out of context.*
- *Don't take extreme positions literally. Words like "never" or "invariably" may be exaggerations for effect.*
- *Don't expect rigorous definitions. Derive meaning from context.*
- *Don't take every statement as profound truth, nor reject others which may seem superficially inane (Holt, 1989, p. 67).*

Imagine yourself as a student of Freud's. Picture the stern, bearded, cigar-smoking master of psychoanalysis as he delivers his final lecture to his students. Note Freud's modest air, tinged with a sense of confidence in his convictions. The lecture is a beautiful example of the thought, logic, and genius of Sigmund Freud. Accept the challenge this lecture presents.

References
Holt, R. (1989). *Freud Reappraised: A Fresh Look at Psychoanalytic Theory.* New York: The Guilford Press.

Ladies and Gentlemen,[1]—You know what we are going to talk about to-day. You asked me why we do not make use of direct suggestion in psychoanalytic therapy, when we admit that our influence rests essentially on transference—that is, on suggestion; and you added a doubt whether, in view of this predominance of suggestion, we are still able to claim that our psychological discoveries are objective. I promised I would give you a detailed reply.

Direct suggestion is suggestion aimed against the manifestation of the symptoms; it is a struggle between your authority and the motives for the illness. In this you do not concern yourself with these motives; you merely request the patient to suppress their manifestation in symptoms. It makes no difference of principle whether you put the patient under hypnosis or not. Once again Bernheim, with his characteristic perspicacity, maintained that suggestion was the essential element in the phenomena of hypnotism, that hypnosis itself was already a result of suggestion, a suggested state;[2] and he preferred to practise suggestion in a waking state, which can achieve the same effects as suggestion under hypnosis.

Which would you rather hear first on this question—what experience tells us or theoretical considerations?

Let us begin with the former. I was a pupil of Bernheim's, whom I visited at Nancy in 1889 and whose book on suggestion I translated into German.[3] I practised hypnotic treatment for many years, at first by prohibitory suggestion and later in combination with Breuer's method of questioning the patient. I can therefore speak of the results of hypnotic or suggestive therapy on the basis of a wide experience. If, in the words of the old medical aphorism, an ideal therapy should be rapid, reliable and not disagreeable for the patient ['*cito, tuto, jucunde*'], Bernheim's method fulfilled at least two of these requirements. It could be carried through much quicker—or, rather, infinitely quicker—than analytic treatment and it caused the patient neither trouble nor unpleasantness. For the doctor it became, in the long run, monotonous: in each case, in the same way, with the same ceremonial, forbidding the most variegated symptoms to exist, without being able to learn anything of their sense and meaning. It was hackwork and not a scientific activity, and it recalled magic, incantations and hocus-pocus. That could not weigh, however, against the patient's interest. But the third quality was lacking: the procedure was not reliable in any respect.

It could be used with one patient; but not with another; it achieved a great deal with one and very little with another, and one never knew why. Worse than the capriciousness of the procedure was the lack of permanence in its successes. If, after a short time, one had news of the patient once more, the old ailment was back again or its place had been taken by a new one. One might hypnotize him again. But in the background there was the warning given by experienced workers against robbing the patient of his self-reliance by frequently repeated hypnosis and so making him an addict to this kind of therapy as though it were a narcotic. Admittedly sometimes things went entirely as one would wish: after a few efforts, success was complete and permanent.[4] But the conditions determining such favorable outcome remained unknown. On one occasion a severe condition in a woman, which I had entirely got rid of by a short hypnotic treatment, returned unchanged after the patient had, through no action on my part, got annoyed with me; after a reconciliation, I removed the trouble again and far more thoroughly; yet it returned once more after she had fallen foul of me a second time. On another occasion a woman patient, whom I had repeatedly helped out of neurotic states by hypnosis, suddenly, during the treatment of a specially obstinate situation, threw her arms round my neck.[5] After this one could scarcely avoid, whether one wanted to or not, investigating the question of the nature and origin of one's authority in suggestive treatment.

So much for experiences. They show us that in renouncing direct suggestion we are not giving up anything of irreplaceable value. Now let us add a few reflections to this. The practice of hypnotic therapy makes very small demands on either the patient or the doctor. It agrees most beautifully with the estimate in which neuroses are still held by the majority of doctors. The doctor says to the neurotic patient: 'There's nothing wrong with you, it's only a question of nerves; so I can blow away your trouble in two or three minutes with just a few words.' But our views on the laws of energy are offended by the notion of its being possible to move a great weight by a tiny application of force, attacking it directly, without the outside help of any appropriate appliances. In

so far as the conditions are comparable, experience shows that this feat is not successfully accomplished in the case of the neuroses either. But I am aware that this argument is not unimpeachable. There is such a thing as a 'trigger-action'.

In the light of the knowledge we have gained from psychoanalysis we can describe the difference between hypnotic and psychoanalytic suggestion as follows. Hypnotic treatment seeks to cover up and gloss over something in mental life; analytic treatment seeks to expose and get rid of something[6]. The former acts like a cosmetic, the latter like surgery. The former makes use of suggestion in order to forbid the symptoms; it strengthens the repressions, but, apart from that, leaves all the processes that have led to the formation of the symptoms unaltered. Analytic treatment makes its impact further back towards the roots, where the conflicts are which give rise to the symptoms, and uses suggestion in order to alter the outcome of those conflicts. Hypnotic treatment leaves the patient inert and unchanged, and for that reason, too, equally unable to resist any fresh occasion for falling ill. An analytic treatment demands from both doctor and patient the accomplishment of serious work, which is employed in lifting internal resistances. Through the overcoming of these resistances the patient's mental life is permanently changed, is raised to a high level of development and remains protected against fresh possibilities of falling ill. This work of overcoming resistances is the essential function of analytic treatment; the patient has to accomplish it and the doctor makes this possible for him with the help of suggestion operating in an *educative* sense. For that reason psychoanalytic treatment has justly been described as a kind of *after-education*.[7]

I hope I have now made it clear to you in what way our method of employing suggestion therapeutically differs from the only method possible in hypnotic treatment. You will understand too, from the fact that suggestion can be traced back to transference, the capriciousness which struck us in hypnotic therapy, while analytic treatment remains calculable within its limits. In using hypnosis we are dependent on the state of the patient's capacity for transference without being able to influence it itself. The transference

of a person who is to be hypnotized may be negative or, as most frequently, ambivalent, or he
may have protected himself against his transference by adopting special attitudes; of that we
learn nothing. In psychoanalysis we act upon the
transference itself, resolve what opposes it, adjust
the instrument with which we wish to make our
impact. Thus it becomes possible for us to derive
an entirely fresh advantage from the power of
suggestion; we get it into our hands. The patient
does not suggest to himself whatever he pleases:
we guide his suggestion so far as he is in any way
accessible to its influence.

But you will now tell me that, no matter
whether we call the motive force of our analysis
transference or suggestion, there is a risk that the
influencing of our patient may make the objective certainty of our findings doubtful. What is
advantageous to our therapy is damaging to our
researches. This is the objection that is most often
raised against psychoanalysis, and it must be
admitted that, though it is groundless, it cannot be
rejected as unreasonable. If it were justified, psychoanalysis would be nothing more than a particularly well-disguised and particularly effective
form of suggestive treatment and we should have
to attach little weight to all that it tells us about
what influences our lives, the dynamics of the
mind or the unconscious. That is what our opponents believe; and in especial they think that we
have 'talked' the patients into everything relating
to the importance of sexual experiences—or even
into those experiences themselves—after such
notions have grown up in our own depraved
imagination. These accusations are contradicted
more easily by an appeal to experience than by
the help of theory. Anyone who has himself carried out psychoanalyses will have been able to
convince himself on countless occasions that it is
impossible to make suggestions to a patient in
that way. The doctor has no difficulty, of course,
in making him a supporter of some particular theory and in thus making him share some possible
error of his own. In this respect the patient is
behaving like anyone else—like a pupil—but this
only affects his intelligence, not his illness. After
all, his conflicts will only be successfully solved
and his resistances overcome if the anticipatory
ideas he is given tally with what is real in him.

Whatever in the doctor's conjectures is inaccurate drops out in the course of the analysis;[8] it has
to be withdrawn and replaced by something more
correct. We endeavor by a careful technique to
avoid the occurrence of premature successes due
to suggestion; but no harm is done even if they do
occur, for we are not satisfied by a first success.
We do not regard an analysis as at an end until all
the obscurities of the case are cleared up, the gaps
in the patient's memory filled in, the precipitating
causes of the repressions discovered. We look
upon successes that set in too soon as obstacles
rather than as a help to the work of analysis; and
we put an end to such successes by constantly
resolving the transference on which they are
based. It is this last characteristic which is the
fundamental distinction between analytic and
purely suggestive therapy, and which frees the
results of analysis from the suspicion of being
successes due to suggestion. In every other kind
of suggestive treatment the transference is carefully preserved and left untouched; in analysis it
is itself subjected to treatment and is dissected in
all the shapes in which it appears. At the end of
an analytic treatment the transference must itself
be cleared away; and if success is then obtained
or continues, it rests, not on suggestion, but on
the achievement by its means of an overcoming
of internal resistances, on the internal change that
has been brought about in the patient.

The acceptance of suggestions on individual
points is no doubt discouraged by the fact that
during the treatment we are struggling unceasing-
ly against resistances which are able to transform
themselves into negative (hostile) transferences.
Nor must we fail to point out that a large number
of the individual findings of analysis, which
might otherwise be suspected of being products
of suggestion, are confirmed from another and
irreproachable source. Our guarantors in this case
are the sufferers from dementia praecox and paranoia, who are of course far above any suspicion
of being influenced by suggestion. The transla-
tions of symbols and the phantasies, which these
patients produce for us and which in them have
forced their way through into consciousness,
coincide faithfully with the results of our investigations into the unconscious of transference neurotics and thus confirm the objective correctness

of our interpretations, on which doubt is so often thrown. You will not, I think, be going astray if you trust analysis on these points.

I will now complete my picture of the mechanism of cure by clothing it in the formulas of the libido theory. A neurotic is incapable of enjoyment and of efficiency—the former because his libido is not directed on to any real object and the latter because he is obliged to employ a great deal of his available energy on keeping his libido under repression and on warding off its assaults. He would become healthy if the conflict between his ego and his libido came to an end and if his ego had his libido again at its disposal. The therapeutic task consists, therefore, in freeing the libido from its present attachments, which are withdrawn from the ego, and in making it once more serviceable to the ego. Where, then, is the neurotic's libido situated? It is easily found: it is attached to the symptoms, which yield it the only substitutive satisfaction possible at the time. We must therefore make ourselves masters of the symptoms and resolve them—which is precisely the same thing that the patient requires of us. In order to resolve the symptoms, we must go back as far as their origin, we must renew the conflict from which they arose, and, with the help of motive forces which were not at the patient's disposal in the past, we must guide it to a different outcome. This revision of the process of repression can be accomplished only in part in connection with the memory traces of the processes which led to repression. The decisive part of the work is achieved by creating in the patient's relation to the doctor—in the 'transference'—new editions of the old conflicts; in these the patient would like to behave in the same way as he did in the past, while we, by summoning up every available mental force [in the patient], compel him to come to a fresh decision. Thus the transference becomes the battlefield on which all the mutually struggling forces should meet one another.

All the libido, as well as everything opposing it, is made to converge solely on the relation with the doctor. In this process the symptoms are inevitably divested of libido. In place of the patient's true illness there appears the artificially constructed transference illness, in place of the various unreal objects of his libido there appears a single, and once more imaginary, object in the person of the doctor. But, by the help of the doctor's suggestion, the new struggle around this object is lifted to the highest psychical level: it takes place as a normal mental conflict. Since a fresh repression is avoided, the alienation between ego and libido is brought to an end and the subject's mental unity is restored. When the libido is released once more from its temporary object in the person of the doctor, it cannot return to its earlier objects, but is at the disposal of the ego. The forces against which we have been struggling during our work of therapy are, on the one hand, the ego's antipathy to certain trends of the libido —an antipathy expressed in a tendency to repression—and, on the other hand, the tenacity or adhesiveness of the libido, which dislikes leaving objects that it has once cathected.

Thus our therapeutic work falls into two phases. In the first, all the libido is forced from the symptoms into the transference and concentrated there; in the second, the struggle is waged around this new object and the libido is liberated from it. The change which is decisive for a favourable outcome is the elimination of repression in this renewed conflict, so that the libido cannot withdraw once more from the ego by flight into the unconscious. This is made possible by the alteration of the ego which is accomplished under the influence of the doctor's suggestion. By means of the work of interpretation, which transforms what is unconscious into what is conscious, the ego is enlarged at the cost of this unconscious; by means of instruction, it is made conciliatory towards the libido and inclined to grant it some satisfaction, and its repugnance to the claims of the libido is diminished by the possibility of disposing of a portion of it by sublimation. The more closely events in the treatment coincide with this ideal description, the greater will be the success of the psychoanalytic therapy. It finds its limits in the lack of mobility of the libido, which may refuse to leave its objects, and the rigidity of narcissism, which will not allow transference on to objects to increase beyond certain bounds. Further light may perhaps be thrown on the dynamics of the process of cure if I say that we get hold of the whole of the libido which has been withdrawn from the dominance of the ego by attracting a portion of it on to ourselves by means of the transference.

It will not be out of place to give a warning that we can draw no direct conclusion from the distribution of the libido during and resulting from the treatment as to how it was distributed during the illness. Suppose we succeeded in bringing a case to a favourable conclusion by setting up and then resolving a strong father-transference to the doctor. It would not be correct to conclude that the patient had suffered previously from a similar unconscious attachment of his libido to his father. His father-transference was merely the battlefield on which we gained control of his libido; the patient's libido was directed to it from other positions. A battlefield need not necessarily coincide with one of the enemy's key fortresses. The defense of a hostile capital need not take place just in front of its gates. Not until after the transference has once more been resolved can we reconstruct in our thoughts the distribution of libido which had prevailed during the illness.

From the standpoint of the libido theory, too, we may say a last word on dreams. A neurotic's dreams help us, like his parapraxes and his free associations to them, to discover the sense of his symptoms and to reveal the way in which his libido is allocated. They show us, in the form of a wish-fulfilment, what wishful impulses have been subjected to repression and to what objects the libido withdrawn from the ego has become attached. For this reason the interpretation of dreams plays a large part in a psychoanalytic treatment, and in some cases it is over long periods the most important instrument of our work. We already know that the state of sleep in itself leads to a certain relaxation of the repressions. A repressed impulse, owing to this reduction in the pressure weighing down upon it, becomes able to express itself far more clearly in a dream than it can be allowed to be expressed by a symptom during the day. The study of dreams therefore becomes the most convenient means of access to a knowledge of the repressed unconscious, of which the libido withdrawn from the ego forms a part.

But the dreams of neurotics do not differ in any important respect from those of normal people; it is possible, indeed, that they cannot be dis-

tinguished from them at all. It would be absurd to give an account of the dreams of neurotics which could not also apply to the dreams of normal people. We must therefore say that the difference between neurosis and health holds only during the day; it is not prolonged into dream-life. We are obliged to carry over to healthy people a number of hypotheses which arise in connection with neurotics as a result of the link between the latter's dreams and their symptoms. We cannot deny that healthy people as well possess in their mental life what alone makes possible the formation both of dreams and of symptoms, and we must conclude that they too have carried out repressions, that they expend a certain amount of energy in order to maintain them, that their unconscious system conceals repressed impulses which are still cathected with energy, and that *a portion of their libido is withdrawn from their ego's disposal.* Thus a healthy person, too, is virtually a neurotic; but dreams appear to be the only symptoms which he is capable of forming. It is true that if one subjects his waking life to a closer examination one discovers something that contradicts this appearance— namely that this ostensibly healthy life is interspersed with a great number of trivial and in practice unimportant symptoms.

The distinction between nervous health and neurosis is thus reduced to a practical question and is decided by the outcome—by whether the subject is left with a sufficient amount of capacity for enjoyment and of efficiency. It probably goes back to the relative sizes of the quota of energy that remains free and of that which is bound by repression, and is of a quantitative not of a qualitative nature. I need not tell you that this discovery is the theoretical justification for our conviction that neuroses are in principle curable in spite of their being based on constitutional disposition.

The identity of the dreams of healthy and neurotic people enables us to infer thus much in regard to defining the characteristics of health. But in regard to dreams themselves we can make a further inference: we must not detach them from their connection with neurotic symptoms, we must not suppose that their essential nature is exhausted by the formula that describes them as a translation of thoughts into an archaic form of expression, but we must suppose that they exhibit to us allocations of the libido and object-cathexes that are really present.[9]

We shall soon have reached the end. You are perhaps disappointed that on the topic of the psychoanalytic method of therapy I have only spoken to you about theory and not about the conditions which determine whether a treatment is to be undertaken or about the results it produces. I shall discuss neither: the former because it is not my intention to give you practical instructions on how to carry out a psychoanalysis, and the latter because several reasons deter me from it. At the beginning of our talks, I emphasized the fact that under favourable conditions we achieve successes which are second to none of the finest in the field of internal medicine; and I can now add something further—namely that they could not have been achieved by any other procedure. If I were to say more than this I should be suspected of trying to drown the loudly raised voices of depreciation by self-advertisement. The threat has repeatedly been made against psychoanalysts by our medical 'colleagues'—even at public congresses—that a collection of the failures and damaging results of analysis would be published which would open the suffering public's eyes to the worthlessness of this method of treatment. But, apart from the malicious, denunciatory character of such a measure, it would not even be calculated to make it possible to form a correct judgement of the therapeutic effectiveness of analysis. Analytic therapy, as you know, is in its youth; it has taken a long time to establish its technique, and that could only be done in the course of working and under the influence of increasing experience. In consequence of the difficulties in giving instruction, the doctor who is a beginner in psychoanalysis is thrown back to a greater extent than other specialists on his own capacity for further development, and the results of his first years will never make it possible to judge the efficacy of analytic therapy.

Many attempts at treatment miscarried during the early period of analysis because they were undertaken in cases which were altogether unsuited to the procedure and which we should exclude today on the basis of our present view of the indications for treatment. But these indications, too, could only be arrived at by experiment. In those days we did not know *a priori* that paranoia and dementia praecox in strongly marked forms are inaccessible, and we had a right to make trial of the method on all kinds of disorders. But most of the failures of those early years were due not to the doctor's fault or an unsuitable choice of patients but to unfavourable external conditions. Here we have only dealt with internal resistances, those of the patient, which are inevitable and can be overcome. The external resistances which arise from the patient's circumstances, from his environment, are of small theoretical interest but of the greatest practical importance. Psychoanalytic treatment may be compared with a surgical operation and may similarly claim to be carried out under arrangements that will be the most favourable for its success. You know the precautionary measures adopted by a surgeon: a suitable room, good lighting, assistants, exclusion of the patient's relatives, and so on. Ask yourselves now how many of these operations would turn out successfully if they had to take place in the presence of all the members of the patient's family, who would stick their noses into the field of the operation and exclaim aloud at every incision. In psychoanalytic treatments the intervention of relatives is a positive danger and a danger one does not know how to meet. One is armed against the patient's internal resistances, which one knows are inevitable, but how can one ward off these external resistances? No kind of explanations make any impression on the patient's relatives; they cannot be induced to keep at a distance from the whole business, and one cannot make common cause with them because of the risk of losing the confidence of the patient, who—quite rightly, moreover—expects the person in whom he has put his trust to take his side. No one who has any experience of the rifts which so often divide a family will, if he is an analyst, be surprised to find that the patient's closest relatives sometimes betray less interest in his recovering than in his remaining as he is. When, as so often, the neurosis is related to conflicts between members of a family, the healthy party will not hesitate long in choosing between his own interest and the sick party's recovery. It is not to be wondered at, indeed, if a husband looks with disfavour on a treatment in which, as he may rightly suspect, the whole catalogue of his sins will be brought to light. Nor do we wonder at it; but we cannot in that case blame ourselves if our efforts remain unsuccessful and the treatment is broken off prematurely because the husband's resistance is added to that of his sick wife. We had in fact undertaken something which in the prevailing circumstances was unrealizable.

Instead of reporting a number of cases, I will tell you the story of a single one, in which, from considerations of medical discretion, I was condemned to play a long-suffering part. I undertook the analytic treatment—it was many years ago—of a girl who had for some time been unable, owing to anxiety, to go out in the street or to stay at home by herself. The patient slowly brought out an admission that her imagination had been seized by chance observations of the affectionate relations between her mother and a well-to-do friend of the family. But she was so clumsy—or so subtle—that she gave her mother a hint of what was being talked about in the analytic sessions. She brought this about by changing her behaviour towards her mother, by insisting on being protected by no one but her mother from her anxiety at being alone and by barring the door to her in her anxiety if she tried to leave the house. Her mother had herself been very neurotic in the past, but had been cured years before in a hydropathic establishment. Or rather, she had there made the acquaintance of the man with whom she was able to enter into a relation that was in every way satisfying to her. The girl's passionate demands took her aback, and she suddenly understood the meaning of her daughter's anxiety: the girl had made herself ill in order to keep her mother prisoner and to rob her of the freedom of movement that her relations with her lover required. The mother quickly made up her mind and brought the obnoxious treatment to an end. The girl was taken to a sanatorium for nervous diseases and was demonstrated for many years as 'a poor victim of psychoanalysis'. All this time, too, I was pursued by the calumny of responsibility for the unhappy end of the treatment. I kept silence, for I thought I was bound by the duty of medical discretion. Long afterwards I learnt from one of my colleagues, who visited the sanatorium and had seen the agoraphobic girl there, that the *liaison* between her mother and the well-to-do friend of the family was common knowledge in the city and that it was probably connived at by the husband and father. Thus it was to this 'secret' that the treatment had been sacrificed.

In the years before the war, when arrivals from many foreign countries made me independent of the favour or disfavour of my own city, I followed a rule of not taking on a patient for treatment unless he was *sui juris*, not dependent on anyone else in the essential relations of his life. This is not possible, however, for every psychoanalyst. Perhaps you may conclude from my warning against relatives that patients designed for psychoanalysis should be removed from their families and that this kind of treatment should accordingly be restricted to inmates of hospitals for nervous diseases. I could not, however, follow you in that. It is much more advantageous for patients (in so far as they are not in a phase of severe exhaustion) to remain during the treatment in the conditions in which they have to struggle with the tasks that face them. But the patients' relatives ought not to cancel out this advantage by their conduct and should not offer any hostile opposition to the doctor's efforts. But how do you propose to influence in that direction factors like these which are inaccessible to us? And you will guess, of course, how much the prospects of a treatment are determined by the patient's social *milieu* and the cultural level of his family.

This presents a gloomy prospect for the effectiveness of psycho-analysis as a therapy—does it not?—even though we are able to explain the great majority of our failures by attributing them to interfering external factors. Friends of analysis have advised us to meet the threatened publication of our failures with statistics of successes drawn up by ourselves. I did not agree to this. I pointed out that statistics are worthless if the items assembled in them are too heterogeneous; and the cases of neurotic illness which we had taken into treatment were in fact incomparable in a great variety of respects. Moreover, the period of time that could be covered was too short to make it possible to judge the durability of the cures.[10] And it was altogether impossible to report on many of the cases: they concerned people who had kept both their illness and its treatment secret, and their recovery had equally to be kept secret. But the strongest reason for holding back lay in the realization that in matters of therapy people behave highly irrationally, so that one has no prospect of accomplishing anything with them by rational means. A therapeutic novelty is either received with delirious enthusiasm—as, for instance, when Koch introduced his first tuberculin against tuberculosis to the public[11] or it is treated with abysmal distrust—like Jenner's vaccination, which was in fact a blessing and which even today has its irreconcilable opponents. There was obviously a prejudice against psychoanalysis. If one had cured a severe case, one might hear people say: 'That proves nothing. He would have recovered on his own account by this time.' And when a woman patient, who had already passed through four cycles of depression and mania, came to be treated by me during an interval after an attack of melancholia and three weeks later started on a phase of mania, all the members of her family—and a high medical authority, too, who was called in for consultation—were convinced that the fresh attack could only be the result of my attempted analysis. Nothing can be done against prejudices. You can see it again today in the prejudices which each group of nations at war has developed against the other. The most sensible thing to do is to wait, and to leave such prejudices to the eroding effects of time. One day the same people begin to think about the same things in quite a different way from before; why they did not think so earlier remains a dark mystery.

It is possible that the prejudice against analytic treatment is already diminishing. The constant spread of analytic teachings, the increasing number of doctors practicing analysis in a number of countries seems to vouch for this. When I was a young doctor, I found myself in a similar storm of indignation on the doctors' part against treatment by hypnotic suggestion, which is now held up in contrast to analysis by people of 'moderate' views.[12] Hypnotism, however, has not fulfilled its original promise as a therapeutic agent. We psychoanalysts may claim to be its legitimate heirs and we do not forget how much encouragement and theoretical clarification we owe to it. The damaging results attributed to psychoanalysis are restricted essentially to passing manifestations of increased conflict if an analysis is clumsily carried out or if it is broken off in the middle. You have heard an account of what we do with our patients and can form your own judgement as to whether our efforts are calculated to lead to any lasting damage. Abuse of analysis is possible in various directions; in particular, the transference is a dangerous instrument in the hands of an unconscientious doctor. But no medical instrument or procedure is guaranteed against abuse; if a knife does not cut, it cannot be used for healing either.

I have finished, Ladies and Gentlemen. It is more than a conventional form of words if I admit that I myself am profoundly aware of the many defects in the lectures I have given you. I regret above all that I have so often promised to return later to a topic I have lightly touched on and have then found no opportunity of redeeming my promise. I undertook to give you an account of a subject which is still incomplete and in process of development, and my condensed summary has itself turned out to be an incomplete one. At some points I have set out the material on which to draw a conclusion and have then myself not drawn it. But I could not pretend to make you into experts; I have only tried to stimulate and enlighten you.

NOTES:

1. This lecture contains Freud's fullest account of the theory of the therapeutic effects of psychoanalysis. His later discussion of the question in his paper on 'Analysis Terminable and Interminable' (1937) seems in some respects to be at variance with it. Freud published very little on the details of psychoanalytic technique. See, however, the technical papers in Volume XII of the *Standard Edition*, where a list of his other writings on the subject will be found.

2. Freud subsequently expressed his disagreement with this view of Bernheim's. See footnote at the end of Chapter X of Group Psychology (1921).

3. In fact Freud translated two of Bernheim's books: *De la suggestion et de ses applications a la therapeutique* (1886 translated 1888-9) and *Hypnotisme, suggestion et psychotherapie* (1891, translated 1892).

4. An instance of this kind was reported by Freud in an early paper, 'A Case of Successful Treatment by Hypnotism' (1892-3).

5. Freud described this episode again at the end of Chapter 11 of his *Autobiographical Study* (1925), (Norton, 1963).

6. This distinction is developed at some length in an early paper of Freud's 'On Psychotherapy' (1905).

7. See the paper 'On Psychotherapy' (1905) where, incidentally, the German word 'Nacherziehung' ('after-education') is wrongly translated 're-education'.

8. Freud gives a small example of this in the 'Wolf Man' case history (1918).

9. Some interesting remarks on the dreams of psychotic patients will be found in Section B of 'Some Neurotic Mechanisms' (1922).

10. Freud recurrs to this question in the New Introductory Lectures, p. 616, where the therapeutic value of psychoanalysis is again discussed.

11. In 1890. Its promise was not fulfilled.

12. Some striking evidence of the medical opposition to hypnotism will be found in an early review by Freud of a book on the subject by the well-known Swiss psychiatrist, August Forel (Freud, 1889).

Figure 7-7. Erik H. Erikson, March 4, 1970, after winning the National Book Award. (UPI/Corbis-Bettmann.)

ERIK ERIKSON'S EIGHT AGES OF MAN

David Elkind

In 1905, Freud published Three Essays on the Theory of Sexuality, *which according to editor James Strachey, "...stand ...beside his* Interpretation of Dreams *as his most momentous and original contributions to human knowledge." (p. 126). In it, he describes a series of stages through which children pass in the process of psychosexual development. In each stage there is a primary erogenous zone; a part of the body where skin meets mucous membrane. Gratification from stimulation of the erogenous zone is required for normal development. A psychosexual conflict is centered at the erogenous zone, and is dealt with in the context of the relationship between the caretakers and the child. If the conflict is adequately dealt with, personality development remains on course. If the conflict has been inadequately or excessively dealt with, fixation results.*

> *...the libido behaves like a stream whose main bed has become blocked. It proceeds to fill up collateral channels which may hitherto have been empty. ...[This diversion brings] about perversions in persons who might perhaps otherwise have remained normal (p. 170).*

Adult psychopathology is assumed to result from childhood fixation. Freud was generally pessimistic and deterministic.

> *...deviations from normal sexual life which are later observed both in neurotics and in perverts are thus established from the very first by the impressions of childhood... [They] can become fixated as a permanent disorder (p. 242).*

Although technically psychosexual theory is comprised of five stages, we will consider the first three as they are the most significant. Freud's description of the psychosexual stages are not sequential, direct, or clear. This invites a myriad of interpretations of what he meant.

Oral Stage: (Birth to 18 months)
The mouth is the erogenous zone and children derive gratification through sucking, eating, and other forms of oral stimulation. Adequate parental attention and nurturance satisfies the oral needs. Undergratification results in compensatory oral behaviors such as excessive eating, alcoholism, and smoking. Overindulgence results in acceptance, dependence, and naivety.

Anal Stage: (18 months to 3 years)
The anus becomes the erogenous zone and the dilemma is toilet training. Firm but patient encouragement results in best resolution. Lack of attention by parents results in anal expulsive personality; messy, unkempt, tardy, and slovenly. Harsh and punitive toilet training results in anal retentive personality. Since the child was cruelly scolded for informing parents after the fact and being dirty, he symbolically compensates as an adult by being compulsively punctual, clean, and fastidious. For a child to witness sexual intercourse may lead to sadistic tendencies, as the act is perceived as a form of ill-treatment or subjugation (p. 196).

Phallic Stage: (3 to 5 years)

The genitals now become the erogenous zone. Self manipulation and exploration produce pleasure. Children develop a naive infatuation with sexuality; they are intrigued by it, yet do not understand it. This is the time of the Oedipus (boys) and Electra (girls) complexes, in which the child "falls in love" with the opposite-sex parent and becomes ambivalent to the same-sex parent, an object of dependence and competition.

Parents who view the Oedipal/Electra drama as a "cute, but temporary phase" of development, foster in their children a sense of comfort and ease in loving one of the opposite sex, albeit a parent. This "first love" is the prototype for adult relationships. Rebuke for loving his mother by a "castrating" father and excessive identification with the mother, will cause diversion of libido into a collateral channel, such as homosexuality. Indulgence by the father of a daughter in the Oedipal drama (sexual abuse) could result in "penis envy." She may become promiscuous and seductive in symbolic efforts to possess a penis; or deceive, embarrass, or hurt men as an attempt to "castrate" them (Hergenhahn, 1984, p. 29). Perhaps an offensive insinuation; these are core traits of borderline personality disorder, common in women who have been abused.

Freud's psychosexual theory became the paradigm for other theorists. Neo-Freudians were writers who endorsed Freud's theories in general, yet rejected, modified, or extended certain aspects of it. Carl Jung, an early disciple of Freud, painfully parted ways with him because of disagreement on Freud's sexual emphasis. Alfred Adler, who coined the term "inferiority complex" based upon his own insecurity, was a staunch ally of Freud for a decade. They parted bitterly over differences about repression, infantile sexuality, and the unconscious. Freud, intolerant of deserters, cynically remarked, "I made a pigmy great." (Hergenhahn, 1984, p. 65).

Erik Erickson remained loyal to Freud despite creating his own theory of personality development. It is in many ways similar to psychosexual theory. However, it places greater emphasis on social factors, is more optimistic, and is a life span theory. Erickson had no college degrees, a clear example of Freud's contention that one need not be a medical doctor to be a psychoanalyist. He originated the term "identity crisis." He was blond haired, blue eyed and of Scandinavian heritage, and raised by his mother and Jewish stepfather. In temple, he was called a "goy" (Yiddish for gentile); in school he was a Jew (Hergenhahn, 1984, p. 163). He died in May of 1994 in a nursing home.

The following article, originally published in 1970, was written by prolific psychology author David Elkind. It is a concise synopsis of Erickson's psychosocial theory. As you read the article, compare and contrast it with Freud's psychosexual theory.

References

Breuer, J. and Freud, S. (1955). *The Complete Psychological Works of Sigmund Freud, Vol. VII, Three Essays on Sexuality.* London: The Hogarth Press.

Hergenhahn, B.R. (1984). *An Introduction to Theories of Personality.* New Jersey: Prentice-Hall.

At a recent faculty reception I happened to join a small group in which a young mother was talking about her "identity crisis." She and her husband, she said, had decided not to have any more children and she was depressed at the thought of being past the child-bearing stage. It was as if, she continued, she had been robbed of some part of herself and now needed to find a new function to replace the old one.

When I remarked that her story sounded like a case history from a book by Erik Erikson, she replied, "Who's Erikson?" It is a reflection on the intellectual modesty and literary decorum of Erik H. Erikson, psychoanalyst and professor of developmental psychology at Harvard, that so few of the many people who today talk about the "identity crisis" know anything of the man who pointed out its pervasiveness as a problem in contemporary society [five] decades ago.

Erikson has, however, contributed more to social science than his delineation of identity problems in modern man. His descriptions of the stages of the life cycle, for example, have advanced psychoanalytic theory to the point where it can now describe the development of the healthy personality on its own terms and not merely as the opposite of a sick one. Likewise, Erikson's emphasis upon the problems unique to adolescents and adults living in today's society has helped to rectify the one sided emphasis on childhood as the beginning and end of personality development. . . .

It is important to emphasize that Erikson's contributions are genuine advances in psychoanalysis in the sense that Erikson accepts and builds upon many of the basic tenets of Freudian theory. In this regard, Erikson differs from Freud's early co-workers such as Jung and Adler who, when they broke with Freud, rejected his theories and substituted their own.

Likewise, Erikson also differs from the so-called neo-Freudians such as Horney, Kardiner and Sullivan who (mistakenly, as it turned out) assumed that Freudian theory had nothing to say about man's relation to reality and to his culture. While it is true that Freud emphasized, even mythologized, sexuality, he did so to counteract the rigid sexual taboos of his time, which, at that point in history were frequently the cause of neuroses. In his later writings, however, Freud began to concern himself with the executive agency of the personality, namely the ego, which is also the repository of the individual's attitudes and concepts about himself and his world.

It is with the psychosocial development of the ego that Erikson's observations and theoretical constructions are primarily concerned. Erikson has thus been able to introduce innovations into psychoanalytic theory without either rejecting or ignoring Freud's monumental contribution.

The man who has accomplished this notable feat is a handsome Dane, whose white hair, mustache, resonant accent and gentle manner are reminiscent of actors like Jean Hersholt and Paul Muni. Although he is warm and outgoing with friends, Erikson is a rather shy man who is uncomfortable in the spotlight of public recognition. This trait, together with his ethical reservations about making public even disguised case material, may help to account for Erikson's reluctance to publish his observations and conceptions (his first book appeared in 1950, when he was 48). . . .

The course of Erikson's professional career has been as diverse as it has been unconventional. He was born in Frankfurt, Germany, in 1902 of Danish parents. Not long after his birth his father died, and his mother later married the pediatrician who had cured her son of a childhood illness. Erikson's stepfather urged him to become a physician, but the boy declined and became an artist instead—an artist who did portraits of children. Erikson says of his post-adolescent years, "I was an artist then, which in Europe is a euphemism for a young man with some talent and nowhere to go." During this period he settled in Vienna and worked as a tutor in a family friendly with Freud's. He met Freud on informal occasions when the families went on outings together.

These encounters may have been the impetus to accept a teaching appointment at an American school in Vienna founded by Dorothy Burlingham and directed by Peter Blos (both now well known on the American psychiatric scene). During these years (the late nineteen-twenties) he also undertook and completed psychoanalytic training with Anna Freud and August Aichhorn. Even at the outset of his career, Erikson gave evidence of the breadth of his interests and activities by being trained and certified as a Montessori teacher. Not surprisingly, in view of that training, Erikson's first articles dealt with psychoanalysis and education.

It was while in Vienna that Erikson met and married Joan Mowat Serson, an American artist of Canadian descent. They came to America in 1933, when Erikson was invited to practice and teach in Boston. Erikson was, in fact, one of the first if not the first child-analyst in the Boston area. During the next two decades he held clinical and academic appointments at Harvard, Yale and Berkeley. In 1951 he joined a group of psychiatrists and psychologists who moved to Stock-bridge, Mass., to start a new program at the Austen Riggs Center, a private residential treatment center for disturbed young people. Erikson remained at Riggs until 1961, when he was appointed professor of human development and lecturer on psychiatry at Harvard. Throughout his career he has always held two or three appointments simultaneously and has traveled extensively.

Perhaps because he had been an artist first, Erikson has never been a conventional psychoanalyst. When he was treating children, for examples he always insist on visiting his young patients' homes and on having dinner with the families. Likewise, in the nineteen-thirties, when anthropological investigation was described to him by his friends Scudder McKeel, Alfred Kroeber and Margaret Mead, he decided to do field work on an Indian reservation. "When I realized that Sioux is the name which we [in Europe] pronounced "See ux" and which for us was the American Indian, I could not resist." Erikson thus antedated the anthropologists who swept over the Indian reservations in the post-Depression years. (So numerous were the field workers at that time that the stock joke was that an Indian family could be defined as a mother, a father, children and an anthropologist.)

Erikson did field work not only with the Oglala Sioux of Pine Ridge, S. D. (the tribe that slew Custer and was in turn slaughtered at the Battle of Wounded Knee), but also with the salmon-fishing Yurok of Northern California. His reports on these experiences revealed his special gift for sensing and entering into the world-views and-modes of thinking of cultures other than his own.

It was while he was working with the Indians that Erikson began to note syndromes which he could not explain within the confines of traditional psychoanalytic theory. Central to many an adult Indian's emotional problems seemed to be his sense of uprootedness and lack of continuity between his present lifestyle and that portrayed in tribal history. Not only did the Indian sense a break with the past, but he could not identify with a future requiring assimilation of the white culture's values. The problems faced by such men, Erikson recognized, had to do with the ego and

with culture and only incidentally with sexual drives.

The impressions Erikson gained on the reservations were reinforced during World War II when he worked at a veterans' rehabilitation center at Mount Zion Hospital in San Francisco. Many of the soldiers he and his colleagues saw seemed not to fit the traditional "shell shock" or "malingerer" cases of World War I. Rather, it seemed to Erikson that many of these men had lost the sense of who and what they were. They were having trouble reconciling their activities, attitudes and feelings as soldiers with the activities, attitudes and feelings they had known before the war. Accordingly, while these men may well have had difficulties with repressed or conflicted drives, their main problem seemed to be, as Erikson came to speak of it at the time, "identity confusion."

It was almost a decade before Erikson set forth the implications of his clinical observations in "Childhood and Society." In that book, the summation and integration of 15 years of research, he made three major contributions to the study of the human ego. He posited (1) that, side by side with the stages of psychosexual development described by Freud (the oral, anal, phallic, genital, Oedipal and pubertal), were psychosocial stages of ego development, in which the individual had to establish new basic orientations to himself and his social world; (2) that personality development continued throughout the whole life cycle; and (3) that each stage had a positive as well as a negative component.

Much about these contributions—and about Erikson's way of thinking can be understood by looking at his scheme of life stages. Erikson identifies eight stages in the human life cycle, in each of which a new dimension of "social interaction" becomes possible—that is, a new dimension in a person's interaction with himself, and with his social environment.

Trust vs. Mistrust

The first stage corresponds to the oral stage in classical psychoanalytic theory and usually extends through the first year of life. In Erikson's view, the new dimension of social interaction that emerges during this period involves basic trust at the one extreme and mistrust at the other. The degree to which the child comes to trust the world, other people and himself depends to a considerable extent upon the quality of the care that he receives. The infant whose needs are met when they arise, whose discomforts are quickly removed, who is cuddled, fondled, played with and talked to, develops a sense of the world as a safe place to be and of people as helpful and dependable. When, however, the care is inconsistent, inadequate and rejecting, it fosters a basic mistrust, an attitude of fear and suspicion on the part of the infant toward the world in general and people in particular that will carry through to later stages of development.

It should be said at this point that the problem of basic trust-versus-mistrust (as is true for all the later dimensions) is not resolved once and for all during the first year of life. It arises again at each successive stage of development. There is both hope and danger in this. The child who enters school with a sense of mistrust may come to trust a particular teacher who has taken the trouble to make herself trustworthy; with this second chance he overcomes his early mistrust. On the other hand the child who comes through infancy with a vital sense of trust can still have his sense of mistrust activated at a later stage, if, say, his parents are divorced and separated under acrimonious circumstances.

This point was brought home to me in a very direct way by a 4-year-old patient I saw in a court clinic. He was being seen at the court clinic because his adoptive parents, who had had him for six months, now wanted to give him back to the agency. They claimed that he was cold and unloving, took things and could not be trusted. He was indeed a cold and apathetic boy but with good reason. About a year after his illegitimate birth, he was taken away from his mother, who had a drinking problem and was shunted back and forth among several foster homes. Initially he had tried to relate to the persons in the foster homes but the relationships never had a chance to develop because he was moved at just the wrong times. In the end he gave up trying to reach out to others because the inevitable separations hurt too much.

Like the burned child who dreads the flame,

this emotionally burned child shunned the pain of emotional involvement. He had trusted his mother but now he trusted no one. Only years of devoted care and patience could now undo the damage that had been done to this child's sense of trust.

Autonomy vs. Doubt

Stage two spans the second and third years of life, the period which Freudian theory calls the anal stage. Erikson sees here the emergence of autonomy. This autonomy dimension builds upon the child's new motor and mental abilities. At this stage the child can not only walk but also climb, open and close, drop, push and pull, hold and let go. The child takes pride in these new accomplishments and wants to do everything himself, whether it be pulling the wrapper off a piece of candy, selecting the vitamin out of the bottle or flushing the toilet. If parents recognize the young child's need to do what he is capable of doing at his own pace and in his own time, then he develops a sense that he is able to control his muscles, his impulses, himself and, not insignificantly, his environment—the sense of autonomy.

When, however, his caretakers are impatient and do for him what he is capable of doing himself, they reinforce a sense of shame and doubt. To be sure, every parent has rushed a child at times and children are hardy enough to endure such lapses. It is only when caretaking is consistently overprotective and criticism of "accidents" (whether these be wetting, soiling, spilling or breaking things) is harsh and unthinking that the child develops an excessive sense of shame with respect to other people and an excessive sense of doubt about own abilities to control his world and himself.

If the child leaves this stage with less autonomy than shame or doubt, he will be handicapped in his attempts to achieve autonomy in adolescence and adulthood. Contrariwise, the child who moves through this stage with his sense of autonomy buoyantly outbalancing his feelings of shame and doubt is well prepared to be autonomous at later phases in the life cycle. Again, however, the balance of autonomy to shame and doubt set up during this period can be changed in either positive or negative directions by later events.

It might be well to note, in addition, that too much autonomy can be as harmful as too little. I have in mind a patient of 7 who had a heart condition. He had learned very quickly how terrified his parents were of any signs in him of cardiac difficulty. With the psychological acuity given to children, he soon ruled the household. The family could not go shopping, or for a drive, or on a holiday if he did not approve. On those rare occasions when the parents had had enough and defied him, he would get angry and his purple hue and gagging would frighten them into submission.

Actually, this boy was frightened of this power (as all children would be) and was really eager to give it up. When the parents and the boy came to realize this, and to recognize that a little shame and doubt were a healthy counterpoise to an inflated sense of autonomy, the three of them could once again assume their normal roles.

Initiative vs. Guilt

In this stage (the genital stage of classical psychoanalysis) the child, age 4 to 5, is pretty much master of his body and can ride a tricycle, run, cut and hit. He can thus initiate motor activities of various sorts on his own and no longer merely responds to or imitates the actions of other children. The same holds true for his language and fantasy activities. Accordingly, Erikson argues that the social dimension that appears at this stage has initiative at one of its poles and guilt at the other.

Whether the child will leave this stage with his sense of initiative far outbalancing his sense of guilt depends to a considerable extent upon how parents respond to his self-initiated activities. Children who are given much freedom and opportunity to initiate motor play such as running, bike riding, sliding, skating, tussling and wrestling have their sense of initiative reinforced. Initiative is also reinforced when parents answer their children's questions (intellectual initiative) and do not deride or inhibit fantasy or play activity. On the other hand, if the child is made to feel that his motor activity is bad, that his questions are a nuisance and that his play is silly and stupid, then he may develop a sense of guilt over self-initiated activities in general that will persist through later life stages.

Industry vs. Inferiority

Stage Four is the age period from 6 to 11, the elementary school years (described by classical psychoanalysis as the latency phase). It is a time during which the child's love for the parent of the opposite sex and rivalry with the same sexed parent (elements in the so-called family romance) are quiescent. It is also a period during which the child becomes capable of deductive reasoning, and of playing and learning by rules. It is not until this period, for example, that children can really play marbles, checkers and other "take turn" games that require obedience to rules. Erikson argues that the psychosocial dimension that emerges during this period has a sense of industry at one extreme and a sense of inferiority at the other.

The term industry nicely captures a dominant theme of this period during which the concern with how things are made, how they work and what they do predominates. It is the Robinson Crusoe age in the sense that the enthusiasm and minute detail with which Crusoe describes his activities appeals to the child's own budding sense of industry. When children are encouraged in their efforts to make, do, or build practical things (whether it be to construct creepy crawlers, tree houses, or airplane models—or to cook, bake or sew), are allowed to finish their products, and are praised and rewarded for the results, then the sense of industry is enhanced. But parents who see their children's efforts at making and doing as "mischief," and as simply "making a mess," help to encourage in children a sense of inferiority.

During these elementary-school years, however, the child's world includes more than the home. Now social institutions other than the family come to play a central role in the developmental crisis of the individual, (there Erikson introduced still another advance in psychoanalytic theory, which heretofore concerned itself only with the effects of the parents behavior upon the child's development).

A child's school experiences affect his industry-inferiority balance. The child, for example, with an I.Q. of 80 to 90 has a particularly traumatic school experience, even when his sense of industry is rewarded and encouraged at home he is "too bright" to be in special classes, but "too slow" to compete with children of average ability. Consequently he experiences constant failures in his academic efforts that reinforces a sense of inferiority.

On the other hand, the child who had his sense of industry derogated at home can have it revitalized at school through the offices of a sensitive and committed teacher. Whether the child develops a sense of industry or inferiority, therefore, no longer depends solely on the caretaking efforts of the parents but on the actions and offices of other adults as well.

Identity vs. Role Confusion

When the child moves into adolescence (Stage Five—roughly the ages 12-18), he encounters, according to traditional psychoanalytic theory, a reawakening of the family-romance problem of early childhood. His means of resolving the problem is to seek and find a romantic partner of his own generation. While Erikson does not deny this aspect of adolescence, he points out that there are other problems as well. The adolescent matures mentally as well as physiologically and, in addition to the new feelings, sensations and desires he experiences as a result of changes in his body, he develops a multitude of new ways of joking at and thinking about the world. Among other things, those in adolescence can now think about other people's thinking and wonder about what other people think of them. They can also conceive of ideal families, religions and societies which they then compare with the imperfect families, religions and societies of their own experience. Finally, adolescents become capable of constructing theories and philosophies designed to bring all the varied and conflicting aspects of society into a working, harmonious and peaceful whole. The adolescent, in a word, is an impatient idealist who believes that it is as easy to realize an ideal as it is to imagine it.

Erikson believes that the new interpersonal dimension which emerges during this period has to do with a sense of ego identity at the positive end and a sense of role confusion at the negative end. That is to say, given the adolescent's new-found integrative abilities, his task is to bring together all of the things he has learned about himself as a son, student, athlete, friend, Scout, newspaper boy, and so on, and integrate these different images of himself into a whole that makes sense and that shows continuity with the past while preparing for the future. To the extent that the young person succeeds in this endeavor, he arrives at a sense of psychosocial identity, a sense of who he is, where he has been and where he is going.

In contrast to the earlier stages, where parents play a more or less direct role in the determination of the result of the developmental crises, the influence of parents during this stage is much more indirect. If the young person reaches adolescence with, thanks to his parents, a vital sense of trust, autonomy, initiative and industry, then his chances of arriving at a meaningful sense of ego identity are much enhanced. The reverse, of course, holds true for the young person who enters adolesecnce with considerable mistrust, shame, doubt, guilt or inferiority. Preparation for a successful adolescence and the attainment of an integrated psychosocial identity must, therefore, begin in the cradle.

Over and above what the individual brings with him from his childhood, the attainment of a sense of personal identity depends upon the social milieu in which he or she grows up. For example, in a society where women are to some extent second-class citizens, it may be harder for females to arrive at a sense of psychosocial identity. Likewise at times, such as the present, when rapid social and technological change breaks down many traditional values, it may be more difficult for young people to find continuity between what they learned and experienced as children and what they learn and experience as adolescents. At such times young people often seek causes that give their lives meaning and direction. The activism of the current generation of young people may well stem, in part at least, from this search.

When the young person cannot attain a sense of personal identity, either because of an unfortunate childhood or difficult social circumstances, he shows a certain amount of role confusion—a sense of not knowing what he is, where he belongs or whom he belongs to. Such confusion is a frequent symptom in delinquent young people. Promiscuous adolescent girls, for example, often seem to have a fragmented sense of ego identity. Some young people seek a negative identity, an identity opposite to the one prescribed for them by their family and friends. Having an identity as a delinquent, or as a hippie, or even as an "acid head," may sometimes be preferable to having no identity at all.

In some cases young people do not seek a negative identity so much as they have it thrust upon them. I remember another court case in which the defendant was an attractive 16-year-old girl who had been found "tricking it" in a trailer located just outside the grounds of an Air Force base. From about the age of 12, her mother had encouraged her to dress seductively and to go out with boys. When she returned from dates, her sexually frustrated mother demanded a kiss-by-kiss, caress-by-caress description of the evening's activities. After the mother had vicariously satisfied her sexual needs, she proceeded to call her daughter a whore and a dirty tramp. As the girl told me, "Hell, I have the name, so I might as well play the role."

Failure to establish a clear sense of personal identity at adolescence does not guarantee perpetual failure. And the person who attains a working sense of ego identity in adolescence will of necessity encounter challenges and threats to that identity as he moves through life. Erikson, perhaps more than any other personality theorist, has emphasized that life is constant change and that confronting problems at one stage in life is not guarantee against the reappearance of these problems at later stages, or against the finding of new solutions to them.

Intimacy vs. Isolation

Stage six in the life cycle is young adulthood; roughly the period of courtship and early family life that extends from late adolescence till early middle age. For this stage, and the stages described hereafter, classical psychoanalysis has nothing new or major to say. For Erikson, however, the previous attainment of a sense of personal identity and the engagement in productive work that marks this period gives rise to a new interpersonal dimension of intimacy at the one extreme and isolation at the other.

When Erikson speaks of intimacy he means much more than love-making alone; he means the ability to share with and care about another person without fear of losing oneself in the process. In the case of intimacy, as in the case of identity, success or failure no longer depends directly upon the parents but only indirectly as they have contributed to the individual's success or failure at the earlier stages. Here, too, as in the case of identity, social conditions may help or hinder the establishment of a sense of intimacy. Likewise, intimacy need not involve sexuality; it includes the relationship between friends. Soldiers who have served together under the most dangerous circumstances often develop a sense of commitment to one another that exemplifies intimacy in its broadest sense. If a sense of intimacy is not established with friends or a marriage partner, the result, in Erikson's view, is a sense of isolation—of being alone without anyone to share with or care for.

Generativity vs. Self-Absorption

This stage—middle age—brings with it what Erikson speaks of as either *generativity or self-absorption*, and stagnation. What Erikson means by generativity is that the person begins to be concerned with others beyond his immediate family, with future generations and the nature of the society and world in which those generations will live. Generativity does not reside only in parents; it can be found in any individual who actively concerns himself with the welfare of young people and with making the world a better place for them to live and to work.

Those who fail to establish a sense of generativity fall into a state of self-absorption in which their personal needs and comforts are of predominant concern. A fictional case of self-absorption is Dickens's Scrooge in "A Christmas Carol." In his one-sided concern with money and in his disregard for the interests and welfare of his young employee Bob Cratchit, Scrooge exemplifies the self-absorbed, embittered (the two often go together) old man. Dickens also illustrated, however, what Erikson points out: namely, that unhappy solutions to life's crises are not irreversible. Scrooge, at the end of tale, manifested both a sense of generativity and of intimacy which he had not experienced before.

Integrity vs. Despair

Stage eight in the Eriksonian scheme corresponds roughly to the period when the individual's major efforts are nearing completion and when there is time for reflection—and for the enjoyment of grandchildren, if any. The psychosocial dimension that comes into prominence now has integrity on one hand and despair on the other.

The sense of integrity arises from the individual's ability to look back on his life with satisfaction. At the other extreme is the individual who looks back upon his life as a series of missed opportunities and missed directions; now in the twilight years he realizes that it is too late to start again. For such a person the inevitable result is a sense of despair at what might have been.

These, then, are the major stages in the life cycle as described by Erikson. Their presentation, for one thing, frees the clinician to treat adult emotional problems as failures (in part at least) to solve genuinely adult personality crises and not, as heretofore, as mere residuals of infantile frustrations and conflicts. This view of personality growth, moreover takes some of the onus off parents and takes account of the role which society and the person himself play in the formation of an individual personality. Finally, Erikson has offered hope for us all by demonstrating that each phase of growth has its strengths as well as its weaknesses and that failures at one stage of development can be rectified by successes at later stages.

The reason that these ideas, which sound so agreeable to "common sense," are in fact so revolutionary has a lot to do with the state of psychoanalysis in America. As formulated by Freud, psychoanalysis encompassed a theory of personality development, a method of studying the human mind and, finally, procedures for treating troubled and unhappy people. Freud viewed this system as a scientific one, open to revision as new facts and observations accumulated.

The system was, however, so vehemently attacked that Freud's followers were constantly in the position of having to defend Freud's views. Perhaps because of this situation, Freud's system became, in the hands of some of his followers and defenders, a dogma upon which all theoretical innovation, clinical observation and therapeutic practice had to be grounded. That this attitude persists is evidenced in the recent remark by a psychoanalyst that he believed psychotic patients could not be treated by psychoanalysis because "Freud said so". Such attitudes, in which Freud's authority rather than observation and data is the basis of deciding what is true and what is false, has contributed to the disrepute in which psychoanalysis is widely held today.

Erik Erikson has broken out of this scholasticism and has had the courage to say that Freud's discoveries and practices were the start and not the end of the study and treatment of the human personality. In addition to advocating the modifications of psychoanalytic theory outlined above, Erikson has also suggested modifications in therapeutic practice, particularly in the treatment of young patients. "Young people in severe trouble are not fit for the couch," he writes. "They want to face you, and they want you to face them, not as a facsimile of a parent, or wearing the mask of a professional helper, but as a kind of over-all individual a young person can live with or despair of."

Erikson has had the boldness to remark on some of the negative effects that distorted notions of psychoanalysis have had on society at large. Psychoanalysis, he says, has contributed to a widespread fatalism—"even as we were trying to devise, with scientific determinism, a therapy for the few, we were led to promote an ethical disease among the many". . . .

There is now more and more teaching of Erikson's concepts in psychiatry, psychology, education, and social work in America and in other parts of the world. His description of the stages of the life cycle are summarized in major textbooks in all of these fields and clinicians are increasingly looking at their cases in Eriksonian terms.

Research investigators have, however, found Erikson's formulations somewhat difficult to test. This is not surprising, inasmuch as Erikson's conceptions, like Freud's, take into account the infinite complexity of the human personality. Current research methodologies are, by and large still not able to deal with these complexities at their own level, and distortions are inevitable when such concepts as "identity" come to be defined in terms of responses to a questionnaire.

Likewise, although Erikson's life-stages have an intuitive "rightness" about them, not everyone agrees with his formulations. Douvan and Adelson in their book, "The Adolescent Experience," argue that while his identity theory may hold true for boys, it doesn't for girls. This argument is based on findings which suggest that girls postpone identity consolidation until after marriage (and intimacy) have been established. Such postponement occurs, says Douvan and Adelson, because a woman's identity is partially defined by the identity of the man whom she marries. This view does not really contradict Erikson's, since he recognizes that later events, such as marriage, can help to resolve both current and past developmental crises. For the woman, but not for the man, the problems of identity and intimacy may be solved concurrently,

Objections to Erikson's formulations have come from other directions as well. Robert W. White, Erikson's good friend and colleague at Harvard, has a long standing (and warm-hearted) debate with Erikson over his life-stages. White believes that his own theory of "competence motivation," a theory which has received wide recognition, can account for the phenomenon of ego development much more economically than can Erikson's stages. Erikson has, however, little interest in debating the validity of the stages he has described. As an artist he recognizes that there are many different ways to view one and the same phenomenon and that a perspective that is congenial to one person will be repugnant to another. He offers his stage-wise description of the life cycle for those who find such perspectives congenial and not as a world view that everyone should adopt.

It is this lack of dogmatism and sensitivity to the diversity and complexity of the human personality which help to account for the growing recognition of Erikson's contribution within as well as without the helping professions. Indeed, his psycho-historical investigations have originated a whole new field of study which has caught the interest of historians and political scientists alike. (It has also intrigued his wife, Joan, who has published pieces on Eleanor Roosevelt and who has a book on Saint Francis in press.) A recent issue of *Daedalus*, the journal for the American Academy of Arts and Sciences, was entirely devoted to psycho-historical and psycho-political investigations of creative leaders by authors from diverse disciplines who have been stimulated by Erikson's work. . . .

Although Erikson, during his decade of college teaching, has not seen any patients or taught at psychoanalytic institutes, he maintains his dedication to psychoanalysis and views his psycho-historical investigations as an applied branch of that discipline. While some older analysts continue to ignore Erikson's work, there is increasing evidence (including a recent poll of psychiatrists and psychoanalysts) that he is having a rejuvenating influence upon a discipline which many regard as dead or dying. Young analysts are today proclaiming a new "freedom" to see Freud in historical perspective—which reflects the Eriksonian view that one can recognize Freud's greatness without bowing to conceptual precedent.

Accordingly, the reports of the demise of psychoanalysis may have been somewhat premature. In the work of Erik Erikson, at any rate, psychoanalysis lives and continues to beget life.

Pavlov investigates classical conditioning with his dog, "Brains," circa 1927. (Corbis-Bettmann.)

Chapter 8

THE LEARNING PERSPECTIVE

A movement to make psychology more scientifically rigorous began during the early part of the twentieth century. Critics of psychology argued that it did not warrant status as a science, in comparison to hard sciences like physics, biology and chemistry. Structuralism, an early school of psychology, attempted to understand consciousness by breaking it down into its constituent parts for analysis. Consciousness could not be directly observed and structuralism was therefore deemed unscientific by its critics. Psychoanalysis was also criticized as unscientific. If the validity of the conscious mind was questioned, the psychoanalytic construct of the unconscious mind was even more suspect.

American John B. Watson became the leader of the behavioristic movement. The prime objective of behaviorism was to place psychology on equal footing with other sciences. In his classic 1913 paper, *Psychology as the Behaviorist Views It*, Watson boldly proclaimed, "Psychology . . . is a purely objective experimental branch of natural science. Its theoretical goal is the prediction and control of behavior. The behaviorist . . . recognizes no dividing line between man and brute" (Watson, 1913).

The object of study in behaviorism is overt, observable behavior. Science conducts research under laboratory conditions and its findings apply beyond the laboratory setting. Ivan Pavlov, a contemporary of Watson's, was a Russian physiologist who conducted early research on classical conditioning with dogs under laboratory conditions. Pavlov was a rigorous scientist. During the Russian Revolution, he disciplined an assistant who arrived late because he had to dodge bullets, and would fire assistants who questioned "why" rather than "what" happened (Fancher, 1990). Psychology was now being studied using the same laboratory methods as the other sciences. The findings of science can be applied outside the laboratory setting. Watson was dismayed that if you, "Ask any physician or jurist [of 1913] whether scientific psychology plays a practical part in his daily routine and you will hear him deny that the psychology of the laboratories finds a place in his scheme of work" (Watson, 1913, p. 168). Thus, Watson attempted to apply the findings of psychology beyond the laboratory setting. Today, application of psychology beyond the laboratory is much more conspicuous.

Watsonian behaviorism relied heavily on the notion that organisms reliably and predictably make specific responses to specific stimuli. Thus, if control over man's environment (the stimulus) could be accomplished, so could prediction and control of his behavior (the response). Watson was so convinced of the importance of environmental factors on behavior that he stated:

> Give me a dozen healthy infants, well-formed and my own specified world to bring them up in and I'll guarantee to take any one at random and train him to become any type of specialist I might select—doctor, lawyer, artist, merchant-chief, and yes, even beggar-man and thief, regardless of his talents, penchants, tendencies, abilities, vocations, and race of his ancestors. (Watson, 1929/1919.)

In essence, Watson perceived the infant as highly malleable and sensitive to environmental influences; a lump of clay to be molded by the environment. This notion was not new. British empiricist John Locke had stated more than two hundred years earlier that the mind at birth was a *tabula rasa*, a blank slate upon which experience writes. Watson's boast, although never realized, was indicative of his degree of conviction, and rallied support for behaviorism.

Watson's personal involvement in behaviorism ended prematurely during the early 1920s, for reasons that will be discussed later in the chapter. Pavlov's research on conditioning, emphasizing abnormal behavior, continued until his death in 1936.

Burrhus Frederic Skinner emerged to fill the void left by the departure of Watson in American behaviorism. His impact began with the publication of *The Behavior of Organisms* in 1938. What Watson lacked in discretion, Skinner possessed in persuasion and tact. In reconciliation of Watson's "dozen healthy infants" claim, Skinner commented:

> Watson was not denying that a substantial part of behavior is inherited. . . . Yet he is probably responsible for the persistent myth of what has been called "behaviorism's counterfactual dogma." And it is a myth. No reputable student of animal behavior has ever taken the position "that the animal comes into the laboratory as a virtual tabula rasa, that species differences are insignificant, and that all responses are about equally conditionable to all stimuli (Skinner, 1966\1969).

Skinner's acknowledgement of the differences in operant capabilities among species, and systematic cultivation of them, endeared potential critics, rather than alienate them. This enabled him to ultimately develop a powerful behavioral technology, and make a contribution to the field of psychology comparable to that of Freud.

The theoretical bases of the illness and psychoanalytic perspectives are distinctly different from that of the learning perspective. The illness perspective is primarily concerned with treating behavioral pathology that results from general medical conditions. The learning perspective identifies improper environments that lead to faulty learning as the culprit. Whereas Freud believed that adult pathology could be linked to childhood conflicts of a sexual nature, the behaviorists believe that adult disturbances could be traced to maladaptive patterns of behavior learned earlier in life.

The behaviorist views abnormal behavior as learned in much the same manner as normal behavior. The behavioral symptoms of the disorder are the disorder, and are not reflective of any deeper, unresolved conflict. Amelioration of the symptoms is the therapeutic objective. Since abnormal behavior is learned, it can also be unlearned. Through environmental manipulation, the organism can learn normal, adaptive behaviors as substitutes for abnormal, maladaptive behaviors.

The traditional learning perspective postulates that human learning is accomplished primarily through two learning models. These models, classical and operant conditioning, will be described later in the chapter. They are stimulus-response models. They are only concerned with the specific relationship between responses and the stimuli that provoke them.

The systematic application of learning models for therapeutic benefit is called behavior modification. To be effective, behavior modification requires the ability to control the environment of the individual so that the conditions of reinforcement can be restructured in a way that is conducive to the learning of adaptive behavior, or to the unlearning of maladaptive behavior. Although behavior therapy is very effective, it does require control and manipulation of the environment of the subject. Proponents of the perspective argue that benefits gained through behavior therapy outweigh any loss of autonomy of those treated.

The Gestalt school was discussed in Chapter 6, The Holistic Perspective. In 1925, its founder, Wolfgang Köhler, published *The Mentality of Apes*. It described eight years of work at his ape station on Tenerife, one of the Canary Islands located off the western coast of Africa. Köhler presented apes with problems to solve. For example, he suspended a bunch of bananas from the ceiling of a room. Among objects in the room were three wooden boxes, which if stacked, would enable Grande to reach them. Stimulus-response theorists would argue that the ape randomly attempted solutions until stumbling upon the correct one. Instead, Köhler argued, Grande attempted no unsuccessful solutions. After contemplating elements of the problem, the solution emerged in a sudden flash of insight. Thus, a thought process occurred between the stimulus and response. Köhler emigrated to the United States and became president of the American Psychological Association. In his presidential address of 1959 he argued for the coalescence of the behavioral and Gestalt schools. Cognitive psychology, which emphasizes the role of thought in mediating behavior, emerged. Presently, cognitive-behavioral therapy has become a very popular and successful method of treatment.

This chapter begins with *Behavior Modification With Children*. It was written by Dr. D.G. Brown, and it is a primer on behavior therapy. Next will appear, *Conditioned Emotional Reactions* by John B. Watson and Rosalie Rayner. Third will be *The Operant Side of Behavior Therapy* by B.F. Skinner. Fourth, *Behavioral Treatment and Normal Educational and Intellectual Functioning in Young Autistic Children* by O. Ivar Lovaas, describes some astounding behavior therapy research. Finally, *Fall Into Helplessness*, by Martin E.P. Seligman, offers a cognitive-behavioral explanation for depression.

References

Fancher, R.E. (1990). *Pioneers of Psychology*. New York: W.W. Norton.

Schwartz, S. (1986). *Classic Studies in Psychology*. Mountainview, California: Mayfield Publishing Company.

Skinner, B.F. (1969). The Phylogeny and Ontongeny of Behavior. In B. F. Skinner, *Contingencies of Reinforcement: A Theoretical Analysis* (pp. 172-217). New York: Appleton-Century-Crofts. (Original work published in *Science*, 1966).

Watson, J.B. (1929/1919). *Psychology from the Standpoint of a Behaviorist*. Philadelphia: Lippincott.

Watson, J.B. (1913). Psychology as the Behaviorist Views It. *Psychological Review*, Volume 20, (2).

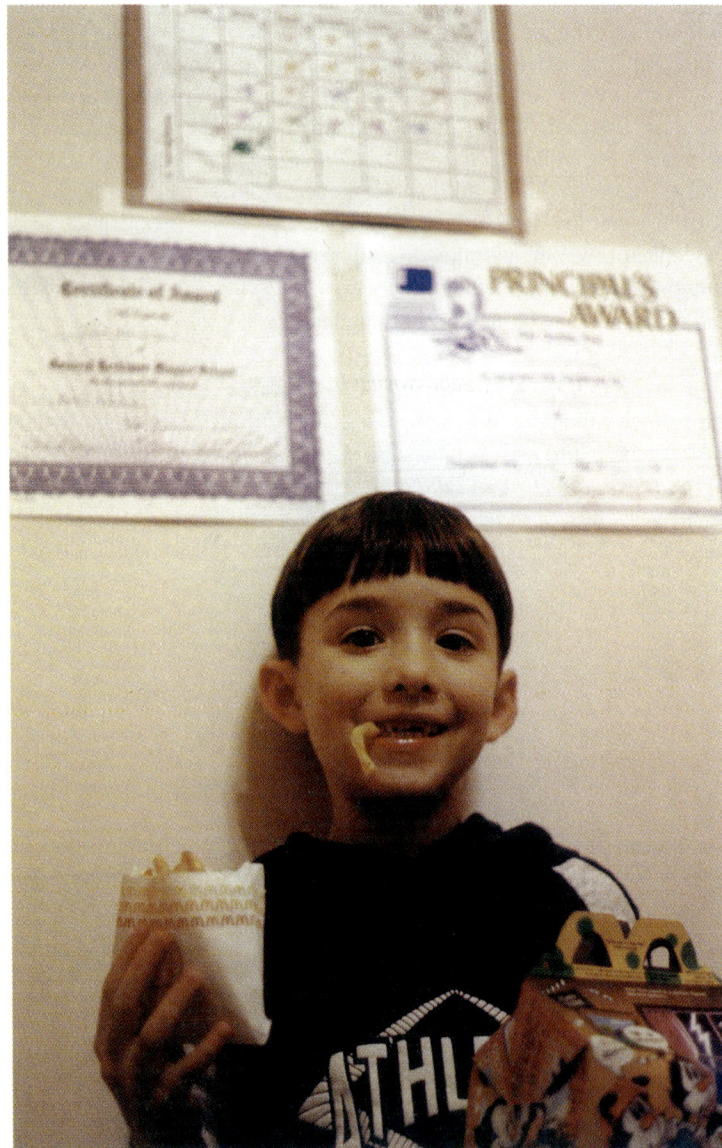

Figure 8-1. "Happy Meal." Potent primary reinforcers strengthen adaptive operants. (Photograph by Jim Rooney.)

READING 8A

BEHAVIOR MODIFICATION WITH CHILDREN

Daniel G. Brown

In the following article, Dr. D.G. Brown provides an excellent overview of the theory, goals, and orientation of behavior therapy. It is presented first to provide basic concepts and terminology to prepare you for the rest of the chapter. In addition to providing behaviorism's explanation of the origin of abnormal behavior, classical and operant conditioning, the basic learning models upon which behavior therapy is based, are described. The value of behavioristic approaches in the treatment of a wide range of behavioral problems is indicated. Dr. Brown also discusses criticisms that are commonly made of the behavioral model. As you read the article, think of how the goals, orientation, and techniques of behavioral psychology are different from those of psychoanalysis.

Although written in 1972, many of the issues presented regarding behavior therapy remain relevant. An additional two decades of research verify the claims made about behavior therapy in the article.

There are indications that the establishment of behavioral analysis and the behavior modification approach may, in time, be considered comparable to such milestones in mental health as the reforms in the treatment of the mentally ill by Pinel in France in the last century; the establishment of psychoanalysis and psychodynamic therapy during the first half of the present century; the psychopharmacological advances of the past twenty years; and the current comprehensive community mental health center movement. And as each of these developments has affected the entire field, it may be predicted that developments in behavior modification will also have significant effects in treatment, training, research and prevention in mental health.

What exactly is meant by such terms as behavior therapy, operant and classical conditioning therapy, reinforcement therapy? Basically, the terms involve the *systematic* application of learning theory and principles of conditioning to the modification of deviant or disordered behavior

and the strengthening of desired behavior toward the goal of establishing more adaptive behavior in human beings. It has been long recognized that the *present environment* of an individual exerts a strong influence on the response or behavior of that individual. For example, a child may acquire a fear of a small, playful rabbit if the rabbit is presented with a sudden and painfully loud noise—the noise being an unconditioned stimulus. This example illustrates the phenomenon of *classical* or *Pavlovian* or *respondent conditioning* and is the basis for many fears, anxieties and phobias as well as other emotional and motivational states in adults as well as in children. The child, however, may gradually lose his fear if the rabbit is presented slowly at a distance and paired with such pleasant activities as eating, playing, etc. Reconditioning is the basis for some of the major therapeutic procedures used in behavior therapy.

Another kind of learning situation is involved when a person acts or responds in some way and a particular *consequence* follows his

Daniel G. Brown, "Behavior Modification With Children," *Mental Hygiene*, 1972. Reprinted with permission of the National Mental Health Association.

action or response. If the consequence that follows results in an increase in the probability of the same action or response occurring again, the consequence is referred to as a *reinforcement.* For example, a child cries for a lollipop, is given one by the parent and then stops crying; the crying is an *operant* behavior, i.e., operates on the environment (parent) in such a way to secure a particular outcome or result, namely a lollipop, and it is this reinforcement that makes more likely the occurrence of similar behavior in the future. This example illustrates the phenomenon of *operant or instrumental conditioning,* which is the basis for much human behavior in children and adults, both adaptive and maladaptive. Thus, the deviant behavior of many emotionally disturbed children may be understood as having been learned and supported by contingencies in the present environment, whether in the home, school, hospital, clinic, camp, or wherever. In this connection, a major therapeutic procedure in behavior modification involves changing the environmental conditions or removing the reinforcements that have maintained a child's maladaptive behavior. The conceptualization of behavior in terms of reinforcement learning theory places adaptive and maladaptive behavior on a single continuum, i.e., both kinds of behavior are learned or unlearned on the basis of the same learning process.

Conditioning

The fundamental nature of classical and operant conditioning has been recognized for over half a century, but only with the last several years have systematic applications been made in the modification of various deviant and disordered behaviors in humans. Why has it taken so many years to utilize in practice what has been known for so long a time? Part of the answer would seem to be in the priorities or emphases of traditional approaches to the mentally and emotionally disturbed. In the past, many mental health professionals were primarily concerned with extensive psychodiagnostic appraisals, with protracted psychiatric interviews, with overly detailed case histories, and with focusing on intrapsychic dynamics and conflicts, with undue emphasis on insight as a presumed requirement

for meaningful behavioral change, and with an overevaluation of the alleged superiority of long-term, dynamically-oriented, reconstructive therapies. In any event it is a sobering experience to reflect on the fact that now, after a half-century, the systematic, applied use of principles of learning and conditioning in psychotherapeutic work both with children and adults is only now getting underway in substantial numbers of mental health centers, institutions, etc.

Concomitant with demonstrations of the general applicability and efficacy of approaches in behavior modification, it might be predicted that increasing numbers of mental health professionals will begin to focus more on the *present* environment and symptoms of a person than on the past history or the original factors that may have been responsible for the symptoms. In this connection, the following four questions provide a functional frame of reference in mental health work with children based on behavior modification:

1. What is the behavior of the child that should be changed or developed? i.e., specify the behavior. Is it mute, autistic behavior? Acting-out destructive behavior? Fearful, immobilized or phobic behavior? Learning to talk or read? What exactly is the behavior to be developed or modified?
2. What is the rate or frequency of this behavior? When and how often does it occur?
3. What are the current environmental contingencies or conditions that support the child's behavior that is to be modified?
4. How can the child's present environment be changed, contingencies altered, and reinforcements utilized to decrease his maladaptive and increase his adaptive behavior?

Behavioral analysis and modification, then, involves the following systematic procedures: 1) specify or pinpoint the behavior to be modified; 2) record the behavior and establish a baseline of its frequency; 3) determine the contingencies that affect or maintain the behavior; and 4) modify the relevant contingencies to increase adaptive and decrease maladaptive behavior.

There are two major directions or outcomes in work involving operant behavior modification:

1. *Developing, strengthening, accelerating or maintaining desirable behaviors.* For example, a child learns to talk, brush his teeth, dress himself, follow directions, mind his parents better, work or play more cooperatively with others, do more things for himself, increase his vocabulary, become a better swimmer, etc. These are behaviors that may be developed or accelerated through the use of appropriate contingencies involving positive reinforcements.

2. *Weakening, decelerating or eliminating undesirable behaviors.* For example, a child learns not to throw tantrums, not to hit his sister, not to suck his thumb, not to bang his head, not to steal from others, not to be late to school, not to disrupt the classroom, etc. These are behaviors that may be decelerated or eliminated through the use of appropriate contingencies involving: 1) *positive reinforcement* for the *non-occurrence* of the undesirable behavior; 2) *negative* or aversive *reinforcement* (e.g., punishment, time-out procedures, etc.) for the *occurrence* of the undesirable behavior; or 3) *no reinforcement of any kind,* positive or negative, for the *occurrence* of the undesirable behavior, e.g., completely ignoring such behavior.

Summed up: behavior is developed, strengthened, weakened, or eliminated by the consequences or effects of the behavior, i.e., behavior is determined by the consequences that follow that behavior, hence, the acceleration or deceleration of a given behavior is based on altering its consequences.

Review of Literature

Now, in order to gain a better understanding of what has been reported in the literature relative to the application of behavior modification as a therapeutic procedure, a content analysis was made of all of the articles that have been published in the two principal journals devoted to work in behavior modification. These are: *Behavior Research and Therapy,* published since 1963, and *The Journal of Applied Behavior Analysis,* published since 1968. As of June 1969, approximately 300 articles had been published in

these journals which may be grouped in terms of application to children, adolescents and adults. Among children and adolescents, applications of behavior modification therapy have been made to the following problems, symptoms, deficits, disturbances or developments:

1) autism, psychosis, and schizophrenia; 2) enuresis, encopresis, and related disturbances; 3) tantrums, destructive, antisocial, predelinquent behaviors; 4) school problems, learning deficits and disabilities, failures, disruptive and other maladjustive behaviors in a school setting; 5) phobias, anxieties and fears; 6) psychosomatic disturbances, e.g., anorexia, obesity, etc.; 7) speech development and disturbances; 8) sexual disturbances; 9) nervous habits, e.g., nail biting, thumb sucking, nightmares, etc.; 10) mental retardation and other handicapped conditions; 11) self-injurious behaviors; 12) development of social skills, cooperative play, and other socially adaptive behaviors, etc.

While not all of the children and adolescents reported on in these studies responded to behavior modification therapy with 100% improvement, in the majority of instances, substantial gains were made and, in many cases, marked improvement was realized. This was true in a number of cases in which other therapeutic approaches had been used but without success. As the above examples indicate, applications of behavior modification have not been confined to a restricted portion of the population but cover a very wide range of disturbances, deficits and developmental problems in children and youth. An indication of the increasing amount of work and research using a behavioral approach is seen in the fact that four new journals concerned primarily with behavior modification or behavior therapy began publication in 1969-1970.

What are some implications of the behavior modification model for the mental health field as a whole? It is evident that this model represents a departure from the traditional conception of mental illness as a manifestation of disease within a child or adult, hence, as consisting of symptoms of underlying psychopathology. In contrast, the assumption is made in the behavioral model that much that is labeled mental illness consists of nothing more than learned ways of adjusting to the environment. There is, thus, considerable controversy among differing theorists and therapists as to the adequacy or inadequacy of the disease model versus the learning-disorder model of mental illness. And there are significant implications in terms of assumptions and approaches for modifying disturbed behavior. The traditional or psychodynamic therapist essentially views the symptoms of an emotional disturbance as "surface phenomena," as indicative of unconscious processes and unresolved conflicts, and the main task of dynamic psychotherapy, therefore, is to deal with these underlying pathological conditions rather than with the overt symptoms and behaviors themselves. The focus is on the reconstruction and analysis of an individual's *past* history, on the antecedents of his present behavior, on covert behavior, internal states, or subjective processes. On the other hand, the behavior therapist holds that most emotional disorders and neuroses are essentially learned behavior patterns and that there is no underlying illness, but rather the symptoms themselves constitute the disorder. Here the focus is on the construction and analysis of the individual's *existing* life situation, on the *consequences* of his present behavior, on what can be objectively observed and recorded. These two conceptualizations of emotional disorders quite clearly involve a fundamental difference with significant implications in terms of assumptions and approaches for modifying disturbed behavior.

Although the behavioral analysis approach in psychotherapeutic work is a very recent development, about 95% of the literature having been published in the last six or seven years, there are indications that compared to other approaches, it has several important advantages that may be summarized as follows: 1) greater *effectiveness* as a treatment method, i.e., for some of the deviant behaviors previously listed in this paper, the results are often clearly superior; 2) greater *efficiency* as a treatment method, i.e., in general, it may take less time and fewer sessions to bring about desired changes in the patient's life adjustment; 3) greater *specificity* in establishing goals and outcome of therapy, i.e., the specific end result of therapy is specified at the beginning of

therapeutic work; 4) greater *applicability* to a wider segment of the population, i.e., the behavioral approach seems to cover the broad spectrum of maladaptive behaviors and is applicable to all social classes, age groups, intellectual and educational levels, etc., rather than, for example, being limited more or less to adult, middle class neurotic patients with above average intelligence, etc.; and 5) greater *utilization* as a treatment method by various groups, i.e., the behavioral approach can be used not only by the core mental health disciplines themselves but by public health nurses, case workers, teachers, etc., and even by parents. In short, there is reason to believe that, compared to traditional therapies, the behavior modification approach may be more effective, more efficient, more specific in therapeutic outcomes, applicable to more people, and may be used by all of the mental health-helping professions and related groups.

Manpower Problems

As suggested above, developments in the use of behavioral procedures have important implications for increasing mental health manpower resources in relation to the mental health needs of children and youth. There are approximately 70 million children and youth under 18 years of age in this country and of this number, between 10% and 22%, depending on the criteria of psychological-psychiatric handicapped conditions, have emotional and behavioral difficulties that require assistance. This involves 7 to 15 million children and youth. To what extent are the manpower resources of the mental health disciplines capable of meeting directly the needs of these millions of children and youth? The answer is: very little. Thus, for each psychiatrist, social worker, nurse and psychologist in mental health programs for children, there are thousands of children with emotional and behavioral difficulties. To be more specific, what about the manpower capability of child psychiatry to cope with the problem? Since there are only about *1,000* child psychiatrists in the United States, this means that for each one, there are between 7 and 15 thousand children and youth who need mental health assistance. These data make dramatically clear a simple fact: that mental health professionals have not, are not, and cannot meet *directly* the needs of overwhelming numbers of children with emotional and behavioral difficulties in this country. When help for mental health problems is sought or needed, for most children, unfortunately, it has not been and is not available. A significant part of the solution to this problem seems obvious: that community care-giving and mental health-related groups such as public health and other nurses, non-psychiatric physicians and social workers, welfare workers, counselors, rehabilitation personnel, clergymen, etc., can and must provide more of the services traditionally considered more or less the exclusive responsibility of the mental health disciplines, i.e., psychiatry, psychology, psychiatric nursing and psychiatric social work. In particular, parents and teachers should be increasingly utilized as mental health resources. Their number, accessibility and availability in relation to the population of children and youth make parents and teachers vital resources both for treatment and prevention in mental health. Thus, while there are thousands of children for every mental health professional who works with children, there are only about 25 children for every school teacher and about 10 or 15 children for every special education teacher and usually one or two parents for each child. Teachers and parents, then, should receive much more attention than they have from the standpoint of the potential contributions they are capable of making in mental health. Mental health professionals can and must provide more training and consultation for these groups who are the ones actually in contact with the vast majority of children in need of help. A number of references are now available that are specifically concerned with helping parents and teachers manage many kinds of behavior problems in their children and pupils. Fortunately, given proper training, instruction and backup help, these groups can learn to carry out behavior modification procedures. This does not mean that teachers, already overburdened with instructional and other demands, would be expected to become psychotherapists for their disturbed or disturbing pupils. But it does mean that many teachers would be able to reduce the incidence of deviant behaviors and facilitate more effective learning among their pupils. This is in contrast to the more traditional approaches

in counseling and psychotherapy in which only professional persons with years of education and advanced training are considered qualified to work with children with disturbed or disordered behavior.

Criticism of Behavioral Conditioning

An attempt has been made in this paper to point up the fact that in very recent years, the development of the behavioral approach has provided the mental health and related professions with new and more effective ways of helping children with various emotional and behavioral problems. There are three remaining observations that may be made relative to this discussion. The first has to do with the fact that there are resistances and misunderstandings, on the part of professionals and laymen alike, concerning the use of behavioral procedures. Like most other major innovations and new conceptualizations in science that were resisted when they first appeared, there have been and will continue to be strong objections to behavior modification. Another example of this in the field of mental health is the initial opposition and rejection of the contributions of Freud and the development of his system for attempting to understand the human mind and modify behavior. The psychoanalytic approach was resisted, misinterpreted, and opposed, but nevertheless survived; and the same outcome may be predicted for the behavior analytic approach despite various attacks that have been made on it. For example, some critics say that behavior modification is "superficial" and not effective with "deep-rooted psychopathological conditions," even though there is now convincing evidence in the literature that shows this approach is capable of bringing about extensive changes in individuals with various behavioral disturbances. Other critics say that the behavioral approach is doomed to failure because "only symptoms" are modified which results in the subsequent development of substitute symptoms, some of which may be worse than the original ones, despite the fact that an increasing number of reports in the literature refute this argument. Still other critics say that behavior modification is "dangerous" and nothing but a form of "brainwashing," despite the fact that, properly used, it may bring about more flexible, adaptive behavior and free a person from fixated or self-defeating patterns. Of course, like any other procedure or tool or treatment in the helping professions, behavior modification should be carried out competently in accordance with high ethical principles and with primary concern for the individual patient or client's welfare. Another criticism of behavior modification is that it is too "mechanical" and "dehumanizing," despite the fact that results in the literature indicate that for the first time in their lives, some children began to make a relatively normal adjustment and some adults, for the first time in many years, were able to resume a relatively normal life after the use of behavior modification therapy. In short, despite considerable opposition and resistance as well as misunderstanding of the basic rationale and application of behavior modification in mental health work, results in the literature suggest that this new development will not only survive but will gradually become an increasingly adopted and respected approach. To paraphrase Charles Kettering, inventor of the electric starter for automobiles, relative to resistance to new ideas and innovations:

First, the critics say that behavior modification is ineffective and they can prove it; failing in this, then they say it may be effective but it is superficial, has very limited application and is insignificant. Finally, the critics acknowledge that behavior modification is both effective and important but they say it is not anything new—they have known about it all along and have been doing "more or less the same thing" for years!

Similarity to Re-Education

The second observation has to do with the fact that behavior modification is entirely compatible with another major advancement in the mental health field, namely the Re-Education Treatment of emotionally disturbed children that has been developed in Tennessee. The Re-Ed approach has demonstrated the effectiveness of a nonclinical program that is essentially a school rather than a hospital and one that provides re-educational and new learning experiences for disturbed children. Such children are seen, not as suffering from "mental disease," but as having learned unproductive and unacceptable behaviors that constitute their emotional disturbance. Behavior modification provides a behavioral management system for the Re-Education approach to child mental health and, as such, can function as an integral component of the total Re-Ed program.

Lack of Training

The third observation has to do with the fact that the mental health disciplines in the past have not included basic course work and experience in behavior modification in their training programs of mental health personnel. This means that the tens of thousands of mental health and related professionals in the field today have been trained in programs that offered no instruction or practicum in the behavioral procedures described in this discussion. Thus, there is a need for staff development and continuing education opportunities that would enable mental health and related personnel to learn and be able to carry out these procedures. A beginning effort in this direction might be to develop a library of basic readings in this area. In this connection Annotated Bibliographies on Behavior Modification have been prepared which provide a representative listing of some of the significant contributions in the professional literature.

In conclusion, it may be predicted that recent, current and continuing developments in behavior modification will bring about substantial advancements in therapeutic work with children and help usher in a new era in the understanding and guidance of children. There is now reason to believe that many emotionally disturbed and mentally handicapped children can be helped more effectively and efficiently than has been possible in the past. As a result the present can be faced with more confidence and the future with more hope.

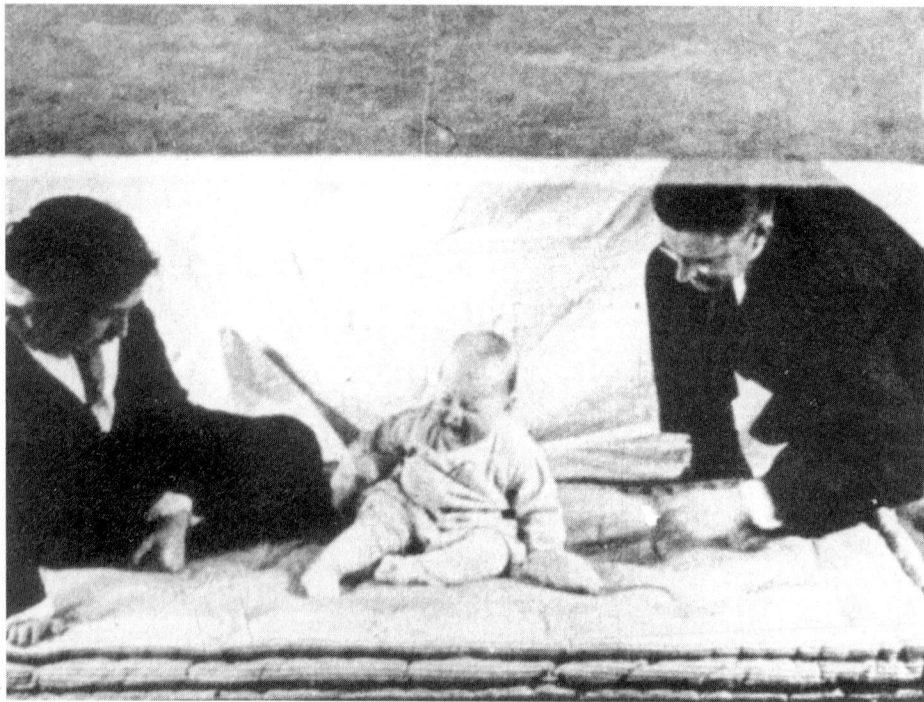

Figure 8-2. Rosalie Rayner, Albert B. and John B. Watson. Through classical conditioning, Little Albert developed a fear of rats and other furry objects—even Santa's face. (Photograph courtesy of Benjamin Harris, Ph.D.)

CONDITIONED EMOTIONAL REACTIONS

John B. Watson and Rosalie Rayner

Cantankerous and irascible describe behaviorism's founder John B. Watson. A wild and impulsive youth, he was often in trouble with police for fighting and firing guns. While at Furman University, he handed in a term paper in reverse order. He failed the course and it took him an additional year to graduate. He vowed his professor would some day come for help. Ultimately, the professor applied to study under him (Schwartz, 1986, pp. 23-24).

Behaviorism became increasingly more popular following the 1913 publication of Psychology as the Behaviorist Views It. Watson quickly became famous and was elected president of the American Psychological Association in 1915 at the age of thirty seven. This position afforded him a powerful forum from which to promote behaviorism.

Spreading behaviorism was one of Watson's primary objectives; discrediting Freud another. The allegation that psychoanalysis was unscientific motivated Watson to dissociate behaviorism from it. In 1909, Freud published the Analysis of a Phobia in a Five-year-old Boy. Little Hans had developed a phobia of horses. He refused to leave the house for fear he would encounter one. Freud reasoned that Hans' phobia really represented a fear of his father. As an expression of the Oedipus complex, Hans feared castration by his father because of competition for the affection of his mother. His father was unavoidable, so his fear was displaced onto horses.

Watson disdained Freud's explanation. Instead, he believed that phobias are conditioned emotional responses. If frightened by an unconditional stimulus (one that elicits fear without prior conditioning) in the presence of an originally neutral stimulus, the neutral stimulus becomes a conditioned stimulus, which will evoke fear by itself. He set about to prove it.

Reference

Schwartz, S. (1986). *Classic Studies in Psychology*. California: Mayfield Publishing Company.

In recent literature various speculations have been entered into concerning the possibility of conditioning various types of emotional response, but direct experimental evidence in support of such a view has been lacking. If the theory advanced by Watson and Morgan[1] to the effect that in infancy the original emotional reaction patterns are few, consisting so far as observed of fear, rage and love, then there must be some simple method by means of which the range of stimuli which can call out these emotions and their compounds is greatly increased. Otherwise, complexity in adult response could not be accounted for. These authors without adequate experimental evidence advanced the view that this range was increased by means of conditioned reflex factors. It was suggested there that the early home life of the child furnishes a laboratory situation for establishing conditioned emotional responses. The present authors have recently put the whole matter to an experimental test.

Reprinted from *Journal of Experimental Psychology*, Vol. 111, no. 1, February 1920, pp. 1-15.

Experimental work has been done so far on only one child, Albert B. This infant was reared almost from birth in a hospital environment; his mother was a wet nurse in the Harriet Lane Home for Invalid Children. Albert's life was normal: he was healthy from birth and one of the best developed youngsters ever brought to the hospital, weighing twenty-one pounds at nine months of age. He was on the whole stolid and unemotional. His stability was one of the principal reasons for using him as a subject in this test. We felt that we could do him relatively little harm by carrying out such experiments as those outlined below.

At approximately nine months of age we ran him through the emotional tests that have become a part of our regular routine in determining whether fear reactions can be called out by other stimuli than sharp noises and the sudden removal of support. Tests of this type have been described by the senior author in another place.[2] In brief, the infant was confronted suddenly and for the first time successively with a white rat, a rabbit, a dog, a monkey, with masks with and without hair, cotton, wood burning, newspapers, etc. A permanent record of Albert's reactions to these objects and situations has been preserved in a motion picture study. Manipulation was the most usual reaction called out. *At no time did this infant ever show fear in any situation.* These experimental records were confirmed by the casual observations of the mother and hospital attendants. No one had ever seen him in a state of fear and rage. The infant practically never cried.

Up to approximately nine months of age we had not tested him with loud sounds. The test to determine whether a fear reaction could be called out by a loud sound was made when he was eight months, twenty-six days of age. The sound was that made by striking a hammer upon a suspended steel bar four feet in length and three-fourths of an inch in diameter. The laboratory notes are as follows:

One of the two experimenters caused the child to turn its head and fixate her moving hand; the other, stationed back of the child, struck the steel bar a sharp blow. The child started violently, his breathing was checked and the arms were raised in a characteristic manner. On the second stimulation the same thing occurred, and in addi-

tion the lips began to pucker and tremble. On the third stimulation the child broke into a sudden crying fit. This is the first time an emotional situation in the laboratory has produced any fear or even crying in Albert.

We had expected just these results on account of our work with other infants brought up under similar conditions. It is worth while to call attention to the fact that removal of support (dropping and jerking the blanket upon which the infant was lying) was tried exhaustively upon this infant on the same occasion. It was not effective in producing the fear response. This stimulus is effective in younger children. At what age such stimuli lose their potency in producing fear is not known. Nor is it known whether less placid children ever lose their fear of them. This probably depends upon the training the child gets. It is well known that children eagerly run to be tossed into the air and caught. On the other hand it is equally well known that in the adult fear responses are called out quite clearly by the sudden removal of support, if the individual is walking across a bridge, walking out upon a beam, etc. There is a wide field of study here which is aside from our present point.

The sound stimulus, thus, at nine months of age, gives us the means of testing several important factors. I. Can we condition fear of an animal, e.g., a white rat, by visually presenting it and simultaneously striking a steel bar? II. If such a conditioned emotional response can be established, will there be a transfer to other animals or other objects? III. What is the effect of time upon such conditioned emotional responses? IV. If after a reasonable period such emotional responses have not died out, what laboratory methods can be devised for their removal?

I. The establishment of conditioned emotional responses. At first there was considerable hesitation upon our part in making the attempt to set up fear reactions experimentally. A certain responsibility attaches to such a procedure. We decided finally to make the attempt, comforting ourselves by the reflection that such attachments would arise anyway as soon as the child left the sheltered environment of the nursery for the rough and tumble of the home. We did not begin this work until Albert was eleven months, three days of age. Before attempting to set up a conditioned response we, as before, put him through all of the regular emotional tests. Not the slightest sign of a fear response was obtained in any situation.

The steps taken to condition emotional responses are shown in our laboratory notes.

11 Months 3 Days

1. White rat suddenly taken from the basket and presented to Albert. He began to reach for rat with left hand. Just as his hand touched the animal the bar was struck immediately behind his head. The infant jumped violently and fell forward, burying his face in the mattress. He did not cry, however.

2. Just as the right hand touched the rat the bar was again struck. Again the infant jumped violently, fell forward and began to whimper.

In order not to disturb the child too seriously no further tests were given for one week.

11 Months 10 Days

1. Rat presented suddenly without sound. There was steady fixation but no tendency at first to reach for it. The rat was then placed nearer, whereupon tentative reaching movements began with the right hand. When the rat nosed the infant's left hand, the hand was immediately withdrawn. He started to reach for the head of the animal with the forefinger of the left hand, but withdrew it suddenly before contact. It is thus seen that the two joint stimulations given the previous week were not without effect. He was tested with his blocks immediately afterwards to see if they shared in the process of conditioning. He began immediately to pick them up, dropping them, pounding them, etc. In the remainder of the tests the blocks were given frequently to quiet him and to test his general emotional state. They were always removed from sight when the process of conditioning was under way.

2. Joint stimulation with rat and sound. Started, then fell over immediately to right side. No crying.

3. Joint stimulation. Fell to right side and rested upon hands, with head turned away from rat. No crying.

4. Joint stimulation. Same reaction.

5. Rat suddenly presented alone. Puckered face, whimpered and withdrew body sharply to the left.

6. Joint stimulation. Fell over immediately to right side and began to whimper.

7. Joint stimulation. Started violently and cried, but did not fall over.

8. Rat alone. *The instant the rat was shown the baby began to cry. Almost instantly he turned sharply to the left, fell over on left side, raised himself on all fours and began to crawl away so rapidly that he was caught with difficulty before reaching the edge of the table.*

This was as convincing a case of a completely conditioned fear response as could have been theoretically pictured. In all, seven joint stimulations were given to bring about the complete reaction. It is not unlikely had the sound been of greater intensity or of a more complex clang character that the number of joint stimulations might have been materially reduced. Experiments designed to define the nature of the sounds that will serve best as emotional stimuli are under way.

II. When a conditioned emotional response has been established for one object, is there a transfer? Five days later Albert was again brought back into the laboratory and tested as follows:

11 Months 15 Days

1. Tested first with blocks. He reached readily for them, playing with them as usual. This shows that there has been no general transfer to the room, table, blocks, etc.

2. Rat alone. Whimpered immediately, withdrew right hand and turned head and trunk away.

3. Blocks again offered. Played readily with them, smiling and gurgling.

4. Rat alone. Leaned over to the left side as far away from the rat as possible, then fell over, getting up on all fours and scurrying away as rapidly as possible.

5. Blocks again offered. Reached immediately for them, smiling and laughing as before.

The above preliminary test shows that the conditioned response to the rat had carried over completely for the five days in which no tests were given. The question as to whether or not there is a transfer was next taken up.

6. Rabbit alone. The rabbit was suddenly placed on the mattress in front of him. The reaction was pronounced. Negative responses began at once. He leaned as far away from the animal as possible, whimpered, then burst into tears. When the rabbit was placed in contact with him he buried his face in the mattress, then got up on all fours and crawled away, crying as he went. This was a most convincing test.

7. The blocks were next given him, after an interval. He played with them as before. It was observed by four people that he played far more energetically with them than ever before. The blocks were raised high over his head and slammed down with a great deal of force.

8. Dog alone. The dog did not produce as violent a reaction as the rabbit. The moment fixation occurred the child shrank back and as the animal came nearer he attempted to get on all fours but did not cry at first. As soon as the dog passed out of his range of vision he became quiet. The dog was then made to approach the infant's head (he was lying down at the moment). Albert straightened up immediately, fell over to the opposite side and turned his head away. He then began to cry.

9. The blocks were again presented. He began immediately to play with them.

10. Fur coat (seal). Withdrew immediately to the left side and began to fret. Coat put close to him on the left side, he turned immediately, began to cry and tried to crawl away on all fours.

11. Cotton wool. The wool was presented in a paper package. At the end the cotton was not covered by the paper. It was placed first on his feet. He kicked it away but did not touch it with his hands. When his hand was laid on the wool he immediately withdrew it but did not show the shock that the animals or fur coat produced in him. He then began to play with the paper, avoiding contact with the wool itself. He finally, under the impulse of the manipulative instinct, lost some of his negativism to the wool.

12. Just in play W. put his head down to see if Albert would play with his hair. Albert was completely negative. Two other observers did the same thing. He began immediately to play with

their hair. W. then brought the Santa Claus mask and presented it to Albert. He was again pronouncedly negative.

11 Months 20 Days

1. Blocks alone. Played with them as usual.

2. Rat alone. Withdrawal of the whole body, bending over to left side, no crying. Fixation and following with eyes. The response was much less marked than on first presentation the previous week. It was thought best to freshen up the reaction by another joint stimulation.

3. Just as the rat was placed on his hand the rod was struck. Reaction violent.

4. Rat alone. Fell over at once to left side. Reaction practically as strong as on former occasion but no crying.

5. Rat alone. Fell over to left side, got up on all fours and started to crawl away. On this occasion there was no crying, but strange to say, as he started away he began to gurgle and coo, even while leaning far over to the left side to avoid the rat.

6. Rabbit alone. Leaned over to left side as far as possible. Did not fall over. Began to whimper but reaction not so violent as on former occasions.

7. Blocks again offered. He reached for them immediately and began to play.

All of the tests so far discussed were carried out upon a table supplied with a mattress, located in a small, well-lighted dark-room. We wished to test next whether conditioned fear responses so set up would appear if the situation were markedly altered. We thought it best before making this test to freshen the reaction both to the rabbit and to the dog by showing them at the moment the steel bar was struck. It will be recalled that this was the first time any effort had been made to directly condition response to the dog and rabbit. The experimental notes are as follows:

8. The rabbit at first was given alone. The reaction was exactly as given in test (6) above. When the rabbit was left on Albert's knees for a long time he began tentatively to reach out and manipulate its fur with forefingers. While doing this the steel rod was struck. A violent fear reaction resulted.

9. Rabbit alone. Reaction wholly similar to

that on trial (6) above.

10. Rabbit alone. Started immediately to whimper, holding hands far up, but did not cry. Conflicting tendency to manipulate very evident.

11. Dog alone. Began to whimper, shaking head from side to side, holding hands as far away from the animal as possible.

12. Dog and sound. The rod was struck just as the animal touched him. A violent negative reaction appeared. He began to whimper, turned to one side, fell over and started to get up on all fours.

13. Blocks. Played with them immediately and readily.

On this same day and immediately after the above experiment Albert was taken into the large well-lighted lecture room belonging to the laboratory. He was placed on a table in the center of the room immediately under the skylight. Four people were present. The situation was thus very different from that which obtained in the small dark room.

1. Rat alone. No sudden fear reaction appeared at first. The hands, however, were held up and away from the animal. No positive manipulatory reactions appeared.

2. Rabbit alone. Fear reaction slight. Turned to left and kept face away from the animal but the reaction was never pronounced.

3. Dog alone. Turned away but did not fall over. Cried. Hands moved as far away from the animal as possible. Whimpered as long as the dog was present.

4. Rat alone. Slight negative reaction.

5. Rat and sound. It was thought best to freshen the reaction to the rat. The sound was given just as the rat was presented. Albert jumped violently but did not cry.

6. Rat alone. At first he did not show any negative reaction. When rat was placed nearer he began to show negative reaction by drawing back his body, raising his hands, whimpering, etc.

7. Blocks. Played with them immediately.

8. Rat alone. Pronounced withdrawal of body and whimpering.

9. Blocks. Played with them as before.

10. Rabbit alone. Pronounced reaction. Whimpered with arms held high, fell over backward and had to be caught.

11. Dog alone. At first the dog did not produce the pronounced reaction. The hands were held high over the head, breathing was checked, but there was no crying. Just at this moment the dog, which had not barked before, barked three times loudly when only about six inches from the baby's face. Albert immediately fell over and broke into a wail that continued until the dog was removed. The sudden barking of the hitherto quiet dog produced a marked fear response in the adult observers!

From the above results it would seem that emotional transfers do take place. Furthermore it would seem that the number of transfers resulting from an experimentally produced conditioned emotional reaction may be very large. In our observations we had no means of testing the complete number of transfers which may have resulted.

III. The effect of time upon conditioned emotional responses. We have already shown that the conditioned emotional response will continue for a period of one week. It was desired to make the time test longer. In view of the imminence of Albert's departure from the hospital we could not make the interval longer than one month. Accordingly no further emotional experimentation was entered into for thirty-one days after the above test. During the month, however, Albert was brought weekly to the laboratory for tests upon right and left-handedness, imitation, general development, etc. No emotional tests whatever were given and during the whole month his regular nursery routine was maintained in the Harriet Lane Home. The notes on the test given at the end of this period are as follows:

1 year 21 Days

1. Santa Claus mask. Withdrawal, gurgling, then slapped at it without touching. When his hand was forced to touch it, he whimpered and cried. His hand was forced to touch it two more times. He whimpered and cried on both tests. He finally cried at the mere visual stimulus of the mask.

2. Fur coat. Wrinkled his nose and withdrew both hands, drew back his whole body and began to whimper as the coat was put nearer. Again

there was the strife between withdrawal and the tendency to manipulate. Reached tentatively with left hand but drew back before contact had been made. In moving his body to one side his hand accidentally touched the coat. He began to cry at once, nodding his head in a very peculiar manner (this reaction was an entirely new one). Both hands were withdrawn as far as possible from the coat. The coat was then laid on his lap and he continued nodding his head and whimpering, withdrawing his body as far as possible, pushing the while at the coat with his feet but never touching it with his hands.

3. Fur coat. The coat was taken out of his sight and presented again at the end of a minute. He began immediately to fret, withdrawing his body and nodding his head as before.

4. Blocks. He began to play with them as usual.

5. The rat. He allowed the rat to crawl towards him without withdrawing. He sat very still and fixated it intently. Rat then touched his hand. Albert withdrew it immediately, then leaned back as far as possible but did not cry. When the rat was placed on his arm he withdrew his body and began to fret, nodding his head. The rat was then allowed to crawl against his chest. He first began to fret and then covered his eyes with both hands.

6. Blocks. Reaction normal.

7. The rabbit. The animal was placed directly in front of him. It was very quiet. Albert showed no avoiding reactions at first. After a few seconds he puckered up his face, began to nod his head and to look intently at the experimenter. He next began to push the rabbit away with his feet, withdrawing his body at the same time. Then as the rabbit came nearer he began pulling his feet away, nodding his head, and wailing "da da." After about a minute he reached out tentatively and slowly and touched the rabbit's ear with his right hand, finally manipulating it. The rabbit was again placed in his lap. Again he began to fret and withdrew his hands. He reached out tentatively with his left hand and touched the animal, shuddered and withdrew the whole body. The experimenter then took hold of his left hand and laid it on the rabbit's back. Albert immediately withdrew his hand and began to suck his thumb.

Again the rabbit was laid in his lap. He began to cry, covering his face with both hands.

8. Dog. The dog was very active. Albert fixated it intensely for a few seconds, sitting very still. He began to cry but did not fall over backwards as on his last contact with the dog. When the dog was pushed closer to him he at first sat motionless, then began to cry, putting both hands over his face.

These experiments would seem to show conclusively that directly conditioned emotional responses as well as those conditioned by transfer persist, although with a certain loss in the intensity of the reaction, for a longer period than one month. Our view is that they persist and modify personality throughout life. It should be recalled again that Albert was of an extremely phlegmatic type. Had he been emotionally unstable probably both the directly conditioned response and those transferred would have persisted throughout the month unchanged in form.

IV. "Detachment" or removal of conditioned emotional responses. Unfortunately, Albert was taken from the hospital the day the above tests were made. Hence the opportunity of building up an experimental technique by means of which we could remove the conditioned emotional responses was denied us. Our own view, expressed above, which is possibly not very well grounded, is that these responses in the home environment are likely to persist indefinitely, unless an accidental method for removing them is hit upon. The importance of establishing some method must be apparent to all. Had the opportunity been at hand we should have tried out several methods, some of which we may mention. (1) Constantly confronting the child with those stimuli which called out the responses in the hopes that habituation would come in corresponding to "fatigue " of reflex when differential reactions are to be set up. (2) By trying to "recondition" by showing objects calling out fear responses (visual) and simultaneously stimulating the erogenous zones (tactual). We should try first the lips, then the nipples and as a final resort the sex organs. (3) By trying to "recondition" by feeding the subject candy or other food just as the animal is shown. This method calls for the food control of the subject.

(4) By building up "constructive" activities around the object by imitation and by putting the hand through the motions of manipulation. At this age imitation of overt motor activity is strong, as our present but unpublished experimentation has shown.

INCIDENTAL OBSERVATIONS

(a) Thumb sucking as a compensatory device for blocking fear and noxious stimuli. During the course of these experiments, especially in the final test, it was noticed that whenever Albert was on the verge of tears or emotionally upset generally he would continually thrust his thumb into his mouth. The moment the hand reached the mouth he became impervious to the stimuli producing fear. Again and again while the motion pictures were being made at the end of the thirty-day rest period, we had to remove the thumb from his mouth before the conditioned response could be obtained. This method of blocking noxious and emotional stimuli (fear and rage) through erogenous stimulation seems to persist from birth onward. . . . If the finger gets into the mouth crying ceases at once. The organism thus apparently from birth, when under the influence of love stimuli is blocked to all others.[3] This resort to sex stimulation when under the influence of noxious and emotional situations, or when the individual is restless and idle, persists throughout adolescent and adult life. Albert, at any rate, did not resort to thumb sucking except in the presence of such stimuli. Thumb sucking could immediately be checked by offering him his blocks. These invariably called out active manipulation instincts. It is worth while here to call attention to the fact that Freud's conception of the stimulation of erogenous zones as being the expression of an original "pleasure" seeking principle may be turned about and possibly better described as a compensatory (and often conditioned) device for the blockage of noxious and fear and rage producing stimuli.

(b) Equal primacy of fear, love and possibly rage. While in general the results of our experiment offer no particular points of conflict with Freudian concepts, one fact out of harmony with them should be emphasized. According to proper Freudians sex (or in our terminology, love) is the principal emotion in which conditioned responses arise which later limit and distort personality. We wish to take sharp issue with this view on the basis of the experimental evidence we have gathered. Fear is as primal a factor as love in influencing personality. Fear does not gather its potency in any derived manner from love. It belongs to the original and inherited nature of man. Probably the same may be true of rage although at present we are not so sure of this.

The Freudians twenty years from now, unless their hypotheses change, when they come to analyze Albert's fear of a seal skin coat—assuming that he comes to analysis at that age—will probably tease from him the recital of a dream which upon their analysis will show that Albert at three years of age attempted to play with the pubic hair of the mother and was scolded violently for it. (We are by no means denying that this might in some other case condition it). If the analyst has sufficiently prepared Albert to accept such a dream when found as an explanation of his avoiding tendencies, and if the analyst has the authority and personality to put it over, Albert may be fully convinced that the dream was a true revealer of the factors which brought about the fear.

It is probable that many of the phobias in psychopathology are true conditioned emotional reactions either of the direct or the transferred type. One may possibly have to believe that such persistence of early conditioned responses will be found only in persons who are constitutionally inferior. Our argument is meant to be constructive. Emotional disturbances in adults cannot be traced back to sex alone. They must be retraced along at least three collateral lines—to conditioned and transferred responses set up in infancy and early youth in all three of the fundamental human emotions.

Notes

[1]Emotional Reactions and Psychological Experimentation,' *American Journal of Psychology*, April, 1917, Vol. 28, pp. 163-174.

[2]'Psychology from the Standpoint of a Behaviorist,' p. 202.

[3]The stimulus to love in infants according to our view is stroking of the skin, lips, nipples and sex organs, patting and rocking, picking up, etc. Patting and rocking (as when not conditioned) are probably equivalent to actual stimulation of the sex organs. In adults, of course, as every lover knows, vision, audition and olfaction soon become conditioned by joint stimulation with contact and kinaesthetic stimuli.

Postscript

I have seen the motion picture study of the conditioning of Albert A. The sound of the bar must have been very thunderous, as it caused an extreme reaction in him.

Admittedly, Watson made no attempt to uncondition the fear of Albert. In 1924, with the advice of Watson, Mary Cover Jones unconditioned the fear of a rabbit in a child named Peter by gradually bringing the animal closer to him. Besides defusing criticism of Watson for purposely conditioning fear in a child, Jones' study showed fears can also be unlearned and provided the theoretical basis for systematic desensitization, a commonly used type of behavior therapy.

In 1920, shortly after the Albert study, Watson began to study the physiological aspects of sexual behavior under laboratory conditions. He attached electrodes to couples engaged in sex to "directly measure" arousal. As a dedicated scientist, Watson wished to participate. However, his wife refused. Rosalie Rayner, co-author of the present article and his research assistant, volunteered. The officials of Johns Hopkins University took a dim view of Watson's research, and he was forced to resign.

A public divorce trial left him economically and emotionally drained. He married Rosalie Rayner. He never held an academic position thereafter, and sold rubber boots door to door and Yuban coffee (Schwartz, 1986, pp. 28-29). He developed an advertising campaign using sex appeal to promote Pebeco Toothpaste (Buckley, 1982). We can only speculate what further impact Watson might have had.

Mariette Hartley is an actress who had a television series, appeared on numerous talk shows, and made award-winning Polaroid commercials with James Garner. John B. Watson was her grandfather. Hartley's mother, Polly, suffered from alcoholism and depression and made frequent suicide attempts. Watson treated her without sentiment or expression of physical affection, which he felt would cripple a child's sense of independence. Mariette was treated the same way by her mother. Despite her sunny screen personality, Hartley has also battled with alcohol and depression. Her story is told in her 1990 book, Breaking the Silence. *The same scientific detachment Watson employed with success in the lab resulted in parental disaster.*

Nearly a decade after the original publication of the "dozen healthy infants" claim, a disheartened Watson remarked in The Ways of Behaviorism *(1928), "I used to feel quite hopeful of reconditioning even adult personalities. ... But ... the zebra can as easily change his stripes as the adult his personality." Despite Watson's premature departure, his legacy was that behaviorism virtually dominated psychology at the time of his death in 1958.*

References

Buckley, K. W. (1982). The Selling of a Psychologist: John Broadus Watson and the Application of Behavioral Techniques to Advertising. *Journal of the History of the Behavioral Sciences*, 18, 207-221.

Schwartz, S. (1986). *Classic Studies in Psychology*. California: Mayfield Publishing Company.

Figure 8-3. B. F. Skinner delivers the keynote address at the American Psychological Association convention, August 10, 1990. He then finished writing his last article for the *American Psychologist,* and died the day after, August 18, 1990. (Photograph copyright © Ellen Shub, 1996. All rights reserved.)

READING 8C

THE OPERANT SIDE OF BEHAVIOR THERAPY

B.F. Skinner

The leadership vacancy created by the exit of Watson was ultimately filled by Burrhus Frederic Skinner. His first major work, The Behavior of Organisms, *was published in 1938. He was a graduate of Hamilton College in New York State, and majored in English. There, in addition to academics, he participated in mischief and pranks. He started a rumor that Charlie Chaplin, famous actor and comedian, would visit the campus. Much to his delight, "everyone" came, with the exception of Chaplin. He did his graduate work at Harvard University and was a professor there for nearly forty years. He returned frequently to lecture at his beloved Hamilton. He died in 1990.*

Skinner's greatest contributions were the development of operant conditioning and its applications. An operant is a voluntary behavior demonstrated by an organism. If followed by a pleasurable stimulus, called a positive reinforcer, the operant will become strengthened. Only the "target" operant will receive positive reinforcement. Through shaping procedures, complex operants, which would not be spontaneously emitted by the organism, can be developed.

Skinner boxes, containers in which experimenters could readily control the contingencies of reinforcement for rats and pigeons, were used to derive the principles of operant conditioning. Capitalizing on the operant tendency of pigeons to swipe, he taught them to play ping-pong. During World War II, he developed the Pelican missile. It employed pigeons which were reinforced to peck at images of enemy targets, making on-course corrections ("Skinner's", 1971). His daughter Deborah's bedroom was highly comfortable and controlled, leading critics to claim she was raised in a Skinner box.

He published Walden Two *in 1948. The novel describes a utopian community built on the findings derived from laboratory experimentation on conditioning. Although contingencies of reinforcement are highly controlled, Walden is a place where contented people operate in the environment in an adaptive and harmonious way.* Beyond Freedom and Dignity *(1971) was a scientific version of Walden Two. In it, he describes freedom and dignity as illusions. Everyone has contingencies of reinforcement controlled by others; all the world is a Skinner box. Control must be used for human betterment:*

> *...we may not really help others by doing things for them. This is often the case when they are learning to do things for themselves. We watch a child tying a shoelace and grow jittery, and to escape from our jitteriness we "help" the child tie the lace. In doing so we destroy one chance to learn to tie shoelaces.*

The same applies for the elderly, recipients of governmental assistance, or those who are given aid because their style of living is not socially prescribed. Skinner depicted how the Danish government implemented a program of "modern reformatory guidance" for Eskimos of Greenland, who were

"The Operant side of Behavior Therapy" by B.F. Skinner. Reprinted with permission from *Journal of Behavior Therapy and Experimental Psychiatry*, Vol. 19, no. 3, pp. 171-179, 1988. Reprinted with permission of Elsevier Science Ltd., Pergamon Imprint, Oxford, England.

actively engaged in fishing. They were now provided for, non-contingent on behavior. Good social relations yielded to drunken brawls in "an alarming chaos of human frustration" (Skinner, 1976).

Skinner was criticized by humanists as being cold and detached for his advocacy of control and behavior technology. O. Ivar Lovaas, a contemporary behaviorist whose work will be described following this article, wrote an eulogy for Skinner. Ironically, it was published in the Journal of Humanistic Psychology. When Skinner put his daughter, Julie, now a psychologist, to bed, Lovaas related, he "would squeeze her hand before leaving, and there would be tears in his eyes." When asked if he would like to live in Walden Two, he replied, "My wife would not let me" (Lovaas, 1991, p. 114).

The following article demonstrates Skinner's views on the therapeutic application of operant conditioning.

References

Lovaas, O. I. (1991, Spring). Reflections on Fred Skinner's Death. *Journal of Humanistic Psychology, 31*(2).
_____(1971, September 20). Skinner's Utopia: Panacea, or Path to Hell? *Time.*
Skinner, B. F. (1976, January/February). The Ethics of Helping People. *Humanist.*

In 1913 John B. Watson issued his famous manifesto: The subject matter of psychology was behavior. It is easy to forget how radical that must have seemed. Psychology had always been the science of mental life, and that life was to be studied through introspection, a process of self-examination borrowed from the philosophers, who had used it for more than twenty-four hundred years. People were seen to behave in given ways because of what they were feeling or thinking about, and feeling and thoughts were therefore the things to study. If animals sometimes behaved rather like people, they probably had feelings and some kind of mental life, although they might not know they had.

Seventy-five years have seen a great change. Introspection has been returned to the philosophers. There are no longer any "trained observers" in the Wundtian tradition, and cognitive psychologists no longer observe the mental processes they talk about. The processes are hypotheses, to be confirmed either by inferences from the behavior they are said to explain or by a different kind of observation—namely, of the nervous system.

Meanwhile, two flourishing sciences of behavior have appeared. Ethology is one of them. The behavior of animals in a natural environment is no longer explained by imagining what the animals are feeling or thinking about but by the contributions the behavior may have made to the future of their genes. In the other science, the experimental analysis behavior, animals are observed in the laboratory, where many of the conditions of which their behavior is a function can be controlled. Most of the behavior is traced to operant reinforcement, a different kind of selective consequence acting during the lifetime of the individual.

As more and more of the variables of which behavior is a function are identified and their role analyzed, less remains to be explained in mentalistic ways. There are proportionate gains in the application of the analysis. It has always been difficult to do very much with feelings and states of mind because of their inaccessibility. The environmental variables are often within reach. Contact between the basic analysis and its applications is therefore important. Although new facts often turn up in the course of applying a science, the science itself usually moves more rapidly into new territory. In what follows I review some well known practices in behavior therapy from the point of view of behavior analysis and discuss a few current theoretical issues. I do so, not to correct or instruct practitioners, but to reassure them. The experimental analysis of behavior is developing rapidly, and at every step the principles of behavior therapy gain authority. Troublesome behavior is due to troublesome contingencies of reinforcement, not to troublesome feelings or states of mind, and to correct the trouble we should correct the contingencies.

Respondent Behavior Therapy

Psychotherapy has often been concerned with feelings—with anxiety, fear, anger and the like. An early step toward behavior therapy was the realization that what was felt was not a "feeling" but a state of the body. The point was made before the advent of behaviorism by William James and Carl Lange. Lange looked for possibly relevant states, but James put the argument in its best known form: we do not cry because we are sad, we are sad because we cry.

A further step was needed, however. We do not cry *because* we are sad or feel sad, *because* we cry, we cry *and* feel sad because something has happened. Perhaps a friend has died. We must know something about the earlier event if we are to explain either the crying or the state felt. That is the behavioristic position: turn to environmental antecedents to explain what one does and, at the same time, what one feels while doing it. For every state felt and given the name of a feeling there is presumably a prior environmental event of which it is the product. Behavior therapy addresses the prior event rather than the feeling.

What are felt as emotions are largely the responses of glands and smooth muscle. Efforts were once made to define a given emotion as a particular pattern of such responses. The variables of which the behavior is a function are a more promising alternative. Some aggressive behavior, for example, is genetic; it has evolved because of its contribution to the survival of the species. Variables of that sort are largely out of reach in dealing with the behavior of an individual, although aggressive behavior can often be allowed to adapt out. Much more can be done when emotional responses result from respondent (Pavlovian) conditioning. Troublesome behavior can then often be extinguished or other behavior can be conditioned to replace it. Both adaptation and extinction have fewer unwanted side effects when stimuli are presented with gradually increasing intensities. The process is called, of course, desensitization.

Operant Behavior Therapy

Therapists have been as much concerned with what people do as with what they feel. Behavior therapists trace what is done to two kinds of selective consequences, innate behavior to natural selection and learned behavior to operant reinforcement. A given instance is usually a joint product of both. There is an operant side to emotion, for example. Fear is not only a response of glands and smooth muscle, it is a reduced probability of moving toward a feared object and a heightened probability of moving away from it. The operant side of anger is a greater probability of hurting someone and a lesser probability of acting to please. Where the bodily state resulting from respondent conditioning is usually called a feeling, the state resulting from operant conditioning, observed through introspection, is called a state of mind.

Important distinctions are obscured, however, when behavior is attributed to a state of mind. An operant is strengthened, for example, when a response has reinforcing consequences, but subsequent responses occur because of what has happened, not what is going to happen. When we say that we do something "with the intention of having a given effect," for example, we attribute our behavior to something that lies in the future, but both the behavior and the state introspectively observed at the time are due to what has happened in the past. "Expectation" misrepresents the facts in the same way. To take an operant example, when a reinforcing consequence has followed something we have done, we are said to expect that it will follow when we do it again. What is introspectively observed is the bodily state resulting from the past occurrence. When one stimulus has often followed another, regardless of anything we may have done, we are said to expect the second whenever the first occurs. That expectation is a bodily state resulting from respondent conditioning.

Terms for states of mind have never been very consistently used. The nervous systems which bring our behavior into contact with various parts of our own body are not very efficient because they evolved for other reasons, and we cannot observe the bodily states of other people at all, at least while they are alive. In any case explanations of that sort must themselves be explained. We make no progress by explaining one state of mind as the effect of another; we must get back to something that can be directly observed and, if possible, put to use. That means, of course, the genetic and personal histories responsible both for the behavior and, in passing, the states of the body introspectively observed.

Some Examples

The operant side of behavior therapy can be illustrated by considering a few characteristic problems, in each of which behavior is traced to a contingency of natural selection or operant reinforcement rather than to a state of mind. Positively reinforced behavior is often accompanied by a state which we report by saying that we are doing "what we want to do,""like to do,"or "love to do." There is a special reason why such behavior is often troublesome. The reinforcing effect of a particular consequence may have evolved under conditions which no longer prevail. For example, most of us are strongly reinforced by salty or sweet foods, not because large quantities are good for us now, but because salty and sweet foods were in short supply in the early history of the species. Those who, thanks to genetic variations, found them especially reinforcing were more likely to eat them and survive. The increased susceptibility to reinforcement then led to the discovery and processing of vast quantities of salty and sweet foods, and we now eat too much of them and may turn to therapy for help.

An increased susceptibility to reinforcement by sexual contact would also have had great survival value in a world subject to famine, pestilence, and predation, and it now raises problems, not only for individuals but for an already over-populated world. A strong susceptibility to reinforcement by signs that one has hurt another person could also have evolved because such signs shape and maintain skillful combat. (The boxer who shows that he has been hurt has taught his opponent how to hurt.) Hence, the strong reinforcement of aggressive behavior which, like that of sexual behavior, raises problems both for the individual and the world.

Problems also arise from reinforcers which have never had any evolutionary advantage. Homo sapiens is not the only species to have discovered them. The reinforcing effects of alcohol, heroin, cocaine and other drugs are presumably

accidental. They are particularly troublesome when their use leads to the powerful negative reinforcers we call withdrawal symptoms. The craving from which an addict is said to suffer is a bodily state which accompanies behavior due to an anomalous reinforcer.

A different problem arises when a repertoire of behavior conditioned in one environment undergoes extinction in another. The relevant bodily state may be called discouragement, a sense of failure, helplessness, a loss of confidence, or depression. A different kind of depression follows when, having acquired a large and effective repertoire in one place, one moves to another in which it cannot be executed. The behavior is not extinguished: there are things one still wants to do, but appropriate occasions are lacking. The student who has acquired an effective repertoire in college may find no place for it in the world to which he moves upon graduation. The person who moves to a new city may suffer the same kind of depression when a repertoire appropriate to the old city does not work well in the new.

The addiction due to anomalous reinforcers is quite different from the addiction due to certain schedules of reinforcement. The so-called variable-ratio schedule is especially likely to cause trouble. It is a useful schedule because it maintains behavior against extinction when reinforcers occur only infrequently. The behavior of the dedicated artist, writer, businessman, or scientist is sustained by an occasional, unpredictable reinforcement. We play games because our behavior is reinforced on a variable ratio schedule, and for the same reason we gamble. In the long run gamblers lose because those who maintain the contingencies must win. As with the behavior due to anomalous reinforcers, gambling is an addiction in the sense that there is no ultimate gain, at least for most of those who gamble.

Many problems calling for therapy arise from a fault in operant conditioning itself. The process presumably evolved because behavior was strengthened when it produced important consequences for both individual and species. The process could not, however, take into account the manner in which the consequences were produced. It was enough that consequences usually followed because they were produced by what was done. Conditioning nevertheless occurs when reinforcing consequences follow for any reason whatsoever. Accidental consequences yield the behavior we call superstition. We fall ill, take a pill or perform a ritual, and get well: we then are more likely to take a pill or perform the ritual when we fall ill again, regardless of whether there was any actual effect. The superstition may stand in the way of a better measure. Therapy is often a matter of destroying the reinforcing effects of adventitious consequences.

Aversive consequences are responsible for many kinds of problems. As negative reinforcers they can have the faults we have just seen in positive reinforcers. As punishment, their side effects may be severe. We learned to crawl, walk, run and ride a bicycle because getting around the world reinforced our correctly doing so but also because we were hurt when we made mistakes. That sort of punishment is immediately contingent on behavior and may reduce its probability of occurrence, but it can also suppress behavior in a different way through respondent conditioning. The situation in which the behavior occurs or some aspect of the behavior itself becomes aversive and it can then negatively reinforce alternative forms of behavior. The punished person remains as strongly inclined to behave in the punished way as ever but escapes from the threat of punishment by doing something else instead. When punishment is imposed by other people, as it often is, it is seldom immediately contingent on what is done and works via respondent conditioning.

The bodily state resulting from the threat of deferred punishment is named according to its sources. When punished by one's peers it is called shame, when by a government guilt, and when by a religious agency a sense of sin. One way to escape is to confess and take the punishment, but when the behavior upon which a deferred punishment was contingent is not clear, escape can be difficult. Merely accidental aversive contingencies generate unexplained feelings of shame, guilt or sin, and a person may then turn to a therapist for help in escaping.

Here, then, are a few examples of troublesome contingencies of operant reinforcement, together with a few "states of mind" to which the behavior is often attributed. Other examples could be given (the list seems endless), but these are perhaps enough to show the precision and potential of the operant analysis. It does not follow, however, that behavior therapists should never ask their clients what they are feeling or thinking about. From their answers something may be inferred about genetic or personal histories. Asking such questions is, in fact, often the only way in which therapists can learn about a personal history. They lack facilities for direct investigations, and to investigate without permission is regarded as unethical. But asking about feelings and thoughts is only a convenience—the very convenience, in fact, which explains why people have asked about them for so many centuries—and we must turn to more accessible variables if we are to have a scientific analysis or use it to do something about personal problems.

The argument for operant behavior therapy is essentially this: What is felt as feelings or introspectively observed as states of mind are states of the body, and they are the product of certain contingencies of reinforcement. The contingencies can be much more easily identified and analyzed than the feelings or states of mind, and by turning to them as the thing to be changed, behavior therapy gains a special advantage. An important question remains to be answered, however. How are contingencies to be changed?

Changing The Contingencies

The conditions of which behavior is a function are under control in homes, for example, and in schools, workplaces, hospitals and prisons. Therapists may change them for their own purposes if they are part of a family or if they teach, employ workers, or administer hospitals or prisons. Professionally, they advise those who do so. They help parents with their children or spouses with their spouses: they advise teachers: they suggest new practices in hospitals and prisons. They can do so because some of the conditions under which people live can be controlled.

The word control raises a familiar issue. What right has a therapist to manipulate the conditions of which a person's behavior is a function? The question is more often asked about the use of punitive consequences by governments or positive reinforcers by business and industry. If it is not so often asked of psychotherapists, perhaps it is because they have not demonstrated any threatening power or because, like Carl Rogers, they insist that they are not exercising control at all. The question is more likely to be asked of behavior therapists because their practices are more often effective. Token economies in hospitals or prisons, for example, have been challenged precisely because they work. Food, even institutional food, is a reinforcer and can often be made contingent on behavior. That can be done to the advantage of those who are reinforced, but it is perhaps more often done to solve problems of management. The ethical question would seem to be *cui bono*, who profits? Control is ethical if it is exerted for the sake of the controlled.

That principle could play a greater part in current demands for legislative action to prohibit the use of aversive measures by therapists. It is easy to argue for banning the use of aversives because they are unpleasant things. By definition they are things we turn away from, and as punishment they interfere with things we want to do. But who eventually profits? The dentist's drill is aversive, but we accept it to escape from a toothache. We accept the punitive practices of governments and religions in return for some measure of order, security, and peace of mind. When aversive stimuli are used to stop the bizarre behavior of autistic people long enough to bring them under the control of nonaversive practices, they would seem to be justified. But only if no other measure can be used. Too ready an acceptance of aversive measures blocks progress along other lines. It is only recently that strong sanctions have been imposed upon child abuse and the battering of spouses and corporal punishment is only now being strongly challenged in schools. We are not yet ready to replace a police force or close the Pentagon. Applied behavior analysis has contributed to alternative measures, however, and we may hope that the problems of the autistic will soon be solved in better ways.

The Clinic

Homes, schools, workplaces, hospitals and prisons are environments in which people spend a great deal of their time. Face-to-face therapy in the clinic is different. Only a small part of the client's life is spent in the presence of a therapist. Only a few reinforcers can be used, and most of the time only to reinforce social, especially verbal behavior. There is a great deal of mutual shaping of behavior in face-to-face confrontations; some of it possibly harmful.

What the client does in the clinic is not of immediate concern, however. What happens there is preparation for a world which is not under the control of the therapist. Instead of arranging current contingencies of reinforcement, as in a home, school, workplace or hospital, therapists give advice. Modeling behavior to be copied is a kind of advice, but verbal advice has a broader scope. It may take the form of an order ("Do this, stop doing that") or it may describe contingencies of reinforcement ("Doing this will probably have a reinforcing effect." "If you do that the consequences may be punishing.").

Traditionally, advice has been thought of as communication. Something called knowledge of the world is said to pass from speaker to listener but a useful distinction has been made between knowing by acquaintance and knowing by description. Knowing because something you have done has had reinforcing consequences is very different from knowing because you have been told what to do. It is the difference between contingency-shaped and rule-governed behavior.

But why is advice taken? Children often do as they are told because they have been punished when they have not done so, and something of the sort is suggested in therapy when it is said that the therapist should become an authority figure, perhaps that of a father or mother. But children also do as they are told because positive reinforcers have followed. Parents who contrive consequences having that effect are said to reward their children for doing as they are told. Teachers contrive similar reinforcing consequences, such as commendation or good grades, to induce their students to study. There is no natural connection between the behavior and its consequence, but the practice is justified on the grounds that genuine consequences will take over in the world at large. Very little of that sort of thing is suitable in therapy. The only reinforcing consequences which induce clients to continue to take advice are largely to be found outside the clinic.

Therapists who resemble people whose advice has often proved to be worth taking have an advantage. Those who do not must work in other ways. In traditional terms, they must build "confidence" or "trust." That can sometimes be done by giving bits of advice which are not only easily followed but will almost certainly have reinforcing consequences.

Face-to-face advice may also take the form of rules for effective action. The proverbs and maxims of cultures are rules of that sort. Rules are especially useful because therapists may not be available to help in solving future problems. Not every problem can be solved by applying a rule, however, and therapists may need to take a further step and teach their clients how to construct their own rules. That means teaching them something about the analysis of behavior. It is usually easier than teaching them how to change their feelings or states of mind.

Health

Psychotherapy is said to promote mental health in the sense of helping people "feel well" and "think clearly." Behavior therapy promotes behavioral health in the sense that it helps people behave well, not in the sense of politely, but successfully. Is there an effect on physical health?

What people do may have obvious medical consequences—what they eat, how much they exercise, how carefully they avoid accidents, whether they smoke, drink, or take drugs, how often they expose themselves to infection, what medicines they take, how well they follow medical advice, and so on. Operant behavior therapists can improve medical health by helping people manage themselves in beneficial ways. But is there an additional, perhaps direct, effect?

Something of the sort is suggested when it is said that a given type of personality or neurosis is associated with a given type of physical health. If psychotherapists can change personalities or neuroses, they should be able to change health. But personality explains nothing until we have explained personality, and as an internal correlate of behavior a neurosis is no more useful here than

elsewhere. The "person" in personality once meant the mask worn by an actor in a Greek play. It defined him as a persona dramatis. The word "neurology" was invented in the early 19th century at about the same time as "phrenology." Phrenologists claimed to locate traits of character in the gross structure of the skull. Neurology went further inside to the gross structure of the nervous system. The important facts, then as now, were what people did. Behavior therapists turn to the contingencies of reinforcement responsible for the behavior that personality, neuroses and the like are said to explain.

To say that physical illness is due to stress, for example, does not explain the illness or point to any way to treat it until stress has been explained. If people are under stress because, for example, there are too many things they must do, the things they must do are the things to be changed. To do anything about an illness due to anxiety we must change the aversive circumstances responsible for what is thus felt. Some of the illness said to be due to discouragement or despair may be alleviated by restoring lost reinforcers, and illness due to hostility or fear by eliminating aversive consequences, especially at the hands of other people. Assertions of this sort do not imply a neglect of genetic factors. Behavior therapy is limited to changes which can be made during a person's lifetime.

A very different relation between behavior and health is implied when it is said that a critically ill patient simply "refuses to die" or that one with a favorable prognosis loses the "will to live." Examples of that sort are, of course, said to show the power of mind over matter. They suggest that being healthy is something one does. An ancient metaphor of the medical profession may be responsible. We "catch" a cold or "get" the measles. Engaged in a war with disease, we are attacked (we have a "heart attack") or struck down (we have a "stroke"). When infections invade us, much depends upon our "resistance." But good health is not contingent upon behavior in such a way as to reinforce "being healthy" as a kind of action.

How contingencies of operant reinforcement affect physiological processes is no doubt an important question. Can immunological reactions be conditioned in the Pavlovian manner, for example? But should the behavior therapist try to find out? Physiology has a special appeal to those who explain behavior in mentalistic terms; it seems to show what is really going on inside, what one is really talking about. Cognitive psychologists have turned to brain science for that reason. Behavior therapists may also turn to physiology if they lack confidence in their own methods, but those methods are equally objective. One cannot quarrel with the choice of medical science as a professional field, or even with philosophers who wish to examine their minds through introspection, but for every behavior therapist who, upon discovering some fact about behavior, then looks for a physiological explanation, there is one therapist the fewer to make further discoveries about behavior itself.

Feeling Well And Feeling Good

People usually seek both medical and behavior therapy because of how they feel. The physician changes what they feel in medical ways; behavior therapists change the contingencies of which what is felt is a function. The distinction between medical and behavior therapy resembles the distinction between feeling well and feeling good. One feels well who feels a healthy body, free of aches or pains. One feels good who feels a body which has been positively reinforced. Positive reinforcers please. We call them pleasant and the behavior they reinforce a pleasure. They please even when they are accidental. ("Happy" first meant "lucky").

What is felt in that way is apparently a strong probability of action and a freedom from aversive stimuli. We are "eager" to do things which have had reinforcing consequences and "feel better" in a world in which we do not have to do unpleasant things. We say that we are enjoying life or that life is good. We have no complaints because complaining is negatively reinforced behavior, and there are no negative reinforcers. Successful therapy builds strong behavior by removing unnecessary negative reinforcers and multiplying positive ones. Whether those whose behavior is thus strengthened live any longer than other people, they can be said to live well in another sense.

Finding a world in which one can live well in spite of infirmities is the theme of Enjoy Old Age, a little book written with the collaboration of Margaret Vaughan. There are medical imperfections in old age which cannot be avoided. Aversive consequences are more likely to follow whatever one does and reinforcing consequences less often. But the world of old people can often be changed so that, in spite of imperfections, one can enjoy more of one's life and perhaps even live a little longer.

Can something of the sort be done for everyone? My utopian novel, Walden Two published forty years ago, was a kind of fictional anticipation of what came to be called applied behavior analysis. It described a community in which governmental, religious and capitalistic agencies are replaced by face-to-face personal control. New members begin by following simple rules, with the help of instruction and counseling, and their behavior is soon taken over by carefully designed social contingencies. Both operant and respondent conditioning are used in therapy. Children learn to manage their emotions, for example, through desensitization. There is little or no negative reinforcement or punishment. (Curiously enough, many critics complained that the citizens of Walden Two are too happy).

Like all utopians, Walden Two tries to solve the problems of a culture all at once rather than one by one. We shall probably not move very rapidly toward that kind of a better world but it is, I think, worth considering as a model. Every advance in behavior therapy moves in that direction because it begins by changing the world in which people live and then, only indirectly, what they do and feel.

For thousands of years philosophers have talked about the behavior of people with whom they have had no contact and about whose feelings or states of mind they could not ask. Instead they have disembodied mental events and discussed them quite apart from anyone in whom they occur. They have said that frustration breeds aggression, that greed overrides caution, that jealousy destroys affection, and so on. Statements of that sort are fairly common in current discussions of government, religion, economics and the other so-called (but in that case miscalled) behavior sciences. By rejecting feelings and states of mind as the initiating causes of behavior, and turning instead to the environmental conditions responsible both for what people do and feel while doing it, behavior analysts, and with them behavior therapists, can approach the larger problems of human behavior in a much more effective way.

A problem of great importance remains to be solved. Rather than build a world in which we shall all live well, we must stop building one in which it will be impossible to live at all. That is wholly a problem in human behavior. How are people to be induced to consume no more than they need, refrain from doing things which unnecessarily pollute the environment, have only

enough children to replace themselves, and solve international problems without risking a nuclear war? The contingencies under which people now live are maintained by governments, religions and economic enterprises, but they in turn are controlled by fairly immediate consequences which are increasingly incompatible with the future of the world. We need to construct relatively immediate consequences of human behavior which will act as the remoter ones would act if they were here now. That will not be easy, but at least we can say that we have a science and a technology which are addressing themselves to the basic problem.

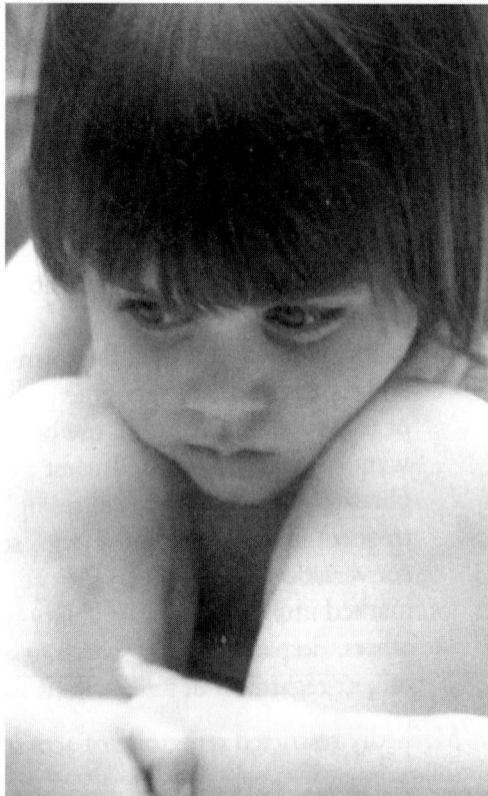

Figure 8-4. Avoidance of eye contact is an initial target behavior in the operant treatment of autism. (Craig Hammell/The Stock Market.)

READING 8D

BEHAVIORAL TREATMENT AND NORMAL EDUCATION AND INTELLECTUAL FUNCTIONING IN YOUNG AUTISTIC CHILDREN

O. Ivar Lovaas

As described in Chapter 4, autism is is an extremely serious childhood mental disorder. Its positive symptoms (maladaptive behavioral excesses) include nonfunctional stereotypic rituals, repetitive motor mannerisms, hand flapping, spinning, and self-injury. Negative symptoms (maladaptive behavioral deficiencies) include language absence or delay, lack of social involvement, and failure to imitate adaptive models. Various treatments have been attempted by many perspectives with limited success. Symptomatic improvement has often been the objective of treatment; "cure", an elusive abstraction.

O. Ivar Lovaas, of the University of California at Los Angeles, has been a prominent and controversial behavior therapist for more than thirty years. Lovaas' work gained notoriety in 1969. Three severely retarded, institutionalized children were referred to him. They were reputed to be the worst cases of self-destructiveness in Southern California, and had caused serious injury through the slamming of their bodies, banging of their heads, and tearing of their flesh. Lovaas theorized that the children were largely unattended by the staff, except for when they were harming themselves. Self-destructive behavior was being unintentionally reinforced.

He instructed the staff to "catch the children being good." Minor self-destruction was to be ignored. However, severe self-destruction was followed by the administration of an aversive electric shock. A 1-second jolt was delivered by a "hand-held inductorium"('Hot-shot', by Hot-shots Products Company, Inc., Savage, Minnesota), more commonly employed to motivate recalcitrant cattle. The shock felt "like a dentist drilling on an unanesthetized tooth". However, the self-destructive behavior of Greg, John, and Linda was virtually eliminated (Lovaas and Simmons, 1969). Aversion remains controversial today.

Lovaas began a treatment program for autistic children at UCLA in 1970. The program involved intensive behavior therapy, primarily operant. The results of some of this work, published in the following article, were astonishing. Behavior therapy proved to benefit even the most severely impaired children, conventionally thought to be beyond habilitation. Lovaas brought to fruition the optimism expressed by Skinner in the previous article. He surpassed Watson's unfulfilled boast to shape the development of "a dozen healthy infants" by successfully treating nine children with autism.

References

Lovaas, O. I. and Simmons, J .Q. (1969, Fall). Manipulation of Self-Destruction in Three Retarded Children. *Journal of Applied Behavior Analysis*, 3(2), 143-157.

Kanner (1943) defined autistic children as children who exhibit (a) serious failure to develop relationships with other people before 30 months of age, (b) problems in development of normal language, (c) ritualistic and obsessional behaviors ("insistence on sameness"), and (d) potential for normal intelligence. A more complete behavioral definition has been provided elsewhere (Lovaas, Koegel, Simmons, & Long, 1973). The etiology of autism is not known, and the outcome is very poor. In a follow-up study on young autistic children, Rutter (1970) reported that only 1.5% of his group ($n = 63$) had achieved normal functioning. About 35% showed fair or good adjustment, usually required some degree of supervision, experienced some difficulties with people, had no personal friends, and showed minor oddities of behavior. The majority (more than 60%) remained severely handicapped and were living in hospitals for mentally retarded or psychotic individuals or in other protective settings. Initial IQ scores appeared stable over time. Other studies (Brown, 1969; DeMyer et al., 1973; Eisenberg, 1956; Freeman, Ritvo, Needleman, & Yokota, 1985; Havelkova, 1968) report similar data. Higher scores on IQ tests, communicative speech, and appropriate play are considered to be prognostic of better outcome (Lotter, 1967).

Medically and psychodynamically oriented therapies have not proven effective in altering outcome (DeMyer, Hingtgen, & Jackson, 1981). No abnormal environmental etiology has been identified within the children's families (Lotter, 1967). At present, the most promising treatment for autistic persons is behavior modification as derived from modern learning theory (DeMyer, et al., 1981). Empirical results from behavioral intervention with autistic children have been both positive and negative. On the positive side, behavioral treatment can build complex behaviors, such as language, and can help to suppress pathological behaviors, such as aggression and self-stimulatory behavior. Clients vary widely in the amount of gains obtained but show treatment gains in proportion to the time devoted to treatment. On the negative side, treatment gains have been specific to the particular environment in which the client was treated, substantial relapse has been observed at follow-up, and no client has

been reported as recovered (Lovaas et al., 1973).

The present article reports a behavioral intervention project (begun in 1970) that sought to maximize behavioral treatment gains by treating autistic children during most of their waking hours for many years. Treatment included all significant persons in all significant environments. Furthermore, the project focuses on very young autistic children (below the age of 4 years) because it was assumed that younger children would be less likely to discriminate between environments and therefore more likely to generalize and to maintain their treatment gains. Finally, it was assumed that it would be easier to successfully mainstream a very young autistic child into preschool than it would be to mainstream an older autistic child into primary school.

It may be helpful to hypothesize an outcome of the present study from a developmental or learning point of view. One may assume that normal children learn from their everyday environments most of their waking hours. Autistic children, conversely, do not learn from similar environments. We hypothesized that construction of a special, intense, and comprehensive learning environment for very young autistic children would allow some of them to catch up with their normal peers by first grade.

METHOD

Subjects

Subjects were enrolled for treatment if they met three criteria: (a) independent diagnosis of autism from a medical doctor or a licensed PhD psychologist, (b) chronological age (CA) less than 40 months if mute and less than 46 months if echolalic, and (c) prorated mental age (PMA) of 11 months or more at a CA of 30 months. The last criterion excluded 15% of the referrals.

The clinical diagnosis of autism emphasized emotional detachment, extreme interpersonal isolation, little if any toy or peer play, language disturbance (mutism or echolalia), excessive rituals, and onset in infancy. The diagnosis was based on a structured psychiatric interview with parents, on observations of the child's free-play behaviors, on psychological testing of intelligence, and on access to pediatric examinations. Over the 15 years of the project, the exact wording of the diagnosis changed slightly in compliance with changes in the *Diagnostic and Statistical Manual of Mental Disorders* (DSM—III: American Psychiatric Association, 1980). During the last years, the diagnosis was made in compliance with DSM—III criteria (p. 87). In almost all cases, the diagnosis of autism had been made prior to family contact with the project. Except for one case each in the experimental group and Control Group 1, all cases were diagnosed by staff of the Department of Child Psychiatry, University of California, Los Angeles (UCLA) School of Medicine. Members of that staff have contributed to the writing of the DSM—III and to the diagnosis of autism adopted by the National Society for Children and Adults with Autism. If the diagnosis of autism was not made, the case was referred elsewhere. In other words, the project did not select its cases. More than 90% of the subjects received two or more independent diagnoses, and agreement on the diagnosis of autism was 100%. Similarly high agreement was not reached for subjects who scored within the profoundly retarded range on intellectual functioning (PMA of 11 months); these subjects were excluded from the study.

Treatment Conditions

Subjects were assigned to one of two groups: an intensive-treatment experimental group (*n* = 19) that received more than 40 hours of one-to-one treatment per week, or the minimal treatment Control Group 1 (*n* = 19) that received 10 hours or less of one-to-one treatment per week. Control Group I was used to gain further information about the rate of spontaneous improvement in very young autistic children, especially those selected by the same agency that provided the diagnostic work-up for the intensive treatment experimental group. Both treatment groups received treatment for 2 or more years. Strict random assignment (e.g., based on a coin flip) to these groups could not be used due to parent protest and ethical considerations. Instead, subjects were assigned to the experimental group unless there was an insufficient number of staff members available to render treatment (an assessment made prior to contact with the fami-

ly). Two subjects were assigned to Control Group 1 because they lived further away from UCLA than a 1-hr drive, which made sufficient staffing unavailable to those clients. Because fluctuations in staff availability were not associated in any way with client characteristics, it was assumed that this assignment would produce unbiased groups. A large number of pretreatment measures were collected to test this assumption. Subjects did not change group assignment. Except for two families who left the experimental group within the first 6 months (this group began with 21 subjects), all families stayed with their groups from beginning to end.

Assessments

Pretreatment mental age (MA) scores were based on the following scales (in order of the frequency of their use): the Bayley Scales of Infant Development (Bayley, 1955), the Cattell Infant Intelligence Scale (Cattell, 1960), the Stanford-Binet Intelligence Scale (Thorndike, 1972), and the Gesell Infant Development Scale (Gesell, 1949). The first three scales were admin-istered to 90% of the subjects, and relative usage of these scales was similar in each group. Testing was carried out by graduate students in psychology who worked under the supervision of clinical psychologists at UCLA or licensed PhD psychologists at other agencies. The examiner chose the test that would best accommodate each subject's developmental level, and this decision was reached independently of the project staff. Five subjects were judged to be untestable (3 in the experimental group and 2 in Control Group 1). Instead, the Vineland Social Maturity Scale (Doll, 1953) was used to estimate their MAs (with the mother as informant). To adjust for variations in MA scores as a function of the subject's CA at the time of test administration, PMA scores were calculated for a CA at 30 months (MA/CA $\times$ 30).

Behavioral observations were based on videotaped recordings of the subject's free-play behavior in a playroom equipped with several simple early-childhood toys. These videotaped recordings were subsequently scored for amount of (a) *self-stimulatory behaviors,* defined as prolonged ritualistic, repetitive, and stereotyped behavior such as body-rocking, prolonged gazing at lights, excessive hand-flapping, twirling the body as a top, spinning or lining of objects, and licking or smelling of objects or wall surfaces; (b) *appropriate play behaviors,* defined as those limiting the use of toys in the playroom to their intended purposes, such as pushing the truck on the floor, pushing buttons on the toy cash register, putting a record on the record player, and banging with the toy hammer; and (c) *recognizable words,* defined to include any recognizable word, independent of whether the subject used it in a meaningful context or for communicative purposes. One observer who was naive about subjects' group placement scored all tapes after being trained to agree with two experienced observers (using different training tapes from similar subjects). Interobserver reliability was scored on 20% of the tapes (randomly selected) and was computed for each category of behavior for each subject by dividing the sum of observer agreements by the sum of agreements and disagreements. These scores were then summed and averaged across subjects. The mean agreement (based both on occurrences and nonoccurrences) was 91% for self-stimulatory behavior, 85% for appropriate play behavior, and 100% for recognizable words. A more detailed description of these behavioral recordings has been provided elsewhere (Lovaas et al., 1973).

A 1-hr parent interview about the subjects' earlier history provided some diagnostic and descriptive information. Subjects received a score of 1 for each of the following variables parents reported: no recognizable words; no toy play (failed to use toys for their intended function); lack of emotional attachment (failed to respond to parents' affection); apparent sensory deficit (parents had suspected their child to be blind or deaf because the child exhibited no or minimal eye contact and showed an unusually high pain threshold); no peer play (subject did not show interactive play with peers); self-stimulatory behavior; tantrums (aggression toward family members or self); and no toilet training. These 8 measures from parents' intake interviews were summed to provide a sum pathology score. The intake interview also provided information about abnormal speech (0 = normal and meaningful language, however limited; 1 = echolalic language used meaningfully (e.g., to express needs); 2 = echolalia; and 3 = mute); age of walking; number of siblings in the family; socioeconomic status of the father; sex; and neurological examinations (including EEGs and CAT scans) that resulted in findings of pathology. Finally, CA at first diagnosis and at the beginning of the present treatment were recorded. This yielded a total of 20 pretreatment measures, 8 of which were collapsed into 1 measure (sum pathology).

A brief clinical description of the experimental group at intake follows (identical to that for Control Group 1): Only 2 of the 19 subjects obtained scores within the normal range of intellectual functioning; 7 scored in the moderately retarded range, and 10 scored in the severely retarded range. No subject evidenced pretend or imaginary play, only 2 evidenced *complex* (several different or heterogenous behaviors that together formed one activity) play, and the remaining subjects showed *simple* (the same elementary but appropriate response made repeatedly) play. One subject showed minimal appropriate speech, 7 were echolalic, and 11 were mute. According to the literature that describes the developmental delays of autistic children in general, the autistic subjects in the present study constituted an average (or below average) sample of such children.

Posttreatment measures were recorded as follows: Between the ages of 6 and 7 years (when a subject would ordinarily have completed first grade), information about the subjects' first-grade placement was sought and validated; about the same time, an IQ score was obtained. Testing was carried out by examiners who were naive about the subjects' group placement. Different scales were administered to accommodate different developmental levels. For example, a subject with a regular educational placement received a Wechsler Intelligence Scale for Children—Revised (WISC—R; Wechsler, 1974) or a Stanford-Binet Intelligence Scale (Thorndike, 1972), whereas a subject in an autistic/ retarded class received a nonverbal test like the Merrill-Palmer Pre-School Performance Test (Stutsman, 1948). In all instances of subjects having achieved a normal IQ score, the testing was eventually replicated by other examiners.

The scales (in order of the frequency of usage) included the WISC—R (Wechsler, 1974), the Stanford-Binet (Thorndike, 1972), the Peabody Picture Vocabulary Test (Dunn, 1981), the Wechsler Pre-School Scale (Wechsler, 1967), the Bayley Scales of Infant Development (Bayley, 1955), the Cattell Infant Intelligence Scale (Cattell, 1960), and the Leiter International Performance Scale (Leiter, 1959). Subjects received a score of 3 for *normal functioning* if they received a score on the WISC—R or Stan-ford-Binet in the normal range, completed first grade in a normal class in a school for normal children, and were advanced to the second grade by the teacher. Subjects received a score of 2 if they were placed in first-grade in a smaller *aphasia* (language delayed, language handicapped, or learning disabled) class. Placement in the aphasia class implied a higher level of functioning than placement in classes for the autistic/retarded, but the diagnosis of autism was almost always retained. A score of 1 was given if the first-grade placement was in a class for the autistic/retarded and if the child's IQ score fell within the severely retarded range.

Treatment Procedure

Each subject in the experimental group was assigned several well trained student therapists who worked (part-time) with the subject in the subject's home, school, and community for an average of 40 hr per week for 2 or more years. The parents worked as part of the treatment team throughout the intervention; they were extensively trained in the treatment procedures so that treatment could take place for almost all of the subjects' waking hours, 365 days a year. A detailed presentation of the treatment procedure has been presented in a teaching manual (Lovaas et al., 1980). The conceptual basis of the treatment was reinforcement (operant) theory; treatment relied heavily on discrimination-learning data and methods. Various behavioral deficiencies were targeted, and separate programs were designed to accelerate development for each behavior. High rates of aggressive and self-stimulatory behaviors were reduced by being ignored; by the use of time-out; by the shaping of alternate, more socially acceptable forms of behavior; and (as a last resort) by the delivery of a loud "no" or a slap on the thigh contingent upon the presence of the undesirable behavior. Contingent physical aversives were not used in the control group because inadequate staffing in that group did not allow for adequate teaching of alternate, socially appropriate behaviors.

During the first year, treatment goals consisted of reducing self-stimulatory and aggressive behaviors, building compliance to elementary verbal requests, teaching imitation, establishing the beginnings of appropriate toy play, and promoting the extension of the treatment into the family. The second year of treatment emphasized teaching expressive and early abstract language and interactive play with peers. Treatment was also extended into the community to teach children to function within a preschool group. The third year emphasized the teaching of appropriate and varied expression of emotions; preacademic tasks like reading, writing, and arithmetic; and *observational learning* (learning by observing other children learn). Subjects were enrolled only in those preschools where the teacher helped to carry out the treatment program. Considerable effort was exercised to mainstream subjects in a normal (average and public) preschool placement and to avoid initial placement in special education classes with the detrimental effects of exposure to other autistic children. This occasionally entailed withholding the subject's diagnosis of autism. If the child became known as autistic (or as "a very difficult child") during the first year in preschool, the child was encouraged to enroll in another, unfamiliar school (to start fresh). After preschool, placement in public education classes was determined by school personnel. All children who successfully completed normal kindergarten successfully completed first grade and subsequent normal grades. Children who were observed to be experiencing educational and psychological problems received their school placement through Individualized Educational Plan (IEP) staffings (attended by educators and psychologists) in accordance with the Education For All Handicapped Children Act of 1975.

All subjects who went on to a normal first grade were reduced in treatment from the 40 hr per week characteristic of the first 2 years to 10 hr or less per week during kindergarten. After a subject had started first grade, the project maintained a minimal (at most) consultant relationship with some families. In two cases, this consultation and the subsequent correction of problem behaviors were judged to be essential in maintaining treatment gains. Subjects who did not recover in the experimental group received 40 hr or more per week of one-to-one treatment for more than 6 years (more than 14,000 hr of one-to-one treatment), with some improvement shown each year but with only 1 subject recovering.

Subjects in Control Group 1 received the same kind of treatment as those in the experimental group but with less intensity (less than 10 hr of one-to-one treatment per week) and without systematic physical aversives. In addition, these subjects received a variety of treatments from other sources in the community such as those provided by small special education classes.

Control Group 2 consisted of 21 subjects selected from a larger group ($N = 62$) of young autistic children studied by Freeman et al. (1985). These subjects came from the same agency that diagnosed 95% of our other subjects. Data from Control Group 2 helped to guard against the possibility that subjects who had been referred to us for treatment constituted a subgroup with particularly favorable or unfavorable outcomes. To provide a group of subjects similar to those in the experimental group and Control Group 1, subjects for Control Group 2 were selected if they were 42 months old or younger when first tested, had IQ scores above 40 at intake, and had fol-

low-up testing at 6 years of age. These criteria resulted in the selection of 21 subjects. Subjects in Control Group 2 were treated like Control Group 1 subjects but were not treated by the Young Autism Project described here.

RESULTS

Pretreatment Comparisons

Eight pretreatment variables from the experimental group and Control Group 1 (CA at first diagnosis, CA at onset of treatment, PMA, sum pathology, abnormal speech, self-stimulatory behavior, appropriate toy play, and recognizable words) were subjected to a multivariate analysis of variance (MANOVA; Brecht & Woodward, 1984). The means and F ratios from this analysis are presented in Table 1. As can be seen, there were no significant differences between the groups except for CA at onset of our treatment (p <.05). Control subjects were 6 months older on the average than experimental subjects (mean CAs of 35 months vs. 41 months, respectively). These differences probably reflect the delay of control subjects in their initiation into the treatment project because of staff shortages; analysis will show that differential CAs are not significantly related to outcome. To ascertain whether another test would reveal a statistically significant difference between the groups on toy play, descriptions of the subjects' toy play (taken from the videotaped recordings) were typed on cards and rated for their developmental level by psychology students who were naive about the purpose of the ratings and subject group assignment.

Table 1
Means and F Ratios From Comparisons Between Groups on Intake Variables

Group	Diagnosis CA	Treatment CA	PMA	Recognizable words	Toy play	Self stimulation	Sum pathology	Abnormal speech
Experimental	32.0	34.6	18.8	.42	28.2	12.1	6.9	2.4
Control 1	35.3	40.9	17.1	.58	20.2	19.6	6.4	2.2
F[a]		1.58	4.02*	1.49	.92	2.76	3.37	.82	.36

Note. CA = chronological age; PMA = prorated mental age; Experimental group $n = 19$; Control Group 1 $n = 19$.
[a]$df = 1.36$ *$p < .05$

The ratings were reliable among students (r = .79, $p < .001$), and an F test showed no significant difference in developmental levels of toy play between the two groups.

The respective means from the experimental group and Control 1 on the eight variables from the parent interview were .89 and .74 for sensory deficit, .63 and .42 for adult rejection, .58 and .47 for no recognizable words, .53 and .63 for no toy play, 1.0 and 1.0 for no peer play, .95 and .89 for body self-stimulation, .89 and .79 for tantrums, and .68 and .63 for no toilet training. The experimental group and Control Group 1 were also similar in onset of walking (6 vs. 8 early walkers; 1 vs. 2 late walkers), number of siblings in the family (1.26 in each group), socioeconomic status of the father (Level 49 vs. Level 54 according to 1950 Bureau of the Census standards), boys to girls (16:3 vs. 11:8); and number of subjects referred for neurological examinations (10 vs. 15) who showed signs of damage (0 vs. 1). The numbers of favorable versus unfavorable prognostic signs (directions of differences) on the pretreatment variables divide themselves equally between the groups. In short, the two groups appear to have been comparable at intake.

Follow-Up Data

Subjects' PMA at intake, follow-up educational placement, and IQ scores were subjected to a MANOVA that contrasted the experimental group with Control Groups 1 and 2. At intake, there were no significant differences between the experimental group and the control groups. At follow-up, the experimental group was significantly higher than the control groups on educational placement ($p < .001$) and IQ ($p < .01$). The two control groups did not differ significantly at intake or at follow-up. In short, data from Control Group 2 replicate those from Control Group 1 and further validate the effectiveness of our experimental treatment program. Data are given in Table 2 that show the group means from pretreatment PMA and posttreatment educational placement and IQ scores. The table also shows the F ratios and significance levels of the three group comparisons.

Table 2

Means and F Ratios for Measures at Pretreatment and Posttreatment

Group	Intake PMA	Follow-up EDP	IQ
Means			
Experimental	18.8	2.37	83.3
Control 1	17.1	1.42	52.2
Control 2	17.6	1.57	57.5
F ratios[a]			
Experimental x Control 1	1.47	23.6**	14.4**
Experimental x Control 2	0.77	17.6**	10.4*
Control 1 x Control 2	0.14	0.63	0.45*

Note: PMA = prorated mental age; EDP = educational placement; Experimental group, n = 19; Control Group 1, n = 19; Control Group 2, n = 21.

[a] df = 1.56   *$p < .01$.   **$p < .001$.

In descriptive terms, the 19-subject experimental group shows 9 children (47%) who successfully passed through normal first grade in a public school and obtained an average or above average score on IQ tests (M = 107, range = 94-120). Eight subjects (42%) passed first grade in aphasia classes and obtained a mean IQ score within the mildly retarded range of intellectual functioning (M = 70, range = 56-95). Only two children (10%) were placed in classes for autistic/retarded children and scored in the profoundly retarded range (IQ < 30).

There were substantial increases in the subjects' levels of intellectual functioning after treatment. The experimental group subjects gained on the average of 30 IQ points over Control Group 1 subjects. Thus the number of subjects who scored within the normal range of intellectual functioning increased from 2 to 12, whereas the number of subjects within the moderate-to-severe range of intellectual retardation dropped from 10 to 3. As of 1986, the achievements of experimental group subjects have remained stable. Only 2 subjects have been classified: 1 subject (now 18 years old) was moved from an aphasia to a normal classroom after the sixth grade; 1 subject (now 13 years old) was moved from an aphasia to an autistic/retarded class placement.

Table 3

Educational Placement and Mean and Range of IQ at Follow-Up

Group	Recovered	Aphasic	Autistic/Retarded
Experimental			
N	9	8	2
M IQ	107	70	30
Range	94-120	6-95	_[a]
Control Group I			
N	0	8	11
M IQ	–	74	36
Range	–	30-102	20-73
Control Group 2			
N	1	10	10
M IQ	99	67	44
Range	–	49-81	35-54

Note: Dashes indicate no score or no entry. [a]Both children received the same score.

The MA and IQ scores of the two control groups remained virtually unchanged between intake and followup, consistent with findings from other studies (Freeman et al., 1985; Rutter, 1970). The stability of the IQ scores of the young autistic children, as reported in the Freeman et al. study, is particularly relevant for the present study because it reduces the possibility of spontaneous recovery effects. In descriptive terms, the combined followup data from the control groups show that their subjects fared poorly: Only 1 subject (2%) achieved normal functioning as evidenced by normal first-grade placement and an IQ of 99 on the WISC—R; 18 subjects (45%) were in aphasia classes (mean IQ = 70, range = 30-101); and 21 subjects (53%) were in classes for the autistic/retarded (mean IQ = 40, range = 20-73). Table 3 provides a convenient descriptive summary of the main follow-up data from the three groups.

One final control procedure subjected 4 subjects in the experimental group (Ackerman, 1980) and 4 subjects in Control Group 1 (McEachin & Leaf, 1984) to a treatment intervention in which one component of treatment (the loud "no" and occasional slap on the thigh contingent on self-stimulatory, aggressive, and non-compliant behavior) was at first withheld

and then introduced experimentally. A within-subjects replication design was used across subjects, situations, and behaviors, with baseline observations varying from 3 weeks to 2 years after treatment had started (using contingent positive reinforcement only). During baseline, when the contingent-aversive component was absent, small and unstable reductions were observed in the large amount of inappropriate behaviors, and similar small and unstable increases were observed in appropriate behaviors such as play and language. These changes were insufficient to allow for the subjects' successful mainstreaming. Introduction of contingent aversives resulted in a sudden and stable reduction in the inappropriate behaviors and a sudden and stable increase in appropriate behaviors. This experimental intervention helps to establish two points: First, at least one component in the treatment program functioned to produce change, which helps to reduce the effect of placebo variables. Second, this treatment component affected both the experimental and control groups in a similar manner, supporting the assumption that the two groups contained similar subjects.

Analyses of variance were carried out on the eight pretreatment variables to determine which variables, if any, were significantly related to outcome (gauged by educational placement and IQ) in the experimental group and Control Group 1. Prorated mental age was significantly ($p < .03$) related to outcome in both groups, a finding that is consistent with reports from other investigators (DeMyer et al., 1981). In addition, abnormal speech was significantly ($p < .01$) related to outcome in Control Group 1. Chronological age at onset of our treatment was not related to outcome, which is important because the two groups differed significantly on this variable at intake (by 6 months). The failure of CA to relate to outcome may be based on the very young age of all subjects at onset of treatment.

Conceivably, a linear combination of pretreatment variables could have predicted outcome in the experimental group. Using a discriminant analysis (Ray, 1982) with the eight variables used in the first multivariate analysis, it was possible to predict perfectly the 9 subjects who did achieve normal functioning and no subject was predicted to achieve this outcome who did not. In this analysis, PMA was the only variable that was significantly related to outcome. Finally, when this prediction equation was applied to Control Group I subjects, 8 were predicted to achieve normal functioning with intensive treatment; this further verifies the similarity between the experimental group and Control Group I prior to treatment.

DISCUSSION

This article reports the results of intensive behavioral treatment for young autistic children. Pretreatment measures revealed no significant differences between the intensively treated experimental group and the minimally treated control groups. At follow-up, experimental group subjects did significantly better than control group subjects. For example, 47% of the experimental group achieved normal intellectual and educational functioning in contrast to only 2% of the control group subjects.

The study incorporated certain methodological features designed to increase confidence in the effectiveness of the experimental group treatment:

1. Pretreatment differences between the experimental and control groups were minimized in four ways. First, the assignment of subjects to groups was as random as was ethically possible. The assignment apparently produced unbiased groups as evidenced by similar scores on the 20 pretreatment measures and by the prediction that an equal number of Control Group 1 and experimental group subjects would have achieved normal functioning had the former subjects received intensive treatment. Second, the experimental group was not biased by receiving subjects with a favorable diagnosis or biased IQ testing because both diagnosis and IQ tests were constant across groups. Third, the referral process did not favor the project cases because there were no significant differences between Control Groups I and 2 at intake or follow-up, even though Control Group 2 subjects were referred to others by the same agency. Fourth, subjects stayed within their groups, which preserved the original (unbiased) group assignment.

2. A favorable outcome could have been caused not by the experimental treatment but by the attitudes and expectations of the staff. There are two findings that contradict this possibility of treatment agency (placebo) effects. First, because Control Group 2 subjects had no contact with the project, and because there was no difference between Control Groups 1 and 2 at follow-up, placebo effects appear implausible. Second, the within-subjects study showed that at least one treatment component contributed to the favorable outcome in the intensive treatment (experimental) group.

3. It may be argued that the treatment worked because the subjects were not truly autistic. This is counterindicated by the high reliability of the independent diagnosis and by the outcome data from the control groups, which are consistent with those reported by other investigators (Brown, 1969; DeMeyer et al., 1973; Eisenberg, 1986; Freeman et al., 1985; Havelkova, 1968; Rutter, 1970) for groups of young autistic children diagnosed by a variety of other agencies.

4. The spontaneous recovery rate among very young autistic children is unknown, and without a control group the favorable outcome in the experimental group could have been attributed to spontaneous recovery. However, the poor outcome in the similarly constituted Control Groups 1 and 2 would seem to eliminate spontaneous recovery as a contributing factor to the favorable outcome in the experimental group. The stability of the IQ test scores in the young autistic children examined by Freeman et al. (1985) attests once again to the chronicity of autistic behaviors and serves to further negate the effects of spontaneous recovery.

5. Posttreatment data showed that the effects of treatment (a) were substantial and easily detected, (b) were apparent on comprehensive, objective, and socially meaningful variables (IQ and school placement), and (c) were consistent with a very large body of prior research on the application of learning theory to the treatment and education of developmentally disabled persons and with the very extensive (100-year-old) history of psychology laboratory work on learning processes in man and animals. In short, the favorable outcome reported for the intensive-treatment experimental group can in all likelihood be attributed to treatment.

A number of measurement problems remain to be solved. For example, play, communicative speech, and IQ scores define the characteristics of autistic children and are considered predictors of outcome. Yet the measurement of these variables is no easy task. Consider play. First, play undoubtedly varies with the kinds of toys provided. Second, it is difficult to distinguish low levels of toy play (simple and repetitive play associated with young, normal children) from high levels of self-stimulatory behavior (a psychotic attribute associated with autistic children). Such problems introduce variability that needs immediate attention before research can proceed in a meaningful manner.

The term *normal functioning* has been used to describe children who successfully passed normal first grade and achieved an average IQ on the WISC—R. But questions can be asked about whether these children truly recovered from autism. On the one hand, educational placement is a particularly valuable measure of progress because it is sensitive to both educational accomplishments and social-emotional functions. Also continual promotion from grade to grade is made not by one particular teacher but by several teachers. School personnel describe these children as indistinguishable from their normal friends. On the other hand, certain residual deficits may remain in the normal functioning group that cannot be detected by teachers and parents and can only be isolated on closer psychological assessment, particularly as these children grow older. Answers to such questions will soon be forthcoming in a more comprehensive follow-up (McEachin, 1987).

Several questions about treatment remain. It is unlikely that a therapist or investigator could replicate our treatment program for the experimental group without prior extensive theoretical and supervised practical experience in one-to-one behavioral treatment with developmentally disabled clients as described here and without demonstrated effectiveness in teaching complex behavioral repertoires as in imitative behavior and abstract language. In the within-subjects studies that were reported, contingent aversives were isolated as one significant variable. It is therefore unlikely that treatment effects could be replicated without this component. Many treatment variables are left unexplored, such as the effect of normal peers. Furthermore, the successful mainstreaming of a 2-4-year-old into a normal preschool group is much easier than the mainstreaming of an older autistic child into the primary grades. This last point underscores the importance of early intervention and places limits on the generalization of our data to older autistic children.

Historically, psychodynamic theory has maintained a strong influence on research and treatment with autistic children, offering some hope for recovery through experiential manipulations. By the mid-1960s, an increasing number of studies reported that psychodynamic practitioners were unable to deliver on that promise (Rimland, 1964). One reaction to those failures was an emphasis on organic theories of autism that offered little or no hope for major improvements through psychological and educational interventions. In a comprehensive review of research on autism, DeMyer et al. (1981) concluded that "[in the past] psychotic children were believed to be *potentially* capable of normal functioning in virtually all areas of development . . . during the decade of the 1970s it was the rare investigator who even gave lip-service to such previously held notions . . . infantile autism is a type of developmental disorder accompanied by severe and, to a large extent, permanent intellectual/behavioral deficits" (p. 432).

The following points can now be made. First, at least two distinctively different groups emerged from the follow-up data in the experimental group. Perhaps this finding implies different etiologies. If so, future theories of autism will have to identify these groups of children. Second, on the basis of testing to date, the recovered children show no permanent intellectual or behavioral deficits and their language appears normal, contrary to the position that many have postulated (Rutter, 1974; Churchill, 1978) but consistent with Kanner's (1943) position that autistic children possess potentially normal or superior intelligence. Third, at intake, all subjects evidenced deficiencies across a wide range of behaviors, and during treatment they showed a broad improvement across all observed behaviors. The kind of (hypothesized) neural damage that mediates a particular kind of behavior, such as language (Rutter, 1974), is not consistent with these data.

Although serious problems remain for exactly defining autism or identifying its etiology, one encouraging conclusion can be stated: Given a group of children who show the kinds of behavioral deficits and excesses evident in our pretreatment measures, such children will continue to manifest similar severe psychological handicaps later in life unless subjected to intensive behavioral treatment that can indeed significantly alter that outcome.

These data promise a major reduction in the emotional hardships of families with autistic children. The treatment procedures described here may also prove equally effective with other childhood disorders, such as childhood schizophrenia. Certain important, practical implications in these findings may also be noted. The treatment schedule of subjects who achieved normal functioning could be reduced from 40 hr week to infrequent visits even after the first 2 years of treatment. The assignment of one full-time special-education teacher for 2 years would cost an estimated $40,000, in contrast to the nearly $2 million incurred (in direct costs alone) by each client requiring life-long institutionalization.

References

Ackerman, A. B. (1980). *The contribution of punishment to the treatment of preschool aged children.* Unpublished doctoral dissertation. University of California, Los Angeles.

American Psychiatric Association. (1980). *Diagnostic and statistical manual of mental disorders* (3rd ed.). Washington, DC: Author.

Bayley, N. (1955). On the growth of intelligence. *American Psychologist 10,* 805-818.

Brecht, M.L., & Woodward J.A. (1984). MANOVA: A univariate/multivariate analysis of variance program for the personal computer. *Educational and Psychological Measurement 44,* 169-173.

Brown, J. (1969). Adolescent development of children with infantile psychosis. *Seminars in Psychiatry 17,* 9-89.

Cattell, P. (1960). *The measurement of intelligence of infants and young children.* New York: Psychological Corporation.

Churchill, D. W. (1978). Language: The problem beyond conditioning. In M. Rutter & E. Schopler (Eds.), *Autism: A reappraisal of concepts and treatment* (pp. 71-85). New York: Plenum.

DeMyer, M. K., Barton, S., DeMyer, W. E., Norton, J. A., Allen, J., & Steele, R. (1973). Prognosis in autism: A follow-up study. *Journal of Autism and Childhood Schizophrenia 3,* 199-246.

DeMyer, M. K., Hingtgen, J. N., & Jackson, R. K. (1981). Infantile autism reviewed: A decade of research. *Schizophrenia Bulletin 7,* 388451.

Doll, E. A. (1953). *The measurement of social competence.* Minneapolis, MN: Minneapolis Educational Test Bureau.

Dunn, L. M. (1981). *Peabody Picture Vocabulary Test.* Circle River, MI: American Guidance Service.

Education for All Handicapped Children Act of 1975. Washington, DC: *Congressional Record.*

Eisenberg, L. (1956). The autistic child in adolescence. *American Journal of Psychiatry 11,* 2607-612.

Freeman B. J., Ritvo, E. R., Needleman, R., & Yokota, A. (1985). The stability of cognitive and linguistic parameters in autism: A 5-year study. *Journal of the American Academy of Child Psychiatry 24,* 290-311.

Gesell, A. (1949). *Gesell Developmental Schedules.* New York: Psychological Corporation.

Havelkova, M. (1988). Follow-up study of 71 children diagnosed as psychotic in preschool age. *American Journal of Orthopsychiatry 38,* 846-857.

Kanner, L. (1943). Autistic disturbances of affective contact. *Nervous Child 2,* 217-250.

Leiter, R. G. (1959). Part I of the manual for the 1948 revision of the Leiter International Performance Scale: Evidence of the reliability and validity of the Leiter tests. *Psychology Service Center Journal 11.*

Lotter, V. (1967). Epidemiology of autistic condition in young children: II. Some characteristics of parents and children. *Social Psychiatry, 1,* 163-173.

Lovaas, O. I., Ackerman, A. B., Alexander, D., Firestone, P., Perkins, J., & Young, D. (1980). *Teaching developmentally disabled children. The me book.* Austin, TX: Pro-Ed.

Lovaas, O. I., Koegel, R. L., Simmons, J . Q ., & Long, J. (1973). Some generalization and follow-up measures on autistic children in behavior therapy *Journal of Applied Behavior Analysis 6*, 131-166.

McEachin, J. J. (1987) *Outcome of autistic children receiving intensive behavioral treatment: Residual deficits.* Unpublished doctoral dissertation University of California, Los Angeles.

McEachin, J. J., & Leaf, R. B. (1984, May). *The role of punishment in motivation of autistic children.* Paper presented at the convention of the Association for Behavior Analysis. Nashville, TN.

Ray, A. A. (1982). *Statistical Analysis System user's guide: Statistics, 1982 edition.* Cary, NC: SAS Institute.

Rimland, B. (1964). *Infantile autism.* New York: Appleton-Century-Crofts.

Rutter, M. (1970). Autistic children: Infancy to adulthood. *Seminars in Psychiatry 2*, 435-450.

Rutter, M. (1974). The development of infantile autism. *Psychological Medicine 4*, 147-163.

Stutsman, R. (1948). *Guide for administering the Merrill-Palmer Scale of Mental Tests.* New York: Harcourt, Brace & World.

Thorndike, R. L. (1972). *Manual for Stanford-Binet Intelligence Scale.* Boston: Houghton Mifflin.

Wechsler, D. (967). *Manual for the Wechsler Pre-School and Primary Scale of Intelligence.* New York: Psychological Corporation.

Wechsler, D. (1974). *Manual for the Wechsler Intelligence Scale for Children—Revised.* New York: Psychological Corporation.

Postscript

The experimental subjects continue to be studied. McEachin, et al (1993), reported that the gains made were preserved at a mean age of 11.5 years. Furthermore, these subjects are indistinguishable from normal children on tests of intelligence, getting along with others, ability to function independently, and adequate socialization. Also absent were typical positive symptoms such as stereotypic or bizarre mannerisms. One enrolled in a junior college.

Behavioral Treatment of Autistic Children *is a video which explains and demonstrates the intensive behavioral treatment program for young autistic children. Particularly compelling is a scene in which the viewer is challenged to select a previously autistic child from a group of normal adolescents. I could not. Further research by others using Lovaas' methods is being conducted in New Jersey, Japan, Norway, and Canada (Sleek, 1994, p. 30). A body of research is accumulating to demonstrate that a cure of autism can be accomplished through behavioral technology.*

References

McEachin, J. J., et al. (1993). Long-Term Outcome for Children With Autism Who Received Early Intensive Behavioral Treatment. *America Journal on Mental Retardation, 97*(4), 359-372.

Sleek, S. (1994, January). Many Methods Employed to Breach Autism's Walls. *American Psychology Association Monitor*, 30-31.

Figure 8-5. Long-confined bird remains despite opportunity for flight. (Photograph by Jim Rooney.)

FALL INTO HELPLESSNESS

Martin E.P. Seligman

Cognitive psychology is concerned with the thought process that occurs between a stimulus and a response. Skinner, earlier in the chapter, wrote, "We do not cry because we are sad or feel sad because we cry, we cry and feel sad because something has happened" (Skinner, 1988, p. 172). How we interpret what has happened effects how we feel.

The following article, originally published in 1973, offers a cognitive-behavioral explanation for depression. Seligman describes learned helplessness—a condition that results when we come to believe that gratification will not occur regardless of what we do. If nothing we do works; we learn to do nothing. He notes many interesting parallels between learned helplessness and depression. He explains that the successful treatment of depression lies in the person's realization that what he does matters, that he can succeed, and influence his fate.

Nearly three decades ago, Seligman, Maier, and Overmier made a casual observation about dogs subjected to inescapable shock. That observation stimulated years of fruitful research on the causes and treatment of depression.

References

Skinner, B.F. (1988). The Operant Side of Behavior Therapy. *Journal of Behavior Therapy and Experimental Psychiatry,* 171-179.

Depression is the common cold of psychopathology, at once familiar and mysterious. Most of us have suffered depression in the wake of some traumatic event—some terrible loss—in our lives. Most of these depressions, like the common cold, run their course in time.

Serious forms of depression afflict from four to eight million Americans. Many of these depressive Americans will recover. Some of them won't; they'll just give up, becoming like T.S. Eliot's hollow men, a ". . . shape without form, shade without color. Paralyzed force, gesture without motion. . ." Many of those who are hospitalized will simply turn their heads to the wall. Others, at least one out of 200, will take their own lives. Yet we know there are some individuals who *never* succumb to depression, no matter how great their loss.

The *Wall Street Journal* has called depression the "disease of the '70s," and perhaps it is part of the character of our times. It is not a new malady, however. Physicians have been describing depression since the days of Hippocrates; he called it melancholia. The 2,500 years since Hippocrates have added little to our knowledge of the cure and prevention of depression. Our ignorance is due not to lack of research on the problem, but, I believe, to a lack of clearly defined and focused theory. Without a theory to organize what is known about the symptoms and cause, predictions about the cure and prevention of depression are, at best, haphazard.

A Cogent Theory

I think such a theory is possible, and my belief is based on the phenomenon known as "learned helplessness." [See "For Helplessness: Can We Immunize the Weak?," by Martin E. P. Seligman, *PT*, June 1969.] There are considerable parallels between the behaviors that define learned helplessness and the major symptoms of depression. In addition, the types of events that set off depression parallel the events that set off learned helplessness. I believe that cure for depression occurs when the individual comes to believe that he is not helpless and that an individual's susceptibility to depression depends on the success or failure of his previous experience with controlling his environment.

So the focus of my theory is that if the symptoms of learned helplessness and depression are equivalent, then what we have learned experimentally about the cause, cure and prevention of learned helplessness can be applied to depression.

Inescapable Shock

A few years ago, Steven F. Maier, J. Bruce Overmier and I stumbled onto the behavioral phenomenon of learned helplessness while we were using dogs and traumatic shock to test a particular learning theory. We had strapped dogs into a Pavlovian harness and given them electric shock—traumatic, but not physically damaging. Later the dogs were put into a two-compartment shuttlebox where they were supposed to learn to escape shock by jumping across the barrier separating the compartments.

A nonshocked, experimentally naive dog, when placed in a shuttlebox, typically behaves in the following way: at the onset of the first electric shock, the dog defecates, urinates, howls, and runs around frantically until it accidentally scrambles over the barrier and escapes the shock. On the next trial, the dog, running and howling, crosses the barrier more quickly. This pattern continues until the dog learns to avoid shock altogether.

But our dogs were not that naive. While in a harness from which they could not escape, they had already experienced shock over which they

had no control. That is, nothing they did or did not do affected their receipt of shock. When placed in the shuttlebox, these dogs reacted at first in much the same manner as a naive dog, but not for long. The dogs soon stopped running and howling, settled down and took the shock, whining quietly. Typically, the dog did not cross the barrier and escape. Instead, it seemed to give up. On succeeding trials, the dog made virtually no attempts to get away. It passively took as much shock as was given.

After testing alternative hypotheses, we developed the theory that it was not trauma per se (electric shock) that interfered with the dog's adaptive responding. Rather, it was the experience of having *no control* over the trauma. We have found that if animals can control shock by any response—be it an active or a passive one—they do not later become helpless. Only those animals who receive uncontrollable shock will later give up. The experience in the harness had taught the dog that its responses did not pay, that his actions did not matter. We concluded that the dogs in our experiments had learned that they were helpless.

Our learned helplessness hypothesis has been tested and confirmed in many ways with both animal and human subjects. Tests with human beings revealed dramatic parallels between the behavior of subjects who have learned helplessness and the major symptoms exhibited by depressed individuals.

Reactive Depression

Depression, like most clinical labels, embraces a whole family of disorders. As a label it is probably no more discriminating than "disease of the skin," which describes both acne and cancer. The word "depressed" as a behavioral description explicitly denotes a reduction or depression in responding. The reactive depressions, the focus of this article, are most common. As distinguished from process depression, reactive depression is set off by some external event, is probably not hormonally based, does not cycle regularly in time, and does not have a genetic history. The kind of depression experienced by manic-depressives is process depression.

Some of the events that may set off reactive

depression are familiar to each of us: death, loss, rejection by or separation from loved ones, physical disease, failure in work or school, financial setback, and growing old. There are a host of others, of course, but those capture the flavor. I suggest that what all these experiences have in common—what depression is—is the belief in one's own helplessness.

Goodies From the Sky

Many clinicians have reported an increasing pervasiveness of depression among college students. Since this is a generation that has been raised with more reinforcers—more sex, more intellectual stimulation, more buying power, more cars, more music, etc.—than any previous generation, why should they be depressed? Yet the occurrence of reinforcers in our affluent society is so independent of the actions of the children who receive them, the goodies might as well have fallen from the sky. And perhaps that is our answer. Rewards as well as punishments that come independently of one's own effort can be depressing.

We can mention "success" depression in this context. When an individual finally reaches a goal after years of striving, such as getting a Ph.D. or becoming company president, depression often ensues. Even the disciplined astronaut, hero of his nation and the world, can become depressed after he has returned from walking on the Moon.

From a learned helplessness viewpoint, success depression may occur because reinforcers are no longer contingent on present responding. After years of goal-directed activity, a person now gets his reinforcers because of who he is rather than because of what he is *doing*. Perhaps this explains the number of beautiful women who become depressed and attempt suicide. They receive abundant positive reinforcers not for what they do but for how they look.

Symptoms in Common

Consider the parallels between depression and learned helplessness: the most prominent symptom of depression, passivity, is also the central symptom of learned helplessness. Joseph Mendels describes the slowdown in responding associated with depression: ". . Loss of interest,

decrease in energy, inability to accomplish tasks, difficulty in concentration and ambition all combine to impair efficient functioning. For many depressives the first signs of illness are in the area of their increasing inability to cope with their work and responsibility. . ." Aaron T. Beck describes "paralysis of the will" as a striking characteristic of depression:

". . . In severe cases, there often is complete paralysis of the will. The patient has no desire to do anything, even those things which are essential to life. Consequently, he may be relatively immobile unless prodded or pushed into activity by others. It is sometimes necessary to pull the patient out of bed, wash, dress and feed him. . ."

Experiments in learned helplessness have produced passivity in many kinds of animals, even the lowly cockroach, and in human subjects. Donald Hiroto subjected college students to loud noise. He used three groups: group one could not escape hearing the loud noise; group two heard the loud noise but could turn it off by pressing a button; group three heard no noise.

In the second part of the experiment, Hiroto presented the students with a finger shuttlebox. Moving one's fingers back and forth across the shuttlebox turned off the loud noise. The students in group two, who had previously learned to silence the noise by pushing a button, and those in group three, who had no experience with the loud noise, readily learned to move their fingers across the shuttlebox to control the noise. But the students in group one, whose previous attempts to turn off the noise had been futile, now merely sat with their hands in the shuttlebox, passively accepting the loud noise. They had learned that they were helpless.

Hiroto also found out that "externals" [see "External Control and Internal Control," by Julian B. Rotter, PT, June 1971] were more susceptible to learned helplessness than "internals." Externals are persons who believe that reinforcement comes from outside themselves; they believe in luck. Internals believe that their own actions control reinforcement.

Born Losers

Depressed patients not only make fewer responses, but they are "set" to interpret their own responses, when they do make them, as failures or as doomed to failure. Each of them bears an invisible tattoo: "I'm a Born Loser." Beck considers this negative cognitive set to be the primary characteristic of depression:

". . . The depressed patient is peculiarly sensitive to any impediments to his goal-directed activity. An obstacle is regarded as an impossible barrier, difficulty in dealing with a problem is interpreted as a total failure. His cognitive response to a problem or difficulty is likely to be an idea such as 'I'm licked,' 'I'll never be able to do this,' or 'I'm blocked no matter what I do' . . ."

This cognitive set crops up repeatedly in experiments with depressives. Alfred S. Friedman observed that although a patient was performing adequately during a test, the patient would occasionally reiterate his original protest of "I can't do it," "I don't know how," etc. This is also our experience in testing depressed patients.

Negative cognitive set crops up in both depression and learned helplessness. When testing students, William Miller, David Klein and I found that depression and learned helplessness produced the same difficulty in seeing that responding is successful. We found that depressed individuals view their skilled actions very much as if they were in a chance situation. Their depression is not a general form of pessimism about the world, but pessimism that is specific to their own actions. In animal behavior this is demonstrated by associative retardation: animals don't catch on even though they make a response that turns off shock; they have difficulty in learning what responses produce relief.

Maier and I found in separate experiments, that normal aggressiveness and competitiveness become deficient in the subjects who have succumbed to learned helplessness. In competition, these animals lose out to animals who have learned that they control the effects of their responses. Further, they do not fight back when attacked.

Depressed individuals, similarly, are usually less aggressive and competitive than nondepressed individuals. The behavior of depressed patients is depleted of hostility and even their dreams are less hostile. This symptom forms the basis for the Freudian view of depression. Freud claimed that the hostility of depressed people was directed inward toward themselves rather than outward. Be this as it may, the *symptom* corresponds to the depleted aggression and competitiveness of helpless dogs and rats.

The Balm of Time

Depression also often dissipates with time. When a man's wife dies he may be depressed for several days, several months, or even several years. But time usually heals. One of the most tragic aspects of suicide is that if the person could have waited for a few weeks, the depression might well have lifted.

Time is also an important variable in learned helplessness. Overmier and I found that the day after they received one session of inescapable shock, dogs behaved helplessly in the shuttlebox. However, if two days elapsed between the inescapable shock and testing, the dogs were not helpless; their helplessness, like the widower's depression, had run its course. Unfortunately, helplessness does not always respond so well to the elixir of time. We found that multiple sessions of inescapable shock made the animals' learned helplessness virtually irreversible. We also found that animals that had been reared from birth in our laboratories with a limited history of controlling reinforcers also failed to recover from learned helplessness over time.

Often when we are depressed we lose our appetites and our zest for life. Jay M. Weiss, Neal E. Miller and their colleagues at Rockefeller University found that rats that had received inescapable shock lost weight and ate less than rats who had been able to escape from shock. In addition, the brains of the rats subjected to inescapable shock are depleted of norepinephrine, an important transmitter substance in the central nervous system. Joseph J. Schildkraut and Seymour S. Kety have suggested that the cause of depression may be a deficiency of norepinephrine at receptor sites in the brain. This is because reserpine, a drug that depletes norepinephrine, among other things, produces depression in man. Moreover, antidepressant drugs increase the brain's supply of norepinephrine. Therefore, there may be a chemical similarity between depression and learned helplessness.

Weiss found that rats subjected to uncontrollable shock got more stomach ulcers than rats receiving no shock or shock they could control.

No one has done a study of ulcers in depression, so we don't know if human experience will correspond to ulceration in helpless rats. However, anxiety and agitation are sometimes seen along with depression. It is my speculation, however, that anxiety persists as long as the depressed person believes there might still be something he can do to extract himself from his dilemma. When he finally comes to believe that no response will work, depression wholly displaces anxiety.

The Chances For Cure

As arrayed above, there are considerable parallels between the behaviors which define learned helplessness and the major symptoms of depression. We have also seen that the cause of learned helplessness and reactive depression is similar: both occur when important events are out of control. Let me now speculate about the possibility of curing both.

In our animal experiments, we knew that only when the dog learned to escape the shock, only when it learned that it could control its environment, would a cure for its learned helplessness be found.

At first, we could not persuade the dog to move to the other side of the box, not even by dropping meat there when the dog was hungry. As a last resort, we forcibly dragged the dog across the barrier on a leash. After much dragging, the dog caught on and eventually was able to escape the shock on its own. Recovery from helplessness was complete and lasting for each animal. We can say with confidence that so far only "directive therapy"—forcing the animal to see that it can succeed by responding—works reliably in curing learned helplessness. However, T.R. Dorworth has recently found that electro-convulsive shock breaks up helplessness in dogs. Electro-convulsive shock is often used as a therapy for depression and it seems to be effective about 60 percent of the time.

Although we do not know how to cure depression, there are therapies that alleviate it, and they are consonant with the learned helplessness approach. Successful therapy occurs when the patient believes that his responses produce gratification, that he is an effective human being.

Against the Grain

In an Alabama hospital, for instance, E.S. Taulbee and H.W. Wright have created an "anti-depression room." They seat a severely depressed patient in the room and then abuse him in a simple manner. He is told to sand a block of wood, then is reprimanded because he is sanding against the grain of the wood. After he switches to sanding with the grain, he is reprimanded for sanding with the grain. The abuse continues until the depressed patient gets angry. He is then promptly led out of the room with apologies. His outburst, and its immediate effect on the person abusing him, breaks up his depression. From the helplessness viewpoint, the patient is forced to vent his anger, one of the most powerful responses people have for controlling others. When anger is dragged out of him, he is powerfully reinforced.

Other methods reported to be effective against depression involve the patient's relearning that he controls reinforcers.

Expressing strong emotions is a therapy that seems to help depressed patients, as self-assertion does. In assertive training, the patient rehearses asserting himself and then puts into practice the responses he has learned that bring him social reinforcers.

Morita therapy puts patients in bed for about a week to "sensitize them to reinforcement." Then the patients progress from light to heavy to complicated work [see "Morita Therapy," by Takehisa Kora and Kenshiro Ohara, PT, March 1973].

The Lift of Success

Other forms of graded-task assignments also have been effective. Elaine P. Burgess first had her patients perform some simple task, such as making a telephone call. As the task requirements increased, the patient was reinforced by the therapist for successfully completing each task. Burgess emphasized how crucial it is in the graded-task treatment that the patient succeed.

Using a similar form of graded-task assignment, Aaron Beck, Dean Schuyler, Peter Brill and I began by asking patients to read a short paragraph aloud. Finally, we could get severely depressed patients to give extemporaneous speeches, with a noticeable lifting of their depression. What one patient said was illuminating: "You know, I used to be a debater in high school and I had forgotten how good I was."

Finally, there is the age-old strategy adopted by individuals to dispel their own minor depressions: doing work that is difficult but gratifying. There is no better way to see that one's responses are still effective. It is crucial to succeed. Merely starting and giving up only makes things worse.

Dramatic successes in medicine have come more frequently from prevention than from treatment, and I would hazard a guess that inoculation and immunization have saved more lives than cure. Surprisingly, psychotherapy is almost exclusively limited to curative procedures, and preventive procedures rarely play an explicit role.

In studies of dogs and rats we have found that behavioral immunization prevents learned helplessness. Dogs that first receive experience in mastering shock do not become helpless after experiencing subsequent inescapable shock. Dogs that are deprived of natural opportunities to control their own rewards in their development are more vulnerable to helplessness than naturally immunized dogs.

The Masterful Life

Even less is known about the prevention of depression than about its cure. We can only speculate on this, but the data on immunization against learned helplessness guide our speculations. The life histories of those individuals who are particularly resistant to depression or who are resilient from depression may have been filled with mastery. Persons who have had extensive experience in controlling and manipulating the sources of reinforcement in their lives may see the future optimistically. A life without mastery may produce vulnerability to depression. Adults who lost their parents when they were children are unusually susceptible to depression and suicide.

A word of caution is in order. While it may be possible to immunize people against debilitating depression by giving them a history of control over reinforcers, it may be possible to get too much of a good thing. The person who has met only success may be highly susceptible to depression when he faces a loss. One is reminded, for example, of the stock market crash of 1929: it was not the low-income people who jumped to their deaths, but those who had been "supersuccessful" and suddenly faced gross defeat.

One can also look at successful therapy as preventative. After all, therapy usually does not focus just on undoing past problems. It also should arm the patient against future depressions. Perhaps therapy for depression would be more successful if it explicitly aimed at providing the patient with a wide repertoire of coping responses. He could use these responses in future situations where he finds his usual reactions do not control his reinforcements. Finally, we can speculate about child rearing. What kind of experiences can best protect our children against the debilitating effects of helplessness and depression? A tentative answer follows from the learned helplessness view of depression: to see oneself as an effective human being may require a childhood filled with powerful synchronies between responding and its consequences.

	Learned Helplessness	**Depression**
SYMPTOMS	1. passivity 2. difficulty learning that responses produce relief 3. lack of aggression 4. dissipates in time 5. weight loss and undereating anorexia; sexual deficits 6. norepinephrine depletion 7. ulcers and stress	1. passivity 2. negative cognitive set 3. introjected hostility 4. time course 5. loss of libido 6. norepinephrine depletion 7. ulcers (?) and stress 8. feelings of helplessness
CAUSE	learning that responding and reinforcement are independent	belief that responding is useless
CURE	1. forced exposure to responding producing reinforcement 2. electroconvulsive shock 3. pharmacological agents (?) 4. time	1. recovery of belief that responding produces reinforcement 2. electroconvulsive shock (?) 3. pharmacological agents (?) 4. time
PREVENTION	inoculation with mastery over reinforcement	inoculation (?)

Postscript

Recently, Seligman has expanded the learned helplessness theory by emphasizing how people attribute their failures. Depressed people, overwhelmed by hopelessness and helplessness, are likely to attribute their failures as stable (enduring), and global (pervasive) (Seligman, 1988). People can be taught to change their explanatory style from pessimistic to optimistic:

> *bolstering self-esteem without changing hopelessness, without changing passivity, accomplishes nothing.... There are almost no findings that self-esteem causes anything at all... Rather, self esteem is caused by a whole panoply of successes and failures...What needs improving is not self-esteem but improvement of our skills [for dealing] with the world"* (*quoted in Azar, 1994, p. 4*).

Thus, successful treatment of depression lies in helping people to behave in a more successful manner, which catalyzes the justified modification of their cognitive appraisal of reality.

References

Azar, B. (1994, October). Seligman Recommends a Depression 'Vaccine.' *American Psychological Association Monitor*, p. 4.

Seligman, M. (1988, October). Boomer Blues. *Psychology Today*, p 50-55.

The Holocaust inspired a new psychology. *Top:* The execution of prisoners in the forest near Buchenwald concentration camp, 1938-1940. (Courtesy of the United States Holocaust Memorial Museum.) *Bottom:* Wild flowers. (Photograph by Jim Rooney.)

Chapter 9

THE HUMANISTIC PERSPECTIVE

The Nazi regime of Adolf Hitler was highly proficient at manipulating reinforcement contingencies to control behavior. Obedience brought rewards; disobedience death. After World War II, some psychologists argued that there was too great a similarity between the control techniques of Hitler and those employed by behaviorists. A major goal of behaviorism, as stated by its founder, John B. Watson, is "the prediction and control of behavior" (Watson, 1913). This is not to imply that behaviorists would use their technology for deleterious purpose; nevertheless, the potential for abuse exists.

The atrocities of the Holocaust led to much soul searching. Psychologists sought to understand this horrible event and prevent similar events in the future. Psychoanalyst Viktor Frankl survived Auschwitz and other death camps. His grueling experience is graphically detailed in his classic *Man's Search for Meaning* (1959). Through reading this compelling book, one can approximate empathy with those who experienced the horror. Upon entering Auschwitz, he made three vows: to survive, to use his medical talents to help others, and to learn something from the experience.

A major objective of the Third Reich was to make Europe "Judenfrei" (free of Jews). Historically, oppressive regimes have defined outgroups as less than human. Nazi Propoganda Minister Joseph Goebbels used the term "Untermenschen" (subhuman) to describe those with more than one-fourth Jewish blood, as well as other undesirable non-Aryans (Wallbank, et al, 1992, p. 841). The Nazi's "final solution to the Jewish question" was genocide. Steven Speilberg's 1993 masterpiece *Schindler's List* vividly portrays death camp existence. Sadistic Nazi Officer Amon Goeth would shoot exhausted prisoners from his balcony.

Frankl concluded that despite all adversity, he must maintain his dignity. He must believe he will survive. He remembered Nietzsche's words, "He who has a *why* to live for can bear with almost any *how*" (Frankl, 1959, p. 76). No matter what the circumstance, man still has choice. "Man can preserve a vestige of spiritual freedom, of independence, even in such conditions of psychic and physical stress" (Frankl, 1959, p. 65). Often, the only choice left to the prisoner was whether to look down upon entering the gas chamber, perceived as an admission of inferiority by the executioner, or to look him straight in the eye with a haunting glance that he would carry to his grave. We all have much greater options than these. Frankl's experience provides a good antidote for self-pity.

Others who would become leaders of a new psychology had also suffered existential crises. Fredrick Perls fled Germany for Holland in 1933, anticipating what was to come. Ultimately, he came to the United States and emerged as a leader of the human potential movement during the politically volatile 1960s at the Big Sur-Esalen Institute in California. His gestalt prayer became the anthem for the era:

> I do my thing, and you do your thing.
> I am not in this world to live up to your expectations
> And you are not in this world to live up to mine.
> You are you and I am I,
> And if by chance we find each other, it's beautiful.
> If not, it can't be helped.   (Perls, 1969, p. 4)

Rollo May was trained in religion and psychoanalysis. However, in 1942 he contracted tuberculosis. His confrontation with death during eighteen months at a Saranac Lake, New York sanatorium resulted in him assuming an existential orientation. "It was a valuable experience to face death," said May many years later, "for in the experience, I learned to face life" (May, 1970). May was fascinated with ancient Greek civilization and noted parallels between Greece during its decline and contemporary America. He strenuously argued that there is a dearth of heroes and myths with which we can identify. Excessive reliance on technology has left us diminished as humans. While we may benefit materially by living in a technological society, our lives may become emotional and spiritual vacuums. We may feel insignificant, alienated from our fellow man, powerless, lonely, and lost. There is a human cost to rampant technology.

During the period following World War II, a diverse group of scholars began writing and communicating among themselves. Initially, all that united them was a dissatisfaction with the prevailing schools; psychoanalysis and behaviorism. In 1963, the fledgling Association for Humanistic Psychology was composed of 200 members. They came from many disciplines: psychology, religion, existentialism, and personality theory. Many were considered dissidents by the dominant schools.

A new psychology took form. Its focus was on human experience and emphasized man's innate goodness. Unlike psychoanalysis, which was pessimistic and deterministic, it was optimistic and advocated freedom. Unlike behaviorism, which according to Watson recognized "no dividing line between man and brute" (Watson, 1913), this evolving school stressed the unique nature of man as a species and individual. It stressed the inherent value and worth of every human being. It became known as humanism.

The formal beginning of the perspective can perhaps be traced to a meeting held in 1964 in a country inn at Old Saybrook, Connecticut. It was attended by those who would later emerge as the pillars of humanism—Carl Rogers, Abraham Maslow, James Bugental and Rollo May (DeCarvalho, 1990). May remarked:

> That conference developed out of the groundswell of protest against the theory of man
> of behaviorism on the one side and orthodox psychoanalysis on the other. That is why
> we are often called the Third Force. There was a feeling on all sides among different
> psychologists that neither of these two versions dealt with human beings as human. Nor
> did they deal with real problems of life. . . . At that conference we discussed what the
> chief elements of humanistic psychology would be.   (May, in Gilbert, 1975, p. 4).

Today, humanism is a vital force in psychology. Its main publication is the Journal of Humanistic Psychology. It has division status within the American Psychological Association. Many colleges have graduate programs in it. Humanists relish the criticism of others, like behaviorists, who consider it more a philosophy or poetic psychology.

The first article in this chapter is entitled *The Treatment of Autism: A Human Protest*, by Dr. Mike Murray. It describes an autistic child's reaction to his treatment in a behavior modification program. The second is entitled *The Third Force in Psychology,* by James F. T. Bugental. It outlines the basic premises of humanism. The third article is entitled *A Theory of Human Motivation* by Abraham Maslow. It is the original statement of his need hierarchy. The fourth selection is taken from Carl Rogers' classic, *On*

Becoming a Person. Its title is *Some Hypotheses Regarding the Facilitation of Personal Growth.* Rogers describes the type of therapeutic atmosphere that he attempts to create to help his troubled clients. Fifth is *Plight of the Ik and Kaiadilt Is Seen as a Chilling Possible End for Man.* It was written by John B. Calhoun and is a sobering account of how man can "cease being human" under conditions of debasement, overcrowding, and degradation. The final selection is *What Does a Man Want?* by Stanley R. Graham. He makes poignant existential observations about America's past and present, and offers optimistic hope for the future.

References

DeCarvalho, R. (1990, Fall). A History of the "Third Force" in *Psychology: Journal of Humanistic Psychology,* 30(4), p. 22-44.

Frankl, V.E., (1959). *Man's Search for Meaning.* Boston: Beacon Press.

Gilbert, R., ed. (1975, April 4-6). Edited Transcript, *AHP Theory Conference Tucson, Arizona.* San Francisco, California: Association for Humanistic Psychology.

May, R. (1970, June 22). Interview. *Time,* p. 66.

Perls, F.S. (1969). *Gestalt Therapy Verbatim.* California: Real People Press.

Wallbank, T.W., et al (1992). *Civilization Past & Present, Vol. II Since 1648,* 7th ed. New York: Harper Collins Publishers.

Watson, J.P., (1913). Psychology as the Behaviorist Views It. *Psychological Review,* 20(2).

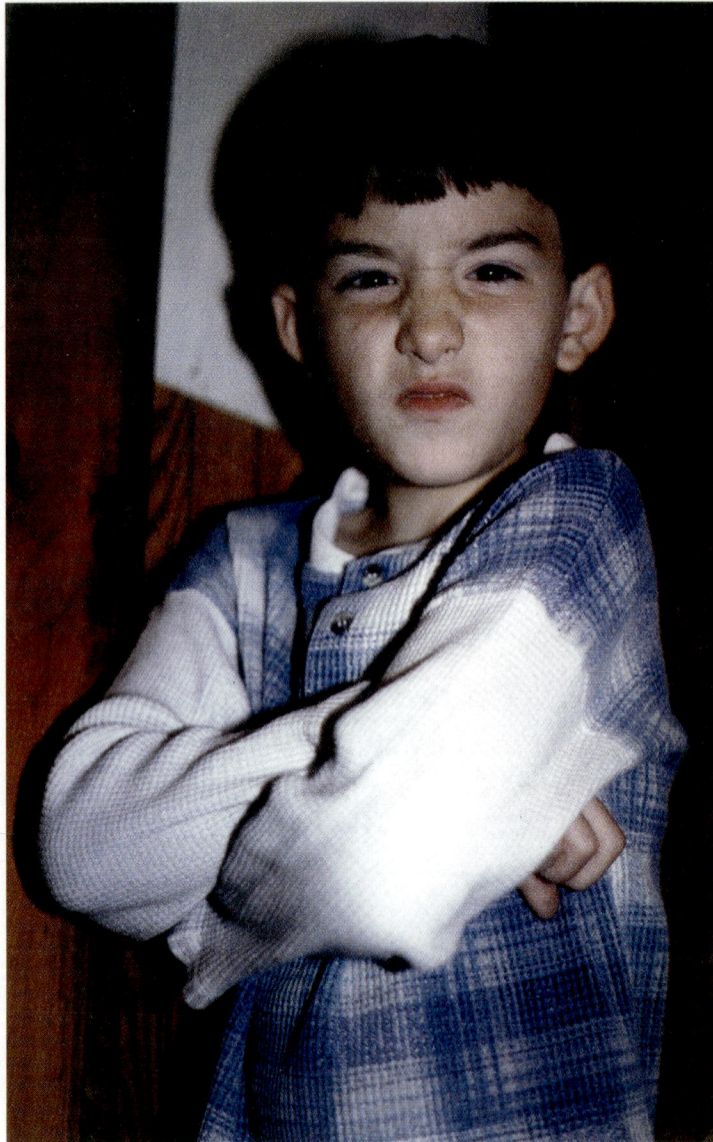

Figure 9-1: David. (Photograph by Jim Rooney.)

READING 9A

THE TREATMENT OF AUTISM: A HUMAN PROTEST

Mike Murray

The success of behavior therapy relies upon the ability of the therapist to manage reinforcement contingencies. Stringent measures, like aversion, may be employed in highly controlled environments. Behavior therapists argue that the therapeutic ends justify the means by which attained. Therefore, behavior therapy is often criticized as mechanistic and dehumanizing. Humanistic psychologists are those who are most likely to make these criticisms. Because people are not broken and defective, they inherently possess the ability to make important decisions themselves. They do not believe that behavior therapists should arbitrarily determine what is best for any individual.

Dawn was a young woman with anorexia nervosa. She became a patient in a hospital that employed rigid behavior modification procedures. Her normal weight was 105 pounds; upon admission she was 65. Contingencies were such that if she gained a sufficient amount of weight during the week, she would be rewarded by being allowed to go home for the weekend. She disliked the hospital greatly. She made some progress for a brief period of time, but one week failed to gain the necessary weight. Despite her protest, she was not allowed to leave. Over the weekend, she attempted suicide by slashing her wrist. Could this have been her way of protesting the treatment?

In the following article, Dr. Mike Murray describes the reaction of an autistic child whom he feels was artificially manipulated by the control techniques of behavior therapy. It is a reminder that therapists must recognize that human beings, no matter how severe their condition, are individuals with free will, rights, and integrity.

In recent years techniques for treating the behavioral deficits of autistic children have become more refined and effective through the use of behavior modification procedures (Bandura, 1969). This is particularly true regarding the acquisition of imitative language (Lovaas, Berberich, Perloff, & Schaeffer, 1966). Treatment usually involves establishing responsiveness to modeling cues and to attentive behavior, as well as developing the effectiveness of social reinforcements in shaping behavior. Procedures include the use of both aversive and positive consequences, depending on the behavior of the child (Lovaas, 1966; Lovaas, 1967; Risley & Wolf, 1967).

While these procedures have proven useful in establishing basic speech patterns, behavior modification techniques are seen by some critics as dehumanizing and overly mechanistic. Humanistic psychologists have criticized the strictly behavioral approaches for being limited in scope and for failing to encompass the full

"The Treatment of Autism: A Human Protest" by Mike Murray, from the *Journal of Humanistic Psychology*, pp. 200-202. Reprinted by permission of Sage Publications, Inc.

range of human misery and potential. In order to facilitate more adequate socialization and growth, alternate plans for treating autistic children have been formulated (Bettelheim, 1967). Interestingly, these psychologists are not alone in their criticism of mechanistic treatment. The following case illustrates the human protest against being artificially manipulated, and is a strong reminder of the limitation of our knowledge about psychopathology and personality development.

Case Study

David is a nine-year-old student at a local mental health and retardation center. He has been diagnosed as autistic and shows the typical patterns of avoidance of interpersonal contact and failure to develop meaningful speech. Verbalizations include generally meaningless babbling with an occasional word thrown in that appears meaningless in terms of its context and situation. His parents report that David has never learned to talk or use language effectively.

Recently the staff at the center has been exposed to the theory and use of operant procedures. Having achieved success in teaching another previously nonverbal, autistic child to ask for food through the use of positive reinforcement, the staff decided that David was to be the next candidate.

The modification procedure consisted of asking David if he wanted a cookie each day during snack times. If he responded by saying "yes," he would receive a cookie, and if he made no response, he received nothing. During the first two and a half days of conditioning, David failed to respond and actively engaged in nonattentive and interpersonally disruptive behaviors when asked if he wanted a cookie. On the third day, during afternoon snack time, David's persistent teacher took David's shoulders in order to try to get his attention and asked him if he wanted a cookie. Suddenly, David ceased his struggling and focused his attention on the teacher.

"No," he replied, "and I'm getting tired of this shit!"

Discussion

Several comments seem in order regarding this case study. The psychodynamic interpretation of this incident is based upon the premise that David's response was meaningful, conscious, and goal-directed. It is not unusual for autistic children to make delayed echolalic responses, and occasionally, merely by chance, such a response may appear to be a meaningful statement. However, the particular situational context and the appropriateness and style of the response are critical to functional interpretation. In the present case report, David's speech is seen as a frustration response to a mechanistic environment.

Upon examination, several aspects of this situation point to the sentence as being a protest rather than echolalia. First, there is the fact that David's response was delayed. It followed the teacher's verbal cue and was not a reaction to being held. Second, the response showed appropriate affect. David focused his attention on the teacher and stated in an assertive and angry manner that he was getting tired of the procedure. This type of statement is, of course, in striking contrast to the normally flat, sing-song sounds of the autistic child's echolalic speech. Finally, David's response did not follow the typical echolalic pattern. As Kanner (1943) states in his original paper, autistic speech is repetitious and parrot-like. There is no conversational give-and-take. The child very rarely answers "yes" or "no," but simply echoes the question. In this vein, personal pronouns are repeated as heard. Thus, the autistic child wrongly refers to himself as "you" and to others as "I." David's response both answered the question with a "no" and correctly used personal pronouns. The appropriateness of the response to the situation, the delayed reaction time, the appropriate affect, and the normal speech pattern strongly argue for this statement's being a very human protest.

References

Bandura, A. *Principles of behavior modification.* New York: Holt, Rinehart and Winston, 1969.

Bettelheim, B. *The empty fortress.* New York: The Free Press, 1967.

Kanner, L. Autistic disturbances in affective contact. *Nervous Child,* 1943, 2, 217-250.

Lovaas, O. I. *Reinforcement therapy.* Philadelphia: Smith, Kline, and French Laboratories, 1966. (16 mm. sound film.)

Lovaas, O. I. A behavior therapy approach to the treatment of childhood schizophrenia. In I. Hill (Ed.) *Minnesota symposia on child psychology.* Vol. 1. Minneapolis: University of Minnesota Press, 1967.

Lovaas, O. I., Berberich, J., Perloff, B., & Schaeffer, B. Acquisition of imitative speech by schizophrenic children. *Science.* 1966, 151, 705-707.

Risley, T., & Wolf, M. Establishing functional speech in echolalic children. *Behavior Research and Therapy.* 1967, 5, 73-88.

Figure 9-2. The Castle Inn on Cornfield Point, Old Saybrook, Connecticut, lies at the junction of the Connecticut River and Long Island Sound. Its ambience nurtured the germination of humanistic notions during the 1964 conference. Humanists continued to meet at the Inn until the late 1970s.

READING 9B

THE THIRD FORCE IN PSYCHOLOGY

James Bugental

The Old Saybrook Conference provided the forum for the coalescence of ideas and notions about humanism. The participants were united in their disdain for psychoanalysis and behaviorism; "low-ceiling psychology" as Abraham Maslow described them. For years, people had already been writing about what form humanism should take. Yet, what could this diverse group, composed of "practitioners, social/political activists, academic/theoretical thinkers, and 'touchy-feely' growth seekers" agree upon? (DeCarvalho, 1990)

James F.T. Bugental was becoming increasingly involved in the movement. In 1963 he published Humanistic Psychology: A New Breakthrough. *He also addressed groups of psychologists on his views. The following article summarizes them. It was published in the Spring of 1964, prior to the November Old Saybrook Conference.*

This reading outlines the basic postulates and orientation of humanism, which, when embraced, become part of the person. It becomes a philosophy for life. It is entwined with the person's attitudes, morals, and beliefs. It stands in stark contrast with the technical, procedural aspects of behaviorism.

Bugental expresses his enthusiasm for the emergence and blossoming of humanistic psychology. The article is written in a hopeful, prophetic manner. Ultimately, Bugental appointed a theory committee for the conference and was a participant. Today, Bugental's hopes and predictions have been largely fulfilled. Appropriately, the Fall, 1996, edition of the Journal of Humanistic Pscyhology is devoted to works honoring James Bugental.

References:

DeCarvalho, R.J. (1990). A History of the "Third Force" in *Psychology. Journal of Humanistic Psychology*, 30, 22-44.

Last week, thinking about our meeting here, I was reminded of a kind of peak-experience of the previous winter. Then, I had a fresh look at the familiar scene of professional psychology. As may happen when one catches a new perspective on his usual environment, I recognized with a quickening of feeling that something was importantly different in that scene.

I remember years ago climbing a mountain, endlessly following the trail through forest, through rocky channels. Each point was interesting and had its own beauty, but all sense of where on the path I was in relation to the peak gradually faded as the altitude pulled at my lungs and the demands of each new stretch of hiking pulled at my muscles and mind. Then suddenly—startlingly—I emerged above the timber line on a narrow shoulder and saw ahead of me the summit, and all around the vista spread out for miles. The sense of discovery restored perspective, was as breathtaking as were the altitude and the view. It is an experience such as this that I want to describe to you now.

Much has been happening in our field in the postwar years: the establishment of our new professional life, the battles for legal recognition, the

James Bugental, "The Third Force in Psychology," *Journal of Humanistic Psychology*, pp. 204-209. Reprinted by permission of Sage Publications, Inc.

concerns with new topics such as habit strength, ideal image, gestalt therapy, games theory, human factors engineering, and so on. Yet many of us have cried alarm that our concerns are still trivial, that the sciences of man are so badly outdistanced by the sciences of things that the very race of man is in jeopardy. We have hoped for and sought a "breakthrough."

What I recognized quite simply was this: a major breakthrough is occurring right now in psychology. Like many another such major change processes—the end of feudalism, the introduction of electricity, the beginnings of the laboratory method in psychology—its presence and potentialities are difficult to recognize for us who are so deep among the stress of daily concerns. Yet I am convinced that the parallels I cite are not vainglorious. I think we are on the verge of a new era in man's concern about man which may—if allowed to run its course—produce as profound changes in the human condition as those we have seen the physical sciences bring about in the past century.

Now I don't mean to tease you unduly by delaying specification of the breakthrough I have in mind. However, l do need to say a few words to prepare you to grasp my meaning. I don't want too many of you to say "Oh, that!" and turn away. You see, I think that we are prisoners of our own involvement with our work. It would be much easier for us to appreciate the report of a breakthrough in historical scholarship or in space physics than in our own familiar domain. Yet I imagine historians and physicists would have the same difficulties in their own provinces. So listen, if you can and will, with the perspective of psychology's whole development in the past 100 years.

Psychology is at last becoming the study of man. Psychology is recognizing that man, as man, has eluded our segmental approaches, our attempts to deal with part-functions, and is beginning to face up to the task of recognizing that no amount of additional findings about parts will ever yield an appreciation or understanding of man in the world.

Now, I'm pretty sure that a majority of you are saying the equivalent of "Oh, that!" I know I would be. Stay with me a bit, and I'll try to show

you that this is no small thing I'm trying to depict.

Recall your undergraduate course in the history of psychology: Wundt, Titchner, Watson, Hull; psychophysics, mental elements, conditioned response, factor analysis, habit strength; Stanford-Binet, Kohs Blocks, Porteus Mazes, Wechsler, Iowa Tests.

All along we had had this implicit assumption as foundation: Discover the basic components and from these we can synthesize the whole person. Concurrently, we have rigorously disciplined ourselves to avoid the subjective and the poetic.

Listen to Clark Hull (1943), a near saint of pre-breakthrough psychology (p. 27):

> A device much employed by the author has proved itself to be a far more effective prophylaxis. This is to regard, from time to time, the behaving organism as a completely self-maintaining robot, constructed of materials as unlike ourselves as may be.

Contrast this with the following:

> A man can understand astronomy only by being an astronomer; he can understand entomology only by being an entomologist (or perhaps, an insect); but he can understand a great deal of anthropology merely by being a man. He is himself the animal which he studies. Hence arises the fact which strikes the eye everywhere in the records of ethnology and folk-lore—the fact that the same frigid and detached spirit which leads to success in the study of astronomy or botany leads to disaster in the study of mythology or human origins. (G. K. Chesterton, *Science and the Savages*, 1909; quoted in Cantril and Bumstead, 1960, p. 12.)

Or this:

> . . . a poem, a painting, or a prayer should be regarded as a psychological datum just as much as the establishment of a sensory threshold in the laboratory or the measurement of an I.Q.

The last quotation is from Cantril and Bumstead's exciting book *Reflections on the*

Human Venture (1960), itself an evidence of the change process I am trying to characterize. Other books that are part of this wave have come from Rogers (1961), Maslow (1962), May (1961), Buhler (1962), Cohen (1962), and so on.

Another way of describing what is happening is to say that two great human traditions are converging, and from their convergence we may expect a tremendous outpouring of new awareness about ourselves in our world. One such tradition is that of science; the other is the humanities. It is as though we are suddenly made heirs to a tremendous storehouse of data which has been but little utilized scientifically before or—to use a different analogy—as though a whole new hemisphere of our globe had been discovered by some new Columbus. Certainly much exploration and development must be done, but at last we are reaching its shores.

There is another evidence—a kind of validation—of the significance of the breakthrough I am trying to depict. An ancient and vast body of human experience has for centuries been accumulating in the Eastern countries. Our Western contacts with this have been chiefly to treat it as a curiosity, as pagan error to be destroyed, or as material for ignorant distortion in melodramas. Now we are beginning to appreciate the tremendous amount of wisdom and insight which has been achieved along routes quite different than those we have traveled. Zen and Taoism and other Oriental cultural traditions have much to say to us, much that we can begin to hear now that our separate ways have drawn close in the evolution of men's thoughts about man (Fingarette, 1963; Watts, 1961).

As an aside let me point out that there is tremendous encouragement for the hope of some achievement of an eventual citizenship of humanity in this start on a genuine dialogue between these two great heritages of man's thought, the Oriental and the Occidental.

You will have observed, I am optimistic about our field. A year or two ago, as some of you may recall, I spoke in less hopeful terms to our California State Psychological Association. Then I feared we were on our way to fossilhood (Bugental, 1962). Today this fate seems less likely, I'm pleased to report. Certainly there are still

dangers, but I think psychology—or perhaps I should say, humanity—has proven itself hardier than once seemed to me to be the case. l mean by this last to say that I believe the renewed psychology of which I speak is but a phase of an evolutionary process which is arising as a survival response to the biology-threatening forces of nuclear destruction. Just as in a single organism, invasion by disease evokes a counter process of antibody production in defense, so do I think it is with the total evolutionary process.

Basic Postulates and Orientation of Humanistic Psychology

Humanistic psychology is an emerging orientation to the study of man (Bugental, 1963; Cantril, 1955; Maslow, 1956; Rogers,1963). Sometimes referred to as "the third force" in psychology, the humanistic orientation endeavors to go beyond the points of view of behaviorism or psychoanalysis, the two most dominant perspectives presently discernable within the broad area of psychology. Humanistic psychology generally does not see itself as competitive with the other two orientations; rather, it attempts to supplement their observations and to introduce further perspectives and insights.

To date it has been hard to designate just what is meant by humanistic psychology, since it is a movement with diverse spokesmen and widely ranging contents and perspectives. The *Journal of Humanistic Psychology* founded in 1961, has brought together a wide spectrum of papers and a distinguished, though diverse, editorial panel, and it is only through inspection of such publications and of the views of the editorial panel that an implicit definition of the field may be arrived at. Similarly, the American Association for Humanistic Psychology (Sutich, 1962) has found it necessary to use a catalogue type of description of just what it is the Association seeks to represent:

Humanistic Psychology may be defined as the third main branch of the general field of psychology (the two already in existence being the psychoanalytic and the behaviorist) and as such, is primarily concerned with those human capacities and potentialities that have little or no systematic place, either in positivist or behaviorist theory or in classical psychoanalytic theory: e.g., love, creativity, self, growth, organism, basic need-gratification, self-actualization, higher values, being, becoming, spontaneity, play, humor, affection, naturalness, warmth, ego-transcendence, objectivity, autonomy, responsibility, meaning, fair-play, transcendental experience, psychological health, and related concepts. This approach can also be characterized by the writings of Allport, Angyal, Asch, Buhler, Fromm, Goldstein, Horney, Maslow, May, Moustakas, Rogers, Wertheirmer, etc., as well as by certain aspects of the writings of Jung, Adler, and the psychoanalytic ego-psychologists, existential and phenomenological psychologists.

The present paper will make a beginning on an affirmative statement of the nature of the humanistic orientation in psychology. We will undertake to do this by setting forth five postulates of humanistic psychology which may represent common elements in the perspectives of most writers identifying with this field. We will also attempt to make some defining statements about the humanistic orientation in psychology. These defining statements will be of the nature of process descriptions as opposed to the substantive or content descriptions provided by our postulates. In setting forth these postulates and these characteristics of the humanistic orientation, the writer is well aware of the very tentative nature of these statements. We are only now beginning really to discover the commonalities in the diverse spokesmen in the humanistic perspective. It is probable and highly desirable that the list of postulates that follows be criticized, revised, and supplemented many times.

Five Basic Postulates for Humanistic Psychology

Man, as man, supersedes the sum of his parts

When we speak of "man" in humanistic psychology, we do so with the intent of characterizing a person rather than an "organism." Humanistic psychology is concerned with man at his most human or, to say it differently, with that which most distinguishes man as a unique species.

Our first postulate states the keystone posi-

tion that man must be recognized as something other than an additive product of various part-functions. Although part-function knowledge is important scientific knowledge, it is not the knowledge of man as man, but knowledge of the functioning of parts of an organism.

Man has his being in a human context

We postulate second that the unique nature of man is expressed through his always being in relationship with his fellows. Humanistic psychology is always concerned with man in his interpersonal potential. This is not to say that humanistic psychology may not deal with such issues as man's aloneness, but it will be evident that even in so designating it "aloneness," we are speaking of man in his human context. The psychology of part-functions is a psychology which ignores this relatedness (actual or potential) of the human experience.

Man is aware

A central fact of human experience is that man is aware. Awareness is postulated to be continuous and at many levels. By so viewing it, we recognize that all aspects of his experience are not equally available to man, but that, whatever the degree of consciousness, awareness is an essential part of man's being. The continuous nature of awareness is deemed essential to an understanding of human experience. Man does not move from discrete episode to discrete episode, a fact overlooked by experiments of the behavioristic orientation when they treat their subjects as though they had no prior awareness before coming into the experimental situation. Our postulation also provides for unconsciousness as a level of awareness in which there is not direct apprehension, but in which awareness is nevertheless present though denied. This is not the same as the Freudian concept of the unconscious, but it is probably more valid within the humanistic orientation.

Man has choice

There is no desire here to resume the hoary debate regarding free will versus determinism. Phenomenologically, choice is a given of experience. When man is aware, he is aware that his choices make a difference in the flow of his awareness, that he is not a bystander but a participant in experience. From this fact flows man's potential to transcend his creatureliness (Fromm, 1959). Also from this postulation we derive man's capability of change.

Man is intentional

In his experience, man demonstrates his intent. This does not mean "striving," but it does mean orientation. Man intends through having purpose, through valuing, and through creating and recognizing meaning. Man's intentionality is the basis on which he builds his identity, and it distinguishes him from other species.

The characteristics of man's intentionality need to be specified. Man intends both conservation and change. Mechanistic views of man frequently deal only with drive-reduction and homeostatic conceptions. Humanistic psychology recognizes that man seeks rest but concurrently seeks variety and disequilibrium. Thus we may say that man intends multiplely, complexly, and even paradoxically.

The Orientation of Humanistic Psychology

In the following statements we will specify some of the characteristics of the humanistic orientation in psychology, trying to articulate and identify those characteristics which are distinguishing of this point of view.

Humanistic psychology cares about man

Humanistic psychology disavows the sort of scientific detachment pretended to or achieved at great cost by other orientations. Humanistic psychology recognizes that man cannot help but be invested in his study of his own condition. Accepting this as a given, humanistic psychology is founded on man's concern about man and is an expression of that concern.

Humanistic psychology values meaning more than procedure

Although humanistic psychology must find its own methods and must validate those methods as providing dependable knowledge about the human condition, humanistic psychology would be untrue to itself were it to become preoccupied with methodology to the loss of concern with meaningful issues in the human condition.

Humanistic psychology looks for human rather than nonhuman validations

It seems to be a basic tenet of the humanistic position that only that validation which is borne out by human experience can ultimately be counted upon. Humanistic psychology does not disavow the use of statistical methods or of experimental tests. However, it does insist that these are but means and that the ultimate criterion must be that of human experience.

Humanistic psychology accepts the relativism of all knowledge

Humanistic psychology postulates a universe of infinite possibility. Thus it recognizes that all knowledge is relative and subject to change. This tenet does much to free humanistic psychology to use the imaginative and creative potential of its orientation.

Humanistic psychology relies heavily upon the phenomenological orientation

What has been said above about the importance of meaning and about human validation will have indicated the centrality of the phenomenological orientation to the humanistic approach. This is not to deny the merits of other orientations but to insist that the ultimate focus of our concern is in the experience of the human being.

Humanistic psychology does not deny the contributions of other views, but tries to supplement them and give them a setting within a broader conception of the human experience

Let me make a few concluding remarks and then I will welcome your discussion. I have tried to give one man's view of what I think is a tremendously exciting development in our field of psychology. If I see it correctly, we are leaving the state of preoccupation with part-functions and getting back to what psychology seemed to us to mean when we first entered the field. We are returning to what psychology still seems to mean to the average, intelligent layman—that is, the functioning and experience of a whole human being. I have chosen to make my statements in somewhat dogmatic fashion, hoping that you will join me in discussion, hoping that this will prove stimulating to your thinking and observation. 1 am sure I am not right in all details; I sincerely hope that I do correctly assess the general trend.

This is a bare initial statement for our third force in psychology. We will need much thought, much imagination, much discussion and argument, much creativity—in short, much of being human to bring our perspective to the place it must have as an affirmation of man's respect for man.

References

Bugental, J. F. T. Precognitions of a Fossil, *Journal of Humanistic Psychology*, Vol. 2 (1962), No. 2, pp. 38-46.

Humanistic Psychology: A New Break-Through, *American Psychologist*, Vol. 18 (1963), pp. 563-567.

Buhler, Charlotte. *Values in Psychotherapy*. New York Free Press of Glencoe, 1962.

Cantril, H. Toward a Humanistic Psychology, *Etc.*, Vol. 12 (1955), pp. 278-298.

_____ and Bumstead, C. H. *Reflections on the Human Venture*, New York: New York University Press, 1960.

Cohen, J. *Humanistic Psychology*. New York: Collier, 1962.

Fingarette, H. *The Self in Transformation*. New York: Basic Books, 1963.

Fromm, E. Value, Psychology, and Human Existence, in A. H. Maslow (ed.), *New Knowledge in Human Values*. New York: Harper, 1959; pp. 151-164.

Hull, C. L. *Principles of Behavior.* New York: Appleton-Century, 1943; p. 27.

Maslow, A. H. Toward a Humanistic Psychology, *Etc.*, Vol. 13 (1956), pp. 10-22.

_____. *Toward a Psychology of Being*. Princeton, N.J.: Van Nostrand, 1962.

May, R. *Existential Psychology*. New York: Random House, 1961.

Rogers, C. R. *On Becoming a Person*. Boston: Houghton Mifflin, 1961.

_____. Toward a Science of the Person, *Journal of Humanistic Psychology*, Vol. 3 (1963), No. 2.

Sutich, A. American Association for Humanistic Psychology: Progress Report. Palo Alto, California, November 1, 1962; mimeographed.

Watts, A. *Psychotherapy East and West*. New York: Pantheon, 1961.

Figure 9-3. Abraham Maslow in 1968. (Photograph by Ted Polumbaum, *Life* Magazine © 1968 Time Inc.)

A THEORY OF HUMAN MOTIVATION

A. H. Maslow

Among the most extensively applied psychological theories is Abraham H. Maslow's hierarchy of human needs. Because the model enhances our ability to understand human motivation and behavior, it has been utilized by business, industry, marketing, the health professions, education, and the military. Its ubiquitous use has invited reinterpretation, sometimes resulting in misinterpretation, and in applications of which Maslow would disapprove.

Maslow was born in Brooklyn, New York in 1908. He was a son of Russian Jewish immigrants and had a lonely, unhappy childhood. His father once asked at a large family gathering, "Isn't Abe the ugliest kid you've ever seen?" Abe sought empty subway cars to spare others his sight. He detested his mother, who kept the refrigerator bolted shut. Reflecting on his childhood without parental love, he said ". . . the whole thrust of my life-philosophy and all my research and theorizing . . . has its roots in a hatred for and revulsion against everything she stood for" (Lowry, 1979, p. 958).

Maslow claimed that his life did not really start until he married his childhood sweetheart and first cousin, Bertha Goodman. He was fascinated with John B. Watson and behaviorism. He went to the University of Wisconsin where he concentrated on behavioral research with animals under experimental psychologist Harry Harlow.

Maslow's enchantment with behaviorism abruptly ended upon the birth of his first child; an event over which he had no control. He was incredibly moved by this "peak-experience," and concluded that behaviorism was woefully inadequate to help comprehend it. ". . . I'd say anyone who had a baby couldn't be a behaviorist" (Hall, 1968, p. 55).

His emphasis now became the study of healthy people. ". . . the study of crippled, stunted, immature, and unhealthy specimens can yield only a cripple psychology and a cripple philosophy" (Maslow, 1970, p. 80). German psychiatrist Kurt Goldstein studied severely injured war survivors. He marveled at the capability of the organism to reorganize after injury and evolve into a new unit that incorporated the damages. It was different from before, but not necessarily marred. He called this tendency self-actualization (DeCarvalho, 1990a). Maslow used the term more broadly to describe people who are healthy, creative, autonomous, achieve full potential, and contribute to the welfare of humanity.

His major professorships were at Brooklyn College and Brandeis University. He was appalled by the horror of World War II and directed his life to discovering a psychology for peace. During the mid-1960s, a growing counterculture sought a leader. Maslow was perhaps too conservative to fill this role. He dismissed overt pacifism as too simplistic, resigned from the American Civil Liberties Union because it defended criminals, and openly disagreed with Harvard University Professor Timothy Leary's advice to "tune in, turn on, and drop out" with drugs (Hergenhahn, 1994, p. 524). Despite his resistance to social trend, he emerged as a leader of the Third Force and was elected president of the American Psychological Association in 1966.

The following selection is an edited version of his 1943 classic A Theory of Human Motivation. *He explains the hierarchal model that has since been the subject of noteworthy attention. The model is logical, clear, and concise. Today, its application is so pervasive that critics dismiss it as "common sense."*

A.H. Maslow, A Theory of Human Motivation. *Psychological Review,* vol. 50, 1943, pp. 370-396. Reprinted with permission of the author.

References

DeCarvalho, R.J. (1990a). The Growth Hypothesis and Self-actualization: An Existential Alternative. *The Humanistic Psychologist*, 18, 252-258.

Hall, M.H. (1968, July). A Conversation with Abraham Maslow. *Psychology Today*, pp. 35-37, 54-57.

Hergenhahn, B.R. (1994). *An Introduction to Theories of Personality*. New Jersey: Prentice-Hall, Inc.

Lowry, R.J. (1979). *The Journals of A.H. Maslow*, Vols 1 & 2. Monterey, CA: Brooks/Cole.

Maslow, A.H. (1970). *Motivation and Personality* (2nd ed.). New York: Harper & Row.

The present paper is an attempt to formulate a positive theory of motivation which will satisfy theoretical demands and at the same time conform to the known facts, clinical and observational as well as experimental. It derives most directly, however, from clinical experience. This theory is, I think, in the functionalist tradition of James and Dewey, and is fused with the holism of Wertheimer (19), Goldstein (6), and Gestalt Psychology, and with the dynamicism of Freud (4) and Adler (1). This fusion or synthesis may arbitrarily be called a 'general-dynamic' theory.

It is far easier to perceive and to criticize the aspects in motivation theory than to remedy them. Mostly this is because of the very serious lack of sound data in this area. I conceive this lack of sound facts to be due primarily to the absence of a valid theory of motivation. The present theory then must be considered to be a suggested program or framework for future research and must stand or fall, not so much on facts available or evidence presented, as upon researches yet to be done, researches suggested perhaps, by the questions raised in this paper.

The Basic Needs

The physiological needs.—The needs that are usually taken as the starting point for motivation theory are the so-called physiological drives. Two recent lines of research make it necessary to revise our customary notions about these needs, first, the development of the concept of homeostasis, and second, the finding that appetites (preferential choices among foods) are a fairly efficient indication of actual needs or lacks in the body.

Homeostasis refers to the body's automatic efforts to maintain a constant, normal state of the blood stream. Cannon (2) has described this process for (1) the water content of the blood, (2)

salt content, (3) sugar content, (4) protein content, (5) fat content, (6) calcium content, (7) oxygen content, (8) constant hydrogen-ion level (acid-base balance) and (9) constant temperature of the blood. Obviously this list can be extended to include other minerals, the hormones, vitamins, etc.

Young in a recent article (21) has summarized the work on appetite in its relation to body needs. If the body lacks some chemical, the individual will tend to develop a specific appetite or partial hunger for that food element.

Thus it seems impossible as well as useless to make any list of fundamental physiological needs for they can come to almost any number one might wish, depending on the degree of specificity of description. We can not identify all physiological needs as homeostatic. That sexual desire, sleepiness, sheer activity and maternal behavior in animals are homeostatic, has not yet been demonstrated. Furthermore, this list would not include the various sensory pleasures (tastes, smells, tickling, stroking) which are probably physiological and which may become the goals of motivated behavior.

In a previous paper (13) it has been pointed out that these physiological drives or needs are to be considered unusual rather than typical because they are isolable, and because they are localizable somatically. That is to say, they are relatively independent of each other, of other motivations and of the organism as a whole, and secondly, in many cases, it is possible to demonstrate a localized, underlying somatic base for the drive. This is true less generally than has been thought (exceptions are fatigue, sleepiness, maternal responses) but it is still true in the classic instances of hunger, sex, and thirst.

It should be pointed out again that any of the physiological needs and the consummatory behavior involved with them serve as channels for all sorts of other needs as well. That is to say, the person who thinks he is hungry may actually be seeking more for comfort, or dependence, than for vitamins or proteins. Conversely, it is possible to satisfy the hunger need in part by other activities such as drinking water or smoking cigarettes. In other words, relatively isolable as these physiological needs are, they are not completely so.

Undoubtedly these physiological needs are the most prepotent of all needs. What this means specifically is, that in the human being who is missing everything in life in an extreme fashion, it is most likely that the major motivation would be the physiological needs rather than any others. A person who is lacking food, safety, love, and esteem would most probably hunger for food more strongly than for anything else.

If all the needs are unsatisfied, and the organism is then dominated by the physiological needs, all other needs may become simply non-existent or be pushed into the background. It is then fair to characterize the whole organism by saying simply that it is hungry, for consciousness is almost completely preempted by hunger. All capacities are put into the service of hunger-satisfaction, and the organization of these capacities is almost entirely determined by the one purpose of satisfying hunger. The receptors and effectors, the intelligence, memory, habits, all may now be defined simply as hunger-gratifying tools. Capacities that are not useful for this purpose lie dormant, or are pushed into the background. The urge to write poetry, the desire to acquire an automobile, the interest in American history, the desire for a new pair of shoes are, in the extreme case, forgotten or become of secondary importance. For the man who is extremely and dangerously hungry, no other interests exist but food. He dreams food, he remembers food, he thinks about food, he emotes only about food, he perceives only food and he wants only food. The more subtle determinants that ordinarily fuse with the physiological drives in organizing even feeding, drinking or sexual behavior, may now be so completely overwhelmed as to allow us to speak at this time (but only at this time) of pure hunger drive and behavior, with the one unqualified aim of relief.

Another peculiar characteristic of the human organism when it is dominated by a certain need is that the whole philosophy of the future tends also to change. For our chronically and extremely hungry man, Utopia can be defined very simply as a place where there is plenty of food. He tends to think that, if only he is guaranteed food for the rest of his life, he will be perfectly happy and will never want anything more. Life itself tends to be defined in terms of eating. Anything else will be defined as unimportant. Freedom, love, community feeling, respect, philosophy, may all be waved aside as fripperies which are useless since they fail to fill the stomach. Such a man may fairly be said to live by bread alone.

It cannot possibly be denied that such things are true but their *generality* can be denied. Emergency conditions are, almost by definition, rare in the normally functioning peaceful society. That this truism can be forgotten is due mainly to two reasons. First, rats have few motivations other than physiological ones, and since so much of the research upon motivation has been made with these animals, it is easy to carry the rat picture over to the human being. Secondly, it is too often not realized that culture itself is an adaptive tool, one of whose main functions is to make the physiological emergencies come less and less often. In most of the known societies, chronic extreme hunger of the emergency type is rare, rather than common. In any case, this is still true in the United States. The average American citizen is experiencing appetite rather than hunger when he says " I am hungry." He is apt to experience sheer life-and-death hunger only by accident and then only a few times through his entire life.

Obviously a good way to obscure the 'higher' motivations, and to get a lopsided view of human capacities and human nature, is to make the organism extremely and chronically hungry or thirsty. Anyone who attempts to make an emergency picture into a typical one, and who will measure all of man's goals and desires by his behavior during extreme physiological deprivation is certainly being blind to many things. It is quite true that man lives by bread alone— when there is no bread. But what happens to man's desires when there is plenty of bread and when his belly is chronically filled ?

At once other (and 'higher') needs emerge and these, rather than physiological hungers, dominate the organism. And when these in turn are satisfied, again new (and still 'higher') needs emerge and so on. This is what we mean by saying that the basic human needs are organized into a hierarchy of relative prepotency.

One main implication of this phrasing is that gratification becomes as important a concept as deprivation in motivation theory, for it releases the organism from the domination of a relatively more physiological need, permitting thereby the emergence of other more social goals. The physiological needs, along with their partial goals, when chronically gratified cease to exist as active determinant or organizers of behavior. They now exist only in a potential fashion in the sense that they may emerge again to dominate the organism if they are thwarted. But a want that is satisfied is no longer a want. The organism is dominated and in behavior organized only by unsatisfied needs. If hunger is satisfied, it becomes unimportant in the current dynamics of the individual.

This statement is somewhat qualified by a hypothesis to be discussed more fully later, namely that it is precisely those individuals in whom a certain need has always been satisfied who are best equipped to tolerate deprivation of that need in the future, and that furthermore, those who have been deprived in the past will react differently to current satisfactions than the one who has never been deprived.

The safety needs.—If the physiological needs are relatively well gratified, there then emerges a new set of needs, which we may categorize roughly as the safety needs. All that has been said of the physiological needs is equally true, although in lesser degree, of these desires. The organism may equally well be wholly dominated by them. They may serve as the almost exclusive organizers of behavior, recruiting all the capacities of the organism in their service, and we may then fairly describe the whole organism as a safety-seeking mechanism. Again we may say of the receptors, the effectors, of the intellect and the other capacities that they are primarily safety-seeking tools. Again, as in the hungry man, we find that the dominating goal is a strong determinant not only of his current world-

outlook and philosophy but also of his philosophy of the future. Practically everything looks less important than safety, (even sometimes the physiological needs which being satisfied, are now underestimated). A man, in this state, if it is extreme enough and chronic enough, may be characterized as living almost for safety alone.

Although in this paper we are interested primarily in the needs of the adult, we can approach an understanding of his safety needs perhaps more efficiently by observation of infants and children, in whom these needs are much more simple and obvious. One reason for the clearer appearance of the threat or danger reaction in infants, is that they do not inhibit this reaction at all, whereas adults in our society have been taught to inhibit it at all costs. Thus even when adults do feel their safety to be threatened we may not be able to see this on the surface. Infants will react in a total fashion and as if they were endangered, if they are disturbed or dropped suddenly, startled by loud noises, flashing light, or other unusual sensory stimulation, by rough handling, by general loss of support in the mother's arms, or by inadequate support.

In infants we can also see a much more direct reaction to bodily illnesses of various kinds. Sometimes these illnesses seem to be immediately and *per se* threatening and seem to make the child feel unsafe. For instance, vomiting, colic or other sharp pains seem to make the child look at the whole world in a different way. At such a moment of pain, it may be postulated that, for the child, the appearance of the whole world suddenly changes from sunniness to darkness, so to speak, and becomes a place in which anything at all might happen, in which previously stable things have suddenly become unstable. Thus a child who because of some bad food is taken ill may, for a day or two, develop fear, nightmares, and a need for protection and reassurance never seen in him before his illness.

Another indication of the child's need for safety is his preference for some kind of undisrupted routine or rhythm. He seems to want a predictable, orderly world. For instance, injustice, unfairness, or inconsistency in the parents seems to make a child feel anxious and unsafe. This attitude may be not so much because of the injustice *per se* or any particular pains involved, but rather because this treatment threatens to make the world look unreliable, or unsafe, or unpredictable. Young children seem to thrive better under a system which has at least a skeletal outline of rigidity, in which there is a schedule of a kind, some sort of routine, something that can be counted upon, not only for the present but also far into the future. Perhaps one could express this more accurately by saying that the child needs an organized world rather than an unorganized or unstructured one.

The central role of the parents and the normal family setup are indisputable. Quarreling, physical assault, separation, divorce or death within the family may be particularly terrifying. Also parental outbursts of rage or threats of punishment directed to the child, calling him names, speaking to him harshly, shaking him, handling him roughly, or actual physical punishment sometimes elicit such total panic and terror in the child that we must assume more is involved than the physical pain alone. While it is true that in some children this terror may represent also a fear of loss of parental love, it can also occur in completely rejected children, who seem to cling to the hating parents more for sheer safety and protection than because of hope of love.

Confronting the average child with new, unfamiliar, strange, unmanageable stimuli or situations will too frequently elicit the danger or terror reaction, as for example, getting lost or even being separated from the parents for a short time, being confronted with new faces, new situations or new tasks, the sight of strange, unfamiliar or uncontrollable objects, illness or death. Particularly at such times, the child's frantic clinging to his parents is eloquent testimony to their role as protectors (quite apart from their roles as food-givers and love-givers).

From these and similar observations, we may generalize and say that the average child in our society generally prefers a safe, orderly, predictable, organized world, which he can count on, and in which unexpected, unmanageable or other dangerous things do not happen, and in which, in any case, he has all-powerful parents who protect and shield him from harm.

That these reactions may so easily be observed in children is in a way a proof of the fact that children in our society, feel too unsafe (or, in a word, are badly brought up). Children who are reared in an unthreatening, loving family do *not* ordinarily react as we have described above (17). In such children the danger reactions are apt to come mostly to objects or situations that adults too would consider dangerous.

The healthy, normal, fortunate adult in our culture is largely satisfied in his safety needs. The peaceful, smoothly running, 'good' society ordinarily makes its members feel safe enough from wild animals, extremes of temperature, criminals, assault and murder, tyranny, etc. Therefore, in a very real sense, he no longer has any safety needs as active motivators. Just as a sated man no longer feels hungry, a safe man no longer feels endangered. If we wish to see these needs directly and clearly we must turn to neurotic or near-neurotic individuals, and to the economic and social underdogs. In between these extremes, we can perceive the expressions of safety needs only in such phenomena as, for instance, the common preference for a job with tenure and protection, the desire for a savings account, and for insurance of various kinds (medical, dental, unemployment, disability, old age).

Other broader aspects of the attempt to seek safety and stability in the world are seen in the very common preference for familiar rather than unfamiliar things, or for the known rather than the unknown. The tendency to have some religion or world-philosophy that organizes the universe and the men in it into some sort of satisfactorily coherent, meaningful whole is also in part motivated by safety-seeking. Here too we may list science and philosophy in general as partially motivated by the safety needs (we shall see later that there are also other motivations to scientific, philosophical, or religious endeavor).

Otherwise the need for safety is seen as an active and dominant mobilizer of the organism's resources only in emergencies, e.g., war, disease, natural catastrophes, crime waves, societal disorganization, neurosis, brain injury, and chronically bad situations.

Some neurotic adults in our society are, in many ways, like the unsafe child in their desire for safety, although in the former it takes on a somewhat special appearance. Their reaction is often to unknown, psychological dangers in a world that is perceived to be hostile, overwhelming and threatening. Such a person behaves as if a great catastrophe were almost always impending, i.e., he is usually responding as if to an emergency. His safety needs often find specific expression in a search for a protector, or a stronger person on whom he may depend, or perhaps, a Fuehrer [as Hitler was called].

The neurotic individual may be described in a slightly different way with some usefulness as a grown-up person who retains his childish attitudes toward the world. That is to say, a neurotic adult may be said to behave 'as if' he were actually afraid of a spanking, or of his mother's disapproval, or of being abandoned by his parents, or having his food taken away from him. It is as if his childish attitudes of fear and threat reaction to a dangerous world had gone underground, and untouched by the growing up and learning processes, were now ready to be called out by any stimulus that would make a child feel endangered and threatened.

The neurosis in which the search for safety takes its clearest form is in the compulsive-obsessive neurosis. Compulsive-obsessives try frantically to order and stabilize the world so that no unmanageable, unexpected or unfamiliar dangers will ever appear (14). They hedge themselves about with all sorts of ceremonials, rules and formulas so that every possible contingency may be provided for and so that no new contingencies may appear. They are much like the brain injured cases, described by Goldstein (6), who manage to maintain their equilibrium by avoiding everything unfamiliar and strange and by ordering their restricted world in such a neat, disciplined, orderly fashion that everything in the world can be counted upon. They try to arrange the world so that anything unexpected (dangers) cannot possibly occur. If, through no fault of their own, something unexpected does occur, they go into a panic reaction as if this unexpected occurrence constituted a grave danger. What we can see only as a none-too-strong preference in the healthy person, e.g., preference for the familiar, becomes a life-and-death necessity in abnormal cases.

The love needs.—If both the physiological and the safety needs are fairly well gratified, then there will emerge the love and affection and belongingness needs, and the whole cycle already described will repeat itself with this new center. Now the person will feel keenly, as never before, the absence of friends, or a sweetheart, or a wife, or children. He will hunger for affectionate relations with people in general, namely, for a place in his group, and he will strive with great intensity to achieve this goal. He will want to attain such a place more than anything else in the world and may even forget that once, when he was hungry, he sneered at love.

In our society the thwarting of these needs is the most commonly found core in cases of maladjustment and more severe psychopathology. Love and affection, as well as their possible expression in sexuality, are generally looked upon with ambivalence and are customarily hedged about with many restrictions and inhibitions. Practically all theorists of psychopathology have stressed thwarting of the love needs as basic in the picture of maladjustment. Many clinical studies have therefore been made of this need and we know more about it perhaps than any of the other needs except the physiological ones (14).

One thing that must be stressed at this point is that love is not synonymous with sex. Sex may be studied as a purely physiological need. Ordinarily sexual behavior is multi-determined, that is to say, determined not only by sexual but also by other needs, chief among which are the love and affection needs. Also not to be overlooked is the fact that the love needs involve both giving and receiving love.

The esteem needs.—All people in our society (with a few pathological exceptions) have a need or desire for a stable, firmly based, (usually) high evaluation of themselves, for self-respect, or self-esteem, and for the esteem of others. By firmly based self-esteem, we mean that which is soundly based upon real capacity, achievement and respect from others. These needs may be classified into two subsidiary sets. These are, first, the desire for strength, for achievement, for adequacy, for confidence in the face of the world, and for independence and freedoms. Secondly, we have what we may call the desire for reputation or prestige (defining it as respect or esteem from other people), recognition, attention, importance or appreciations. These needs have been relatively stressed by Alfred Adler and his followers, and have been relatively neglected by Freud and the psychoanalysts. More and more today however there is appearing widespread appreciation of their central importance.

Satisfaction of the self-esteem need leads to feelings of self-confidence, worth, strength, capability and adequacy: of being useful and necessary in the world. But thwarting of these needs produces feelings of inferiority, of weakness and of helplessness. These feelings in turn give rise to either basic discouragement or else compensatory or neurotic trends. An appreciation of the necessity of basic self-confidence and an understanding of how helpless people are without it, can be easily gained from a study of severe traumatic neurosis (8).

The need for self-actualization.—Even if all these needs are satisfied, we may still often (if not always) expect that a new discontent and restlessness will soon develop, unless the individual is doing what he is fitted for. A musician must make music, an artist must paint, a poet must write, if he is to be ultimately happy. What a man *can* be, he *must* be. This need we may call self-actualization.

This term, first coined by Kurt Goldstein, is being used in this paper in a much more specific and limited fashion. It refers to the desire for self-fulfillment, namely, to the tendency for him to become actualized in what he is potentially. This tendency might be phrased as the desire to become more and more what one is, to become everything that one is capable of becoming.

The specific form that these needs will take will of course vary greatly from person to person. In one individual it may take the form of the desire to be an ideal mother, in another it may be expressed athletically, and in still another it may be expressed in painting pictures or in inventions. It is not necessarily a creative urge although in people who have any capacities for creation it will take this form.

The clear emergence of these needs rests upon prior satisfaction of the physiological, safety, love and esteem needs. We shall call people who are satisfied in these needs, basically satis-

fied people, and it is from these that we may expect the fullest (and healthiest) creativeness. Since, in our society, basically satisfied people are the exception, we do not know much about self-actualization, either experimentally or clinically. It remains a challenging problem for research. . .

Further Characteristics of the Basic Needs

The degree of fixity of the hierarchy of basic needs.—We have spoken so far as if this hierarchy were a fixed order but actually it is not nearly as rigid as we may have implied. It is true that most of the people with whom we have worked have seemed to have these basic needs in about the order that has been indicated. However, there have been a number of exceptions.

(1) There are some people in whom, for instance, self-esteem seems to be more important than love. This most common reversal in the hierarchy is usually due to the development of the notion that the person who is most likely to be loved is a strong or powerful person, one who inspires respect or fear, and who is self confident or aggressive. Therefore such people who lack love and seek it, may try hard to put on a front of aggressive, confident behavior. But essentially they seek high self-esteem and its behavior expressions more as a means-to-an-end than for its own sake; they seek self-assertion for the sake of love rather than for self-esteem itself.

(2) There are other, apparently innately creative people in whom the drive to creativeness seems to be more important than any other counter-determinant. Their creativeness might appear not as self-actualization released by basic satisfaction, but in spite of lack of basic satisfaction.

(3) In certain people the level of aspiration may be permanently deadened or lowered. That is to say, the less prepotent goals may simply be lost, and may disappear forever, so that the person who has experienced life at a very low level, i.e., chronic unemployment, may continue to be satisfied for the rest of his life if only he can get enough food.

(4) The so-called 'psychopathic personality' is another example of permanent loss of the love-needs. These are people who, according to the best data available (9), have been starved for love

in the earliest months of their lives and have simply lost forever the desire and the ability to give and to receive affection (as animals lose sucking or pecking reflexes that are not exercised soon enough after birth).

(5) Another cause of reversal of the hierarchy is that when a need has been satisfied for a long time, this need may be under-evaluated. People who have never experienced chronic hunger are apt to underestimate its effects and to look upon food as a rather unimportant thing. If they are dominated by a higher need, this higher need will seem to be the most important of all. It then becomes possible, and indeed does actually happen, that they may, for the sake of this higher need, put themselves into the position of being deprived in a more basic need. We may expect that after a long-time deprivation of the more basic need there will be a tendency to reevaluate both needs so that the more prepotent need will actually become consciously prepotent for the individual who may have given it up very lightly. Thus, a man who has given up his job rather than lose his self-respect, and who then starves for six months or so, may be willing to take his job back even at the price of losing his self-respect.

(6) Another partial explanation of *apparent* reversals is seen in the fact that we have been talking about the hierarchy of prepotency in terms of consciously felt wants or desires rather than of behavior. Looking at behavior itself may give us the wrong impression. What we have claimed is that the person will want the more basic of two needs when deprived in both. There is no necessary implication here that he will act upon his desires. Let us say again that there are many determinants of behavior other than the needs and desires.

(7) Perhaps more important than all these exceptions are the ones that involve ideals, high social standards, high values and the like. With such values people become martyrs; they will give up everything for the sake of a particular ideal, or value. These people may be understood, at least in part, by reference to one basic concept (or hypothesis) which may be called 'increased frustration-tolerance through early gratification.' People who have been satisfied in their basic needs throughout their lives, particularly in their

earlier years, seem to develop exceptional power to withstand present or future thwarting of these needs simply because they have strong, healthy character structure as a result of basic satisfaction. They are the 'strong' people who can easily weather disagreement or opposition, who can swim against the stream of public opinion and who can stand up for the truth at great personal cost. It is just the ones who have loved and been well loved, and who have had many deep friendships who can hold out against hatred, rejection or persecution. . . .

Degrees of relative satisfaction—So far, our theoretical discussion may have given the impression that these five sets of needs are somehow in a step-wise, all-or-none relationships to each other. We have spoken in such terms as the following: "If one need is satisfied, then another emerges." This statement might give the false impression that a need must be satisfied 100 percent before the next need emerges. In actual fact, most members of our society who are normal, are partially satisfied in all their basic needs and partially unsatisfied in all their basic needs at the same time. A more realistic description of the hierarchy would be in terms of decreasing percentages of satisfaction as we go up the hierarchy of prepotency. For instance, if I may assign arbitrary figures for the sake of illustration, it is as if the average citizen is satisfied perhaps 85 percent in his physiological needs, 70 percent in his safety needs, 50 percent in his love needs, 40 percent in his self-esteem needs, and 10 percent in his self-actualization needs.

As for the concept of emergence of a new need after satisfaction of the prepotent need, this emergence is not a sudden, saltatory phenomenon but rather a gradual emergence by slow degrees from nothingness. For instance, if prepotent need A is satisfied only 10 percent then need B may not be visible at all. However, as this need A becomes satisfied 25 percent, need B may emerge 5 percent, as need A becomes satisfied 75 percent need B may emerge 50 percent, and so on. . . .

The role of gratified need.—It has been pointed out above several times that our needs usually emerge only when more prepotent needs have been gratified. Thus gratification has an important role in motivation theory. Apart from this, however, needs cease to play an active determining or organizing role as soon as they are gratified. . . .

A man who is thwarted in any of his basic needs should be envisaged simply as a sick man. This is a fair parallel to our designation as 'sick' of the man who lacks vitamins or minerals. Who is to say that a lack of love is less important than a lack of vitamins? Since we know the pathogenic effects of love starvation, who is to say that we are invoking value-questions in an unscientific or illegitimate way, any more than the physician does who diagnoses and treats pellagra or scurvy? If I were permitted this usage, I should then say simply that a healthy man is primarily motivated by his needs to develop and actualize his fullest potentialities and capacities. If a man has any other basic needs in any active, chronic sense, then he is simply an unhealthy man. He is as surely sick as if he had suddenly developed a strong salt-hunger or calcium hunger.

If this statement seems unusual or paradoxical the reader may be assured that this is only one among many such paradoxes that will appear as we revise our ways of looking at man's deeper motivations. When we ask what man wants of life, we deal with his very essence.

SUMMARY

(1) There are at least five sets of goals, which we may call basic needs. These are briefly physiological, safety, love, esteem, and self-actualization. In addition, we are motivated by the desire to achieve or maintain the various conditions upon which these basic satisfactions rest and by certain more intellectual desires.

(2) These basic goals are related to each other, being arranged in a hierarchy of prepotency. This means that the most prepotent goal will monopolize consciousness and will tend of itself to organize the recruitment of the various capacities of the organism. The less prepotent needs are minimized, even forgotten or denied. But when a need is fairly well satisfied, the next prepotent ('higher') need emerges, in turn to dominate the conscious life and to serve as the center of organization of behavior, since gratified needs are not active motivators.

Thus man is a perpetually wanting animal. Ordinarily the satisfaction of these wants is not altogether mutually exclusive, but only tends to be. The average member of our society is most often partially satisfied and partially unsatisfied in all of his wants. The hierarchy principle is usually empirically observed in terms of increasing percentages of non-satisfaction as we go up the hierarchy. Reversals of the average order of the hierarchy are sometimes observed. Also it has been observed that an individual may permanently lose the higher wants in the hierarchy under special conditions. There are not only ordinarily multiple motivations for usual behavior, but in addition many determinants other than motives.

(3) Any thwarting or possibility of thwarting of these basic human goals, or danger to the defenses which protect them, or to the conditions upon which they rest, is considered to be a psychological threat. With a few exceptions, all psychopathology may be partially traced to such threats. A basically thwarted man may actually be defined as a 'sick' man, if we wish. . .

References

1. Adler, A. *Social interest*, London: Faber & Faber, 1938.
2. Cannon, W. B. *Wisdom of the Body*. New York: Norton 1932.
3. Freud, A. *The ego and the mechanisms of defense*. London: Hogarth, 1937.
4. Freud, S. *New introductory lectures on psychoanalysis*. New York: Norton, 1933.
5. Fromm, E. *Escape from Freedom*. New York: Farrar and Rinehart 1941.
6. Goldstein, K. *The organism*. New York: American Book Co., 1939.
7. Horney, K. *The neurotic personality of our time*. New York: Norton, 1937.
8. Kardiner, A. *The traumatic neuroses of war*. New York: Hoeber, 1941.
9. Levy, D. M. Primary affect hunger. *Amer. J. Psychiat.*, 1937, 94, 643-652.

10. Maslow, A. H. Conflict, frustration, and the theory of threat. *J. Abnorm. (Soc.) Psychol.*, 1943, 38, 81-86.

11._____. Dominance, personality and social behavior in women. *J. Soc. Psychol.*, 1939, 10, 3-39.

12._____. The dynamics of psychological security-insecurity. *Character & Pers.*, 1942, 10, 331-344.

13._____. A preface to motivation theory. *Psychosomatic Med.*, 1943, 585-92.

14._____ & Mittleman, B. *Principles of abnormal psychology*. New York: Harper & Bros., 1941.

15. Murray, H. A., et al. *Explorations in personality*. New York: Oxford University Press, 1938.

16. Plant, J. *Personality and the cultural pattern*. New York: Commonwealth Fund, 1937.

17. Shirley, M. Children's adjustments to a strange situation. *J. Abnorm. (Soc.) Psychol.,* 1942, 37, 201-217.

18. Tolman, E.C. *Purposive behavior in animals and men*. New York: Century, 1932:

19. Wertheimer, M. Unpublished lecture at the New School for Social Research.

20. Young, P.T. *Modification of behavior*. New York: John Wiley & Sons, 1936.

21. _____.The experimental analysis of appetite *Psychol. Bull.,* 1941, 38, 129-164.

Figure 9-4. Carl Rogers, center, with a group of workshop students at the Adirondack Humanistic Center, Upper Jay, New York, in 1972. Third from right, top row, is Professor Emeritus Joseph E. Riley. (Personal photograph of Professor Riley.)

READING 9D

SOME HYPOTHESES REGARDING THE FACILITATION OF PERSONAL GROWTH

Carl Rogers

Carl Rogers championed many integral notions of humanism more than two decades before its formal beginning. In 1928, he helped delinquent children at the Child Study Department of the Society for the Prevention of Cruelty to Children in Rochester, New York. In 1942 his first book, Counseling and Psychotherapy, *was published. In 1956, Rogers engaged his nemesis, B.F. Skinner, in a classic symposium at the annual conference of the American Psychological Association. The battlelines between behaviorism and humanism were drawn.*

His major professorships were at the Universities of Chicago and Wisconsin. From 1968 until his death in 1987, he was a resident fellow at the Center for Studies of the Person in La Jolla, California (Nye, 1992, p. 96). There, he was a leader of the encounter group movement of the 1970s. Encounter groups are small groups that, through intense interaction, help people gain self-insight, and solve common problems.

Early in his career, Rogers called his psychotherapy client-centered, later to become person-centered. Either indicates the essence of his therapy. The illness, behavioristic, and psychoanalytic perspectives use doctor-patient terminology, implying illness. Rogers views the person with whom he is involved as normal and competent, and perceives his role as helping the person grow and actualize. As a person seeking legal help contracts a lawyer, a person seeking psychological help contracts a therapist.

Rogers feels that the success of therapy depends upon the therapeutic rapport created between himself and the person. Under proper conditions this relationship can be used by the client to enhance growth.

Carl Rogers died suddenly in 1987. He was still active at the Center for the Study of the Person. When he was over eighty, he was still leading peace workshops in Europe, South Africa, and the Soviet Union. One session held in the Soviet Union was to emphasize humanistic education and creativity. As commonly practiced, the group was allowed to take its own course. However, vicious hostility, accusations, and resentment among group members resulted. Rogers, stating his genuine reaction, told the group he was "horrified" by the way it was acting (Nye, 1992, p. 123).

Rogers' obituary in the American Psychologist was written by his friend and colleague Eugene T. Gedlin. He wrote, "He cared about each person—but not about the institutions. He did not care about appearances, roles, class, credentials, or positions, and he doubted every authority including his own." The last time the two met was at a video-recorded panel. An argument began between those who supported pure client-centered therapy and those who supported other techniques. Apparently dismayed by the counterproductive intrusion, Rogers said, "I didn't want to find a client-centered way. I wanted to find a way to help people." (Gedlin, 1988).

The following selection from On Becoming a Person, *describes the conditions under which Rogers believes maximum beneficial therapeutic change can occur. As you read the article you may perceive that Rogers is overly optimistic. Some consider him naive. However, optimism is a core characteristic of the humanist.*

References
Gedlin, E.T. (1988, February). Obituary for Carl Rogers. *American Psychologist*, 43(2), 128-129.
Nye, R.D. (1992). *Three Psychologies: Perspectives from Freud, Skinner, and Rogers,* 4th ed. California: Brooks/Cole Publishing Company.

To be faced by a troubled, conflicted person who is seeking and expecting help, has always constituted a great challenge to me. Do I have the knowledge, the resources, the psychological strength, the skill—do I have whatever it takes to be of help to such an individual?

For more than twenty-five years I have been trying to meet this kind of challenge. It has caused me to draw upon every element of my professional background: the rigorous methods of personality measurement which I first learned at Teachers' College, Columbia; the Freudian psychoanalytic insights and methods of the Institute for Child Guidance where I worked as interne; the continuing developments in the field of clinical psychology, with which I have been closely associated; the briefer exposure to the work of Otto Rank, to the methods of psychiatric social work, and other resources too numerous to mention. But most of all it has meant a continual learning from my own experience and that of my colleagues at the Counseling Center as we have endeavored to discover for ourselves effective means of working with people in distress. Gradually I have developed a way of working which grows out of that experience, and which can be tested, refined and reshaped by further experience and by research.

A General Hypothesis

One brief way of describing the change which has taken place in me is to say that in my early professional years I was asking the question, How can I treat, or cure, or change this person? Now I would phrase the question in this way: How can I provide a relationship which this person may use for his own personal growth?

It is as I have come to put the question in this second way that I realize that whatever I have learned is applicable to all of my human relationships, not just to working with clients with problems. It is for this reason that I feel it is possible that the learnings which have had meaning for me in my experience may have some meaning for you in your experience, since all of us are involved in human relationships.

Perhaps I should start with a negative learning. It has gradually been driven home to me that I cannot be of help to this troubled person by means of any intellectual or training procedure. No approach which relies upon knowledge, upon training, upon the acceptance of something that is *taught*, is of any use. These approaches seem so tempting and direct that I have, in the past, tried a great many of them. It is possible to explain a person to himself, to prescribe steps which should lead him forward, to train him in knowledge about a more satisfying mode of life. But such methods are, in my experience, futile and inconsequential. The most they can accomplish is some temporary change, which soon disappears, leaving the individual more than ever convinced of his inadequacy.

The failure of any such approach through the intellect has forced me to recognize that change appears to come about through experience in a relationship. So I am going to try to state very briefly and informally, some of the essential hypotheses regarding a helping relationship which have seemed to gain increasing confirmation both from experience and research.

I can state the overall hypothesis in one sentence, as follows. If I can provide a certain type of relationship, the other person will discover within himself the capacity to use that relationship for growth, and change and personal development will occur.

The Relationship

But what meaning do these terms have? Let me take separately the three major phrases in this sentence and indicate something of the meaning they have for me. What is this certain type of relationship I would like to provide?

I have found that the more that I can be genuine in the relationship, the more helpful it will be. This means that I need to be aware of my own feelings, in so far as possible, rather than presenting an outward facade of one attitude, while actually holding another attitude at a deeper or unconscious level. Being genuine also involves the willingness to be and to express, in my words and my behavior, the various feelings and attitudes which exist in me. It is only in this way that the relationship can have *reality*, and reality seems deeply important as a first condition. It is only by providing the genuine reality which is in me, that the other person can successfully seek for the reality in him. I have found this to be true even when the attitudes I feel are not attitudes with which I am pleased, or attitudes which seem conducive to a good relationship. It seems extremely important to be real.

As a second condition, I find that the more acceptance and liking I feel toward this individual, the more I will be creating a relationship which he can use. By acceptance I mean a warm regard for him as a person of unconditional self-worth—of value no matter what his condition, his behavior, or his feelings. It means a respect and liking for him as a separate person, a willingness for him to possess his own feelings in his own way. It means an acceptance of and regard for his attitudes of the moment, no matter how negative or positive, no matter how much they may contradict other attitudes he has held in the past. This acceptance of each fluctuating aspect of this other person makes it for him a relationship of warmth and safety, and the safety of being liked and prized as a person seems a highly important element in a helping relationship.

I also find that the relationship is significant to the extent that I feel a continuing desire to understand—a sensitive empathy with each of the client's feelings and communications as they seem to him at that moment. Acceptance does not mean much until it involves understanding. It is only as I *understand* the feelings and thoughts which seem so horrible to you, or so weak, or so sentimental, or so bizarre—it is only as I see them as you see them, and accept them and you, that you feel really free to explore all the hidden nooks and frightening crannies of your inner and often buried experience. This *freedom* is an important condition of the relationship. There is implied here a freedom to explore oneself at both conscious and unconscious levels, as rapidly as one can dare to embark on this dangerous quest. There is also a complete freedom from any type of moral or diagnostic evaluation, since all such evaluations are, I believe, always threatening.

Thus the relationship which I have found helpful is characterized by a sort of transparency on my part, in which my real feelings are evident; by an acceptance of this other person as a separate person with value in his own right; and by a deep empathic understanding which enables me to see his private world through his eyes. When these conditions are achieved, I become a companion to my client, accompanying him in the frightening search for himself, which he now feels free to undertake.

I am by no means always able to achieve this kind of relationship with another, and sometimes, even when I feel I have achieved it in myself, he may be too frightened to perceive what is being offered to him. But I would say that when I hold in myself the kind of attitudes I have described, and when the other person can to some degree experience these attitudes, then I believe that change and constructive personal development will invariably occur—and I include the word "invariably" only after long and careful consideration.

The Motivation For Change

So much for the relationship. The second phrase in my overall hypothesis was that the individual will discover within himself the capacity to use this relationship for growth. I will try to indicate something of the meaning which that phrase has for me. Gradually my experience has forced me to conclude that the individual has within himself the capacity and the tendency, latent if not evident, to move forward toward maturity. In a suitable psychological climate this tendency is released, and becomes actual rather than potential. It is evident in the capacity of the individual to understand those aspects of his life and of himself which are causing him pain and dissatisfaction, an understanding which probes beneath his conscious knowledge of himself into those experiences which he has hidden from himself because of their threatening nature. It shows itself in the tendency to reorganize his personality and his relationship to life in ways which are regarded as more mature. Whether one calls it a growth tendency, a drive toward self-actualization, or a forward-moving directional tendency, it is the mainspring of life, and is, in the last analysis, the tendency upon which all psychotherapy depends. It is the urge which is evident in all organic and human life—to expand, extend, become autonomous, develop, mature—the tendency to express and activate all the capacities of the organism, to the extent that such activation enhances the organism or the self. This tendency may become deeply buried under layer after layer of encrusted psychological defenses; it may be hidden behind elaborate facades which deny its existence; but it is my belief that it exists in every individual, and awaits only the proper conditions to be released and expressed.

The Outcomes

I have attempted to describe the relationship which is basic to constructive personality change. I have tried to put into words the type of capacity which the individual brings to such a relationship. The third phrase of my general statement was that change and personal development would occur. It is my hypothesis that in such a relationship the individual will reorganize himself at both the conscious and deeper levels of his personality in such a manner as to cope with life more constructively, more intelligently, and in a more socialized as well as a more satisfying way.

Here I can depart from speculation and bring in the steadily increasing body of solid knowledge which is accumulating. We know now that individuals who live in such a relationship even for a relatively limited number of hours show profound and significant changes in personality, attitudes, and behavior, changes that do not occur in matched control groups. In such a relationship the individual becomes more integrated, more effective. He shows fewer of the characteristics which are usually termed neurotic or psychotic, and more of the characteristics of the healthy, well-functioning person. He changes his perception of himself, becoming more realistic in his views of self. He becomes more like the person he wishes to be. He values himself more highly. He is more self-confident and self-directing. He has a better understanding of himself, becomes more open to his experience, denies or represses less of his experience. He becomes more accepting in his attitudes toward others, seeing others as more similar to himself.

In his behavior he shows similar changes. He is less frustrated by stress, and recovers from stress more quickly. He becomes more mature in his everyday behavior as this is observed by friends. He is less defensive, more adaptive, more able to meet situations creatively.

These are some of the changes which we now know come about in individuals who have completed a series of counseling interviews in which the psychological atmosphere approximates the relationship I described. Each of the statements made is based upon objective evidence. Much more research needs to be done, but there can no longer be any doubt as to the effectiveness of such a relationship in producing personality change.

A Broad Hypothesis of Human Relationships

To me, the exciting thing about these research findings is not simply the fact that they give evidence of the efficacy of one form of psychotherapy, though that is by no means unimportant. The excitement comes from the fact that these findings justify an even broader hypothesis regarding all human relationships. There seems every reason to suppose that the therapeutic relationship is only one instance of interpersonal relations, and that the same lawfulness governs all such relationships. Thus it seems reasonable to hypothesize that if the parent creates with his child a psychological climate such as we have described, then the child will become more self-directing, socialized, and mature. To the extent that the teacher creates such a relationship with his class, the student will become a self-initiated learner, more original, more self-disciplined, less anxious and other-directed. If the administrator, or military or industrial leader, creates such a climate within his organization, then his staff will become more self-responsible, more creative, better able to adapt to new problems, more basically cooperative. It appears possible to me that we are seeing the emergence of a new field of human relationships, in which we may specify that if certain attitudinal conditions exist, then certain definable changes will occur.

Conclusion

Let me conclude by returning to a personal statement. I have tried to share with you something of what I have learned in trying to be of help to troubled, unhappy, maladjusted individuals. I have formulated the hypothesis which has gradually come to have meaning for me—not only in my relationship to clients in distress, but in all my human relationships.

I have indicated that such research knowledge as we have supports this hypothesis, but that there is much more investigation needed. I should like now to pull together into one statement the conditions of this general hypothesis, and the effects which are specified.

If I can create a relationship characterized on my part:

- by a genuineness and transparency, in which I am my real feelings;
- by a warm acceptance of and prizing of the other person as a separate individual;
- by a sensitive ability to see his world and himself as he sees them;

then the other individual in the relationship:

- will experience and understand aspects of himself which previously he has repressed;
- will find himself becoming better integrated, more able to function effectively;
- will become more similar to the person he would like to be;
- will be more self-directing and self-confident;
- will become more of a person, more unique and more self-expressive;
- will be more understanding, more acceptant of others;
- will be able to cope with the problems of life more adequately and more comfortably.

I believe that this statement holds whether I am speaking of my relationship with a client, with a group of students or staff members, with my family or children. It seems to me that we have here a general hypothesis which offers exciting possibilities for the development of creative, adaptive, autonomous persons.

Figure 9-5. Population density causes pathology in Calhoun's mouse colony. (Photograph by Bunji Tagawa from "Population Density and Social Pathology" by John B. Calhoun (*Scientific American*, February, 1962). Copyright © 1962 by *Scientific American*. All rights reserved.)

Figure 9-6. Blind Logwara found humor in being trampled by fellow Ik who fought him for putrid hyena meat. The Ik represent an unfortunate analogue of the mouse colony. (Reprinted with the permission of Simon & Schuster from *The Mountain People* by Colin M. Turnbull. Copyright © 1972 by Colin M. Turnbull.)

READING 9E

PLIGHT OF THE IK AND KAIADILT IS SEEN AS A CHILLING POSSIBLE END FOR MAN

John B. Calhoun

In June of 1979, 18-year-old Renee Katz, a gifted flutist, was maliciously, and without provocation or motive, pushed in front of a moving New York City subway train. Her hand was severed in the incident, but was miraculously reattached. A man charged with the crime was acquitted in January of 1980. In April of 1989, the "Central Park Jogger" was savagely assaulted and left for dead by a gang of attackers. In August of 1995 in Detroit, a young woman was brutally beaten on a bridge before an allegedly cheering crowd. She ultimately jumped to her death. Unfortunately, cases of wanton violence such as these are not uncommon. What could possibly motivate such cruel, heinous behavior? Perhaps an examination of the nature of contemporary American society can provide us with an answer.

Humanistic psychologists have stressed that people need to perceive purpose, significance, and meaning in their existence to become self-actualized. Carl Rogers long maintained that people need to be valued and prized as unique, inherently good individuals to develop positive self-concepts.

Erik Erikson's work with Native Americans on reservations and hospitalized disabled war veterans has added to our understanding of the adjustment problems of people who have suffered existential crises. Their problems were related to the fact that they had been uprooted from their normal life style and cut off from what was meaningful in their lives. They had lost the sense of who and what they were. They had been robbed of their sense of identity.

What happens to people when they live under conditions that make self-actualization impossible, are stripped of identity, and perceive no significance or meaning in their existence? The unfortunate answer may be that they lack integral human qualities. They lose the ability to enjoy living and the capacity to love, share with, and care for others. As opposed to being self-actualized, they become self-absorbed. They may gain a sense of perverted significance through recognition received by being cruel to others.

In 1962, John B. Calhoun, author of this article, conducted controversial research that received severe criticism. He created rat colonies in which the population became greater than the environment could support. Overcrowding, pollution, and debasement resulted in cannibalism and pathological behavior (Calhoun, 1962). His critics claimed that his study was unnecessary and cruel. Calhoun maintained that similar pathology can also occur in humans. The following article relates the experiences that anthropologist Colin M. Turnbull had with a human equivalent to Calhoun's rat colonies. It is Calhoun's opportunity to say "I told you so" to those who criticized his work.

The article can help us understand what might motivate violence. It also helps us understand the human cost of overcrowding, dehumanization, and degradation which often coexist with unprecedented affluence and technology in our larger cities.

John B. Calhoun, "Plight of the Ik and Kaiadilt is seen as a Chilling Possible End for Man," *Smithsonian*, November, 1972. Reprinted with permission of Edith G. Calhoun.

The Mountain—how pervasive in the history of man. A still small voice on Horeb, mount of God, guided Elijah. There, earlier, Moses standing before God received the Word. And Zion: "I am the Lord your God dwelling in Zion, my holy mountain."

Then there was Atum, mountain, God and first man, one and all together. The mountain rose out of a primordial sea of nothingness—Nun. Atum, the spirit of life, existed within Nun. In creating himself, Atum became the evolving ancestor of the human race. So goes the Egyptian mythology of creation, in which the Judaic Adam has his roots.

And there is a last Atum, united in his youth with another mountain of God, Mt. Morungole in northeasternmost Uganda. His people are the Ik, pronounced eek. They are the subject of an important new book, *The Mountain People,* by Colin M. Turnbull (Simon and Schuster). They still speak Middle-Kingdom Egyptian, a language thought to be dead. But perhaps their persistence is not so strange. Egyptian mythology held that the waters of the life-giving Nile had their origin in Nun. Could this Nun have been the much more extensive Lake Victoria of 10 to 50 millenia ago when, near its borders, man groped upward to cloak his biological self with culture?

Well might the Ik have preserved the essence of this ancient tradition that affirms human beginnings. Isolated as they have been in their jagged mountain vastness, near the upper tributaries of the White Nile, the Ik have been protected from cultural evolution.

What a Shangri-la, this land of the Ik. In its center, the Kidepo valley, 35 miles across, home of abundant game; to the south, mist-topped Mt. Morungole; to the west the Niangea range; to the north, bordering the Sudan, the Didinga range; to the east on the Kenya border, a sheer drop of 2,000 feet into the Turkanaland of cattle herdsmen. Through ages of dawning history few people must have been interested in encroaching on this rugged land. Until 1964 anthropologists knew little of the Ik's existence. Their very name, much less their language, remained a mystery until, quite by chance, anthropologist Colin M. Turnbull found himself among them. What an opportunity to study pristine man! Here one should encounter the basic qualities of humanity unmarred by war, technology, pollution, overpopulation.

Turnbull rested in his bright red Land Rover at an 8,000-foot-high pass. A bit beyond this only "navigable" pass into the Kidepo Valley, lay Pirre, a police outpost watching over a cluster of Ik villages. There to welcome him came Atum of the warm, open smile and gentle voice. Grayhaired at 40, appearing 65, he was the senior elder of the Ik, senior in authority if not quite so in age. Nattily attired in shorts and woolen sweater—in contrast to his mostly naked colleagues—Atum bounced forward with his ebony walking stick, greeted Turnbull in Swahili, and from that moment on took command as best he could of Turnbull's life. At Atum's village a plaintive woman's voice called out. Atum remarked that that was his wife—sick, too weak to work in the fields. Turnbull offered to bring her food and medicine. Atum suggested he handle Turnbull's gifts. As the weeks wore on Atum picked up the parcels that Turnbull was supplying for Atum's wife.

One day Atum's brother-in-law, Lomongin, laughingly asked Turnbull if he didn't know that Atum's wife had been dead for weeks. She had received no food or medicine. Atum had sold it. So she just died. All of this was revealed with no embarrassment. Atum joined the laughter over the joke played on Turnbull.

Another time Atum and Lojieri were guiding Turnbull over the mountains, and at one point induced him to push ahead through high grass until he broke through into a clearing. The clearing was a sheer 1,500-foot drop. The two Iks rolled on the ground, nearly bursting with laughter because Turnbull just managed to catch himself. What a lovable cherub this Atum! His laughter never ended.

New Meaning of Laughter

Laughter, hallmark of mankind, not shared with any other animal, not even primates, was an outstanding trait of the Ik. A whole village rushed to the edge of a low cliff and joined in communal laughter at blind old Lo'ono who lay thrashing on her back, near death after stumbling over. One evening Iks around a fire watched a child as it crawled toward the flames, then writhed back screaming after it grasped a gleaming coal. Laughter erupted. Quiet came to the child as its mother cuddled it in a kind of respect for the merriment it had caused. Then there was the laughter of innocent childhood as boys and girls gathered around a grandfather, too weak to walk, and drummed upon his head with sticks or pelted him with stones until he cried. There was the laughter that binds families together: Kimat, shrieking for joy as she dashed off with the mug of tea she had snatched from her dying brother Lomeja's hand an instant after Turnbull had given it to him as a last token of their friendship.

Laughter there had always been. A few old people remembered times, 25 to 30 years ago, when laughter mirrored love and joy and fullness of life, times when beliefs and rituals and traditions kept a bond with the "millions of years" ago when time began for the Ik. That was when their god, Didigwari, let the Ik down from heaven on a vine, one at a time. He gave them the digging stick with the instruction that they could not kill one another. He let down other people. To the Dodos and Turkana he gave cattle and spears to kill with. But the Ik remained true to their instruction and did not kill one another or neighboring tribesmen.

For them the bow, the net and the pitfall were for capturing game. For them the greatest sin was to over-hunt. Mobility and cooperation ever were part of them. Often the netting of game required the collaboration of a whole band of 100 or more, some to hold the net and some to drive game into it. Between the big hunts, bands broke up into smaller groups to spread over their domain, then to gather again. The several bands would each settle for the best part of the year along the edge of the Kidepo Valley in the foothills of Mt. Morungole. There they were once again fully one with the mountain. "The Ik, without their mountains, would no longer be the Ik and similarly, they say, the mountains without the Ik would no longer be the same mountains, if indeed they continued to exist at all."

In this unity of people and place, rituals, traditions, beliefs and values molded and preserved a continuity of life. All rites of passage were marked by ceremony. Of these, the rituals sur-

rounding death gave greatest meaning to life. Folded in a fetal position, the body was buried with favorite possessions, facing the rising sun to mark celestial rebirth. All accompanying rituals of fasting and feasting, of libations of beer sprinkled over the grave, of seeds of favorite foods planted on the grave to draw life from the dust of the dead, showed that death is merely another form of life, and reminded the living of the good things of life and of the good way to live. In so honoring the dead by creating goodness the Ik helped speed the soul, content, on its journey.

Such were the Ik until wildlife conservation intruded into their homeland. Uganda decided to make a national park out of the Kidepo Valley, the main hunting ground of the Ik. What then happened stands as an indictment of the myopia that science can generate. No one looked to the Ik to note that their hunter-gatherer way of life marked the epitome of conservation, that the continuance of their way of life would have added to the success of the park. Instead they were forbidden to hunt any longer in the Kidepo Valley. They were herded to the periphery of the park and encouraged to become farmers on dry mountain slopes so steep as to test the poise of a goat. As an example to more remote villages, a number of villages were brought together in a tight little cluster below the southwest pass into the valley. Here the police post, which formed this settlement of Pirre, could watch over the Ik to see that they didn't revert to hunting.

These events contained two of the three strikes that knocked out the spirit of the Ik. *Strike No. 1*: The shift from a mobile hunter-gatherer way of life to a sedentary farming way of life made irrelevant the Ik's entire repertoire of beliefs, habits and traditions. Their guidelines for life were inappropriate to farming. They seemed to adapt, but at heart they remained hunters and gatherers. Their cultural templates fitted them for that one way of life.

Strike No. 2: They were suddenly crowded together at a density, intimacy and frequency of contact far greater than they had ever before been required to experience. Throughout their long past each band of 100 or so individuals only temporarily coalesced into a whole. The intervening breaking up into smaller groups permitted realignment of relationships that tempered conflicts from earlier associations. But at the resettlement, more than 450 individuals were forced to form a permanent cluster of villages within shouting distance of each other. Suppose the seven million or so inhabitants of Los Angeles County were forced to move and join the more than one million inhabitants of the more arid San Diego County. Then after they arrived all water, land and air communication to the rest of the world was cut off abruptly and completely. These eight million people would then have to seek survival completely on local resources without any communication with others. It would be a test of the ability of human beings to remain human.

Such a test is what Dr. Turnbull's book on the Mountain People is all about. The Ik failed to remain human. I have put mice to the same test and they failed to remain mice. Those of you who have been following *Smithsonian* may recall from the April 1970 and the January 1971 issues something about the projected demise of a mouse population experiencing the same two strikes against it as did the Ik.

Fate Of a Mouse Population

Last summer I spoke in London behind the lectern where Charles Darwin and Alfred Wallace had presented their papers on evolution—which during the next century caused a complete revision of our insight into what life is all about and what man is and may become. In summing up that session of 1858 the president remarked that nothing of importance had been presented before the Linnean Society at that year's meeting! I spoke behind this same lectern to a session of the Royal Society of Medicine during its symposium on "Man in His Place." At the end of my paper, "Death Squared: The Explosive Growth and Demise of a Mouse Population," the chairman admonished me to stick to my mice: the insights I had presented could have no implication for man. Wonderful if the chairman could be correct—but now I have read about the Mountain People, and I have a hollow feeling that perhaps we, too, are close to losing our "mountain."

Turnbull lived for 18 months as a member of the Ik tribe. His identity transfer became so strong that he acquired the Ik laughter. He laughed at

seeing Atum suffer as they were completing an extremely arduous journey on foot back across the mountains and the Kidepo Valley from the Sudan. He felt pleasure at seeing Lokwam, local "Lord of the Flies," cry in agony from the beating given him by his two beautiful sisters.

Well, for five years I have identified with my mice, as they lived in their own "Kidepo Valley"—their contrived Utopia where resources are always abundant and all mortality factors except aging eliminated. I watched their population grow rapidly from the first few colonizers. I watched them fill their metal "universe" with organized social groups. I watched them bring up a host of young with loving maternal care and paternal territorial protection—all of these young well educated for mouse society. But then there were too many of these young mice, ready to become involved in all that mice can become, with nowhere to go, no physical escape from their closed environment, no opportunity to gain a niche where they could play a meaningful role. They tried, but being younger and less experienced they were nearly always rejected.

Rejecting so many of these probing youngsters overtaxed the territorial males. So defense then fell to lactating females. They became aggressive. They turned against their own young and ejected them before normal weaning and before adequate social bonds between mother and young had developed. During this time of social tension, rate of growth of the population was only one third of that during the earlier, more favorable phase.

Strike No. 1 against these mice: They lost the opportunity to express the capacities developed by older mice born during the rapid population growth. After a while they became so rejected that they were treated as so many sticks and stones by their still relatively well-adjusted elders. These rejected mice withdrew, physically and psychologically, to live packed tightly together in large pools. Amongst themselves they became vicious, lashing out and biting each other now and then with hardly any provocation.

Strike No. 2 against the mice: They reached great numbers despite reduced conceptions and increased deaths of newborn young resulting from the dissolution of maternal care. Many had early been rejected by their mothers and knew little about social bonds. Often their later attempts at interaction were interrupted by some other mouse intervening unintentionally as it passed between two potential actors.

I came to call such mice the "Beautiful Ones." They never learned such effective social interactions as courtship, mating and aggressive defense of territory. Never copulating, never fighting, they were unstressed and essentially unaware of their associates. They spent their time grooming themselves, eating and sleeping, totally individualistic, totally isolated socially except for a peculiar acquired need for simple proximity to others. This produced what I have called the "behavioral sink," the continual accentuation of aggregations to the point that much available space was unused despite a population increase to nearly 15 times the optimum.

All true "mousity" was lost. Though physically they still appeared to be mice, they had no essential capacities for survival and continuation of mouse society. Suddenly, population growth ceased. In what seemed an instant they passed over a threshold beyond which there was no likelihood of their ever recouping the capacity to become real mice again. No more young were born. From a peak population of 2,200 mice nearly three years ago, aging has gradually taken its toll until now there are only 46 sluggish near-cadavers comparable to people more than 100 years old.

It was just such a fading universe Colin Turnbull found in 1961. Just before he arrived, *Strike No. 3* had set in: starvation. Any such crisis could have added the coup de grace after the other two strikes. Normally the Ik could count on only making three crops every four years. At this time a two-year drought set in and destroyed almost all crops. Neighboring tribes survived with their cultures intact. Turkana herdsmen, facing starvation and death, kept their societies in contact with each other and continued to sing songs of praise to God for the goodness of life.

By the beginning of the long drought, "goodness" to the Ik simply meant to have food—to have food for one's self alone. Collaborative hunts were a thing of the past, long since stopped by the police and probably no longer possible as

a social effort, anyway. Solitary hunting, now designated as poaching, became a necessity for sheer survival. But the solitary hunter took every precaution not to let others know of his success. He would gorge himself far off in the bush and bring the surplus back to sell to the police, who were not above profiting from this traffic. Withholding food from wife, children and aging parents became an accomplishment to brag and laugh about. It became a way of life, continuing after the government began providing famine relief. Those strong enough to go to the police station to get rations for themselves and their families would stop halfway home and gorge all the food, even though it caused them to vomit.

Village of Mutual Hatred

The village reflected this reversal of humanity. Instead of open courtyards around each group of huts within the large compound, there was a maze of walls and tunnels booby trapped with spears to ward off intrusion by neighbors.

In Atum's village a whole band of more than 100 individuals was crowded together in mutual hostility and aloneness. They would gather at their sitting place and sit for hours in a kind of suspended animation, not looking directly at each other, yet scanning slowly all others who might be engaged in some solitary task, watching for someone to make a mistake that would elicit the symbolic violence of laughter and derision. They resembled my pools of rejected withdrawn mice. Homemaking deteriorated, feces littered doorsteps and courtyard. Universal adultery and incest replaced the old taboo. The beaded virgins' aprons of eight-to-twelve-year-old girls became symbols that these were proficient whores accustomed to selling their wares to passing herdsmen.

One ray of humanity left in this cesspool was 12-year-old, retarded Adupa. Because she believed that food was for sharing and savoring, her playmates beat her. She still believed that parents were for loving and to be loved by. They cured her madness by locking her in her hut until she died and decayed.

The six other villages were smaller and their people could retain a few glimmers of the goodness and fullness of life. There was Kuaur, devoted to Turnbull, hiking four days to deliver mail, taunted for bringing food home to share with his wife and child. There was Losike, the potter, regarded as a witch. She offered water to visitors and made pots for others. When the famine got so bad that there was no need for pots to cook in, her husband left her. She was no longer bringing in any income. And then there was old Nangoli, still capable of mourning when her husband died. She went with her family and village across Kidepo and into the Sudan where their village life turned for a while back to normality. But it was not normal enough to keep them. Back to Pirre, to death, they returned.

All goodness was gone from the Ik, leaving merely emptiness, valuelessness, nothingness, the chaos of Nun. They reentered the womb of beginning time from which there is no return. Urination beside the partial graves of the dead marked the death of God, the final fading of Mount Morungole.

My poor words give only a shadowy image of the cold coffin of Ik humanity that Turnbull describes. His two years with the Ik left him in a slough of despondency from which he only extricated himself with difficulty, never wanting to see them again. Time and distance brought him comfort. He did return for a brief visit some months later. Rain had come in abundance. Gardens had sprung up untended from hidden seeds in the earth. Each Ik gleaned only for his immediate needs. Granaries stood empty, not refilled for inevitable scarcities ahead. The future had ceased to exist. Individual and social decay continued on its downward spiral. Sadly Turnbull departed again from this land of lost hope and faith.

Last summer in London I knew nothing about the Ik when I was so publicly and thoroughly chastised for having the temerity to suspect that the behavioral and spiritual death my mice had exhibited might also befall man. But a psychiatrist in the audience arose in defense of my suspicion. Dr. Geoffrey N. Bianchi remarked that an isolated tribe of Australian Aborigines mirrored the changes and kinds of pathology I had seen among mice. I did not know that Dr. Bianchi was a member of the team that had studied these people, the Kaiadilt, and that a book about them was in preparation, *Cruel, Poor and Brutal Nations* by John Cawte (The University Press of Hawaii). In galley proof I have read about the Kaiadilt and find it so shattering to my faith in humanity that I now sometimes wish I had never heard of it. Yet there is some glimmer of hope that the Kaiadilt may recover—not what they were but possibly some new life.

A frail, tenacious people, the Kaiadilt never numbered more than 150 souls where they lived on Bentinck Island in the Gulf of Carpentaria. So isolated were they that not even their nearest Aboriginal neighbors, 20 miles away, had any knowledge of their existence until in this century; so isolated were the Kaiadilt from their nearest neighbors that they differ from them in such heredity markers as blood type and fingerprints. Not until the early years of this century did an occasional visitor from the Queensland Government even note their existence.

For all practical purposes the first real contact the Kaiadilt had with Western "culture" came in 1916 when a man by the name of McKenzie came to Bentinck with a group of male mainland Aborigines to try to establish a lime kiln. McKenzie's favorite sport was to ride about shooting Kaiadilt. His helpers' sport was to commandeer as many women as they could, and take them to their headquarters on a neighboring island. In 1948 a tidal wave poisoned most of the fresh-water sources. Small groups of Kaiadilt were rounded up and transported to larger Mornington Island where they were placed under the supervision of a Presbyterian mission. They were crowded into a dense cluster settlement just as the Ik had been at Pirre.

Here they still existed when the psychiatric field team came into their midst 15 years later. They were much like the Ik: dissolution of family life, total valuelessness, apathy. I could find no mention of laughter, normal or pathological. Perhaps the Kaiadilt didn't laugh. They had essentially ceased the singing that had been so much a part of their traditional way.

The spiritual decay of the Kaiadilt was marked by withdrawal, depression, suicide and tendency to engage in such self-mutilation as ripping out one's testes or chopping off one's nose. In their passiveness some of the anxiety ridden children are accepting the new mold of life forced upon them by a benevolent culture they do not understand. Survival with a new mold totally obliterating all past seems their only hope.

So the lesson comes clear, and Colin Turnbull sums it up in the final paragraph of his book: "The Ik teach us that our much vaunted human values are not inherent in humanity at all, but are associated only with a particular form of survival called society, and that all, even society itself, are luxuries that can be dispensed with. That does not make them any the less wonderful or desirable, and if man has any greatness it is surely in his ability to maintain these values, clinging to them to an often very bitter end, even shortening an already pitifully short life rather than sacrifice his humanity. But that too involves choice, and the Ik teaches us that man can lose the will to make it."

Blind Lo'ono almost died in a fall on the mountain, to the glee of Ik neighbors. They abandoned her.

Reference

John B. Calhoun, "Population Density and Social Pathology." *Scientific American*, 206, (1962).

Postscript

This article was published in 1972. Its message becomes more poignant with time. Massive famine has occurred in the African countries of Ethiopia, Somalia, the Sudan, Rwanda, and Zaire since the mid 1980s.

Since antiquity, small groups of hunters and gatherers had wrested a dependable, albeit poor existence from this arid and unforgiving environment. Western colonialists arbitrarily created countries whose boundaries were often incompatible with tribal migrations, alliances, and animosities. Accustomed to fertile soil, and ample rainfall, the Westerners had developed an efficient agricultural technology. Perhaps with "heart in right place," or more cynically, the desire for new markets for their technology, the hunters and gatherers were encouraged to abandon their way of life to become farmers. Population grew as the tribes became sedentary. Lack of knowledge about farming and machinery maintenance, combined with drought, resulted in crop failure, desertification, and famine. The arbitrary creation of countries invited civil war. Knowing how to survive in a harsh environment by hunting and gathering will be foreign to children reared in refugee camps.

Figure 9-7. Stanley R. Graham, Ph.D. (Photograph courtesy of Dorothy Graham.)

READING 9F

WHAT DOES A MAN WANT?

Stanley R. Graham

Earlier in the chapter it was pointed out that one reason humanism emerged was because of the other schools' failure to appreciate the real problems and issues of daily life. Existential issues absorb our psychological strength and energy, often manifesting themselves clinically in mood or anxiety disorders. Gender is a major component of our self-concept and changes in gender identity over the past few decades has created ambiguity about what it means to be a man or woman.

Stanley R. Graham has had a distinguished career teaching and practicing psychotherapy. He won American Psychological Association Distinguished Psychologist Awards in 1983 and 1985, and was elected president of the organization in 1990.

The following is Dr. Graham's presidential address to the American Psychological Association on August 17, 1991 in San Francisco. He was sixty-five years old at the time. He reflected on his life, changes in our society, the impact of historical events, and gender attributions. Phenomenology implies the ability to share the experience of another. An editor's note accompanying the article stated, "This address is a very personal reflection on the author's life and experiences; the term man should not be construed to apply to humankind or to men in general." Regardless of your gender or experience, the phenomenological challenge is to comprehend Dr. Graham's worldview, then reflect.

APA presidential addresses, like APA presidents, come in many sizes and shapes. Some presidents have spoken of their research, others have addressed public policy issues, and still others have endeavored to predict the future. My presentation will be somewhat different. I have long since abandoned any hope of predicting the future. At this stage of my life, I am much more interested in understanding the past and how it has shaped the present.

This convention represents the beginning of psychology's centennial year. As our discipline has grown and prospered for 100 years, our society has undergone drastic changes that affect all of us. More people were born in this century than in all previous centuries, and most of the people who ever lived are alive today. Psychology has grown up in a remarkable period of history. Vast numbers of people have experienced wars, a technological revolution, and massive social change. What we have become, as a people and as a discipline, has been deeply influenced by these changes, and it is on this that I wish to reflect today.

I hope you will understand why I must be quite personal in my presentation. I can best understand the changes that our society has undergone by reflecting upon what I have experienced. To do so, I must tell you something about myself. I will not pretend that my experiences are typical or even representative of the lives of all of the men of this century. Nor will I assert that the question "What does a man want?" can be answered by saying what this particular man wants. But I hope my account of how the environment in which I have lived and my attempts to define myself as a man will strike some common chords in the men and women—my colleagues and friends—who have so kindly come to hear me today.

My father's father was born in 1868 and lived to be 92 years old. My father lived to be 89, and so, with a little luck, I hope to extend the patrilineage into a third century. I cannot claim great wisdom, but in three generations my family has accumulated a lot of experience. Spanning horse-drawn wagons and intercontinental missiles, my grandfather, my father, and I have lived through interesting times. Many things have changed in the 123 years we've been around. The meaning of what it is to be a man has only recently become a popular topic of discussion. I will talk today about the generations of men that have lived as adults in the 20th century. Although the modern interpreters of myths tell us that in some ways manhood is independent of culture, how one lives as a man has changed greatly.

The television shows of the past 20 years often portray father as fool. In contrast, the role of the father was taken very seriously in the decades immediately preceding the past two. Whether a husband or father was rich or poor, he was looked upon as wise and strong and so wielded an enormous amount of authority and garnered a great deal of respect. Any important problem or life decision was submitted to him for his judgment. His opinion was sought, and he exerted a pretty effective veto on most actions of which he did not approve.

There have always been good and bad men, but the model of a man during the first half of this century had a great deal to do with integrity and hard work. Men married young, raised families, and held themselves responsible for the conduct and well-being of their children. They were implanted in their community and tied by custom, religion, and the extended family to a code of behavior that was fairly rigid. A man was expected to support his family, and there was no such thing as public assistance if he failed to do so. For men as well as for women, there were widely accepted standards of conduct. Of course there were men who abused their wives and children and men who drank and philandered. Laziness and irresponsibility are not recent inventions. However, such a man lost respect in his own community and felt the pressure of peer disapproval. The community and the extended family enforced community standards and served as a brake on the most untoward behavior.

Today, people living next to each other in urban centers know little, if anything, about each other. The walls have grown thinner, but family violence goes unattended unless the noise disturbs the neighbors. On a city block in an economically well-to-do neighborhood in New York, a man, over a period of months, beat his six-year-old adoptive daughter to death and so mutilated his domestic partner that she came to resemble a concentration camp survivor in body and mind. On that same block lived several hundred residents of the community, and there were two mental health clinics with approximately 300 practicing psychotherapists. The man, the woman, and the child were unknown to anyone on the block.

That could not have happened in the community in which I grew up. In the ghetto of the Lower East Side of New York where l lived in the 1920s and 1930s, I knew of no one who had been divorced, and the few adults who were single were regarded as unusual. When I was a child, most of my family lived within walking distance. Like many Americans, we lived in enclaves of isolated ethnicity. Some of my teachers in public school were Irish, and there was an Irish family on the block that we regarded with wonder. l believe I met my first identifiable Protestant at the age of 18, when I attended the College of the City of New York. Today, one of the things that pains my wife greatly is the fact that she must travel 3,000 miles to see her five grandchildren. Whereas I spent much of my childhood in my grandparents' home and saw them almost every day, she sees her grandchildren once or twice a year.

My grandfathers were each in their own way patriarchs. They firmly believed that a man's home was his castle and a woman's place was in the home. The dominant view of society was that women worked until they were fortunate enough to find a "breadwinner," and then they became "housekeepers." The authority of my grandfathers in the home was never questioned. Unlike their wives, they left home every day to conduct their business; they voted; and they were educated, to some extent. They were the family's contact with the "outside world." The Depression changed everything for my generation. My father ran a successful gas station and a garage until history seized us by the throat in 1929. In a matter of a year or two, we went from affluence to poverty.

For millions of American families, the story was similar, and for some the descent into poverty deeply affected family relationships. The father was home, but he had no functional place in that home. He was simply not working. This happened to many men—almost one in three was unemployed. The diminished status of men was demonstrated by their helplessness. Mothers struggled to make do. This was difficult but at least they were functioning in a customary role, whereas most were not. The man who could not maintain his position as breadwinner was seen as a failure. The woman who maintained her role under great stress was a heroine. If she found a way to contribute to the family's well-being financially, she was performing even more than was expected of her. The husbands lost much of their identity.

John Steinbeck's classic novel, *The Grapes of Wrath* (1939), told about the Joad family, who were farmers in the Southwest. The dust storms of the mid-1930s destroyed their farm and induced them to migrate to California and become itinerant farm laborers. Amidst the poverty and exploitation of the migrant camps, the men of the Joad family were rendered impotent by the economic forces that crushed them. The dominating spirit was Ma Joad, whose faith and strength maintained a family that was disintegrating under the chaotic economic and social pressures.

The economic decline that so greatly affected my generation lasted for a decade. Men continued to lose status during this period because many of them were unemployed for long periods of time. Family structure deteriorated. Women could sometimes obtain jobs, but they were usually paid less than men would have been paid for the same work. For many millions during this period, federal assistance programs replaced the father as the breadwinner, and the country was overflowing with itinerant men seeking employment, or at least sustenance, separate from their families.

In 1941, the nation went to war. Fifteen million men left their homes, and women found themselves in the unusual position of being totally responsible for the management of the home, children, and the social milieu. Technology provided muscle and permitted women to do work that had been reserved for men. Women took all kinds of occupational positions and demonstrated a level of competence and stability that surprised employers. My wife's mother got up at four in the morning and, after stoking the furnace, traveled 3 hours to Poughkeepsie, spent 8 to 10 hours riveting airplane parts, then 3 hours returning home, arriving in time to put the children to bed.

All wars promote increased sexual freedom for both men and women. Men away from home and women separated from the normal structures of social interaction became freer in their sexual behavior. It was a period of time in which the respective responsibilities of men and women were altered. Many men and women took on different roles and for several years lived lives that diminished the importance of the patriarch and vastly expanded the roles of women.

The end of World War II was followed by a period of readjustment. Many women gave up their jobs and returned to more traditional homemaker roles. Higher education flourished as veterans used the GI Bill to get a college education. Thousands of new families moved to the suburbs and began to have children. The country, starved for material things, began to produce goods in abundance. As the technology accelerated, it required the participation of more and more women in the workplace. By the mid-1950s, the stereotype of the typical American family composed of a breadwinner, a housekeeper, and two children began to break down as more young women sought advancement through education and more housekeepers entered the labor force. This increased women's worldly sophistication and economic autonomy.

The theme of the 1960s was freedom, and Americans sought it in a variety of ways. The increasing independence of women and the greater accessibility of higher education contributed to a change of climate throughout the country. In the context of a violent and unstable time for society in general, individuals and families were confronted by fundamental changes in the relationships between men and women. The availability of more methods of contraception removed some of the barriers to sexual activity, especially for women. Reducing the likelihood of pregnancy lifted a tremendous burden from women and offered men diminished responsibility. For the first time in history, women could admit to an involvement in an active sexual life and still retain a respectable position among their peers. The tenet that a man was honor-bound to marry a woman he had gotten pregnant fell by the wayside.

As it became common for young people to form relationships and live together without marrying, women gained more responsibility for themselves and men less responsibility for anything. Politics, which had been the preserve of White men, was acted upon by the energies of millions of women—and an emerging African-American presence—demanding a role in reshaping the world. Freedom was also the theme in the burgeoning civil rights movement. Martin Luther King, Jr., became the symbol and the voice of people no longer willing to quietly accept segregation and restricted access to opportunity.

The nuclear family became much less common, and the single-parent home, usually a woman with one or more children, was accepted as an alternative. One aspect of this situation was poverty and its concomitant disintegration of social structures. But more and more, we began to see the abandonment of wife and children by fathers of the middle class as well. Even when legal requirements of separation and divorce stipulated financial terms, large numbers of men discontinued financial support of their families in the second and third years following the dissolution of their marriages. According to the National Survey of Children, one half of all divorced men stop seeing their children regularly after the first year (Cherlin & Furstenberg, 1984). The emancipation of women was paralleled by the abandoning of responsibility by men. What I am saying is that the social and economic revolution as it pertained to women gave them a lot more work, a lot more responsibility, and sexual freedom to some degree, but it gave men much more sexual free-

dom, at least until the spread of herpes and acquired immunodeficiency syndrome (AIDS) in the 1980s.

In the workplace, many men found it uncomfortable to compete with women. Competing with other men was part of the games they had played from childhood. Competing with women at work was a new experience for which they were unprepared. One consequence was that they developed a pervasive tendency to diminish and confine the achievements of women (Morrison & Von Glinow, 1990) as a way of maintaining male supremacy. Women had attained freedom—but only up to a point.

Decades after the emergence of the women's movement, we have the beginnings of a men's movement. I think it has evolved in a very different way. It is aimed more at internal than external change. One of the shapers of the men's movement is Robert Bly, a poet who seems, in his writing, to be seeking to resolve a relationship with an abusive, alcoholic father. Bly describes and analyzes the unavailability and the distance that many men have felt from their fathers. That was not my experience—my father and I were very close when I was growing up—but it seems to be a prevalent problem. I believe it was the men of my generation, rather than my father's, that had less time for their children. Many men of my generation single-mindedly pursued the rewards of success, enjoying the opportunities of money, sexual freedom, and mobility as no previous generation could have contemplated. Ultimately caught between the two choices of overwhelming responsibility and absolute irresponsibility, they established ever more distance from their women and children than did previous generations.

In Bly's book *Iron John* (1990), one of the touchstones of the men's movement, a boy helps a primitive, beastlike man escape from the adults who are holding him prisoner and goes with him into the woods. There the boy grows to manhood. Bly speaks of father hunger stemming from the contemporary separation of boys from their fathers. He describes how our culture separates boys from their fathers, and he believes that one result is men who lack a well-developed masculine identity. He encourages men to recover their lost manhood by escaping the confines of contemporary culture and reforming their masculine identity.

Another prominent leader of the men's movement is Sam Keen (1991), whose *Fire in the Belly* is subtitled *On Being a Man*. Keen believes that men's problems stem from the "primal power that women wielded over men because of the imperfect separation of man from the mother." He, too, teaches that a break with the present configuration of men's and women's roles is necessary if men are to define themselves more completely and affirmatively.

My own observation of the generation between the 1960s and the 1980s is that the more women accepted the role of breadwinner and provider, the less responsibility men felt for providing for their wives and children. The more women accepted the responsibility for their own sexuality and contraception, the less responsibility men took. The more competitive women became in business and the professions, the more confused men became in their relationships with women. Among professional men and women, the increasing tendency for both parents to take on jobs even beyond the traditional workday hours meant that both parents were increasingly unavailable and kids were growing up with a lot less definition from either parent.

For a time, the avenue to happiness seemed to be becoming the so-called sensitive man. The actor Alan Alda was the model, and he may well have been the only really successful sensitive man. The sensitive-man model was accepted and emulated by few men, and it did not seem that many women found it completely satisfying. Bly contends that the image of the sensitive man as fostered by feminism has robbed men of their righteous anger and their ability to act decisively and has disconnected them from their identity, self-assurance, and creative instinct.

On the social level, many women have achieved more intimate communication with other women than with men. In truth, there are fewer barriers between women. Under most conditions they confide in each other more than men do. One of the chief complaints of women has always been that men are occupied with matters of business and sport and rarely talk about intimate topics. Unfortunately, men talk as little to other men as they do to women. If a man confides intimacies to another man, it is apt to embarrass both of them. Most often, a man chooses to keep his own counsel and keep his problems within himself, so that the closest of male friends may not be privy to each other's difficulties and may suffer alone the deepest and most extensive of problems.

It is remarkable that men and women sometimes can only speak with intimacy about the same things in the aftermath of a quarrel or in the middle of the night when neither can sleep and they are completely detached from that sense of immediacy that seems to absorb them in every waking moment. It is then that they fear the loss of one another and cut through the rationalizations and defenses that obscure their need for one another. Strangely enough, the times when communication between men and women seems most difficult are when they are thrown most closely together, as at the dinner table, where there should be time to talk, and in the aftermath of sexual intimacy, when they should be at their closest. The man will complain that what she wants to talk about is insubstantial, but the man talking about matters that are not his personal focus feels held to account and wants to curtail or cut short what, for the woman, is an element of intimacy.

For the man, feeling caught in a position he does not control is uncomfortable. In the sexual engagement his wanting to get away from the reality of the intimacy and all it implies allows him to devalue the uncomfortable time when emotion is all important and logic is a minor bystander. His is the discomfort of a boy being required to attend to matters beyond his preferred focus. He feels he is being held against his will and must conform with good manners to somebody else's standards. As the woman is the maestro of emotion, the man struggles against inheriting a universe of values that are not his own.

The task-oriented man in his pursuit of success is entirely focused on completion and achievement. Coming home, he often sees nothing to complete or achieve with his wife and children and so reads and watches television, not recognizing that the woman needs communion on a continuous basis. Men complain that the affinity of a mother and child blocks out any sense of primacy that the father may have for his children, and so his usual image is very often that of a pallid pseudomother. More important, but less observed, is the unconscious tendency on the part of the man to see himself as the oldest child of the wife and, as such, the one who really requires less care and attention. I think that adds up to a perception of being less loved: It is hard to be last in line.

I am ready to tell you, at least from my own perspective, what a man wants. He wants his children to grow and mature to be wise and capable, independent and self-reliant, and yet he longs to hold them in the palm of his hand as he did on the day of their birth. He wants to be able to subdue his pride and forgive their brusqueness so he can remain close to them until they see his caring. He wants to be free to express his caring as David did when he cried "Absalom, my son, my son, would that I had died for thee" (I Samuel 18:33). Although father and son seem made for contention, they derive their highest sense of pride from one another. He wants to admire his daughter's beauty and grace, for each girl child's beauty is unique in the eyes of her father. At the same time, he wants to honor her wit and intellect so that the complete human being that she becomes is not obscured by artificial sentimentality.

He wants his mate's love and caring without having to ask for it, and he wants to be able to show his love for her without having to be concerned that it undermines the image of his manhood. He hates to see himself as a tearful, weak creature, dependent on others for his sense of affirmation. But he is tired of hiding his tears and turning away to preserve some traditional image of manhood.

I will be more explicit. I am tired of wars. I do not want to be killed or maimed, and I do not enjoy other people dying or being maimed. I want to accept responsibility for what I do and not be blamed for what I did not do. I have always judged my fellow human beings one at a time on the merits of their own behavior, and I demand to be judged as one person on the basis of my own faults and virtues. As such, my race, religion, politics, and sexual preference are nobody's business. I have gotten used to calling myself a man. The title is not pejorative; it is something I have done for half a century, and I am comfortable with it. If you choose to call yourself something else, that is all right with me, but please leave my definition of myself to me. Any thinking man continues to evolve philosophically—influenced by every person, circumstance, and concept that he is exposed to. I want to continue this growth and come to be what I want to be.

I will not have my values dictated by football coaches. The maxim "Winning is everything" leaves out too much. I will not give up the joy and excitement of competition, but I am joined to all of humanity, so that if I am the victor, then so I am the vanquished. To deny this is to go through life as half a person.

I resent being categorized, and I resent people who place people in categories. To say that men have certain characteristics is valid in a general sense. To say that a man has certain characteristics is only valid with comprehensive knowledge of the individual. To attribute something to that person on the basis of stereotyping is disruptive of the essential human rights of that individual.

I believe that life is a ship in distress, and the true task of humanity is to get everyone into the lifeboat. It is unfortunate that so many people divide humanity into *us* and *them*, so that the us is somehow better, more easily forgiven and accepted. *Them* is forever below the salt, clothed in the darker garments of evil. We are currently in the midst of a great revolution, and the half of the human race called *female* has, after countless centuries of oppression and exploitation, stood up and cried "Nonsense!" The good that will accrue to all of us is immeasurable. The lies and distortions relative to the nature of women have diminished the entire human race. The sooner they are lost in antiquity, the better.

Psychology has given us an expanded understanding of the differences between men and women. Healing techniques attempt to bridge the gap. We have sensitivity training to help men acquire women's skills, and we have assertiveness training to help women acquire men's skills. I hope some innovator will evolve some procedures that can teach the archaic practices of good manners, decency, and good will.

I am convinced that following the wars of

ambition—the striving and the stolidness, the silences and the shrugging off of uncomfortable sentiment—a man wants to be seen as good. The term *a good man* was once a welded unity, a thoughtful caring person who touches the lives of all around him. To quote Mark Antony (Shakespeare, 1599/1919, *Julius Caesar,* act 5, sc. 5, line 73), "His life was gentle and the qualities so mixed in him that nature might stand up and say to all the world—this was a man."

References

Bly, R. (1990). *Iron John*. New York: Vintage Books.

Cherlin, A., & Furstenberg, E. (1984, April 13). Fathers Who Don't Pay. *The Washington Post*, p. 23.

Keen, S. (1991). *Fire in the Belly: On Being a Man*. New York: Bantam Books.

Morrison, A. M.. & Von Glinow, M. A. (1990). Women and Minorities in Management. *American Psychologist*, 45, 200-208.

Shakespeare, W. (1919). *Julius Caesar*. New Haven, CT: Yale University Press. (Original work written ca. 1599).

Steinbeck, J. (1939). *The Grapes of Wrath*. New York: Viking Penguin.

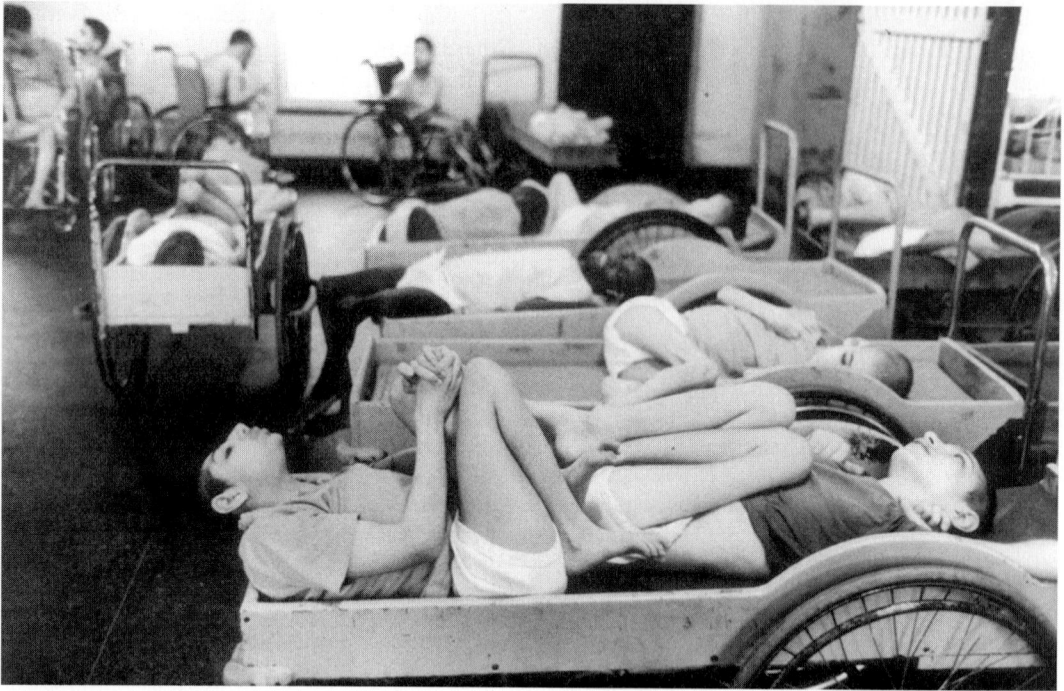

Top: Retarded and handicapped children at Willowbrook State School, 1972. (Copyright © Bill Pierce/*Time* Magazine.) *Bottom*: Homeless people sleep beneath benches and worldly belongings across Pennsylvania Avenue from the White House, January 20, 1994. (Bruce Young, Reuters/Corbis-Bettmann.)

Chapter 10

THE SOCIAL PERSPECTIVE

The last perspective to be covered is the social perspective. Unlike the others, which had their roots in medicine or psychology, the genesis of this perspective can be traced to a conglomerate of sources. Other perspectives identify general medical conditions or psychological factors as causes of mental disorders. This perspective views them from a social context. It has been a vital political force for nearly four decades and has had a tremendous impact on the delivery of mental health services; ultimately affecting society at large.

The 1960s were a politically volatile and fertile period. Tradition was challenged across arenas. A movement called antipsychiatry evolved. It was critical of the illness perspective, conventional psychiatry, and mental hospitals. Its message had strong emotional appeal. Mental hospitals were dehumanizing institutions for people who were not really sick. They were prisons for people who had broken no laws. Their crime was that they behaved in unconventional ways and their presence made dominant society ill at ease. Psychiatry's validity was questioned.

Psychiatrist Thomas Szasz, one of his profession's most vocal critics, argued against calling abnormal behavior mental illness. Since most of what is called mental illness lacks a general medical condition for explanation, the medical model does not apply. Mental illness is a bad metaphor. It would be more beneficial and productive for the individual and society to say the person is having "problems in living" (Szasz, 1960).

Another dissident psychiatrist, E. Fuller Torrey called for the abolition of his profession in *The Death of Psychiatry:*

> Psychiatry is an emperor standing naked in his new clothes. It has worked and striven for 70 years to become an emperor, a full brother with the other medical specialties. And now, it stands there resplendent in its finery. But it doesn't have any clothes on; and even worse, nobody has told it so (Torrey, 1974, preface).

In *Asylums* (1961), sociologist Irving Goffman created a piercing comparison of "total institutions," which include prisons, concentration camps, and mental hospitals. He portrayed patients as inmates who are maltreated and ascribed inferior status. Sociologist Thomas J. Scheff argued that schizophrenics were chronic violators of society's residual rules; those that go without saying, but are not articulated in any code or law. For example, people typically make eye contact in face to face interaction. A schizophrenic may scrutinize another's ear (Scheff, 1970). Theodore Sarbin, R.D. Laing, and Jay Haley wrote on similar themes.

Films were also influential. In 1965 Senator Robert Kennedy observed the deplorable conditions at Willowbrook, an institution for the mentally retarded on Staten Island, New York. Geraldo Rivera's initial reports for WABC-TV, New York were in 1972. His reports were compiled in *Willowbrook*, which was closed in 1975. Frederick Wiseman's *Titicut Follies* (1967) was a scathing indictment of the treatment of the criminally insane in the Massachusetts Correctional Institution at Bridgewater. It was the only American film whose showing was restricted for reasons other than obscenity or national security. Ken Kesey's novel, *One Flew Over the Cuckoo's Nest* (1962) described the abuse of patients under the care of the diabolical Nurse Ratched. It was the basis for the 1975 award winning film. A 1977 ABC News documentary, *Madness and Medicine*, criticized the institutions, drugs, electroshock, and psychosurgery. The result of all of the preceding was to inform psychiatry that "it did not have any clothes on."

The movement to dramatically reform the delivery of mental health services officially began in 1963 with the passage of the Community Mental Health Centers Act; President John Kennedy's "bold new approach" to mental illness. Kennedy's concern was inspired by what happened to his allegedly retarded sister, Rosemary. She was placed in an institution away from the family in 1941, and ultimately received a lobotomy, performed by Watts and Freeman. Under Kennedy's plan, smaller mental health centers (one for every 50,000 people) would replace large institutions. Patients would no longer have to leave their community to receive treatment.

Deinstitutionalization and normalization were offered as alternatives to the mental hospital. With the closing of many large institutions and population reduction in others, patients were released for treatment in the community. Controversy persists. What has been the result of deinstitutionalization? What is the status of community mental health? Has its focus changed? Has the condition of the mentally ill improved? Hopefully, some answers to these questions will be revealed as the chapter unfolds.

The first two articles illustrate the orientation of the perspective at its inception. Initially, an *Interview with Dr. Thomas Szasz*, critic of psychiatry, is presented. Then comes *The Art of Being Schizophrenic* by Jay Haley. It is an intriguing portrayal of complex social factors that he perceives are instrumental in producing schizophrenia. The third article is entitled *The Principle of Normalization and Its Implications to Psychiatric Services* by Wolf Wolfensberger. Written at the beginning of the movement, it provided guidelines for effective implementation. The fourth, *Brief Report: Innovative Programming in a Community Service Center*, by Edith Cunnane, M.A., et al, describes a sound, multifaceted community based program. The final article, *The Sleep of Reason: How the Insane Were Turned into the Homeless*, by David Gutmann, provides somber commentary on the present status of community mental health.

References

Scheff, T.J. (1970, Fall). Schizophrenia as Ideology. *Schizophrenic Bulletin*, 1.
Szasz, T., (1960). The Myth of Mental Illness. *American Psychologist*, 15, 113-118.
Torrey, E.F., (1974). *The Death of Psychiatry*. Radnor, Pennsylvania: Chilton Book Company.

Figure 10-1. *Top*: **Dr. Thomas Szasz**, who allows patients the option of suicide. (The Syracuse Newspapers, photograph by C.W. McKeen, copyright © The Syracuse Newspapers.) *Bottom*: **Dr. Jack Kevorkian**, who assists the suicide of terminally ill patients. (Blake Discher/Sygma.)

AN INTERVIEW WITH DR. THOMAS SZASZ

Richard Ballad

The following interview of Thomas Szasz by Richard Ballad appeared in the October 1973 edition of Penthouse. *However, Dr. Szasz has remained consistent over time. In a conversation with him in 1993 he said, "Mental illness is a myth. My perspective is totally logical. Just like two plus two equals four; my views have not changed in thirty years."*

In the introduction to this chapter reference was made to an antipsychiatry movement that emerged during the 1960s. Dr. Szasz has long been associated with this movement, although he denies he is against all psychiatry. He complains about involuntary psychiatry; voluntary participation is "alright between consenting adults." He rejects a psychiatric vocabulary that portrays personal problems as disease, prisons as hospitals, and conversation as treatment. He perceives psychiatrists as "travel agents disguised as mechanics."

*Dr. Szasz makes poignant remarks concerning the relationship between medicine and each of the following: government, confidentiality, individual rights in psychiatric treatment, and the insanity plea. Of John Hinckley, who successfully plead not guilty by reason of insanity for the shooting of President Reagan, he said, "It's useful to Mr. and Mrs. Hinckley to think of their son as schizophrenic when he's really just a bum." (*Time, *1923-1988, p. 75). His ideas have attracted and maintain a large following.*

References

Time Retrospective: Psychology 1923-1988. *Time.*

Dr. Thomas Szasz sent shock and rage through the psychiatric fraternity in 1961 with his book *The Myth of Mental Illness.* He has remained the most stinging gadfly of his profession. He acknowledges brain disease, brain damage, brain defects, but not mental illness. "Disease," he says, "cannot be cured by conversation." What so many doctors call mental disease, Szasz calls human conflict expressed in ways society can't live with. He has become this country's leading spokesman for the newest trend in behavioral science— the belief that science belongs on the side of the people it studies, rather than aligning itself with a society that wants to control differentness. Szasz is opposed to all involuntary hospitaliza-

tion, and he has wakened America's conscience to many "crimes" committed in the name of "mental health," from abuses in private practice to our system of criminal justice.

Within a year after *The Myth of Mental Illness* appeared, the New York State Commissioner of Mental Hygiene called for Szasz's resignation as a professor at the state university's Upstate Medical Center at Syracuse, a position Szasz has held since 1956. After great turmoil, including the resignation of the chairman of the department of psychiatry, the rebellious Szasz emerged secure in his job. He is still there.

Yesterday's shock artist is today's authority. Many of Szasz's aphorisms have become slogans

Richard Ballard: "An Interview with Dr. Thomas Szasz, *Penthouse* Magazine, October, 1973, pp. 228-236. Reprinted with permission.

for Young Turks in medicine who stand with the patient rather than the hospitals and the jails. The following are excerpts from his book *The Second Sin,* published in 1973:

- "If a man says he is talking to God we say he is praying. If he says God is talking to him we say he is a schizophrenic."
- "Treating addiction to heroin with methadone is like treating addiction to Scotch with bourbon."
- "Mental hospitals are the POW camps of our undeclared and unarticulated civil wars."

Szasz pours them out, and they inspire retaliation. The late Dr. Manfred Guttmacher, a distinguished forensic psychiatrist, wrote: "A bird that fouls its nest courts criticism. Dr. Szasz doubtless enjoys the contentions he is creating."

Dr. Guttmacher was right: Szasz gets a huge kick out of twisting tails. He criticized Dr. Bernard Diamond, chief psychiatrist for Sirhan B. Sirhan, who assassinated Robert F. Kennedy. He ridiculed the idea of Sirhan's being portrayed as unaware of what he'd done because he was presumably insane at the time. Dr. Diamond, in turn, called some of Szasz's ideas on psychiatry and the law "irresponsible, reprehensible, and dangerous."

But now Szasz has many defenders. Some have joined the American Association for the Abolition of Involuntary Mental Hospitalization, of which Szasz is co-founder and chairman of the board. The American Humanist Association named him the 1973 Humanist of the Year. Far-out admirers have talked of forming "The Insane Liberation Front" in his honor.

Szasz was born in Hungary in an upper-middle-class Jewish family. His father had a law degree and was overseer of several estates. In 1938, young Szasz came to the U.S. to avoid the impending Nazi take-over. He was an honors graduate of the University of Cincinnati in 1941, with a major in physics, and three years later he was graduated at the top of his class from that university's medical school. He interned at Boston City Hospital, took his residence in psychiatry at the University of Chicago Clinics, and his analytic training at the Chicago Institute for

Psychoanalysis. He has maintained a private psychiatric practice since that time.

Dr. Szasz has written more than two hundred articles and eight books and has recently edited an anthology called *The Age of Madness* (1973).

Some of his better-known works are Psychiatric Justice (1965), *The Ethics of Psychoanalysis* (1965), *The Manufacture of Madness* (1970) and *Ideology and Insanity* (1970).

Penthouse: What do psychiatrists do when they are said to be treating mental illness?

Szasz: In my view, when psychiatrists "treat" so-called mental illness, they actually intervene, in one way or another, in a conflict. Now, in the face of a conflict, there are three alternatives: you side with one party, side with the other, or try to remain neutral and act as an arbitrator or judge. Psychiatric interventions—which is the term I prefer to "psychiatric treatments"—are actually a confused and confusing mixture of these three kinds of social actions.

Penthouse: Give us some examples.

Szasz: Let's first take the case of a person who goes of his own accord to a private psychiatrist— say, someone like Dr. Daniel Ellsberg. Such a person hires the psychiatrist to help him with whatever he, the so-called patient, considers to be his problem, and to help him deal with it the way he, the client, wants to deal with it. Such a person is likely to have secrets—from his wife, his employer, the government—which he may share with his psychiatrist, but which the psychiatrist is expected to keep confidential. In Ellsberg's case, for example, the psychiatrist may have come into the possession of information which the U.S. government wanted to have. In short, in the conflict between Ellsberg and the American government, Ellsberg's psychiatrist acted as an agent of his client— protecting his client's interests, even where these might have been in conflict with the interests of the government.

Penthouse: But, isn't this an exceptional case?

Szasz: Only insofar as government agents burglarized the psychiatrist's office—which, I assume, is not yet common practice. For the principle it illustrates, however, it is not unusual at all; it is typical. In the less sensational case, the patient may confide secrets to the therapist that have to do with his conflicts with his wife, or a wife may confide her conflicts with her husband; the therapist will then be acting for the interests of one marital partner and against those of the other.

Penthouse: Give us some examples of other things psychiatrists do.

Szasz: In my first example, the psychiatrist did something *for* the patient. In the case of the husband and wife—which is economically and statistically more important than the first—the psychiatrist does something to the patient: for example, a husband contacts a psychiatrist, tells him that his wife has delusions or is depressed, and the psychiatrist then commits the wife to a mental hospital. The wife, the ostensible patient, does not want to be in the hospital; she wants to be left alone. Here then, the psychiatrist acts not as the patient's agent, but as his or her adversary. Finally, when a psychiatrist is hired and paid to "evaluate" individuals—for example, for a court, a draft board, the Peace Corps, an insurance company, and so forth—he acts as an arbitrator or judge. He is, in principle, neither the patient's agent nor his adversary; he is the agent of whoever hires him and pays him—assuming that he does his job honestly.

Penthouse: How can people tell what sort of thing a psychiatrist will do; whether he will act for or against what you call the patient's "self-defined interests?"

Szasz: They often can't. That's why I have gone to such great pains, in several books, to try to show that there are a minimum of two very different kinds of psychiatry—voluntary and involuntary, and that the difference is at least as important as the difference between say, psychotherapy and organic therapy.

Penthouse: Are you opposed to involuntary psychiatry?

Szasz: Indeed I am.

Penthouse: Why?

Szasz: Because I consider all involuntary psychiatric interventions to be punishments. Because I believe that physicians should be healers, not jailers. And because I believe that no one should be punished who did not break the law and who was not duly tried and convicted in court for it.

Penthouse: Not many psychiatrists share your idea that involuntary psychiatry is punishment.

Szasz: Not many psychiatrists. But many writers do. James Thurber described this in *The Unicorn in the Garden.* Of course, the victims of involuntary psychiatry think it's punishment, but their opinion doesn't count; they are considered "crazy." I suspect it's the main reason people are afraid of psychiatrists. After all, dermatologists and gynecologists are not in the business of locking people up, but psychiatrists are. And people know this. So what I am saying is at once shockingly novel, because it is the exact opposite of what medical and psychiatric orthodoxy says; and yet it is terribly obvious, because no one wants to be locked up in an insane asylum. That's why we have commitment laws and closed wards in mental hospitals.

Penthouse: You often complain that psychiatrists do not keep their patients' confidences. You mention, for example, the psychiatrist who released reports on a man who shot and killed several people from a tower at the University of Texas. Why do psychiatrists do that?

Szasz: Because they are no more honest than politicians. They often comply with popular expectations and pressures. There are countless such cases. For example, there was Lee Harvey Oswald, the man who supposedly killed President Kennedy. A psychiatrist saw him when he was in his teens. After Oswald was apprehended and killed—perhaps even before he was killed, I don't remember the exact timing—this psychiatrist gave out the whole story on Oswald; that is, when he saw him, and what he thought was wrong with him, and Oswald's mother, and so forth. An utter breach of confidence, in my opinion.

Penthouse: What about President Nixon's psychiatric record? Didn't he see a psychiatrist in the 1950's?

Szasz: He saw a physician who at the time was said to have specialized in psychosomatic medicine. He subsequently became a psychotherapist. This doctor also talked—perhaps blabbered would be a better term. The very fact that he acknowledged that Mr. Nixon had been his patient was in my opinion a breach of confidence. But that wasn't all; he also published a story in one of the mass magazines in which he went on at length about how mentally healthy Mr. Nixon was. This too was improper. He shouldn't have said anything.

Penthouse: Doesn't the ethics committee of the American Psychiatric Association do anything about this?

Szasz: You must be joking! Ethics committee! You know what such committees are for? To protect the profession—not the patient or the public. This is the whole problem with professions, especially when they manage to instill awe and fear in the public. George Bernard Shaw said that "every profession is a conspiracy against the public." Nowhere is this now more true than with respect to psychiatry.

Penthouse: In your writings, you cite the names of many public figures who have been "psychiatrized against their will." Can you mention some of them and just what happened?

Szasz: The list is a mile long. Ernest Hemingway was involuntarily hospitalized and given electric shock treatment. Secretary of Defense James V. Forrestal was apprehended, supposedly because he was suicidal. He was taken to the Bethesda Naval Hospital and was placed in a room on the top floor—the eleventh, I believe. A few weeks later he was found dead on the pavement in front of his window. Earl Long, the former governor of Louisiana, was incarcerated in a psychiatric hospital in Texas. When he was returned to a Louisiana mental hospital, he freed himself by firing the head psychiatrist of the Louisiana state mental health system. Long was a smart man. He understood psychiatric gangsterism better than most politicians do.

Finally, I want to mention the Goldwater case. During the 1964 presidential race, Senator Goldwater was, as you may recall, called crazy by about one thousand psychiatrists. Now, the interesting thing—and to me the terrible thing—about the aftermath of that affair was that Senator Goldwater sued Ralph Ginzburg, the publisher of *Fact* magazine, where this psychiatric defamation was published. Ginzburg was found guilty of libel and had to pay a substantial sum to Goldwater for damages. But, interestingly, Goldwater didn't sue any of the psychiatrists, even though they were the ones who produced and supplied the libelous material to Ginzburg.

This shows, I think, how afraid politicians are of psychiatrists, of the psychiatric profession as a whole, and that they consider psychiatrists more sacrosanct than Presidents or White House candidates. It's a dangerous situation.

Penthouse: You have criticized the symbiotic relationship between medicine—especially psychiatry—and the state. How did this symbiosis develop?

Szasz: This is a complicated matter, but in a nutshell, as the prestige and popularity of organized religion diminished, following the Enlightenment, medicine took over many of the functions formerly performed by the churches. Physicians became the new priesthood and it has been the psychiatrists especially who have played the roles of priests. They are our secular and "scientific" priests.

In a theocratic society the religious values, as interpreted by the priest, are enforced by the government; for example, you must close your shop on Sunday, or Saturday. In a therapeutic society, the medical values, as interpreted by the physician, are enforced by the government; for example, you must be vaccinated against smallpox and you cannot buy a hypodermic syringe.

Penthouse: If you are so critical of psychiatry, why do you teach and practice it?

Szasz: I am not critical of *all* of psychiatry. I am no more against psychiatry than a 16th century priest who opposed the Inquisition was against Catholicism. Of course, many orthodox Catholics in the 16th century would have said such a priest was against Catholicism, and many orthodox psychiatrists would now say that I am against psychiatry. This proves only that there is a conflict between me and orthodox psychiatrists, which is obvious. It does not prove that I am "against" psychiatry and that they are "for" it. The situation is a lot more complicated than that.

I object to only two things. First, I object to any and all *involuntary* psychiatry; to any kind of psychiatric measure that's imposed on a person against his will. Second, I object to the widespread mislabeling in psychiatry, whether it is voluntary or involuntary psychiatry; that is, calling personal problems "diseases," calling prisons "hospitals," calling conversation "treatment," and so forth.

Penthouse: What do you approve of?

Szasz: I approve of any kind of psychiatry that's voluntary and to which the so-called patient consents, and which is correctly labeled—or at least approximately so. If people want to do it, they should have the right to use all the existing psychiatric measures and any others that anyone wants to add—you name them: psychoanalysis, psychotherapy, group therapy, drugs, hospitalization, electroshock. They are all okay for those who *want* them. If someone like Senator Eagleton wants to go to a hospital and hire a doctor to give him electrically induced convulsions, why shouldn't he? I think he is making a bad mistake in doing so, but that's only my opinion. He is entitled to have his opinion and to act upon it.

Penthouse: You are personally opposed to electroshock. Why?

Szasz: It's a barbarity. I have never used it and never would. I wouldn't dream of recommending it. If someone asked me about it, I would point out that neurologists go to great lengths trying to prevent seizures in persons who have epilepsy, because every time a person has a grand mal seizure, his brain gets damaged. Nevertheless, psychiatrists claim that giving someone a seizure is a form of treatment. But then the history of medicine is full of instances of so-called cures that were actually harmful. You know the old saying, "The cure is worse than the disease." It applies to a lot of things psychiatrists do—electroshock, lobotomy, often the use of drugs, and sometimes even psychotherapy or psychoanalysis.

Penthouse: Despite this you would not want to see these things abolished?

Szasz: Certainly not! In my view of life, the foremost value is individual freedom and responsibility. People should have a chance to make their own choices. I am willing to state my views—for example, that I think that anyone who has electroshock is an idiot, but I would not want to impose my views on anyone. For one thing, I could be wrong. But even being right should not give one the right to impose his views or will on others. I view all this on the model of religion and religious freedom. It isn't only electroshock and lobotomy that I don't think much of. I don't think much of being a Jehovah's Witness or a Christian Scientist; but I certainly think people should have

a right to these religious beliefs and the practices they entail. And I think the same way about medical beliefs and practices.

Penthouse: Then you are not an antipsychiatrist, as so many seem to think?

Szasz: Of course not. I am against psychiatric coercion and deception, but I'm not antipsychiatry! There is now a whole literature on what is called "antipsychiatry," and I am supposed to be one of the originators of this whole movement. Words are very important, especially in psychiatry. So I reject the term "antipsychiatry." It's a bad term. It's misleading. It fails to make the distinction between voluntary and involuntary psychiatry. If one values individual freedom and dignity, then one must, of course, oppose involuntary psychiatry; at the same time, one must not oppose voluntary psychiatry, not try to prevent people from choosing psychiatric interventions that one personally dislikes or disapproves of.

Penthouse: You often refer to religion. Are you religious?

Szasz: Not in any formal sense. In the sense that I hold some values dear, yes. In a sense, everyone is religious. Man is fundamentally a religious being.

Penthouse: What do you think about death? What happens when we die? As a scientist, aren't you curious about it?

Szasz: Not really. This may sound foolish, but I think I know what happens when we die.

Penthouse: What?

Szasz: We are dead. That's it.

Penthouse: But do you accept the *possibility* that you might not know everything that happens when we die?

Szasz: Well, of course. All I am saying is that I don't believe in a life after death—whatever that phrase means. I have just never had the usual hang-ups about death. Life is very precious. But when one dies, one dies. That's the way it is, I think.

Penthouse: You often refer to John Stuart Mill and Ralph Waldo Emerson. What other men do you admire? Who influenced you?

Szasz: The great writers and playwrights—Shakespeare, Moliere, Dostoevsky, Camus, and countless others. Among contemporaries, people like Wittgenstein, Bertrand Russell, Karl Popper.

Penthouse: How about psychoanalysts?

Szasz: I admire all three of the great founders of psychoanalysis; not uncritically, though. Freud, Jung, and Adler were, all three of them, immensely gifted and creative and important people. It's too bad people no longer read them very much—read their original works. They are better than 99 percent of the current stuff.

Penthouse: What do you admire about these men or their work?

Szasz: I admire Freud's brilliance and his systematic style of work; Jung's humaneness and sensitivity to man's moral and religious nature; and Adler's common sense and directness. It seems to me, too, that Jung and Adler must have been superb psychotherapists, which Freud clearly was not.

Penthouse: In your new book, *The Second Sin,* you say that, "The narcotics laws are our dietary laws." Why don't you consider the addict a sick person?

Szasz: Because a bad habit is not a disease. In fact, I maintain that not only is the addict not sick, but that there is no such thing as "addiction" and no such person as an "addict." There are, to be sure, people who take some drugs which some other people do not want them to take; and if the latter have more power than the former, then they can and sometimes do call the former "addicts."

Penthouse: Do you say this for effect or do you really believe it?

Szasz: Both. But look at the similarities between this drug situation and the situation as it was not so long ago with religion. A few hundred years ago, if a person was not a Christian, or was not a Christian in just the right way, he was considered a heretic. Today we know there are no heretics. Heretics were simply people whose religious habits offended those who defined the true faith. I hold that, in the same way, addiction is a sort of pharmacological heresy.

Penthouse: I presume you don't think much of methadone?

Szasz: It's as good a narcotic as another. It's much like heroin—just as Orthodox Judaism is much like fundamentalist Christianity, which is why they make such perfect antagonists.

Penthouse: Isn't methadone a treatment?

Szasz: Of course it's a "treatment." It must be.

The United States government says so. The American Medical Association says so. The American Psychiatric Association says so. So most people are likely to go along and believe this. I don't. But I don't expect most people to agree with me on a thing like this, which is almost entirely a matter of fashion, of fast-changing definition.

Penthouse: At one time heroin was used as a treatment for morphine addiction. You think the same thing may happen to methadone?

Szasz: Yes, l think there is an excellent chance for that. As methadone is used more widely and over a longer period, more and more people will be "abusing" it, and then the medical profession and the government will decide one nice day that it's no longer a "treatment" but a disease!

Penthouse: You are opposed to prescriptions. Wouldn't a lot of people hurt themselves and perhaps hurt others if anyone could buy any drug he wanted?

Szasz: If people buy drugs and hurt themselves, that's their problem. If they hurt somebody else, they should be punished especially hard instead of it being an extenuating circumstance calling for mercy. Under Roman law, a person who committed a crime while intoxicated was punished especially hard. That was two thousand years ago. What we need is a little catching up. But you don't penalize people by stopping them from buying and taking drugs. That is not a crime.

Penthouse: Give us some other examples of this alliance between medicine and the state.

Szasz: There are so many, and we are so embedded in them, that we are unaware of them, as people are unaware of the air they breathe—until they get asthma. A few years ago, abortion was a crime. Now it's a treatment—and Blue Cross pays for it! Pimping is a crime, but when a so-called sex therapist like Dr. Masters gets you a prostitute and calls her a "surrogate wife," then pimping becomes a form of treatment, which you can take off your income tax. Sending your son or daughter through college is not tax-deductible, but "sex-therapy" is. If that doesn't drive home the truth about the alliance between medicine and state, the politicalization of illness and treatment, l certainly don't know what would.

Penthouse: You don't believe there is such a

thing as "mental illness." Well, how does schizophrenia develop, and other behavior conventionally called "mental illness?"

Szasz: I don't want to be difficult, but I must insist that schizophrenia doesn't develop. A certain kind of behavior develops, and that may be called "schizophrenia." Assuming that, and assuming we have the same sort of behavior in mind, this would be my answer. There are two basic ways of being badly screwed up in childhood: by being neglected too much or by being interfered with too much. Being left alone, being left unoccupied, unstimulated—or, on the other hand, being overprotected, intruded upon, overstimulated —both are pretty nearly intolerable for children—as well as for adults. To develop what we in our culture call "properly," we must be able to grow up and live in some middle range between too much aloneness and too much togetherness.

Penthouse: Some researchers claim that diet—and especially some vitamins—can affect schizophrenia and may be used to treat it. Could you comment on this?

Szasz: I can't comment on the biology of this matter, because I don't know what dietary influences or vitamins do for whatever may be physiologically the matter with some "schizophrenics"—if anything. But I do want to emphasize that if schizophrenia is a disease, like diabetes, to which medically oriented psychiatrists often compare it, then the "schizophrenic" patient should have the same rights as those of the diabetic patient. Foremost among these are the right to reject treatment, the right to reject being diagnosed —indeed, the right to reject being a "patient" at all, in the sense of having the right to refuse to submit to medical ministrations. At the same time, as I said before, people should have the right to whatever treatment they want—vitamins, electroshock, even lobotomy; but only if they want it.

Penthouse: Why do you emphasize the right to reject treatment?

Szasz: Because psychiatrists and medically oriented psychiatric researchers make constant claims about this or that being physiologically wrong with "mental patients"—as if establishing the presence of an objectively identifiable disease

would legitimize treating such patients. It wouldn't. Syphilis is an objectively identifiable disease. But there is no law, in New York State, authorizing a physician to treat a person for syphilis who does not want to be treated. In other words, what makes treatment legitimate in medicine is that the patient wants it; whereas what makes it legitimate in psychiatry is that the physician *claims* that the "patient" is "sick." I insist on distinguishing between illness as a biological condition and the act of treating a person— with or without his consent—which is a political event.

Penthouse: Your objection to involuntary mental hospitalization and treatment leaves open the problem of what to do with people who are dangerous, those who commit crimes.

Szasz: Here I must refer you to my two books, *Law, Liberty and Psychiatry* and *Psychiatric Justice*, where I discuss this subject in detail. Briefly, my position is that in a free society, no one should be deprived of liberty without due process of law. And to me, due process implies that the only justification for loss of liberty is the commission of an illegal act. Mental illness can never justify it, just as heresy can't—just as being too fat or too thin can't. In other words, if someone is suspected of breaking the law, he should be accused, tried, and if convicted, sentenced. If the sentence calls for loss of liberty, then the offender should be confined in an institution that's penal, not medical, in character. Of course, in many cases where such sentences are imposed, they really should not be imposed if we are to be truly concerned with the protection of public safety and the maintenance of human dignity. In any event, I don't want doctors to be jailers or torturers. We have already forgotten what doctors did in Nazi Germany, and we don't want to know what they do in Communist Russia.

Penthouse: All right, so we send criminals to jail without considering insanity as an extenuating circumstance. But our jails are very bad. Very few people come out of them fit for society. What good does it do to send them there unless you hold everybody for life terms?

Szasz: Of course our prisons are bad. I didn't say they were good. Nor did I promise to solve all social problems. I am only trying to clarify what psychiatrists do and to identify what I think is good or bad among the things they do, and why. If prisons are bad, and if we want to do something about this, the remedies are obvious enough. We should send fewer people to prison and we should make the prisons better. Placing lawbreakers or suspected lawbreakers—and indeed, innocent persons suspected of being "dangerous," whatever that term might mean—in mental hospitals, which are themselves horrible prisons, is not my idea of prison reform.

Penthouse: You say that committing suicide should be a human right. But suppose I tried to jump out of that window? Wouldn't your impulse be to restrain me?

Szasz: Yes, of course, I would try to stop you, partly because I would assume that that's what you would want me to do; otherwise you wouldn't be trying to kill yourself right in front of me. But the point is that I would not call the police; I would *not* commit you to a mental hospital; I would *not* even try to persuade you to see a psychiatrist. What I might say is, "Look, you are insulting me. You call me on the telephone. You say you want to talk to me, to do an interview. You come and we talk. And then you want to jump out of *my* window. How can you do this to me? Why did you deceive me?'"

Penthouse: Suppose I then told you: "All right, I'm going to get a room of my own, check in, and jump out of my window." Then what?

Szasz: I would offer to talk about it with you. That's all. The rest would be up to you. Perhaps I would also ask you why you tell me that you are going to kill yourself. Why don't you keep it to yourself?

Penthouse: You seem reluctant to say much about the possibilities of altering behavior chemically. Why is that?

Szasz: Because I do not consider myself particularly knowledgeable about biochemistry or pharmacology. Of course, I recognize that it is possible to alter behavior chemically. But I try to focus on the ethical and political aspects of how such alteration is brought about rather than on the alteration itself.

Penthouse: I'm sorry. You'll have to clarify that.

Szasz: I know that chemical substances alter behavior. That's not in dispute. Right now, we are drinking vodka tonics. If we drink enough of the stuff, we shall produce an alteration in our behavior due to alcohol. That's the model. The idea is simple enough; alcohol, nicotine, opium, methadone, barbiturates, amphetamines—it's a long list. All those drugs alter behavior. So I am not denying any of this or that drugs may be useful for what is now called psychiatric treatment.

Penthouse: But shouldn't medical men, chemists, biologists, be working full speed on this? Aren't you excited about the possibilities?

Szasz: I am not particularly excited about this area simply because I happen to believe—and, of course, I could be wrong about this—that most of the things we call "mental diseases" are personal problems, human problems; and there isn't much you can do about human problems by drugging the person who has them. Second, I am not too excited about this area because it seems to me that, by and large, drugs affect mood and behavior in one of two ways: they stimulate or they depress—that is, they make you feel more energetic and awake (at least for a while) or they make you feel less energetic and more sleepy. Now, each of these effects may be useful. In fact, I happen to believe that we have too many restrictions on drugs that have these effects. They should be freely available. And this carries me to my third point, which is the moral and political one. Who now controls, and who will control in the future, the use of these drugs? The government? The medical profession? The free citizen of a free society? It may be foolish to plunge ahead and develop more and more psychopharmacological agents when we can't seem to decide how to use the agents we now have. After all, opium has been around for thousands of years; and we now consider it "progress" to prohibit its use and to replace it with synthetic drugs. And last but not least, I think we should grapple—and I mean politicians, lawyers, civil libertarians and people in general—with the basic question of whether such drugs should ever be used involuntarily, and if so, when, how, by whom, on whom, and what sort of protections will the citizen have against being drug-controlled by physicians and politicians? It's not enough to write science fiction about this. It's necessary to confront it as the political—not medical— problem that it is.

Penthouse: One last question: In many of your

books you are concerned with the dangers of medical oppression, or a kind of therapeutic tyranny. You have coined the term "therapeutic state." Could you clarify what you mean?

Szasz: For nearly twenty years now I have been writing about the fundamental similarities between the persecution of heretics and witches in former days and the persecution of madmen and mental patients in ours. Briefly, my view is that just as a theological state is characterized by the preoccupation of the people with religion and religious matters, and especially with the religious deviance called heresy, so a therapeutic state is characterized by the preoccupation of the people with medicine and medical matters, and especially with the medical deviance called illness. The aim of a therapeutic state is not to provide favorable conditions for the pursuit of life, liberty, and happiness, but to repair the defective mental health of the subject-patients. The officials of such a state parody the roles of physician and psychotherapist. This arrangement gives meaning to the lives of countless bureaucrats, physicians, and mental health workers by robbing the so-called patients of the meaning of their lives. We thus persecute millions—as drug addicts, homosexuals, suicide risks and so forth—all the while congratulating ourselves that we are great healers curing them of mental illness. We have, in short, managed to repackage the Inquisition and are selling it as a new scientific cure-all.

Postscript

Dr. Szasz expressed his belief that committing suicide should be a human right. He expounded on this topic in The Case Against Suicide Prevention *in the July 1986 edition of the* American Psychologist. *He argued that professionals are not necessarily negligent or guilty of malpractice if patients under their care harm themselves. Some consider him the "Dr. Kevorkian" of psychiatry.*

In January of 1992, Hilda B. Klein filed a medical malpractice suit against Dr. Szasz. Her husband, Dr. Michael B. Klein, hanged himself in 1990. Michael Klein had been diagnosed with bipolar disorder and was taking lithium. Dr. Szasz instructed him to stop taking lithium. The suit claimed that suicide was left an option.

The suit was settled out of court in 1994, shortly before going to trial. The terms of the settlement were not disclosed. Szasz did not admit to doing wrong.

Figure 10-2. Jay Haley. (Illustration by Jim Rooney.)

READING 10B

THE ART OF BEING SCHIZOPHRENIC

Jay Haley

Proponents of the social perspective deny that a disease entity, schizophrenia, exists. According to R.D. Laing, a Scottish psychiatrist and a leader of the antipsychiatry movement:

> *. . . behavior that gets labeled schizophrenic is a special sort of strategy that a person invents in order to live in an unlivable situation. In his life situation the person has come to be placed in an untenable position. He cannot make a move or make no move, without being beset by contradictory pressures both internally, from himself, and externally, from those around him. He is, as it were, in a position of checkmate. I must make it clear that this state of affairs may not be perceived as such by any of the people in it. The man at the bottom of the heap may be being crushed and suffocated to death without anyone noticing . . . (Laing, 1964).*

The double bind theory of schizophrenia was originally published by Bateson, Jackson, Haley, and Weakland in 1956. Simply stated, it postulates that schizophrenia results from confusing, complicated and threatening social situations consistently encountered by an individual. Children, who eventually become schizophrenic, are often placed in "no win" situations by their parents. Communication, verbal and nonverbal, is often ambiguous and contradictory. The child learns to be remote, evasive, and withdrawn (negative symptoms of schizophrenia) to avoid conflict and criticism in this confounded and confusing environment. Thus, schizophrenia results from complex social factors.

In the following article, Jay Haley, one of the original authors of the double bind hypothesis, elaborates on some of its basic tenets. He describes the family dynamics likely to produce schizophrenia. He notes parallels between the struggles faced by the schizophrenic when at home and those faced in the mental hospital. As previously stated, the social perspective evolved from its criticism of the illness perspective and psychiatry.

Haley's work was instrumental in providing the foundation upon which contemporary family systems theory is built. Contemporary concepts such as the dysfunctional family, codependency, and enabling can be inferred from this article.

The article may be difficult to understand. No one writes quite like Jay Haley. Much of the article is written in a tongue-in-cheek manner. However, The Art of Being Schizophrenic *is a profound account of Haley's perception of schizophrenia.*

Reference

Laing,R.D. (1964). Is Schizophrenia A Disease? *International Journal of Social Psychiatry,* 10.

Jay Haley, "The Art of Being Schizophrenic." Reprinted from *Voices, the Art and Science of Psychotherapy,* Vol. 1, no. 1, Fall 1965, with permission of the American Academy of Psychotherapists.

It is common today to hear complaints that standards are falling in every field of endeavor. Like most generalizations, this one may not be true, but certainly standards are dropping in the field of psychiatric diagnosis. Where there was once neatness and rigor, one now finds a slipshod, lackadaisical, devil-may-care lumping together of the most diverse maladies as if the need for diagnostic precision no longer existed. The most shocking example is the diagnosis of schizophrenia. At one time it was clear that a man was either schizophrenic or he was not, and the several species were neatly catalogued and appreciated. Today we find that the label of schizophrenia is likely to be applied to just about anyone. A passing temper tantrum by an adolescent can earn a diagnosis of schizophrenia without providing the youth any opportunity to show his true nature and abilities in this line of endeavor. Not only are the wrong sort of people included in this category, but we also find ourselves drowning in the attempts to water down the diagnosis so that just about anyone can be classed in this way. Let us face facts: what on earth is a schizoid, or worse yet a schizo-affective state? Are not such labels merely absurd compromises showing an unwillingness to keep the diagnosis clean and pure in the European, particularly the German, tradition? At this time we should review what is required of a person who truly merits this diagnosis so that we can ruthlessly eliminate the false contenders and draw a sharp line between this and other maladies. To use the term "schizophrenic" loosely for anyone who wanders in the hospital door looking befuddled betrays those individuals who have worked long and hard to achieve the disease.

The Right Sort of Family

To say that not everyone can achieve schizophrenia is to say a great deal. Today any competent diagnostician who is sifting the true schizophrenic from the chaff will include in his observation the environment of the patient. After all, to be schizophrenic it is essential that one be born into the right sort of family and if one can manage that all else may follow. However, we cannot choose our parents, they are a gift of heaven. People who have attempted schizophrenia with-

out the correct family background have universally failed. They can erupt into psychotic-like behavior in combat or when caught in some other mad and difficult situation, but they are unable to sustain that behavior when the environment seems to right itself. The same point applies to the variety of fascinating drugs which are falsely said to induce psychosis. Not only does the drug influence miss the essence of the experience, but the effect wears rapidly off. The occasional goat who manages to be a schizophrenic after the drug has left his system is easily separated from the sheep who go back to normal—he has come from the right sort of family and probably would have achieved schizophrenia even without the benefit of medical research.

The type of family one must come from to become schizophrenic has been extensively described in the professional journals. One can summarize these scientific reports by saying that as individuals the family members are unrecognizable on the street but bring them together and the outstanding feature is immediately apparent—a kind of formless, bizarre despair overlaid with a veneer of glossy hope and good intentions concealing a power-struggle-to-the-death coated with a quality of continual confusion.

Observing such a family one is struck by the central figure, the mother, and notes at once that the schizophrenic owes to her his flexibility and his exasperating skill in frustrating people who attempt to influence him. Just as the child in a circus family learns from his parents how to maneuver on the slack wire, so does the schizophrenic learn from his mother how to maneuver acrobatically in interpersonal relations. To achieve schizophrenia a man must have experienced a mother who has a range of behavior unequalled except by the most accomplished of actresses. She is capable when stung (which occurs when any suggestion is made to her) of weeping, promising violence, expressing condescending concern, threatening to go mad and fall apart, being kind and pious, and offering to flee the country if another word is said. At the minimum, and on an off day, this type of mother is able to reply to an accusation about her alcoholism by saying, "I never drink, at least not often, and then only because it makes me more cheerful for the family's sake." When faced with the dreadful child she has raised, she is able to reply innocently that the fault lies elsewhere since she has done nothing in life for herself but everything for her child. This halo-effect is apparent in the comment of a mother who said, "A mother sacrifices, if you would be a mother yourself you would know this, like even Jesus with his mother, a mother sacrifices everything for her child."

It should be obvious that such mothers are not easy to find and probably don't represent more than twenty percent of the females born. Yet for the true flowering of schizophrenia, even such a mother is not enough. To balance the flexibility provided by mother, the schizophrenic must have a father who will teach him to remain immovable. The father of the schizophrenic has a stubbornness unequalled among men (as well as the skill to keep a woman in the state of exasperated despair which helps mother make use of her full range of behavior). On occasions when present and sober such a father can easily say, "I am right, God in heaven knows I cannot be proven wrong, black is not white and you know it too in your heart of hearts." This sort of father is not easily found in the general population, largely because he is rarely home.

When one considers the odds that this type of uncommon man will find such an uncommon woman, and the even more astonishing odds that two such people could copulate, it is clear at once that the incidence of true schizophrenia could not be high. (Often such parents report that the copulation only occurred when one or both was asleep and that is why they had to get married, but even granting this possibility the odds against schizophrenia being common do not change appreciably.)

Finally, it is important, although not essential, that a schizophrenic have as part of his environment a certain type of brother or sister. This sibling must be the kind of person who is hated on contact—a do-gooder, a good-in-schooler, a sweet, weak, kind bastard of a sibling who can provide the contrast for the future schizophrenic by showing him up to be the complete idiot his family expects him to be.

Given this array of talent around him, one might think the individual raised in such a family constellation would inevitably achieve schizophrenia. However, this is obviously not true since all children in such families do not go clearly mad. The schizophrenic must not only have such a family, but he must hold a certain position in it and serve certain vital functions over an extended period of time. Like any artist, several hours a day of practice over many years are necessary.

Regarding his position, he must be the child the parents choose to focus upon—that special child the parents expect to be remarkable for reasons related to their own dark pasts. Whatever this particular child does is of exaggerated importance to the parents, and he soon learns that touching his nose can set off an earthquake in the family. This parental focus is sufficiently intense that when it is turned from the schizophrenic to the sibling, the sibling begins to disintegrate like a match head placed under a burning glass.

It is the primary function of the schizophrenic to be the representative failure in the family, and in that sense be remarkable. The parents feel themselves to be insignificant wretches, lost souls incapable of any human accomplishment (although many of them make rather good scientists). Therefore for their survival they must have before their eyes the schizophrenic child as an example of a worse failure so they can stand a little higher in the world by that fact. The child can fulfill this function rather easily since he need only fail at whatever he attempts. The average schizophrenic shows his artistry by achieving more than usual ability along this line, while also indicating at regular intervals that he could do quite a good job at succeeding if he wanted to, thus shining in the light of his parents' admiration while giving them sufficient cause for disappointment.

The schizophrenic is not only the focus of his parents' life, but he serves a key position in the wider morass that is the total family network. One is reminded of the vast array of tumblers who stand upon each other's shoulders, all constructed upon one man standing at the bottom holding up the entire edifice. Just as the child is caught up in the conflict between his parents, so is he in the middle of the triangular struggle between his mother and her mother, his father and his mother, and the many other cross-generational conflicts in this type of family. (When the schizophrenic sides with his mother against father, father can only protest weakly since he is joining his mother against his wife.)

The average schizophrenic has had a lifetime balancing conflicting family triangles, each one focussed upon his every action, so that whatever he says and does in one triangle has repercussions in another. If he should please his grandparents, he will displease his parents, and should he agree with any one person he is certain to antagonize several others. Therefore the schizophrenic must learn to communicate in a way that satisfies everyone by saying one thing and disqualifying it with a conflicting statement and then indicating he didn't mean any of it anyhow. This complicated mode of adaptation makes his behavior appear rather peculiar.

The schizophrenic soon learns, of course, that he has a position of extreme power in manipulating triangles to his advantage. The importance of his skill in this essential game cannot be overemphasized. For example, one teenage schizophrenic, precocious as most schizophrenics are, said, "My parents and I are involved in the eternal triangle," and she showed her skill in this game by climbing into bed between her parents and kicking her mother out (while her father protested weakly that mother should have locked the bedroom door). The schizophrenic also takes for granted what social scientists are only beginning to realize—the true disturbance in human life comes when secret coalitions occur across generations or other power hierarchies (this is The Second Law of Human Relations). The schizophrenic is, of course, the master at cross-generation coalitions. He may decline to join his peers, but he will join a parent or a grandparent, and he has even been known to provoke a great grandfather to intrude into the parental conflict.

The primary responsibility of the schizophrenic is to hold the family together. Although social scientists, even family therapists, have not yet the vaguest idea how to prevent a family from disintegrating, the schizophrenic child accomplishes this with ease. It is his duty to use his keen perception and interpersonal skill to maintain the family system in a stable state, even if that state is a mood of constant despair. His importance in

this function appears on those rare occasions when the schizophrenic abandons his disease and becomes normal, succeeding in life and leaving his family. His parents at once individually collapse, losing their sense of purpose in life, and they set about to divorce (weakly apologizing to their parents for being more successful as parents than they were).

The schizophrenic child prevents divorce and family dissolution in a rather simple way; he provides the parents an excuse for staying together by offering himself as a problem. With minor threats of separation, he merely looks unhappy to provide mother and father with an excuse to stay together. When the parents are constantly on the verge of leaving one another, the child must present himself as a more severe problem. Such children learn quickly how to behave; a few odd mannerisms and grimaces in inappropriate moments are helpful, as well as muteness and a kind of twisting, weird waving of the hands accompanied by an occasional idiotic squeal. If of school age, the child must show that he is incapable of existing outside the family and therefore his parents must stay together and comfort him since they are his only source of life. By becoming the family problem, the child requires his parents to stay together to save him, offers himself as an excuse for their misery with each other, and he also challenges them. These parents feel they must be perfect parents and when their child behaves oddly all their determination to cure him is aroused, thus giving them further reason to continue to associate as a family.

The schizophrenic must also act quickly if the parents threaten to come closer together and be more affectionate, thereby provoking a change in the family (as well as panic in the parents). Should father almost reach out a hand to mother, the schizophrenic must promptly wet his pants, or he must say, "Oh, I want to visit Granny," thereby bringing father's mother into the scene, which always provokes an argument between the parents.

When the schizophrenic is old enough to perceive that his family is culturally defiant, he begins to function as the symbol of the family's differentness. The peculiar way he chooses to express himself on this matter will drive the parents closer together and at the same time attract community attention to provide some help for the family. His technique is to use parody. Schizophrenics have long been known as the most skilled people at parody in the world, and it has been said that they parody all the worst aspects of our society. This gives them too much credit; they are merely parodying their families. For example, if the parents insist that they are devoutly religious while behaving in a most unreligious manner, the schizophrenic son will begin to grow a beard and burn holes in the palms of his hands with cigarettes. Should this not attract sufficient attention—some of these parents will consider this only playful behavior—then the schizophrenic will take to strolling about the neighborhood carrying a large cross. The parents do not always take this as action in their best interests, particularly since they have a passion for secrecy about many matters, but in such a case they can hardly accuse the child of misbehavior when he merely is being more religious than they are. In a similar way, if the parents have unsavory minds while insisting that they are terribly puritan, the schizophrenic will loudly condemn dirty words, naming them and even writing them on the front sidewalk.

The skill with which a schizophrenic calls attention to a family problem while simultaneously declining responsibility for doing this is best illustrated by his verbal comments. The ideal comment is one which is as ambiguous as mother could offer—it must reach the parents in their souls but keep them uncertain whether an outsider gets the point. For example, a schizophrenic daughter listened to her parents describe how happy this family was except for this wretched daughter, and she said, "Yes, but wouldn't you and Daddy be happier if you didn't drink so much?" Granting that this calls attention to the parents' need for help, it was also a rather unskillful and crude thrust which does not merit being called schizophrenic. This rude directness might be attributed to the daughter's faulty control of her anger. The more experienced schizophrenic can completely control the expression of his feelings and offer flattened affect even when the doctors are sticking pins into him at medical demonstrations. One can only applaud another daughter who panicked her mother by saying flatly, "I'm

going to call the police and tell them the house is dirty," a son who sent his mother a Mother's Day card which said, "You've always been like a mother to me," and yet another daughter who arrived with her mother and stepfather in a psychiatrist's office and said, with inappropriate affect, "Mother had to get married and now I'm here."

When the family threatens to dissolve, the schizophrenic must be willing to go to any extreme, even insane activity which brings in the neighbors and the police. It is the willingness on his part to fulfill the function of holding the family together which explains why the schizophrenic—despite his skill, wariness, and keen perception—lets himself be cast into a mental hospital. His psychotic behavior is a last resort when a family crisis has reached the point where an unresolvable breach is about to take place. This final extremity drives the parents together because of their common burden of a truly unfortunate child, forces the parents into a common front against the community which is protesting that something must be done, and lets the family make the schizophrenic the patsy for all past and present difficulties. The psychotic episode is merely a more extreme version of other behavior of the schizophrenic at times of family crisis, but this time it precipitates him into a situation which calls forth all his skill—the treatment situation. Before describing the talent necessary for the schizophrenic to survive in the hospital setting, let us summarize the training the schizophrenic has had when he arrives, his face unwashed and his hair uncombed, ready for entrance into the institution which will become his tomb.

In sum, the schizophrenic must have come from the right sort of family, with appropriate parents as models. He must have learned to manipulate and balance complicated, conflicting family triangles, and he must be perceptive enough to keep his feet in a morass of trickery and despair. He must also have learned to deal with intensive attention; other children are ignored at times by their parents, but with the schizophrenic every move and word is taken personally. As a consequence he must become skilled in concealing his emotions, he must learn to indicate that whatever he did just happened and he is not responsible for it, he must perceive the threats in every situation, and he must achieve skill in stabilizing whatever system he is in by being a willing scapegoat to support the inadequacies of those around him. It should be immediately evident that few people can meet the complicated requirements of the world of the average schizophrenic. There is one final requirement which eliminates most contenders. Only certain of the great political and religious leaders of the past have had the character structure, the determination of the schizophrenic. He has the will to devote his life to an absolute and stubborn crusade. His crusade is this: never to let his family off the hook. The hundred million affronts he has suffered are never to be forgiven to the end of his days. Even if the law should force him to separate from his parents, he must continually remind them, by bizarre letters if necessary, that they have driven him mad and he plans to continue in that state. His one risk is cure because if cured this means he has forgiven his family, and the true schizophrenic, his will power forged in the fire of a billion conflicts, will not offer that forgiveness even in the face of the most pitiable pleas. Just as the Crusader tenaciously pursued the Holy Grail over the bodies of the infidels, the true schizophrenic will remain attached to his family at all costs and by any methods so that on their deathbeds his parents still have on their conscience this parental disaster.

The Right Sort of Hospital

Only in the mental hospital can schizophrenia achieve its full flowering. Just as a plant reaches its greatest growth in well manured ground, so does the schizophrenic achieve his full range on the closed wards of mental institutions. Yet oddly enough the first reaction of the schizophrenic to hospitalization is a stout objection. Only when he has been incarcerated for a period of time does he recognize the merit of the establishment. Then he is almost impossible to remove. Nowhere in the world can he find an environment so similar to life at home and yet with opponents so much less skilled than the members of his family.

The average mental hospital has been extensively described in the professional literature. One can summarize these scientific reports by saying that the outstanding feature of a mental institution is a kind of formless, bizarre despair overlaid with a veneer of glossy hope and good intentions concealing a power struggle to the death between patients and staff, coated with a quality of continual confusion. The basic art of schizophrenia lies in a genius for dealing with power struggles, and of course in a mental hospital the problem of power is central. It should not be thought that the struggle between patient and staff is unequal. True, the staff has drugs, tubs, cold packs, shock treatments (both insulin and electric), brain operations, isolation cells, control of food and all privileges, and the ability to form in gangs composed of aides, nurses, social workers, psychologists and psychiatrists. The schizophrenic lacks all these appurtenances of power, including the use of gang tactics since he is essentially a loner, but he has his manner and his words and a stout and determined heart. He also has had extensive training in a family made up of the most difficult people in the world. A normal person might disintegrate or capitulate on any issue in the face of the organized assault by the staff of a mental hospital, but the schizophrenic at one glance can size up the situation and seize upon his opportunities. Even though disconcerted by being betrayed into the hospital, as he usually is, the schizophrenic can have family and staff embroiled in an argument before he has been stripped of his civilian clothes and had his money and driver's license confiscated.

The first lesson the schizophrenic learns in the hospital is that he must do what the aides tell him to do. His initial reaction is to decline, since he has never in his life done what he was told, it is against family tradition. However, the aides cannot permit recalcitrance since it is their duty to keep the hospital functioning. Therefore when the schizophrenic refuses to obey an order, the aide hits him as hard as he can in the gut. This astonishes the patient, and he muses over how to turn it to his advantage. He soon learns that he cannot, because being hit in the gut receives no publicity. Should the patient complain, the aide denies that it happens and the doctor pretends to believe him. That night the aide hits the schizophrenic as hard as he can in the gut twice more and calls him a squealer. From that time on the schizophrenic obeys the aide, although his courage is apparent even in these circumstances because he does what he is told in a desultory manner as if he has not heard a command and is only happening to follow it. In more modern and progressive mental hospitals the aides are not allowed to beat up on the patients. It is necessary for the aide to report that the patient cannot control his hostility so that the doctor can bang the patient in the head with a shock machine. This procedure maintains the proprieties for medical investigating boards who know medical treatment when they see it. Recently institutions have attempted to incapacitate the schizophrenic by pouring drugs into him until his eyeballs float and he is uncertain what is up and what down. Drowned in sufficient powerful drugs, the schizophrenic's keen perception becomes impaired and he is less skillful in the hospital power struggle. However, over time immunity to the drugs begins to set in, and recently there has been a trend in hospitals to return to the shock machine.

After his first encounter with the brute force of the hospital structure, the wise schizophrenic casts his dull and calculating eye upon the basic game he must play to survive and keep his self respect. He soon learns that little is new; all is like life at home.

The first weakness the schizophrenic discovers in the hospital structure is the same one he found in his family; the hospital can be hoisted on its own pretense of benevolence. Just as mother defined all she did as done for his sake, so does the hospital define all it does to be for the benefit of the schizophrenic. Arrangements which suited mother's convenience were said to be for her child's best interests, and all hospital activity which is for the efficient operation or convenience of the staff, whether forcing patients to rise at six in the morning or cutting out random portions of the brain, must be said to be for the sake of the schizophrenic. It is when he is offered such benevolence that the schizophrenic manifests his most skillful appearance of confusion, disorientation, and delusion. If he is told he must be in bed at nine in the evening because of his need for rest (and not the convenience of the ward staff) the schizophrenic will experience night terrors which keep the ward in turmoil until his more reasonable bed time. Having forced the hard fist of the aide or the heavy hand of the psychiatrist on the shock machine to quiet him, the schizophrenic has won the acknowledgement that nine o'clock bedtime is a hospital convenience. Hanging a psychiatrist on his benevolence is best illustrated by the patient who was faced with a doctor who could not tolerate his patients milling about the ward indicting him for his inability to cure them. He therefore announced that for their sakes the patients must be out of the ward all day getting fresh air. This particular schizophrenic declined to leave the ward. When he was forced out the front door, he walked straight ahead until he bumped into a tree, remaining there outside the doctor's window with his forehead against the tree until the exasperated physician retrieved him later in the day.

The hospital also provides the schizophrenic with the comfortable feeling he is still at home with his family by the similarity in power structure. Just as mother maintained the pretense that father was in charge, while ignoring him, so does the nurse pretend the ward psychiatrist is in charge while running things herself. The schizophrenic soon finds that the ward psychiatrist is as unavailable as his father ever was, since of course the psychiatrist never has the time or inclination to talk to the patients. The schizophrenic finds too that his long training in stirring conflict between his parents is unusually valuable in the hospital where nurse and psychiatrist can be played off against each other with minimum maneuvers. The confusion between doctor and nurse over their official and actual power position can be touched off in quite simple ways. For example, when the doctor requires some activity of the patient, the schizophrenic can indicate that the nurse said he was not to do that. The doctor may reply that by God *he is* the one who makes such decisions, but he becomes uncertain in his dealings with the nurse, who feels in turn that she must have antagonized him in some inexplicable way. If necessary to go to extremes because of a dull-witted staff, the patient can begin to scream whenever a particular staff member comes near him, thus making the entire staff look upon that person with suspicion.

The schizophrenic's training in manipulating coalitions across generations comes in appropriately in the hospital. He can join psychiatrist against nurse, nurse against aide, social worker against ward doctor, ward doctor against hospital administrator, staff against family, and so on. More skillful schizophrenics will escape occasionally and join community and police against the hospital. On the rare occasions when the schizophrenic is provided with a psychotherapist, he has the entire confusion in the staff power structure to play upon. The therapist, like mother, can be persuaded to request that the schizophrenic be given special treatment or at least be more fully understood, and the ward psychiatrist, like father, will bluster ineffectually that the patient must do what is expected of him, while the nurse protests that despite what the patient implied she wasn't out of her office for two hours leaving the ward unattended, and the aide will say that it's clearly a paranoid delusion when the patient says he was hit in the gut during the night. These periods of excitement alternate with long days of boredom for the schizophrenic, just as at home.

Whenever he is sufficiently bored, the schizophrenic can provoke action to enliven life on the ward. In fact, many schizophrenics have found they can provide some excitement by *not* doing anything. For example, they can stop eating. Just as mother went into a panic at home if her food was ignored and her poor child was wasting away to her shame, so does the hospital staff develop waves of anxiety if the patient ignores their food. They must have staff conferences, changes of drugs, physical examinations, the ever handy shock machine, extensive efforts to baby him into eating, and finally intravenous feeding. Before reaching the point of no return, the schizophrenic will usually begin to eat again. Some clever schizophrenics will time their resumption of food to coincide with a new drug the doctor has given them. Since the staff is always hoping for a pill which will cure all the staff problems, they rejoice with each success of a new drug— only to discover later that other patients do not respond to it and the responsive schizophrenics have duped them again. The position and function of the schizophrenic in the hospital is identical with his position and function at home. The staff of a mental institution feel themselves to be outcasts in the profession, insignificant wretches incapable of human accomplishment. Therefore it is essential for their survival that they surround themselves with people who are more incompetent than they are. Living among the experts in failure, the schizophrenics, the staff can stand a little higher in the world. From the top administrator of the hospital who kicks his assistant when irritated, down through the hierarchy to the aide who kicks the patient when irritated, the structure requires that final someone that all else can feel superior to—and there we behold the schizophrenic. As at home, the bad feelings and difficulties of the staff members with each other can be excused as a product of dealing with such a difficult person as the schizophrenic, so that his valuable function as a scapegoat binds the entire structure together like an adhesive.

It should not be thought that just anyone, including people with other psychiatric problems, could fulfill the schizophrenic's function. Training, persistence, and ingenuity are required. There is also a need for courage because of the risks. The schizophrenic not only faces the daily possibility of the aide's fist and the psychiatrist's shock machine, but he also lives under the threat of total isolation in solitary confinement as well as the threat that the doctors will plunge a scalpel into his brain as a last resort. These dangers add spice to the schizophrenic's life, and they require a particular style of behavior from him. This style is known medically as symptomatic of the hospitalized person. Since clear rebellion or justifiable outrage against the institution provokes savage punishment for his own good, the schizophrenic must behave like a difficult person while indicating that it's not he who's doing it and besides he cannot help himself— this is the definition of mental illness. The staff is reluctant to give him the business since he cannot help himself and so they must flounder in dealing with him—this is called treatment of the mentally ill. The most basic way to behave in a difficult manner and deny that it is your fault is to say that you are someone else and so aliases are common among schizophrenics. However, the mere alias is not enough, it should be one which is clearly an alias, such as a male patient calling himself Jacqueline

Khrushchev. Alternatively, one can say that the behavior originated elsewhere, and therefore one should not be punished. A nice device to achieve this is to say that a "voice" told one to do it, therefore responsibility lies elsewhere. One can make any criticism of the staff, even accuse a puritanical nurse of unsavory thoughts, if one says that it is really the Lord speaking and one is merely an instrument for that voice. The nurse becomes uncertain about putting the Lord on the shock roster. Another procedure is to act clearly insane so that one is obviously not responsible for needling the staff. A way to do this is to appear to be disoriented in space and time, which is particularly effective if it carries within it an indictment of the staff. To say that the place is really a prison and it is the seventeenth century is to make it clear that one is too insane to be blamed for an act. Yet at the same time the resemblance to a seventeenth century prison is close enough to most hospitals to arouse the guilt feelings of the staff. One thereby can indict while disarming and escaping blame, all neatly in one maneuver. Sometimes the guilt can be aroused by more ironical disorientation; one can say, for example, that the hospital is a palace and the doctor a king, thereby dismaying the doctor with the comparison. A third procedure is to make caustic comments while giving a silly and dilapidated laugh—who can punish such an idiot?—and yet the comments simultaneously reach home. One can also indict by actions without ever saying a word. When a schizophrenic stands against the wall with his head hanging down and his arms outstretched, the staff suspects that they are being told they are crucifying the patient, yet they are told in a way that they cannot accept or deny the accusation, or blame the schizophrenic—here lies the true art of schizophrenia.

These few simple procedures may seem limited, but a skillful schizophrenic can provide tremendous variety in his use of them. Whenever he has finally driven the staff to bring brute force to bear, it could be expected that the staff does so with the guilty feeling that they are taking advantage of a poor, helpless victim who cannot control himself. However, to assume that the staff feels guilty is to underestimate their education. After all, psychiatrists have received a liberal college education, thorough medical training, and a full residency in the science of psychiatry. They are usually good-hearted men attempting to do their best, and they follow civilized rules in dealing with the human beings. Because of their education and knowledge of the history of men, they are able to use a device which has always been used by civilized men caught in a death struggle for power with other men—they define the other men as not human beings, and therefore anything goes. The good-hearted Southerner can give the Negro his lumps and the good-hearted concentration camp guard in Germany can fling people into gas chambers as long as he can define those people as sub-human. Knowledge of this tradition has helped the psychiatrist, particularly those with a European orientation, to define the schizophrenic as not a person but a thing, an organic hulk who is out of contact with reality. Therefore civilized rules do not apply. By adopting this point of view and building it into a theory of psychosis, the staff can agree that the patient is not responsible for the trouble he is causing because he is not really a person and therefore regular bangs in the head with shock or an isolation room is obviously necessary to point the beast in a more amiable direction. Only by arguing that civilized rules do not apply to the schizophrenic can the staff meet the patient on at least equal terms, because the schizophrenic too is unwilling to follow civilized rules. Driven by his terrifying despair, he will go to any extremity of self abasement and therefore has a great advantage in such a struggle. The staff is faced with a person of extraordinary determination and skill in innovations. Even stripped nude and flung into a cell without furniture and soundproofed so that he cannot be heard, the schizophrenic is still not incapacitated. Ordinary people who must rely on friends, furniture to fling, or at least insults when they are in a power struggle would collapse in futile hopelessness in such a situation. Yet locked up alone and unheard, the schizophrenic still finds ways to express his opinion of the staff and arouse them further. He is willing to use the products of his own body and he will pee upon the door and crap upon the floor, cheerfully drawing pictures of the staff upon the wall in what he considers appropriate material.

Since there is some variety in the hospital environment, from reasonably pleasant wards for showing visiting dignitaries to the miserable back wards ruled by sadistic nurses and aides, it is important that the patient learn how to deal with the staff so that he forces them to behave badly to him but only if *he* has arranged it. He does not mind misery which he has provoked, but he does not like people to treat him badly on their own initiative. Therefore the schizophrenic must do a diagnosis of the staff to find the areas which are most suitable for provocations. The staff too must have an estimate of the range of skill of the schizophrenic so they can know what maneuvers to expect of any individual patient in this struggle. The need for a quick estimate of the schizophrenic has produced psychologists who are willing to do psychological testing so that the staff can diagnose the patient's weak points and thereby gain an advantage in dealing with him. Schizophrenics, however, are not put off as normal people would be by the aroma of pseudo-science exuding from the pores of the psychologist. The patients see immediately that this fellow who sits down pleasantly with them and asks them to look at blots of ink and talk about them is indeed a man who does not have their best interests at heart. In fact the schizophrenic knows what he says about the ink blot will be held against him and affect his career in the hospital in ways he cannot predict. Therefore the wise schizophrenic is guarded in his comments about the ink blots. Faced with the same kind of ambiguous situation he was raised in at home, with equally disastrous effects if he should say the wrong thing, the schizophrenic will avoid describing any coherent picture, because he knows this staff member may make ulterior use of the coherence. Instead he will point out little pieces of the ink blot here and there and make no connections between them. He will also avoid mentioning any of the human shapes he sees, even if they look like the psychologist, because he cannot be sure whether the human beings in power over him will take his comments personally. The more self-confident schizophrenic will toy with the test, reaching for bizarre points to see if he can shake the deadpan expression from the psychologist's face, playing with the idea of a bat since he is supposed to be

bats, and occasionally making oblique references to violence to indicate that he knows that this threat lies behind the testing. Only indirectly will he indicate that looking at blots of ink seems rather silly and so he knows there must be some reason for it which is being kept from him. The psychologist is pleased with the schizophrenic's protocol because he can discover that the responses are not common, ignoring the fact that the situation of the schizophrenic is also rather uncommon. It is like the white man in the South who concludes that a Negro is ignorant because the fellow shuffles and scratches his head and says, "Yassah, Boss," ignoring the context which makes it wise for the Negro to behave in that way. Since psychologists have a trained incapacity to examine contexts, they write down in their report that the patient is confused and loose in his associations, has distorted perception, deeply repressed hostility, and a sprained ego. This scientific description of test results is given to the staff which uses it, as the schizophrenic knew they would, to determine where to place him and how to deal with him.

It would seem evident that schizophrenia can be a dangerous game, but it has its lighter side too. Occasionally, for example, the patient is given a chance to have psychotherapy. Although the ward psychiatrists are so flooded with patients they do not have time to talk with them, and would hardly know what to talk with them about if they did take the time, most hospitals report in their publicity brochures that they are not merely prisons because they have a therapy program. This consists of group therapy meetings led by social workers. It is the function of these meetings to (a) turn the schizophrenics upon each other so they will be less occupied with entrapping the staff (this is called the Keseyan function); and (b) provide the social workers with a feeling of being useful while also letting them vent upon the patients the feelings they have developed from attempting to deal with the patient's families. The schizophrenic usually uses these group meetings to sharpen and broaden his techniques of verbal comment. Often he uses them to practice subtle variations in his repetitious behavior; the schizophrenic is, of course, the master at repeating the same behavior until the staff is driven to distraction. A possible record is held by the schizophrenic who, in a period of only two years, said, "I think my thinking is not good," a total of two hundred million, seventy-three times.

Occasionally a hospital will have a psychiatrist training program, and here the schizophrenic might have an opportunity for individual psychotherapy with a resident. The profession considers it wise to start these young fellows out on schizophrenics so that anything they meet later when making their fortunes in private practice will be anticlimactic. Psychiatric residents are a peculiar lot. Either they chose psychiatry because they thought they were going mad and it might help, or they could not develop a passion for some other medical speciality, like proctology, and so they fell into psychiatry by default. Once in training they discover that little of what their teachers say is of any use to them in dealing with a schizophrenic. Their instructors teach only part time and make their living in private practice where they entirely avoid schizophrenics (having had enough of them when *they* were residents). The basic problem of the resident is one of translation. His instructors talk in one bizarre language and the patients in another. While the instructors talk about dark ids flooded with anxiety and the daffodil structure of ego syntonics, the schizophrenics talk about the influence of atomic energy upon the burontonic systems and the difference between he-cocks and she-cocks. It is forbidden for instructors or residents to talk directly about the central theme of hospital life, the power struggle among staff and patients.

A typical beginning interchange between patient and psychotherapist can be presented to illustrate the kind of skill required of the true schizophrenic. The patient is brought to a room by an aide who mumbles something about seeing a doctor and then shuffles away. The schizophrenic waits, uncertain what new tactic the staff is offering and attempts to estimate its degree of savagery. At this point the door opens and a vacant-faced young man enters. He wears a suit and tie to distinguish him from the patients. "Hello," he says with false heartiness, "I'm Dr. Offgamay." The schizophrenic stares at the wall as if he has not noticed the intrusion. "Well," says

the doctor, attempting to ignore being ignored, "I thought we might talk about things." This typical therapeutic gambit, the vague, ambiguous, open-ended statement interests the patient. It may even arouse his admiration since it is a degree of ambiguity he thought only his parents could achieve. He begins to test whether this man is really what he appears to be or is more dangerous by saying something like, "My tail light is on," or perhaps, "My head was bashed in last night."

"Well now," says the young man, uncertain what to do with that sort of statement, "I'd like to know a little about you, won't you tell me about yourself."

The schizophrenic, who knows perfectly well his record has been carefully examined for his history, has already understood the situation and he decides on a further test for confirmation. He says, "I want to do what you do."

The doctor freezes—his status position shaken by this mild remark as if by an earthquake. "Oh," he says, his voice rather cool, "how long have you been a *patient* here?"

The schizophrenic has finished his testing, and he replies, "I was born here." He makes this statement with absolute sincerity, as if he fully believes it.

"Born here?" says the doctor, so confused by the sincerity that he can only inquire, "How old are you?"

"A hundred and eighty-seven," says the schizophrenic. The doctor suddenly has that lost feeling of one who suspects he is being put on and has been provoked into making a fool of himself and yet cannot be sure. The result is continuing suppressed fury and desperation as the game goes on and the doctor finds himself constantly provoked into saying what he would rather not say. He can only grab onto his shaky status position as a passenger holds the door handle on a wild ride down a mountain road.

This illustration of a typical interchange demonstrates the quick perception and interpersonal skill of the schizophrenic. If they had competitions, schizophrenics would vie among themselves to see who could discover most quickly whether he was dealing with a worthy opponent.

Once the therapy is off to this fine start, the only skill required of the schizophrenic is to keep it going. After all, the therapist is usually the only one in the hospital who will speak to him, except for the aides who have more muscle than wit. The schizophrenic must keep the therapy ongoing by not creating too much fear and despair in the therapist while at the same time not allowing anything which might approach success. Since residents change every few months, it is also good to give an impression of almost being cured so that this resident can encourage one of the next crop of residents to continue the treatment. Some schizophrenics can achieve strings of eight to ten psychotherapists over time, each one feeling that he is almost able to "reach" this poor wretch and a few more interviews will bring about a breakthrough.

The skill of the schizophrenic comes into play in several ways in psychotherapy. He must provide stimulation for the therapist and keep him coming, but he must also provide sufficient exasperating difficulties to help the therapist feel that he faces a worthy challenge of his abilities. Keeping the therapist on the hook requires an avoidance of any direct confrontation of the therapist with his miserable incompetence as part of a courtesy procedure. For example, if the therapist is late to an appointment and does not bother to apologize, it is not correct to directly confront him with his rudeness or he is likely to flee, as mother did when directly confronted with her misbehavior. Rather, the schizophrenic must tell a story which allows the therapist to correct himself if he chooses. For example, the patient can say, "I was out on my submarine this morning, and we were to meet the refueling ship off Madagascar, but unfortunately the ship had been struck by an atomic bomb and barely limped in late with its Chinese flagons at half mast." This rather complex statement, which any schizophrenic can quickly devise, allows the therapist an out. He can say, "I'm sorry I was late today," or he can argue, "Now Sam, you know you weren't out on a submarine this morning, you were right here in the hospital." The therapist's recognition that there might be more here than meets the vacant eye is usually represented by his following such an argument with, "Now let's try to get an understanding of why you'd think you were on a submarine. What does a submarine mean to you?"

A further requirement of the schizophrenic is an ability to find out quickly what the current psychiatric ideology is so that he can provide the young therapist with support for the theories he is learning. If it is a period when genital symbolism is the order of the day, the patient must discuss kings being overthrown and virgin queens married and vaguely rub his crotch whenever he mentions his mother. If genital symbolism is passe and oral symbolism is being emphasized in training, the patient must quickly adapt to oral metaphors. He will discuss the cement in his stomach and the whiteness of milk, he can offer drawings which vaguely resemble breasts to the keen psychiatric eye, and he may make occasional sucking motions with his lips to stimulate the therapist. The skillful schizophrenic can read the interests of therapists from minimal cues, such as lighting up of the eyes when some obvious symbol that makes sense in theory is mentioned. The more Sullivanian fads require more skill from the patient. As the therapist struggles to handle his interpersonal defenses and to help the patient discover how he deals with people, the patient must offer interpersonal behavior which is easily enough interpreted by even a novice therapist. For example, he must fold his arms and cross his legs and turn his head away so the therapist can point out that he is building a wall between them and interfering with their interpersonal relationship. However, the patient must not merely help the therapist, he also must occasionally show the novice that he still has a great deal to learn. When the young fellow is feeling rather confident in his therapeutic acumen, the schizophrenic can stare thoughtfully at him and then look away and say, "There are some people in the world who have a homosexual fix." Such a comment will shatter any sensitive resident and leave him dragging through the day wondering about his unconscious desires.

The odds against a schizophrenic in a hospital meeting a skillful therapist of schizophrenics are so great that in the memory of those who keep track of these matters the last time it occurred was in Buffalo in 1947. Should this happen, the full range of schizophrenic genius is necessary. He must play therapist against staff, make a thrust at every weak point in the man, pretend improvement when there is none, and generally fight for his life. After all, if he is inadvertently cured he must go out of the hospital to the family waiting for him at the gate. That family has discovered their child can be the burden which holds the family together while still being in the hospital with a hired staff to deal with the inconvenience, and so they protest how welcome he is without wishing him back. The occasional families who actually wish the patient to return home have marshalled their forces in his absence and plan to make up for lost time in giving him the business. Should the patient go mad and become normal, he also faces a society which will blacklist him for having accepted hospital treatment.

Psychiatry today is going through revolutionary changes, and we owe to the schizophrenic many of the advances being made. It is evident that the schizophrenic is responsible for the recent movement to close down all mental hospitals. The leaders of this movement, the more prominent psychiatrists in the field, are suggesting that rest homes should be created for the aged and emergency wards be set up in general hospitals for people to stay in for a few days during family crisis. Mental hospitals would be discarded with a state law that psychotic patients could not be kept in custody more than a few days unless they had committed a crime. The proponents of this scheme argue that schizophrenics should be returned to the families who deserve them and psychiatrists should be forced to deal with the insane and not avoid them.

Enthusiasts for the mental hospital, a group composed of families of patients, psychiatrists in peaceful practice, and those people employed in such institutions, argue that such a radical change is fantastic. These patients are diseased and need medical care, they say, and besides they don't make sufficient income to pay psychiatrists for treatment. The moral wing of this faction also point out that it would be unfair to loose psychotics upon the profession of psychiatry. Just as one would not put a man who runs the mile in four hours in the same race with a man who runs it in four minutes, so it is unfair to face the average psychiatrist with a schizophrenic or his family.

However, enthusiasts for closing down the hospitals argue in turn that such an act is necessary because of the skills of the true schizophrenic. As one proponent put it, "When patients were confined at home, it was thought they would improve with hospital treatment. Now let us admit defeat. Despite all attempts at reform and promising new methods of approach, the schizophrenic has beaten us. We should concede that fact and find other ways to deal with him." More active advocates of closing down mental institutions have created a slogan which can be seen on the signs they carry as they picket mental hospitals, "Let's get the patients off the back wards and back home into the back rooms!"

Figure 10-3. A community residence of the New York State Office of Mental Retardation and Developmental Disabilities provides services consistent with those described by Wolfensberger. (Photograph by Jim Rooney.)

READING 10C

THE PRINCIPLE OF NORMALIZATION AND ITS IMPLICATIONS TO PSYCHIATRIC SERVICES

Wolf Wolfensberger

In the concluding paragraphs of the preceding article, Jay Haley referred to a national movement to close down large mental hospitals. As presented initially, deinstitutionalization described the movement to 1) provide appropriate mental health services in community-based systems, 2) assure accurate matching of client needs to available services, and 3) assure that potential benefits of deinstitutionalization justify the expenditure of community resources. The intention of this liberal movement was to empower and benefit the nation's mentally ill and retarded.

In 1955 there were 558,922 residential patients in public mental hospitals. In 1975 this number had been reduced to about 193,000. In 1984, a point-in-time census of all state and county mental hospitals, there were 118,647 patients (Geller, 1992). According to the Statistical Abstract of the United States (1994) there were 98,400 in 1990.

The following article was published in 1970 when much deinstitutionalization was being planned and implemented. Syracuse University Professor Wolf Wolfensberger, a leader of the movement, outlined the basic theory of normalization and described how it should be conducted. The plan described is logical, clear, and appealing. To emotionally advocate the closing of large institutions without concrete, fiscally responsible plans for community care would be hollow rhetoric, reckless, and counterproductive.

Community mental health generated tremendous controversy. Proponents argued that treating in the community would allow patients to live autonomously and to blend in with society. Critics protested the "dumping" of sick, deviant people into the community without adequate care and support. Both views were extreme. The conduct of policy would determine which was closer to the truth. The guidelines contained in this article provide practical standards for assessing community mental health.

Reference

Geller, J. L. (1992, November). A Historical Perspective on the Role of State Hospitals Viewed From the Era of the "Revolving Door." *American Journal of Psychiatry,* 149 (11).

The "normalization principle" formulated by Scandinavian workers in mental retardation aims at eliciting and maintaining culturally normative behavior and using culturally normative means to this end. The principle is simultaneously simple and comprehensive, and it can constitute a unifying ideology for all human management areas. It provides guidance for decisions from the lowest clinical to the highest systems levels. Some specific implications for psychiatry are discussed.

The President's Committee on Mental Retardation recently sponsored a searching reappraisal of residential services for the mentally retarded.[1] In this report the history and evolution of residential models in retardation were traced; present practices were documented, assessed, and largely rejected; and a number of sweeping proposals were offered for the future. It is noteworthy that in the concluding and synthesizing chapter, Dybwad[2] identified the "normalization principle" as the keystone of a new approach not only to residential services specifically, but also to all services for the retarded. I submit that the field loosely referred to as "mental health" can profit as much from utilization of the normalization principle as the field of mental retardation.

The Normalization Principle

The normalization principle was first fully formulated in Scandinavia, and it has received little discussion thus far in the American literature. Yet the principle is consistent with and subsumes a number of concepts and principles that have gained ascendancy in sociological theory and human management practices and are widely known in the United States.

As a theoretical construct, the normalization principle is remarkably elegant and parsimonious and has profound implications for the management of persons who are likely to be viewed as "deviants" in a culture. In Scandinavia, especially in Denmark and Sweden, the normalization principle has not only become a dominant theme in clinical practices but is also expressed and accepted increasingly by the citizenry. The principle has been incorporated most extensively in the area of mental retardation and has found its most recent legal expression in a new, comprehensive Swedish law (effective since July 1, 1968) about provisions and services for the mentally retarded (3)[2]. Its expression in concrete service structures and delivery systems has recently been documented by Bank-Mikkelsen (5) for Denmark and Grunewald (6) for Sweden.

The principle of normalization is deceptively simple. Reduced to its essentials, it states that human management practices should enable a deviant person to function in ways considered to be within the acceptable norms of his society; by the same token, human management practices should enable a person who is not a deviant to continue being able to function within the acceptable norms of his society. As much as possible,

the means employed should be culturally normative ones.

In terms of human management practices the principle has innumerable specific implications, some of which will be discussed later in this paper. However, the specifics can be classed into three broad categories:

1. Deviant persons should be helped to be able to become less deviant and nondeviant people to remain nondeviant; however, it should be noted that the goal is not to impose social conformity but to prevent or reverse involuntary or unconscious deviancy.

2. Deviant persons should be presented and interpreted to society in such a way as to emphasize their similarities to rather than differences from other people, and their positive aspects rather than negative ones. The use of culturally normative rather than esoteric means is intended to minimize the appearance of separateness of deviant individuals.

3. The attitudes and values of society should be shaped to be more accepting and tolerant of harmless types of differentness, such as differentness in appearance, demeanor, intelligence, speech and language, nationality, education, race, skin color, ethnic background, and dress.

My first response to exposure to the normalization principle was "So what is new?" and I have found that most people respond as I first did, wholeheartedly endorsing the principle. However, I have also found that neither I nor most other professionals in the human management field could immediately grasp the sweeping implications of the principle, much less change daily human management practices so as to bring them into conformity with it. It is for this reason that I will spell out some specific management implications of the normalization principle.

Specific Human Management Implications

Normalization means that deviant persons should be exposed to experiences that are likely to elicit or maintain normative (accepted) behavior. These experiences can be derived from one's physical activities and from one's interaction with the physical environment (such as one's residence and its furnishings) and one's physical neighborhood. They can also be derived from one's interaction with the social environment, such as one's family, neighbors, fellow citizens, group members, and human managers. Social interaction with typical citizens under typical life conditions brings with it innumerable occasions and role expectancies that are likely to elicit normative behavior and normative role performance. Thus both physical and social environments must be structured in such a manner as to weigh their normalizing and de-normalizing elements, as well as those elements that are irrelevant to normalization.

Normalization has many subtle implications that require appreciation of other socio-behavioral processes. For instance, a common phenomenon in human management is for deviant persons to drift into employment where they work with clients who are deviant themselves. Thus the teacher who cannot cope with regular pupils is put in charge of a special education class; the physician who does not have a license to practice in the community (usually because of inadequate training or skill, language problems, alcoholism, drug addiction, or physical or mental problems) is permitted to practice in institutions for the retarded or disordered; prisoners may be placed into training or work with the mentally retarded; retarded workers may be placed as orderlies in homes for the aged; and so forth.

Usually human managers defend these practices on narrow clinical grounds: The deviant worker can make a contribution by such an arrangement; he can be habilitated by it; and so forth. However, attention rarely is given to certain important and broad sociological considerations that lead back to the normalization principle. Three such considerations come to mind in this context.

1. When a deviant "reject" from society is employed to administer services to other deviants, it is inevitable that members of the larger society conclude consciously or unconsciously that the deviants who are served are of low value. For instance, a person not good enough to teach my normal child may be good enough to teach someone else's retarded child. Thus a juxtaposition of deviant workers with deviant clients devalues both of them even more, but particularly so the client. Inevitably, this devaluing perception will lead fellow citizens to behave toward the deviant client group in a way that is more likely to be "dehabilitating"(7) than normalizing.

2. When deviants work for and with deviants, almost inevitably a subculture of deviancy is created that exacerbates rather than reverses the deviancy of those within the subculture.

3. At a given time, a person generally has the potential of forming a limited number of social ties and meaningful relationships. Usually he will fill his "relationship vacancies" with the people he encounters in his social system(s). The likelihood of filling one's relationship needs with deviant persons probably stands in direct proportion to the percentage of deviants in one's social system(s). Thus, by surrounding a deviant client with deviant workers, or vice versa, the chances of each group to socialize with nondeviant persons is lowered. Both the real and perceived deviancies of both groups are likely to be increased; and the chances of habilitation for either group, especially the much larger client group, are likely to be reduced.

It follows that instead of there being mutual benefits, both groups may actually lose—if not in each concrete instance, then at least in the long run of societal processes. Normalization principles would thus not only prohibit the juxtaposition of deviant workers with deviant clients but would dictate that as much as possible, deviant individuals be surrounded by nondeviant ones.

Let us return to the clinical considerations for a moment. Actually, juxtaposing deviant workers with deviant clients has been primarily a matter of convenience. If normalization principles were clearly understood and accepted and if a commitment were made to the discovery or creation of alternatives, such alternatives capable of optimizing normalization of all involved could be found, developed, and/or utilized.

Exposure to Normative Experiences

Since exposure to normative experiences is a crucial aspect of normalization, every effort should be made to avoid conditions that are apt to inhibit or even prohibit normalizing behavior. Thus psychiatric services should be structured so as to bring about the most feasible maximum integration of the deviant into society.

It follows that in a psychiatric service that purports to be habilitational, deviant persons should never be congregated in numbers larger than the surrounding community (usually even neighborhood) social system can readily absorb and integrate. How large such a number might be is ultimately an empirical question and depends much on local community factors. There is probably no neighborhood that can integrate 2,000 deviants, although there are some that might be able to integrate 100 to 200. Generally, a psychiatric residential service or similar facility should probably not congregate more than 25 to 50 deviant persons. This implies a major rethinking and reorganization in regard to our residential psychiatric services, especially those that are defined as habilitation-oriented.

Generally, people in our society engage in age-specific associations and activities, and many activities and services are specifically identified in the minds of the public as appropriate for one age group and less appropriate or even inappropriate for another. Thus it is abnormalizing if we place persons into a context of activities or services perceived as age-atypical by a significant portion of the public.

This means that adults should not be housed closely adjacent to children and should ordinarily not be engaged in activities that are not considered appropriate for a typical adult. Thus while American society approves of recreation after work, it does not approve of recreation instead of work; the latter is viewed as childlike play activity.

A prime implication is that endless "recreational therapy" as well as the often euphemistically labeled "occupational therapy" of our psychiatric facilities are not culturally normative means and may have an effect opposite to their stated and intended one: They may dehabilitate and denormalize. Even if one were not willing to agree with this interpretation, one might consider whether meaningful work in a typical work routine would not be more culturally normative and therefore more effective than the ambiguously structured, defined, perceived, and valued recreational and occupational "therapies."

The conclusions that have been reached here can also be derived by considering other points that will be discussed shortly, such as the meaning of work in our culture and the nature of a normal rhythm of daily, weekly, and monthly activities of adults.

Normalization means that a person should live in a normal routine of life. In our culture most people live in one place, work or attend school in another, receive their medical treatments somewhere other than their residence (unless they are bed-bound), and partake of a variety of recreational activities outside their homes and places of work. Thus when we offer residence, treatment, work, religious nurture, and recreation all under one roof (as we usually do in residential treatment and service centers), we often denormalize.

To offer all services under one roof is convenient—although not always as economical as claimed. However, this convenience should be sacrificed if a useful principle is at stake. We should ask ourselves at all times whether any service provided in conjunction with a residential service could not be provided in a more normalizing fashion by drawing on extraresidential and community resources, thereby increasing the resident's integration and habilitation. Obviously, a community mental health center attempting to offer "comprehensive" services under one roof is likely to violate the normalization principle.

Most adults work eight or more hours a day, usually between 8 a.m. and 5 p.m., and usually outside their place of residence. Thus we should strive to provide a similar rhythm and arrangement and to involve adults in meaningful work, in as near a meaningful workday as possible. The idleness forced upon many of the consumers of our psychiatric services, especially residential ones, is clearly denormalizing; only slightly less denormalizing is "occupation" or work that is meaningless. This consideration argues strongly for the establishment of sheltered workshops that can be used by residents of psychiatric facilities—except that for most psychiatric residents these shops should not be on the grounds of the residential facility, as this would not be normalizing.

A normal rhythm of the day also means that most people under treatment should not have to rise significantly earlier than typical fellow citizens or have to go to bed at odd hours. It also means that they should be able to eat their meals at normal hours; few citizens eat their supper at 4:30 or 5:00 p.m., as do residents in many of our treatment facilities.

Most people go on a vacation trip once a year, which breaks up the routine of life. Few things are as monotonous as long-term residence in a psychiatric facility. It is thus normalizing to provide annual trips for such residents to the usual tourist and vacation places. In Scandinavia even the severely retarded are taken on vacation trips—often abroad. Although cost may be a problem, at least some arrangements can be made, even if it is only a trip of two to three days' duration to a vacation home owned by the facility.

Normalization implies that generally, a person under psychiatric management lead an economic existence that is typical of the larger society. Once more, this implies that clients should have an opportunity to work and earn some income so as to exercise adult control over pocket money (not merely scrip or credit) and minor, everyday purchases. In Danish and Swedish human management services, clients who are impecunious or cannot earn money are provided generous allowances so as to increase dignity, assist in realistic social training, and foster independent choice behavior (6). "Poverty in a mental hospital is no less dehumanizing than in a slum"(8).

Although the normalizing nature of work has long been recognized in psychiatric practice, it has been greatly underutilized. One reason may be that in the acute stages of a client's dysfunctioning, the psychiatric manager may be impressed by the fact that the client's behavior has decreased or even eliminated his ability to carry out his ordinary work. The manager may then conclude that the same would be the case with all work, overlooking the possibility that the client may be capable of working, and being normalized by some other type of work activity. For instance, the certified public accountant, although momentarily too distraught to handle his ordinary job, may be effective in and normalized by the workshop assembly of relay switches.

Another reason may be that when work was assigned to psychiatric clients, it usually was work associated with the maintenance of the facility, e.g., in the laundry or library, on the farm or living unit. Such work has suffered from two aspects that have diminished its normalizing value. Such work was often exploitative, involving little or no pay and perhaps even leading to institutional peonage(9) rather than habilitation; conversely, work was often contrived or viewed with such an indulgent paternalistic ("therapeutic"?) attitude that it lost much of its work nature, thereby its sociocultural meaning, and consequently much of its normalizing effect.

Normalization also dictates that a person should be as independent, free to move about, and empowered to make meaningful choices as are typical citizens of comparable age in the community. As much as possible, his wishes and desires should carry the same weight as they would under ordinary circumstances outside of a human management context.

This means that unless it is essential, a person should not be submitted to a "mortification" process upon attaining "patienthood" (e.g., stripped of clothes and possessions, locked up) and that generally he should not be prevented by even nonphysical (e.g., social and psychological) means from exercising normal freedom of movement. Furthermore, a person generally should have reasonable control over his physical environment, including freedom to turn lights on and off, to open and close windows, to regulate the temperature in his room, and to decide whether he wants another person to enter or not. A nurse or other manager sweeping abruptly into a resident's room commits an act of denormalization. No person should be deprived of his physical freedom or his freedom of choice because he is housed in a facility with other people who appear incapable of exercising these freedoms.

A secondary implication is that residential facilities should achieve a greater degree of specialization of function. Instead of congregating the mildly disordered and the severely disordered together, as we commonly do at least during some (usually the initial) phases of a typical residential treatment course, we should group clients so that each group can be served with the minimum feasible number of restrictions and even personnel. Thus contrary to stereotype, a high staff ratio can imply an interpretation of the client as being more deviant than he is and can thus be denormalizing under certain circumstances.

Normalization means living in a bisexual world. In residential facilities this means that the building and the social structure should produce at least as much mingling of sexes as in a hotel, a mixed boarding house, or a home in which there live adults other than a married couple. For models, one need only think back to the extended households of some decades ago when families sometimes shared their homes with aunts, uncles, grandparents, housekeepers, governesses, etc. A bisexual environment also means that there should be both men and women working with the clients.

Finally, an important aspect of normalization is to apply health, safety, comfort, and similar standards to mental health facilities as they are applied to comparable facilities for other citizens. This has implications primarily to residential facilities such as institutions and even more specifically to state-operated services that, in many states, may and do operate below the standards prescribed by law for private facilities. However, it also has implications to clinics. For instance, reception and waiting areas should be as comfortable, attractive, and private as typical citizens might encounter in comparable community services. By this criterion, the reception areas of many of our (psychiatric) clinics are not normalizing.

There are, of course, innumerable other implications from the clinical level to the level of large social systems. The examples given here represent only a selected and arbitrary sampling. However, they underline that many major and minor practices that are currently accepted and not found objectionable by proponents of other human management systems are, in fact, quite inconsistent with the principle of normalization.

Normalization Versus Other Management Systems

The normalization principle has powerful theoretical force *vis-à-vis* other human management systems, and despite its late emergence, considerable empirical evidence—primarily from social psychology and related fields—can be marshalled in support of it (10). However, upon first superficial exposure to the principle, one

may well ask how it differs from a number of other approaches, as, for example, the therapeutic community.

The difference lies in the simplicity, parsimony, and comprehensiveness of the principle. The principle requires no assumptions that the consumer of human management services is, or is not, "sick" or a "patient." The principle is applicable not only to psychiatric populations and practices, both residential and nonresidential, but to many aspects of societal functioning and human management services as well[3]. The principle subsumes many current human management theories and measures—but goes beyond them in stipulating other measures that have been neglected so far. And the principle is easily understood once one has opened one's mind to it.

Occasionally, psychiatric orientations have been classified as being somatotherapeutic, psychotherapeutic, and sociotherapeutic. Although the normalization principle transcends psychiatry, it can be viewed as being most consistent with a sociotherapeutic approach in that it uses concepts and constructs rooted primarily in sociology. The emergence of this principle appears particularly timely now, both because of the apparent confusion and disagreement in the field in regard to human management ideologies and because the field appears to be ready to orient itself increasingly toward sociotherapeutic concepts (11, 12). While some management concepts, such as the therapeutic community, constituted a big step from a medical to a social model, the very word "therapeutic" still symbolizes medical model thinking. Now we should advance in our thinking from a "therapeutic community" to a "normalizing community."

A noteworthy aspect of the normalization principle is that it suggests action on three levels: clinical, public interpretation, and societal change. In addition to suggesting specific practices on all three levels, the principle also has relevance to the balance between them. At present, most mental health professionals work on the first level, very few work on the third. The normalization principle presents a powerful rationale for a redistribution of psychiatric priorities so that the second and third levels will receive at least as much attention as the first. After all, fellow citizens are the ones who ultimately define a person's behavior as deviant, and thus much deviancy is of our own making. Furthermore, by his involvement in sociosystemic action, a professional can often be instrumental in bringing about more individual benefits in a short time than he could in a lifetime of traditional clinical service.

From the larger viewpoint of how to move society toward effective support of necessary social action measures, the normalization principle has many advantages. Our society apparently has an inadequate understanding of current management measures in mental health (much less so than in mental retardation, for example), and this is an area where societal understanding will probably have to precede effective societal support. On the other hand, the normalization principle makes sense; it can be explained in a matter of minutes to an average citizen and usually finds at least partial acceptance. Thus it would appear that to the degree that the mental health field explicitly embraces this principle and its concrete implications, it may not only become more effective in its management and practices, but will also be able to marshal the necessary societal support for the action that is so urgent.

Notes

[1] The Webster's dictionary definition of management is "judicious use of means to accomplish an end." For the purposes of this paper I will define a concept of "human management" and of "human management services" as entry of individuals and/or agencies, acting in societally sanctioned capacities, into the functioning spheres of individuals, families, or larger social systems in order to bring about changes intended to benefit such individuals, their families or larger social systems, or society in general.

[2] The law is dated December 15, 1967, and is printed in the Swedish Code of Statutes, 1967(4).

[3] The principle can even be incorporated into some existing management theories, purifying and yet preserving them. For instance, the medical model is highly appropriate for certain types of problems, but it could be considerably improved by being suffused with the normalization principle.

Figure 10-4. Aptly named, "Provisions" is a restaurant run by mental health consumers. It provides employment and an asylum from the cold streets of Syracuse, New York. (Photograph by Carmelita Lomeo.)

READING 10D

BRIEF REPORT: INNOVATIVE PROGRAMMING IN A COMMUNITY SERVICE CENTER

Edith Cunnane, William Wyman, Ann Rotermund, and Ruth Murray.

In the preceding article, Dr. Wolfensburger described the principles of good normalization. For nearly four decades, successful programs employing sound normalization principles have been implemented across the nation. Since 1965, Community Mental Health Journal has been the premier publication for the dissemination of information about innovative community based treatment programs for the severely, persistently mentally ill. The following article portrays one such program.

Economic, social, and health care changes have resulted in a burgeoning number of homeless and poor people in the United States. Development of comprehensive community services and utilization of the earlier National Institute of Mental Health (1980) guidelines in caring for the homeless mentally ill have been described by Belcher and DiBlasio (1990), Stroul (1986), Eussner, Goldfinger, and White (1990), and Martin (1990).

St. Patrick Center is a social service agency that implements the philosophy of providing comprehensive, flexible, and innovative programming that addresses the immediate and ongoing needs of the homeless and poor population, with a focus on severely, persistently mentally ill (SPMI) and chemically dependent persons. Continuity of services assists clients to make choices and help themselves.

The success of the Center from its inception has been the approach of the Executive Director and staff to problem solving. They educate and involve all sectors of the community, secure funding from a variety of sources, and learn directly from the poor and mentally ill homeless about their perception of problems and the needed services. Volunteers are recruited to work closely with staff. Without the annual contribution of the currently involved, especially oriented 2,500 volunteers it would be impossible for a minimum number of professional staff to daily serve 400 or more clients of diverse background with a comprehensive set of services.

The effectiveness of the Center has evolved from two major foci outreach and employment services. Outreach takes three main forms (a) Shamrock Club Day Treatment Program, (b) the Mobile Outreach Program, and (c) Neighborhood Outreach Services. Employment has three major thrusts: (a) Employment Services, (b) Restaurant

Program. and (c) Employment Reintegration Program. These two major emphases and the related programs of support services are presented in this paper.

OUTREACH PROGRAMS

Shamrock Club: Day Treatment Program

The Center's beginning was based in its original outreach effort, on the Day Treatment Program for chronically mentally ill and chemically dependent homeless persons. It was commissioned by Missouri Department of Mental Health in collaboration with Catholic Charities. The Program, established in June, 1983, and named Shamrock Club, has continuously provided food, shelter, protection, personal hygiene facilities, clothing, and physical necessities. Less obviously, the staff has also provided health screening, crisis intervention, counseling, referral, and placement. The primary mission of Shamrock Club is to increase the probability that this population will gain trust in the staff and seek and accept help for emotional problems. Responding to a rapidly increasing number of clients and expressed client needs, the Day Treatment Program is open every day and has developed a number of other services, such as socialization programs, phone access without charge, and a stable mailing address. Volunteers provide legal aid services, teach ABE/GED courses and arts and crafts, and assist in social skill building. In order to ensure that the clients do not remain indefinitely, a life skills course and employment training are provided. The philosophy of client rehabilitation is the impetus for a number of Programs and services, including Life Skills Center, Employment Services, drug and alcohol counseling, and the Restaurant Program, which will be discussed separately in the following pages.

Daily, from 5 p.m. to the next 6 a.m., the space and facilities of Shamrock Club are utilized, with different staff, for the Women's Night Program, which furnishes housing for 12 chronically mentally ill women who have been refused admission to night shelters because of their disruptive behavior. The Center was approached by the City of St. Louis and Department of Mental Health to establish this program of night-time shelter, food, counseling, and follow-up care during the day. Start-up funding for the Program was initially provided by the American Association of Military Knights of Malta.

The Membership Plan. The staff realizes that the homeless SPMI client, often without any connections, needs to develop feelings of respect, responsibility, and hope. The clients are encouraged, through a membership plan, to participate freely in the Program, to help shape the Program design and activities, to develop a sense of ownership. The staff believe that only then can the person become responsible for self and feel a sense of togetherness and a sense that there will be a future. The supportive environment of the Club and approach of the staff assists the client in pursuing appropriate goals *at the pace set by the client.*

Hot Lunch Program. The need for a more extensive and nutritious food program became obvious soon after opening the Center. Letters were sent to all of the Catholic parishes in St. Louis, asking for their help in setting up a casserole program to feed the clients. The idea was that each parish would choose one day for the month—each month—and deliver and serve a meal consisting of a meat/vegetable casserole, salad, bread and butter, and a dessert. The response was such that by 1993, 59 parishes from the St. Louis area are responsible for feeding over 300 *hot* meals each day of the year, including weekends and holidays, to homeless clients and poor families from the neighborhood. Other groups provide food and entertainment for monthly birthday parties and holidays. In addition to the food, an added benefit for the Day Treatment Program clients is the opportunity to interact with people from the community. In turn, people from the community who are assisting with the lunch service, see the individuality and strengths, not just needs and limits, of each person who is served a meal.

Mobile Outreach Program

By the mid-1980s, it became apparent to Day Treatment Program staff that many of the homeless who slept in the streets were vulnerable to ridicule, robbery, assault of various kinds, physical injury—even death. The staff felt it was imperative to patrol the streets nightly, seeking the mentally ill who did not come to the Day Treatment Program, developing rapport with the street people, inviting them to come to Shamrock Club, and providing food, blankets, clothing, and emergency care or transportation to health care facilities, as needed. A van for the Mobile Outreach Program was initially obtained and supplied through a donation from McDonnell-Douglas Aircraft Corporation. The van is staffed by the Center's social service personnel who take turns on the night-time assignment. The public health nurse who works with the homeless or psychology, social work, or nursing students may accompany the team in the van on its nightly run.

As the Mobile Outreach team encounters some of the same people on the streets each night, individual logs are kept on selected vulnerable persons who remain on the streets over a period of time. Daily updates and therapeutic interventions are suggested to the Mobile Outreach team each night. The two person (one male/one female) team is taught which situations they are to handle and for which situations they should call the police. Typically, the Mobile Outreach team approaches any person who appears mentally ill.

Motivating street-based clients to use Shamrock Club or other services is the main focus of the Mobile Outreach team. Usually just one team member takes the lead in establishing rapport in order not to overwhelm the extremely withdrawn person. The lead-team member uses supplies on the Outreach van to give the street person what is needed and wanted. When the timing feels right, the team member offers to pick up the person during the daytime hours to escort him to Shamrock Club for lunch and then to bring him back to the client's requested location. The non-intrusive approach to the long-term street person works best. Often the person becomes interested in attending other aspects of the Program after having opportunity for lunch, personal hygiene, and clothing for several consecutive days, or weeks.

The van is mandated to respond to emergency calls from the community, and often it transports street people to a night shelter if beds are available. During the day the van is used to transport clients to other referral programs available through local agencies which work with the Center, to medical or psychiatric treatment, to a job site, or the staff use the van to visit former clients placed in independent housing. The mobile outreach staff also visit area businesses that the homeless frequent to give brochures and suggest approaches to take with homeless clients in order to educate the community regarding homelessness.

Skills Center Program

The Skills Center Program began in October, 1989, when the Center was awarded a $108,000 grant by the St. Louis Department of Human Services to operate an educational program for people who are homeless or at-risk for homelessness. The Program has developed into several components. The first is a series of 14 living skills classes. Topics include problem solving, nutrition, parenting, tenant rights and responsibilities, home management, energy conservation, budgeting, career development, preparation for employment, job success, balancing home and career, and an optional session on bus transportation through the metropolitan area. The second component, either case management, vocational counseling, referral to a formal educational program or an employment counselor at the Center, and housing options follows completion of the classes. The Skills Center has suggested a minimum of 12 months for client follow-up. While the client is participating in the Program, he/she is eligible for all the support services at the Center.

EMPLOYMENT PROGRAM

Employment Service

The Employment Service was opened in January, 1985, as the economic recession deepened and there was a need to generate employment opportunities. This Program is designed to place better prepared homeless clients who are either unemployed or under-employed in jobs or to prepare chronically mentally ill unemployed applicants for employment through the following processes: (a) identifying applicant skills, (b) performing a work or school reference check, (c) assisting with resume writing, (d) coaching for job interviewing, (e) counseling for job retention, (f) referring applicants to potential employers, (g) providing work clothes and transportation to and from the job, and (h) referring to other services at St. Patrick Center as needed. Staff members actively recruit job placements. For example, in 1993, the Service placed 611 clients in 379 full-time, 35 part-time, and 197 temporary positions. Staff do follow-up with both the employer and the applicant after placement. The follow-up has ensured continued success of the Program. Over the years, job retention rate for placed clients has averaged 65%. A number of clients have improved their job status and some have passed the GED examination and later have enrolled in a local community college or trade school.

One of the challenges for homeless clients who have become employed and live in independent housing is that they are not stress-free. All problems are not automatically solved because they have employment. They now must learn to cope with a new set of stressors-stressors that people in the work force daily confront. That issue and the surrounding fears and doubts must be worked through before the person is really ready to "graduate" into permanent employment.

The Restaurant Program

In 1988, a restaurant job training program was initiated specifically for the mentally ill and chemically dependent homeless clients. A Department of Labor grant was obtained to establish a luncheon business through an already existing restaurant in St. Louis. Planning for this Program took considerable effort and involved a number of important connections.

For six months, the luncheon business was a successful venture. A Center staff member supervised the Program and SPMI clients were trained to serve as waiters, bus persons, and cooks. However, because the restaurant was not actually owned by the Center, certain unexpected logistical and administrative problems arose. The owner of the restaurant requested that the luncheon service by the homeless be terminated at the restaurant. While this venture had not lasted

as long as the grant application had been awarded, there was still commitment to the venture because the Program had been successful and was well supported by the community.

McMurphy's Grill: The Restaurant Program Reestablished. The Center and Day Treatment Program continued to explore the possibility of reopening a restaurant. Negotiating to obtain a downtown restaurant site continued through 1989 and 1990. The Executive Director approached the co-owners of the Pasta House Company to join in efforts to find and remodel a site. The McDonnell-Douglas Foundation and the McDonnell-Douglas Employee's Community Fund provided more than $100,000 of financial assistance.

Staff in the Day Treatment and Employment Services Programs work with mentally ill clients to assist them in learning skills in all facets of restaurant work. Each client who expresses an interest in the Restaurant Program and who is evaluated as a potential candidate is required to attend a minimum of four classes in order to be taught basics about personal hygiene, such as cleaning and trimming fingernails, and about the basic rules of etiquette. Clients are taught to reach the job on time, use break time effectively, bring no weapons to work, and receive no personal phone calls on the job. Some clients are sleeping in shelters or on the streets when they begin the training program. They shower and dress at the Center and are given the necessary clothing and transportation for work.

With the tips earned, clients are taught how to save as well as spend money. Program staff assist clients in establishing a bank account. As the individual increases earnings, stable housing is obtained. A new identity develops within the person of someone who has job competency, is compliant with an appropriate treatment regimen, has a place to live, and is becoming a contributing member of society. Since 1991, 71 clients have entered the Program; each remains as long as necessary. Thirty-eight clients have completed the Program and are employed full-time or part-time in local restaurants. Some left before finishing the Program and may be employed in the community.

Overcoming Obstacles. The restaurant's success has resulted from combined efforts of the Center and restaurant staff; the homeless client employees; financial support and donated supplies and labor from the community; and the public's patronage. Various obstacles have been overcome in the process of implementing and maintaining this tightly controlled, Center-owned restaurant. Support had to be secured from Catholic Charities, the City alderperson, the urban business community, and nearby neighborhood organizations. Securing funding and a suitable location were paramount. Two philosophies have been balanced by the Board of Directors and staff and community advocates: that of running a business and providing an employment rehabilitation program. Promotion of the Program has had to be done in a way that did not arouse charges of unfair advertising and competition to the business community. In retrospect, having a part-time advertising specialist would have been useful. A staff mix of paid supervisory personnel and volunteers to train clients have been carefully selected to accommodate rehabilitation as well as business aspects. Criteria for selecting and training client employees were developed, and standards to be met by the client-employee were established and are maintained.

Operation of a Restaurant Program is a difficult business at which to succeed. Each year, the Board of Directors has budgeted the restaurant as a Program so that the restaurant does not have to generate a profit, even though all who are involved are working to reach a break-even point. In addition to the luncheon trade, the Program has expanded by selling box lunches and renting McMurphy's Grill for private parties to ensure additional income. The expansion has also promoted diversified training. Fiscal soundness is necessary for effectiveness. Equally important to effectiveness is sound training and placement of client employees.

Employment Reintegration Project (ERP)

ERP was established in October, 1990, to provide an opportunity for homeless recovering chemically dependent clients to gain control over their illness and learn employment skills, build a positive work history, improve self-esteem, become integrated into the labor force, and earn an income.

Employment contracts were negotiated in the community. Jobs included painting, miscellaneous building remodeling and rehabilitation jobs, and lawn mowing and snow shoveling. When the client gained necessary skills and demonstrated job readiness, the person was referred to permanent employment. The Day Treatment Program and on-site AA program and Employment Services provide supportive services to ERP clients; 47 clients have been placed in employment during an 18-month-period.

The cost of ERP was approximately $30,000 for start-up and equipment and supplies the first year. Through a grant of $19,500 from the St. Louis Philanthropic Organization, and United Way Funding for the Coordinator's salary, St. Patrick Center was able to begin the program. Donations of various equipment and supplies, such as hand and power tools, shovels, nails, paint, and even work clothes, aided the Program. Recent funding loss has discontinued the Program.

SUMMARY

For over a decade, a community service Center has been a complex organization and has been creative, resourceful, and successful in its response to needs of poor and homeless individuals, including the severely and persistently mentally ill and chemically dependent. When a problem or need is recognized, a needs assessment and effective response is quickly developed with minimum administrative obstacles and maximum administrative support. Local and national grant awards provide great assistance. Active networking with many groups and individuals throughout the metropolitan area has resulted in solid linkages with the Mayor's Office, the business community, philanthropic groups, various religious groups as well as the Catholic Archdiocese, health care agencies, and several educational institutions. Volunteers have donated not only time, money, and material goods and initiated fundraisers, they have daily shared enthusiasm, hope, caring, commitment, and resourcefulness. Even during economic recessions, donations and funding have remained constant as a result of well-directed efforts.

From a public policy viewpoint, it is

believed that the Day Treatment Program has saved considerable dollars for the State Department of Mental Health and the City of St. Louis. From a human standpoint, considerable suffering has been averted or reduced. The staff have used a gentle unhurried approach, gradually building a trust relationship with the client. They present opportunities for improvement in life and health. The client sees others in the Program moving into an apartment and job and is motivated to get to that point himself. In turn, he/she joins in the Program activities, demands, and responsibilities, thus becoming more responsible, contributing members of their own community.

REFERENCES

Belcher, J., & DiBlasio, F. (1990). The needs of depressed homeless persons: Designing appropriate services. *Community Mental Health Journal,* 26(3), 255-266.

Eusser, E., Goldfinger, S., & White, A. (1990). Some clinical approaches to the homeless mentally ill. *Community Mental Health Journal,* 26(5), 463-480.

Martin, M. (1990). The homeless mentally ill and community-based care: Changing a mindset. *Community Mental Health Journal,* 26(5), 435-447.

National Institute of Mental Health. (1980). *Guidelines for community support systems* (rev.). Rockville, MD: Author.

Stroul, B.A. (1986). *Models of community support services: Approaches to helping persons with long term mental illness in community support programs.* Rockville, MD: National Institute of Mental Health.

Figure 10-5. Several homeless people camp out in front of the State Office Building in downtown Philadelphia, October, 1987. (Reuters/Corbis-Bettmann.)

READING 10E

THE SLEEP OF REASON
HOW THE INSANE WERE TURNED INTO THE HOMELESS

David Gutmann

A book review of *Madness in the Streets: How Psychiatry and the Law Abandoned the Mentally Ill* by Rael Jean Isaac and Virginia C. Armat.

What is the present status of community mental health? Has it been successful? Are the mentally ill being adequately treated? The previous article demonstrates that community programs can serve their consumers well. However, are there sufficient resources and programs to meet the needs of the mentally ill who are in the community?

During the time that deinstitutionalization was implemented, major shifts have occurred in where special needs populations are quartered (cared for), or perhaps, not quartered.

Declining Populations					Change
Public Mental Hospitals:	1955 -	558,922	1990 -	98,400	–82%
State Residential Facilities for the Mentally Retarded:	1970 -	189,956	1991 -	91,239	–52%
Increasing Populations					
State and Federal Prisons:	1960 -	212,957	1990 -	1,115,111	+524%
Nursing Homes:	1970 -	927,514	1990 -	1,772,032	+191%
Homeless:	1960 -	not measured	1990 -	600,000	unknown

Data derived from United States Census of Population published by the Department of Commerce.

Major shifts in large populations are the result of complex interaction among many variables. Regardless, as institutions for the mentally ill and retarded were closed, significant increases in the prison and nursing home populations occurred. Statistics on homelessness were recorded during the Great Depression of the 1930s; then discontinued for decades. Measurements resumed following the implementation of deinstitutionalization.

In 1990, Rael Jean Isaac and Virginia C. Armat wrote Madness in the Streets: How Psychiatry and the Law Abandoned the Mentally Ill. *It is the definitive scholarly work that demonstrates how, on the whole, community mental health has failed. The following is a review of this book.*

Liberal social scientists, radical reformers, and crusading lawyers have in recent years fastened on the "homeless," citing their misery as evidence that the last stages of capitalism are upon us. But Rael Jean Isaac and Virginia C. Armat, in their densely researched and powerful book on de-institutionalization of the insane and its consequences, have shown us that these same experts—self-elected to be society's bad conscience—are themselves in large part responsible for the misery of the mentally ill and for the trashing of our cities. It is they, the crusading psychiatrists, anti-psychiatrists, community mental health experts, patient's rights lawyers, etc., who paved the roads from the asylums to our urban hells with their good intentions—and with the flawed philosophies and programs that flowed from these same good intentions. Isaac and Armat tell us, in rich detail, how these various parties got into the act, under what banners, at what point in the process of de-institutionalization, and with what grim consequences.

First, there were the rogue psychiatrists, the bad boys who became anti-culture heroes: Thomas Szasz, the cranky but eloquent psychiatrist who insisted that there was no such thing as "mental illness," that it was a myth and Ronald Laing, who argued with equally nutty eloquence that schizophrenia, rather than being a mental illness, represented higher and saner form of consciousness—hyper-sanity, no less. Arguing from a libertarian, even right-wing bias, Szasz held that the idea of mental illness was a joint invention of the psychiatrists who needed income and the dogooders who wanted to limit the freedom of strong but unruly people. By contrast, Laing—who romanticized madness—was more in tune with the earnest, high-minded craziness of the sixties radicals and counter-culturists: for them, the ego, the rational psychic establishment, represented a kind of cancer, a metastasis within the head of the life hating social establishment—the "camp of death"—outside the head. Laing helped to move the revolution away from oppressive society to the psychic interior, directing against society's inward metaphor, the ego. The schizophrenic was a noble savage, and madness was in actuality liberation: a Molotov cocktail of the revolution.

Isaac and Armat carefully document how subsequent waves of experts aided in this work, of moving trouble out of the head and relocating it—or the blame for it—in some piece of the ambient society. Thus, the family systems' theorists argued that the emotionally ill patient was in truth a scapegoat, a kind of drainage sump for a larger pathology, of the family as a whole. Going beyond the anti-psychiatry psychiatrists, the sociologists came on line to further the work of externalizing mental trouble, of recasting the patient as a victim of social rather than psychological pathology. Thus, Erving Goffman proposed, in *Asylums,* that madness was a reasonable *political* response to total institutions: any extreme, unnatural situation—for example, mental hospitalization—*demanded* a deviant response. Sociology's "labeling" theorists gave such plea-copping evasions the tonus of high science. According to Howard Becker: "Social groups create deviants by making the rules whose infraction constitutes deviance and by applying those rules to particular people and labeling them as outsiders . . . deviant behavior is behavior that people so label."

Goffman had blamed the asylum, as a special kind of social ecology, for bringing about the condition of madness that it was ostensibly designed to treat. Now the labeling theorists completed the job that he began, of indicting the entire mental health profession. The psychiatrists were revealed as society's hatchet men and women, behavior police who stigmatized and discredited those with the energy and the guts to be unorthodox. In the eyes of the social science establishment, 'mental illness" was becoming an empty term; it referred to no real phenomena in the heads of patients, but only to a misconception lodged in the minds of the psychiatrists and given spurious reality by the asylums that they sponsored. Most sentient humans, from peasants to psychiatrists, regardless of historical period, ethnicity, or society, have recognized the terrible and ubiquitous condition of madness; but with a few strategic texts, the antipsychiatry social scientists had tried to replace this universal awareness with a lumpen-Marxist conspiracy theory.

Thus far I have been mainly summarizing the order and argument of the book. But at this point I should like to interject some ideas of my own concerning the cultural climates— beyond academia and psychiatry—that burgeoned in the sixties and seventies, which guaranteed the wide acceptance of these hectic social philosophies.

The activists of the sixties and seventies are now canonized as secular saints. But I was a young professor in Ann Arbor ("Dope Capital Of the Midwest") and I remember them quite differently not as saints, but as *gluttons*. To be sure, they craved sainthood; but they wanted at the same time to be dramatic sinners. Alternatively, they tried to overcome the stern boundary that distinguishes saints from sinners, or true revolutionaries from posturing dopeheads. They were articulate, over-ideational *kvetchers* whose ultimate struggle was not with their fathers, nor with capitalist society, but with *all* limitations, whatever their source. They rephrased their essential complaint—that their gender, ethnicity, and nationality had been imposed on them without prior consultation— into the language of politics and simplistic Marxism. The burden of their essential complaint read like this: "Not fate, but political repression decrees that we are members of only one species, of only one sex, and that we are born to die." These stern limitations, so long regarded as fixed conditions of our existence, were being deconstructed, blithely redefined as nothing more than labels stamped on passive minds by the "camp of death." A vast political conspiracy kept everybody from their natural birthright of being everything; undo it, and we are free. There is nothing new about such ideas. Dotty old ladies in California, busy fighting water fluoridation, had pioneered equivalent conspiracy theories long before there was a trendy counterculture. The amazing thing is how quickly such erudite delusions were accepted, and by the very psychiatrists who are charged with maintaining the collective immune system against irrationality. But the most influential psychiatrists are social scientists as well as clinicians. Exposed to academic labeling theory and all the rest of it, many psychiatrists forgot their hard-won clinical experience and allowed *themselves* to be labeled—they accepted the mark of the oppressor pasted on them by the sociologists. They were not only the messengers of mental illness, but

also, by implication, became the bad news. In expiation, and aided by the new psychotropic drugs, they set about emptying the state hospitals and the closed wards. Concurrently, many of them signed on to the emerging community mental health philosophy and thereby embraced the major premise of anti-psychiatry: There is no mental illness as such; there are only sick and disordered societies requiring cleansing revolution rather than individual therapy. As the late homeless advocate Mitch Snyder put it: "A psychotic episode is a socio-political event and not a medical event."

But if the responsibility for mental illness was externalized into society, then by the same token the burden of treatment was also externalized into the "community." Like other icons of the sentimental Left—for example, the "environment," or organically grown veggies—the "community" was celebrated as part of the camp of life and the source of natural wholeness and healing. Rather than trained, professional skills, "authenticity" became the first criteria for community mental health workers. We were into the era of the barefoot psychiatrist and of untrained community activists hired to replace psychiatrists. Carried away by the hectic spirit of revolt (perhaps because it was aimed against themselves), over-excited psychiatrists were urging their black or Hispanic workers to sack the center and do away with the psychiatrists.

But Isaac and Armat show very clearly that all this heady stuff was not good for troubled heads. Thus, the dispossessed schizophrenics, newly sprung from the back wards, did not find much welcome in the mental health centers, the clinics that were supposed to smooth their path into the loving, healing community. They found centers that were geared up to organize street theater in favor of some leftist agenda; but they did not find personnel who knew much about severe mental disorder or who were prepared for the mundane, undramatic but essential side of treatment—providing structure, monitoring medications, locating relatives, or finding adequate housing. Predictably, center personnel (uniformly uniformed in their carefully torn blue jeans, tie-dyes, and ponytails) were most congenial with those patients who were most like themselves—

reformed druggies, for example, looking for feel-good encounter groups. But for the chronic schizophrenic, the mental health center was too often only a temporary way station on the long slide from the back ward to the back alley.

Meanwhile, even as the mentally ill were being deprived of the care that they really needed, the lawyers were piling into the scrimmage to defend the "prisoners of psychiatry." Asserting that "psychiatry is a way to get rid of people who annoy others," the patient advocates fought and won precedent-setting court battles against commitment for any patient who was not clearly dangerous to himself or to others. But the determination of psychiatric risk is not a simple matter; detecting a suicidal or homicidal tendency is a job for trained professionals and not for lawyers, however noble their intentions. The patients' advocates were, as Isaac and Armat put it, "practicing medicine with the wrong degree."

But while the patients' advocates were harmful to their disturbed clients in the clinical sense, they nevertheless provided the patient population—particularly the paranoids—with a more palatable view of their own affliction. Masses of experts had by now accredited the patients as bona fide victims—not of their own disordered psyches, but of some faceless conspiracy that had punished them for nonconformity. Rebaptized as victims, discharged mental patients could join the swelling chorus. They, too, along with their lawyers, became the bad conscience of the mental health profession. Psychiatry, which has the task of correcting delusional thinking, had instead helped to generate a worldview that gave new grounding, new legitimacy to its patients' paranoia. The radical lawyers and psychiatrists had taught their patients how to give the coup de grace to the system of care that had, however ineptly, tried to nurture and heal them.

As an ultimate expression of this paradox, the National Institutes of Mental Health now hires ex-patients as expert consultants on treatment regimes, with veto power over financing. Joined with the patient advocates, the ex-patients discredited all somatic treatments: psychosurgery, electro-convulsive therapy ("shock treatment"), and the whole panel of psychoactive drugs used to suppress psychotic symptoms. As

an example of the hyperbole that had replaced clear clinical thinking, all psychotropic drugs were dismissed as being the "chemical equivalent of a lobotomy."

We have all experienced the most disastrous consequences of psychiatric revisionism. Our city centers are showcases for the wildest forms of psychosis, displays no longer seen in the remaining asylums, where patients do take their medicine on schedule. Goffman, it turns out, was wrong. *You can take the madman out of the madhouse, but you do not thereby take the madness out of the madman.* Quite the contrary. Instead of being defined by his surroundings, the madman shapes the world to his measure and turns the city center into a version of the snake pit.

Off the street, the policy of de-institutionalization has had less public, but equally tragic consequences. The authors draw our attention to the nonviolent but disoriented patients who cannot find state-supported inpatient care and to the families that are being literally destroyed by terribly sick children whom they cannot hospitalize and will not consign to the streets. Perhaps worst of all, instead of being redeemed by the community, it turns out that madness has been criminalized. The authors report that the number of deranged individuals in our penitentiaries now equals the number still confined in mental institutions. "Rescued" from relatively protective asylums, the ex-patients end up in real prisons, in settings where they are much more at risk, more liable to sadistic exploitation, than on any locked ward.

For the sake of balance, it should be noted that the authors have located a few bright spots, aftercare centers that live up to the original community mental health idea of comprehensive care for the discharged chronic patient. The authors are particularly impressed by the Thresholds Program, ably directed in Chicago by Dr. Jerry Dincin (a psychologist who also belongs to the Northwestern University Medical School faculty, where I work and teach). Thresholds staff deal with discharged, usually chronic patients in a manner that combines dedication to the individual case with a no-nonsense, unsentimental *professional* attitude. They see to it that patients take their medicines; they provide confrontive, interpretative "talk therapy," and they maintain their patients in the community. The Extended Ambulatory Care Program, also linked to Northwest-ern's Institute of Psychiatry (and not mentioned in the book), is another point of light: a system of aftercare and day hospital settings where severely disturbed patients receive individually titrated doses of medications, psychodynamic psychotherapy, social services, and rehabilitation counseling. Again, as with Thresholds, the staff is professional and dedicated, concerned about individuals, but unsentimental about "the homeless." Unfortunately, programs of this caliber are very much the exception rather than the rule.

I do have one quarrel with the authors of this almost flawless book. Like the schools of thought they oppose, Isaac and Armat diminish the importance of the human psyche as a system in its own right. Thus, the revisionists deny that mental illness exists; instead, they pathologize the larger society. In their turn, and in order to preserve mental illness as a "real" phenomenon, the authors end up by pathologizing the body, particularly the genes, and the neuro-endocrine system. The anti-psychiatrists externalize the responsibility for mental illness into the failings of society; and these authors shift the responsibility in the other direction, toward the frailties of the body. Thus, even as they distance themselves from anti-psychiatry, the authors do sign off on its central and most misguided ideas: that individuals bear no responsibility for their own troubles; that they play no part in shaping their own fate—even a bad one; and that they have no covert investment in their own symptoms.

The authors have bought the latest psychiatric *Zeitgeist:* that somatic, usually genetic, flaws are the independent variables in the pathogenic process—a disordered gene produces a disordered mind or even a particular neurotic symptom. Accordingly, the scientific chase halloos off to find bad genes, not only those responsible for schizophrenia and depression, but also for alcoholism, eating disorders, racism, and white-collar criminality.

But when they buy into the "rogue genes" doctrine, the authors ignore a large body of scientific work that shows that the causal sequences

can also flow the other way, from the mind to the body. Purely psychological conflicts—between reason and emotion, between appetites and ideals—generate anxiety; and the "fight or flight" systems of the body are mobilized in response to the resulting sense of emergency. When conflicts remain unresolved and the stress on physical systems is unabated, the body can develop multiple disorders—ulcers, immune system suppression, high blood pressure, etc.—of the sort that can kill without help from any lethal gene.

The psychodynamic position, which I espouse, takes a more tragic but ultimately more liberating view: that patients, for their own reasons, act so as to find or even create their own purgatories. If patients are in some part responsible for their troubles, then ultimately they have the power to create a better fate. Nowadays, this stern but effective doctrine is called "blaming the victim," but it should be remembered that most psychodynamic psychiatrists and psychologists did not buy into the new, "exculpating the victim" doctrines that have proved so destructive. It is probably significant that the effective, redeeming community mental health services, such as Thresholds and Northwestern's Extended Ambulatory Care Program, are determinedly Freudian—in the broadest sense—in their therapeutic stance.

Besides being wrong, the somatocentric view propagates another version of victimhood. As such, it has bad consequences for the patient and for clinical practice. The anti-psychiatrists taught patients that they were victims of society, and somatic psychiatry teaches that they are victims of their own flesh. In either case, the patient is freed from any responsibility for his condition. Indeed, the somatocentric philosophy provides the patient with new copouts, new reasons for indulging the symptoms: "How can I stop drinking when I am commanded by my alcoholism gene?"

The lessons to be learned from the tragedy of our streets go far beyond the proper treatment of mental illness. The major lesson, for me, is this: Do not trust social scientists, particularly when they attack and try to change long-established, recurrent features of our social life and the common, practical wisdom that supports such arrangements. This bloody century has already taught us what happens when technologists, always for the best of reasons, disturb—without knowing or reckoning the consequences—long-established ecological relationships. Full of zeal to kill insect pests with DDT, we ended by killing the birds as well, bringing on the Silent Spring. The same critique should be leveled against the liberal intellectuals who are not only messing up the mental health system, but are also busily devastating our long-established psycho-ecological arrangements around sex roles, child rearing, and the division of labor by gender, as in warfare. The returns are not yet in, but preliminary results, particularly those having to do with the psychological malaise of our children, strongly suggest that we could be heading towards new social disasters, dwarfing those that Isaac and Armat have already documented.

This powerful book reminds us that we should take very seriously the advice given by Paul Johnson in the last paragraph of his recent book, *The Intellectuals:*

One of the principal lessons of our tragic century, which has seen so many millions of innocent lives sacrificed in schemes to improve the lot of humanity, is—beware intellectuals. Not merely should they be kept well away from the levers of power, they should also be objects of particular suspicion when they seek to offer collective advice ... for intellectuals, far from being highly individualistic and non-conformist people, follow certain regular patterns of behavior. Taken as a group, they are often ultraconformist within the circles formed by those whose approval they seek and value. This is what makes them, *en masse, so* dangerous, for it enables them to create climates of opinion and prevailing orthodoxies, which themselves often generate irrational and destructive courses of action. Above all, we must at all times remember what intellectuals have habitually forgot: That people matter more than concepts and must come first. The worst of all despotisms is the heartless tyranny of ideas.

Even more dangerous, as Isaac and Armat have shown, are grandiose delusions that masquerade as Big Ideas.

Reference:

Isaac, Rael Jean and Virginia C. Armat. (1990). *Madness in the streets: how psychiatry and the law abandoned the mentally ill.* Free Press.

Chapter 11

CLARIFICATION

We have now covered six major perspectives for understanding, explaining, and treating abnormal behavior. I trust it became apparent that the theory and practice of each perspective are unique, and often in conflict. This was to be expected. It is uncommon to find an expert in any field in general agreement with experts in others. If you are still somewhat confused about which perspective is best for conceptualizing and treating abnormality—don't dismay. A major objective of this book has been accomplished. There is no easy answer. I don't ordinarily derive pleasure from helping to confuse people, but for a student of abnormal psychology to appreciate its perplexing and controversial nature is of extreme importance.

However, the situation is not hopeless. We can derive meaning from dissention; from chaos comes order. It is the goal of this chapter to illuminate the relative strengths and limitations of each perspective; to "put the perspectives into perspective."

Patients and their families generally are not very knowledgeable about the various types of treatment available for disorders and their relative merits and faults. They are concerned and anxious, but lack information. They often believe that all treatment is the same, regardless of the clinical setting, or the perspective of the clinician. Clearly this is not the case.

Science is a major source of social authority in America. We turn to science to answer questions of all types. Physicians are the representatives of science with whom most people interact. We often place blind faith in the medical profession, and trust without question its advice or guidance. Obviously, the clinician should be a source of authority, but is not automatically a holder of objective truth. A modicum of skepticism is wise. Patients and families often implore clinicians for cure. To make such pleas indicates their trust, faith, and confidence. However, "magic wands" that offer simple cure are very rare in this field.

Entering a mental hospital following a psychiatric emergency can be a frightening experience for the patient and concerned others. They ask the staff a multitude of questions. Their queries are of immediate concern and importance to them, but may not be germane to the admissions situation. They may ask whether their insurance covers psychiatric hospitalization, how long they will be there, or who will take care of their children. They may worry about how their employer will react upon learning of the situation. Although these are important concerns, those related to the immediate care of the patient should be a greater priority.

As indicated throughout the book, the type of treatment a patient receives is a function of the orientation of the clinician. Patients come under the care of a particular clinician in a variety of ways. Some are referred, or selected by reputation, while others are assigned based upon availability. Little may be known of the theoretical or therapeutic orientation of the provider.

Often clinicians employ the theory and techniques in which they were trained. They may develop "theoretical blinders" which inhibit them from employing alternative treatments of potentially greater benefit. As medical general practitioners are scarce, so are mental health general practitioners. *Eclectic clinicians* are those who are well versed in all of the perspectives and employ the most relevant for the particular patient. They may combine aspects of several perspectives in a comprehensive treatment program. Rather than force the patient into a perspective, treatment is fashioned for the unique patient. Knowing the orientation of the clinician is of extreme importance, as it will likely dictate the type and course of treatment.

The best questions are those that directly relate to diagnosis, prognosis, and treatment options. A reasonable sequence of questions to be asked of the staff follows:

1. *Can you provide a diagnosis?* Even a provisional diagnosis is helpful. To label an ubiquitous condition which seems overwhelming can be beneficial.
2. *Based on research, what types of treatments are available for the diagnosed disorder?*
3. *Do you provide those treatments here?*
4. *If not, where can they be obtained?*
5. *Can you provide general information about prognosis for the diagnosed disorder?*

Recipients of mental health treatments should perceive themselves as consumers of a service—a very expensive one. People who may become enraged if they purchased a defective toaster might passively accept the interpretation and directives of their clinicians. Concerned consumers should expect and demand to be well-informed.

A concise synopsis of each of the perspective's strengths and limitations follows. Scientific research shows that some perspectives offer better explanations and more effective treatments for particular disorders. The following discussion could be of great relevance, should you be a provider or consumer of mental health services.

Figure 11-1. The Clozapine Ball. (Photograph courtesy of Lynn Johnson.)

THE ILLNESS PERSPECTIVE

The illness perspective explains mental disorders as the result of known general medical conditions. These factors may be genetic, infectious, traumatic, or metabolic. It is known that dementia due to syphilis is caused by spirochetal invasion and can be effectively treated by penicillin. Down Syndrome is caused by a superfluous 21st chromosome. Although presently there is no effective treatment, the gene that causes Huntington's disease has been mapped at chromosome 4p16.3 (Cell, 1993).

Janice Egeland's ten year study of the genetically and culturally isolated old-order Amish of Lancaster County, Pennsylvania revealed a possible genetic marker for bipolar disorder near the short end of chromosome 11. Sixty-three percent of those with the marker had bipolar disorder. The Amish elders were not impressed with the findings. They intuitively knew bipolar disorder was "siss im blut" —in the blood (Hostetler, 1987). Genetic explanations for schizophrenia and autism hold promise, but are inconclusive.

Structual abnormalities can cause mental disorders. Demonstrable pathology exists in the brains of boxers and football players with dementia due to head trauma. As described earlier, George Gershwin, one of America's most beloved composers, became depressed the year prior to his death from an undiagnosed brain tumor (Goldberg, 1958, pp. 346-350). Had the tumor been detected earlier, surgery might have helped.

Psychosurgery remains controversial, despite its judicious use and technological improvements. Modified leukotomy, in which two to three centimeters of white matter coursing through the anterior cingulate gyrus is severed, demonstrated promise for the treatment of obsessive compulsive disorder (Tippen and Henn, 1983). Ironically, the analog of this structure regulates nest building in birds. In early 1988, The Associated Press reported that a young man with obsessive compulsive disorder shot himself in the head with a .22-caliber rifle. He survived, and his compulsions stopped, raising speculation that the part of the brain responsible for them had been affected. Cingulotomy, a refined procedure in which a tiny electrode merely heats each cingulate bundle, was shown to be effective in treating obsessive compulsive disorder among patients who failed to respond to medication or behavior therapy (Baer, et.al, 1995).

In 1988, a ban was placed on federal funding for research on transplantation of aborted fetal tissue. It was rescinded during the first days of the Clinton administration in 1993. This allowed research to resume on implanting dopamine synthesizing neurons from six to eight week aborted fetuses in patients with Parkinson's disease. "Live" dopamine is preferable to laboratory manufactured L-Dopa. Promising preliminary findings prompted the National Institutes of Health to provide 9.6 million dollars for further studies (Goldberg, 1995).

Computerized axial tomography and magnetic resonance imaging have allowed neuroscientists to study the brain in new ways. About 20 to 35 percent of schizophrenic patients demonstrate measurable brain impairment. Among these impairments are enlarged ventricles and cerebral atrophy (Seidman, 1983). Not all schizophrenics have these abnormalities, and it is difficult to tell whether they are a cause or effect of schizophrenia.

Electroconvulsive therapy remains a viable treatment option for endogenous depression, particularly if the patient is suicidal. It works more quickly than drugs.

Anti-psychotic drugs are the mainstay of the treatment for schizophrenia. In general, they ameliorate positive symptoms like agitation, hallucinations, and delusions, but do not affect negative symptoms, like social withdrawal. Long-term use of these powerful drugs often results in medication-induced movement disorders, crippling nervous and muscular conditions, like tardive dyskinesia. Tacrine, an anticholinesterase that is used to treat barbiturate and opiate poisoning, helps alleviate some symptoms (Ingram and Newgreen, 1983). Vitamin E helps control involuntary movements and spasams (Adler, et al, 1993).

In 1990, the Food and Drug Administration approved Sandoz Pharmaceuticals to market clozapine (Clozaril) for the treatment of schizophrenia. In 1991, Sandoz reported results of a major clinical trial. Clozaril had offered superior symptomatic control of both positive and negative symptoms in patients who failed to respond to other treatments. There was virtual absence of any medication-induced movement disorders, and no reports of tardive dyskensia. It is estimated to successfully treat thirty percent of treatment-refractory schizophrenic patients. Sixty-four percent of patients respond to high doses, compared to only twenty-two percent for low doses (Perry, et. al., 1991). In 1992, a "Clozapine Ball" was held in Cleveland, Ohio. The event, organized by the staff at Case Westen Reserves affiliated University Hospitals, allowed 175 patients to attend the prom they had missed in their youth due to schizophrenia (Wallis & Willwerth, 1992).

The annual cost for treatment with clozapine is approximately $9,000. Agranulocytosis, a sometimes fatal decrease in white cell count, affects two percent of patients, necessitating frequent blood tests (Baldessarini & Frankenburg, 1991). However, it is still less expensive than institutional or community based care. Claims that it doesn't cause medication-induced movement disorder may be premature.

During the 1970s, Dr. Ronald Fieve pioneered American research on lithium carbonate as a treatment for bipolar disorder. He claimed more than twenty years ago that lithium was "the first specific prophylactic [preventive] treatment ever to come about in the field of psychiatry. It prevents the recurrence of a major mental disease—manic-depression." (The Thin Edge: Depression, 1975.)

Evidence accumulated supporting Fieve's optimism. A summary of fourteen studies revealed that patients treated with lithium had fifty percent fewer recurrences of mania or depression, and that their recurrences were less severe (Consensus Development Panel, 1985). Furthermore, patients with bipolar I disorder (predominant mania) and a family history of mood disorders respond better than those with bipolar II disorder (predominant depression), or rapid cycling (Faedda, et al., 1991).

In 1994, The American Psychiatric Association issued a supplement providing guidelines for the treatment of bipolar disorder. "Lithium is effective in the acute treatment of manic and depressive episodes," and in preventing recurrences. Lithium reduced manic symptoms in eighty percent of reported studies. Discontinuation of treatment is associated with a significant increase in the risk of recurrence (American Psychiatric Association, 1994, pp. 4-5). Lithium approximates a "magic bullet" for the treatment of bipolar I disorder.

A continuing problem in drug therapy is compliance. Some patients do not comply with prescriptions because of carelessness, incompetence, fear of collateral symptoms or perceived wellness.

In other cases, drugs are overprescribed, inviting abuse. During the 1970s, the minor tranquilizer diazepam (Valium) was widely prescribed. An incredible 44.6 million prescriptions were filled in 1978. A request from a family physician for something to help control anxiety and temper around children was often sufficient to obtain a prescription. The Rolling Stones admonished those who ran "for the shelter of this 'mother's little helper.'" Multiple prescriptions were often obtained. Patients became dependent upon legally prescribed medication. Rickels, et al. (1983) found that forty-three percent of patients who had been treated for eight months showed clear symptoms of withdrawal. In 1988, New York State began requiring "triplicate prescriptions" for diazepam; one copy for the doctor, pharmacy and state. Prescriptions declined.

In 1980, Dr. George Nichopoulos had his medical license suspended for three months by the Tennessee Board of Medical Examiners for prescribing more than 10,000 pills to Elvis Presley during the last twenty months of his life. In 1981, he was acquitted on separate charges for overprescribing drugs to Presley, singer Jerry Lee Lewis, and seven others. Nichopoulas surrendered his license again in 1992, under similar charges, as reported by the Gannett News Service.

The most controversial drug of the mid-1990s is fluoxetine hydrochloride. In 1987, the Food and Drug Administration approved Eli Lilly and Company to market the drug as Prozac. It is an antidepressant which inhibits the uptake of serotonin in the central nervous system. Thirty-two thousand subjects took part in more than 3,000 clinical trials.

By 1994, more than eleven million customers had been prescribed Prozac, grossing 1.7 billion for Eli Lilly (Nichols, 1994). About two-thirds of patients are helped with Prozac, with fewer collateral effects than other drugs. The Church of Scientology sued the Food and Drug Administration to ban the sale of Prozac, claiming it caused suicide and anxiety. Lily countered, arguing that depressed patients are the relevant population for suicide. Anxiety could result if Prozac is prescribed to depressed patients without serotonin depletion, or overtaken by the patient, but those are diagnosis and compliance issues (Burton, 1991). On November 19, 1996, the Associated Press reported on the work of Dr. J. John Mann of Columbia Presbyterian Medical Center. He said that serotonin levels are 20-25% lower in patients who are at high risk for suicide and such people are four to six times as likely to complete suicide.

Critics of Scientology argued that Prozac was hurting its business. People were opting for Prozac over readings from an "Electropsychometer," a device which purportedly measures "the mental state or change of state in a person's distress or trevail." The E-Meter bears the trademark of L. Ron Hubbard, Scientology's founder, and appears manufactured by Fisher-Price.

In August of 1991, the American Psychiatric Association issued a news release applauding the Food and Drug Administration's rejection of Scientology's suit, thus "choosing science over sensationalism." Prozac, when "carefully prescribed following a thorough psychiatric evaluation and diagnosis, will continue to be lifesaving for many thousands of people suffering from depression."

Neuropsychiatrist Richard Restak claims that in response to Prozac's success, new "designer drugs" will be produced that enhance intelligence, memory, experience, and moods in people who are already functioning well (Begley, 1994). The new pills will "make us larger," where the old ones (barbiturates and tranquilizers) "made us small."

Despite tremendous advances within the perspective, the vast majority of mental disorders are still considered primary, as definite causes have not been found. The illness perspective can be overapplied by perceiving any human problem an illness and therefore, absolving the individual of any accountability for his condition.

Figure 11-2. Colin Powell, strong in mind, body, and spirit, exemplifies the tenets of holism. (Photograph courtesy of General Colin L. Powell, USA (Ret).)

THE HOLISTIC PERSPECTIVE

Holism is primarily concerned with the prevention of mental disorders through a healthy lifestyle that builds resistance and resilience for physical and mental stress. Overall health management requires the integration of mind and body. Although emphasis is on prevention, there are treatment applications.

Whether employed to prevent or treat, a holistic regimen would likely include elements of diet, exercise, examination of lifestyle, modification of Type A behavior, and stress management.

Hans Selye's general adaptation syndrome was discussed earlier. It describes three stages involved in the body's reaction to stress. In the alarm phase, the organism perceives a demand upon it and summons its resources. In the stage of resistance, the resources are employed to defend against the stressor. However, if the defenses are inadequate or the stress too great, exhaustion occurs. The weakest link in the organism subsequently breaks down. The effects may be minor, severe, or even fatal. They may be primarily mental, as in anxiety or depression; physical, as in stroke or ulcer; or both.

Being stressed is being alive. Life without stress would be dull. However, prolonged, extreme distress can be dangerous. Although we can learn how to cope with it better, it is inevitable. It is a less than perfect world, and life is often unfair. Good does not always prevail over evil, nor does hard work always pay off. Bad things happen to reasonable people at inopportune times. Yet, we can employ a lifestyle that "thickens" our phase of resistance and helps us withstand stress without harm.

Consider hypothetical adult, male, identical twins. They are forty years old, have good jobs, considerable investments, modern homes, and are married with children. Ralph is thirty pounds overweight, drinks excessively, smokes a pack of cigarettes a day, uses illicit substances, subsists on a diet bereft of nutrition and laden with chemicals, doesn't exercise, reacts to conflict with anger, and gets insufficient rest. Jake is normal weight, drinks moderately, doesn't smoke, uses no substances, manages his diet carefully, exercises regularly, is cognizant of his Type *A* tendency and addresses it, and gets sufficient rest.

Suppose that without warning, the stock market crashes. Each brother is fired from his job and informed by his wife that she is leaving him and taking the children, with the exception of the eldest, who was arrested earlier in the day and is now in jail. Each has been subjected to acute, intense, unpredictable distress. All things equal, Jake would be more likely to withstand the stress without damage. Certainly, he will have difficulty adjusting, but his considerable resistance will enable him to adapt without reaching the stage of exhaustion. It is more likely that Ralph's resistance will be penetrated, resulting in exhaustion and some type of breakdown. A fundamental tenet of holism is that we can increase our resilience through voluntary, conscious management of our lifestyle.

Psychoneuroimmunology was discussed earlier. One exciting application is increasing longevity and improving quality of life in individuals infected with the human immunodeficiency virus (HIV), and the acquired immunodeficiency syndrome (AIDS) virus. Evidence is compelling that repeated exposure to the virus through reckless sex, drug use, other infections, and poor nutrition enhance disease progression. Since behavior and cognition can influence immune function, those who modify high risk behavior, receive treatment and psychotherapy, and have supportive interpersonal relationships remain healthy longer (Kielcolt-Glaser and Glaser, 1988). Irvin "Magic" Johnson, National Basketball Association standout, tested positive for HIV in 1991. A holistic regimen has enabled him to remain healthy and physically active. He has been an inspiration to many by enhancing awareness of the disease and promoting the modification of high risk behavior.

Colin Powell described his holistic philosophy and lifestyle, among other things, in his autobiography, *My American Journey*. He was "a black kid of no early promise from an immigrant family of limited means who was raised in the South Bronx..." While in basic training at Fort Benning, Georgia, in 1958, he learned that he could buy what he wanted at Woolworth, so long as he didn't try to eat there or use the men's room. He did not become bitter. He survived a helicopter crash and regular ambushes during two tours in Vietnam. General Powell was the National Security Advisor for Ronald Reagan and Chairman of the Joint Chiefs of Staff during the Gulf War.

He rises at 5:30 a.m., has a workout on the Lifecycle, and a breakfast of raisin bran, a banana, orange juice, and coffee. He is also an avid raquetball player. Raised with a strong religious background, General Powell has strong, clear principles and values.

> Nothing seems to embarrass us; nothing shocks us anymore. [We spend time switching channels on a] parade of talk shows serving up dysfunctional people whose morally vacant behavior offers the worst possible models for others. ... At least in the old days of Amos 'n' Andy, Amos was happily married and hardworking, and he and his wife together were raising sweet little Arabella, who said her prayers every night.

When asked if he would run for the Presidency in 1996, he said, "I think I have the skills to handle the job" (*Time*, 1995). He has not ruled out running in the future. As he demonstrated in the Gulf War, good generals do not reveal their battle plan prematurely.

Holism has an appealing logic. It has inspired many to adapt a healthier lifestyle. Many women are more concerned with optimizing conditions during pregnancy to insure the birth of a healthy baby. Research and publicity about the harmful effects of alcohol and tobacco have changed behavior. Smoking is now restricted in most public places. For many who do not abstain, usage is now moderate. Despite capitalistic motive and dubious taste, television commercials and infomercials convince many to eat better and exercise more.

Critics of the holistic perspective argue that scientific evidence supporting diet, exercise, and lifestyle in the prevention of mental disorders is not compelling. However, it is difficult to know how many people would have developed disorders had it not been for holistic living. Although adhering to a holistic lifestyle may not be a psychiatric panacea, it surely can't hurt.

THE PSYCHOANALYTIC PERSPECTIVE

Psychoanalysis is based on the notion that prior unconscious factors affect present mental life. Patients who intuitively believe that these explanations are plausible are most likely to benefit. Freud's critics have argued against unconscious factors, claiming they cannot be directly measured or observed.

Recent neuropsychological research has shown that the brain allows an additional half-second interval between sensory stimulation and conscious awareness. It seems that the brain functions in a way that can repress a thought or feeling, if it is perceived as too unpleasant (Miller, 1986). A fifty millisecond presentation of a visual stimulus is required for conscious recognition. However, if the Oedipal message "Mommy and I are one," is flashed for a mere four milliseconds, male subjects report feeling happier and less anxious, suggesting unconscious influence (Silverman and Weinberger, 1985). "Recent research has established several empirical results that are widely agreed to merit description in terms of unconscious cognition. ...unconscious cognition is now solidly established in empirical research..." (Greenwald, 1992).

Psychoanalysis stresses that conflicts and traumas from childhood are reflected in adult pathology. The extent to which Freud recanted the seduction theory can be debated. However, consistent with Freud's theory, a review of research on the impact of child sexual abuse showed that damage is most severe when the experience involved the father or father figure, genital contact and force (Browne and Finkelhor, 1986). Freudian theory provides a model from which pathology resulting from abuse can be perceived, understood, and treated. The model provided by Sylvia B. Patten, et.al. in Chapter 7 is excellent and provides treatment guidelines for when to "let sleeping dogs lie" or "open Pandora's box." Verifying that abuse has occurred remains a difficult issue. Educating and sensitizing children to what consitutes improper adult conduct, instilling in them to report immediately such conduct to a most trusted adult, and prompt investigation seeking corroboration can help alleviate the problem.

Freud's critics argued he overestimated the significance of developmental processes like nursing or toileting. However, the way parents deal with these issues likely reflects their overall attitude. A loving parent not only nourishes a child in this way, but interacts in general in the same manner; parents who are harsh and punitive while toilet training are generally the same in other parenting areas. People

Figure 11-3. Brochures. (Photograph by Jim Rooney.)

with disorders often had, have, and will continue to have chaotic disturbances within familial relationships. They readily describe and discuss family problems, perceiving them as significant in their situation. Psychoanalysis is a treatment that is concerned with family dynamics.

Research on the effectiveness of psychoanalysis has not been very convincing. Some studies have reported about a fifty percent success rate in the treatment of neurotic disorders. Critics have said that the success rate is actually lower, because some patients spontaneously improve (this criticism can be made of any therapy). Psychoanalysis does not work well with psychosis. In *An Outline of Psychoanalysis*, originally published in 1940, Freud candidly stated, " . . . we discover that we must renounce the idea of trying our plan of cure upon psychotics—renounce it perhaps forever or perhaps only for the time being, till we have found some other plan better adapted for them." (Freud, 1949, p. 30.) However, schizophrenia has been a major challenge to all other perspectives.

Freud is often perceived as overly pessimistic and deterministic. However, pessimism is justified in some circumstances. Fixation results when libido is diverted from its normal channel into a pathological collateral channel. Logically, the diverted libido cannot return to the proper course. Theoretically, sexual pathology resulting from childhood fixation should be resistant to treatment. It is. Rebecca Roe, head of the Special Assault Unit of the King County, Washington, prosecutor's office, has been extensively involved in the treatment of sex offenders. She said, "There is simply no good evidence that treatment works" (Ostrom, 1989). According to Lee Hazelwood, retired FBI agent who specialized in investigating violent sexual crime, "Our research has showed that there are two types of violent sex criminals that can't be treated: the adult antisocial sadist and the adult antisocial pedophile" (Hazelwood, 1995).

In 1995, *NBC Dateline* reported that FBI research shows that children killed by their mothers without an accomplice will be found within ten miles of home and in an embryonic state—wrapped or under water. Analytically, such behavior would indicate a wish for the children to return to the womb, or to have never been born. This information enabled police to find Susan Smith's children submerged in a lake in South Carolina.

Psychoanalysis was psychology's "First Force." It offered a complex model of psychopathology and its treatment. Later perspectives have been afforded the historical opportunity to criticize this model and advocate their models. Attacks have come on many fronts. A century later, the smoke has cleared and psychoanalysis remains steadfast. Many of the critics have been forgotten. In 1954, sixteen years after his death, a statue was unveiled at his beloved University of Vienna. The inscription read, "Sigmund Freud: who divined the famed riddle and was a man most mighty" (Kassin, 1995, p. 573).

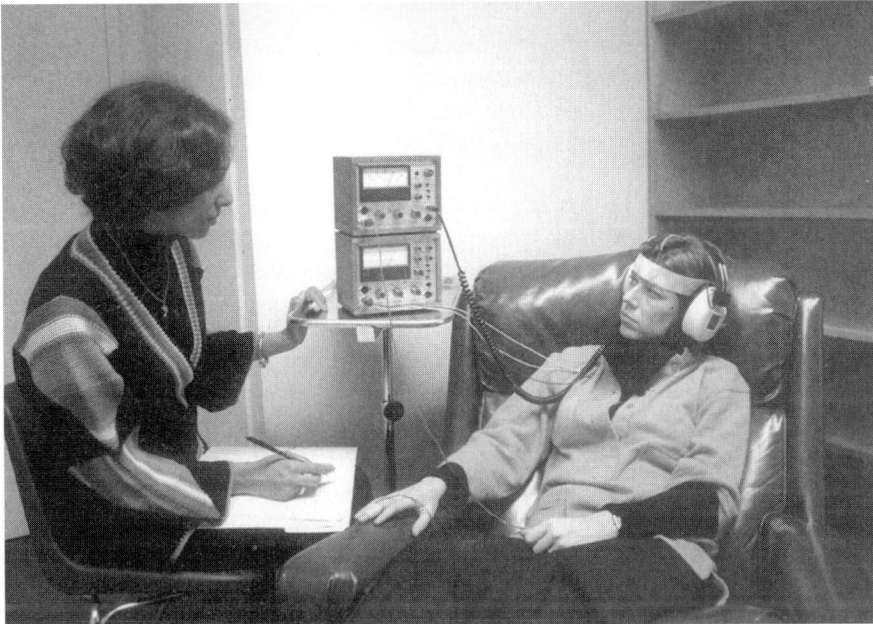

Figure 11-4. Biofeedback. (UPI/Corbis-Bettmann)

THE LEARNING PERSPECTIVE

Basically, behavior therapy is the application of two major learning models; classical and operant conditioning. All behavior is viewed as learned, so all behavior can be modified by changing reinforcement or conditioning contingencies. Daniel G. Brown's *Behavior Modification with Children* (1972) was presented in Chapter 8. An impressive list of disorders behavior therapy had successfully treated was presented. Since then, the list has grown considerably. A convincing literature substantiates its therapeutic effectiveness. It has consistently demonstrated the ability to help patients learn adaptive behaviors, and unlearn maladaptive behaviors. In reviewing research for this book, hundreds of articles were examined attesting to its success. It often successfully treats disorders, regardless of cause. Typically, successful outcomes are obtained in sixty to ninety percent of cases. It works.

Prior to deinstitutionalization, chronic schizophrenics were often treated with behavior therapy in an institution. Severely impaired patients learned daily living skills like eating, personal hygiene, and self-care. With deinstitutionalization, thousands of schizophrenic patients were released from the hospitals, often unable to function and poorly prepared for independent living. Follow-up care consisted of a prescription for antipsychotic medication. They often returned to their families who were ill-prepared to care for or cope with them. Their condition deteriorated. Relapse rates averaged about forty percent in the first year after discharge.

In 1986 Gerard E. Hogarty, et al., demonstrated success in preventing relapse in previously hospitalized schizophrenics. Patients were given intensive training in verbal and nonverbal social skills over a two-year period. Their families were taught: 1) how to better resolve conflicts, 2) specific behavior management skills, and 3) more about schizophrenia. Upon release to their families, the patients continued to take medication. One year later, none of the twenty subjects required readmission. Of seventeen control subjects who were released without training and continued medication, twelve (71 percent) relapsed. Since then, the Community Mental Health Journal has published numerous articles verifying the benefits of social skills training.

Ivar Lovaas' breakthrough research in treating autism was presented in Chapter 8. He was able to obtain normal intellectual and educational function in forty-seven percent of his subjects through intensive behavior therapy. Programs employing Lovaas' methods are being conducted in other areas of the world.

These studies attest to the therapeutic power of behavior therapy. Two of the most intractable disorders were effectively treated.

Biofeedback involves providing subjects with external information about internal physiological function. Typically, one is not aware of his blood pressure. However, if blood pressure is monitored and the person is instructed to lower it, eventually it will spontaneously decrease. A decrease in blood pressure turns on a light. The subject learns to reduce blood pressure by turning on a light. Learning to decrease muscle tension in the facial frontalis muscle with electromyographic biofeedback can be helpful in treating anxiety and headache (American, 1989, p. 2052-2055). The technique has been widely applied.

Cognitive-behavioral therapy has also demonstrated impressive results. Beliefs affect mood and behavior. If a person believes he is helpless and hopeless, he will likely feel and act depressed. Anxiety results from anticipation of perceived impending doom. Cognitive modification can produce beneficial change in mood and behavior. Albert Ellis' rational-emotive therapy was one of the earliest cognitive-behavioral therapies. He believes that irrational beliefs, like the following, are the underpinnings for most forms of maladjustment.

- One should be loved by everyone for everything one does.
- It is horrible when things are not the way we would like them to be.
- Human misery is produced by external causes, or other people, or events, rather than by the view that one takes of these conditions.
- It is better to avoid life problems if possible than to face them.
- One should be thoroughly competent, intelligent, and achieving in all respects.
- Because something once affected one's life, it will indefinitely affect it.
- One must have certain and perfect self-control.
- We have virtually no control over our emotions and cannot help having certain feelings.

Therapy is designed to modify these cognitions (Ellis, 1970).

A meta-analysis reviews a multitude of studies regarding a particular topic and produces a concise compilation of data. Mark W. Lipsey and David B. Wilson (1993) documented the success of cognitive-behavioral therapy and behavior modification in a survey of twenty-three studies conducted between 1983 and 1991. Behavioral methods were successful in treating a wide range of disorders in multiple populations.

Demand for mental health services exceeds supply. The principles of behavior therapy are fairly simple and can be employed by laymen with relatively little technical training. Parents, spouses, siblings, teachers, and hospital staff members are potential behavior therapists.

Behavior therapy often provides simple solutions for what other perspectives consider complex problems. Although attention-deficit/hyperactivity disorder may have a biological basis and can be treated with drugs and diet, it can also be viewed behaviorally. Conduct disorders are diagnosed in children who are extremely aggressive, explosive, destructive, deceitful, and neglectful of the rights and desires of others. ADHD and conduct disorder are often codiagnosed. Children, alledgedly with ADHD, may play video games undistracted for hours. Yet, when a parent directs the child to turn off the game, do homework and get ready for bed, the child recoils with behaviors symptomatic of ADHD. The parent may relent, not demand the child do homework, and again allow video game playing to calm him. Many children diagnosed with ADHD probably have conduct disorders.

Such behavior can be understood through an ABC analysis. A represents the *antecedent* conditions of B, the target *behavior.* C is the *consequence* of B. If A is a child contentedly playing a video game, B is the tantrum thrown when directed to stop, and C is the consequence of the tantrum, being allowed to again play the game, the child is being reinforced for misbehavior. A contingency change is needed. Perhaps the game cartridge should disappear for a week and more adaptive operants reinforced.

Despite its considerable success, the learning perspective has its critics. Some argue that behavior therapy offers only symptomatic improvement and does not constitute cure. Schizophrenics may learn to shave, wash, and improve their social skills, but they still have schizophrenia. Behavior therapists argue that they have been able to bring about symptomatic improvement in the most disturbed patients, and that is preferable to none.

Critics also argue that improvement will continue only as long as the reinforcement contingencies are controlled and will not generalize beyond the treatment setting. Optimistically, it is hoped that intrinsic (internal) reinforcers will ultimately replace extrinsic (external) reinforcers in maintaining behavioral improvements. Hopefully, the patient will realize that feeding himself is enjoyable, enables him to become more autonomous, and is aesthetically preferable to being tube fed.

Perhaps the strongest criticism of the learning perspective is ethical. Behavioral techniques are viewed as mechanistic, manipulative and dehumanizing because they rely on reward and punishment. They deny patients freedom of choice. Behaviorists argue that benefits gained supercede perceived infringements. A child who stops banging his head following aversive conditioning is inherently more human than before treatment. Behaviorists have been willing to assume the responsibility for making such crucial ethical decisions.

As B. F. Skinner indicated in *Walden Two* (1948) and *Beyond Freedom and Dignity* (1971), behavioral control is a reality of life. We all have our conditions of reinforcement controlled to some extent. For example, if we work well at a job, we are reinforced with pay and promotions. However, if our work is unsatisfactory, we may be demoted or fired. The world may well be a complex Skinner box.

In 1989, Douglas Biklen of Syracuse University brought back facilitated communication from a trip to Australia. Facilitated communication involves holding the hand of a nonverbal person by an assistant. This enables the person, also lacking fine-motor skills, to communicate by spelling out words on a keyboard.

Testimonials for the technique were awe-inspiring. Autistic and retarded people who had never effectively communicated were expressing complex and abstract thoughts using advanced vocabulary. For example, Blake Emerson of Houston, Texas was a nonverbal, mentally retarded, autistic sixteen year old. After six months, he "talked" of his dream of studying biology at the University of Houston and finding ways to help other people trapped inside "crazy bodies" (Hamilton, 1992).

Controversy flourished. Advocates extolled its virtues. With faith and anticipation, clinics and schools bought facilitated communication equipment. Critics claimed it was too good to be true. If it did work, the subjects were misdiagnosed. Unfortunately, the critics were right. The following quote was taken from the synopsis of the definitive article entitled *A History of Facilitated Communication: Science, Pseudoscience, and Antiscience*:

> Controlled research using single and double blind procedures in laboratory and nat-

ural settings with a range of clinical populations with which FC is used have determined that, not only are the people with disabilities unable to respond accurately to label or describe stimuli unseen by their assistants, but that the responses are controlled by the assistants (Jacobson, et.al., 1995).

Ultimately, do the positive aspects of the learning perspective outweigh the negative? Perhaps we should ask this question to a once nonverbal, self-injurious, autistic child who is now functioning normally as an adult because of Lovaas' behavior therapy.

Figure 11-5. Mother Teresa is the epitome of humanistic values. (Mark Elias: AP/Wide World Photos.)

THE HUMANISTIC PERSPECTIVE

The major goals of humanistic therapy are to enable the person to discover significance and meaning in his/her existence, to assist in discovering the courses of action that are most appropriate in life, and to guide in the development of fullest human potential. Most other perspectives are treatment-oriented. Holism is prevention-oriented. Humanism is growth-oriented. Humanistic therapists are concerned with the development of a close rapport with the client. Carl Rogers, in Chapter 9, indicated that therapists should be warm, genuine, trusting, and understanding in the therapeutic relationship. They should be empathic, rather than merely sympathetic. They should endeavor to enter the phenomenal world of the person.

Humanistic therapies are most appropriate for YAVIS people. Coined at the beginning of the movement, YAVIS stands for young, attractive, verbal, intelligent, and successful. Such people have many positive attributes. They function in an adaptive manner. However, they are not content with their present lives. They are unfulfilled, and may feel anxious or depressed. They seek change and growth.

Contemporary American society enjoys a technical sophistication and level of affluence unsurpassed in history. We can mass-produce consumer items in a relatively inexpensive, efficient way.

Labor-saving devices do much of our work. Computers can do in an instant what previously required hours. We can put people on the moon, transplant organs, and select among hundreds of television stations via satellite. We can bank with a machine, shop by television, purchase a multitude of products from vending machines, and attend drive-through funeral parlors. Our cars inform us when our lights are left on, fuel is low, seatbelts are unbuckled, or when keys are left in the ignition.

However, there may be a human cost for our technological society. Mechanical interaction has replaced human interaction. People feel less significant. For many, a spiritual and existential emptiness exists in the midst of a technological paradise.

The young, upward-mobile professional signals for the garage door to open from the driver's seat of his Saab as he completes his fifth phone call during his thirty minute ride home. He enters the driveway of a split-level suburban home that is distinguished from those adjacent to it by a different name on the mailbox. He feels exhausted, although he has done no physical work. He tells his wife about the headache he has from squinting at his computer and bucking the traffic. She hears, nods, but doesn't listen. She tells him that Jason has chipped a tooth, the pool filter is clogged, and that she won't be able to work Thursday if she can't find day care for Tiffany. He nods, but continues to watch stock exchange results.

Blaring reruns maintain the attention of the children in the den, who have not been reinforced for acknowledging their father's arrival. Three drinks later, the microwave has produced a bland but effortless dinner. He does some work and goes to bed early. She is accompanied only by television as she reviews overdue bills and notices threatening credit. She notices her Prozac is running out. "Why am I so miserable? I have everything that is supposed to make me happy!" The next day is the same. So is the next. The "American dream" has brought a nightmare of boredom and emptiness. Humanistic therapy and philosophy can help fill this existential void.

In November 1978, our nation was shocked by the suicide-murder in Guyana of nine-hundred thirteen members of the Peoples Temple, a California-based religious cult. In April of 1993, eighty-six people died in the FBI attack on the compound of David Koresh and the Branch Davidian cult in Waco, Texas. Bhagwan Shree Rajneesh was a self-proclaimed guru from India. He established a "new age" community called Rajneeshpuram, near Antelope, Oregon in 1981. He implored his followers to "Surrender to it" (Karlen and Abramson, 1984). "Surrender" referred to his followers' money. When forced to leave the country in 1985, Rajneesh owned eighty-two Rolls-Royces and the commune's sixty-four thousand acres were valued at thirty million dollars (Karlen and Abramson, 1985).

The mental status of people who would surrender their money and autonomy to follow diabolical leaders was questioned. Most followers did not have severe psychopathology. Most were essentially YAVIS people. They were young and seemed intelligent and conscientious. Perhaps they were naive, vulnerable, and misled, but not psychotic.

Dr. Hardat Sukhdeo was chief of psychiatry of the College of Medicine and Dentistry at New Jersey Medical School at the time of Jonestown. He interviewed a number of survivors. He characterized them as "polite, law-abiding, responsible, and intelligent. They all had some humanitarian ideals. They want to work for people, to help people, to work for a just cause." In a study of former cult members, Deutsch and Miller (1983) found they were very idealistic and wished to unite and serve others. Their religious views had magical and mystical overtones. Some cult members were disenchanted with our material, technological society. They felt alienated and alone. Even though they wanted very badly to form meaningful relationships, they didn't fit in. They were often proverbial social "square pegs." Saul Levine (1984), expert on radical departures to cults, has found that ninety percent of cult members abandon them within two years and return home.

Millions find existential purpose and meaning through their religion. Others find them in humanism. They embrace its philosophy and internalize its values. It gives their lives direction. A person does not need to enter formal humanistic therapy. The study of humanism can be embarked upon individually. It offers an alternative to cult membership or social alienation.

Critics of humanism condemn it as overly optimistic and naive. Treating all others with unconditional regard and respect will result in being taken advantage of. However, life involves taking existential risks. The rewards of intimate human relationships are too great not to take them.

Humanism has also been criticized for contributing to an American society perceived as overly permissive, lacking discipline, and fostering irresponsibility. Humanism does stress individual freedom. It also stresses the acceptance of responsibility for one's chosen course of action. Gestalt therapist Frederick Perls wrote the gestalt prayer which contributed to the "do your own thing" philosophy pervasive during the 1970s. However, Perls was very clear on the issue of personal accountability. "Full identification with yourself can take place if you are willing to take full responsibility—*responsibility* for yourself, for your actions, feelings and thoughts . . ." (Perls, in Binderman, 1974.)

Humanistic notions, although often born of pain and suffering, offer great hope. Viktor Frankl, suffering Auschwitz during the sixth winter of the Second World War, optimistically looked forward to a time when the horror would end. What he had gone through would ultimately become an asset. Quoting Nietzsche, he imbued his comrades "Was mich nicht umbringt, macht mich stärker" [That which does not kill me, makes me stronger] (Frankl, 1959).

THE SOCIAL PERSPECTIVE

The social perspective was the driving force behind community mental health. Its proponents argued convincingly against involuntary commitments, large institutions, locked wards, powerful drugs, shock, and lobotomies. This approach advocated normalization and deinstitutionalization as alternatives. Patients were to be released to transitional community environments. The environment was to be the least restrictive; essential services would be provided, while fostering autonomy. It was hoped that former patients would ultimately become fully integrated, productive members of society with dignity. If the true measure of our society is the way in which it cares for its least powerful citizens, the society would by highly evaluated.

The rhetoric of the social perspective had emotional appeal. State governments thought they could close expensive institutions, and treat more cheaply in the community. Retrospectively, this reasoning was short-sighted. Equivalent community care is more expensive than institutional. Initially, public opinion was benign, then the influx of former patients began changing the makeup of communities leading to public outcry.

Today, the homeless population is estimated to be six hundred thousand. As stated in chapter 10, nearly fifty percent of the homeless are severely and persistently mentally ill. A third have been previously hospitalized for mental disorders, fifteen percent abuse drugs and 50 percent abuse alcohol, according to the National Institute of Mental Health. Clearly, existing means for preventing and treating substance abuse do not work. In 1994, the inspector general at the Department of Health and Human Services reported that just one percent of low-income drug addicts and alcoholics ever recover or get jobs. More than eighty thousand drug addicts and alcoholics received monthly disability checks of four hundred forty-six dollars per month until they died or went to jail. In 1996, supplemental security income increased to five hundred fifty-six dollars a month but was limited to three years. In behavioral terms, we potently reinforce pathology.

A study of released patients who were living in board-and-care homes found that one-third of them had been victims of crime during the past year (Lehman, et al., 1984). The number of prison inmates with serious mental disorders today approximates the number of patients in mental hospitals during the 1950s (Isaac and Armat, 1990). Patients who are poorly suited for community life often travel the "golden triangle": from the psychiatric emergency department to the state psychiatric hospital to the county jail (Ciccone and Clements, 1984). The situation became so desperate that communities offered

Figure 11.6. "Kidz'ncoaches" provides emerging children with an opportunity to share prosocial experiences with college student volunteers. (Photograph by Jim Rooney.)

"Greyhound therapy" (one-way bus tickets away from the area) as the solution (Cordes, 1984).

Although treatment is often a euphemism for providing for consumer needs, quality community programs exist. A meta-analysis of social skills training and relapse prevention showed that "Social skills training leads to significant improvements in the social behavior of schizophrenics when specific behavioral measures are used. Similarly, training appears to have a positive impact on schizophrenics' perceptions of themselves..." (Benton and Schroeder, 1990). However, there simply aren't enough good programs. "Slipping through the cracks" is an inappropriate metaphor; "falling through gaping holes" is more appropriate.

I have not presented an optimistic statement on community mental health. The number of mentally ill and retarded people living in imposing community residences, receiving quality treatment and care pales when compared with the homeless mentally ill who receive no treatment or services and sleep on street grates. Should we admit community mental health on the whole has failed, it is unlikely that we could reopen hospitals. We are too busy building prisons.

ECLECTIC APPROACHES

The perspectives have been presented as separate and distinct. This was done to enable you to perceive the unique nature of each. However, clinicians have traditionally viewed disorders and employed treatments consistent with the perspective in which they were trained. "If all you have is a hammer, everything looks like a nail—anything can be fixed with a big enough hammer." Such reasoning has proven faulty in the past. When thorazine was first employed to treat schizophrenia, some patients did not respond. Larger doses did not work any better.

Looking toward the future, eclectic approaches hold bold promise. Highly skilled clinicians, knowledgeable of all perspectives, will employ the perspective, or combination, that best suit the unique needs of the individual. Like the highly skilled craftsman, who selects from a box filled with a variety of quality tools, the clinician will select "the right tool(s) for the job."

The May 1994 edition of Psychiatry was devoted to eclectic treatments. Combined behavioral, medical, and psychosocial approaches demonstrated impressive results in treating a variety of conditions, including phobic, panic, eating, and obsessive-compulsive disorders. The synergy of the combinations was emphasized. Hopefully, eclecticism will flourish.

This chapter has enabled you to evaluate the relative merits of the perspectives. After examining the strengths and limitations of each, you should have a better understanding of abnormal psychology. Should you or a loved one require mental health services, you should be better able to evaluate options. Knowledgeable consumers make wiser decisions. You should know what questions to ask.

However, if you are still somewhat confused about abnormal psychology and can't decide which approach is best—don't dismay. You see, you just can't get the experts to agree.

REFERENCES

Adler, L.A., et.al (1993, September). Vitamin E Treatment of Tardive Dyskinesia. *American Journal of Psychiatry,* 150:9.

American Psychiatric Association (1989). Treatments of Psychiatric Disorder: A Task Force Report of the American Psychiatric Association, volume 3. Washington, D.C.: *American Psychiatric Association.*

American Psychiatric Association (1994, December Supplement) Practice Guideline for the Treatment of Patients with Bipolar Disorder. *American Journal of Psychiatry,* 151:12.

Baer, L. et. al. (1995, May). Cingulotomy for Intractable Obsessive-Compulsive Disorder. *Archives of General Psychiatry,* 52(5), 384-392.

Baldessarini, R.J. and Frankenburg, F.R. (1991, March 14). Clozapine: A Novel Antipsychotic Agent. *The New England Journal of Medicine,* 746-754.

Begley, S. (1994, February 7). One Pill Makes You Larger, and One Pill Makes You Small. *Newsweek,* 36-42.

Benton, M.K. and Schroeder, H.E. (1990, December). Social Skills Training With Schizophrenics: A Meta-Analytic Evaluation. *Journal of Consulting and Clinical Psychology,* 58(6), 741-747.

Binderman, R.M., (1974). The Issue of Responsibility in Gestalt Therapy. *Psychotherapy: Theory, Research and Practice,* 11:3.

Browne, A. and Finkelhor, D. (1986). Impact of Child Sexual Abuse: A Review of the Research. *Psychological Bulletin,* 99(1), 66-77.

Burton, T.M. (1991, August 2). Scientologists Fail to Persuade FDA on Prozac. *The Wall Street Journal.*

Cell (1993, March 26). A Novel Gene Containing a Trinucleotide Repeat That is Expanded and Unstable on Huntington's Disease Chromosomes. *Cell Press,* 72, 971-983.

Ciccone, J.R. and Clements, C. (1984, March). Forensic Psychiatry and Applied Clinical Ethics: Theory and Practice. *American Journal of Psychiatry,* 141:3.

Consensus Development Panel (1985, April). Mood Disorders: Pharmacologic Prevention of Recurrences. *American Journal of Psychiatry,* 142:4.

Cordes, C. (1984, February). The Plight of Homeless Mentally Ill. *APA Monitor,* 15(2).

Deutsch, A. and Miller, M.J. (1983, June). A Clinical Study of Four Unification Church Members. *American Journal of Psychiatry,* 140(6).

Ellis, A. (1970). *Reason and Emotion in Psychotherapy.* New York: Lyle Stuart.

Faedda, G., et.al. (1991, September). Episode Sequence in Bipolar Disorder and Response to Lithium Treatment. *American Journal of Psychiatry,* 148:9.

Frankl, V. (1959). *Man's Search For Meaning.* Boston: Beacon Press.

Freud, S. (1949). *An Outline of Psychoanalysis.* New York: W. W. Norton & Company, Inc.

Goldberg, J. (1995, July). Fetal Attraction. *Discover,* pp. 87-93.

Goldberg, I. (1958). *George Gershwin: A Study in American Music.* New York: Frederick Ungar Publishing Company.

Greenwald, A.G. (1992, June). New Look 3: Unconscious Cognition Reclaimed. *American Psychologist*, 47(6), 766-779.

Hamilton, K. (1992, July 5). Breaking Through. *Houston Chronical,* Houston, Texas, p. 1G+.

Hazelwood, L. (1995, March 2 & 3). *Conference on Sexual Violence.* Fort Lauderdale, Florida.

Hogarty, G.E., et. al. (1986, July). Family Psychoeducation, Social Skills Training, and Maintenance Chemotherapy in the Aftercare Treatment of Schizophrenia. *Archives of General Psychiatry,* 43.

A. J. Hostetler, A.J. (1987, May). Scientists Warn Role of Biology Miscast in Wake of Amish Study. *APA Monitor,* 18(5).

Ingram, N.A.W., and Newgreen, D.B. (1983, December). The Use Of Tacrine for Tardive Dyskinesia. *American Journal of Psychiatry,* 140:12.

Isaac, R.J. and Armat, V.C. (1990). *Madness in the Streets: How psychiatry and the Law Abandoned the Mentally Ill.* New York: The Free Press.

Jacobson, J.W., et.al. (1995, September). A History of Facilitated Communication: Science, Pseudoscience, and Antiscience; Science Working Group on Facilitated Communication. *American Psychologist,* 50(9), 750-765.

Karlen, N. and Abramson, P. (1984, December 3). Bahgwan's Realm: An Indian Guru Transplanted to Oregon Takes Over a Town and Causes a Mighty Culture Clash with Locals. *Newsweek,* 34-38.

_____. (1985, December 9). Rajneeshpuram: Final Days: With Bhagwan Gone, His Commune Comes Apart. *Newsweek,* 30.

Kassin, S. (1995). *Psychology.* Boston: Houghton Mifflin Company.

Kiecolt-Glaser, J and Glaser R. (1988, November). Psychological Influences on Immunity: Implications for AIDS. *American Psychologist,* 43 (11), 892-898.

Lehman, A.F., and Linn, L.S., (1984, February). Crimes Against Discharged Mental Patients in Board-and-Care Homes. *American Journal of Psychiarry,* 141:2.

Levine, S.V. (1984). *Radical Departures: Desperate Detours to Growing Up.* Harcourt, Brace, Jovanovich.

Lipsey, M.W. and Wilson, D.B. (1993, December). The Efficacy of Psychological, Educational, and Behavioral Treatment. *American Psychologist,* 48(12), 1181-1209.

Miller, L. (1986, December). In Search of the Unconscious. *Psychology Today.*

Nichols, M. (1994, May 23). Questioning Prozac: Are Too Many People Popping a Pill to Treat Clinical Depression? *Maclean's Magazine,* Maclean Hunter Ltd., 36-41.

Ostrom, C.M. (1989, June 18). Treating Sexual Deviants. *Seattle Times/Post-Intelligencer*, Seattle, Washington, A1+.

Perry, P.J., et.al. (1991, February). Clozapine and Norcloxapine Plasma Concentrations and Clinical Response of Treatment-Refractory Schizophrenic Patients. *American Journal of Psychiatry,* 148:2.

Powell, C. (1995, September 18). My American Journey. Excerpted from *Time.*

Rickels, K., et.al. (1983, August 12). Long-Term Diazepam Therapy and Clinical Outcome. *JAMA,* 250(6).

Seidman, L.J. (1983). Schizophrenia and Brain Dysfunction: An Integration of Recent Neurodiagnostic Findings. *Psychological Bulletin,* 94(2), 195-238.

Silverman, L. and Weinberger, J. (1985). Mommy and I are one: Implications for Psychotherapy. *American Psychologist*, 40, 1296-1308.

The Thin Edge: Depression. Produced by WNET. New York State Education Department, 1975.

Tippen, J. and Henn, F.A. (1983, December). Modified Leukotomy in the Treatment of Intractable Obsessional Neurosis. *American Journal of Psychiatry*, 139:12.

Wallis, C., and J. Willwerth. (1992, July 6). Schizophrenia: A New Drug Brings Patients Back to Life. *Time*, pp. 53-55.

Glossary

abnormal psychology. The study of relatively rare and unusual human behavior, thought, and emotion.

amnesia. A mental disorder characterized by loss of memory.

anorexia nervosa. An eating disorder characterized by an extreme lack of appetite and weight loss.

autism. A mental disorder characterized by psychological isolation and withdrawal from the environment.

behaviorism. A school of psychology which holds that behavior is learned and can, therefore, be modified.

bipolar disorder. An mood disorder typically characterized by episodes mania and depression.

bulimia nervosa. An eating disorder characterized by episodes of binge eating, in which large amounts of food are consumed.

cultural relativism. The notion that standards of normality vary among different societies.

delirium. A syndrome characterized by a clouded state of consciousness, incoherent speech, disorientation in space and time, and memory lapses.

dementia. A syndrome characterized by a loss of intellectual abilities to the degree that is interferes with social and occupational function.

dependent personality. A personality disorder in which the individual has an extreme need for the company, support, and approval of others.

Diagnostic and Statistical Manual of Mental Disorders (DSM). The official document for the classification of mental disorders in the United States.

DSM—IV-R. The current version of the *Diagnostic and Statistical Manual of Mental Disorders*, published in 1994.

dysthymia. A chronic disturbance characterized by depressed mood.

ethnocentrism. The belief that one's culture is inherently superior and the standard against which others should be judged.

exhibitionism. A mental disorder in which the individual becomes sexually aroused by displaying his genitals to an unsuspecting stranger .

fetishism. A mental disorder in which the individual is sexually aroused by nonliving objects.

Freud, Sigmund. The founder of the psychoanalytic school of psychology.

general adaptation syndrome. Hans Selye's model for describing the way in which the body adapts to stress.

Gestalt psychology. A school of psychology which believes that man can be best understood in his holistic form.

Global Assessment of Functioning Scale. An axis of the DSM—111—R that rates the psychological, social, and occupational function of the individual.

holistic perspective. A perspective for abnormal psychology that is concerned with the prevention of mental disorders through diet, exercise, and psychosomatic means.

humanistic perspective. A perspective for abnormal psychology that appreciates the uniqueness and worth of every human being, and is concerned with man's full existential development.

Huntington's disease. A progressive, degenerative, hereditary nervous disorder that is ultimately fatal.

hyperactivity. A condition in which a person is easily distracted and has great difficulty maintaining attention, presently called attention deficit hyperactivity disorder.

hypochondriasis. A mental disorder in which the individual is obsessed with his health and mistakenly believes that he is seriously ill.

illness perspective. A perspective for abnormal psychology in which abnormal behavior is believed to be the result of organic factors and to require medical intervention.

intelligence quotient (I.Q.). A measure of an individual's ability to function in a specific cultural setting.

kleptomania. A mental disorder characterized by compulsive stealing that is motivated by thrill rather than deprivation.

learning perspective. A perspective for abnormal psychology based upon the theory and goals of behaviorism, in which behavior is thought to be learned and, therefore, modifiable.

malingerer. An individual who feigns a mental disorder in order either to avoid unpleasant circumstances or to put himself in a favorable position.

masochism. A condition in which an individual voluntarily subjects himself/herself to situations of abuse and humiliation.

mental disorder. Any psychological or behavioral condition that is sufficiently abnormal to warrant treatment.

mental illness. The metaphor used by the illness perspective to conceptualize abnormal behavior.

mental retardation. A mental condition characterized by subnormal mental and behavioral function.

metaphor. A figure of speech used to convey a particular perspective's conceptualization of abnormal behavior (for example, "mental illness").

model. An analogy used by a perspective to explain its conceptualization of abnormal behavior (for example, "medical model").

multiaxial evaluation system. A system for evaluating five significant areas of information (axes) about a patient. It is the basis for diagnosis in the DSM.

narcissism. A personality disorder characterized by an exaggerated sense of self-importance, vanity, egocentrism, and attitude of entitlement.

neuroscience. The science that studies physiological factors in behavior. A contemporary term for illness perspective.

neurosis. According to Freud, a group of related mental disorders in which anxiety is the primary symptom.

obsessive-compulsive disorder. A mental disorder characterized by obsessions (persistent thoughts that pervade consciousness) which motivate compulsions (ritualistic behaviors).

paranoia. A mental state characterized by suspicion and delusions of jealousy, persecution, or grandeur.

pedophilia. A mental disorder in which an adult is sexually aroused by prepubescent children.

personality disorder. A chronic, deeply ingrained character defect that results in chronic maladaptive behavior.

perspective. A group of scholars or practitioners who employ a common model, metaphor, vocabulary, and orientation for the study of abnormal behavior.

phobia. An excessive or unreasonable fear that is experienced when specific situations occur or when in the presence of specific objects.

psychiatrist. A medical doctor who specializes in the treatment of mental disorders.

psychoanalysis. The type of psychotherapy developed by Sigmund Freud that uses free association, dream interpretation, and analysis to investigate mental processes.

psychoanalytic perspective. The perspective, based on the theories of Freud, which believes that mental disorders stem from the unconscious level and result from unresolved conflicts from childhood.

psychologist. A nonmedical specialist, trained in psychological testing, theories of personality, and psychotherapy, who specializes in the treatment of mental disorders.

psychosis. A general term for any mental disorder in which the individual has a distorted perception of reality.

psychosurgery. Surgical or electrical alteration of the brain employed to alleviate mental disorders.

psychotherapy. Any type of treatment that primarily employs conversation between a therapist and patient as the therapeutic agent.

pyromania. A mental disorder in which a person is obsessed with fire and compulsively sets fires.

Rogers, Carl. One of the leaders and prominent spokesman of the humanistic perspective.

sadism. A mental disorder which is characterized by sexual gratification that is obtained by subjecting another person to pain and humiliation.

schizophrenia. A serious type of psychosis characterized typically by hallucinations, delusions, disturbed thought, and marked impairment of function.

Selye, Hans. An advocate of the holistic approach to medicine, Selye developed a model for the way in which the body adapts to stress.

social perspective. A perspective for the study of abnormal psychology which holds that long-term hospitalization is denormalizing and advocates community mental health as the alternative.

transsexualism. A mental disorder in which the individual is repulsed by his genitals and desires to be the opposite sex.

transvestic fetishism. A mental disorder in which a heterosexual male is sexually excited by dressing like a female.

Watson, John B. The founder of behaviorism, the theory upon which the learning perspective is based.

Index

Self Tests

SELF-TEST: MEASURING COMPREHENSION
Chapter 2

1. Assume you have a serious mental disorder. During which period of history would you choose to have it? Why? Describe the attribution, social climate, source of social authority, and technology of the chosen period.

2. Reflecting on the criteria for normality and abnormality, analyze yourself. In which ways are you normal? Why? In which ways are you abnormal? Why?

3. Discuss the relationship between mental illness and insanity.

4. Describe the four general criteria for determining insanity, and provide a specific example of what could justify each.

5. Should a condemned prisoner, judged to be incompetent to be executed, be allowed to give his consent for treatment that could enable him to become well enough to be executed? Why or why not?

SELF-TEST: MEASURING COMPREHENSION
Chapter 3

1. Why is the *Diagnostic and Statistical Manual of Mental Disorders* a political document?

2. Describe the effects of various political constituencies on the composition of the *Diagnostic Manual.*

3. Describe the distinctions between neurosis and psychosis.

4. Name the five DSM—IV axes and describe the type of information contained on each.

5. What distinguishes mental disorders from personality disorders?

6. Compare and contrast dependent and avoidant personality disorder.

SELF-TEST: MEASURING COMPREHENSION
CHAPTER 4

1. How can a retarded child be distinguished from an autistic child?

2. What are the distinctions among cognitive syndromes delirium, dementia, and amnesia?

3. How are mental and cognitive symptoms distinguished?

4. What is the correct sequence of progressive substance-related conditions?

5. What distinguishes delusional disorder from schizophrenia?

6. Describe the profile of a potential suicide.

7. What is the difference between specific phobia and generalized anxiety disorder?

8. Differentiate somatization disorder, conversion disorder, and hypochondriasis.

9. What are the major distinctions between the presenting symptoms of factitious and somatoform disorder?

10. Discuss ways that dissociative identity disorder can be distinguished from malingering.

11. Describe the profile of the serial killer and distinguish it from a mass killer.

12. Examine the psychopathological patterns common in anorexia nervosa. Which seems most plausible to you? Why?

13. Explain how specific sleep disorders are likely to coexist with depression and/or post traumatic stress disorder.

14. Distinguish kleptomanics from shoplifters.

15. Discuss the relative severity of adjustment disorder, depression, and post-traumatic stress disorder.

4A SELF TEST: MEASURING COMPREHENSION
A Portrait of Neurosis
Oscar Levant

1. Oscar Levant demonstrated the symptoms of many of the disorders discussed in the chapter. Even though DSM-IV clearly delineates diagnostic criteria sets, Levant is a clinical challenge. Reexamine "A Portrait of Neurosis." Indicate specific symptoms demonstrated by Levant of the following disorders.

   a.   substance use disorder

   b.   obsessive-compulsive disorder

   c.   phobic disorder

   d.   hypochondriasis

   e.   dysthymic disorder

   f.   anorexia nervosa

   g.   dissociative amnesia

   h.   conversion disorder

2. Can you think of any other disorder that Levant demonstrated symptoms of? If so, list the disorder with the symptoms demonstrated by him.

4B SELF TEST: MEASURING COMPREHENSION
A Portrait of Psychosis
Norman Cameron

1. What symptoms did Joan demonstrate that would justify a diagnosis of schizophrenia?

2. Which of Joan's symptoms are of the affective domain?

3. Which of Joan's symptoms are of the cognitive domain?

4. Reexamine the criteria set for schizophrenia. Does Joan satisfy DSM-IV criteria? Why or why not?

5. Does Joan represent a particular subtype of schizophrenia? Which?

5C SELF TEST: MEASURING COMPREHENSION
To Catch a Killer Gene
Susan Katz Miller

1. If you were at risk for Huntington's, would you take a test that could determine whether you have the disease? Why or why not?

2. Assume that you were at risk for Huntington's and declined to take the diagnostic test. However, your child did. What is your risk for the disease if the child tests negative? What is your risk if she tests positive?

3. With present technology, how could Huntington's disease be totally eliminated?

4. Why do the residents of the village on Lake Maracaibo, Venezuela, represent such an important population for Huntington's research?

5. Should diagnostic tests be used if there is no cure for the disease? Why or why not?

6. Describe the relationship among the various Huntington's research teams.

5D SELF TEST: MEASURING COMPREHENSION
Psychosurgery: Damaging the Brain to Save the Mind
Joann Ellison Rodgers

1. What disorders is psychosurgery used to treat today?

2. Describe Matthew's symptoms prior to the operation.

3. Provide an Axis I diagnosis for Matthew.

4. What is the theoretical basis for Matthew's operation?

5. Compare the surgical procedures of Dr. Freeman and Dr. Uematsu.

6. What were the results of the operation?

5E SELF TEST: MEASURING COMPREHENSION
The Blood of Madness
Mary Long

1. What are the basic principles behind Cade's theory advocating dialysis for schizophrenia?

2. Cade and Wagemaker's critics argue that improvement results from placebo effect. What are these arguments?

3. How do Cade and Wagemaker respond to their critics?

4. Considering all the evidence, what conclusion can be drawn about the Cade-Wagemaker regimen for treating schizophrenia?

5F SELF TEST: MEASURING COMPREHENSION
Electroshock: Fifty Years Later
Russ Rymer

1. How do Susan Hale and Leonard Frank differ in their opinions on electroshock therapy?

2. Describe Cerletti's original electroshock procedure.

3. What are the collateral effects of the treatment?

4. On what disorders has shock treatment been used? On which does it work best?

5. What changes have been made in the treatment as it is practiced today?

6. What is your opinion on the use of electroshock therapy? Why?

6A SELF TEST: MEASURING COMPREHENSION
Psychoneuroimmunology:
The Interface Between Behavior, Brain, and Immunity
Steven F. Maier, Linda R. Watkins, and Monika Fleshner

1. What is psychoneuroimmunology?

2. What is the difference between innate and specific immunity?

3. What evidence demonstrates that the brain participates in controlling the immune process?

4. What evidence demonstrates that classical conditioning influences the immune process?

5. According to the section on "stress and immunity," was it defeat or injury that inhibited the stranger rats' antibody reaction?

6. What evidence demonstrates that the immune system can stimulate a stress response?

7. What is the scientific basis for the "licking of wounds" and sleeping when ill or injured?

8. Is present knowledge of psychoneuroimmunology adequate to understand the mechanism by which the course of cancer can be affected? Why or why not?

6B SELF TEST: MEASURING COMPREHENSION
The Mastery of Stress
Hans Selye

1. "Our goal, then, is to strike a balance between the equally destructive forces of hypo- and hyper-stress, to find as much eustress as possible and minimize distress." What does Selye mean?

2. Why is relaxation therapy ineffective in combating hypostress?

3. What is altruistic egoism?

4. What are the basic principles of Selye's code for the mastery of stress?

5. How did he apply this code in dealing with his own life crises?

6C SELF TEST: MEASURING COMPREHENSION
Influence of Aerobic Exercise on Depression
I. Lisa McCann & David S. Holmes

1. According to the authors of this article, what have been the methodological problems with prior studies done on this topic?

2. How was this study designed to avoid these problems?

3. All three groups had lower levels of depression at the completion of the study.
   A) Do you think progressive muscle relaxation and walking were really placebos? Why?

   B) Recall seasonal affective disorder. During which semester was this study likely conducted? Why?

4. What explanations are offered for reduction of depression in the subjects in the aerobic exercise conditioning? Explain.

5. How does your own experience with exercise correspond with the results of this study?

6D SELF TEST: MEASURING COMPREHENSION
Diet for a Small Madman: Food Chemicals and Behavior
Christopher Norwood

1. Which specific ingredients are excluded from the Feingold diet?

2. Describe some of the factors that make it difficult to conduct research on hyperactivity.

3. What foods contain salicylates?

4. What difficulties might be encountered in trying to keep a child on the Feingold diet?

5. Do you think that packages containing food with synthetic additives should be clearly labeled? Why or why not?

6. After reading the article, what effect do you think food additives have on behavior?

6E SELF TEST: MEASURING COMPREHENSION
THE PACE OF LIFE
Robert V. Levine

1. How does the Shiite Muslim concept of time compare to the American?

2. What four variables were measured to indicate the pace of life of United States cities?

3. Which region of the United States has the fastest pace of life?

4. Do fast-paced cities create or attract Type-A people? Why?

5. Based on your Type A-B Personality Test score, select a city where the pace of life best suits your personality.

6. Reflect on your score on the Type A-B personality test. Do you need to make changes in your pace of life? How?

7A SELF TEST: MEASURING COMPREHENSION
Altered States: Peeling Away the Layers of Multiple Personality
Frank W. Putnam

1. Did Anna O. demonstrate distinctly different personality states? If so, describe them.

2. Was one personality state aware of the other?

3. Were the switches spontaneous and unprovoked by cue?

4. Is trauma present in the cases described in the article?

5. If an alter ego is blind yet the executive can see, can a general medical condition be ruled out? Why or why not?

6. Do the personalities of the cases in the article represent foils?

7. How can a promiscuous alter provide gain for an overly modest executive?

8. What is your opinion of dissociative identity disorder? Why?

7B SELF TEST: MEASURING COMPREHENSION
Posttraumatic Stress Disorder and the Treatment of Sexual Abuse
Sylvia B. Patten, Yvonne K. Gatz,
Berlin Jones, Deborah L. Thomas

1. What symptoms indicate a patient "cannot remember" trauma?

2. What symptoms indicate a patient "cannot 'not' remember" trauma?

3. What types of treatments are used if a patient has symptoms of denial?

4. What types of treatments are used if a patient has symptoms of intrusion?

5. Briefly describe the four traumatic effects of sexual abuse as described by Finkelhor and Browne.

6. What did the therapist do to deal with potential stigmatization of Susan?

7. According to the sexual trauma recovery process model, Freud's cathartic treatments did not always work because they primarily dealt with symptoms resulting from _____.

7C SELF TEST: MEASURING COMPREHENSION
Lies of the Mind
Leon Jaroff

1. Initially, how do "recovered memories" of sexual abuse differ from memories of other abuse victims?

2. How can unfounded allegations of abuse "trigger a backlash" against concern for those actually abused?

3. According to Margaret Singer, are memories of trauma likely to be repressed?

4. What does Elizabeth Loftus believe about repressed-memories?

5. Summarize the evidence on the existence of satanic-ritual abuse.

7D SELF TEST: MEASURING COMPREHENSION
The Psychodynamics of Suicide
Herbert Hendin

1. What did Sigmund Freud feel was the primary motive for suicide?

2. What is the major methodological problem of those who study suicide?

3. What technique did Hendin develop to study suicidal motivation?

4. Which of the explanations of suicide offered by Hendin seems most valid to you? Why?

5. Is dream interpretation a valid way of studying suicidal motivation? Why or why not?

7E SELF TEST: MEASURING COMPREHENSION
Lecture XXVIII, Analytic Therapy
Sigmund Freud

1. What were the major reasons why Freud became disenchanted with hypnosis as a therapeutic technique?

2. Describe Freud's ideas regarding how transference can be used to enable the ego to gain control over the libido.

3. Why did Freud feel that the interpretation of a patient's dreams could give important clues toward an understanding of the underlying dynamics of the patient's neurosis?

4. Why did Freud feel that the intervention of the patient's family could be a hindrance to effective psychoanalysis?

5. One major criticism of Freud has been that he failed to provide empirical evidence for the success of psychoanalysis. Why did he feel such evidence was not necessary?

7F SELF TEST: MEASURING COMPREHENSION
Eight Ages of Man
Erik Erikson

1. What experiences lead Erikson to stress social, rather than sexual forces, in producing psychopathology?

2. What three contributions to the study of the human ego did Erikson make in *Childhood and Society*?

3. What additional factors exert influence on personality development during Stage Four (Industry vs. Inferiority)?

4. Should the ages of Stage Five (Identity vs. Role Confusion) and Stage Six (Intimacy vs. Isolation) be modified to reflect the change in modern society? How?

5. Does the theory sound dated in any way? How? What changes would you make?

6. Which psychosocial stage do you feel you are presently in? What are the issues you are dealing with?

8A SELF TEST: MEASURING COMPREHENSION
Behavior Modification with Children
D. G. Brown

1. From the behaviorist's point of view, how does abnormal behavior originate?

2. Of the three techniques described by Dr. Brown to weaken undesirable behavior (positive reinforcement for non-occurrence of undesired behavior, aversive reinforcement for occurrence of undesired behavior, or no reinforcement), which do you feel would work best in trying to stop a four year old child from misbehaving in front of relatives? Why?

3. What does Dr. Brown feel are the major advantages of behavior therapy over other types of therapy?

4. What are some of the commonly made criticisms of behavior therapy?

5. What are some of the major differences between the orientations of behavioristic and psychoanalytic psychology?

8B SELF TEST: MEASURING COMPREHENSION
Conditioned Emotional Reactions
John B. Watson and Rosalie Rayner

1. Why was Albert B. selected for being the subject of the study?

2. What was used as an an unconditioned stimulus to elicit fear?

3. How was the conditioning of fear in Albert B. justified by Watson?

4. How do the conclusions regarding transfer and persistence of conditioned emotional responses help us better understand complex phobias like agoraphobia?

5. Do you feel there were any violations of experimental ethics in the conduct of this study? If so, explain.

6. What comments and conclusions are made in the article comparing/contrasting behaviorism and psychoanalysis?

8C SELF TEST: MEASURING COMPREHENSION
The Operant Side of Behavior Therapy
B.F. Skinner

1. In Skinner's view, what causes troublesome behavior?

2. According to Skinner, why do we cry or feel sad?

3. A child allegedly has attention deficit disorder. Yet, he can play a video game undistracted for hours. Shortly before bedtime, his mother requests that he read a story. He throws a tantrum. His mother relents, allowing him to play the video game until sleepy. Provide a behavioral analysis, and make recommendations for changing contingencies.

4. What are Skinner's views on the ethics of environmental control and use of aversive measures in therapy?

5. How would Skinner advise someone who feels the unpleasant effects of stress?

8D SELF TEST: MEASURING COMPREHENSION
Behavioral Treatment and Normal Educational and Intellectual Functioning in Young Autistic Children
O. Ivar Lovaas

1. Describe the prognosis for autism, according to Rutter (1970).

2. Describe the treatment procedures that were followed for the experimental group. Was aversion employed?

3. What were the results of treatment for the experimental group?

4. Compare the results for the experimental group with the prognosis data of Rutter (1970).

5. What methodological steps were taken to increase confidence in the effectiveness of the experimental group treatment?

6. Intensive behavior therapy is expensive. How can it be financially justified?

8E SELF TEST: MEASURING COMPREHENSION
Fall Into Helplessness
Martin E. P. Seligman

1. What is learned helplessness?

2. What is the difference between process and reactive depression?

3. What is success depression, and how does Seligman feel it is caused?

4. How does Seligman treat learned helplessness and depression?

5. If neurotransmitters, like norepinephrine, are depleted in those who are depressed, how could Seligman's treatment for learned helplessness stimulate neurotransmitter production?

9A SELF TEST: MEASURING COMPREHENSION
The Treatment of Autism: A Human Protest
Mike Murray

1. What are Dr. Murray's criticisms of behavior modification techniques?

2. How do you interpret the verbal response made by David?

3. How might a behavior therapist like O. Ivar Lovaas, who has demonstrated such success with autistic children, defend behavior therapy?

9B SELF TEST: MEASURING COMPREHENSION
The Third Force in Psychology
J. F. T. Bugental

1. What does Bugental mean when he states that "Psychology is at last becoming the study of man?"

2. Bugental states that man is intentional and his behavior is motivated to both conservation and change. Examine your life. In what ways are you conserving? In what ways are you changing?

3. Describe the general orientation of humanism, indicating that you have an understanding of it.

4. How does the overall orientation of the humanistic perspective differ from the learning perspective?

9C SELF TEST: MEASURING COMPREHENSION
A Theory of Human Motivation
A. H. Maslow

1. Concisely describe the five basic types of needs and how each can be satisfied?

2. What does Maslow mean when he states the average American experiences only appetite rather than hunger?

3. What is the relationship between sex and love?

4. According to the model, what happens when a want becomes satisfied?

5.   How does Maslow define a healthy person?

6.   What percentage of each level of need is satisfied in you?

      Physiological

      Safety

      Love

      Esteem

      Self-Actualization

7.   What is your primary level of motivation?

9D SELF TEST: MEASURING COMPREHENSION
Some Hypotheses Regarding the
Facilitation of Personal Growth
Carl Rogers

1. What are the specific elements of the client-therapist relationship that Rogers feels are important for successful therapy?

2. Rogers feels that if he can create the proper therapeutic atmosphere the client will be better able to move toward maturity. What does he feel are the characteristics of the mature individual?

3. What specific changes occur in clients as the result of successful Rogerian therapy?

4. Can you find evidence of psychoanalytic influence in the writing of Rogers? If so, what?

9E SELF TEST: MEASURING COMPREHENSION
Plight of the Ik and Kaiadilt Is Seen
as a Chilling Possible End for Man
John B. Calhoun

1. List some examples of the pathological humor of the Ik.

2. Describe the cultural, religious, and occupational identity of the Ik prior to their uprooting.

3. What were the "three strikes" against the mice that made them lose all of their "mousity"?

4. Describe the similarities between the behavior of the Ik following their uprooting and Dr. Calhoun's mice.

5. Does what happened to the Ik help us understand urban violence? If so, how?

9F SELF TEST: MEASURING COMPREHENSION
What Does a Man Want?
Stanley R. Graham

1. Contemplate Dr. Graham's description of American society during his early life. Compare and contrast your perception of what it was like based on what you have learned from older relatives or friends.

2. According to Dr. Graham, what were the social consequences of the Depression, World War II, and technological advance?

3. How does contemporary society differ from the described earlier period?

4. Reflect on what Dr. Graham wants as a man. Regardless of your gender, restate these desires expressed as "what a woman wants."

5.   What is your reaction to this article?

10A SELF TEST: MEASURING COMPREHENSION
An Interview with Dr. Thomas Szasz
Richard Ballad

1. According to Szasz, what do psychiatrists do when they are said to be treating mental illness?

2. What is your opinion of Dr. Szasz's position on suicide?

3. For what reasons is Szasz against electroshock therapy?

4. Cite examples of what Szasz feels is evidence of an alliance between medicine and the state.

5. Do you feel that his criticisms regarding the alliance between medicine and the state are justified? Why or why not?

6. What is Dr. Szasz' stance on the insanity plea?

10B SELF-TEST: MEASURING COMPREHENSION
The Art of Being Schizophrenic
Jay Haley

1. What are the characteristics of the parents and siblings of the potential schizophrenic?

2. What role does the potential schizophrenic play within the family structure?

3. How is the situation encountered by the schizophrenic in the mental hospital similar to that of his home situation?

4. What criticisms does Haley make of the mental hospital and its staff?

5. In the final analysis, is the schizophrenic manipulated by those around him, or does he do the manipulating? Support your view.

6. What arguments presented in the article served as justifications for deinstitutionalization?

10C SELF TEST: MEASURING COMPREHENSION
The Principle of Normalization and
Its Implications to Psychiatric Services
Wolf Wolfensberger

1. What was the intent of normalization?

2. Cite specific ways by which the normalization of former patients could be enhanced.

3. Based upon your perception of the present status of the mentally ill in the community, assess whether or not guidelines presented in the article have been followed?

4. Cite specific ways by which the normalization of those requiring residential care can be enhanced.

10D SELF-TEST: MEASURING COMPREHENSION
Brief Report: Innovative Programming in a Community Service Center
Edith Cunnane, William Wyman,
Ann Rotermund, and Ruth Murray.

1. What are the two major foci and their components of the St. Patrick Center.

2. Recall Maslow's hierarchy of needs presented in Chapter 9 article C. What levels are addressed by specific elements of the St. Patrick Center?

3. How does the St. Patrick Center demonstrate the philosophy and guidelines presented by Wolfensberger in the previous article?

10E SELF-TEST: MEASURING COMPREHENSION
The Sleep of Reason:How the Insane Were turned Into the Homeless
David Gutmann

1. Describe the various groups/constituencies which advocated the closing of the hospitals.

2. How were those who assumed responsibility for caring for the mentally ill in the community poorly prepared for the task?

3. How was explaining mental illness as a fault of society or the result of defective genes a disservice to the mentally ill?

4. To prevent further social deterioration, why according to Paul Johnson should we be wary of intellectuals?

SELF TEST: MEASURING COMPREHENSION
Chapter 11: Clarification

We have completed our study of abnormal psychology. Now you can apply what you have learned in the analysis of case histories. As you read the following cases, look for information that proponents of various perspectives would consider relevant to their analyses. Also contemplate treatment options.

CASE HISTORY I

Patient's Name: Nancy K.   **Date of Admission:** July 21, 1996

Age: 46   **Religious Preference:** none

Family History:

Parents: Father, John J., age 71, no general medical conditions. He abused alcohol.

                  Mother, Mary J., recently died at age 69 from heart attack. At age 50 she received out-patient treatment by a psychiatrist for manic-depression (bipolar disorder). She was alcohol dependent.

Siblings: Brother, Arthur J., age 49, no mental disorders or general medical conditions.

                  Sister, Eva N., age 47, was treated for dysthymia between the ages of 23 and 26.

Children: Son, Arnold K. Jr., age 23, college graduate, works as a computer engineer in Chicago, no mental disorders or general medical conditions.

                  Daughter, Heather K., age 21, now a junior in college in California, no general medical conditions. Received counseling for a brief period for an adjustment disorder during the first semester of her freshman year.

Relational History:

Nancy has been married to Arnold K. Sr. for 24 years. It has been each spouse's only marriage. Until the last few years, the marriage had been mutually satisfactory. Arnold had an extramarital affair, and the couple were separated for a three week period. He stated that the reason he left her was that he couldn't tolerate Nancy's "crazy" behavior any longer.

Personal History:

Nancy was the youngest of three children in her middle class Caucasian family. During the seventh month of her pregancy with Nancy, her mother had rubella (German measles). This did not apparently impair Nancy's physical or mental development.
Nancy's mother was the dominant person in the family. Her father was relatively passive, and was

seldom home. Nancy had remarked that she felt her parents had always shown preference for her older siblings. Her older brother and sister were viewed as ideal children by the parents. They earned good grades in school, and were seldom discipline problems.

On the contrary, Nancy was viewed as a discipline problem by her parents. She seemed slower to develop than her older siblings. She was not toilet trained until almost four years of age. Her brother recalls their mother angrily scolding Nancy for making mistakes in her toilet training. He recalls her saying she was "fed up with washing diapers after all these years," and that "if Nancy was born first, there would have been no other children."

Nancy did not do well in school. She was a tense and anxious child. When 17 years old, she ran away from home and went to Los Angeles, where she became sexually promiscuous. She became pregnant and had an abortion. She also contracted syphilis. After a year she returned home to "put her life back together." She was treated for syphilis with penicillin. Her parents continually reminded her how she had disgraced them by running away.

Education and Employment:

Upon her return home, she completed high school and a nurse's aide training program. She began working as a nurse's aide, and really enjoyed her work. She stated that for the first time in her life she felt that she was doing something worthwhile, and she found helping others rewarding. She met Arnold Sr. at the hospital, where he was also employed. They married when she was 22 years old, and has not been employed since.

Interaction with Legal System/Crime:

December 4, 1995, Nancy was arrested and charged with disorderly conduct and shoplifting. She was apprehended in a department store. The store manager called the police because Nancy was screaming, crying, and throwing merchandise on the floor. The police discovered that she had filled her purse and coat pockets with cosmetics and jewelry. Nancy later said she didn't know why she had stolen the merchandise. She said she didn't have any need for the things she stole, and that she had enough money to pay for them. She said she just felt compelled to do it. Charges were dropped under the condition that she not return to the store. Arnold Sr. reported that she had probably done this sort of thing before and not been caught, because her bedroom closet was filled with similar merchandise.

Events Leading To Hospitalization:

Until a couple of years before her hospitalization, Nancy had been an ideal mother and wife. She was very meticulous in her house cleaning, and made sure that everything was in its proper place. She would have periodic bursts of energy in which she would thoroughly clean the house.

Shortly after Heather left for college in the Fall of 1993, Nancy's behavior began to change. She became menopausal. She complained of boredom. While she was caring for her children, she was active and fulfilled. Their adolescence presented challenges, but kept her engaged and provided her purpose. After they left, she seldom left the house and spent most of her day watching television, waiting for Arnold to come home at 5 o'clock. She eventually stopped preparing meals and cleaning the house. She had no desire to have sex. She began drinking. Although at first she just drank once in a while, she eventually drank daily. Arnold stated that he found partially empty wine bottles hidden throughout the house. She gained thirty pounds after binging on sweets and packaged snacks. Arnold was sympathetic toward her, assumed many of the household chores, and encouraged the children to call her often.

Arnold became increasingly concerned about Nancy's condition, and suggested that she find a hobby. She began writing poetry. Arnold noticed that her poetry was void of content and made little sense. She did volunteer work at a nursing home briefly, but behaved inappropriately and was asked not to return. She would explain her lack of interest by stating, "What's the use? The kids are gone. Every day is the same. You go to work. You come home. I sit here every day. It doesn't matter what I do. Everything will still be the same."

Nancy drank more heavily. It became common knowledge in the neighborhood that Nancy took daily walks to the liquor store to buy wine The neighborhood children ridiculed and taunted her as she staggered down the street, talking aloud to herself. Arnold criticized her drinking and told her that their reputation in the community had been ruined. She began to express feelings of self pity and persecution. She began blaming Arnold for her condition, and said that if he really wanted to help her, he wouldn't be so critical of her. Arnold relented and assumed more of the household responsibilities.

Arnold became increasingly more frustrated, angry, and dismayed over the deterioration of his marriage and home life. He began an affair with a nurse who worked at the same hospital. Initially, he excused his coming home late by saying that he had to work overtime. Eventually, Nancy became suspicious, and accused Arnold of infidelity. Arnold told Nancy that she was imagining things, and that he thought she was "crazy." Although still despondent, she became extremely anxious and apprehensive. In lucid moments, she feared Arnold was right. She began drinking more heavily.

Arnold stopped coming home at all evenings. He admitted to Nancy that he was having an affair, and that he was going to live with the woman. A tremendous argument followed. As Arnold walked out the door, Nancy slammed it shut behind him with her right hand. Her hand felt numb at first and then was ostensibly paralyzed.

Arnold did not return home for three weeks. His new relationship was not working out, and he felt guilty about leaving Nancy. Not much is known about what happened to Nancy in the meantime, but when Arnold returned home, the house was slovenly and disheveled. Empty wine bottles, snack bags, and wrappers were very conspicuous. He found Nancy laying on a soiled bed, staring at the ceiling, babbling incoherently. She did not acknowledge his presence. Arnold called an ambulance, and Nancy was brought to the hospital. She was admitted to an alcohol detoxification unit. She had bruises on her head and limbs from falling, she was dehydrated, and malnourished. Cognition, affect, and behavior did not improve and she was transferred to the hospital's psychiatric unit.

Condition Since Hospitalization:

Nancy was admitted to the psychiatric unit on July 21, 1996. She evidently experienced auditory hallucinations. She expressed thoughts of extreme self-deprecation and abandonment. "My life is worthless! I gave them the best years of my life and they left me." Her right hand remained partially paralyzed. Her affect was blunt, cognition impaired, and she lacked volition.

During the remainder of July and August, behavioral procedures were employed to help her relearn social/survival skills. She became better able to attend to her personal hygiene and care. However, she remained withdrawn and seldom initiated or allowed social interaction. During incoherent episodes, she repeatedly mumbled, "The dungeon is crawling with lunatics, but we're getting just what we deserve. Please don't let in the lepers, they only keep making things worse." When lucid, she remarked how crazy the other patients were, but how well she fit in.

On September 12th, Nancy attempted suicide by slashing her wrists with her shaver. She stated she wanted to die because her life was worthless and no one cared. She criticized the staff for not helping her, and said that hospitals only make people sicker. A week later, she recalled that the night before her attempt she had a nightmare in which her mother was scolding and beating her for not being as good as her siblings.

Her family visits her periodically, but she is generally not responsive to them. It has been suggested to Arnold that training is available to help him better cope and care for Nancy upon her return home. Arnold is reluctant, and remains uncertain of his plans. Nancy's prognosis is poor.

1. Provide a diagnosis for Nancy.

DSM—IV Multiaxial Evaluation

Axis I: Clinical Disorders

Axis II: Personality Disorders

Axis III: General Medical Conditions

Axis IV: Psychosocial and Environmental Problems

Axis V: Global Assessment of Functioning

GAF = ＿＿＿ Highest level in past year.

GAF = ＿＿＿ Present

2. Each perspective would view Nancy differently. Using the language of the perspective, demonstrate how each might explain and treat her condition.

a. **Illness Perspective**

b. **Holistic Perspective**

c. **Psychoanalytic Perspective**

d. **Learning Perspective**

e. **Humanistic Perspective**

f. **Social Perspective**

CASE HISTORY 2

Patient's Name: Kevin C .

Date of Admission: Admitted to hospital October 27, 1996. Admitted to psychiatric unit November 2, 1996.

Age: 22

Religious Preference: Catholic

Family History:

Parents:

Father, David C., age 53, no mental disorders or general medical conditions. David is a physician with a demanding practice in a large urban area.

Mother, Delores C., age 51. Delores has been periodically treated for depression for the past 20 years. First episode followed the delivery of a stillborn child a couple of years after Kevin was born. Kevin feels that there is nothing wrong with his mother and that she sees a psychiatrist because it is "the fashionable thing to do."

Siblings: None living

Children: None

Relational History:

Kevin has not been married. He dated only his high school girlfriend, Holly, from age 17 to 21. They planned to marry when Kevin completed his bachelor's degree. Kevin became very close friends with his college roommate, Erik L. He was very homesick during his freshman year in college, and Holly was happy that Kevin had found such a good companion in Erik. Because of the distance between Kevin's college and hometown, he could only see Holly about once a month. However, Kevin and Erik came to realize that their attraction for each other was more than platonic. Erik's sexual experience had been limited to ego syntonic homosexuality. He enticed Kevin to experiment with him. Their relationship intensified and lasted for more than two years. Holly was unaware of Kevin's relationship with Erik, but became suspicious during spring recess of Kevin's junior year, when he spent the vacation with Erik rather than come home to be with her. Following spring recess, Holly went to visit Kevin without telling him she was coming. She entered their room and found Kevin and Erik sleeping, wrapped in a lover's embrace.

Later that day Holly told Kevin that she still loved him, but that she would never see him again unless he promised to move into another room and terminate the relationship with Erik. Kevin reluctantly agreed, and Holly promised secrecy.

Holly went home and Kevin began moving his belongings into another room. Erik was extremely disturbed that Kevin was terminating their relationship and told him that if he left, he would kill himself, and it would be his fault. Kevin told Erik that he couldn't "psychologically blackmail" him, and that he didn't want to lose Holly. He left the room. Erik was found dead the next morning after a fall from the dormitory window. Although Erik's death was determined to be accidental, Kevin knew what had happened. Kevin felt extremely guilty. Thereafter, Kevin and Holly's relationship was never the same. Kevin has had no serious relationships since.

Personal History:

Kevin was an only child. His parents were wealthy, and he had every material comfort. His father, David, was a prominent member of the community. Because of his medical practice, David worked long hours and was seldom home to interact with Kevin. Kevin's mother, Delores, was frequently engaged in social activities and was vice-president of the local chapter of Parents Anonymous. She viewed caring for Kevin as demeaning and boring. Kevin was cared for by a nanny during most of his childhood. David seemed to resent Delores spending time with Kevin during the limited occassions the family was together.

Delores suspected that a nanny had sexually abused Kevin when he was three. She came home unexpectedly one afternoon, and found Kevin crying with unexplained bruises on his body. The nanny vehemently denied the allegation, said Kevin had fallen down stairs, but was fired. David convinced Delores not to file charges in order to avoid undesirable publicity.

David and Delores demanded that Kevin do well in school. Both insisted that Kevin would be a doctor. Throughout childhood, his worth was defined by progress toward that pursuit. Kevin received a set of encyclopedias for his fourth birthday, and his parents became angry with him if he did not "study." He did exceptionally well in school, but had few friends. Kevin was hurt by his classmates' ridicule for being a "nerd." Absence of a social life provided him ample time to study.

Kevin began dating Holly during their junior year in high school. They spent most of their free time together at Kevin's house, and became sexually active. They experimented with drugs taken from David's home office. They frequently became intoxicated with inhalants such as lighter fluid, cleaning supplies, and cosmetic aerosol cans. Delores was oblivious to empty containers in Kevin's room. She accused the housekeeper of stealing when the accountant noticed an increase in household expenses. They used cocaine but would not smoke marijuana for fear of its odor being detected. Delores often boasted at social functions that her son did not drink or smoke.

Kevin was valedictorian of his high school class, and voted "most likely to succeed." David bought him an expensive foreign car as a graduation present, but never rode in it with him. Kevin remarked that the only time his father ever showed him any affection was when he shook his hand and put his arm around him at the ceremony.

During the spring of Kevin's senior year, he was accepted into a premedical program at a prestigious eastern college, David's alma mater.

Kevin was successful and reasonably contented in his freshman year. Visits from Holly made him less homesick. Kevin perceived Erik as the best friend he never had in high school. His parents called often to check on his academic progress. David often said, "There's going to be another doctor in the C. family in a few years."

Major problems developed during the spring semester of Kevin's sophomore year. He questioned whether he wanted to be a doctor, and felt unjustly compelled to satisfy the wish of his parents, at the expense of his own. His sexual relationship with Erik had begun, and intensified. He felt increasingly guilty about deceiving Holly. He feared that she and his parents would find out, and that his father would totally reject him.

As he doubted his motives for becoming a doctor, his grades slipped. His use of substances, which had been moderate and episodic, increased. When home on weekends, he took as many drugs from his father's office as he thought he could, without David becoming suspicious. Kevin and Erik took the same classes. As exams approached, they would take amphetamines so they could study all night. However, Kevin could not sleep nights following exams. He began using barbiturates to help him sleep. This cycle of alternative use of amphetamines and barbiturates became common practice for him. He became dependent on both.

Kevin's grades continued to worsen during his junior year. His parents became critical of him. He came to believe that the only reason his parents had been proud of him was that he had been doing well in school, and now that he wasn't, they could not acccept him. He came to resent his parents, his father in particular.

David suspected that Kevin was using drugs. He noticed that his office supply was depleted without explanation. During Christmas vacation, David locked the office door. He caught Kevin trying to break in. Kevin went into substance withdrawal. David secretly treated Kevin at home, preferring that he not be hospitalized for detoxification.

Kevin returned to college in late January for the spring semester of his junior year. He had not taken drugs for a month, but began again, as Erik has returned to school with an ample supply. Kevin's homosexual relationship with Erik remained intense. His interest in school continued to diminish, and his grades were now failing. Following the previously described discovery by Holly of Kevin's relationship with Erik, and Erik's suicide, Kevin dropped out of school and returned home. He felt extremely guilty and viewed himself as a failure.

Kevin's parents were now highly critical and ashamed of him. Holly began to make excuses for not seeing Kevin. They drifted apart and their relationship soon ended. Kevin felt abandoned by her. He continued to grieve for Erik. He resented more and more the competitive, materialistic lifestyle of his parents.

One summer afternoon, as Kevin was walking downtown, he was approached by two young women who asked if he would like to talk to them. They were very friendly and told him that he was a beautiful human being, and they cared for him very much. Kevin was very impressed by the girls, as he felt they were genuinely interested in him. He began making trips downtown purposely to meet them, as they could be found any afternoon in the downtown area. He did not care that they frequently asked him for money to "help them get by."

The girls eventually asked Kevin to come "home" with them at the end of the summer. They described "home" as a place in the country, far away, where a hundred friends live together as a family. He continued to visit them regularly. Toward the end of September, they told him that they were leaving. They told him he had to come immediately, and tell no one. Kevin was so dissatisifed and desperate that he went.

After hitchhiking for days, they arrived "home" —three barrack-like buildings five miles from the nearest road in a remote area of Oregon. Upon arrival, they were greeted by the "family." Members told Kevin they were glad he was there, and they would help in his "education." First of all, he must learn to "Surrender to the flow" and "Obey all guidance from the Enlightened One." During the first week he was taught begging and panhandling techniques. During "truth sessions" he was asked about his family's finances. He noticed there were no telephones, televisions, radios, or newspapers. He remembered one bit of advice from his father, who said "Anyone who asks you to surrender is not concerned with your best interest." He realized he was in a training camp for new converts to a cult. He fled during the night. Exhausted, disillusioned, and feeling duped and betrayed, he returned home.

Education and Employment:

Kevin completed two and a half years of college. He was dismissed for academic reasons following his leaving school during the spring semester of his junior year.

Kevin worked for two summers during college as a clerk in a pharmacy. He was fired when the owner suspected he had been stealing drugs. The owner did not press charges on the condition that Kevin never enter the store again. Kevin admitted that he had been stealing the drugs. He did not tell his parents.

Events Leading to Hospitalization:

Kevin returned home from the commune with his life in shambles. His parents were thoroughly disgusted with him, and continually reminded him how embarrassed they were by his running away. The police had been notified and the community was aware he was missing. He tried to renew his relationship with Holly, but she was dating another man and anticipated getting engaged. Returning to college was out of the question. David said he would no longer finance the education of a "disgrace." Kevin recently learned that Erik's former lover was now seriously ill with AIDS. He is fearful of infection although he is presently HIV-negative. Bizarre, unsigned letters with random post marks arrive daily. They threaten that "no one ever gets away alive."

Kevin became increasingly more despondent. After David began locking his office, Kevin started purchasing illicit drugs. Late one October night, after taking LSD, Kevin crashed his car. He was driving at an unreasonable speed on a familiar, winding road. He was admitted to the emergency room of the hospital with a concussion, numerous contusions, and a broken arm. When he first regained consciousness he said to the attending doctor, "Why didn't you just let me die? I am no good to anyone. I'm a disgrace. Nobody cares about me. The crash was no accident!"

Condition Since Hospitalization:

Kevin was transferred to the psychiatric unit of the hospital when his condition stabilized. He was diagnosed with major depressive disorder and substance dependence.

Kevin's parents have visited him regularly since he entered the hospital. They seem to realize they neglected him emotionally during childhood. They appreciate that Kevin must find something in life that is meaningful to him, and that what he chooses to do may not be compatible with what they want. Holly has come to visit him, although she has no intentions of dating him again. Kevin was very pleased to see her.

Kevin is still depressed, but his outlook seems to be improving. He is contemplating options for when he leaves the hospital. He expresses a commitment to abstain from substances. He has promised to join a support group for substance abusers that meets at his church. Although he does not feel it is realistic to plan on completing medical school, he thinks that he might like to take up nursing at a local community college. He realizes that his recovery process will be difficult. He has reasonable insight regarding his condition. There is reason for cautious optimism.

1. Write a narrative explaining Kevin's condition. You may choose one perspective, or integrate any number of perspectives into an eclectic explanation. Include plans for treatment.